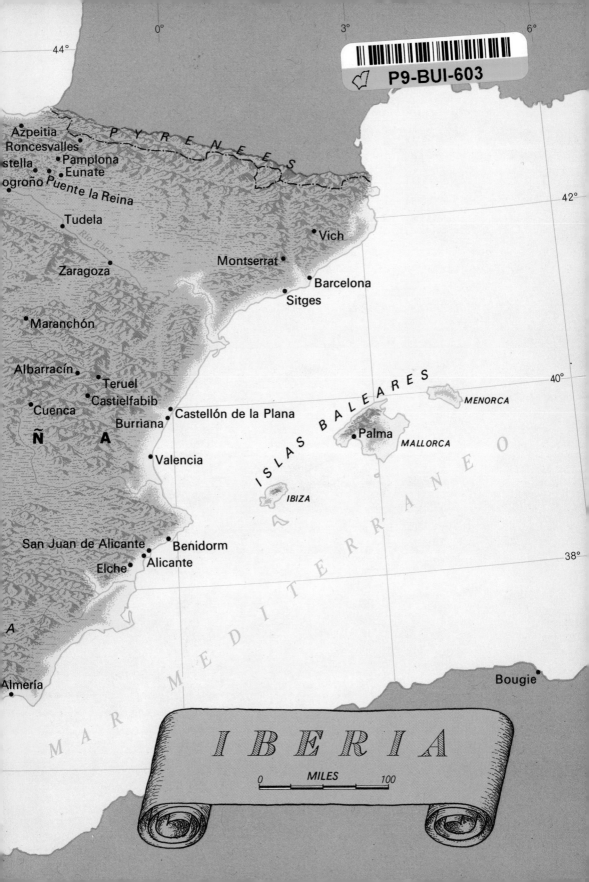

44°

0°   3°   6°

P9-BUI-603

PYRENEES

Azpeitia
Roncesvalles
stella   Pamplona
ogroño Eunate
Puente la Reina

42°

Tudela

Vich

Zaragoza

Montserrat

Barcelona

Sitges

Maranchón

Albarracín

40°

Teruel
Castielfabib

Cuenca

Ñ   A

Castellón de la Plana

Burriana

ISLAS BALEARES

MENORCA

Palma

MALLORCA

Valencia

IBIZA

San Juan de Alicante   Benidorm

38°

Elche   Alicante

A

MAR MEDITERRÁNEO

Almería

Bougie

Río Ebro

MAR MEDITERRÁNEO

IBERIA

0   MILES   100

33

$5.00

Fee

BOOKS BY *James A. Michener*

TALES OF THE SOUTH PACIFIC
THE FIRES OF SPRING
RETURN TO PARADISE
THE VOICE OF ASIA
THE BRIDGES AT TOKO-RI
SAYONARA
THE FLOATING WORLD
THE BRIDGE AT ANDAU
HAWAII
REPORT OF THE COUNTY CHAIRMAN
CARAVANS
THE SOURCE
IBERIA: *Spanish Travels and Reflections*

with A. Grove Day
RASCALS IN PARADISE

IBERIA

Spanish Travels and Reflections

JAMES A. MICHENER

PHOTOGRAPHS BY ROBERT VAVRA

 RANDOM HOUSE   NEW YORK

IBERIA

SPANISH TRAVELS AND REFLECTIONS

Copyright © 1968 by Random House, Inc.
All rights reserved under International and Pan-American Copyright Conventions.
Published in the United States by Random House, Inc., New York, and
simultaneously in Canada by Random House of Canada Limited, Toronto.
Library of Congress Catalog Card Number: 67–22623
Manufactured in the United States of America
Maps by Jean Paul Tremblay
Design by Betty Anderson

Acknowledgments

The balanced view which this book endeavors to maintain regarding the Muslim occupation of Spain was checked against the anti-Muslim point of view expressed in Louis Bertrand and Charles Petrie, *The History of Spain* (London, Eyre and Spottiswoode, rev. ed. 1952).

In my general attitude toward Fernando, Isabel, Carlos V and Felipe II, I was much influenced by R. Trevor Davies, *The Golden Century of Spain 1501–1621* (London, Macmillan, rev. ed. 1958).

All statements made about the Inquisition were weighed against Henry Kamen, *The Spanish Inquisition* (New York, New American Library, 1965).

Data relating to the siege of the Alcázar in Toledo during the Spanish Civil War were checked against Cecil D. Eby, *The Siege of the Alcázar* (New York, Random House, 1965).

All material relating to the Carlist pretenders was checked against Theo Aronson, *Royal Vendetta, The Crown of Spain 1829–1965* (Indianapolis, Bobbs-Merrill, 1966).

The quotation castigating bullfighting comes from Eléna de La Souchère, *An Explanation of Spain* (New York, A. A. Knopf, 1965), a powerful assault on many aspects of contemporary Spain.

The passage illustrating the interlocking relationships between Spain and England is quoted from H. V. Morton, *A Stranger in Spain* (New York, Dodd, Mead & Co., 1955) and that regarding Carlos the Bewitched from John Langdon-Davies, *Carlos, The King Who Would Not Die* (New York, Prentice-Hall, 1963).

Data and opinions in the last chapter were constantly checked against those expressed so felicitously by Walter Starkie in his *The Road to Santiago, Pilgrims of St. James* (London, John Murray, 1957). I used principally the Spanish edition (Madrid, Aguilar, 1958).

For the enumeration of the attendants waiting upon Juana la Loca at Tordesillas I am indebted to Amarie Dennis, *Seek the Darkness* (Madrid, privately published, 1961). Mrs. Dennis also consented to talk with me about various aspects of the Isabel-Juana story, for which I am grateful.

To Mary Elizabeth Brooks I am indebted not only for her excellent study of King Sebastião of Portugal, *A King for Portugal* (Madison, University of Wisconsin, 1964) but also for the instructive dialogue we held in Madrid in which she explained sidelights of this bizarre episode. Where my account differs from hers I have so indicated in the text.

After my manuscript was completed I had the privilege of meeting in person that queen of American bullfight aficionados, Alice Hall of Georgia. Her preferences were

ACKNOWLEDGMENTS

so violent and so persuasive that I modified certain opinions I had previously expressed in the taurine material.

In the text I have expressed my appreciation of the help provided by Don Luis Morenés y Areces, Marqués de Bassecourt, who helped me on three different occasions: in Las Marismas, in Madrid, and on the pilgrimage to Santiago de Compostela. I have never known a better traveling companion nor a man more imbued with his subject, in this case a love of Spain.

During the two months that I concentrated on the question of bullfighting I had the pleasure of Matador John Fulton's company, and while I must not saddle him with any of the heterodox opinions I express about his profession I do wish to thank him for his expert guidance.

For permission to explore the Coto Doñana I am, like naturalists around the world, indebted to José Antonio Valverde, who serves as custodian for this rare corner of Europe. Many of the incidents I report as to the passing of the year in the Coto I owe to Dr. Valverde.

To Patter Winslow Ashcraft I am indebted for some of the finest picnics I have ever had. To wander across Spain without halting for varied picnics would be to miss the best the country has to offer and from this fate I was saved by Mrs. Ashcraft.

To my two old diplomatic friends from Afghanistan days, Steven Baldanza and Osbert Day, I am indebted for their help in guiding me around their new duty posts, Baldanza in Lisboa, Day in Madrid.

I cannot adequately express my dependence upon and appreciation of Professor Kenneth Vanderford, Ripon College, Ripon, Wisconsin. At my request he read the manuscript and checked it against his encyclopedic knowledge. Barely a page escaped his savage eye. On esoteric points he was a prince of debaters. He also assumed responsibility for all translations from Spanish into English, except where historical ones had to be followed.

My deepest gratitude must go to that extraordinary tertulia of the Café León. That a group of distinguished members of the Real Academia de Española should have welcomed me, a stranger, and should have given their time to my questions was a testimony to the warmth of hospitality which Spain extends to the visitor. I am especially indebted to José María de Cossío, whose robust humor and wide spread of interests impressed me, and to that delightful and irreverent scholar from the University of Texas, Ramón Martínez López.

To the scores of other advisors, like Juan Quintana and Virginia Smith on bullfighting, William Frauenfelder on Cataluña, Ignacio Herguete G. de Guadiana on Trujillo, Luis Ybarra González on Las Marismas, Luis Morondo on the music of Victoria, Father Jesús Precedo Lafuente on Santiago de Compostela, Alcalde José Filgueira on Pontevedra, Fernando Zóbel on contemporary Spanish painting, José María Lassaletta on wildlife, Tess LaTouche on daily gossip, Brewster Cross on flamenco, Dr. José María Muguruza on the Prado, David Peace on tourism, and Madelyn Mack on one woman's view of the romance of Spain, I owe a debt which can never be repaid.

January 15, 1968   J A M E S   A .   M I C H E N E R

Contents

IBERIA

Spanish Travels and Reflections

FOLLOWING PAGE: *Hard and dry like the bark of the cork tree is the land of Spain.*

INTRODUCTION

OCEANO
ATLANTICO

MILES
0   100

CABO FINISTERRE

Barcelona

Teruel
Castellón de la Plana
Burriana
Madrid
Valencia

Lisboa

Sevilla

MAR MEDITERRANEO

I have long believed that any man interested in either the mystic or the romantic aspects of life must sooner or later define his attitude concerning Spain. For just as this forbidding peninsula physically juts into the Atlantic and stands isolated, so philosophically the concept of Spain intrudes into the imagination, creating effects and raising questions unlike those evoked by other nations. During the four decades that I have traveled in Spain I have always wanted to describe the impact this vibrant land has had upon me, and now I have an opportunity to do so.

Did any traveler ever enter Spain in a more appropriate manner than I? While a student in Scotland, I had shipped as chart boy aboard a Clydeside freighter which lugged coal to Italy and brought back oranges from Spain to be used in the marmalade factories of Dundee. We sailed from Glasgow, buried in coal dust, as ugly a little tramp steamer as ever skirted the Bay of Biscay. Against headwinds we made only ninety-six miles a day, pitching and tossing the while, so that I was well fed up with the trip before we ever saw land. Then out of the Atlantic we spotted Cabo Finisterre off the port bow, and for much of one stormy day we kept it in view, a tantalizing taste of Spain, solid, dark, mysterious, looming out of the gray waves.

As our freighter rose and fell in the troughs this glimpse of land began to haunt me. More than anything else in the world I wanted to see the Spain of which Finisterre formed the western rampart. Past this point three and a half centuries ago Sir Francis Drake had come to harry Spanish shipping and to burn Spanish ports. Here the Armada had formed for its assault on England, and the headland as I saw it that stormy day was well suited to historic purposes. It was dark, heavy, unlike anything I had previously seen. It was in truth land's end, the western promontory of the European continent, and it challenged the mind.

5

Well, we left Finisterre and plowed our way monotonously south, and a long time later, when I had grown accustomed to the pitching of our uncomfortable freighter, we steamed into the Straits of Gibraltar and I saw, again to port, the sun-drenched uplands of Algeciras, and they were so different from what I had seen in the storm off Finisterre, so inviting and so startling in the vividness of their color, that I again felt the urge to flee that ship and go ashore, forgetting Italy, which had been the purpose for making this trip.

But we left Gibraltar behind us, then Mallorca, then Corsica, and finally we emptied our coal at ancient Civitavecchia, that dreariest of all Italian ports, where Michelangelo had once served as city architect in charge of fortifying the harbor and where Henri Beyle had spent long years as French consul, publishing his reflections under the name of Stendhal. He and Michelangelo distracted me for a while, but often as I traveled over Italy on leave from the coal barge I recalled those two fleeting glimpses of Spain and longed for the day when our empty ship would sail into some distinguished port like Valencia or Barcelona to pick up our oranges. I imagined myself striding ashore to inspect at first hand the greatness which I felt sure existed in that dour land. The captain of the freighter wasn't certain which of the ports we would head for, but trusted Glasgow to advise him by the time we reached Mallorca.

When we were abeam of that island the wireless finally spoke: 'Castellón de la Plana,' and the captain was pleased. 'Beautiful little city,' he said.

I ran to my charts and found that Castellón lay between Barcelona and Valencia, the actual city being some two miles or more inland from the harbor. It was a major port for the shipping of oranges and tradition-ally the scene of Spain's first fair of the year, at which the opening bull-fights of the season were held. 'Castellón is one of the best places in Spain for beginning a visit,' the captain assured me.

During the passage from Mallorca to the mainland I memorized the shipping instructions contained in *Pilot for the East Coast of Spain* and prepared myself spiritually for my entrance to the country by rereading the best passages of *Don Quixote*. But on the last evening we received a wireless directing us to avoid Castellón de la Plana and to proceed instead to the tiny village of Burriana, where oranges were awaiting us.

'Burriana has no harbor!' I protested, for the *Pilot* said: 'Ships anchor in the roads and prudent ones keep a sharp watch on their lines.'

'They barge the oranges out to us,' the captain explained.

'Then we don't land?'

'No.'

My disappointment was so apparent that he added, 'But you can ride ashore on one of the barges and join us next week in Valencia.'

I had rarely heard finer words, and all that night I stayed on deck, waiting to catch my first glimpse of the point at which I would enter Spain, but no lights showed, and finally in the east, over Mallorca, which we had left astern, the sun began to rise and a soft Mediterranean beauty suffused the air.

My first view of Burriana? It wasn't a view. It was a smell, for the offshore breeze carried to our dirty little freighter the odor of orange blossoms, heavy and pungent and inescapably the odor of Spain. Then, in the direction from which this superb aroma came, I saw the low shore begin to rise from the waves and with incredible swiftness present itself. Our ship slowed. The anchor chains went out. Lines were thrown to men in rowboats, who attached them to buoys, and gradually we swung to in the current, ready to receive whatever cargo awaited us.

It was then that I saw the immemorial aspect of Spain, and my introduction in the minutes that followed was so perfect that it still stands for me as a permanent vision of Spain. Later I was to see the bullfights in Ronda and the cathedral at Santiago de Compostela and the roomful of Velázquez paintings at the Prado, and the pass at Roncesvalles where Roland perished and the great, bleak olive orchards of Badajoz and the Holy Week processions in Sevilla. I was to see the Spain that men have written about for two thousand years, but seldom would I see anything so representative of Spain.

Since the little farming village of Burriana had no harbor curving out to protect the shore, it could have no pier; storm waves driving in from the east would periodically destroy attempts to maintain a quay. So the huge barges which conveyed the oranges to the freighter had to be loaded ashore. Each barge was hauled onto dry land and crammed with barrels containing oranges until it must have weighed several tons.

'Why barrels?' I asked, watching the procedure with binoculars. 'They are barrels, aren't they?'

'Steel barrels.'

'Why?'

'You'll see.'

Obviously, when the barges were loaded they had to be dragged back into the water in order to be floated so that they could be rowed out to our ship. How to do it? In Roman times businessmen using this coast for the transfer of freight to Italy had solved the problem. They reared a breed of oxen that thrived in salt water, and now these huge beasts, working in the sea with often only their eyes and horns visible, backed close to a barge while workmen attached chains to their harness. Then with men who also lived mostly in the sea whipping at them and cursing, the great beasts strained while everyone ashore pushed on the barge. Slowly, slowly the near-swimming oxen and the men and the shouting got the barge moving. Slowly it left the shore. The massive oxen moved deeper and deeper into the sea, so that men directing them had to keep afloat by grasping the oxen's horns, and in this way the oranges in their steel barrels were ferried out to our ship.

The first Spaniard I ever met was a workman of Burriana, dressed only in a breechcloth, swimming to meet me with his left hand grasping the horn of an ox. He was a poor man and existed only by this brutal work, which kept him half submerged all day, but he had the face of a satyr rising from a swamp, and when I first saw him he was laughing. His skin was bronzed like leather and he had not shaved for some days. He had enormous arms and very quick eyes and saw at once that I was a stranger, perhaps an American, who might pay for a ride ashore in his barge. In a guttural voice, using a Valencian argot, he grunted at me. Of the first sentences spoken to me in Spain I understood not a single word.

I did understand, of course, that he was proposing to carry me ashore in his barge, for a fee. I agreed and started to climb into the barge, but our captain interrupted. 'There's no point in going ashore now. It's only five o'clock. No buses to Castellón yet.' He was right, so to the disappointment of the bargeman I said I'd wait.

'But only me,' he insisted in words I did understand. 'Not those other . . .' He indicated the next barge coming to our ship, and I wished I had enough command of the Valencian dialect to understand his profane description of his competitors. It must have been extreme, because when he repeated it for the benefit of the incoming crew they threatened him. But he laughed.

Till the sun was high I stayed on deck, watching the nautical oxen of Burriana haul loaded barges, then talking with the rugged men who brought the barges to our freighter, but each time my satyr returned he renewed his contract with me. 'When I go ashore I'll go with you,' I assured him. I would have been afraid to go with another.

I now discovered why the oranges were being delivered in steel drums, for the captain directed that a hose be thrust down into the Mediterranean where the water was clear, then ordered the deck hands, 'Knock out the bungs,' and presently all the drums were opened and I saw that the oranges inside had been cut in half. The resulting juice, of course, did not fill the barrel, and the empty space was now to be filled with sea water.

'What's the idea?' I asked.

'Everything sloshes back and forth, all the way home to Dundee,' the captain said.

'To accomplish what?'

'It prepares the rind for making marmalade.'

There were two schools of thought aboard our ship. The captain held that the action of salt water ate away the pulpy part of the rind and left the skin translucent, as required in the better brands of marmalade. The pulp and juice would be thrown away. 'Nonsense,' one of the deck hands argued. 'Everything in that barrel is mixed with sugar and then boiled down to make that bittersweet taste of a true Dundee marmalade. Without the salt water it wouldn't be worth a damn.'

A tugging at my sleeve reminded me that my laughing satyr was back, and this time I allowed him to lower me into his barge, now empty of drums. He had arms like some prehistoric man, and to him I was a child. His animals were unlike any I had ever seen before, and together we moved toward the shore of Spain. When I saw the process of launching the barges close up I was appalled at the energy required. It was medieval or worse. It was an expenditure that I could not comprehend and it continued all day and all year, men and animals working themselves to death.

But the men thus engaged were so handsome, their smiles so compelling that there was something different about them, something powerful and stoic. This was their lot and they would not complain. Ashore some were having breakfast and they invited me to join. I knew that I was taking someone's share, but I could not resist such an opening meal in my new country and I paid my bargeman for my share of food. I can taste it yet: anchovies, which have always been my delight, hard bread, harder cheese and red wine. How good it was, how honest in its Spanish quality.

I wondered if any previous traveler to Spain had entered through this nonexistent Burriana? Later I was to enter through many different ports, but none has ever compared with the beauty of that first morning, nor with its significance. Because in subsequent years, no matter how superficial my visits might be or my reactions to them, I could rely on the fact that at the beginning, if only for a moment, I had been allowed to see deep into the quality of Spain. I saw the toiling men, the congenial peasants, the straining beasts, the honest food. I smelled the salt of the shore, the oranges of the inland fields, the burning chicory that passed for coffee, the sourness of the red wine, the harsh seductiveness of cheap anchovies. It is this Spain that has been with me through the years, and whenever in subsequent visits I have again come close to that particular vision I have felt at home.

Thirty-five years ago the road from Burriana to Castellón de la Plana ran through orange groves, at the end of which stood the charming little city that was immersed in festival when I saw it for the first time. For two days I enjoyed about as fine an introduction to Spanish life as a young man could have, for it was the custom in Castellón in those years to conduct the traditional evening parade along unique lines. In the center of town, as in all Spanish localities, unattached men walked round and round the plaza in a counterclockwise direction while unmarried girls walked arm-in-arm in the opposite direction, so that in any one complete transit a man who kept to the outer circle was constantly staring into the faces of beautiful girls, each of whom he would encounter twice. I know it is difficult for people who have never courted in this way to believe how easy it is to conclude understandings in two hours of such parading, but when one has actually participated in the constant meeting and judging and winking and nodding that takes place, he knows how effectively the courtship is conducted.

Well, this evening paseo is the same in all Spanish small towns and in some large ones too, but Castellón added a feature which was most attractive. Only half the girls paraded in the square. The other half rested in balconies overlooking the promenade, from which they threw down onto the men passing below small darts trailing colored streamers. Since I had been easily recognized as an American, not many of whom got to a place like Castellón in those days, I found myself the target of many such darts and I brushed them away.

'Stupid!' a harsh laughing voice sounded, and I turned to see that the satyr bargeman who had ferried me ashore that morning was walking behind me and explaining in a proprietary manner who I was. 'Stupid!' he repeated, gathering up the darts which I had brushed from my clothing. He explained that it was not the darts but the colored streamers that were important and must be saved. 'Because,' he said in Spanish that I only half understood, 'at the end of the parade you are entitled to visit any balcony decorated in the colors matching the streamers you hold.'

We paraded as a team, and when I saw my bargeman in ordinary clothes and shaved I realized that he was not much older than I and already his thundering life in the surf hauling immense weights had made him an old man. We collected many darts that first night, and when the music stopped he led me to one balcony after another, and we danced and drank and ate anchovies and met the beautiful and shy girls who had pinned us with their streamers. Since I was a stranger, and what was worse, probably a Protestant, the older women of the houses kept severe watch on me, but the bargeman whispered that any girl of Castellón who had even a little intelligence would know how to slip down into the square, and he was right.

Later that night he led me to a corner where two girls waited, and the four of us went to a vaudeville show, where the bargeman insisted upon paying for the tickets. I tried to prevent this, knowing that I could afford the money better than he, but in true Spanish style, as if he were a nobleman of the grand school, he flashed the money I had paid him that morning for the ferry ride ashore and said loudly, if I understood his Spanish correctly, 'He paid this morning. Tonight I pay.'

I remember the entertainment for two reasons: there I saw my first zarzuela (brief light opera) and was captivated by it; and in the vaudeville portion I watched two robust comedians who, whenever they wanted an extra loud laugh, announced that they had come from Burriana. At each mention of my nonexistent seaport the crowd roared. It was like comedians in New York who coax cheap laughs by saying they're from Brooklyn or those in Chicago who achieve the same effect by being from Peoria. Apparently every community has a neighbor which it regards as ridiculous and I had chosen for my landing place in Spain a town that was the butt of the coast between Castellón and Valencia. My bargeman did not laugh at the jokes nor did I.

What a marvelous fiesta that was, my first in Spain, with a huge workman to guide me and orchestras and girls throwing streamers and comedians making jokes about Burriana, and the great warmth of Spanish hospitality as one knows it in a provincial city.

I cannot remember now how I discovered my technique for exploring a strange land, for I have followed this procedure for as long as I can recall. I enter the country unannounced and without a letter to anyone. I stand back and look at the scene before me, talk with anyone who cares to talk with me, then go to the bus station and buy a ticket for the end of any random line. This drops me in some village out in the country, and there I spend a couple of days just sitting and looking and talking. This produces some very dull days, but also some memorable ones.

At the end of World War II, I did this in Canton and saw enough of China to nourish my imagination for decades. I used the same system in Bali, and later in Japan I skipped out of Tokyo and wound up in Morioka, a small city to the north, where I had a series of experiences through which I gained an understanding of Japan that would have been denied me otherwise. I often forget Tokyo but never Morioka. With its lantern-lit little shops and its sprawling rock-strewn river, Morioka will be with me always. Anything good I have written about Japan stems from Morioka.

Now, in Castellón I went to the bus station and found that my plan wouldn't work. It seemed that the only buses then available ran to Burriana, but there was a railroad which wandered about the countryside, and on the advice of a straggler I purchased a ticket to Teruel, thus projecting myself into a corner of Spain not often visited by strangers.

The train that carried me there consisted only of third-class carriages, a euphemism for boxcars lined with rough-plank benches which were filled before the whistle tooted, so that more than half the passengers had to stand. When started, the train moved quite slowly and threw an unusual amount of cinders through the screenless windows. It was jerky in motion, creaky in sound, antique in appearance and utterly captivating.

For it was filled with human beings of a kind I had not met in my college textbooks on Spain. Here there were no grandees, no industrial giants. There were no caballeros in leather, no beautiful women in mantillas. There was only a jostling crowd of extremely poor people, dressed in the oldest of clothes, huddled together in a dirty boxcar. This was a Spain for which I was unprepared, yet as I settled down and began to make friends with these apparently suspicious and silent people, I found myself among some of the most congenial persons I had so far encountered in

Europe, and the interminable trip developed into exactly what I had hoped for.

For the first hour the train chugged south along the coast toward Valencia and the oppressive smell of the boxcar was offset by the sweet aroma of oranges, but then the line diverged abruptly to the west and we began to climb a steep valley marked by low mountains, a rushing stream and poor forests. Most of that day we climbed slowly upward, so that I became convinced that Teruel must be perched on a considerable mountain, an impression which has never left me. How dull, how tedious that long day's trip could have been, with cinders in my eye and hunger in my stomach. The land was bleak, with scarcely a town or any human element to relieve the monotony, and such stragglers as we did see appeared to be shepherds, incredibly poor. Even their dogs were scrawny and unlovable.

But the more forbidding the terrain the more delightful the peasants in my boxcar. These were tremendous men and women, hard as treated leather, determined as the mountains among which we were traveling. When at a junction I purchased a generous supply of bread and cheese to throw into the common pot, I gained admission to the group, as it were, and the wine bottles were passed to me and the tins of anchovies and the rock-hard ends of sausage. We were all so hungry by now that our odds and ends of food seemed a feast and it was natural that the men and women who sang best should offer us a series of quiet songs, nothing boisterous and nothing to tempt a man into unseemly bellowing, but rather a quiet, forceful series of statements about love and rural life and the fiestas that occur in small towns. I could understand few of the words.

But as the day wore on I talked much with these people of the boxcar. They were peasants, even those who lived in towns like Teruel and Castellón, and their life was indescribably hard; one of the strangest bits of information I gathered in my long conversations was that most of these people were wearing their best clothes. It was something important to be making so long a trip by train and they were wearing the best they had. How pitiful they seemed, with trousers mended four times at the same spot with four different swatches of cloth, with dresses in which whole panels had been replaced by cloth of a different color. Shoes were shabby beyond description and socks were filled with holes even in the nonessential parts that clung about the ankles. The men's caps were mostly torn and the women's shawls were ragged at the edges, and not because of fringes either. Such teeth as had been lost had not been replaced and many of these people showed need for a doctor, to whom apparently they had no access. Speaking only of outward appearances, these people were as poverty-stricken as any I had ever seen.

But about them, in all they did, there was a stolid dignity and a profound joy. When they sang it was as if they were in a cathedral, for they took each note seriously but not pompously, and their voices blended

Peasant.

for powerful effect. When they spoke it was only after weighing each word, not for its effect but for its appropriateness. The volubility which one thinks of in relation to Latin peoples was not evident here, but rather the taciturnity of New Englanders or Scots. But in both the singing and the conversations there was joy, and when a joke was told it brought forth the guffaws common to all rural people.

It was a remarkable day, one of the best I would ever spend in Spain, and at last our tired and cinder-throwing engine chugged up the final hill and brought us into the station at Teruel. 'Adiós, norteamericano!' the passengers said softly as I hauled down my small bag and asked directions for the heart of the city. These people had provided me with a solid introduction to Spain and I would be forever indebted to them. I was loath to separate from them, but the journey was ended and they were now headed for their separate homes. I visualized them going to English-type cottages with hollyhocks about the door, as if they were the ordinary rural people of Europe. Later I would see what kind of homes they actually lived in.

For me Teruel was the introduction into a new world, the hard, remorseless, poverty-stricken world of provincial Spain. The lives I saw in Teruel were terribly confined within some of the narrowest circles I have ever known. The streets were equally narrow, as if hewn out of solid rock. The architecture was not pleasing, like the panoramas shown in my textbooks on Spain. The restaurants were uncongenial, the theaters were ugly and the band in the central plaza played off-key. But there was a compelling durability about this town that one had to admire, and the longer I stayed there the better I liked it. I remember chiefly the acrid smell of roasting chicory or some similar coffee substitute, so that even today whenever I chance upon the smell of burning chicory I think of Teruel.

On my first morning in the city, according to habit, I wandered out past the edges of town to see in what respects it might be different from the Burriana region or from Castellón, and as I was walking along a country road I heard a voice calling, 'Eh, norteamericano!' I turned to find at the doorway to a house one of the men with whom I had shared my bread and cheese on the train the previous day, and he invited me into his home, something that I later wished he had not done, for I can still see it as it was that day, and having seen his home I could no longer preserve storybook myths about this powerful land of Spain.

The walls were of stone unchinked with cement or mortar. They had, however, been tightly packed with clay and were both water- and wind-proof, forming a solid and pleasing barrier against the elements. The floor was of packed earth, worn smooth by centuries of use, for I judged the house to have been built at least three hundred years earlier. No dust rose from the floor and it was surprisingly even, for through the centuries the earth had been leveled until it was now at least as flat as an average flagstone floor. The house had two rooms, the partition between them consisting of some of the poorest lumber I have ever seen, scarcely good enough for the making of a cheap industrial crate in a country like Germany. I could see through the wall at many spots where warping had occurred or the chipping off of fragments, for the boards were paper-thin, and this in an area where forests had once abounded and where to a lesser degree they still existed. If lumber was being harvested in the Teruel district, none of it was filtering down to homes like this.

The house contained one table, one chair, one bed, one cradle. That was about all. There were no cupboards, no shelves, no rocking chairs, no benches, no sideboards, no bathroom, no iron stove, nothing. A man some fifty years old and his wife of about the same age had each worked in Teruel for forty years, for they had begun at the age of ten, and frugally they had saved their money, and at the end of twoscore years of labor this was what they had accumulated.

I was a stranger and was not afraid of rebuffs, so I asked to see everything. What clothes did they have? What eating gear? What food supplies? What books? Books? Neither wife nor husband could read. Clothes? Mainly what they had worn on the train, plus older ones for working, and I have already described what the good ones looked like. Food? They had enough to live on for three days, for they had no refrigerator, and after three days they would go to the store and buy more food, if they had the money. I did not know the Spanish word for hope, but in a roundabout way I asked them what their plans were for the future. The future? What future?

And so I wandered back and forth across Teruel, that austere mountain city, and allowed the reality of Spain to beat in upon me. One evening I went to the cathedral, if I am using the proper word for so mean a church, and there I attended my first religious service in Spain. It was overwhelmingly impressive, with candles and choirs and priests who seemed to bear the weight of this poor settlement upon their necks. The people of Teruel that I saw worshiping that night were devout and to them religion was terribly important, but as I looked about the gloomy church I found in the congregation few of the peasants I had ridden with on the train. This praying group came from a different stratum and I was pleased to have a chance to see it. The church people were better dressed than my earlier acquaintances and better shaved too, but they were equally solid, and when I met them later in cafés or stores they were equally attractive.

I had an exciting time in Teruel, a moving time for a young man trying to discover for himself what Spain was like, and after I had seen several of the better-class houses in the city, finding them to have floors such as we had in Pennsylvania and bookcases and shelves for storing food and colorful patios, I began to wonder if I had been unlucky in first stumbling upon that earthen-floored hut containing almost nothing. Had I by chance been deceived? Was rural Spain better than I had judged?

So I went out into the country in the opposite direction and stopped at three different farmhouses selected at random, and at each I introduced myself and was generously received. The farmers and their wives offered me water and wine, if they had any, and seemed pleased to talk with a norteamericano who had taken the trouble to learn their language, however poorly. They showed me their homes: earthen floors, one table, not enough chairs to entertain formally even one guest, few clothes, no stores of food.

When I returned to Teruel, I was met at the edge of the city by two

From any train window there is the chance of seeing unexpected beauty.

armed men dressed in nineteenth-century uniforms featuring two-cornered patent-leather hats called tricorns after an older version which had three points. They were members of the Guardia Civil, whose job it was to keep watch on everything that happened in rural areas like Teruel, and they traveled in pairs, having learned that it was safer to do so. They did not stop me but fell in beside me as I walked. They were cordial and correct as they asked, 'Looking at the countryside?'

    'Yes.'

    'Visiting friends?'

    'Not friends.'

'And when are you leaving Teruel?'

'In the morning.'

When the train pulled out they were there, extremely pleasant and smiling, their highly polished hats gleaming in the morning sunlight as if they were part of the chorus for a New York production of *Carmen*. They were my last sight of Teruel.

I was to rejoin my ship at Valencia, that powerful and often rebellious capital of the eastern coast, and as my dirty little train chugged into the center of the city I was made aware that Valencia was to be something special. I didn't know it at the time, but I was arriving on the Saturday evening which marked the height of the fiesta that celebrates the end of winter, and as I left the station the sky above Valencia was filled with exploding fireworks and the air with shouts and music and screams of delight. Valencia is the fireworks capital of Europe and outdoes itself at the fallas (bonfires). In the public square enormous wooden structures are raised, representing horses or galleons or Mont Blanc in Switzerland or the leaders of the nation, and each foot of timber is wound with colorful explosives, while chains of smaller firecrackers hang in festoons in all possible directions. I mean that these structures are sometimes as high as three-story buildings and are very solidly constructed.

Well, when the maximum crowd has gathered and the wind is right, these mammoth things are set afire, and as the wood begins to burn and the explosives ignite and the lovely loops of firecrackers explode, it seems as if the whole city of Valencia is going up in flames. It is really something to see, one of the great spectacles of Europe.

And the cafés! They were filled with well-to-do people and the food was excellent, emphasizing fish provided by the Mediterranean. The theaters were crowded and the same comedians who had delighted me in Castellón had arrived to tell the same bawdy jokes about being forced to spend the night in the hotel at guess where . . . Burriana! And as the chambermaid was described and her sexual capacities suggested, the Valencian crowd roared approval. Each time the name Burriana was mentioned the people of Valencia howled. Here the paseo was a wild affair, with some of the best-dressed women I was to see in Spain going with the clock and hordes of young men in fine suits marching in the opposite direction to inspect them. Apparently, in Valencia the people of Spain lived well.

But what I can never forget was the next day, when a tall, heavy man stopping in my hotel said in fine Spanish, 'Sir, I trust you will be attending the bullfight.'

'Is there one?'

'At five,' he said graciously and offered to lead me to where I might buy a ticket. As we paraded through the streets I noticed that the men of Valencia paid deference to my companion and some spoke to him with a kind of reverence. At the ticket window, not at the bullring but at a downtown office, the same respect was paid, and I finally asked, 'Who are you?' and he explained that he was picador for one of the men fighting that afternoon. I was less impressed then than I was to be later.

The cartel that afternoon contained the names of three matadors who were to be remembered in the history of Spanish bullfighting: Marcial Lalanda, Domingo Ortega and El Estudiante. The first was one of the most poetic matadors ever to grace the rings of Spain, and passes which he invented are still being used by his successors. Ortega, an illiterate farmhand often referred to as el de Borox (he from the trivial village of Borox), was to become the cold classicist and the idol of those who love an icy, controlled excellence. On this day in 1932 he was just beginning his career at the advanced age of twenty-four. In the 1950s he was still fighting now and then, a man remarkably durable and never hurried or vulgar. El Estudiante was something special, a young student named Luis Gómez who had graduated from high school but who had given up his studies for glory in the bullring. He was to make a less lasting contribution to the history of bullfighting than either Lalanda or Ortega, but his arrival on the scene and under the conditions I have described was emotionally exciting, and he was to have a series of good years.

I could not have been introduced to bullfighting under more auspicious conditions: a professional picador to choose my seat, a poetic matador to open the fight and an austere classicist to compete with him, followed by the young student whom Spain was taking to her heart. I settled down in my front-row location and waited. The interior gates of the plaza swung open. The band burst into music. Bugles sounded and the opening parade was under way. I did not know enough to identify the matadors, nor the banderilleros, but behind them on horseback rode the man who had helped me buy my ticket, and in his leather pants, cockaded hat and articulated leg armor he looked enormous, as knights must have looked centuries ago when they ventured forth to battle. He nodded to me as he rode past and I felt that I was part of the fight.

Some years before, when still a student in a small Pennsylvania college, I had been cajoled into attending my first symphony concert, at which Arturo Toscanini was to conduct Beethoven's Fifth and Third in that order, and I can truthfully say that in the first minute of this music I understood as much about orchestral music as I was ever to know, even though I studied it avidly during subsequent years. So also, in that first minute in the bullring at Valencia, I understood bullfighting, even though I have been improving my knowledge at rather close range ever since. When Lalanda came out to unfurl his cape and with a series of breath-taking passes bring his bull under control, I understood that I was watching a theatrical display and not a sport. When the bull killed the first horse— because if I remember correctly either pads were not used that day in Valencia or only inadequate ones if they were—I understood that I was participating in a tribal tragedy dating back to prehistoric times and not in a game. At Valencia in those days they still used on cowardly bulls the black banderillas with firecracker heads that exploded harmlessly above the bull's neck muscles, frightening him into action, and when a pair of these went off not ten feet from where I sat, with the bull's face pointed at mine, I saw the effect on the animal, saw him stare at me in amazement, then leap sideways in the air and thunder off, and I was forever after a friend and a student of the fighting bull. And when on his first bull el de Borox took his truncated red cloth for the final act of his fight and dominated a towering bull as if the latter had been a tame puppy, I understood that this spectacle was intended to show puny man engaged in his war with the powerful forces of night. I was never to see Ortega better than he was that day, and I left the ring hopelessly addicted to this short, swarthy, cold perfectionist. I was curiously pleased to discover that my picador belonged to the cuadrilla of Ortega and not to one of the others. Later I was to travel briefly with this cuadrilla and to see Ortega in various plazas, and he was as great a matador as I thought him that first day. I concluded then, and have never changed my mind, that if I were to be a matador I would want to be like Domingo Ortega. Being far too chunky in the bottom to qualify as even a third-rate matador and not being hefty enough to be a picador aboard a horse, I never entertained any illusions in this direction even though at intervals I have spent a lot of time with the bulls and have even fought the smaller calves, but as a writer I have often remembered Ortega and have tried in words to attain some of the controlled effects he achieved with cloth and sword. To me, el de Borox would always be a Spanish archetype.

That Sunday night the picador and I went to a café near our hotel, where we were joined by a gang of Valencian bullfight fans who started to discuss the day's events in an animated dialect which I could little understand, and it was their opinion that Ortega had been exceptional. However, the purpose of the evening was not to rehash the bullfight but to enjoy a famous flamenco team of a woman dancer and a male guitarist. They had come from Madrid, I believe, or possibly Sevilla. At any rate, the smoky hall was crowded and waiters scurried about serving sweet wine and cakes or sour wine and anchovies, and our table chose the latter. Girls provided by the management wandered among the tables and three invited themselves to join us. The picador insisted that they provide one who could speak English, but none was available. They did, however, find one who spoke South American-style Spanish, and her I could understand.

What few lights the café had were dimmed. A single chair was placed on stage to be occupied by a round, fat, baldheaded man carrying a guitar. He was greeted with applause and launched directly into a composition which I would remember as one of the best I was to hear in Spain. I asked the girl beside me to explain the song, and she said that flamenco had more than a dozen standard types of song, like malagueños, fandangos and peteneras. This was a good example of the last. When I asked what words accompanied the music, she said, 'We have many versions. But the best tell the story of a beautiful Jewish girl named Petenera.'

> Where are you going, Petenera?
> Where are you going, Jewish maid?

I suppose that 'Petenera,' as this particular song was called, has become more a part of me than any other piece of folk music I have ever heard, the story of a Jewish girl and her tragic effect upon a small Spanish town. It must be very old, dating back at least to the 1400s, when Jews were common in Spain; the music is not exceptional and the words are arbitrary, but others have testified to the fact that the song as a whole has a powerful effect on them too, so I am not unusual in liking it.

It was obvious that this fat man on the chair was a notable guitarist, for he could make his instrument roar and whisper, laugh and sob. Both he and his music were very Spanish, and I relished each, but in due course he struck a series of commanding chords that sounded much like a machine gun, and onto the stage whirled my first flamenco dancer. She was a woman in her forties, not at all pretty and much fatter than I would have expected, but after that quick inventory I forgot her visible characteristics, for she could dance.

On Monday morning an event occurred that was to come back to me with terrible effect in the years that followed, although when it was happening I could not have anticipated its significance. I was in the central square, or at least one of the central squares, where the ashes of Saturday night's fire were being cleared, when from one of the government buildings I saw a procession crossing toward me. It was composed of many men in fine dark suits, including three or four in formal morning wear. In the center of the front rank was a most ordinary-looking man, apparently in his fifties, undistinguished in face, slightly dumpy in body and awkward in manner. I remember distinctly that even then I thought him to be a man of good though flabby will, and somebody beside me whispered that he was the President of Spain. It was Niceto Alcalá Zamora, the quiet man chosen to head Spain after the departure of King Alfonso XIII, who had slipped out of the country only the year before, thus avoiding the necessity of abdication. In this simple, fumbling man I saw the Republican alternative to the Bourbon dynasty (in Spanish, Borbón) and I was not impressed.

Then, to my astonishment, the cortege of black-suited men came straight at me, and a big crowd gathered behind me, so that I was wedged into position. President Alcalá Zamora—a fussy lawyer who was known, in a mixture of affection and contempt, as Botas (Old High Button Shoes) —spoke casually to several people in the crowd, then stopped and faced me.

'You are a stranger, I believe?'

'An American,' I said.

*How long ago it seems
that I first saw Valencia.*

'Ah, norteamericano. How do you like Spain?'

'The fireworks last night,' was all I could manage.

'What else have you seen?'

'Teruel.'

There was a long silence, and the president softly said, 'Teruel. Not many get to Teruel,' and he was gone.

When I returned to the hotel I found that the picador had departed with Ortega's cuadrilla for a fight in some other part of Spain but had left me an envelope containing a free ticket for the novillada (a bullfight in which novices rather than full matadors appear) scheduled for that afternoon. The young matadors put on a fight of some skill even though facing bulls somewhat smaller than the full matadors had fought. Having tasted the day before the essence of bullfighting in the work of Lalanda and Ortega, I was eager to apply what I had learned to a less professional performance. I saw much that day and have often wondered who the three aspirants were. Did they go on to glory? Were they men whose names I am now familiar with? Or were they merely three more among the hundreds who manage a fight or two in Valencia or Sevilla or Córdoba and then vanish? I suppose there must be some way I could track down their names, because for that one Monday in Valencia they were proficient.

When the time came for me to leave Valencia, I reflected: I've seen the best Spain has to offer. The well-dressed businessmen. The luxurious clubs, they're as good as any in Europe. The gaiety of a first-class fiesta. Good hotels, good restaurants, good entertainment. A substantial city that seems to be well run. I've even seen the president himself, moving unguarded among his people and willing to talk with a norteamericano. I have seen Spain.

But as I rode out to the port of Valencia to rejoin my ship for the long haul back to Scotland, I could not help recalling the peasants of Teruel and the abysmal and almost terrifying poverty that was their lot. Between these two Spains, and remember that I had not yet seen the superarrogant nobility of Sevilla, there existed such a gap that I simply could not bring it into focus. It was like the test the oculist gives you when you have weak eyes: 'You will see before you two halves of a picture. Use all your muscles to make them form one single picture. Try! Try!'

Now, if the two halves are things like a countryman in Scotland as opposed to a banker in Edinburgh, there is at first a discrepancy, but as one exercises his muscles he can bring them together into one fused portrait of Scotland that is not difficult to comprehend. The countryman remains a countryman and the banker a banker, and they can stand side by side with no embarrassment. In the same way you can fuse a coal miner in Johnstown, Pennsylvania, and a storekeeper in Pittsburgh. But to fuse the rural peasant of Teruel and the rich clubman of Valencia lolling in his leather chair after a gorging meal was for me impossible, and I began at that moment to formulate that series of speculations regarding Spain which were to exercise me for the next decades. Whenever I read about Spain it was to find answers to these questions, and remember that they were posed some years before the Civil War disfigured the country. These are the questions of peace, and whenever I traveled in Spain or talked with Spaniards in America or England, I continued to study only these permanent questions. Later, after the war had ended, I applied myself to these speculations and did not torment myself with questions as to who was right or wrong in the war, for I have always regarded Spain as my second home and I have wanted to know about its enduring quality, not its current preoccupations. These are the speculations which have concerned me.

Speculation One. Spain and Italy are both peninsulas that jut out from the mainland of Europe, and in the north each is marked by mountains which formerly cut the inhabitants off from the main intellectual and political movements of the continent, but Italy was able to adjust to those continental movements and even to mold and lead them whereas Spain was not. Why? It is true that for a relatively brief period during the reigns of Carlos V and Felipe II, Spain succeeded in reversing this tradition and in governing much of Europe, but in the long run of her history she was emotionally confined to her peninsula whereas Italy was not. Why?

Speculation Two. In the period of greatness referred to above, Spain faced east toward her possessions in Italy, north toward her important holdings in the Low Countries, west toward her vast empire in the Americas and south toward involvement in Africa, but she never seemed able to make up her mind as to where her basic interests lay and thus frittered them all away. Why this indecision?

Speculation Three. During a period of some four centuries prior to 1492, Spain had shown herself more hospitable to varied cultural, religious and ethnic groups than any other major power, including those in Asia and Africa, and this tolerance appeared to be an established way of life, yet with startling speed she reversed herself and extirpated from Spanish soil all Jews, Muslims, Protestants, Illuminati and Jesuits, transforming herself into one of the most homogeneous and frightened people in the world. What accounted for this dramatic reversal?

Speculation Four. With her drive toward uniformity and centralism, why has it been Spain who has preserved so strongly a regional pattern of life? With her devotion to a royalist theory of government, why has she so persistently produced strong democratic movements? With her love of personal freedom, why has she repeatedly sought her major solutions in dictatorial forms of government, and why do these work so well with the Spanish people?

Speculation Five. Why did Spain, when she was already one of the richest countries in Europe, spend so much energy gaining control of the riches of the New World, then allowing this influx of gold and silver to generate an inflation which converted her into the poorest country in Europe and one of the poorest in the world? This is a perplexing question, for it touches upon one of the real tragedies of history and has implications for present nations. I used to consider this self-impoverishment of Spain a tragedy that could not be explained and assumed that it had occurred without anyone's being aware of the problem; but that is not so. Recent studies have proved that certain Spanish theorists in the sixteenth century understood that a sudden importation of raw wealth which had not been created by productive work within the nation would create an inflation which would bankrupt Spain, and they warned against it. But they were not listened to. Why?

Speculation Six. Prior to the industrial revolution which re-formed the face of Europe, Spain was a leader in the manufacture of quality goods, a leader in world trade and a leader in agriculture. Had she merely projected this leadership at a normal rate of growth and had she been able to make the relatively simple adjustments that were afoot throughout the rest of Europe, she would probably have remained the leader in manufacturing, trade and agriculture and might even have improved her relative position. Instead, almost consciously and with calculated arrogance, she dedicated herself to an opposite course. She hamstrung her manufacturers, restricted her trade and crippled her agriculture. Within a few generations world leadership in these crucial fields had passed into the hands of France, Germany and England, and to a lesser degree, Italy. Who can explain this extraordinary series of wrong decisions?

Speculation Seven. For several centuries Spain was one of the exciting leaders in art, music, drama, poetry, the novel, philosophy—both as producer and consumer. Then abruptly the leadership was abandoned. The traveler to Spain can have no more perplexing an experience than to visit the Prado Museum and see there the paintings of Italians like Titian, of Flemings like Roger van der Weyden and of Germans like Dürer and to realize that during the lifetimes of those men Spain was the art capital of the world, and then to search in vain for a Spanish museum which contains comparable samples of the Frenchman Cézanne, the Italian Modigliani, the Russian Soutine, the Austrian Kokoschka or the German Klee. One fails to find the work of even Spanish-speaking artists like Picasso, Miró, Orozco and Rivera. What can explain this dramatic volte-face?

Speculation Eight. No aspect of Spain is more perplexing to the foreigner than her passionate devotion to the Catholic Church, which she has defended at heavy cost in wealth and manpower, while never being reluctant to oppose the Pope when she considered him in moral or political error. Several times Spanish kings mounted armies to attack the Vatican, and both Carlos V and Felipe II, who are described in Spanish history as the nonpareils of Catholic orthodoxy, were excommunicated because of their anti-Rome behavior. Papal decrees were often refused entrance into Spain; Spanish kings and cardinals simply refused to promulgate them, and even today there is a tendency for the Spanish Church to consider one of its main tasks to 'save Rome from itself.' Such contradictory behavior is one of the continuing anomalies of Spanish history.

Speculation Nine. On my first day in Teruel I found that the contradictions I was becoming aware of could be explained only by reference to what might be termed the central mystery of Spanish psychology. How can the Spaniard, who is so outgoing, so earthy, so in love with the trivia of daily existence, be at the same time so withdrawn and inwardly mystical? In this book the reader will not find an answer to this permanent enigma, but he will find, I hope, certain illustrations of it from which he can draw his own conclusions.

In other words, to travel in Spain is not like traveling elsewhere. The people are exciting, but so are they in Greece; the land is compelling, but so is it in Norway; art forms like flamenco, the bullfight and the decoration of the central plaza are unique, but so are the art forms of Italy; and if reflections on Spanish history drive the stranger to speculation, so do reflections on German history. What makes Spain different is that here these speculations are positively unavoidable. The people are so dramatic in their simplest existence that one must identify with them, and when one does he begins to think like a Spaniard; the art forms are so persuasive that the stranger is sucked into their vortices, even against his will; and the problems of history are so gigantic and of such continuing significance that one cannot escape an intellectual involvement in them. Some travelers, of whom I am one, find also an emotional involvement in Spanish history, and when this happens we are lost, for then Spain forever haunts us as it has haunted our predecessors, Georges Bizet, Henry de Montherlant, George Borrow and Ernest Hemingway.

What I am saying is that Spain is a very special country and one must approach it with respect and with his eyes open. He must be fully aware that once he has penetrated the borders he runs the risk of being made prisoner. I believe I sensed this danger on that silvery dawn many years ago when I stood off the shore of Burriana and watched the heaving men and the straining oxen, dimly aware that in nearby Castellón there was a fiesta which awaited me and in the hills cold Teruel, which would be forever one of the principal cities of my mind. I knew then that Spain was a special land, and I have spent many subsequent trips endeavoring to unravel its peculiarities. I have not succeeded, and in this failure I am not unhappy, for Spain is a mystery and I am not at all convinced that those who live within the peninsula and were born there understand it much better than I, but that we all love the wild, contradictory, passionately beautiful land there can be no doubt.

FOLLOWING PAGE:
Cork harvester.

BADAJOZ

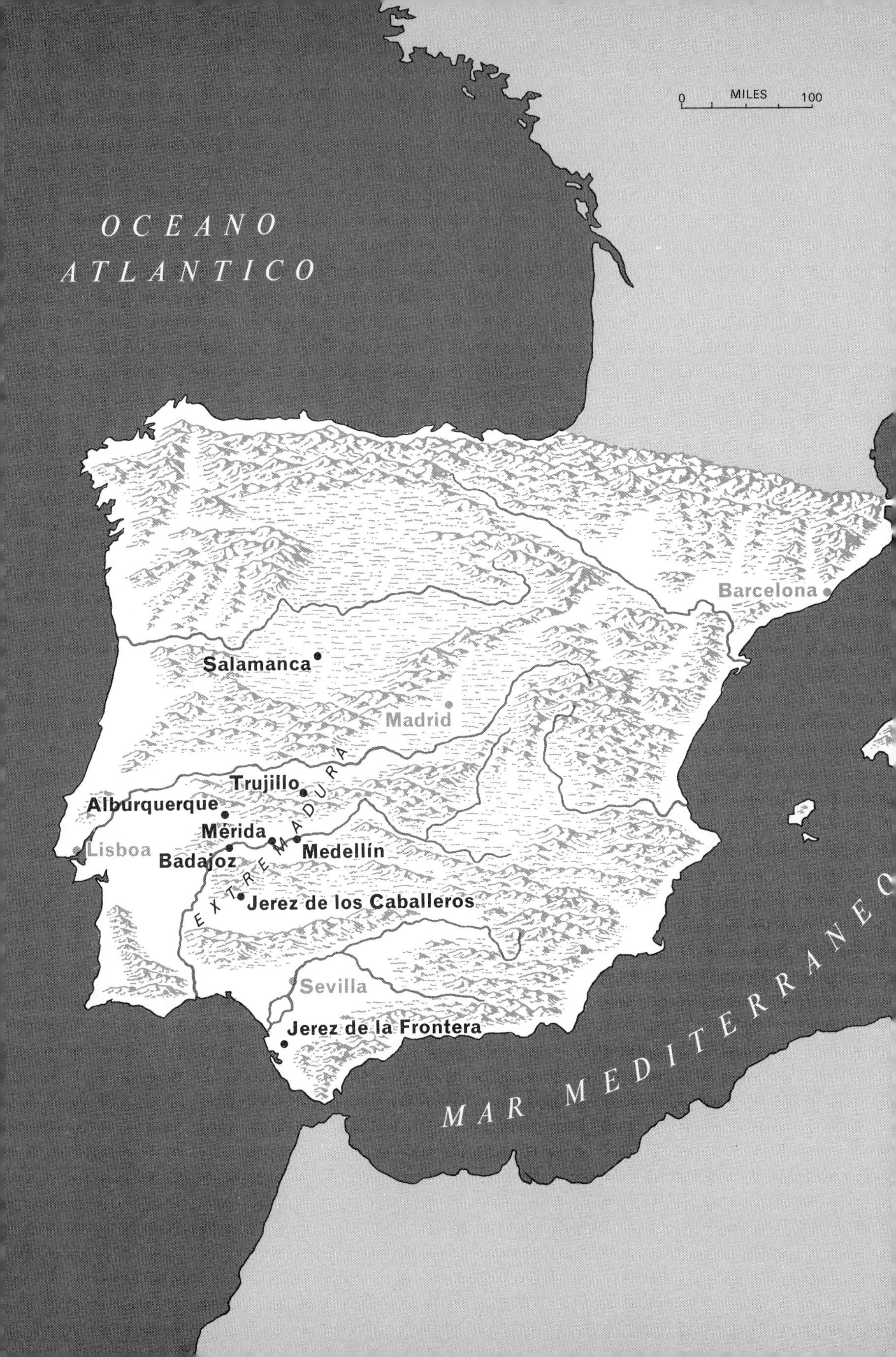

OCEANO
ATLANTICO

MAR MEDITERRANEO

MILES
0   100

Barcelona

Salamanca

Madrid

Trujillo

Alburquerque

Mérida

Lisboa

Badajoz

Medellín

EXTREMADURA

Jerez de los Caballeros

Sevilla

Jerez de la Frontera

B adajoz still lay forty miles to the north. In a hot bus that talked back to itself I was plodding through the vast region called Extremadura, that empty, rocky section of Spain lying southwest from Madrid along the Portuguese border. It was a day of intense heat, with the thermometer well above a hundred and ten. For as far as I could see there were no towns, no villages, only the brassy, shimmering heat rising up from the plains and the implacable sky without even a wisp of cloud. When dust rose, it hung in the motionless air and required minutes to fall back to the caked and burning earth. I saw no animals, no birds, no men, for they refused to venture forth in this remorseless heat.

In fact, the only thing in nature that moved was the sun, terrible and metallic as it inched its way across that indifferent sky. I was relieved therefore when the bus descended a long hill and we came to a meadow-land filled with trees, but such trees I had not seen before. They were not tall like elms, nor copious like maples. They were low, extremely sturdy, with dark gray trunks and gnarled branches that reached wide, so that each tree was given a considerable area to itself. The meadowland in between was filled with small yellow flowers, as if it were a carpet of gold, accented here and there with concentrations of white daisies and punctuated by the massive trees with their dark crowns.

I had barely inspected this pleasing landscape when the trees changed radically. Their trunks, up to a height of perhaps ten feet, turned suddenly bright orange, as if they had been painted that morning. And before I could adjust to orange-colored trees they were replaced by trunks of angry russet, then by trunks of a dark and heavy brown, and finally by trees whose trunks were the original gray I had seen at first; but all the trees, whether orange or gray, sent their limbs twisting and turning in the hot air as if they were gasping for breath.

'What is it?' I asked the driver.

'Cork forest. The bright orange means a tree that was stripped of its cork a few days ago. Enough time and the bark grows gray again.' We saw a low shed back among the spacious trees but no sign of life. 'The cork harvesters are taking a siesta,' the driver explained.

We next came to a grove with quite different trees; the trunks were badly shattered, as if the trees were dying; in some there were holes through which I could see; the branches were low and carried delicate leaves that were dark on top, silvery gray on bottom, with clusters of small black fruit. 'Olive grove,' the driver said. 'When the breeze comes through, the leaves flutter. Beautiful.' But this day there was no breeze.

Most of the land was barren, with no trees at all. The soil was rocky and red from decomposing ferrous elements. At times a stream-bed, empty of water for the past five months, crawled like a wounded snake across the plain, but often there was not even this to watch. I longed for at least a buzzard to mark that merciless sky, but none appeared. 'Sleeping,' the driver said. 'Everything is sleeping.'

We came to a village, a truly miserable collection of adobe huts clustered about an unpaved square. One bar was open, apparently, for its doors were not closed, but no men were visible behind the strands of beads that served as a curtain for keeping out the flies. Farther on there was a town, and since it was now nearly five in the afternoon people were beginning to move about, but the heat was so intense that no work was being done. It was a town that had little to commend it except its longevity; Roman legions had known this town, and when their expeditions had ended in the years before the birth of Christ, Caesar Augustus had allowed the oldest veterans to take up land here. Over the ravine at the edge of town ran a stone bridge that had been used in its present form for more than two thousand years.

'You want to stop for a drink?' the driver asked.

'Not in this town,' and we pushed on.

We came now to fields that looked as if they might have been cultivated and to a series of oak and olive forests that were well tended. 'We're getting close to Badajoz,' he said, pronouncing the word with respect. As evening approached, the heat grew more bearable and in one river valley we actually felt a breeze. We climbed a hill, turned west and saw below us the Río Guadiana, which farther on would form the border between Portugal and Spain, and in its valley stood a city without a single distinction: no towers, no ancient walls, no exciting prospects. The eastern half looked old and unrepaired; the western half, new and unrelated to the rest; and there was no apparent reason why a man in good sense would descend the hill to enter that particular city, for this was Badajoz, the nothing-city of the west. 'Precisely what I wanted,' I said.

In America when I had explained to my friends that I was heading for

Badajoz, they had shrugged their shoulders because they had never heard of it, and when I told my Spanish friends they grimaced because they had. 'For the love of Jesus, why Badajoz? It has absolutely nothing.' In Spanish this last phrase sounds quite final: 'Absolutamente nada,' with the six syllables of the first word strung out in emphasis. They tried to dissuade me from going, explaining that Badajoz was a mere depot town along the border, that it was lost in the emptiness of Extremadura, and that if I was determined to visit a remote town, why not a beauty like Murcia near the Mediterranean, or Jaén in the mountains, or Oviedo, where the relics of Christ were kept? 'Why Badajoz?'

Why indeed? I had not tried to explain, but there was an explanation and a good one. When I heard the word Spain, I visualized not kings and priests, nor painters and hidalgos, nor Madrid and Sevilla, but the vast reaches of emptiness, lonely uplands occupied by the solitary shepherd, the hard land of Spain stretching off to interminable distances and populated by tough, weatherbeaten men with never a ruffle at their throats nor a caparisoned horse beneath them. In short, when I thought of Spain, I thought primarily of Extremadura, the brutal region in the west, of which Badajoz was the principal city.

There was a reason. Apart from my first brief visit to Castellón de la Plana and Teruel as a student, my introduction to Spain had come in the American southwest, in the empty areas of New Mexico, Arizona, Texas and California, where the Spanish impact had been great. To me, a Spaniard was a man like Coronado, who had ventured into Kansas in 1541. Hernando de Soto and Cabeza de Vaca were my Spaniards and the unknown men who settled Santa Fe and Taos. The Spain I had known in western United States was a heroic Spain, the Spanish landscape with which I was familiar reached at least four hundred miles in any given direction over largely empty land. To have been a Spaniard in those early days in New Mexico and Arizona signified, and the closest approach to that Spain in the home country was Extremadura.

My second contact with Spain was different. I had spent considerable time in Mexico and at one period or another had lived in all but two of its states, always seeing Mexico as a land that had been discovered, occupied, developed and ruined by Spaniards. I knew well the routes traveled by Hernán Cortés in his conquest of the Aztecs, and I had studied those haunting plateresque churches built by his followers in towns where silver was mined. There were few Spanish buildings in Mexico that I had not explored, and some of the happiest days of my youth were those spent in drifting across the plateaus of Chihuahua or exploring the jungles west of Vera Cruz. But whenever I looked at Mexico, I saw Spain. Mexican culture was meaningful only as an extension of Spanish culture, and the cyclones of Mexican political history were merely a reflection of the home country.

Early in my study I discovered that most of the Spanish heroes who had operated in the Americas had come from Extremadura. The New World was won for Spain not by gentlemen from Toledo and Sevilla but by a group of uneducated village louts who, realizing that they had no future in their hard homeland, had volunteered for service overseas, where their Extremaduran courage proved the most valuable commodity carried westward by the Spanish galleons.

Extremadura was my Spain, and no one who had missed my experiences in New Mexico and Old could appreciate what Badajoz meant to me, but when I saw this unlovely, battered town, called Pax Augusta by the Romans, and when I saw about me the suspicious, dour Extremadurans, whose ancestors had conquered not cities but whole nations and continents, I felt that I had come back to my own land.

My first experience in the city proved that I was in Extremadura. The hotel to which I had been sent was dark and mean and tucked away on a side street. The clerk growled, 'We can let you have a small room for tonight. Fifty pesetas.' This was eighty-three cents and I judged I could go a little higher, so I said, 'I'll be here for a month, so if you have a larger room . . .'

'A month! In that case the room will be sixty pesetas.'

This confused me, and I started to explain that elsewhere if a man stayed for a month the price went down, not up, but he stopped me. 'We don't want people coming here. We have too many already.' I looked about the dark lobby and saw no one. I was about to point this out when he snapped, 'You can't have a room for a month. Nobody can have a room for a whole month.' He looked at me suspiciously, as if to ask, 'Why would a foreigner want to stay in Badajoz for a month?'

My second experience was one that I look back upon with affection. Through the warm night I walked to the main square and asked a policeman where a hungry man could get a decent meal, and he took me by the arm and said, 'There's only one place—Restaurante Colón. And you'll thank me later.' He led me to an old narrow building whose face had recently been lifted with purple plastic, chrome and neon. I hesitated but he pushed me in, and I found a menu which offered a bewildering selection: green plate, gray plate, black plate, ivory plate and white plate, each for about a dollar twenty. When the waiter came, a very tall, thin Extremaduran, he grabbed the menu away and whispered, 'If you want the best, take the zarzuela.' I was pretty sure I knew what a zarzuela was, so I asked, 'How's that again?' And he growled, 'Take the zarzuela.'

A zarzuela, unless I was out of my mind, was what I had seen in Castellón de la Plana, a short Spanish-type musical comedy in which the songs are closer to opera than those of an American musical. I had seen some good zarzuelas and had enjoyed them, but now I was being asked to eat one.

I must have shown my apprehension, because the waiter said an extraordinary thing: 'My friend, if you trust in the goodness of God, take the zarzuela.' Such advice I could not ignore, so I nodded, fearing the worst.

Instead I got the best: a ramekin containing olive oil, a judicious amount of garlic, some baked potatoes, chopped onions, pimientos, tomatoes and a heavenly assortment of shrimp, crayfish, squid, octopus, hake and filet of sole, all done to a golden brown and served with croutons and an effervescent white wine. It was a savory introduction to Badajoz and I had to agree with the waiter that sometimes the goodness of God must be trusted.

When I finished, it was still light and I had no intention of going back to my gloomy hotel. I decided instead to stroll through the streets of Badajoz and to see with a fresh eye how a Spanish city looked. I wanted, as it were, to build a base of understanding to which I could add as I visited the nine other cities of my projected tour, and in retrospect I am glad that I did this, because if one understands Badajoz he will understand Spain.

The Restaurante Colón stood on the main plaza, and as I left it I faced the cathedral, a low, squat ugly building built many centuries ago and one of the least attractive in Spain. It carried a square tower of no distinction, decorated by nine urns on each side, looking like the battlements of a fortress and not a cathedral. Eight bells hung in the tower, but during my stay I did not hear them ring. The massive walls had no Gothic windows, nor did they carry any ornamentation to relieve their drabness. The building was entered by a sadly inappropriate door flanked by four Ionic columns which some architect had added in the eighteenth century in an attempt to dress up the façade, and on the great slab-sided front facing the plaza appeared the two words which I would see carved into the walls of churches all across Spain: JOSE ANTONIO. The letters were accompanied by seventeen laurel wreaths cast in rusting iron.

Although the cathedral was unusually ugly it conveyed a sense of dignity, for it was a frontier church-fortress, and only the security which it provided had allowed Badajoz to survive its sieges and attacks. It was then and remained now the center of Badajoz life, and the society which it supervised was much like it: ancient, unornamented, solid and well able to protect itself.

The plaza which the cathedral dominated was small and awkward and as undistinguished a main square as I would see in Spain. There were old buildings of no quality and others like the Restaurante Colón whose face-lifted façades gleamed garishly in plastic and neon. The Banco Mercantil had recently been redone in ultramodern style and looked rather handsome. Its windows were low, and to keep idlers from sitting on the sills, the latter were decorated with sharp, tall spikes. The six white columns of the Palacio Municipal supported a balcony ready for an orator who never came.

What was the chief characteristic of the plaza? That it was jammed with automobiles and had the same parking problem as Rome, London or New York. The parking of cars was supervised by a corps of crippled war veterans who collected their fee whenever a car drew up to the curb. Traffic through the very narrow streets leading into the plaza was constant and was guided by policemen with a good sense of humor. Every four or five minutes large buses passed through the square on various routes which took them to all parts of the suburbs. The buses hauled large numbers of passengers, as they did throughout Spain.

Having completed a rapid survey of the plaza, I closed my eyes and asked, 'Is there anything here that would prove I am in Spain?' I looked again, and apart from the obvious signs in Spanish, saw nothing that would betray the origin of this city. It could have been Italy, or southern France, or even rural Texas. I want to make this point secure because travelers often expect strange cities to look a certain way, but with modern technology, architecture and traffic most of them look alike. If I had tried this test of 'Where am I?' in the plazas of the villages and towns of southern Extremadura the answer would have been, 'This can only be Spain,' but in the cities, no. They are international.

Yet even as I said this I saw two minor things that would have betrayed a Spanish origin. At the far end of the plaza stood a statue to the painter Luis Morales (1509–1586) and in the next small square another statue to another painter, Francisco Zurbarán (1598–1664). Spain is inordinately proud of its painters and writers. The Spanish jet which had brought me from New York bore the name *El Greco* and I tried to imagine an American plane, patronized by our businessmen, bearing the name *Jackson Pollock*. And on one of the plaza walls stood the type of marble plaque common in Spain. This one recalled the salient event of recent Spanish history, the Civil War:

SPAIN

CONQUEROR OF COMMUNISM

IN THE CRUSADE WHICH BEGAN THIS DAY

TO ENSURE PEACE FOR THE EMPIRE.

FOR UNITY, FOR GREATNESS, FOR LIBERTY

IN THE SIGN OF FRANCO, THE CAUDILLO.

¡ARRIBA ESPAÑA!

17–18–19 JULY 1936

When I left the plaza I entered the old part of Badajoz, and was delighted with the narrow streets and the memories of Spain as it used to be. This was a pleasing part of town and here I was not in Rome or Texas. This was authentic Spain, but when I moved to the west and to the area of big new buildings, sprawling schools and hospitals, I might once more have been in any modern European city. Taken building by building, Badajoz was a respectable-looking city, clean, well organized and modern. Homes, stores, theaters, the lesser churches and the public offices were about what one would expect in a city of similar size in Italy or France. Beauty there was not, but solidity there was. There was also evidence that the citizens had money, for whenever in my tour I reached a high point of ground, I saw numerous television aerials; sets in the city could bring in both Portuguese and Spanish programs.

What kind of people lived in Badajoz? I returned to the main plaza and found an outdoor table, where I sat for some hours simply looking at the passers-by, and as the cooler temperatures of evening arrived a good many people appeared for their nightly stroll. As to the girls, they looked exactly like girls of similar age in New York or London. They wore the same amount of make-up, the same length of dress, the same hairdos. They giggled in the same way at private jokes, and when they walked with young men they held hands and sometimes kissed in public. If the young women gave no signs of being Spanish, certain of the older women did, but only because they wore much more black than I would have found in England or America.

Young men looked exactly like their cousins around the western world. In dress they were wholly indistinguishable from boys their age in Chicago or Mexico City, except that not many wore their hair long. They did, however, carry transistor radios, which they used as abusively as young people elsewhere. Spaniards are conservative in dress and this became especially noticeable when I studied the older men, for of all groups they alone did betray the fact that they were Spanish, but only because they wore extremely somber clothes. I saw not a single sport shirt, nor a blazer, nor even a light-colored suit of any kind.

In facial appearance I could not detect among the young any characteristics that would brand them as Spanish, but as both the girls and boys grew older a certain Spanish look did seem to appear; I mentioned this to an Englishman whom I met later, and he said, 'You're wrong. If you put a hundred of the older people in various European cities, you'd not be able to identify them. France, Italy, Greece, Turkey would absorb them without your knowing. Sweden and Finland? No. The Spaniards are a little darker than the European average and against the blonds of those two countries they'd be conspicuous.'

One point I must make clear. You could sit in the plaza at Badajoz for three months and see no women trailing by in mantillas. You'd see no castanets, no high ivory combs, no colorful shawls tied about the waist. Nor would you see any men dressed like Don Quixote or conquistadors. No bands of guitarists gather at midnight, wrapped in cloaks, to serenade women behind iron grilles, and the Spanish types one sees in *Carmen* are visible only in the bullring, where in the infrequent fights matadors dress as they did a century ago.

Yet certain trivial customs create a Spanish atmosphere. There being little public assistance as we know it in America, it is traditional for blind people to roam the streets selling lottery tickets; cripples park cars or peddle things, and consequently one sees more deformity in Spain than he would elsewhere. There is, however, no begging. Shoeshine boys are also more numerous, but usually they are grown men who move endlessly from one café table to the next, calling '¿Limpia?' (Shall I clean?), so that in the course of two hours one could have his shoes shined by ten or fifteen different men.

One of the sure signs that this is Spain is the number of young married women who have allowed themselves to get fat. On my first night in Badajoz, I estimated that Spanish women of thirty years and older weighed about twenty pounds more than American or French women of comparable age and social background. I commented on this to a Spaniard, and he said approvingly, 'It's one of the most beautiful sights in Spain. To sit in the plaza at dusk and watch the fat married women roll by with their husbands and children. It's beautiful because in Spain, once a woman is married, she never again has to fight the dinner table. She has her man and nothing on earth can take him away from her, so she doesn't give a damn how fat she gets. In Spain there's no divorce and her children cannot be taken away nor her home either. She's safe. Of course, her husband will probably take a mistress. Three-fourths of the fine Spanish gentlemen you've been meeting and enjoying so much have mistresses. But they'd have them whether their wives were slim or fat. So our women eat and love their children and go to the movies and gossip and put their faith in the Church, and to hell with dieting, and you won't find a more contented group of women in the world.'

The newspapers for sale in the plaza were a strange lot. Generalísimo Franco, the country's dictator, was an old man and his successor had not been determined, and this was a matter which might decide the fate of Spain, but public discussion of this vital problem was forbidden, and to read the papers in Badajoz one would have felt that the general was going to live forever. I am speaking here of 1961, shortly after the inauguration of President Kennedy, when American newspapers were already speculating on what might happen in the 1964 election, and especially the 1968, but of Spain's greater problem there was no discussion. In place of political news the papers offered reams of fine writing on sports, many columns on the Church, emphasizing the activities of the Pope, and because the men who owned the newspapers were monarchists, a constant stream of stories about how European countries that lived under kings were better off than those that didn't.

The marriage of Prince Carlos of Bourbon to Princess Ana, daughter of the Count of Paris, was characterized by its simplicity.

Will Princess Benedicta of Denmark never find a husband? There is still hope, but available men are few and for the present she loves only horses.

Queen Isabel of England, on her forthcoming visit to Germany, will decide what shall be served at state banquets. Even though Prince Felipe of Edinburgh loves lobsters, none will be served because Isabel prefers little German sausages.

One got the feeling that the Spaniards would have enjoyed arguing politics in their papers, but it was forbidden, so they satisfied themselves with sports and religion and the doings of distant royalty.

And so it went. Badajoz was Spain, and no place else. It was sharply different from Portugal, which lay only four miles away, but it was not an exaggerated Spain, not a musical-comedy land at all.

In the morning I set out to visit random stores to see for myself what it would cost a Spaniard to live in Badajoz as compared with what I paid at home. I started by listing the dinner I'd had at the Colón:

Item	*Badajoz*	*U.S.A.*
First-class dinner	$ 1.20	$ 4.50
Hotel room	.83	14.00
Man's shoes	8.00	10.00
Child's schoolbag	.50	1.50
Woman's slip	1.60	4.00
Two-piece woman's suit	30.00	75.00
Kelvinator refrigerator	235.00	160.00
Woman's blouse	6.50	8.00
Man's suit	37.00	75.00
Wash-and-dry shirt	8.00	6.00
Slide rule	11.50	22.50
Fine girl's sweater	5.00	12.00
Man's haircut	.25	2.50
Calico dress	7.50	10.00
Girl's cosmetic kit	1.30	1.50
Cheap ball-point pen	.07	.29

When one considers that the average wage in Spain is sharply lower than that in the United States, these prices are on the high side, but remember that recurring costs like food and lodging are much cheaper in Spain. Also, practically anything available anywhere in the world is available in Spain. I saw Norwegian sweaters, Italian shoes, Argentinian wool, German scissors and French encyclopedias—all within a few minutes.

Consider the case of the fish market where I spent a morning talking with the proprietor and his stream of customers. It was run by Armando

Olivera and stood at the busy corner of Sepúlveda and López Prudencio. At first sight it looked as if it would offer three or four kinds of inexpensive fish; in fact, it had more than thirty. Señora Gutiérrez wanted some hake, brought that morning by truck from Huelva on the Atlantic. Señora Meléndez plumped her shopping bag on the marble counter and said she wanted a bagful of backbone joints from the huge swordfish that had come from Portugal. She was making a fish stew and the joints contained much meat, but when the package was weighed and paid for, sixteen cents, Olivera chucked in an extra slice of pure meat, for which he was thanked.

At least half the fish available in this shop was frozen, much of it coming from Norway and Germany. I was surprised to see in the freezer a large selection of whole frozen chickens from Denmark, butter from Ireland and frozen meat pies from England, all at prices sharply lower than they would have been in America.

Spain makes it easy for the foreigner to convert his dollars into pesetas. In even the smallest town, if it has a bank, one can cash his traveler's checks with ease. In Badajoz there were, I judged, about fifteen banks or offices which performed this service. I used the Banco Mercantil, the exterior of whose building had impressed me during my survey of the plaza. Inside, it was as brisk and bright as a new branch bank in Omaha and much more so than one in Glasgow. I presented my check and passport to a young man, who greeted me in English. In less than a minute he typed out slip #453, handed half to me and passed the other half along to three different officials, who initialed it and handed it to the teller, a very busy man. I waited in a long line while the teller dealt with slips #440 to 452. Finally he called, 'Cuatro cientos cincuenta y tres.' I presented my matching half of the slip and he counted out the money. 'We are pleased to have you in Spain,' he said in Spanish.

I was eager to find out what an average day for a Spanish businessman consisted of, and on one of my walks I came upon the Casino de Badajoz, a distinguished men's club whose broad plate-glass windows, fronting on the main street, were always occupied by gentlemen who seemed to do nothing but ogle the passing girls. Without any kind of introduction I entered the club and explained my problem to the major-domo, who grasped the situation at once, offered me a beer and summoned a club official, a delightful talker whose monologue I shall repeat as he gave it:

'This club is the heart of Badajoz. Very old, very honorable. It costs thirty dollars to join and twenty dollars a year dues, but the waiting list is so long you'd not have a chance right now. As a foreign visitor, however, you would be most welcome on a temporary basis. On the second floor, the big television room. Next to it our enormous ballroom. These red and white

This fat pig, fed on acorns from the forests of Extremadura, has been dead for two years and may hang proudly in the butcher's window for another two before it is eaten. Price in Spain, twenty-three cents a pound.

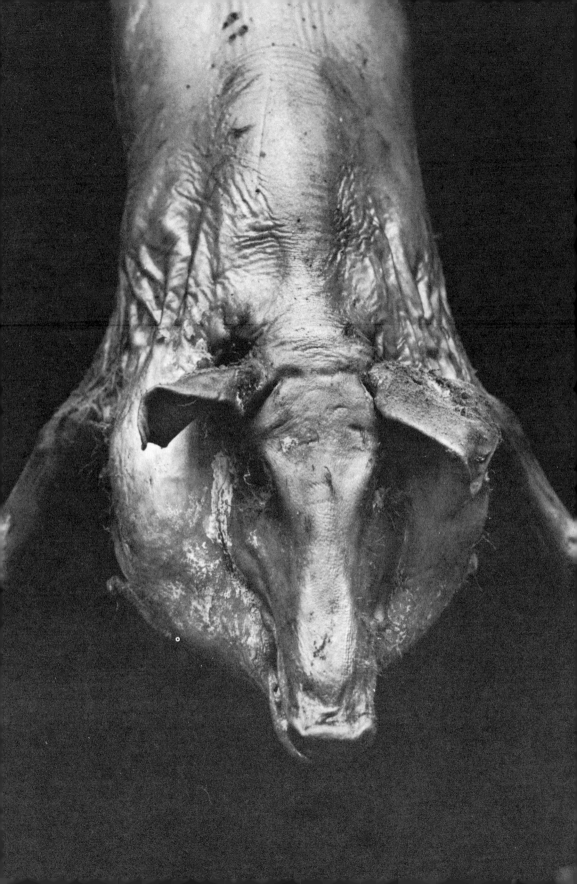

furnishings, the mirrors, the red plush boxes, the stucco figures on the ceiling . . . we think these lend a touch of elegance. I don't know who carved that "Venus Holding a Mirror" or the huge "Judgment of Paris," but they're old and familiar and lend a sense of permanence. We have four floors here, all marble, a barbershop, billiards. At the green tables in this game room a lot of money has been won and lost. The bar, the library. We get papers from all over Spain and Paris too. Our restaurant used to do a large trade, now the snack room does more. We offer much to attract children and in the evening women are welcomed too. But, as you can guess, it's this big front room that establishes the quality of the club. In the course of a week you'll see in this room all the men who run Badajoz. You might almost say Extremadura. Even the soldiers and the priests you'll see here. It is marble, has those five impressive front windows, the big comfortable leather chairs. The large painting shows a country wooing. I think the man is playing an oboe. But this is the heart of the club. This is the room that means more than home to the men of Badajoz.

'No, the man you ask about is not from Badajoz. You see, each city in Spain has one top club like this, and if you belong to it in your home town, you automatically have privileges in all the others. The man you're looking at is from Sevilla.

'You want to know what the average day of a club member is? You must remember that these are well-to-do men, the leaders of Badajoz, and this is an agricultural region. So your average man would have to be a farmer. Let's take that one in the big chair, staring out the window. His name is . . . we'll call him Señor Don Pedro Pérez Montilla. He lives about twenty miles south of here. Has one large plantation of cork trees, another where he grows wheat, some pigs and sheep. About two thousand acres altogether. Has three cars. An English Land Rover to get about the plantation, a Spanish SEAT 1500 for his own driving and a SEAT 600 for the rest of his family. Of course, he never drives himself. Has a driver who does that. He must rise rather early, for in the morning, after breakfast of a roll, some coffee and a glass of anís (anisette), he supervises his farms. But every day he reaches this club not later than twelve-thirty. Plays dominoes in the back room. Talks with his friends. About two-thirty in the afternoon he drives back to his farm, makes his lunch on soup, eggs and potatoes, meat and fruit and takes his siesta. He's back at the club by six-thirty and always sits in the chair you see him in now.

'At that time he's joined by three other men, whom he's known for forty years. They form what we call a tertulia. That's an informal club that meets every day to gossip. What about? Don Pedro's tertulia are all farmers, so they talk about cork and olives and sheep and whether a Land Rover is better than a Jeep. Yes, every day for forty years that's what they've talked about. Politics not very often. Religion never, because all four men in the tertulia know what the others think on those subjects.

Sometimes no one speaks for forty minutes. When that happens they all look out the window at the pretty girls in the paseo. The tertulia meets in those four chairs till about ten at night, when Don Pedro drives back to the farm for his dinner of consommé and tortilla [in Mexico, a flat unleavened bread of maize; in Spain, a potato omelet]. A man like Don Pedro would never eat in a restaurant, but one night four years ago he did invite a guest to the farm for dinner.

'Don Pedro reads the *ABC* each morning, but nothing else. He goes to the movies only when they show Gary Cooper or John Wayne. He has two fine daughters who went for a while to the convent school, but now they're waiting for someone to marry them. Don Pedro would probably not allow them to marry a man whose family did not belong to our club. Otherwise where would the new family fit in?'

A word about Spanish names. To explain the tradition fully would require many pages, for it is unbelievably complicated, but ideally every Spaniard, male or female, has two surnames, the first and more important being the father's and the second the mother's. Thus Pedro Pérez Montilla can properly be referred to as Señor Pérez Montilla or simply as Señor Pérez, but to refer to him as Señor Montilla would be a real gaffe. Spanish also has the handy little words Don and Doña, which have no equivalent in English and cannot be translated; they are used only preceding a given name, allowing one to refer to a man or woman by the given name with no presumption of intimacy. Thus our friend can be called Don Pedro or Señor Don Pedro Pérez Montilla. When he married, let us say to Leocadia Blanco Alvarez, his wife did not surrender her surnames but merely added his, preceded by the preposition de (of), so that her name became Señora Leocadia Blanco Alvarez de Pérez Montilla, and she may properly be addressed as Doña Leocadia, or as Señora Blanco, or as Señora Blanco Alvarez, or as Señora Blanco Alvarez de Pérez Montilla, or as Señora de Pérez Montilla. Frequently the paternal and maternal surnames are joined by either a hyphen or an y (and), which means that Don Pedro's son could be named Antonio Pérez Blanco, or Antonio Pérez-Blanco, or Antonio Pérez y Blanco, although in recent years the last has become less frequent. Many Spaniards today, in common usage, simply omit the maternal surname entirely or abbreviate it to a single letter. On the other hand, if Don Pedro and Doña Leocadia belong to the nobility or the aristocracy (or if they want to put on airs) the son will adopt the name Señor Don Antonio Pérez Montilla y Blanco Alvarez.

The problem is further complicated when a man has a family name which is unusually common and a maternal name which is less so, for then he becomes known by the more distinctive of his two names, which is only sensible. The five most common Spanish surnames, in order of frequency, are García, Fernández, López, González and Rodríguez, and just as the Englishman named Smith or Jones is accustomed to adding a

hyphenated second name, such as Smith-Robertson, so the Spaniard becomes García Montilla, sometimes with the hyphen. It is in conformity
with this custom that the great Spanish poet Federico García Lorca is so
often referred to simply by his maternal name. Anglo-Saxon readers encounter difficulties with the names of such historical figures as Spain's two
cardinals who exercised political leadership, Mendoza and Cisneros; in
history books you will find many pages about them, and they were at least
as famous as Richelieu in France and Wolsey in England, yet if you try to
look them up in a Spanish encyclopedia you will find nothing unless you
happen to know that the former was born Pedro González de Mendoza
and the latter Gonzalo Jiménez de Cisneros. In each of these instances,
however, the distinctive name is not maternal but merely a place name
added in hopes of making a common name distinctive. So far I have
discussed only the simple cases; the complicated ones I had better skip.

In a small Spanish city to which a friend had sent me a postal money
order I had a rueful introduction to this problem of names. My friend had
assured me by phone that the money had been sent, and the post office had
advised me that it had arrived and that upon presentation of my passport
it would be paid. Accordingly, I went to the post office, but before telling the
clerk my name, handed him my passport. He studied it, consulted his file
of incoming money orders and said, 'Nothing here.' I explained that I knew
it was in hand, so with much politeness he searched his papers again and
said, 'Nothing here.' This time I noticed that he was looking in the *A* file,
so I suggested, 'Perhaps if you look in the . . .'

'Please, Señor Albert,' he said. 'I know my business.'

In my passport he had seen that my name was James Albert Michener
and he was smart enough to know from that who I was, and he had no
cash for any Señor Albert. When I tried to explain what my name really
was he became angry, and I was not able to get my money until Spanish
friends came from the hotel to the post office and explained who I was.
When the money was paid, the clerk took my passport again, studied my
name and shook his head. When he handed back my papers he said, 'I am
sorry for your inconvenience, Señor Albert.'

The nightly paseo which Don Pedro watches from his window is
common to most Spanish cities, but in Badajoz it has special features because the city has not one main plaza but two. Plaza San Juan, which faces
the cathedral, we've seen, but Plaza Generalísimo Franco, the larger of the
two, we have not. They are connected by the street that runs past the big
windows of Don Pedro's Casino de Badajoz, so that what in other cities is
called 'a turn about the plaza' becomes in Badajoz a substantial march:
back and forth along Plaza San Juan, down the long street past the Casino,
then around the Plaza Franco, where band concerts are held from eight to
ten.

Badajoz, as seen from this latter plaza at night, is a delightful city.

'These gardens are for all and are to be cared for by all,' states a large sign beneath which iron tables are set out for groups of eight or ten teen-agers. Nursemaids in starched uniforms parade up and down with infants in carriages, and a host of children under six play among the trees till midnight. 'They've been taking a siesta all afternoon,' a mother explains. At the corners of the park semicircular benches made of bright tile are occupied by soldiers and their dates, while at the tables along the outer edges men sit in groups talking about the same topics that are being discussed in the Casino. At ten-thirty or eleven the older people wander home for dinner, and the long day ends.

In all but one of the cities discussed in this book I will be drawing upon recollections of more than one visit. I have been to Badajoz four different times, to Madrid about twenty, to Sevilla a dozen, to Teruel two; it was not until my last visit to Spain that I saw Barcelona for the first time. Of the various things I was to see in Badajoz, I think the most meaningful occurred during my first visit when I was standing idly in Plaza Franco toward midnight as the stragglers were heading home. A married couple named Serrano were seated at the table next to mine, and as I rose to go back to my hotel the man said, 'You're not going to miss the cathedral?' I asked why not, and he said, 'Because it's May 13.' I asked what was special about that date, and he said, 'Come and see.'

We walked back to the cathedral, where families were entering the ugly main portal accompanied by more than a hundred young people. I entered the dark interior; little boys in robes were handing out lighted candles that produced marvelous shadows across the low-vaulted ceiling. The interior of the cathedral was even more depressing visually than the exterior, for late in the life of the church some enthusiastic canon had built a choir and plastered its walls with a cheap stucco that was supposed to look like cut stone. The four bottom rows were painted a dirty beige, the nine top, a sickly puce. But spiritually the interior had the same bold force that I had observed in the cathedral as a whole; I was inside a great fortress which contained no nonsense or embellishment. In time of peace worshipers came here to pray; in time of war to defend themselves.

At midnight bells tolled and five dignitaries of the church in full regalia conducted a service which I could not understand. 'It's not a mass,' the Serranos told me. 'It's an invocation to the Virgin.' There was a moment of silence as the hundreds of candles flickered, and then Señor Serrano whispered, 'It's May 13. The Virgin of Fátima. We're very close to Portugal, you know.'

When the praying stopped I assumed that the services were over, but they were just beginning, for now a procession formed at the altar and left the cathedral, entering the dark city, and all who bore candles fell in line and began a solemn march down Calle del Obispo San Juan de Ribera, through the silent Plaza Franco and out into the suburbs lying to the northwest. The procession consisted of some four or five hundred worshipers, perhaps as many as a thousand, for it stretched a long distance. At the head marched a priest with an electronic bullhorn, through which he sang endlessly in a husky voice,

'Ave, Ave, Ave Maria,
Ave, Ave, Ave Maria . . .'

until all marchers took up the chant and Badajoz echoed with praises of the Virgin.

Through the darkness we approached a tall building some seven or eight stories high which was used as a girls' school; it was-dark and silent, but as the priests at the head of our column reached its doors, suddenly from the roof several hundred girls in white lit their candles and began chanting, 'Ave, Ave, Ave Maria.' The effect was stunning. The marchers stopped. The priest with the bullhorn sang no more, but the girls' voices, drifting through the night, lent the procession a religious quality that was profoundly moving. Quietly word passed along the column, 'Proceed,' and in silence we left the school, from which the echoes of chanting could long be heard.

Now we were in the country, toward two o'clock in the morning, and a three-quarter moon lit our way, so that we could see the trees and the towers of some building about a mile distant. The priest with the bullhorn resumed his chant and finally we came to a halt before a building, which I never did identify. Its front contained many balconies which were jammed with monks and nuns, and everyone bared his head as the priests who had led us from the cathedral began a service in praise of Our Lady of Fátima. It was a solemn, deeply moving moment, and many knelt.

In the days that followed I was reminded again of the first essential for anyone who wishes to understand Spain: in every manifestation of life Spain is a Catholic country, and if citizens are willing to march several miles at midnight to honor the Virgin, they are equally willing to abide her surveillance in daily life. Down the street from the Casino de Badajoz stands an old palace at present converted into the offices of the diocese, from which the schools of Badajoz are supervised. The walls contain graduation pictures from the College of Our Lady of Carmen, in which, by Spanish tradition, the boys are dressed as admirals of the fleet and the girls as queens with tiaras, except that the boy who gained top grades is dressed as a fifteenth-century grandee with lace ruffs. There is no education not under the control of the Church and its orientation is to the past.

On the door of the parish church nearby hangs a poster classifying the motion pictures to be shown in Badajoz this week:

The National Catholic Confederation of Heads of Families.
Remember these classifications:
Class 1.   For everyone, including children
Class 2.   For those fourteen and above

Class 3.   For those eighteen and above
Class 3-R. For those eighteen and above, but watch out
Class 4.   Gravely perilous to morals

These restrictions apply in all dioceses and cannot be changed by any officials in those dioceses.

Of the forthcoming pictures only one was in Class 1, *The Sound of Music*, called in Spanish *Smiles and Tears*. *Return from the Ashes*, with Samantha Eggar and Maximilian Schell, was condemned for stressing 'lust, adultery, illicit relations, crime and sadism. On one church door I saw this condemnation of an especially bad show: 'This should be seen only by those ninety-four and above.'

One experience especially demonstrated the force of Catholicism in Spain. I had taken a long walk out into the country on a narrow road that led to Olivenza, and on the way back I stopped to inspect a group of clean, good-looking buildings called the Maternity Hospital of the Virgin of Solitude, and as I stood at the gate a man came out whose wife had just been admitted and we spoke of the good work such hospitals did.

'Who runs them?' I asked.

'The Church. Who else?'

'Are there any public hospitals?'

'I don't know what you mean. The Church gives us our hospitals and schools. Don't they give you hospitals and schools in your country?'

'We provide such things with taxation.'

He pondered this for some moments, then asked, 'You mean the government taxes you for what the Church gives us? You have to pay for them out of your own pocket?'

I tried to explain that in many countries, England and Germany for instance, taxes provided schools, but he interrupted, grabbing me by the arm. 'Tell me, would sensible men trust politicians to run a hospital? The Church you can trust.' He was unable to imagine a society which operated on a system of taxation, and his final question was, 'You mean to say you allow politicians to teach your children? The Church you can trust, but not those others.'

In Badajoz I also learned something about the government of Spain. At the post office I purchased ten air-letter forms and paid six pesetas (ten cents) each for them. I went back to the cathedral plaza and spent most of one morning writing ten letters, a job I find difficult, for words do not come easily to me. The next day I took the ten letters to the post office to mail, but a clerk refused them, saying, 'The price of air-letter forms went up this morning from six pesetas to ten.'

'All right. Give me ten four-peseta stamps and I'll stick them on the letters.'

'We can't do that, sir, because it states very clearly on the form that if anything whatever is enclosed in the form or added to it, it will be sent by regular post.'

45

'Then let me give you the difference, and you stamp them as having ten pesetas.'

'There's no provision for that, sir.'

'Then what can I do? Mail them as they are and let them go regular mail?'

'No, because they're no longer legal. They've been declassified.'

'It took me a long time to write these letters. How can I mail them?'

'Take each one. Place it inside an airmail envelope. Readdress the envelope and place twelve pesetas' worth of stamps in the corner and mail it as a regular air-mail letter.'

This I did, and the letters were delivered in various countries, but I was so astounded by the procedure that I called upon a high government official to ask how such things could happen. His answer was revealing. 'The clerk did right. The forms you bought were valid yesterday. Today they're not. Each form states clearly that nothing may be added, so there was no way to mail the old forms.'

I pointed out that in half a dozen different countries, including my own, I'd faced this problem and it had always been a simple matter to paste on the additional postage, at which he said, 'In other countries, yes. But no nation in the world is so difficult to govern as Spain. No people are so fundamentally anarchistic as the Spanish. Therefore, when we say that nothing may be stuck on the envelope we have got to mean it. If we fluctuated on this point, we might be driven to fluctuate on others. The Spaniard understands when the clerk stands fast. If the clerk once wavered, he might be dead the next day.'

'But it's so unfair! You sell the forms one day and cancel them the next, with no redress.'

'My friend. The whole affair cost you what? Ten times six pesetas. About one dollar American. That's money lost, and it's too bad. But you will talk about this everywhere in Spain and word will filter out to many people. And they'll say, "See! Our government means just what it says, even with foreigners." Your loss will do much good, by friend. Because we Spaniards are devils to govern.'

That is why, throughout Spain, one sees so many members of the Guardia Civil, always in pairs, as I had seen them in Teruel. No truth in Spain is more difficult for the traveler to ascertain than that regarding these men, who are in effect the masters of rural Spain and men of tremendous power in all society. I shall recite seven stories for which I can personally vouch, having either witnessed the incident or known the persons involved.

An American couple working at a United States Navy base could not find quarters on the base but did find a comfortable house in a nearby town. They had a thirteen-year-old daughter who went to the local school. One Thursday the parents arranged for her to be picked up by friends at the base and to stay with them overnight. At five o'clock that afternoon two officers of the Guardia Civil appeared, saying, 'Señora, your daughter has not passed our headquarters this day. Is there trouble?' It is said that every human being who lives in the Spanish countryside must be personally known to the guardia, who are able to report on that person's movements, ideas and behavior.

An Englishman driving a small car of British make had a breakdown on a lonely road out of Salamanca. A pair of guardia walked by, ascertained his trouble, walked on to a telephone, called their headquarters twenty miles away, directed the guardia there to find at some garage a part for the British car, then walked back to the Englishman and stayed with him until a passing truck driver dropped off the part.

An Englishwoman staggered into an Extremaduran town with a terrifying tale. She had been in a little village where a gang of gypsies had molested her, trying to steal her purse. Two officers came on the scene and began to rough the gypsies up, whereupon the latter, fed up with previous pressure from the Guardia Civil, cut their throats to the neckbone. Someone from the village ran to report the murders to a neighboring Guardia station, whereupon four pairs of guardia climbed into a truck, drove to the scene of the murder, threw a cordon around the gypsy encampment and proceeded to machine-gun every human being therein.

The weekly bullfight at Sevilla was going badly and a riot started. The local police who attend all bullfights tried to control things, but the crowd laughed at them. The riot looked as if it were going to get out of hand, so the squad of guardia who are kept in reserve at all such functions started quietly down from their seats high in the rafters. As they descended men began to whisper, 'The Guardia Civil.' Slowly the guardia moved into the arena, taking up positions facing the unruly mob. They drew their revolvers and quietly looked at the rioters. There was not a man in the mob who doubted that within the next minute the guardia would begin to fire, and the riot collapsed.

An American working in a bar along the Mediterranean coast got drunk and slugged a guardia. He was hauled off to a military jail, where he was held incommunicado for six weeks, for the guardia are under military rule and offenses against them are judged by court-martial. Efforts of a most extraordinary kind were made to gain the young man's release, but to no avail. 'We can't allow anyone to strike a member of the Guardia Civil,' his friends were told. 'No one.' Finally he was brought to secret trial and sentenced to seven years in military prison. That was four years ago. The night before I wrote this paragraph I was advised by an American who knew the young man that word had been quietly passed that he could have his freedom if he could scrape together a fine of $7,000. Word of this affair traveled widely among the hordes of young Europeans and Americans barging into Spain in the summer: 'No matter what you do, no matter what happens, never touch a guardia.'

A New York woman, lost in the outskirts of Madrid at midnight, was escorted to her hotel by two members of the Guardia. When we asked her why she was in the Madrid countryside at midnight, she explained, 'In New York or Chicago or San Francisco, I would be mortally afraid to go out alone after dark. A woman simply isn't safe in the United States after dark. But in Spain, with the Guardia Civil on the job, I am safe to go anywhere. No one is going to abuse me. So when I come to Spain the thing I like to do most is to walk at night. Tonight I got lost.'

An intelligence officer of the United States Navy told me, 'We had this incident in which one of our kids in uniform committed a major crime. No question about it. But we didn't know whether he'd had accomplices or not, so we put our best brains on the job, and when we were through we checked with the Guardia Civil and they'd done the same thing we were doing, but they had a dossier on this kid that was unbelievable. They knew everything he'd done for months past, who all his gang were, who was involved. In the States I've cooperated with our F.B.I. on similar cases, but in thoroughness they don't compare with the Guardia.'

About such an organization opinions can vary. Conservatives believe the Guardia to be the agency which permits Spain to exist and that without these pairs of police Spain would fall apart in anarchy. Liberals recall García Lorca's harsh phrase, 'those patent-leather men with their patent-leather souls.' At the outbreak of Civil War in 1936 one of the first things that happened in small villages across Spain was the slaughter of the Guardia Civil, so in the ensuing war they fought on the side of General Franco, revenging themselves for the outrages committed against their brothers. I have heard many foreign travelers arguing that the Guardia Civil was an invention of the Franco regime; actually they are well over a century old, having been created in 1844 to replace the militia, which had proved to be politically unreliable, and since then, no matter what form of government has ruled Spain, the guardia have been needed to keep order. In recent years the Franco government, in an effort to popularize the Guardia, has encouraged the press always to refer to them as La Benemérita (the well-deserving) in much the same way that Manhattan police are called 'New York's finest,' and it is common to see stories in which the brave Benemérita captured a bandit or the compassionate Benemérita helped a widow. A Spaniard told me, 'We Spaniards are really bastards to govern. If we didn't have the Guardia we'd have no country. And remember this. If the Communists had won in 1939, every guardia you see today would still be a guardia. Only he'd be a Communist guardia. For to rule Spain without them would be impossible.' He then used a phrase I had not heard before: 'We have the old spirit of Viva yo. In Spain you must always take into account Viva yo.'

I must explain Viva yo because the phrase is essential, but before I get

Afoot, on bicycle or on horseback, officers of the Guardia Civil in pairs move back and forth across Spain.

to it I would like to introduce a few other words which I shall be using frequently. When I was in college I mowed the lawn of Professor J. Russell Smith, a Quaker geographer who wrote a series of books about foreign lands. During the academic year Professor Smith was usually absent, for he taught at Columbia University, but in the summers he often spoke to me, and one evening he mentioned some of the principles which governed his work. I forget all of them but one: 'James, if thee ever has cause to write about a foreign land, remember this. Don't pepper the page with foreign words printed in italic. That's pedantry and accomplishes little. But when thee has compiled a list of foreign words which thee thinks necessary, identify those which thee will be using at least three times in the chapter at hand or a dozen times in the book as a whole. These are the words thee really needs. Use them. But define them very carefully when thee first introduces them. Then define them by allusion on second use.' The significance of this advice was somewhat lost on me at the moment because of the extraordinary thing he said next: 'I discovered this principle by necessity. I was trying to teach graduate students about strange lands and I could see they were being drowned in words. So I asked myself, "What is the most successful expository material available today?" And I read the Bible to see how St. Paul expounded his ideas and I read the Tarzan books to find out why people who knew nothing of Africa were finding them so easy. I studied other works as well, but those were the two that taught me how to write.'

In dealing with Spain one is especially tempted to scatter italics. Spanish words are easy to pronounce, are often self-explanatory and do have an attractive power of suggesting to the reader that he is listening to castanets. I have never considered this an honorable way of writing and have followed Dr. Smith's advice, but in writing of Spain certain words are inescapable. Without them I do not see how one can come even close to explaining this country or his reactions to it. Herewith, then, the words which I intend to use throughout this book, for they relate to the soul of Spain and are indeed of its essence.

Duende. In my recent visits to Spain I have heard no other word so frequently used to express important ideas, whereas years ago I did not hear it at all. In fact, my rather large Spanish-English dictionary, compiled originally in 1852, does not even contain the word, and one issued as late as 1959 offers several irrelevant meanings like *elf, ghost, hobgoblin, hypochondriac, the restless one, glazed silk, small copper coin,* but no connotation resembling the one which now dominates Spanish conversation. I find myself unable to define duende, yet it seems to have become the sine qua non of Spanish existence. Without duende one might as well quit the game, and I mean this seriously. To say that a friend or performer has duende is the highest praise one can bestow, and an experience which I prized came one night in Badajoz when we had been drinking late in the

public square before the ugly cathedral and I made a painstaking observation in garbled English-Spanish, at the conclusion of which a student
said solemnly, 'Sir, you may be a norteamericano but you have duende.'
What was it I had? Let me refer to Japan in an attempt to explain. The
Japanese have a word which summarizes all the best in Japanese life,
yet it has no explanation and cannot be translated. It is the word *shibui*,
and the best approximation to its meaning is 'acerb good taste.' For example, a bright yellow could never be shibui but a dusty purple might be.
A kimono decorated with golden dragons would not have the slightest
chance of being shibui, but a gray-black one with a single silver crest the
size of a half-dollar might have. Architecture, landscaping, theater, art
forms, total personal appearance, conduct—all can be shibui if they are
properly acerbic, restrained and in the great tradition of Japan, but what
the word finally means no one can say, for it relates to the soul of Japan,
which is itself undefinable. Duende is a word like that, but since Spain
is not a country given to acerb restraint, the connotation is different.
The dictionary of the Real Academia de la Lengua (language) defines it
as 'mysterious and ineffable charm.' A night club has duende if all things
are in proportion, all properly Spanish, and if a sense of lovely, swinging
motion pervades. A singer possesses duende if suddenly she can tilt her
voice in such a way that everyone automatically cries '¡Ole!' (Bravo!). A
bullfighter has duende when he displays not bravery but unmistakable
class. The essence of the word lies in its peculiar usage, as in the sentence
I heard not long ago describing a dancer, 'My God! He has duende upon
him.' I judge from this that duende is something that no man can will
upon himself, but occasionally, when he is one with the spirit of a place
or with the inherent quality of Spain, it rises from some deep reserve
within him. I am aware of its presence when I see it, and I would suppose
that the indulgent scholar at Badajoz was wrong when he conferred duende
upon me. I know of no foreigner in Spain who has ever shown me duende
except that extraordinary American John Fulton Short, whom we shall
meet later. In areas where he yearned for duende, I suspect he did not
achieve it, but one night during the fair in Sevilla, in a high attic where
some dancers, guitarists and singers had gathered, Short danced in such
a way that duende shone upon him. It was something to see. I'm sure that
when Hemingway was young and in the first blush of his exploration
of Pamplona he had duende. In his last crumbling years when he was trying
to retrace his steps he wasn't even close. García Lorca compiled a considerable essay on duende in which he suggested that the best definition was
one given accidentally by Goethe when speaking of other matters: 'Paganini
had that mysterious power which all sense but no one can explain.' Lorca
cites other quotations which indicate an understanding of the word. Of
Manuel de Falla's music: 'Whenever it is composed of black sounds it has
duende.' And of a flamenco singer: 'You have the voice, you have the style,

but you will never triumph because you have no duende.' Duende, then, is the essence that makes something Spanish.

Gracia. This is a lovely word, which my Spanish friends use a good deal and which for a long time I was unable to understand. 'Does it mean grace?' I asked. That and much more. 'Is it a sense of humor?' Without one you could not have gracia, but it would have to be a very gentle sense of humor, one that smiled quietly at the inanities of the world. 'Sometimes you use the word as if it meant good judgment or breeding.' It includes all of that and much more. Spaniards are fond of saying, 'Our coins state that Franco is caudillo by the grace of God. Fact is, Franco is caudillo because God has a sense of gracia.' I didn't catch the implication, and then one day while I was wasting time in the plaza at Pamplona, waiting for the bullfight to begin, I saw a fat girl with almost no neck and strangely cocked eyes, a girl one would not normally bother with, except that she had some peculiar charm that was immediately apparent to all who saw her, and the young man who sat with her knew this, for obviously he loved her. She radiated a warmth that made itself felt across the plaza, and I was so captivated that I had to raise my glass to her and nod. She must have thought that I was making fun of her, although that was not my intention, for she looked at me with a frank and melting charm that many beautiful women never attain, and smiled at me and raised her glass with an awkward gesture, making fun of me in her way. To my friends who had been trying to explain words, I said, 'That girl has gracia,' but they corrected me. 'That one is gracia.' We saw her often during the fair and noticed that she was never without male companions who seemed to find her fascinating. When the feria ended and was gone, my friends and I never referred to the beautiful Swedish girls we'd seen nor the German blondes who had decorated the city, but we often recalled the fat girl with no neck, for she had gracia, and when a girl has this she illuminates a plaza and gives it character. There is much in Spain that has a gracia which cannot be found elsewhere.

Ambiente. I once hired a car and took a Badajoz family for a picnic. I provided the wine, the cheese and the anchovies. They brought the bread, the meat, the cake, the utensils and the blankets. We were in high spirits and the countryside was beautiful. This was bound to be a great picnic in a land where picnics are a way of life. We drove first toward the Portuguese border and I saw several spots that were, to my thinking, ideal for an outing, but the wife, who was by no means the head of this family and who usually kept silent, said firmly each time, 'No hay ambiente,' which meant that the spot I was suggesting had no ambiance. Well, with the aid of the driver I uncovered some half-dozen other spots, but in the opinion of the woman none had ambiente, so we turned around, retraced our route and headed south, where a series of equally desirable spots unfolded, each to be dismissed with that scornful 'No hay ambiente.' Finally we came to

As a beautiful young girl this woman was, of course, kept behind iron bars to protect her from young men.

an old farm beside a stream, with large olive trees, a grassy meadow, ducks on the water and cattle in the opposite field. Immediately we saw this spot, so gracious in the midday sun, with shade for all and room to move about in, we realized that our critical woman had been right. The other spots had not had the proper ambiente for a picnic. This one did. It longed for people to enter into it and spread their blankets beside its stream and upon its flowers. A Spaniard would willingly travel an extra fifty miles to find a spot with ambiente. Let word get around that a restaurant has ambiente and it is filled. If a vacation spot has ambiente its registration is crowded. The antique bullring at Ronda has ambiente, so that even though it lies perched in almost inaccessible mountains, people from all over Spain willingly travel long distances to see a fight there. The entire city of Sevilla has ambiente and is loved therefor. Madrid is too young to have achieved ambiente yet, but since it has power it is respected. What bestows ambiente upon a place? I don't know. But I have often been with Spaniards who have walked into what outwardly appeared to be a rather ordinary place and have been struck instantly by its charm. 'This place has ambiente!' they have cried, and in that split second I have known that it did. How did they know? How did I know? No one can explain, but without ambiente a thing can scarcely be Spanish. With ambiente it needs little else.

Pundonor. Many languages have cultivated special meanings for the word honor, and nations using those languages have developed particular connotations for this word. I think one would agree that in France, with its tradition of dueling, the concept of honor has had a rather more delicate definition than in America. In imperial Germany, where the dishonored infantry officer was left with a revolver as the only solution for having transgressed the code, the definition was also specialized, and no other nation has been able to enforce the strict interpretations that England observes regarding a businessman's word of honor. In Japan a whole culture, the samurai's, grew up around this word. However, in other countries in which I have lived but had better not name, none of the above concepts has any currency, and in the United States we have been rather more lax in our application than Germany and France and markedly more lax than England and Japan. But it has been left to Spain to cultivate not only the world's most austere definition of honor but also to invent a special word to cover that definition. Of course, Spanish has the word honor, which means roughly what it does in French, but also the word pundonor, which is a contraction of punta de honor (point of honor). At any rate, it is not sufficient for a meticulous Spaniard to worry about his honor. Many things that an American man can in all decency forgive, the Spaniard cannot. If he is a man of pundonor, he must take action against insult. A young man with four unmarried sisters had better cultivate a nice sense of pundonor. A politician, a businessman engaged in intricate dealings, a stage idol and above all a bullfighter must be studious of their pundonor, and in this book, where I deal with several men noted for their pundonor, I shall make use of this uniquely Spanish word, for I have found that whenever I am perplexed about what a Spaniard might do under certain circumstances, or the nation as a whole for that matter, it is instructive to ask, 'Under these circumstances what would a man do who subscribed to an acute or even a preposterous sense of honor?' And from endeavoring to answer this question I often find clues as to what the Spaniard will do. After all, *Don Quixote* is an engaging study of Spanish traits not only because it lampoons the concept of pundonor but also because it demonstrates that no man ever possessed pundonor to a greater degree than the doleful knight.

Sinvergüenza. Sin = without. Vergüenza = shame. A sinvergüenza is a man the precise opposite of one with pundonor. In no country of the world except Japan is it so damaging to a man to charge him with being a sinvergüenza, and when one throws this accusation against another he must be prepared to defend his judgment.

Estupendo, including other such extravagant words as *maravilloso, fantástico* and *magnífico.* Few Americans and no Englishmen have ever mastered these peculiarly Spanish expressions, for we have reserved them for things like Cecil B. De Mille movies and the circus. But observe my experience in Madrid. I had rented a car and like others found much difficulty in parking it, but at a restaurant nearby I became acquainted with a doorman who seemed to have psychic powers in determining where empty parking spaces would be. For this service I tipped him rather generously, I thought, about a quarter in American money, which he accepted grudgingly. Against my better judgment I raised the tip to thirty-five cents, with no appreciable modification of his manners, and then to forty cents, which brought only the same surly acknowledgment. However, one day I went to this restaurant with Víctor Olmos, the ebullient *Reader's Digest* editor for Spain, who wheeled into the parking area, slammed on his brakes, leaped from the car and left it. When we returned, the attendant hurried for the car (he dawdled disgracefully when getting mine) and cried, 'Señor, I found you a place.' 'Estupendo!' Olmos said as he gave the man a six-cent tip. The attendant's face was wreathed in smiles. 'Fantástico!' Olmos added. 'Simply maravilloso.' The attendant nodded and I could see that he felt good all over. When I next parked there I gave him a twenty-cent tip and cried 'Estupendo!' and he beamed. Later on it was fantástico and extraordinario, and I had built myself a secure place in his attentions. My car came promptly now, for like a good Spaniard he needed words as much as he needed money, and the words he wanted had to be the most expansive and inflated available. In Spain words form a kind of currency which must be spent freely, and to do this is not easy for an American, yet not to do it in Spain is to miss the spirit of human relationships. For this purpose I prefer estupendo. Its four syllables, properly pronounced, ripple off the tongue, and if one drags out the *pen* for four or five seconds, the effect can be seductive. For the American it can also be corrupting. For example, when I showed Robert Vavra, whose photographs illustrate this book, the first completed chapter, he cried, 'Don Jaime! Estupendo!' For a moment I was delighted that my work had found favor in his expert eye, but before I had a chance to make an ass of myself I realized that he had been living in Spain for a long time. What he meant was that the material was not wholly offensive. Estupendo, properly used, means 'It might get by.'

Viva yo. This phrase will not be found in dictionaries. Some time ago there was a competition for the cartoon which best expressed the Spanish character, and the winner, without a close second, was one showing an arrogant little boy urinating in the middle of the street and spelling out the words 'Viva yo,' which could be translated as 'Hurray for me,' except that the guts of the phrase is the implied second half, 'and to hell with everyone else.' A comprehension of the Spaniard's addiction to Viva yo will help anyone trying to make his way in Spain. When the little car barrels right down the middle of the highway, forcing everyone else into the ditch, you don't swear at the driver. You say 'Viva yo' and you understand what happened and why. When you pay seven dollars for a seat at the bullfight and find it occupied by a man who will not move, you don't punch him. You say 'Viva yo' and steal someone else's seat. The spirit of Viva yo animates groups as well as individuals and sometimes the entire nation. It crops up in unexpected places and accounts for some very funny newspaper stories: 'Last night the music lovers of San Francisco, California, stormed the box office and paid up to fifty dollars for seats to hear the great Spanish tenor Alfredo Kraus make his debut in that city. Also in the cast was the Australian soprano Joan Sutherland.' When a group of Spaniards who had emigrated to Australia changed their minds after a year and came scuttling back to Spain, an editorial announced: 'They said that they had returned because they loved Spain better than any other country on earth, they wanted to live within the embrace of the Catholic Church, which was their spiritual home, and they had learned that if they didn't leave right away they would be drafted into the Australian army for service in Viet Nam.' The little boy spelling out his philosophy on the street grows up to be a man determined to live by that philosophy, and at times he can be aggravating. Even the poorest Spaniard subscribes to the spirit of Viva yo and is prepared to act upon it. This makes for some trying times, but with gracia they can be weathered. If, however, one finds that the constant exhibition of Viva yo irritates him, he should stay out of Spain and probably Texas too.

As for the other Spanish words that one would naturally want to use, most of them have found their way into the English language and can be adopted without definition. Some of the more common are: agua, alcalde, blanco, caballero, conquistador, flamenco, fiesta, mantilla, paseo, patio, plaza, rojo, sierra, siesta, tortilla and such bullfight terms as banderilla, banderillero, cartel, cuadrilla, matador, picador, toro and torero. The word toreador is also in the English dictionary but no one in Spain uses it any longer, for it is held to be archaic.

While assembling the above list I discovered to my surprise that pundonor has also become a good English word, although in our language it identifies a specific point of honor rather than a general attribute. And of course it does not carry the philosophical connotations which it has in Spanish.

It was my intention when visiting the major cities of my itinerary to make certain side trips to smaller towns and villages which held points of unusual interest, and Badajoz presented an opportunity for four such expeditions, all within Extremadura. One of the side trips was not an opportunity; it was an obligation, but of it I shall speak later.

The first trip took me into Roman Spain. How had Rome gained control of the peninsula? By 15,000 B.C. indigenous Iberians were well established along the coasts and had probably wandered inland, following rivers like the Guadiana. By 1300 B.C. Celtic invaders from the north had begun to displace them and had pretty surely reached Extremadura. By 1120 B.C. Phoenicians were building lighthouses on prominent peninsulas and founding the city of Gades (Cádiz), making it the oldest continuously occupied city in Europe. By 630 B.C. Greeks had arrived, and two centuries later the Carthaginians had taken charge of much of the peninsula. Historic names such as Hamilcar and Hannibal then appeared in Spanish history, the latter taking a Spanish wife and commanding territory as far inland as the site of Mérida, but the Second Punic War, 218–201 B.C., determined that Spain would pass under the control of Rome. This control was easier to establish along the coasts than it was inland, so what Rome could not gain in battle she tried to win by guile, and it was in 147 B.C. that the part of Extremadura surrounding the future site of Mérida became important.

Then Viriathus, a brilliant uneducated shepherd of the region, decided that the continued pressures and treacheries of Rome could no longer be tolerated. He led an uprising of Extremadurans that was subdued only because the Romans invented some new treachery which cost 9,000 Extremaduran dead and 20,000 men sold into slavery, among them Viriathus. As a Roman slave he learned much, and when through heroism he escaped, it was to raise fresh troops and to lead a major war against the Romans. At one point he controlled most of central Spain and even laid siege to Cádiz. He inflicted heavy defeats on Rome, and an army of magnitude was sent from Italy to subdue him once and for all, but he outmaneuvered it and killed many. He became the first hero of Spanish history, a native-born Extremaduran who had repulsed Roman armies.

But then Scipio Aemilianus, adoptive son of the house that had defeated Carthage, was dispatched with a major expedition to put an end to the business. Refusing to fall into the kind of military trap that Viriathus had sprung against previous Roman armies, Scipio baited a trap of his own. He entertained three of Viriathus' envoys and discussed peace with them, but while doing so he suborned them with wine and gold and sent them back to their leader, bedazzled by promises. The three ambassadors did not report to Viriathus but lingered outside the camp until he was asleep, then slipped into his tent and murdered him. Thus died Spain's first hero, a self-taught general of marked courage and considerable skill; after his death Scipio pacified the peninsula, and Spain became as much a part of the Roman Empire as Italy was. In fact, the first two Roman settlements established outside Italy and conferring citizenship were located in Spain.

The importance of Spain is illustrated by that unbroken chain of Spaniards, that is to say, men born in Spain or of Spanish parents, who made significant contributions to the Roman Empire. Three emperors who

FOLLOWING FACING PAGES:
Roman bridge, Romany folk.

well exemplified the glory of Rome—Trajan, Hadrian and Theodosius— were Spaniards. So were the two Senecas (in Spanish, Séneca), the second of whom we shall meet in more detail at Córdoba. Lucan the historian, Quintilian the master of rhetoric, Martial of the epigrams, men of foremost rank in Roman literature, were also Spaniards. There were others who served Rome well, the latest family being one that came long after the empire, the Borjas (Borgias) from Valencia, who supplied two popes, Calixtus III and the infamous Alexander VI, father of Lucrezia and Cesare, and one saint, Francis Borgia, third general of the Jesuits.

To see Roman Spain at its best, one must visit Mérida, thirty-six miles up the Río Guadiana from Badajoz. Its history began only in 25 B.C., when the Emperor Augustus authorized the veterans of his Fifth and Tenth Legions to retire from active service and take farms in the area, to be known henceforth as Augusta Emerita (Augustus' Veteran Colony), whence Mérida. A long bridge was then built over the Guadiana, and Mérida became a chief link in communication between Hispalis (Sevilla) in the south and Salmantica (Salamanca) to the north.

Rome built greater cities in Spain than Mérida, but it was the one whose monuments have been best preserved, and a visit to its museum and excavations is like a trip to ancient Rome. It has a wealth of important structures: an immense circus seating 30,000, where chariot races were held and where flooding enabled boats to engage in naval battles; a well-preserved amphitheater of 14,000 seats, where slaves were fed to wild beasts; an aqueduct of giant proportions; and numerous arches and memorials. Three sites, however, are of special attraction. The theater, which we know to have been built during the second year of the city's existence, must have been a thing of marked beauty; it was a perfect semicircle with four separate flights of seats reaching high in the air. The proscenium utilized the full diameter of the circle and was backed by five double-tiered pulpits, or forums, supported by innumerable white marble columns. For about sixteen hundred years the theater lay forgotten beneath rubble, which preserved it, so that when serious excavations started in this century most of the stones and pillars still existed and had only to be raised to their original positions. Today the theater is a masterpiece of imperial architecture, and one can sit in its lovely semicircle and imagine how it must have looked when Plautus or Terence was being presented. Or he can climb onto the central forum, where statues of gods once more decorate the rostrum, and imagine what it was to have been a Roman actor touring the provinces. This theater is a national treasure of Spain and is again being used for dramatic presentations.

The museum housed in an old church in the center of the city is more informative in that it contains a fine cross section of the art uncovered in Mérida in the last two hundred years. Its massive heads and clean-limbed statues are some of the best that have reached us from Roman times, including an especially provocative head of Augustus as a god, wearing a mysterious cowl over his marble locks, but I preferred two smaller heads which legend claims are his adoptive son and grandson, Tiberius and Claudius. The statue of the former shows a fleshy young man with heavy jowls, thick neck and flat-topped imperial hair. The face is handsome but the mouth is thin and cruel, and if this is indeed a portrait of Tiberius, it catches the spirit of that difficult man. Claudius, on the other hand, shows a frail and narrow face, slight neck and small ears. The hair is done in a more poetic manner and is less flat. The marble face has a thoughtful look that could be taken perhaps as vacant, and the mouth is weak like that of a stammerer. Again, the essential personality of Claudius has been captured.

But the glory of Mérida lies in the Roman bridge, a half-mile long, composed of eighty-one huge arches. It crosses the two arms of the Guadiana and today carries autobuses on its ample roadway where two thousand years ago it carried marching legions and their carts. It is a splendid construction, and those solid pillars that bear the brunt of any flood are pierced by a small narrow arch to permit the passage of excess waters. It was built of granite, perhaps before the birth of Christ, and has this curiosity: the arches are numbered beginning at the Mérida end and records have been kept as to what happened to which. Thus we know that Arches 11–16 were rebuilt by a Visigothic king in 686. Arches 21–22 were blown up by Spanish-English forces in 1811 to prevent Napoleon from using the bridge during the siege of Badajoz. Arches 29–31 were washed away during the flood of 1860, and 32–33 were lost in 1877. The Roman bridge was so important to this part of Spain that in Extremaduran documents it was referred to simply as 'the bridge.' It remains a majestic structure.

The arches have long served a double purpose, for they not only support the bridge but also offer protected camping sites for gypsy caravans that travel this road. I used to walk out across the bridge and descend to the meadows on the far side, and there under the arches I would see gypsy families, their beds spread out beneath the arches, their tables set with spiced food, their women in bright costumes, their men in more somber dress but each with a rattan cane which was his badge as a horse trader. Beyond the arch I would see groups of cattle, and I suppose that these camping sites have been used in this way for the five hundred years the gypsies have been in Spain. They are an undigested element in Spanish life, beyond control of state and Church alike. Up to a few years ago they were not even allowed in the armed forces, and when Spaniards argued with me about discrimination in the United States, I used to ask them about gypsies in Spain. Their answer was, 'Gypsies! They're different.'

During my wanderings in Mérida I stayed at the Parador Nacional, and because I shall be tempted to describe so many of these paradors scattered about Spain, I had better describe this one fully and have done with it. The noun parador is derived from the verb parar (to stop). A parador is therefore a stopping place, an inn, and these have been established by the government in recent years to help meet the sudden and enormous influx of tourists. They stand in spots which tourists would like to visit but where private capital either could not or would not build adequate accommodations, and in the opinion of travelers they are the best system of inns in the world. Their charges are unusually low, about a half or two-thirds of what one would normally pay for a good hotel in Spain, and the plan seems to be for the government to operate them only as long as necessary and when they have proved their feasibility to sell them to private operators.

Where practical, the paradors are housed in ancient buildings, such as old convents, monasteries, castles no longer in use, hospitals dating back to the age of the Catholic Kings or inns in which Columbus may have slept. One characteristic distinguishes them all. In Spain interior decoration is apt to be pretty bad, favoring dark massive objects unfitted to the human eye or fundament, but the paradors have been decorated by some of the most skilled art connoisseurs in Spain so that each is an experience in good design; each contains handsome old furniture and is embellished with paintings and brocades centuries old. The food is exceptionally good; the personnel is trained centrally and then sent out to the remote areas where the paradors are located. To travel across Spain by halting each night at a parador is to know travel at its best and most reasonable.

At Mérida the parador is housed in the Convento de los Frailes de Jesús, which stands in the heart of town and dates back to sometime around the year 1500. The numerous air-conditioned rooms stand on several different levels, which indicate how the old convent was added to as the number of friars increased, and as one climbs extremely old stone stairs to his room, with its floor of hand-hewn planks eighteen inches wide, it takes no imagination to picture oneself in Spain four centuries ago. But the chief beauty of this parador is the cloister of the convent, now used as a kind of salon. It exists unchanged from its original days, a quiet, beautiful square outlined by columns and arches. The former are very old, but the capitals which top them are something you may not see again in your travels, for they go back to Visigothic days, that period during which raiders from the north of Europe swept over Spain, drove out the Romans and established Christianity as the state religion. The central part of the cloister is now a garden filled with flowers and fine shrubs and with a well so old no one knows its date.

During the year of which I shall be speaking I should be visualized as living in such surroundings. Many of the paradors I stayed in were more beautiful than the one in Mérida; some were larger; others were in older buildings; and in still others the food was so good as to qualify as some of the best in Spain. Of course, large cities like Madrid, Sevilla and Barcelona

have no paradors, for there they are not needed, but in most areas of the country they are within striking distance and represent the best value in Spain.

I especially enjoyed the parador at Mérida because from it I could walk to the Basílica de Santa Eulalia, and I want to spend a few moments discussing this stalwart old medieval church, since it establishes certain themes which will recur in this book. In either A.D. 303 or 304, when Christianity was fighting for a foothold in Spain, a group of children in Mérida became infected with the new religion, held to be both infamous and treasonous by the priests of Rome's official paganism, and much effort was spent in trying to win the children away from Jesus, but they were truly inspired with the new religion and refused to apostatize. One day when a high official pleaded with special force, the girl Eulalia, then twelve or thirteen years old, reared back and spit in his eye. To teach the others a lesson she was burned at the stake. Her tomb is reputed to be somewhere within the area covered by the present basilica; however, when we get to Barcelona we will find that certain partisans of that region are convinced that her remains were translated there, where she is also the patron saint, but serious students believe that two different saints are involved, the Barcelona one being a literary version of the Mérida. At any rate, their saint's days are different, December 10 in Mérida and February 12 in Barcelona. Much bitterness has been spent on this issue, complicated by the fact that the city of Oviedo claims that Eulalia's tomb was moved there in 783.

On the ancient wall of the church appears in huge letters the name JOSE ANTONIO, and beside the main entrance stands a very old Roman temple. As I entered the basilica I had the good fortune to meet a priest whose life had centered upon Mérida, Father Juan Fernández López. From a very small village he had come here to school at the age of six, had gone to Badajoz for his seminary training and then returned to Mérida to work. He looked as if he were still in his twenties, with a squarish face, dark complexion and bubbling enthusiasm. He was an exciting guide and I mention him in such detail because wherever I went in Spain I was to meet either by accident or plan such men. They are scholars in a quiet way, enthusiasts for their city or their church, willing sharers of what they know. I shall not list them all as I go along; let Father Fernández of the Basílica de Santa Eulalia represent them, for they are one of the chief adornments of Spain, a country where education is not widespread and where the truly educated man is a kind of monument to himself.

Father Fernández was especially eager that I see two things: the pair of old and friendly chapels flanking the main altar, for they showed all the ancient grace of line and structure that I had missed in the cathedral at Badajoz, and the pulpit. At the latter Father Fernández wanted me to note particularly the bas-relief scenes depicting the saints

Servandus and Germanus, because he had a tale to relate about how these boys who he claimed were from a nearby village, but who were actually from Sevilla and Cádiz respectively, had attained sainthood. I did not hear what he said because I was attracted by a quite different saint carved on the pulpit, and since he is to form the leitmotif of this book and the subject of the last chapter, I had better introduce him properly at this first appearance.

He was Santiago (St. James), the patron of Spain. He was presented as a squat, sturdy man holding a staff, and a big-bellied gourd and wearing a large-brimmed hat decorated with cockleshells. He was a pilgrim, and judging from this first statue of many that we shall see, a doughty traveler prepared for whatever he met on the way. This was the famous Santiago. My heart warmed to meet him, for he had played an intimate role in the building of Spain.

Before I left Mérida I went to the two final buildings that help summarize its history. The first was a gangling, ugly fortress at the end of the Roman bridge. It was a square structure, much longer than a football field on each side, and had been built originally in 835 by Moors who had by then thrown out the Visigoths and established Islam as Spain's religion. In 1230 Christians again occupied the city, and the fortress passed into the hands of that para-military organization, the Knights of Santiago, who ruled it as their personal domain, a misrule which lasted to 1500.

The final building was something quite different. Atop a small hill at the south end of town stood a modern bullring, where bullfights were held occasionally in the summer, and normally I would not have bothered with what appeared to be an ordinary modern edifice that could be duplicated in any of a dozen small cities. The unique thing about the bullring in Mérida was that by accident it stood precisely upon the spot where in Roman times a great Mithraeum had stood, that mysterious and dark temple to the rock-born Persian god Mithras, who had killed the divine bull from whose body sprang all plants and animals on which man exists. In any Roman garrison town, and at its height Mérida housed 90,000 legionnaires, the Mithraeum was the most important temple, because in its subterranean caverns occurred the taurobolium, the ritual in which soldiers banded together to purchase a pristine bull, then huddled beneath a grating on which the bull was ceremoniously slaughtered so that the hot blood of the animal could run down over them, conferring invincibility in battle. How many bulls must have been slain in the Mithraeum of Mérida in those years when Spain was the manpower reservoir for the empire!

Today, on the spot where these sacrifices occurred, other bulls of that same breed are sacrificed for somewhat similar emotional reasons: their mysterious power confers immortality on those who fight them and on those who participate in the spectacle. I did not see any bullfights in Mérida because prior to my departure from home, Conrad Janis, son of the well-known New York art dealer, had taken me aside and said, 'The one thing you must see when you get to Spain is this new matador Curro Romero. Hottest thing to come along in many years. The greatest.' He spoke with a certain intensity. 'Curro cites the bull from a distance, seems to mesmerize him. Brings him forward very slowly, as if he were a lap dog, then wraps the bull around him to form a magnificent piece of sculpture. He's enchanting—and remember his name. Curro Romero. No matter how far you have to travel to see him, take my word. He'll be worth it.'

Young Janis was a hard-headed witness, not given to hyperbole, and if he spoke so highly of a new matador, the man merited attention, so I studied the posters that appeared in Mérida, but unfortunately Romero was not scheduled to fight and I did not see him performing at the Mithraeum, where bulls had been worshiped two thousand years ago.

I was now ready for my second expedition. East of Mérida, in a bleak landscape commanded by a low hill on which cowers a crumbling castle, stands the miserable village of Medellín, a collection of low houses strung along unpaved streets. In midsummer the heat is unbearable and the dust as copious as the flies. The church, whose thick old walls seem to be falling down, is closed most of the time, and the main plaza is as empty and unrewarding as any in Spain. Here is Extremadura at its most unforgiving, yet this little town is a shrine to which a few devoted travelers come each year from overseas to pay homage to one of the molders of history: Hernán Cortés, conqueror of Mexico and archetype of the conquistador. Born of poor parents and foreseeing no opportunity in a village like Medellín, where life was dominated by whatever family happened to occupy the castle on the hill, Cortés struck out for the New World, where his harsh Extremaduran training enabled him, with a bare handful of men like himself, to conquer the Aztec empire and deliver it to Spain. His achievement was heroic, for he brought not only the gold and silver mines to the king but also a new race of people to the Church.

In the weed-grown plaza of Medellín, above the spare white houses with their tiny windows and red-tiled roofs, stands one of Spain's uglier statues. Cortés in bronze looks over the land he deserted and he is brutal in his arrogance. His right leg is rigid and pushed back, so that his hip is high, while his left leg is cocked and resting on some vanquished object. His right arm, holding the baton of authority, is drawn back, while the left holds the unfurled flag of conquest. He wears an ornate helmet and his heavily bearded face is grim with determination. Behind his legs dangles the scabbard of a huge sword, and he might well be called 'The Spirit of Extremadura.'

The heavy base is adorned by shields bearing the local spellings of the names of those strange places where the emigrants from this town gave their lives: 'Méjico, Tebasco, Otumba, Tlascala.' At the site of the cottage from which he left for conquest stands the plaque: 'Here stood the house where Hernán Cortés was born in 1484.' (Most scholars say 1485.) But one looks in vain for the school established with the wealth he won, or the library, or the hospital, or the university, or even the factory set up for personal gain. The richness of Medellín, her men, was exported and nothing came back. No nation in history ever won so much wealth for itself in so short a time as did Spain in that half-century from 1520–1570, nor did any other nation ever retain so little for itself. Gold came by the shipload from Mexico and Peru, paused briefly in Spain and, having accomplished nothing, sped on to Italy and the Low Countries. Again and again in mournful repetition this will be the story of Extremadura, and when I see a defrauded village like Medellín, I am appalled at the bad deal Spain accepted in that crucial era. In fact, she ended up worse off than she had been when it began, for all the bright young men who might have developed Spain were gone. One might argue, I suppose, that the social system in Spain was such that if an energetic man like Cortés had stayed in Medellín he would have been submerged by the reactionary force of the castle on the hill, and that in escaping to Mexico he at least accomplished something. But whether that argument is valid or not, the fact is that when he succeeded in Mexico some of the fruits of his conquest should have filtered back to his homeland, but that did not happen and today Medellín stands as one of the most mournful places in Europe.

A brief explanation regarding historical and geographical names in this book. It is not just to refer to Spaniards by their English names. The Catholic Kings, whom we shall meet later, were not Ferdinand and Isabella; the great emperor who will dominate the next chapter was not Charles the Fifth; and the mighty and complex man who married Queen Mary of England was not Philip the Second. They were, respectively, Fernando and Isabel, Carlos V and Felipe II. I once put this problem to a tertulia of savants, whom we shall meet later in Madrid, and they, having faced the problem in their own writings, proposed a sensible rule: 'What name would you have used when speaking to the man face to face?' The conquistador we know as Cortez was surely Cortés. Therefore I shall use Spanish names, except in the case of Cristóbal Colón; after all, he was an Italian who did not get to Spain until 1484, when he was in his late thirties, so that Colón is as much a perversion of his name as is Columbus. The same rule will govern geographical names, which means Extremadura not Estremadura; Sevilla not Seville; Zaragoza not Saragossa; and La Coruña not Corunna; also, in Portugal, Lisboa and Porto. However, in the case of adjectives derived from place names, special problems arise. Strictly speaking, a man from Extremadura is an extremeño, a man from Madrid a madrileño, a man from Andalucía an andaluz, and one from the Basque Provinces a vascongado, all, you will notice, without capital letters. Some of these forms are so difficult to identify that I have preferred to use standard English forms, which in the cases cited above are Extremaduran,

Andalusian and Basque; but in Spanish cultural life the word madrileño carries with it such specific meanings that I shall keep it, with a capital letter.

At Trujillo, farther north, I had the good luck to know Don Ignacio Herguete García de Guadiana, grandson of a famous doctor who had served the last two kings of Spain. Himself a businessman in Madrid, his aunt lived in Trujillo, where she occupied one of the noble houses fronting the main plaza. Don Ignacio was a short man, handsome in appearance, and the most rapid speaker I have ever known; he seemed a volcano of ideas and I could understand why he had prospered in Madrid. He had a countryman's sense of humor and a deep appreciation of Spanish history. He also had three beautiful daughters, each destined to be taller than himself and representative of the young people of Spain.

'It's the plaza that counts,' he said as he finished showing me his aunt's house, with its tall ceilings and fifteenth-century adornment. 'Come out on the balcony and see the best small plaza in Spain.' We stood there for a long time as he pointed out the features of this architectural gem, so beautiful and compact that it ought to be preserved as a kind of museum. 'Up there, as a solid backdrop, the old castle. Marvelously preserved. You must imagine it in 1470, when a famous gentleman of these parts, Colonel Gonzalo Pizarro, used to prowl the streets of this town on romantic forays. He sired a chain of illegitimate sons, the most famous of which was Francisco, who left here to conquer Peru. In the background you see a chain of fortress churches, each a rough jewel rich in memories. Now look at how that side of the plaza is composed entirely of flights of stairs interlocking at different levels and at different angles. It's like music in brick. We used to block off the plaza and hold great bullfights, with people sitting on the flights of stairs. The pillared arcades which line the plaza are necessary in a place like Trujillo, because our noonday heat can be pretty strong. I know other towns have arcades too, but have you ever seen any that were more exactly suited to their setting than ours? That large house over there with the huge iron chain across the front? It dates back to the twelfth century and belonged to a noble family who befriended the Emperor Carlos Quinto, who stopped here on his way to marry Isabel of Portugal in 1526. The chain indicates that Carlos granted immunity from taxes to the owner. It belonged to the Orellana family, one of whom discovered the Amazon. My cousin owns it now, but this one over here is more famous. The big shield shows that it belonged to the Pizarro family. Long after the conquest of Peru, Pizarro's descendants took the title Marqués de la Conquista and that building was where they lived.

'The statue on horseback? You'll be interested in that. It's Pizarro in the uniform of a conquistador. It was sculpted by either the wife or the daughter, I've never known which, of the famous Spanish expert from New York, Archer M. Huntington.'

For some time Don Ignacio continued to point out the marvels of this little plaza; there were seven or eight old homes with Ionic pillars and severe ornament which were works of art, but I lost my heart to a small building tucked away in a corner beyond the Pizarro palace and now serving as the town hall. Its façade consisted of three tiers of arches, each of the same width but diminishing in height, so that the top ones were very wide and flat, the middle wide and fairly flat and the bottom wide and properly tall. The combination was unique and vivacious, and during all the time I was in Trujillo I kept looking back to that delightful building, one of the most charming things I saw in Spain.

The castle of Trujillo consists of great cubes of masonry formed into towers and long, blank walls. It is magnificently preserved and bleakly empty. Throughout Spain we shall see many castles; in fact, the nation has adopted as its tourist symbol the legendary 'Castle in Spain,' and there are many fine examples, but nowhere one properly fitted out as it was in the fifteenth century. They are always either empty, or being used for grain storage, or redecorated into hotels, or perverted altogether, but nowhere can one see a castle as a castle, and I think this regrettable. At Medina del Campo, where Isabel the Catholic died, there is one which could easily be restored, and at Almodóvar del Río, west of Córdoba, one of the finest castles in the world, but it will be no use to visit either. If I suffered any major disappointment in Spain, it was that a country which had such great treasure in castles did so little with them, for I believe that if one were properly restored, travelers would come great distances to see it, as a reminder of an age that has gone.

While sitting in the plaza one day I had an unexpected glimpse of rural life. Earlier I had noticed a truck fitted out with seats which seemed to contain an unusual number of passengers, but I had thought no more about it. Now this same truck drew up to the plaza and disgorged fourteen primly dressed rural people, including a bride and groom. There was no jollity in the group, although a wedding had apparently taken place and I supposed that the celebrants were headed for some kind of banquet, but they were very poor people, very poor indeed, and as they passed I saw that the groom was a sunburned, stolid, square-faced peasant of about forty and his bride a particularly ungainly spinster about five years older. I cannot recall ever having seen a woman so unlike a bride, so ill at ease in chiffon. As she passed my table I smiled, and she returned the stare of one who had worked very hard and had come not to a celebration but to a one-day respite, after which the work would resume. They were not headed for a banquet but to an ice cream stand, where the groom stood beside the clerk dispensing the cream and counted out his guests, one at a time, and each received a small ice cream sandwich costing four cents. That was fourteen times four or fifty-six cents for his wedding feast. The country people stood in the sunlight eating their sandwiches, then climbed back into the truck. 'Where are you from?' I asked one of the men. 'Medellín,' he said, 'we've come here to celebrate.' He then added gratuitously a statement the significance of which I would understand later: 'He came home from Germany to marry her.'

The most domineering building on the plaza was the Pizarro palace, an uninspired baroque construction whose baronial shield was unlike any I'd so far seen. Counting its pedestal, it was three stories high, covered the corner of its building and wrapped around a considerable expanse of each wall. 'I'm glad at least one of the conquistadors returned home to grandeur,' I said, but Don Ignacio corrected me. 'That wasn't the home of the Pizarro you know. It was the palace of Hernando, and his story is perhaps even more interesting.'

As I sat in the plaza talking with Don Ignacio and his friends I learned much about the Pizarros of Trujillo. Fiery old Gonzalo Pizarro, who lived to be ninety-eight according to legend, seventy-seven according to history, had been a hero at the conquest of Granada and had also served with that master Spanish soldier known simply as el Gran Capitán, who had disciplined Italy in the age of Columbus. Some claim that the old colonel lived in the castle that dominates Trujillo, others give him a smaller castle in the neighborhood, but the likelihood is that he lived in a house that formerly stood on the site of the present Pizarro mansion. Of one thing we are sure. Between wars he had a penchant for visiting his elderly Aunt Beatriz, who had taken orders in a convent, and after paying his respects to the old lady he liked to climb into bed with one or another of her maids. In this manner he had one son, Francisco, another Juan, and a third Gonzalo, each by a different mother, plus a daughter María, a second daughter Francisca, a third Graciana and a fourth Catalina, all by the mother of his third son. He also had two legitimate daughters and a son, Hernando Pizarro, a clever and prudent lad who wound up with the big house.

There being no future in the Pizarro family for seven bastards, the first two girls became nuns, the last two married men from the region and the three boys became soldiers. When Francisco led his pitiful little army to the conquest of Peru, the first thirty-seven positions were occupied by men from Trujillo, and the five top positions were held by himself, his legitimate brother, his two bastard brothers and a half brother who was the son of his mother but not of the old colonel. The remainder of his army of 167 were from other parts of Extremadura. The manner in which Pizarro led his clan to victory is a saga of heroism and brutality, for it seems inconceivable that so few Spaniards could conquer a land so vast and a civilization so advanced; perhaps only men trained in the hardness of Extremadura could have done it.

In the fighting, Pizarro and his illegitimate brothers were usually in the forefront, with legitimate Hernando in the rear looking after business

Conquistador.

affairs, and in victory the same division of labor was observed. The Pizarro men were well advanced in years for such adventures, Francisco being in his fifties, but their sagacity offset their age and they became rulers of a vast part of South America. Then one by one the bastard brothers fell on evil times; there were betrayals and assassinations, so that it was only the canny bookkeeper Hernando who survived. His brother Francisco had married an Inca princess, Inés Yupanqui, and they had had a lovely daughter Francisca, who was Hernando's niece and whom he married. In 1629 the grandson of Hernando (and also the great-grandson of Francisco) applied for the right to inherit the title originally granted to the conquistador, and this was approved, so that the house on the square became the seat of the Marqués de la Conquista. To look at its massive shield is to recall the history of both Spain and Peru, for the statues which grace it represent Francisco, his wife Inés, their daughter Francisca and her husband, canny Hernando, who was also her uncle.

Judged from today's perspective, the conquistadors of Extremadura seem monstrous men devoid of pity, cruel destroyers of civilizations as splendid as their own, and as hard as the barren land from which they sprang. Their crimes against Aztec and Inca can be understood, for the conquistadors were few and the enemy were many; but the callous manner in which they betrayed their fellow Spaniards was appalling. Typical is the history of Pizarro: he did not try to defend his protector Balboa when the latter was hounded to execution by the venality of his friends, but later he found himself accused the way Balboa had been and was assassinated by his friends. To us he seems to have been false to every promise he made, and his offenses against common decency comprise a catalogue; but from Spanish historians the judgment is otherwise, largely because Pizarro did bring into the Christian Church thousands of pagan Indians. As Presbítero Clodoaldo Naranjo wrote in 1929:

> Pizarro was the genius brooding over a vast empire, subduing enemy pueblos, founding cities, organizing institutions, sacrificing his own interests, loving his soldiers as if they were his sons, exact in discipline, faithful to his king, yielding to no man in pundonor, to no man in just administration of the public welfare, to no man in the high religious propriety of his actions. With the Cross raised high he commenced his enterprise, with the Cross aloft he founded his cities, and with the Cross sealed with his own blood he gave up his life.

Louis Bertrand, leading French expert on Spain, in the fine historical summary he wrote with the Englishman Charles Petrie, supports the Spanish judgment:

> These conquerors have also been accused of destroying, through ignorance and barbarism, precious civilisations like those of the Aztecs and the Incas. This is making civilisation a laughing-stock. Let me repeat once more: those rudimentary civilisations have been overestimated in the most ridiculous

way, with the object of lowering and defaming the Spaniards and Catholicism, held as responsible for this alleged destruction. Can one regard as civilised the Peruvians, who did not know how to write, and who reckoned years and centuries by knots tied in cords; or the Mexicans, who used infantile hieroglyphics for history and chronology; peoples who had neither draught beasts nor beasts of burden, neither cows, cereals, nor vines; peoples who were not acquainted with the wheel, and had not reached the Iron Age; peoples among whom man was reduced to the role of a quadruped, whose bloody religion admitted human sacrifices, and who had markets for human flesh? If the conquistadors destroyed much and practised needless cruelties—destruction and cruelties which are as nothing beside those of modern war—they blazed the trail for the missionaries who saved for history everything that was essential in those embryonic civilisations, and but for whom we should know absolutely nothing about pre-Columbian America.

The final judgment, however, is the pragmatic one made by Mexico, whose citizens, remembering the brutalities of Cortés, still refuse to permit statues of the conquistador within their country.

My reflections were broken by Don Ignacio, who ran off to intercept a friend, whom he brought to our table. 'Dr. Ezequiel Pablos Gutiérrez,' he said, introducing a lively red-headed man in his early fifties. 'Medical graduate of Salamanca and alcalde [mayor] of Trujillo.'

'How do you like our city?' the alcalde asked, after introducing his wife and daughter.

'I've fallen in love with that little building over there.'

'The one with the three tiers of arches? That's my office.'

'You're lucky,' I said.

'We're thinking of converting it into a parador.'

'When it opens, reserve me a room for a month.' I could imagine nothing better than to have a room in such a parador and from it to survey the pageant that unfolded in the plaza.

'Right now we have other plans,' the alcalde said, 'so jump in the car.' He drove rather spiritedly along a country road leading east of Trujillo and soon we were in the heart of Extremadura, the low hills, the flat burning land and here and there the olive groves.

'I like this land very much,' I said. 'I think I must be an Extremaduran.'

'If a man is tough enough to love this land, he will never forget it,' the alcalde said. 'Never. I see men who go away. Big jobs in Madrid. Buenos Aires. But always they come back to the barren soil of Extremadura.'

We drove for a dozen miles, it seemed, and Señor Pablos turned down a lane and headed for what looked like an Arizona ranch house. 'This is my ranch,' he said. 'I raise fighting bulls here. Look!' On the horizon I saw a herd of perhaps thirty sleek black bulls. In the setting sun they were handsome beasts, watching us with disdain as they continued their feeding. Between us and them there appeared to be no fences, but they were so far away that they presented no danger. 'They never attack if they're kept in a group,' the mayor explained. 'Only when they're alone and insecure.'

Don Ignacio's car pulled up beside ours and we descended to enjoy a long, easy evening in the country. I noticed that Señora Pablos disappeared rather quickly, but her lively daughter and a young man who obviously hoped to marry her took charge of bringing horses for those who wanted to ride. Workmen from the ranch came with reports of what had been happening, and there seemed to be a good deal of muffled talking and arranging going on, centering upon a tall, very graceful young man who had joined the party, but I failed to detect what was under way.

After the sun had set, leaving a fine reddish haze over the ranch, the alcalde said, 'We're going to ride back up in the hills. Horses or automobiles.' At the head of our column rode six horsemen from the ranch, but before long they left us and cut across country toward the bulls we had seen earlier. Without disturbing the bulls they rode on to a fenced ravine where young heifers were grazing, and in a neat concentration of effort they cut out eight or ten and began herding them toward us. I still didn't understand what was happening, but at the top of the hill we came upon a clean, pure little building, totally whitewashed and built in the form of a circle. It was a private bullring maintained by the alcalde for testing his animals. The tall young man was a matador, and the herdsmen were in the process of driving three heifers into the corrals for testing with the cape.

It was almost dark when we finally took our places atop the wall of the ring, and the red of sunset had been replaced by a purple that already obscured the hills. Birds who normally nested in the ring flew gracefully back and forth as if trying to drive us away. The voices of the herdsmen were guttural as they reassured the heifers moving into the corrals, and the alcalde was excited as he directed the opening and closing of gates that shut each heifer off into its own small pen from which it would later catapult into the ring. It was so dark that I wondered if it would be possible to fight the heifers or even to see them.

A moment of silence, then the alcalde's reassuring voice, 'Open that one!' and as the gate to the ring swung open a heifer, from whom fighting bulls are reputed to inherit their bravery, erupted into the ring, raised a cloud of golden dust and began charging at anything that moved. Three workmen without capes provoked her by jumping out from behind barriers, then ducking back in as she charged headlong at them. Finally the matador stepped out with his magenta-and-yellow cape, at which the heifer dashed as if it were a lifelong enemy. Three times, four times, five, she doubled back on herself and slashed at the offending cape. In the darkness she seemed like a mysterious thunderbolt hurtling across space, and I could understand why it was popularly said that 'the cow determines the bull.' Such fury, if applied to a full-grown bull of a thousand pounds, with widespread horns and powerful neck, could make a formidable enemy.

The darkness deepened rapidly, so that the moving figures on the sand, bound together by a swirling cape, became ghostlike and the shadowy matador as strange a creature as the animal he was fighting. Birds, startled by the unfamiliar scene, now began to cry, and from behind the barrier the foreman of the work crew called out, 'That's enough.' The matador withdrew; a gate was opened; the heifer leaped at something that moved beyond the gate; the gate closed and the arena was still.

'Shall we let in another?' the alcalde called down.

'We can't see to cape it,' the matador called back.

'We'll let her run through anyway,' the alcalde shouted, and the ropes were pulled to make the various doors swing open. A heifer, larger than the first, ripped into the arena; obviously she could see in darkness better than the men opposing her, for within a few seconds she had bowled over three men, one after the other, and had ripped the cape out of the matador's hand. He prudently fled behind the barrier and called, 'Get her out of here. She has radar.' The gates swung open and the little cyclone swept majestically from sight, having defended her terrain against all comers. The ring was closed down and the birds settled into the nests of which we had deprived them.

When the matador joined us he said, 'I'd like to have seen that last one in daylight. She charged like a thunderbolt.'

'She comes from a good strain,' the alcalde said proudly, and we trailed back from the testing plaza to the ranch house, where Señora Pablos had laid out a vast country-style supper lit with torches, and under the starry Extremaduran sky we began to eat the crisp salad, the rugged potato omelette and something I was not often to taste in Spain, a good cheese. It was tangy and of excellent texture, and the men asked for seconds and I for thirds. 'Where did you find such a good cheese?' I asked, and the alcalde's wife replied, 'I make it. I came from a farm family and we always had good cheese.' The night grew cooler, so the workmen started a fire and we finished our supper with sparks flying into the air and transforming themselves into stars. I took this opportunity to get an expert opinion from the matador. 'In New York a young man told me there was a new star in bullfighting, Curro Romero. Is he any good?'

Matadors are notoriously envious, but this one said, 'You should go to much pains to see Romero, for he is special. He is very slow with the cape, like a guitarist who is sure of himself and doesn't have to stamp and whistle. At the end of the fight he is a genius, wrapping the bull around him as if it was a blanket. Never have you seen anything so slow. If you're going toward Sevilla, watch out for him. He's worth seeing.'

We then spoke of Trujillo during the various wars of succession and of how it so often backed the wrong contender, and of the conquistadors wandering across the Americas, and the alcalde repeated a prediction from Clodoaldo Naranjo's local history. 'I am not afraid to assert, almost prophetically, that the day is not far distant when the greater part of America will feel for Trujillo the same veneration that in its religious life it feels for those spots which were the birthplaces of messiahs and prophets.'

Thus ended my three casual expeditions out of Badajoz: to Mérida and its Romans, to Medellín and Cortés, and to Trujillo and its Pizarros. Now the obligatory trip was to begin and I headed south to the little town with the lovely name, Jerez de los Caballeros. In Spain, as in the United States, where we have several Portlands and many Springfields, names of towns are apt to be repeated in the various provinces, so some kind of distinguishing phrase is frequently added. Thus there is the great Jerez of the wine industry; it lies south of Sevilla on the old Christian-Muslim frontier and is called Jerez de la Frontera; and there is Jerez de los Caballeros on a hill commanding a large section of the Extremaduran plains. Who were the knights of the name? Originally they were a band of murderously tough Knights Templars who owned the city and were responsible for guarding the town against Islam; in the last chapter of this book, when visiting a similar city in the north, we shall learn what happened to these unfortunate Templars. When they vanished the rugged little city passed into the ownership of the Knights of Santiago, who used it as an anchor in their assaults on the infidel. Jerez de los Caballeros was an embattled city, and when I first saw its towers from a creaking autobus bouncing over dusty, unpaved roads, it seemed like a haven whose protection I would enjoy, but as the bus crawled closer I began to have doubts, yet it was imperative that I visit Jerez, for I was drawn there by a kind of pilgrimage.

The only thing I knew about Jerez came from a travel book written by an Englishwoman. She had had a miserable time, finding nothing to commend, but even her savage condemnation of the place—poor food, inhospitable people, bad beds, foul climate—had contained a whisper of attraction, as if to say, 'If you want to see Spain at its worst, test yourself on Jerez de los Caballeros.' English writers have a particular knack for describing a strange place in terms that are both repellent and attractive, especially when they write about Spain.

It is difficult to explain why the best writing on Spain has usually been done by Englishmen, but that seems to be the case. I have sometimes thought that it was because the sherry trade required Englishmen to live in Spain, but I could find no one directly connected with that trade who had written with any charm of the peninsula. I've also suspected that it might be the Englishman's intuitive yearning for the sun which accounted for his preoccupation with Spain, but that doesn't seem to stand inspection either. Whatever the reason, if you want good reading on Spain, read the English.

Richard Ford's classic account remains unsurpassed. It came into being because Ford, son of the man who created London's mounted police, married the daughter of the Earl of Essex and gained thereby a yearly income and a sickly wife whose doctor ordered her to travel in a warmer climate. In 1830 Ford took her to Spain, where they lived for three years and where she regained her health.

As a result of this stay, Ford acquired an immense library on Spain, and in 1839 when the London publisher John Murray happened to remark that he was looking for a guidebook on Spain, Ford volunteered. Five years later he delivered the manuscript for his famous *Handbook for Travellers in Spain,* but after it was printed in 1845 Murray grew apprehensive that it was too outspoken and suppressed it. Later an expurgated version was published and it became a classic. Finally, in 1846, a supplementary volume titled *Gatherings from Spain* was issued, and the two taken together are the foundation of Ford's reputation.

I prefer George Borrow's strange narrative *The Bible in Spain,* in which he recounts his experiences in 1836–1840 as an itinerant peddler of Bibles. As the book's editor said: 'It was in an atmosphere of hatred, intrigue and adventure that Borrow lived, striving manfully to print and propagate an alien gospel among the fanatical Spaniards.' It is a robust book, opinionated, specialized and often infuriating. It is written in an apocalyptic style which recalls Doughty's similar writing on Arabia and remains indispensable for anyone wanting to dig below the surface into Spanish matters, but I would think that Catholics might find it irritating. Two facts about the book interest me. Borrow too saw Spain first at Finisterre: 'On the morning of the 10th of November, 1835, I found myself off the coast of Galicia, whose lofty mountains, gilded by the rising sun, presented a magnificent appearance.' And he too started his journey at Badajoz, on January 5, 1836: 'In a moment I was on Spanish soil, and having flung the beggar a small piece of silver, I cried in ecstasy, "Santiago y cierra España!" ' (This is the traditional battle cry of the nation. Its literal translation is 'St. James and close Spain.' Its meaning is 'Help us, Santiago, and let's go, Spaniards, in closed ranks.') Then Borrow adds: 'I was now at Badajoz in Spain, a country which for the next four years was destined to be the scene of my labors. The neighborhood of Badajoz did not prepossess me much in favor of the country which I had just entered.'

Ford and Borrow are classics, but they are garrulous. For a short, highly condensed view of Spain one can do no better than V. S. Pritchett's *The Spanish Temper* (1954). It requires only a few hours to read but is of such high specific gravity as to provide enough hard material to keep the mind working for weeks. Constantly Pritchett throws out challenging observations: 'The very day when Fernando VII closed the university in Sevilla, he opened a school for bullfighters there.' 'Spaniards are born disciples of Seneca, natural stoics who bear and forbear.' 'If El Greco painted out of the day and the land, Goya paints out of the night.' 'It was a Spaniard who founded the first order of Commissars in Europe, the Society of Jesus (Jesuits).'

For the essential romanticism of Spain, I suppose one should rely upon Somerset Maugham's sardonic *Don Fernando* (1935), for although the great storyteller never wrote a novel about Spain, it haunted his life, and it was to this country that his alter ego Philip Carey in *Of Human Bondage* dreamed of escaping, a dream which was truncated by his involvement with Mildred. The essays in *Don Fernando* are exasperating, and some of them seem unduly precious, but they are fun and throw such an oblique light on Spain that the reader will often find himself discovering a new set of meaningful shadows.

A good analysis of Spanish character is Havelock Ellis' *The Soul of Spain* (1908). Neither systematic nor complete, the little book contains so much wry comment and so many particular judgments that it constitutes one of the best approaches to matters Spanish. On a recent rereading of this pivotal work I was impressed by something that had escaped me the first two times around. Ellis, like me, had made his basic acquaintance with Spain not through the mother country but through the colonies, in his case Peru. He thus saw the peninsula reflected, as it were, in the shield of Theseus, and apparently this is a good way to approach Spain, for then certain fundamental characteristics stand forth which might otherwise be missed. At any rate, Ellis loved Spain and wrote of it with deep affection, whereas many who approach it more directly fail to do either.

If the reader finds my account too favorable to Spain, I direct him to *Silk Hats and No Breakfast* (1957) by Honor Tracy, in which this witty Irish woman presents a bittersweet account of her travels in 1955. She saw little that was not contemptible and expressed her contempt by citing one pejorative incident after another. No aspect of Spanish life was sacred and none was accorded charity. It is an old-fashioned book in that everything foreign is held up to ridicule, and I would suppose that Spaniards despise it.

Finally, since the Spanish Civil War of 1936–1939 was a major historical event of the first half of the twentieth century and since I am not going to belabor it, I recommend two books: for the background, Gerald Brenan's *The Spanish Labyrinth* (1943), and for the war itself, Hugh Thomas' *The Spanish Civil War* (1961). With typical British impersonality and with a high regard for truth, Thomas picks his way magisterially through the debris of this anguished period to produce what will long be the classic account of the war. It seems to me that he writes the general truth concerning these sad events, and the fact that his book has been unofficially adopted by the Spanish people as the legitimate narrative of the war signifies that the winners at least do not consider it offensively wrong.

For light reading, and as an antidote to the acerb quality of Honor Tracy's work, one could profitably look into H. V. Morton's *A Stranger in*

Spain (1955), in which this professional traveler relates Spanish history to events occurring simultaneously in England. This presupposes the hypothesis that real history was occurring in England, but that interesting by-plays were occurring at the same time in Spain. This makes England the universal measuring stick, but since Americans tend to know English history better than they do American, and certainly better than Spanish, there is an advantage to Morton's system:

> I never really grasped what a good claim Philip II had to the English throne. I suppose a Catholic genealogist at the time of the Armada would have infinitely preferred his blood-relationship with the House of Lancaster to Elizabeth's tenuous Tudor connexion with the House of York; and perhaps had the Armada been invincible we might have heard a great deal about this. . . .
>
> John of Gaunt's adventures in Spain are an odd and fascinating little chapter in Anglo-Spanish history. . . . John of Gaunt, whose first wife was dead, married Constance of Castile, while his brother, Edmund of Langley, married her sister Isabel. In twelve years' time John of Gaunt and Constance took an English army to Spain to claim the throne of Castile, though the expedition ended not in war but in wedding bells. They gave up all claim to the throne upon the marriage of their daughter Catherine to Henry III of Castile. This is the Catherine who is buried in Toledo, a woman who, as a little girl, lived in the Savoy and saw the Strand in those days when London was
>
> > . . . *small and white and clean,*
> > *The clear Thames bordered by its gardens green.*
>
> She knew Geoffrey Chaucer, who must have taken her on his knee many a time, and she probably had as governess that much-maligned woman, Catherine Swynford, Chaucer's sister-in-law and her father's mistress. She would have remembered the turmoil of Wat Tyler's rebellion and the sacking of her father's place in the Strand. . . .
>
> Catherine could not have had a happy life in Spain. Her husband was an invalid, and like so many queens of Spain she was left with an infant heir and lived in terror that he might be taken away from her. But he was not. He became John II of Castile and the father of Spain's greatest queen, Isabel the Catholic. It is interesting to think that Isabel's grandmother was the daughter of John of Gaunt. . . .
>
> Important as this marriage was, it is surpassed in interest by that of Catherine's younger sister, the flighty Isabel, with John of Gaunt's younger brother, Edmund of Langley. They became the ancestors of Edward IV, Edward V, Richard III and Elizabeth of York, who was eagerly married by Henry VII to bolster up his weak claim to the throne by linking himself with the House of York. So Spanish blood, fairly thin by this time no doubt, passed to Henry VIII and Elizabeth.

Not widely known is the fact that one of the first English writers to deal with Spain was Samuel Pepys, who made an official navy trip to Tangier in 1683–1684 and wrote a secret report of the matter when he got home. His *Tangier Report* was not distributed generally until 1935, when it appeared in the official papers of the Navy Records Society, and the following excerpts will explain why:

A Spaniard says, 'Go with God' and not 'God go with you.'

Rather a hole in a suit than a patch.

Won't piss in the streets, but will against your door.

They shit in pots and wipe their arses with linen cloths.

The laboring Spaniard eats five meals a day. And the greater part of Spain eat nothing but what they make of water, oil, salt, vinegar, garlic and bread, which last is the foundation of all.

Wear spectacles abroad, and some only to seem readers.

You may starve and tax them as you please so you do not beat them, but give them good words; while we English fill our bellies and you can do or say what you will to us.

The bus dropped me at the edge of Jerez de los Caballeros and I walked up Avenida José Antonio toward the central plaza, which was as ugly as the one in Badajoz. There I made inquiries, and at first no one knew what I was talking about and I was afraid that my long pilgrimage was to be fruitless, but finally a bartender understood and said, 'Cross the plaza, pass the bank and look for Calle Capitán Cortés.'

'It isn't Cortés I'm looking for,' I explained.

'You go to house Number 10. That's it.'

I followed his directions and found the Calle Cortés to be narrow, attractive and clean, but there was no indication that what I was seeking might lie in such a street. I wandered along, looking at the houses, which seemed like a row of individual forts, until I came to Number 10. It was low, smaller than its neighbors, and bore no sign or distinguishing marks except that it was immaculately clean, having been freshly whitewashed. I doubted that this could be the house I sought, so I asked a woman who was passing by. She was most charming, and with a reassuring smile said, 'This is it. You norteamericanos never believe it, but this is it. You must be the fiftieth I've told this year.' She banged on the red door, pushed it open and called, 'Señora Ordóñez. Visitor from América del Norte.'

A very old woman, with gray hair and all her teeth, came to the door, saying softly, 'Come in. It is my pleasure.'

She led me into a small entranceway decorated with colored photographs of Egypt taken from an air-line calendar, and stopped before a dark alcove the size of a closet. 'He was born in that corner, the great Vasco Núñez, who discovered your Pacific Ocean.'

'You mean Balboa?'

'If you want to call him that.'

I wished to stay in the alcove to pay my respects to the first European to find the ocean which had meant so much to me, but she insisted that I see her kitchen, a delightful room with open beams, rickety doors, windows that didn't quite fit, stairways built of uneven stones and a characteristic that I had read about but had never seen: the whole had been whitewashed so many times—say twice a year for five hundred years—the limestone had built up to such thickness that all corners were conquered by a softly undulating cocoon of white stone. The doorjambs were rounded; the crevices where upper walls met the floors had become delicate quarter-circles, and nowhere in this room could I see a harsh edge or a straight line, as if much living had smoothed out the roughness. At three spots in the white room flowers stood, more brilliant than French wallpaper, and outside in a very small garden I could see where the old lady kept two fig trees, an arbor of grapes and six or seven hens.

The house looked as if it had been built to illustrate a child's fairy tale, but Ana Ordóñez assured me it had long served as an ordinary home. 'My husband and I worked on a farm, but about forty years ago we decided to move into town and bought this place. At the time we didn't know it was the house in which Núñez was born.' I was to find that in Jerez there was no Balboa, the name we know him by, but there was a Núñez, which was his official name. 'After we had been here a while . . . remember this was forty years ago when there weren't so many travelers. Well, people began to stop by to see where Núñez was born. People on this street remembered the family, and this tiny alcove is where the birth took place. No, I charge nothing to see it. I've had a good life and my children watch out for me. I am honored to mind the house where Núñez lived.'

I looked again at the alcove, thinking of my debt to this poverty-stricken man of Jerez who had left Extremadura, tried to make a go of it in the islands of the New World, but found himself so deeply in debt that he had to smuggle himself to the mainland at Panama in a cask of provisions. There his fortunes improved, for his quick ear caught two bits of rumor: beyond the mountains swept a vast ocean not yet seen by white men, and far to the south along the shores of that ocean lay a land called Peru, heavy with gold. Due solely to the determination and courage of Balboa, an expedition forced its way through the jungle to the crest of the mountains and from there looked down on the Pacific. Among the soldiers was Francisco Pizarro, who first heard of Peru from Balboa.

On his return to the Atlantic side Balboa dispatched enthusiastic reports back to Spain, plus samples of his booty. His promise of much gold excited the home government and he was made admiral of the South Sea, but he was a driving man who aroused the envy of others, and before long his superiors grew bitter over his grandiose plans for conquering Peru. The governor of Panama waited and watched and one day trapped him. A drumhead court-martial convicted him of treason, not against Spain but against the local governor. With no show of justice, Balboa was sentenced to death. Like a common criminal he was publicly beheaded in 1517, but his enthusiasm for Peru found refuge in the mind of Pizarro.

In spite of this mournful history, Balboa's birthplace caused me to chuckle over a bit of delightful nonsense that occurred years ago when I was a student in Scotland. One of the first newspaper columnists, an Englishman with an irreverent sense of humor, announced a poetry contest for schoolboys. He said that he had heard so much adverse comment on boys of the current generation, he wanted to show the people of Britain that some at least were interested in things of the mind. For weeks he reported the contest daily, with clergymen praising his effort and judges saying that this was the sort of thing Britain needed. Finally the winner was announced, somebody like Malcolm McGrory from a rural school, and his poem was printed with pride:

> Much have I travelled in the realms of gold,
> And many goodly states and kingdoms seen;
> Round many western islands have I been
> Which bards in fealty to Apollo hold.
> Oft of one wide expanse had I been told
> That deep-browed Homer ruled as his demesne;
> Yet did I never breathe its pure serene
> Till I heard Chapman speak out loud and bold:
>
> Then felt I like some watcher of the skies
> When a new planet swims into his ken;
> Or like stout Cortez when with eagle eyes
> He stared at the Pacific—and all his men
> Looked at each other with a wild surmise—
> Silent, upon a peak in Darien.

The columnist ended with a condescending paragraph in which he said that this poem, uneven though it was, showed promise for a boy of fourteen and that if young McGrory applied himself he might one day be entitled to call himself poet.

Well, the roof fell in. From all over the British Isles people wrote in, pointing out that Malcolm McGrory had filched his prize-winning sonnet right out of the collected works of John Keats. The columnist, as I remember, played it straight and tried to place the blame for this fiasco on the judges, who should have known better than to be hoodwinked in this way. He was then off for another dozen columns bewailing the lack of honor in the younger generation, and especially in Malcolm McGrory, who would try to fob off onto the British public, many of whom read books, a cheap theft of this sort. He predicted a very bad end for Malcolm.

It is strange that Keats should have immortalized the wrong man, so

With inherent grace this Spanish family poses naturally
before their cracked and ancient oven.
The boys will probably go to Germany.

that even in death Vasco Núñez was cheated. In Jerez de los Caballeros, I could find no statue to him, nor to the town's other outstanding conquistador, Hernando de Soto. (The nearby town of Barcarrota claims De Soto, but this is an error.) There was, however, a Plaza Vasco Núñez, an odd-shaped square at the end of Avenida José Antonio, marked only by a watering trough for horses and a large metallic sign: Coca-Cola.

Friends came to Jerez to drive me back to Badajoz, and as we were passing through a cork forest, whose silence was broken only when a herd of pigs, grubbing for acorns, grunted at us, we came to a clearing which housed a small village, from which two members of the Guardia Civil ran out to halt us. Wondering what law we had broken, we pulled to the side of the road.

'What's wrong?' the driver asked.

The Benemérita pointed to where four villagers were bearing the inert body of a man. 'He fell from the church steeple,' a guardia said. 'He was cleaning it. May God have mercy on him.'

'What do you wish of us?'

'Turn the car around. We've got to take him to Jerez.' To me, the man seemed quite dead, but the second guardia put his hand over the man's heart and said, 'He's still alive.'

Since the two guardia would not split up, it was arranged that they would occupy the back of the car with the unconscious body and that the man's wife would ride in front. That meant that I would have to wait in the village until the car returned, and this I volunteered to do, so the car sped back down the road to Jerez and I was left alone with a group of disturbed villagers.

A tall, very thin man in his late forties and his almost equally tall wife, also thin, suggested that I come to their house in the village and wait there. They led me about a quarter of a mile from the road, accompanied by eight or ten villagers, and took me to an immaculate cottage with a dirt floor, one table, a rope bed and one chair. Although I offered the wife the chair, I was forced to take it, and while I waited there for a couple of hours the villagers sat on the floor about me and we talked of many things.

'Is América del Norte really as rich as they say?'

'We have many poor people. And even those who are not poor have to work hard.'

'As poor as Spain?'

'Our worst, yes. Farmers like you, it's better in America.'

'Can black men live in América del Norte wherever they want?'

'No, but things are getting better.'

'Are there also Catholics in América del Norte?'

'Many. In the little town where I live there are many.'

They sent for a neighbor who had some cigarettes and he arrived to offer me one, very formally, and when I said I didn't smoke, he carefully folded back the top of his pack and returned it to his pocket. Another neighbor brought a bottle of wine and two badly chipped glasses and he and I had a drink.

'How much a day do you make in the fields?' I asked, because it was obvious that these people wanted to talk about important things.

'Forty pesetas a day.' (Sixty-seven cents)

'For grown men?'

'Yes.' They told me that they stripped cork for the man I had watched in the Casino de Badajoz, Don Pedro Pérez Montilla, and they spoke well of him. 'He has three automobiles,' they said, forming their hands into fists, about a foot apart, and moving their elbows sharply up and down to simulate a chauffeur driving a car.

'How do you feed yourselves? Clothe yourselves?'

'The credit goes to our wives.' The man who said this nodded slightly, not to his own wife but toward the mistress of this house, and when I looked at her grave, dark face I could better understand that wedding feast at Trujillo, when the rural bridegroom had spent fifty-six cents, most of a day's income, to honor his stalwart bride with ice cream sandwiches.

The men and women who sat with me in the bare kitchen were a handsome lot, rich in gracia. Their faces were strong and deeply lined, but their eyes shone with humor. Their rough corduroy clothes were cleaner than one would have thought possible under the circumstances. I recalled the list of prices I had collected at the stores in Badajoz, and now, against a wage of sixty-seven cents a day for the head of a family, they seemed appallingly high. A man's suit of clothes for thirty-seven dollars. That would be two months' wages, and no wonder the men about me wore homespun.

Then as I looked into the sober faces of the men who worried about their friend who had fallen from the steeple, I had the sensation that I was back in that farmhouse which I had visited in Teruel, more than thirty years before, and it was apparent that no matter how much urban Spain had prospered in the intervening decades, little wealth had filtered down to the farms. I could not recall any land other than India where the discrepancy between the rich and the poor was so great. Don Pedro, who owned the cork forest in which these men worked, drove three cars but his workmen earned sixty-seven cents a day. In Badajoz, during the nightly paseo, I had seen hundreds of people dressed as well as my neighbors dressed in Pennsylvania, but in no part of America could I find farmers living at the miserable level that these Spanish farmers lived. It was a miracle, I thought, that Spain maintained its tranquillity when such conditions prevailed, and I could understand why the Guardia Civil patrolled the villages.

'Is it true,' one of the villagers asked, 'that in América del Norte you eat corn?'

I nodded, and they burst into laughter. 'We grow corn . . . for pigs.' They laughed again and asked if it were the same kind of corn. I nodded, for in the fields of Extremadura I'd seen some corn which if eaten young would have been as good as what we ate at home. 'Corn is for pigs and Mexicans,' they said, and I wondered if that was why Spain refused this food. When the conquistadors invaded Mexico they found the Indians eating tortillas, and in their pride, turned their backs on this major source of food. Viva yo.

'How many people live in your village?' I asked.

This was the question that unlocked the floodgates of communication, for there was much they wanted to tell me. Forty years ago, when the speakers were young . . . 'we had more than two hundred people here. You can see the church, it's rather fine. But in recent years it's been impossible to live in Extremadura. The wages are just too low. So, many of our young men go to Germany and work there for six or seven years.'

'How many from this village?'

The doleful litany began. 'My two sons, and the son of Gómez, and her two cousins, and the priest's nephew.'

I judged there must have been about fifty men of the village absent. 'How many would you say?' I asked again.

'Well, maybe sixty.'

A woman interrupted. 'But you understand, they're not all in Germany. A good many have gone to Barcelona.'

At this name the group grew silent, as if it were a worse fate to go to the Spanish city of Barcelona than to the German city of Düsseldorf. A woman explained why. 'When our men go to Germany we know they'll come back. In Germany they find no Catholics, no girls to marry. So as they work they remember life back home, some girl in this village. And they come home.'

'Barcelona?'

'It's Spain,' a man said. 'My younger brother went to Barcelona. He found a girl there. Life in Barcelona . . .'

He spoke of the city as if it held the Holy Grail. 'I tell you,' another villager said, 'in Barcelona it's as good as it is in New York. He was there one week and found a job at a hotel on the Costa Brava. Tourists. Now he speaks French . . . my brother.'

'It would be a lot better,' his wife said, reflecting a family argument, 'if we could all go to Barcelona.'

'Do your men like Germany?' I asked.

The villagers pointed to a man who had spent five years there, and he did not speak, but he did make three most informative gestures which I was to see often. With his right hand he fed himself, signifying, 'In Germany you eat well.' With the thumb and forefinger of his right hand he felt the cloth of his shirt, meaning, 'In Germany you can dress decently.'

And with two hands he made the sign of a man driving an automobile. These were the universal comments on Germany.

'You mean to say you had an automobile in Germany?' The man nodded. 'Then why did you come back to Extremadura?' The man blushed and pointed with his head toward his wife.

'Aren't your women allowed to go to Germany, too?'

I didn't understand the answer to this question and my Spanish was not good enough to pursue the nuances. Either the Spanish government would not allow women to go or the pressure of Spanish rural society was so great that any female who dared to leave was considered as good as dead. From what happened next I suppose it was the latter, for the villagers, seeing that it was going to be some time before my car returned, took me on a tour of their village, and I heard a lament that I was to hear often in rural Spain. 'This house is closed. They went to Barcelona.' Or, 'This house is closed. The sons went to Germany.' One man said, 'I used to work in Jerez de los Caballeros. There were twenty thousand people there then. Now there's only fourteen thousand. You must have seen the shuttered houses.'

They were taking me to the church from whose steeple the injured man had fallen, and on the rude oaken door of the church I read a poster in which some bishop of the diocese had long ago laid down the rules which were to govern local life:

1. Women shall not appear on the streets of this village with dresses that are too tight in those places which provoke the evil passions of men.
2. They must never wear dresses that are too short.
3. They must be particularly careful not to wear dresses that are low-cut in front.
4. It is shameful for women to walk in the streets with short sleeves.
5. Every woman who appears on the streets must wear stockings.
6. Women must not wear transparent or network cloth over those parts which decency requires to be covered.
7. At the age of twelve girls must begin to wear dresses that reach to the knee, and stockings at all times.
8. Little boys must not appear in the streets with their upper legs bare.
9. Girls must never walk in out-of-the-way places because to do so is both immoral and dangerous.
10. No decent woman or girl is ever seen on a bicycle.
11. No decent woman is ever seen wearing trousers.
12. What they call in the cities 'modern dancing' is strictly forbidden.

July 11, 1943

The church was not open because with the sharp decline in population it was no longer possible to provide a full-time priest. In fact, I judged from what I was told here and elsewhere that priests were in rather short

87

supply. On one side of the church, carved deeply into the stones of the wall and whitewashed, was the name JOSE ANTONIO.

Wherever we went in that village the story was the same: 'He went to Germany,' and I reflected that in the Golden Age of Spain the men of Extremadura had gone out to Mexico and Peru to build civilizations there, and none of their work had profited Spain; now their descendants were leaving to build up Germany, not Spain, and the creative energy of the land was once more being perverted.

'No,' a woman reproved me when I raised this question, 'the men do send home money. There are many of us who would die if it were not for the money from Germany. It's not all loss.'

As she said this I came upon that sign which had blossomed across Spain in recent months. The Franco government, always alert to remind Spaniards of their blessings, had pasted on fifty thousand vacant walls posters reading: 'Twenty-five years of peace.' I pointed to the sign, and a man said, 'He's the only leader in the world who can say that to his people. He did bring us a quarter of a century of peace.'

Back in Badajoz, I sought out the structure which for a few weeks in 1936 focused the eyes of the world upon this city. I was told that plans were under way to tear it down and I trust this will be done, for while it stands it is a monument to evil. If you go to the cathedral and stand at the main entrance, you will see off to one side the narrow and lovely Calle de Ramón Albarrán. 'Who was he?' I asked half a dozen men from Badajoz. No one knew, but several said, 'Oh, that was a family well known in these parts.' If you follow this street, looking at the fine doorways on either side with their marble stoops which women wash each morning, you will pass a neat barbershop and then the impressive entrance to the College of Pharmacy, and at the far end, where the street terminates before a massive red building, you will find yourself facing the bullring. It is this building that is the terror and shame of Badajoz.

Today it is simply another plaza de toros, round in shape and with a billboard from which hangs a tattered poster announcing the latest motion picture to be shown inside: Gregory Peck, Ann Blyth and Anthony Quinn in *El mundo en sus manos.* Spanish is defective in that in such a construction you don't know in whose hands the world is, because *su* stands for his, her, its, your, their or one's, and you must guess which. The interior is rather attractive, in a nineteenth-century sort of way, for the tiers of seats are made of rough stone and the slender columns supporting the partial roof are of a handsome ironwork, with intricate grillwork serving as capitals. On the grayish yellow sand, where the bull would normally be fought, stands a forest of folding metal chairs facing a very large improvised screen for outdoor movies. A rusty yellow band of paint runs around the wooden barrier that encloses the fighting area, while off in the distance to the left rises a tall new office building of many floors.

89

Bullring at Badajoz.

America started here.

On the morning of August 15, 1936, this bullring served as the setting for one of the early climaxes of the Spanish Civil War. At the outbreak of the rebellion of General Franco's rightist army forces against the legally constituted Republic, Badajoz like most of Extremadura had come out in defense of the Republic, but General Franco's disciplined army units, beefed up with crack Moorish troops from Africa, swept northward along the Portuguese border, ducking into sanctuary in Portugal when necessary, and by a flanking movement isolated Badajoz and defeated the Republicans. The Spanish war now faced its first public test: How would the Franco forces, when the world was watching, deal with the citizens of a city that had surrendered after fighting in defense of the government?

On that morning of August 15 Moorish troops swept through the city, arresting any men suspected of having aided the government, and many old grudges were paid off. Estimates vary as to the number of prisoners thus collected, but Jay Allen, of the Chicago *Tribune*, who reached the city some days later, says that after interrogating as many witnesses as possible he reached the conclusion that there must have been about eighteen hundred, including a fair number of women. They were herded into the ugly plaza, marched past the cathedral doors and chased down the Calle de Ramón Albarrán, where spectators on balconies jeered at them as they scurried by. Into the bullring they were herded while the seats in the stands filled with citizens eager to see what was going to happen to their neighbors. Then soldiers of the rebellion, infuriated by reports of atrocities which government troops were supposed to have committed against captured rebels, turned their machine guns on the mass of prisoners and shot them down as they huddled against the yellow striped fence. Those who tried to escape by running were shot in the way partridge and deer are potted in the field. Of the massacre Allen said, 'There is more blood than you would think in eighteen hundred bodies.'

Later researchers, working upon a matter which has always been shrouded in mystery and shame, concluded that the figure given by Allen was too high. They pointed out that he did not reach Badajoz until August 23, eight days after the massacre, and that he relied only on the reports of excited and confused witnesses, whose estimates would have to be guesswork. It is now believed that the number who so died may not have been above four hundred, and some question the event altogether. I have never spoken to a man who would admit that he had been in the bullring that day, but once at a café in Sevilla I was shown a man who admitted to having been there. I asked if I could speak with him, and friends approached him, but he stared at me across the tables and shook his head no. Men in the bar said, 'He told us it was the worst thing a man could see on earth.'

I cannot permit the bullring at Badajoz to be my last memory of Extremadura. I left the city one morning for a trip to Alburquerque, with the blazing sun overhead in an unmarked sky. There seemed no living thing abroad, neither insects nor birds nor lizards, and when I was thinking that this was a man's land and that if a young Norwegian or Englishman or American really wanted to test himself he should leave Cádiz in July and proceed slowly up through Extremadura to Salamanca, and then he would know whether he was man enough to challenge Spain, I saw across the drought-stricken field an old man riding on a two-wheeled cart behind a slow-moving horse. I hailed him and asked how things were, and he said, 'I'm getting by. My two sons are in Germany. But they'll come back. Men always come back to Extremadura.'

FOLLOWING PAGE:
The passion of Spain.

III

TOLEDO

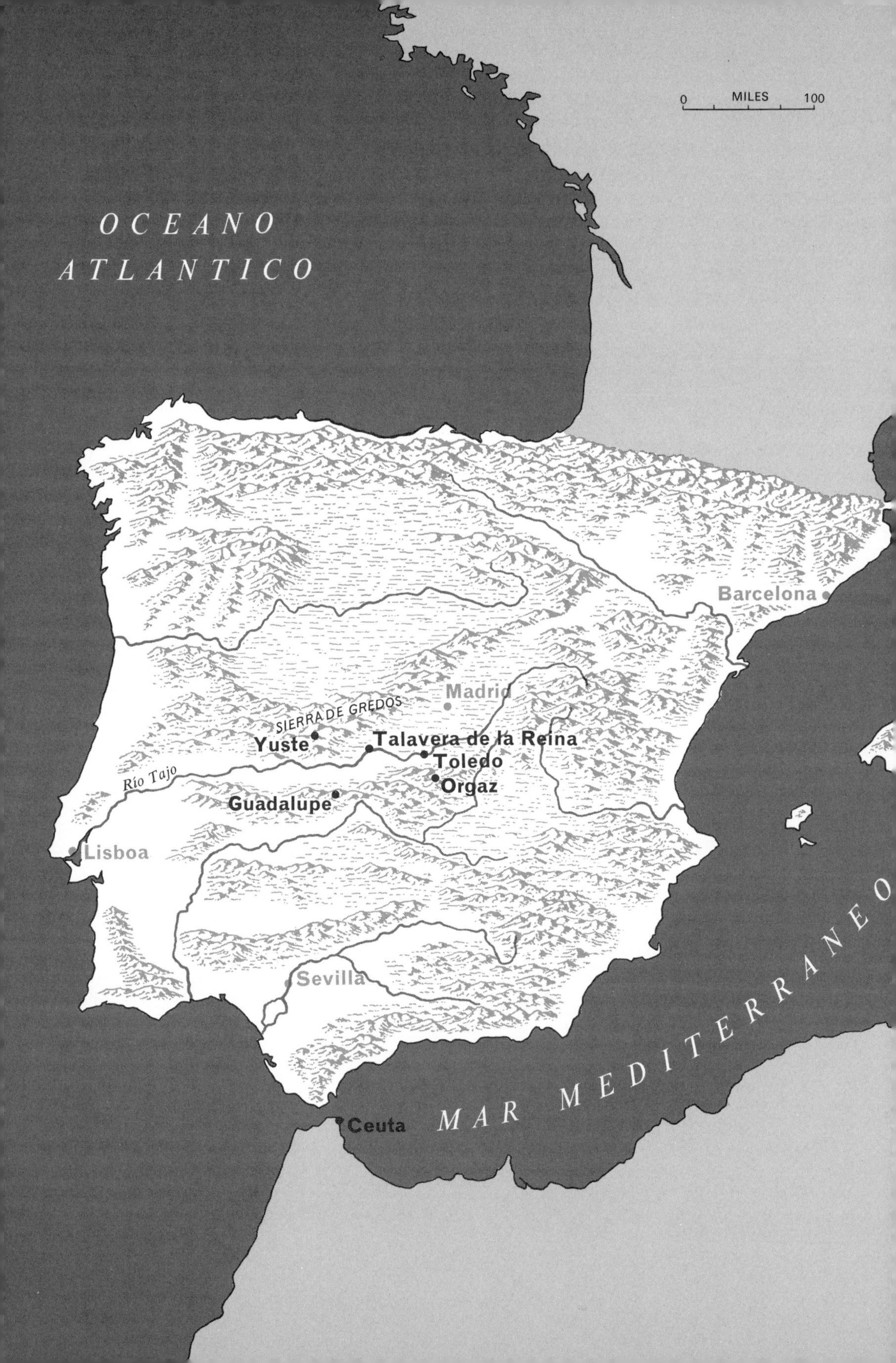

0 MILES 100
OCEANO ATLANTICO
Barcelona
Madrid
SIERRA DE GREDOS
Yuste
Talavera de la Reina
Toledo
Río Tajo
Orgaz
Guadalupe
Lisboa
Sevilla
Ceuta
MAR MEDITERRANEO

The city of Toledo, a bejeweled museum set within walls, is a glorious monument and the spiritual capital of Spain; but it is also Spanish tourism at its worst. Anyone who remains in this city overnight is out of his mind, and I was scheduled to stay four weeks.

I was checked into a ratty hotel whose desk crew must have been trained in the gorilla cage of a second-rate zoo, except that if they had treated animals as they did humans, some society would have prosecuted them. Throwing a key at me they snarled, 'Room 210.' They should have said, 'Cell 210.'

It was cramped, poorly designed and hot. These inconveniences I could have adjusted to, but in addition it was noisy. In fact, it was so noisy that the clang of ordinary traffic, such as I had heard at Badajoz, was like the muted dress rehearsal of an orchestra lacking drums, cymbals or trumpets.

The lone window of my narrow room looked out upon a cramped courtyard occupied by a garage specializing in the repair of motorcycles, none of which had mufflers, and there must have been an epidemic of faulty ignition systems in Toledo, for never had I heard such coughing, choking and spitting as came up from that nest of cycles. The noise was magnified, of course, by the restricted area in which it took place and by the reflecting walls which hemmed in the court.

Some twenty children played about the doors of the garage, engaged in a game requiring three boys to hold hands while making a dash through the opposition in an effort to touch a truck whose motor was being disassembled by means of hammer blows which struck resisting metal and echoed through the court. The game had three parts: Those holding hands screamed as they ran. The defense screamed encouragement to one another. And the workmen hammering the truck hurled curses at both.

95

From a nearby doorway a mother, determined that her son not become a delinquent, screamed an unceasing series of cautions: 'Diego, stay away from the truck!' 'Diego, stay away from the motorcycle!' 'Diego, stay away from the big boys!' Diego, whoever he was, paid no attention.

Just when I concluded that I had come upon a kind of absolute noise, two additional motorcycles roared into the compound with exploding motors, whereupon the children left their game and screamed approval of the new machines while the workmen banging at the truck bellowed warnings to stay clear of the machines and Diego's mother issued, at the top of her voice, a new volley of instructions.

Under these circumstances a siesta was impossible and even resting with my eyes open was forestalled, so I left the clamorous room and decided to explore the city, but when I reached the elevator it was ominously dark. It was out of order, so I walked downstairs and searched for the Zocodover, the lively central plaza which I had enjoyed in years past, and there in relative peace I watched as long-distance motorbuses from Milan, Amsterdam and Stockholm poured tourists into the city. In addition, scores of local buses brought Spaniards to Toledo, so that on this day Toledo must have been one of the busiest tourist cities in Europe. Foreigners came to see the cathedral and the El Grecos; Spaniards came to pay silent homage at their national shrine, the Alcázar, and there were so many people in town it was difficult to find a seat at any of the attractive cafés, and I began to comprehend what a tourist crush had enveloped Spain in recent years.

If I left the Zocodover, I was confronted, wherever I went, by rows of little shops selling acres of the cheapest tourist junk: damascened ash trays, inlaid penknives, letter openers that tried to make you believe they were ancient Moorish daggers, florid ceramics showing a wan knight tilting at a windmill, and gaudy banners woven with iridescent colors. These graceless shops numbered not in the dozens but in the hundreds, and it was depressing to think that the once-great crafts of Toledo, which had supplied the medieval world with splendid wares, had so degenerated.

In the early evening I returned to the hotel to try a tardy siesta, but the elevator wasn't working and when I reached my room the noise from the courtyard was simply unbelievable. New children had joined the games; new motorcycles were being tested; and Diego's mother had returned to her monitory job with new energy. It was difficult to believe that the taciturn Spaniard of history could make so much noise, but apparently his repression of centuries found voice whenever he came into contact with an internal-combustion engine. No man, I was to discover, derives so much pleasure from racing an engine with the exhaust open as a Spaniard; it is a national characteristic.

In a kind of numb despair I walked back downstairs, the elevator still being inoperative, and sought a restaurant for dinner. By bad luck I fell into the hands of a restaurant dedicated to the business of gypping foreigners, most of whom appeared in the city for only one day and were gone, so that they could be outraged with impunity. I was about to witness an example of this policy.

The Spanish government, aware that the golden rewards of tourism could evaporate as quickly as they appeared, has taken sensible steps to protect the tourist; the chain of paradors is proof of this. Restaurants are required to offer, in addition to their à la carte menus, a special tourist menu from which one can get a good meal and a bottle of wine at a fixed price. By ordering from this menu one can eat really well in Spain and at about half the price he would expect to pay in either France or Italy.

But. I sat down, looked at the menu and said, 'I'll take fish soup, Spanish omelet and flan.'

'And what wine?'

'Whatever comes with the meal.'

'Nothing comes with the meal.'

'But it says right here . . .'

'You have to order that. Then it's extra.'

'But the menu says . . .'

'You're pointing at the tourist menu.'

'That's what I ordered.'

'Oh, no! You didn't mention the tourist menu.'

'I'm mentioning it now.'

'You can't mention it now. You've got to mention it when you sit down.'

'But you haven't even given the order to the kitchen.'

'True. But I've written it in my book. And it's the writing that counts.'

'You mean that if I'd said "tourist menu" at the start, my meal would have cost me a dollar and sixty cents?'

'Clearly.'

'But since I delayed three minutes the same meal is going to cost me two-sixty?'

'Plus sixty cents for the wine.'

I tried to point out how ridiculous such a situation was, but the waiter was adamant, and soon the manager came up, looked at his waiter's book and shrugged his shoulders. 'If you wanted the tourist menu you should have said so,' he grumbled.

'I'm saying so now.'

'Too late.'

I rose and left the restaurant, with the waiter abusing me and the manager claiming loudly that I owed him for having soiled a napkin, which I admit I had unfolded.

I escaped but projected myself into an even worse mess, for I chose what seemed to be the best restaurant in Toledo, where I announced quickly and in a clear voice that I wanted the tourist menu.

'What a pity! With the tourist menu you can't have partridge.'

'I don't believe I'd care for partridge.' I had had it on a previous visit and was not too taken with it. 'Just the tourist menu.'

'But on the tourist menu you get only three dishes.'

'That's exactly what I want.'

'But on that menu you don't get special wine, and I know you Americans prefer a special wine.'

'I'll drink whatever you Spaniards drink.'

'We drink the special wine.'

I insisted that I be served from the tourist menu, and grudgingly the waiter handed me a menu which offered an enticing choice of five soups, eleven egg or fish dishes, seven meat courses and six promising desserts, but of the twenty-nine dishes thus available, twenty-six carried a surcharge if ordered on the tourist menu. Technically, one could order a dinner that would cost the price advertised by the government, but if he did so he would have two soups, one cheap fish and no dessert. Madrid had laid down the law, but Toledo was interpreting it.

As a traveler I work on the principle which I commend to others: No man should ever protest two abuses in a row. Few men can be right twice running, and never three times straight, so I ordered three dishes, each of which carried a surcharge: soup, roasted chicken, flan. The soup was delicious and the ordinary wine was palatable and I sat back to enjoy the meal which had started off so badly.

Unfortunately, I had chosen a table that put me next to a good-looking, ruddy-faced Englishman whose tweed suit gave the impression that he must at home have been a hunting man. As he finished his soup he said to his wife, 'First class, absolutely first class.' He had, as I suspected he might, ordered the partridge, but when the waiter deposited the steaming casserole before him, the Englishman looked at it suspiciously, waited till the waiter had gone, then asked his wife quietly, 'Do you smell something?'

'I think I do,' she replied.

'And do you know what it is?'

Without speaking she pointed her fork at the partridge, whereupon her husband nodded silently and brought his nose closer to the casserole. 'My goodness,' he said in a whisper, 'this is fairly raunchy.' In gingerly manner he tasted the bird, folded his hands in his lap and said, 'My goodness.'

His wife got a piece of the bird onto her fork and tasted it, looked gravely at her husband and nodded.

'What to do?' he asked.

'You obviously can't eat it.'

'I wonder should I call the waiter.'

'I think you'd better.'

I was now in a relaxed mood and had no desire to see the Englishman make a fool of himself, because obviously he wanted to avoid a scene. 'With your permission, sir,' I said, waiting for him to acknowledge me.

'Of course.'

'I'm afraid there's nothing wrong with your partridge, sir. It's how they serve it in Spain. A delicacy. Well hung.'

With admirable restraint the Englishman looked at me, then at the offending bird and said, 'My good man, I've been accustomed to well-hung fowl all my life. Gamy. But this bird is rotten.'

'May I, sir?' I tasted the partridge and it was exactly the way it should have been by Toledo standards. Gamy. Tasty. A little like a very strong cheese. Special taste produced by hanging the bird without refrigeration and much admired by Spanish hunters and countrymen. 'It's as it should be,' I concluded.

The Englishman, not one to make a scene, tasted the bird again but found it more objectionable than before. 'I've shot a good many birds in my lifetime,' he said, 'but if I ever got one that smelled like this I'd shoot it again.' He picked at the casserole for a moment and added, 'This poor bird was hung so long it required no cooking. It had begun to fall apart of its own weight.'

Once more I tried to console him: 'I've had Toledo partridge twice before, and I promise you, it tasted just like yours.'

'And you lived?' He pushed his plate away but refrained from complaining to the waiter. He did, however, look rather unpleasantly at me, as if to reprimand me for trying to convince him that he should eat such a bird.

At this point the waiter brought my chicken, and I am embarrassed to report that it smelled just like the partridge. It was one of the worst-cooked, poorly presented and evilest-smelling chickens I had ever been served and was obviously inedible. I tried cutting off a small piece, but blood ran out the end and the smell increased. I followed through and tasted it, but it was truly awful and I must have made a face, for the Englishman reached over, cut himself a helping, cut it into pieces and tried one while giving the other to his wife. Neither could eat the sample, whereupon the Englishman smiled indulgently and said very softly, 'See what I mean?'

When I tried to erase the taste of that dreadful chicken with a drink in the Zocodover, the effect of the lively square was killed by a couple at the next table who had with them that curse of the modern world, a very loud-playing transistor radio which ground out exactly the kind of cheap jazz I could have heard if I had traveled not to Spain but to Waco, Texas. And when I got back to my hotel the elevator still wasn't working but the mechanics below me were. Diego and his mother had gone to bed, thank God, but an older set of delinquents were now playing with motorcycle throttles and I was still not asleep.

I was kept awake not by the motorcycles, which did shut down before

midnight, but by television, which from five or six nearby sets, all emp-
tying into my enclosed courtyard, offered the Spanish-language version of
Bonanza, one of the reigning favorites on Spanish television. I doubt if
there is any country in Europe which has the unremitting noise quotient of
Spain, and on this night I was to understand why. Anyone who has a
television set must play it at top volume to let his neighbors know he has
it. Anyone who has a motorcycle must run it open-throttle to impress those
who aren't so lucky. And now a family down the alley, who had neither TV
nor motorcycle, showed the world what they did have by playing their
radio full-blast, with Mahalia Jackson, to whom I am normally partial,
bellowing 'He's Got the Whole World in His Hands.' How I got to sleep I
don't know, but early in the morning I was awakened by a dishwasher
serenading me with 'Cielito lindo' while he dropped cups and saucers.

And yet it was Toledo that would reveal the essence of Spanish
history. It was a city crammed with meaning, and in exploring it I
experienced a kind of schizophrenia: my routine living was as unpleasant
as I would know in Spain, for the noise grew as the service declined, but
the significance of Toledo increased until I felt it to be a spiritual home in
which I was a privileged guest. It remains the city which I recall with
greatest frequency if not the most affection.

To appreciate Toledo one must see it from afar, for it is a mighty
fortress on a rock. It is practically unassailable and its history has been a
succession of sieges, some of which the insolent city withstood for years.
From the east the Río Tajo (Tagus) comes wandering out of the plain and
bumps into the rock of Toledo. Rebuffed, it turns south, runs almost
completely around the rock, then meanders off toward Portugal to enter
the Atlantic at Lisboa. It thus protects Toledo on three sides, and to think
of the city without the river would be meaningless.

The northern flank of the city has no river, but an escarpment
provides a natural bulwark which armies could not overcome. Within
these defenses a considerable settlement grew up in ancient times to serve
as the capital of Spain throughout the greater part of its history. The
general pattern of the city today is roughly what it was two thousand years
ago, for as an official told me, 'Forty years ago we had a population of
about forty thousand. Today we have the same. And forty years from now
it will still be the same, unless we build skyscrapers. For we have used up
our rock.'

To remind myself of Toledo's unique posture, I walked one day out of
the city, across the bridge over the Tajo and up onto that road that swings
to the south, and when I had climbed to a high point I stopped to look
back. How magnificent Toledo was, with its two salient bulwarks: to the
right, the blunt, four-square Alcázar, a gigantic fortress with no artistic
grace whatever, and in the center the glory of Toledo, the Gothic cathedral,
whose spire and extended walls can best be appreciated from where I
stood.

On the city side of the river, dwellings and monuments crowded together like animals in a storm, but on the country side the land stood practically empty. The Tajo was a line demarcating civilization from nothingness, and until Toledo was captured no invading general could claim that he had subdued Spain. This was the sequence of occupation with the approximate dates when Toledo fell into new hands:

Prehistoric	Iberians
Early Historic	Celtiberians
192 B.C.	Romans
A.D. 411	Wandering Germanic Tribes
A.D. 453	Visigoths
A.D. 712	Muslims
A.D. 1085	Spaniards

At Mérida we have witnessed the impact of Roman rule; in the next chapter we shall see the Muslims at Córdoba; and in all parts we can observe Spaniards, but it is only in Toledo that we can glimpse that nebulous period of three centuries when tribes from northern Europe dominated the peninsula.

The first Germanic tribes that spilled over into Spain after the debacle of the Roman Empire were mere adventurers and brought little except fire and disruption. Vandals, Alans, Suevi, they left no mark on either the culture or the population of Spain and were so disorganized that it was relatively easy for the superior Visigoths (the name means Noble Goths and refers to the West Goths) to supersede them. The Visigoths played an important role in the civilization of Spain. They brought a vigorous if heretical Christianity, and when on May 8, 589, King Reccared finally abjured his heresy and pledged allegiance to the Catholic Church of Rome, he installed Spain's most prized possession.

The Visigoths also introduced a codified law, a sensible tax system, a centralized government and an element of strength in the Spanish character. Since these Goths ruled Spain for nearly three hundred years and stayed on after their final defeat, they must also have made a strong contribution to Spanish blood, and it is they who account for the large number of blue-eyed Spaniards. On the other hand, they left almost no literature, little art and no substantial architecture. I recall few mass movements of people that left behind so little visual proof that they had occupied a country.

Toledo was probably an imposing city when it served as their capital, but the only echo of its grandeur is found in the Santa Cruz Museum, a few steps east of the Zocodover, where a few Visigothic remains are on display. In a corner room downstairs stands a typical example, a tombstone from the sixth century, carved in a soft limestone which should have been easy to work; but its letters are so puerile, its design so trivial and its effect so unsatisfying that one can see that it was carved by a man who had no sense of proportion or art. It is one of the few ancient stones I know that must be called ugly; yet in the next room stand beautifully carved Roman stones of about the same period, and these were surely available to the Visigoths as examples.

As one moves from room to room the conviction grows that the Visigoths were ungracious men; the capitals they used to top their columns are crude and the columns are poorly carved, as if a shaggy bear had done the job with his claws.

And yet, in the far room on the second floor, when I had about given up on the Visigoths, I came upon a piece of stone, number 196, which was positively superb, and having seen it, I had a new appreciation of the Visigoths. I commend it as one of the best things in Spain.

It is about eight inches high and was once square, about thirty inches on the side, but now one of the corners has been damaged, which does little harm; indeed, it lends a feeling of history. The four sides of the stone, a rather soft, whitish limestone, are sloped inward and decorated with rude square crosses of the kind known as formée. Broad at the ends and tapering to a point where the vertical and the lateral bars meet, the four triangular parts give the impression of a huge stone Iron Cross, as if this early work of the Goths had served as the pattern for present-day Germans, which it probably did. The crosses are accompanied by rows of massive and ungainly fleurs-de-lis plus other odds and ends, the whole decoration producing a feeling of combined awkwardness and significance. The stone is not inspired, but it is devout; it is not beautiful, but it does evoke a sense of primitive worship.

On top it has been hollowed to form a basin, and through one side, the cutting having been performed crudely, a drainpipe issues, for this is a baptismal font, and here the Goths committed themselves and Spain to the Christian religion. I never tired of looking at this stone; it seemed to me to have the rude force attained by our best modern sculpture, and I suppose if Henry Moore or Richard Stankiewicz were called upon to produce a baptismal font for a contemporary church it would look something like this. Of all the Visigothic stones I have seen in Spain, this one speaks most clearly and purely of that shadowy age when these northern barbarians fumbled and grumbled their way to victory and defeat.

Legend says that the Visigoths lost Spain because a voyeur king spied on a naked princess. Roderick, fated to be the last king of Toledo, had assumed the throne in 709. A married man, he conceived a great passion for the daughter of his friend and counselor, Count Julian, who governed Ceuta in Africa. King Roderick used to secrete himself in the bushes near a cave, still shown to tourists, on the other side of the Tajo near where I had stopped to see the city, and from this hidden spot he watched Florinda bathe. One day, while doing so, his passion overcame him and he leaped from his hiding place and raped the girl. Count Julian, seeking a revenge which would repair his daughter's honor, was ridiculed by the king much as Rigoletto, the father of Gilda, was ridiculed by his count. Rigoletto missed his revenge; Count Julian did not. He fled Toledo, went south to Gibraltar, crossed over to Ceuta, and there invited the Muslims to help him teach Roderick a lesson. He led the Moors into Spain, where they defeated Roderick, and then he brought them to Toledo and showed them how to cross the Tajo and penetrate the defenses. Of Roderick, when the battle ended, there remained only a kingly scarf and a glove; his fate was never known, but the rule of the Goths was ended and they left behind only that litany of strange and un-Spanish names used by their kings: Reccared, Witeric, Wamba, Witiza, Quindasvinto. The long dominance of the Muslims had begun.

The heart of Toledo is the Gothic cathedral, begun in 1227 and finished more than two hundred and fifty years later. It is so beautiful that one could never exhaust its variety, so evocative of the religious and civil history of Spain that it can never be fully understood. It is a masterpiece of concept and execution.

I care little for the exterior, what I have been able to see of it, for the façade is so uneven it looks as if Visigoths had planned it. The left spire is marred by three curious circles of projecting flanges such as boats use on their pier lines to prevent wharf rats from climbing aboard; it therefore looks as if it were prepared to repulse an assault of angels. The right spire was never finished, and what exists of its base was severely mutilated by a late addition. The various doors leading into the cathedral have been admired by some, but they are poor things compared to what we shall see in the north. But even if the exterior were a masterpiece it wouldn't matter, because you can't really see it. Houses and shops are jammed against it, and only from across the river can one see the part that soars above the surrounding roofs and gain an idea of what the building must have been before it was so sadly encroached upon.

But inside, it is quite a different matter. One does not enter through the main façade but through a cloister that stands off to one side. Whenever I step into the cathedral itself, I go to the first closed door on my right, lean back against it and allow my eye to wander the full length of the left aisle to remind myself of how enormous this church is. One morning I stepped it off, about a yard to a step, and it measured 136 paces, well beyond the length of a football field.

From my vantage point at the door I can see three things: the immense sweep of the aisle; the massive structure in the center of the cathedral, which houses the choir and the altar; and at the far end the Capilla de Santiago, which terminates the aisle. This chapel is something very special.

Seen from where I stand, the ground-level part of the chapel is

*The joy of first communion, at which time
the young Spaniard joins her ancient Church,
is a memory that abides
through a lifetime.*

composed of an iron grille which provides a lovely tracery and a subtle movement which invites the eye to look past the great bulk of the altar and around into the ambulatory. Above the grille, stained-glass windows lend color and variation to the scene. Aloft, the vaulting crisscrosses in various angles and planes, creating a polyphonic counterpoint whose intricacies never end. This distant conjunction of elements is like a perpetuum mobile placed at the end of a long line of stone trees whose trunks are the majestic pillars of the cathedral, and although there will be much for me to see in this subtle building, nothing will excel this simple yet complicated

view down the aisle to the distant chapel. With this view one gains an insight into what a cathedral is supposed to be.

Let us walk from my door down the length of the church to the Capilla de Santiago. A quarter of the way down on the left stands a small golden chapel, put there to break the long sweep; it is placed exactly right, for it lends a touch of color without creating confusion: this cathedral is surprisingly free of clutter or the kind of garbage that often mars the minor churches of Spain. Now on the right we see the heavy walls of the choir and altar. Light strikes us as we cross the transept, a small cathedral in itself, and at the end we face the chapel whose components I have described.

It contains two works of note. High on the wall Santiago rides a brightly colored merry-go-round horse caparisoned in gold and shells. This is the same Santiago we saw as a pilgrim in Mérida, but in this evocation he is Santiago Matamoros (Moor-slayer), brandishing the enormous sword with which he slays Muslims, one of whom we see beneath the horse's hooves getting his head slashed off. We will meet this ferocious Matamoros riding over much of Spain but never in a more stylish presentation.

On the pavement of the chapel stand a pair of splendid marble tombs, each supported by four kneeling knights of the Order of Santiago, and from looking at them one can appreciate how grand and powerful that order was. The tombs form the end of a story both tragic and amusing, for they contain the bodies of the Conde Alvaro de Luna and his wife. The conde was born in 1388 as the illegitimate son of a rural family. Having no family prospects, he maneuvered himself into position as the confidant of Isabel the Catholic's father King Juan II, whom we have already met as the grandson of John of Gaunt, and so charmed him that he, Alvaro, became the effective ruler of Spain and the most notorious legal thief in history. His appetite for land and money was so voracious that after a few years he had amassed a million and a half coins of Spanish gold, eighty million lesser coins of Castilla and Aragón and seven trunks of Italian gold coins. He was Master of Santiago, which made him one of the most powerful lay forces in religion, and Condestable de Castilla, which empowered him to control the countryside. By one clever trick or another he acquired outright ownership of one hundred and twenty different towns. In the days when Colonel Pizarro was a boy in Trujillo, for example, Don Álvaro owned the city. His end was sardonic. Always loyal to the king, he engineered for Juan a most favorable second marriage to Isabel of Portugal (who would become the mother of Isabel the Catholic), but no sooner had she become Queen of Spain than she decided that the Conde de Luna must go. 'He is stealing the nation,' she told her husband as she organized a cabal of nobles who arrested the conde on some irrelevant charge, gave him a drum-head court-martial and sped him to the execution block. He was buried in the Capilla de Santiago, and that is where the humor comes in, for his family erected over his grave a life-sized portrait statue so articulated that when Mass was being said at the main altar some twenty yards away, a servant who followed the motions of the priest could manipulate a series of underground chains which made the statue stand, sit or genuflect at the proper points of the service, creaking loudly as it did so. So far as we know, this was the world's first mechanical man and it became so notorious that more people watched it than the priest. This continued for some thirty years until one day Queen Isabel said sternly, 'Get that thing out of here!' What became of the praying statue no one remembers.

Toledo's cathedral has a score of similar focal points, each laden with historical and spiritual significance; I wonder if there is another church in the world whose interior is so rich and at the same time so beautiful. I propose to speak of only four of the treasures: the choir, the main altar, a preposterous thing called the Transparente and the sacristy, which may be the most rewarding of all because of two paintings it contains.

In the center of the cathedral, facing the main altar, has been set down a very large masonry cube whose outer walls of stone are tastefully carved. It is the inside which is noteworthy, a symphony of dark beige alabaster and oil-stained wood, accented here and there by fine statues in marble, bronze and a lighter alabaster. To appreciate the quality of this noble structure, large enough to hold a chorus of up to eighty priests who chant during celebration of Mass, you must visualize the five layers of art which fit together, one on top of the other, to form the stalls in which the singing priests sit. At the lowest level, of course, are the carved misericords, those half-seats which can be quietly propped up when the service is long and leaned against so that the singer seems to be standing up while he is actually sitting down. 'Cheater-seaters,' I heard an American girl explain to a friend. Since misericords were used by the human fundament, custom allowed them to be carved to represent devils, fiends, vices and other low forms of life, so that in some cathedrals the misericords present scenes of sexual malpractice and abomination. The second layer is formed by the backs of the choir stalls, where a series of fifty-four carved wooden panels depict scenes from the Conquest of Granada. The third tier consists of misericords for an upper row of choir stalls and above them the great treasure of the choir, a series of wooden panels depicting standing figures from the Bible, and these are magnificently carved. And at the top, above the two ranks of choir stalls, runs a fine series of standing figures carved in pale alabaster that shines so as to make the faces of these noble figures seem alive. Any one of these five components would have made this choir notable; taken together they form one of the chief treasures of Spanish art.

I should like to comment briefly on only three of the components. The battle scenes by Rodrigo the German are an extraordinary production insofar as magnitude is concerned, for each of the panels is large and contains dozens and sometimes scores of separate figures. Since they were carved shortly after the Conquest of Granada the observation of armies and weaponry is of historic value. I am not so sure about the art. There is a decided monotony of design; in panel after panel a set of identical towers appears off-center left or right, against which an army moves with a confrontation of sorts between heroic Christians and abject Moors, all the warriors presenting a sameness of figure and face. This is one war in which the Muslims, who had defeated the Spaniards for some seven hundred years, fail to win a battle. On the other hand, these repetitious panels do contain much delightful observation on the wildlife of the countryside, and some of this work is of merit. Taken as a whole, the panels are delightful, and what they lack in art they compensate for in their ability to convince the viewer that he is seeing the Conquest of Granada, not as it happened, but as Fernando and Isabel desired it to be remembered.

The topmost parade of alabaster warriors used to please me very much, for it presented the heroic figures of Bible story in the dress of German knights of the fifteenth century, and I especially liked old Roboam (where does he appear in the Bible and under what name, I used to wonder; later I found that he was a link in the genealogy of Christ as given in Matthew), who stands tenth in on the right-hand side, next to King Solomon. He strides ingratiatingly, with a military sash pulled about his body, reminding me of Lohengrin. But in later years as I have grown to know the figures better I have concluded that they are fairly ordinary, possibly because the wooden figures below them now seem so wonderful.

This endless line of Biblical figures, carved in the darkest wood, is probably the most important Renaissance work in Spain, and was completed between 1539 and 1543 by two men with contrasting styles, the figures on the right as you enter the choir being by the Frenchman Felipe Vigarní de Borgoña and those on the left by the Spaniard Alonso de Berruguete. At first acquaintance the work of the former is easier to appreciate, especially panels like the one near the middle showing Jacob wrestling with the angel, in which the intertwining of figures is done with invention and grace. Vigarní's share of the work contains another half-dozen panels of high merit, particularly the one in the corner showing a man with an ox.

But as I grew to know the panels my taste inclined more and more to the remarkable portraits carved by Berruguete. They are sometimes heavy but always inspired; they are decidedly awkward but always moving; they are particularly tortured, like the late work of El Greco, but never tedious. A good panel with which to start an appreciation of Berruguete is the one to the left of the alabaster relief in the central wall, for this shows St. Peter and is not successful: the chair is grotesquely done, the keys and book are out of balance and the savage distortion of the figure produces no artistic gain. In fact, the whole idea misses. The four evangelists who appear next to Peter are ordinary, for they seem not to know what to do with the books they carry, and even John the Baptist, who comes next, emphasizes a tortured distortion rather than an artistic form.

So far Berruguete shows less talent than Vigarní, but on the left-hand wall he offers a series of figures that are explosive in their excellence. Jerome and his lion are magnificent; I have never seen a better Abraham preparing to sacrifice Isaac; Eve, as she stands nude plucking the apple, is wonderfully seductive, her eyes closed in rapture, her face wreathed in an enigmatic smile; a blindfolded old Sibyl with her prophetic tablets seems to have been carved by Michelangelo, so reminiscent is the weather-beaten face. The panels are not well designed and display a clutter that a purist would not have indulged in, but they are powerful and speak with the clear, strong voice of the Renaissance.

Before leaving the choir you should look at the rare marble statue of the standing Virgin and Child which graces the altar. She wears a white robe and is known as the White Virgin. (Legend says she was the gift of St. Louis, King of France, some time in the thirteenth century, but most art historians are satisfied that she was carved no earlier than the fourteenth, which knocks that legend in the head.) Her title is curious in that both she and Jesus have very dark faces; indeed, He looks like an adorable little Negro baby. I mentioned this once to a Spanish friend, who was outraged, so I asked him how otherwise he explained the darkness of the pair, and he replied, 'It's difficult but they're not Negroes.' Later when we meet the Virgin of Montserrat and the Virgin of Guadalupe we will find that they too are dark, as is San Fermín, the saint after whom the yearly feria at Pamplona is named. There I was warned, 'We will forever damn you if you say Fermín was a Negro. Dark, yes. Moorish, yes. Negro, never.'

Facing the choir, but separated from it by the full width of the transept, is a second structure containing the high altar, and this area is so lavish that books have been written about it alone, but I shall refer only to the reredos because the rest of the place overwhelms me and I doubt that I could do it justice. To approach the reredos you must pass through the wrought-iron screen which cuts it off from the main body of the church. It is an exquisite piece of work, so classically proportioned and so intricately executed that it allows the worshipers outside the altar area to participate as if they were inside, yet it marks them off as not being priests. This is one of the most delicate screens ever forged of iron and is ideally suited for this cathedral. It was authorized at the late date of 1548 and was wrought by Francisco de Villalpando, who took ten years for the job. Today the hinges of its great gates swing as easily as they did when installed, and Americans who are not familiar with screens ought to see this masterpiece.

The gold-leafed reredos which soars above the tabernacle is so intricate and ornate as to be more like a fantasy than reality. Immensely high, its upper figures seem to be trying to escape through the roof of the cathedral. It is composed of tier upon tier of religious tableaux carved in high relief on larch wood, then covered with gold leaf. One panel, for example, might contain as many as five life-sized figures set off from nearby panels by yards of intricate filigree work, but the construction is so gigantic that one has no sense of clutter but rather of a heavenly pageant which one is permitted to glimpse through a golden frieze. There are fourteen such scenes, any one large enough for an average church, plus ten huge figures of patriarchs and prophets, all topped by an enormous

Crucifixion featuring a mammoth Jesus surrounded by the two thieves on their crosses and the two Marys in red. A predella offers a series of smaller panels, also crowded with gold figures, and a fine Virgin and Child. In the center of the reredos stands an enormous tabernacle used in the Mass; each inch is ornamented in gold and encrusted in jewels.

What I have failed to convey is the effect of this intricate flowering of Late Gothic: it is so resplendent and dazzling that in a lesser building it would be overpowering if not preposterous, but in the far reaches of this cathedral it seems necessary. It was put together—that is the only phrase to describe its construction—within the brief period of two and a half years by a team of craftsmen whose names indicate how artisans moved about in Europe at the beginning of the sixteenth century: Rodrigo the German, Petijean of France, Diego Copín of Holland, Juan and Felipe de Borgoña, Francis of Antwerp, and two Spaniards who designed the whole, Enrique de Egas and Pedro Gumiel. When I was younger I did not care much for the confection this team threw together, and I amused myself by imagining Egas shouting one afternoon, 'Petijean, we need six more statues just like the last ones.' But when I saw it recently I was awed by the sheer bravado of the thing; its mass is overpowering; its intricacy is as well planned as a Bach fugue. If Egas did indeed call for carved saints by dozen lots, he knew where to put them when he got them.

The reredos is so placed that the tabernacle, which is the raison d'être for the whole, is in shadow, and in the early days of the eighteenth century it was decided that a shaft of light should be brought through the rear wall of the cathedral and then through the back of the reredos so as to illuminate the tabernacle. This might also solve another problem; just as Queen Isabel had objected to people's staring at the articulated statue of the Conde de Luna during Mass, so two centuries later devout Catholics were objecting to the fact that others less devout were wandering about the ambulatory during service, and it was thought that if they could see the tabernacle from the rear they would respect it and be silent when Mass was being read. The result of these two needs was the Transparente, so named because light would pass through solid walls. It is one of architecture's cleverest juggling feats, if not one of art's successes.

Into the back of the high altar a circle was cut so that persons in the ambulatory could see through to the tabernacle and know when it was being used. At the same time, high on the opposite wall of the cathedral, a very large hole was cut, perhaps twenty to thirty feet across, to admit a shaft of light that would fall upon the tabernacle thus exposed. It was a bold solution, made possible only because the outside walls of the cathedral, erected about 1227, were strong and could withstand being pierced, and because the altar had been so solidly built that it did not collapse when a fairly large hole was driven through. Thus, in the mornings when Mass was being said and when the sun stood in the eastern heavens, shafts of sunlight came unimpeded to illuminate the filigreed tabernacle when seen from either front or back.

Of course, two gaping holes resulted and it was the steps taken to mask them that constituted the marvel of the Transparente, known in Spain as 'the eighth wonder of the world.' Tastes of the time were on the florid side, and the Transparente became the most florid baroque accomplishment of its period. It is a fantastic thing. The clue to its bewildering opulence comes with the identification of the team who built it: the Spanish architect Narciso Tomé assisted by his four sons, two of whom were architects, one a sculptor and the last a painter. Tomé put his whole family to work, and when the holes were completed, the sculptor and the painter, aided by teams of assistants, began producing a whole company of saints, angels, prophets and cardinals. Some were painted flat on the walls of the openings but in wonderful perspective, so that from the great distance at which they were seen, and from below, they appeared to be sculptures. Most were sculpted in marble or bronze and some of these were polychromed. Intricate abstract designs suggesting flowing robes and foliage were created to hang over corners so that the architectural details of the piercing could be masked. And splendid groups of figures, so intricate that the eye could hardly unravel them, were put together so that the opening leading to the tabernacle could be hidden and yet permit light to pass through unimpeded. As a jigsaw puzzle, the Transparente of Toledo is without peer, and the pieces are full-sized human beings.

Now to fit the puzzle together. It is apparent, I hope, that we are speaking about two rather large holes separated by a considerable distance, the first low down at the back of the main altar, the second across the ambulatory very high up and on the outside wall. Well, Narciso Tomé and his four sons solved this by posting along the edges of the outside cut a stunning array of Biblical figures who seem to pour into the cathedral from the heavens. They twist and tumble, clutch at one another and raise their hands in prayer, fall and slide, gesticulate and grimace, forming a veritable cascade of heavenly figures from which we slowly pick out the significant fact: at the outer edge of the opening sits Jesus Himself, on a bank of clouds and surrounded by the angels of paradise.

This upper half of the Transparente is the lesser of the two parts and the more restrained, for the whole back of the reredos has been converted to a tower of marble which reaches from floor to ceiling. When it was finished a problem arose: 'How to join the two halves?' and here Tomé and his sons showed ingenuity. The painter provided a mural which crosses the top of the cathedral and ties the two halves together. It is a daring and successful device, in which painted and sculptured forms unite to make one vast procession, but to try to pick out the various parts from below makes one dizzy. We can, however, enjoy the massive structure that backs the high altar, for it is composed of four identifiable parts: at the bottom a

FOLLOWING FACING PAGES: *Left, the Transparente: upper hole.*
Right, the wedding of sculpture and fresco.

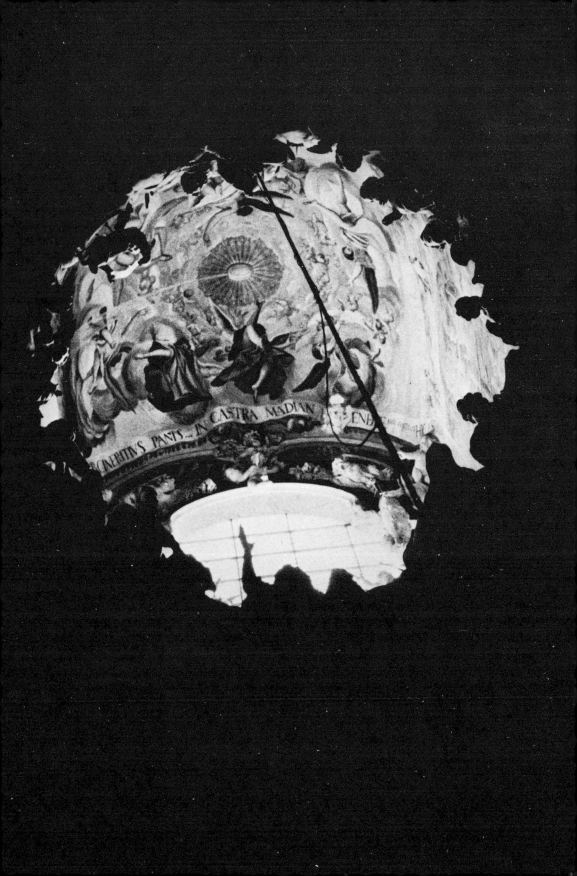

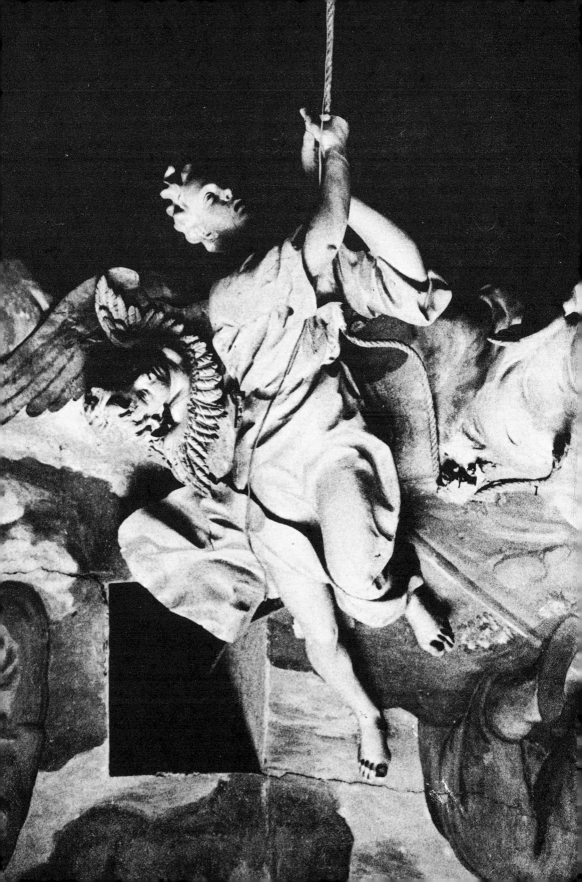

beautiful enthroned Mother and Child; quite high up so that most visitors miss it, a Last Supper with thirteen full-sized polychromed marble celebrants; at the very top, so that her head almost touches the muraled ceiling, the Virgin Mary ascending into heaven; and in the center, masking the opening to the tabernacle, a whirlwind of angels and clouds, one of the most successful depictions of wild movement ever to have been achieved in marble.

That's the Transparente, save for some score of separate standing figures and a forest of highly ornamented pillars that lend a pattern to the whole. It is blatantly a work of the early eighteenth century and could have been created, I suppose, only by a man who had four sons who could paint, carve, cast bronze and work upside down while suspended from ropes which passed through the ceiling.

Art of a different quality is to be found at our last stop, the sacristy, a long hall which one enters through an avenue of sixteen El Grecos, depicting the twelve disciples, Jesus, Mary, Santo Domingo and an extra portrait of St. Peter. Any one of these, appearing by itself in a foreign museum, would become a famous work; it is interesting to study the second portrait of Peter, one of the finest of its size El Greco ever did, for it shows Peter weeping and reminds one that the artist must have had a special fondness for him. He always painted him with such love.

Our purpose in visiting the sacristy, however, is to see two paintings more important than the portraits. They are among the finest examples of Spanish art, and with their help we shall discover something about the soul of Spain.

The first is the more conspicuous and more easily grasped. At the far end of the long hall, framed as an altarpiece, stands the 'Spoliation of Christ' by El Greco, depicting the mysterious figure of Jesus draped in flaming red as he is taunted by the rabble while in the foreground a carpenter in a yellow smock prepares the cross. Gaunt, ethereal faces stare out from the crowd; a woman in ochre robe and purple dress, her back to the viewer, raises her hand dramatically as a Roman guard, posed by some man brought in from the streets of Toledo, stands in polished armor. Flags and spears and plumed helmets fill the top of the picture. One sees the passion and terror of sixteenth-century Spain. It is a stunning picture and El Greco must have liked it, for a nearby museum has a smaller copy, but it lacks the vitality of this great presentation.

A few yards away, set so far back in a niche that the unobservant might miss it, is a slightly smaller picture by Goya, 'The Arresting of Jesus on the Mount of Olives,' a vigorous night scene, earthy and with no sense of mystery. Christ is shown as a faltering man robed in a curious pinkish white, while the soldiers who surround him are counterparts of those depicted in Goya's series of etchings 'The Disasters of War.' They are not Romans, but rather peasants from the central plateau of Iberia, and their leering faces can be seen even today in the villages outside Madrid. The picture is a haunting thing, a country scene of torment in which Jesus appears to be actually suffering the indignities being thrown at him by the mob, and those hurried visitors who miss this fine work miss something very good and very Spanish.

In neither of these powerful pictures do I find anything of Jesus the religious figure nor of the Holy Land as I knew it in Israel and Jordan; I doubt that in the strictest sense they ought to be called religious pictures. But in each I find an infinite amount of Spain in its basic manifestations, the mystical of El Greco and the practical of Goya. The former, with its tortured figures and demonic faces, recalls the agonies which Spain has always inflicted upon itself, the self-condemnation, the religious fervor, the leaping of inspired minds directly to the throne of heaven, the impassioned singing and violence. These things I can see in the El Greco, where flaming red dominates and leads the eye to colors no other artist would dare place in juxtaposition, just as no sensible man laying out the history of a nation would dare give one country the contradictory experiences that Spain has known. In the Goya, on the other hand, I see the earthiness of Spain, the robust animal-like characteristic of the soil and the men who work it. These ugly, extremely human and likable faces remind me of the Spaniards who cursed as they pulled the oars at the Battle of Lepanto, who cursed as they mounted a guerrilla resistance against Napoleon, who suffered through the sad mismanagement of their country and who have survived whatever defeats and humiliations have been visited upon them. It is not by accident that in this canvas, which shows one of the most solemn moments of Biblical history, when the first physical step toward the Crucifixion was being taken, a goodly number of the participants are laughing. As one reads this book he must not forget that at the most solemn moments of Spanish history someone is laughing, sardonically perhaps, but laughing.

I never leave the cathedral at Toledo without paying my respects to two contrasting figures, now shadowy but once of earth-moving power, who ruled from this building and whose confrontation continues throughout Spanish history, for they are so dramatic that they seem to have been created by a playwright rather than by the chances of history. They are the two fiery cardinals, Mendoza and Cisneros, who had large roles in governing Spain, Mendoza from 1482 till 1495, Cisneros from 1495 till 1517. Pedro González de Mendoza (1428–1495) was the fourth (some say fifth) son of a noble family and his presence in the church was an accident: he was really a confirmed layman pushed by his relatives into a position from which he could exercise power. In clerical robes he led the armies of Fernando and Isabel and helped them gain the crown. He was first into Granada at the end of the conquest, served as civil governor of Castilla in the footsteps of Don Alvaro de Luna, and was one of the few at

court who understood what Columbus was talking about. Taking his religious vows lightly, he sought Rome's forgiveness for having sired illegitimate children, but being prudent as well as lecherous he made his appeals in group lots. He was cast in heroic mold and maintained his own court and armed guard, and he left behind him in Toledo so many monuments that he seems as alive today as he did in that period when he was helping usher Spain into its period of maximum greatness. His tomb stands at the left of the main altar and is a fantastically pompous affair of pillars, arches, statues, niches plus a gaudy marble casket in which he lies in regal splendor befitting his nickname, 'third King of Spain.' When I studied Mendoza in books I never cared much for him, but it was not until I saw his tomb that I understood why.

To me the best thing he did was to sponsor as his successor Gonzalo Jiménez de Cisneros (1436–1517), who had begun his life as a poor boy in a town near Madrid and who when entering orders changed his name to Francisco in honor of his patron. Of a shy retiring nature, he hid himself in a convent, where his piety commended itself to Queen Isabel, who made him her confessor. The better she knew him the more she respected him, and one day she handed him a letter from the Pope appointing him Archbishop of Toledo, but he refused the honor, an impasse which she solved by appointing him anyway. Soon Fernando, desiring some strong administrators at the head of the Spanish Church, connived to have him made cardinal, and one of the first things this quiet, bookish man did was to conscript an army of twenty thousand soldiers to invade Oran and Tripoli to teach the Muslims a lesson. There is a touching account of how, on the eve of a great battle in which he would lead the troops, he reflected upon the irony of a fate which had made him, a seeker after retreat and silence, the general of an invading army.

Much more was in store for him. When Fernando died in 1516, Cisneros found that he had been appointed in the king's will to serve as regent of Castilla until Fernando's grandson, Carlos I of Spain and V of the Holy Roman Empire, should reach Spain, which he had not yet seen. That year Cisneros was eighty, and without hesitation he launched upon one of the miraculous years of Spanish history. He challenged the power of Adrian of Utrecht, the tutor of young Carlos, and frustrated his plans to make Spain an appendage of Austria. He battled the nobles and recovered from them powers which he felt Carlos ought to exercise when he became king. He put down the intrigues of the courtiers who wanted to pass the throne of Aragón along to Carlos' younger brother, Fernando of Austria, who had been brought up in Spain. Under his own supervision he built several buildings that are notable still. He strengthened farming and initiated steps which would have ensured Spain great agricultural wealth

Except for the worm holes through his forehead,
this saint seems as alive today as he did
three hundred years ago. He is for sale
on the streets of Toledo.

had they been pursued. He armed the nation's ships against the pirates of the Mediterranean and the freebooters of the Atlantic, thus establishing himself as the father of the navy which seventy-two years later culminated in the Armada. He spent much time furthering the development of the new university which he had founded at Alcalá de Henares. He watched over the publication of one of the world's premier examples of scholarship, the *Biblia Poliglota Complutense* (the Polyglot Bible of Alcalá de Henares, completed in 1514–1517 but not set into type until 1522), which he had fathered and in which, for the Old Testament, the Hebrew, Greek and Latin texts were printed side by side, 'with the Latin in middle,' as the preface pointed out, 'like Jesus between the two thieves at the Crucifixion.' For the Pentateuch, that is, the first five books, a fourth column was provided, giving the Aramaic text of the Targum of Onkelos; for the New Testament, of course, only two columns were needed, Greek and Latin. All subsequent Biblical scholarship would be dependent upon this great work. And most important of all, Cisneros quietly rebuffed every attempt to put on the throne of Spain the rightful heir, Juana la Loca (Mad Joanna), daughter of Fernando and Isabel and mother of Carlos I. He argued that even though Juana had divine right to the throne—which fact none denied—she was so incompetent that she could rule only through a regency, and this he feared would be so prolonged that only evil could result. (He was right; in her virtual prison Juana lived for another thirty-nine years.) Quiet, relentless in pursuit of all he believed in and champion of the rights of the boy king whom he had never seen, Cisneros by force of character held Spain together on the eve of its greatness.

His last act as regent was to leave Toledo and move in wearying stages to one monastery after another so as to be ready to consult with Carlos as the youth entered Spain for the first time, but the trip was so arduous that Cisneros fell ill. Fable claims that he died from anguish after reading a letter, which Carlos had sent ahead, rebuking him for assumption of powers and dismissing him from all offices. But historians believe that Cisneros had died before the letter arrived.

The cathedral at Toledo contains a strange memorial to Cisneros, and it contrasts favorably, I think, with the flamboyant tomb of Mendoza. At the southwest corner of the cathedral stands the Capilla Mozárabe. When the Moors overran Toledo they offered the conquered two alternatives: convert to Islam or remain Christians and pay certain special taxes. The Mozárabes (would-be Arabs) were those who followed the second course. They remained Christians and through the centuries developed their own peculiar style of celebrating the Mass. In 1085, when Alfonso VI conquered the city, his wife and his religious advisor, both of them French, prevailed upon him to enforce throughout his realm the newly proposed Cluniac reforms, which required the adoption of the Roman type of Mass. The Mozárabe was thus frowned upon, which was right because it was through the various consolidations of power and uniformity proposed by the Cluniac reforms that the Catholic Church attained the cohesion it needed for the tasks ahead, and a single form of the Mass, understandable in all lands, was one of the greatest unifying forces. On the other hand, it was sardonic that the Mozárabes, having been allowed to practice their form of Mass by the Arabs, should now be in danger of losing it to Catholics. Stubbornly they held onto their version for four hundred years, from 1085 to 1485 and beyond, in spite of real pressure from Rome; finally Cardinal Cisneros decreed that if any people were so devoted to their form of worship their wishes should be respected, and at the southwest corner of the cathedral he authorized a chapel to be built for perpetual observance of the Mozárabe rite. It is this chapel, ugly on the outside, lovely inside, that disfigures the right side of the façade, but the spirit that animated Cisneros to this generous act is considered his finest memorial. Today only one hundred and fifty families still follow the Mozárabe rite, and they remember Cisneros with affection.

Obviously Cisneros is a hero of mine, for wherever one meets his trail one finds greatness. It is my duty, therefore, to report that he undertook two additional responsibilities: he served as head of the Holy Inquisition for all Spain and many of its worst excesses were committed under his leadership. When Carlos, writing from Flanders prior to his arrival in Spain, suggested to Cisneros that reforms in the inquisitorial process might be advisable, the cardinal wrote back: 'The Inquisition is so perfect that there will never be any need for reform and it would be sinful to introduce changes.' It was also Cisneros who supported Isabel's expulsion of the Jews from Spain, but later, when planning his Poliglota, he searched Europe for Jewish scholars expert in Hebrew and brought them to Alcalá de Henares, where he protected them as they taught.

While renewing my acquaintance with the cathedral I continued to experience Toledo tourism, and I began to appreciate why personal services were so bad. Each morning as I walked downstairs, for the hotel elevator still didn't work, I found fifty or sixty suitcases stacked in the lobby and buses waiting at the door. Foreigners streamed down the stairs, checked their luggage with bleary eyes and crawled into the buses, not to return. It reminded me of herding Texas cattle, and there was no reason why the overworked men behind the desk should bother to identify as individuals the animals moving in and out. In fact, I was surprised that the service was as good as it was, except that I was somewhat irritated one morning when the desk man looked up with surprise and said, 'Dios mío, are you still here?' Finally, one afternoon as I returned weary from a long walk through the city, the elevator was working. It lifted me to floor two-and-a-half and there conked out altogether, leaving me suspended for thirty minutes.

On the other hand, I had found a good restaurant and a waiter who actually laughed. Once when I tipped him rather more than usual, he confided, 'I'm saving this to get to Madrid.'

'You taking a job there?'

'No. I love bullfights and Curro Romero is fighting on Sunday. He's the best. Care to come along?'

I was much tempted, because I had not yet seen Romero, but I had reached the point where my extended walks into out-of-the-way places were beginning to produce an affection for Toledo which I did not want to imperil. 'You go,' I said. 'I'll see Romero later.'

'Don't delay,' the waiter warned me, 'because he does such things with the bull that any day he might get hurt.'

My walks took me into many corners of Toledo, one of the most interesting being the south side of the city, where the poor lived. I had not intended going there, but a donkey came by hauling a milk cart and I followed it for some time and found myself in a warren of medieval streets that led down the cliffs to the banks of the Tajo. In a few instances I saw the kind of poverty I had seen in the farm villages in Extremadura, but most of the houses I stopped at were those of what one might call the respectable poor, with adequate clothing and good food but not quite enough of either; and no matter how poor the house it usually was next to one with a television aerial. I spent some time with a pauper who made his living by walking into the country and collecting reeds which he bound into whisk brooms, tying their ends together with a rope he made from vines. He worked at the base of a tree near the river. 'This is my factory,' he said. It consisted of one very old knife for cutting his materials and a stick on which he wound his rope, with room at each end for him to stand on, so that when the time came to bind his reeds he could pull very hard against the stick held down by his toes; old beggars must have used this system in Egypt two thousand years before the birth of Christ. 'I make enough to live on,' he said. When I asked him how much, he said, 'I can make three of these brooms a day, when the weather's good, and I sell them for eight cents apiece.' I asked if he could live on twenty-four cents a day, and he said, 'I beg too.' When his whisk was finished he showed me how to bang it against the tree. 'Women appreciate it when you've knocked out the seeds.'

I now came upon a courtyard which explained much about Toledo's noise, for a group of six or seven young men were preening their motorcycles as carefully as men in London preen their Jaguars. The motorcycles were of a kind new to me, for although each had one front wheel, it had two rear wheels on which was slung a trucklike body capable of carrying, I should judge, about a quarter-ton. It was these motorcycles which made the noise and moved the cargoes of modern Spain. The rich in Spain have

In Spain one has a constant image
of suspicious people peering out
from half-opened doors to check upon
who or what is passing.

always loved automobiles; recently the middle class have been able to afford them too; but the poor can afford only their motorcycle trucks, and the government would face revolution if it passed laws forbidding them. If I were dictator of Spain, I would certainly not restrict the motorcycles, but I would earmark a large budget for the development of a muffler system.

I was often stopped by Spaniards who wanted to talk about foreign countries or their own, and if the newspapers were afraid to talk politics, the people were not. Jokes were common. Generalísimo Franco was traveling through the countryside when his coach broke down. Desiring to know what his people thought, he walked alone to a farmer and said, 'How're things?' and the farmer said, 'Lousy. The government doesn't know its ass from its elbow.' Franco became angry and said, 'Don't you know who I am?' and the farmer said, 'I've seen your face somewhere before,' and Franco said, 'You'll find my name on all the principal streets, everywhere.' The farmer dropped his hoe, looked up with delight and cried, 'Oh! Señor Coca-Cola!'

When I say that 'I talked with this man or that,' I am using the verb in a restricted sense. I read Spanish fluently, understand it partially and speak it poorly, but I have memorized some twoscore old-style phrases of considerable gentility and these I can rattle off, so my speaking consists of something like this: 'My esteemed señor, would you do me the favor of seeing . . .' I begin rapidly, thus creating the impression that I know what I'm talking about, but I end like this: 'if . . . you have . . . one . . . beer . . . cold . . . very?' Encouraged by the speed of my opening, my listener responds at a natural rate, and when he does I understand about two-thirds of what he says, especially if it concerns a subject on which I know the basic vocabulary. Of course, in philosophical discussions I am often at a loss in critical moments because I fail to catch whether Miguel de Unamuno said that Spain was lost or that Spain was inspired. But I do not hold back because of my ineptness, and I have talked for many hours with many different kinds of Spaniards.

I had now descended to the Tajo at the spot where a dam constructed centuries ago created a waterfall, and here I stayed through twilight; always before, I had seen the fall from the top of a cliff, distant and silent and lovely, and I was now surprised at how much noise it made. An old man came to sit with me and we looked for some minutes in silence at the ruins of the mill that jutted into the river. 'You from América del Norte? Must be a great place.' I asked him why he thought so, and he said, 'Our newspapers say so many bad things about it.' I asked him if he'd want to go to America, and he said, 'For the money, yes. Here it's hard for a man to earn enough. But for the life over there . . . the speed . . . the noise . . . no, thank you.' I asked him if Spain were easier now. 'Much better. At last they're getting some sense into their crazy heads in Madrid.' Something moved close to me in the darkness and I jumped. 'What's that?' 'My cows,' he said. And there, on an edge of Toledo I'd not seen before, a farmer was herding five black-and-white cows who apparently found a good living among the thickets that grew along the riverbanks.

Whenever I wandered back toward the center of town I found myself engulfed in the deluge of tourists and I resolved to find out how Toledo copes with this industry. Leaving the cathedral one morning and keeping the cardinal's palace on my right and the city hall on my left, I followed a narrow path to the beautiful Plaza del Consistorio, from which ran the Pasadizo del Ayuntamiento, a covered footway running through the heart of a store specializing in stones from early Christian times. Leaving this I walked along a chain of pleasant streets that brought me to Santo Tomé, the church which holds El Greco's 'The Burial of Count Orgaz,' and a little farther on I stopped at San Juan de Dios, 20, at the damascene shop of Luis Simón, a handsome, fleshy man in his forties, with prematurely gray hair. He said business was slow at the moment and he'd be glad to show me around his factory, and from what I saw I judged that he specialized in good workmanship applied to the kinds of things that were bound to sell: penknives, ash trays, brooches, decorative swords. Taking a piece of steel and a blowtorch, he softened a mixture of wax, resin, red earth and olive oil and set the steel into it. As soon as the flame was withdrawn the mixture hardened and Simón was ready to work. 'I employ fourteen people throughout the year. It took me five years to learn the trade, another five to become good, but now in Toledo we have a school of applied arts, and young men can speed the process. If they have skill they earn a good living. You'll notice my men are all young. During the Crusade of 1936 we lost a whole generation of artists. Older men were killed off. Younger men were not trained. The steel I'm using, as you can see, is very soft. They make it for us specially in the mills at Bilbao.'

As he spoke he was scoring the steel with a sharp-pointed knife, laying down a series of fine lines with burred edges about 1/120th of an inch apart. When he had completed a section running in one direction he turned the steel and worked across the lines, so that in the end he had an area completely covered by crisscross lines of the finest delicacy. Luis Simón was obviously a master workman, but in answer to my question he said, 'Of course, I could make any object you see in the shop. But today I'm too busy selling. The manufacturing I must leave to my men. This gold I'm using comes to us from Madrid but I believe they buy it from Germany.' Across the burred edges of the steel he was running a strand of very thin gold wire of great brilliance, and when he had laid out an ancient Arabic design consisting of triangles and solid spaces, he gently tapped each wire into position, and as he did so the roughened edges of the lines caught at the gold and held it fast. He then picked up a small mallet and a blunt-headed instrument and with some force hammered the gold wires into permanent position, closing the edges of the lines about them. 'That gold

FOLLOWING FACING PAGES:
Waiting for the bus.

can never be pulled out now. Try it,' and when I had unsuccessfully tried, he said, 'We now bake the steel so that the gold forms a permanent bond and the empty spaces of steel become jet black. That's what damascene work is.' He showed me his salesroom, where an ash tray seven inches across, decorated in a gold-and-silver Moorish design of considerable intricacy, sold for twenty-seven dollars. 'Twenty-four karat gold and pure silver,' he explained, 'but we have others of less complicated design, same size, for as low as sixteen dollars.'

He was proud of the swords made in his shop, immense things with braided-steel handles. 'We have our own forge, and water-temper the steel just the way they did in this street when a Toledo blade was famous throughout the world. The sword you're holding is five feet long with a woven handle and we can sell it for nine dollars. But this one, smaller size, gold inlaid, is an exact copy of a sword used ceremonially by Queen Isabel . . . Try it, it's completely flexible. Costs three hundred dollars. We also make fencing swords. This one for beginners, only four-sixty and completely flexible. Best fencing sword with inlaid handle, sixteen dollars. This one, of course, we're proud of. The bullfighter's sword. Heavy. Very strong. For beginners this one for six dollars., For the real thing, maybe fifty dollars. When my father worked here, all matadors' swords came from Toledo, because we were the world's finest sword makers, but starting about 1910 a firm named Luna in Valencia took away the business, and they did make good swords. Today most matadors get theirs from Bermeja in Madrid, and so it goes.'

As to tourists, Señor Simón was in favor of them. 'They are our existence. We can survive if we get twenty good customers a day. I try to meet each one because I have a funny sense about what people want and what they'll be willing to pay. More than half our customers are French, but the norteamericanos come second and they tend to buy more when they do come. I speak French, English, Italian and a little German. My two daughters work with me. One speaks French and English; the other, French and German. I learned my languages by listening, when I was a boy working at the benches, while others did the selling. I'd repeat each word over and over. I used to work in a pretty big factory. Forty people. We had a deal with travel agencies. They'd steer their tourists to us and we'd sell a two-dollar bracelet for three dollars and give the agency a split. They watched us like hawks to see how much we were selling, and we'd try to work it so that the tourists wouldn't buy then but would come back later on. I got tired of such business and started my own. No guides, no agencies, no runners. We pay commissions to no one. I emphasize this because Toledo has been badly hurt by the last printing of Mr. Fielding's book on travel in Europe. He warns the norteamericanos, "Don't buy anything in Toledo. You can get it cheaper in Madrid." One norteamericano after another tells me, "Mr. Fielding told me to buy in Madrid, so I'm going to wait." I say, "Can't you make up your own mind?" but they say, "Sure, but who wants to be robbed?" Fact is, Mr. Fielding was right. The shops to which the guides take you do rob you, and you can buy the same thing cheaper in Madrid. But the truth is that if you come to shops like mine, and there are dozens like me in Toledo, even near the Zocodover, you get bargains that no one in Madrid can match. Look at my prices and compare. The guides know this and they have to protect themselves, so now they tell the norteamericanos, "Sure, Señor Simón's price is a little lower. Why shouldn't it be? Everything he sells is machine-made." This is a tough business but we make our way.'

As he spoke, an American woman came into the store to conclude a bargaining session that had extended over three days. 'In spite of what Fielding says, I'm going to buy from you.' She was satisfied that Señor Simón's prices were about as good as she was going to find and she was prepared to place her order: 'Six of the larger ash trays, four pairs of scissors, four penknives, six water jugs, six small swords for letter openers, one large plate, one larger sword . . .' I understood what Simón meant when he said that with twenty customers a day he could get by. This woman's bill was going to be close to two hundred dollars and she was delighted with the things she was getting. 'This store is so clean and well lighted it's a pleasure to do business here,' she said. When she was gone, Simón said, 'It ought to be clean. The municipal government sends an inspector here once a month to be sure the shop looks appealing. In Toledo, tourism is a big business . . . the biggest we have, and we've got to do everything we can to offset the bad blow Mr. Fielding gave us.'

On my way to inspect the damascene factory I had noticed, at Calle de Santo Tomé, 6, an attractive restaurant whose main dining room was the patio of an old convent. It was run by a vigorous young man named Mariano Díaz and his robust, handsome wife Sagrario. 'And seven others, all members of the family,' Don Mariano explained. He was proud of his restaurant and wanted to talk about it. 'I'm from Toledo. My father has a restaurant of his own on the other side of town and I've always wanted to be in the business. It was Sagrario's father who started this one, and I took over when I married Sagrario. Her father came from Valencia, during the Crusade. He couldn't stand the Communists who were in control of the city, so he fled. Started a bar on this corner, but the big growth came when Sagrario and I took over. We have 225 seats now and during most of the summer they're filled every noon. We pay commission to no one . . . no guides, no tourist agencies, no runners. We don't want that kind of business. You look at us and if you like the way we look . . . We spend a lot of time keeping this place clean and attractive, and all of our business comes from walking tourists who say, "That old convent looks interesting. Let's eat there." It used to be a Franciscan convent. We rent it.'

Señor Díaz was the kind of man I enjoy meeting in any field of

endeavor, because he loved his work and took pride in explaining its tricks and triumphs. He was a big, tall man with an expressive face, a young man, too, barely in his thirties, filled with plans for a better Toledo. 'Some of us younger people wanted to put up a hotel, a real fine place where you wouldn't be ashamed to stay. We figured about sixteen thousand dollars a room and we could have financed it, but then we asked ourselves, "what will we do about the winter?" And the more we studied, the more we realized that any money we made in summer would be lost in winter, when nobody comes here. Maybe we'll work out something else. I'm not worrying. I have enough to keep me busy trying to make this a fine restaurant. Did you see where the French guide gave us a two-fork rating? You can get a fine meal with us and not spend too much money. We offer three different menus. A la carte, and you can get a good meal from it for a dollar eighty-five. Special lunch of the house, a dollar thirty. And of course, the tourist menu at one fifty-five. How do the customers choose? A la carte forty percent, house special thirty percent, tourist thirty percent. Our very best meal, I would say, was partridge Toledo-style. Estupendo! There's a farm not far from here that kills two or three thousand partridges a day in season. The French, who know good cooking, always go for partridge because at two-twenty it's a sensational bargain. The norteamericanos? Well, they don't understand that game has to be hung. Sometimes they say it smells, so we take it back and serve them boiled chicken. They say it doesn't smell.'

I spent a long time with the Díaz family, nine of them including the wife's sister, who must be the most beautiful waitress in Spain. Kitchen, washrooms, tables and crockery were all immaculate. 'The government's smart,' Díaz said. 'They have one corps of restaurant inspectors who live in Toledo, another in Madrid. They send the Toledo men to inspect Madrid and the Madrid men out here to inspect us. You could be one of the Madrid men, for all I know. They pull tricks like that on us, but they have no problem with me because we police ourselves. We try to do everything possible to make tourists happy, and the disgraceful business you had when you ordered from the tourist menu too late would never happen here. The girls speak a lot of languages. French is most important, especially in a restaurant, because a norteamericano sits down and says, "Bring me that," but the Frenchman wants to know does it have a sauce, are the vegetables fresh, is the cream chilled. Frankly, the French are more fun, but we do everything we can to make the norteamericanos feel at home. They will spend money if they're encouraged.'

As to the food in El Plácido, as the quiet place was appropriately named, it was among the best I had in Spain. Don Mariano and his wife tried to push the stewed partridge, but when I resisted, they shrugged their shoulders and he said, 'It's the French who know how to eat. I suppose you want boiled chicken?' I took the mixed salad, which was crisp and delicious.

Tourist wares.

Right across the street, at Calle de Santo Tomé, 5, stood an element of the tourist industry which had always fascinated me, the marzipan factory of Rodrigo Martínez, who ran the big retail shop on the Zocodover where trays of marzipan in various shapes have seduced generations of travelers. In Spain this delicacy is called mazapán and has many distinctive qualities which differentiate it from brands sold elsewhere in the world. Señor Martínez was a small, conservative man in his fifties, cautious in all he did and said, and quite unable to understand why a stranger would be interested in anything so Spanish as a mazapán factory. Gingerly, as if I were a commercial spy, he released one bit of classified information after another in what was one of the most painstaking interviews I have ever conducted.

'If it weren't for the oil contained in the seed kernel of the almonds,' he began in the middle, 'mazapán would last indefinitely, like the dried meat they chop up in northern countries.' I must have shown my bewilderment at such a beginning, for he added slowly, 'You're probably like all other strangers and think that we get our almonds from Andalucía in the south. But we don't. The almonds that do grow down there aren't very good. We get ours from orchards along the Mediterranean coast. South of Valencia. Some of the best almonds in the world and to my taste much better than those grown in Arab countries. More consistent. Almonds and oranges grow in the same kind of soil and the same climate, so they compete.'

He must have concluded that that was all I needed to know about mazapán because he stopped. After some moments of silence he added cautiously, 'If you did want to make mazapán you'd get the best almonds you could find and dip them in boiling water, then run them through this friction machine, which scrapes off the skin. Look at that pile of skins. It has no commercial use whatever, doesn't even burn well. When the almonds are clean and shining white you move them over to this machine, but be careful to set the grinding wheels fairly far apart. Into the hopper you put one part almonds, one part cane sugar, and this machine breaks the almonds into pieces and mixes the sugar with them. Almonds cost about eighty-five cents a pound and sugar about ten cents a pound, so you can see that there's a great temptation to put in a lot of sugar and a little almond, but that makes wretched mazapán. Watch out for the man who puts in less than half almonds. You now throw the whole mass back into the grinder, but this time you set the wheels very close together, so that the almonds are pulverized. Then you press the paste into forms and bake it in a moderate oven for about fifteen minutes, take it out, paint it with a glaze of water and sugar and finish it off for another ten minutes to give that lovely brownish crust. That's the best mazapán you can get in the world.'

Señor Martínez was still suspicious, but he asked softly, 'Would you care to see what we do for Christmas?' I tried to show the enthusiasm I was feeling, and he brought down from a high shelf a set of empty circular boxes covered with bright decorations. 'Into these round boxes we coil long lengths of mazapán made in the shape of eels. They have scales of sugar, eyes of candy, and are filled with crystallized cherries, candied sweet potato, apricot jam and sweetened egg yolks. This big box sells for about four dollars, and lots of children think the thing inside is a real serpent, but of course it's only mazapán. I supply stores all over Spain and some in América del Norte, too.'

I said that I was especially fond of marzipan and frequently bought small samples in America, at which his face took on the glazed look that overtakes a Frenchman when you praise California wine. 'I'm afraid that in América del Norte you've never tasted real mazapán. Friends have sent me samples and it's mostly sugar. Very bad. But wait a minute. In Mexico City there's a man who learned how to make mazapán here in Toledo. During the Crusade he was on the other side, and when peace came he didn't want to live in Spain any longer, so he went to Mexico.' He paused, evidently remembering his long-absent friend, exiled from Toledo by the Civil War. 'I've heard some very good things about the quality of mazapán he's making in Mexico, but I'm sure you don't get any of it in New York.'

The interview had ended, and I was about to leave when I saw a sign which read: 'Exquisite paste for making the classic almond soup, in packages of any weight, eighty-seven cents a pound.' 'Is that how you make almond soup?' I asked with some excitement. 'Do you know our great almond soup?' he asked, his face brightening. 'I was introduced to it the other day. Best soup I ever tasted. Like angels' wings.' He became positively animated and said, 'Even better. We make a paste . . .' as if he could not believe my sincerity, he asked, 'Do you really like almond soup? Norteamericanos don't usually like it. It's the French who know something good when they taste it.' I assured Señor Martínez that from the first moment I had tasted this delicious soup, fragrant and heavy with flavor, I had delighted in it. 'The first bowlful they gave me had a rose petal floating in it. One rose petal, deep red against snowy white.' He realized that I knew what I was talking about and said, 'We don't use rose petals much any more. But we make this paste. You take two hundred grams of the paste and one liter of very cold, rich milk. You add a little handful of sweet biscuits well flavored and a small touch of carnela.' I asked him what carnela was, thinking that he must mean caramelo. No, he meant carnela. Everybody knew what carnela was, but my dictionary didn't give the word, so I didn't find out. 'You put these together and beat them thoroughly. Then serve ice-cold . . . or if it's Christmas, when we use almond soup a lot, you can heat it. Like our sign says, it's classic.'

As we talked we were surrounded by trays full of marzipan, some plain, some shaped in little cups and filled with apricot jam, and now Don Rodrigo offered me samples, delighted to have found someone who appreciated his art. As I ate, he said, 'After the battle of Navas de Tolosa in the year 1212 there was famine in many parts of Spain, so the monks of San Clemente convent, here in Toledo, developed the secret upon which our industry is founded. How to crush almonds so they will stay good to eat after four or five months. We sent our paste throughout Spain and that's how Toledo became famous for this delicacy. The secret? Well, when I was telling you how to make mazapán . . . the wheels and the sugar and the hot water . . . well, I didn't tell you everything.'

Much later, when I happened to have a bowl of almond soup in Madrid, the host sprinkled it with cinnamon. 'Canela,' he said. 'The final touch.'

When I left the marzipan factory I wandered to the west and came to a promenade that ran along the top of a cliff, from which I could look down into the river below. As I strolled along I came to a notable old building which stood hidden behind a high brick wall, as if it were a jewel under protection. A creaking gate let me into a Moorish garden which could have existed in that spot a thousand years ago when the Moors still occupied Toledo. Palm trees and lemon and orange grew in lovely patterns. In one corner a fountain bubbled, sending echoes across the graveled walks, and there were benches from which I could study at leisure the low and unimpressive building. I could not identify it: possibly it had been a mosque, or a synagogue or a church, for it seemed to partake of many characteristics. At the bottom it was built of unfinished brick; at the top, of a muddy stucco, which had begun to peel. The windows were off-center and the entrance was notable principally for a very old wooden door decorated in Moorish design.

I pressed against the door and it opened slowly to reveal a most beautiful building which looked like a mosque. The interior was filled by twenty-four octagonal columns, each topped by a capital of Arabic design supporting Moorish arches, but when I looked for the Muslim mihrab which would show worshipers the direction of Mecca, I found instead a Christian altar, for this was the famous Santa María la Blanca church and its origin was one of the compelling stories of Toledo.

To understand it we must leave Santa María and go to another part of Toledo, where in the Plaza Santo Domingo el Real we find imbedded in a wall a plaque which reads: 'Memorial to the fiestas which the Valencian colony of Toledo held in honor of San Vicente Ferrer solemnizing the Fifth Centennial of his glorious death, May 1919.' Vicente Ferrer was an inspired Dominican orator who operated around Valencia at the end of the fourteenth century. His preaching was so persuasive that he was credited with the conversion of thousands in lands as remote as Ireland and Italy. He was especially famed for his ability to convince Jews of their error and was responsible for converting many. In 1405 he came to Toledo to deliver a series of sermons against the Jews, which caused one historian to describe him as 'the bloodthirsty enemy of the Jews, intolerant and vehement, with an oratorical style both vibrant and tempestuous and a destructive eloquence without par.'

Following one inflamed sermon, his audience became so infuriated with the obstinacy of Toledo's Jews who refused to heed the words of Ferrer that they swarmed out of church, ran through the streets gathering a mob and burst into the Moorish building which I have been describing. It was then operating as a synagogue, from which the mob hauled all Jews they could find, dragged them to the promenade overlooking the river, cut their throats and threw them onto the rocks below. In one tremendous spasm the Jews of Toledo were practically eliminated, and no sooner were they gone than their synagogue was consecrated a church, and so it remains to this day.

One would suppose that after such tragedy the Jews would have had enough of Toledo, but a few years later the quota was again about normal. Jewish traders flourished, and although their original synagogue had been lost to them, since a building once consecrated could not revert to a prior use, they were encouraged to worship in another building nearby, which still stands as Spain's finest example of a synagogue. Thus matters stood until 1492, when Queen Isabel, acting under guidance and pressure from Cardinal Cisneros, decreed that all Jews in her kingdom must either convert to Christianity or go into exile. It is strange, in this day, to read on the interior wall of the cathedral a huge sign which commemorates the expulsion:

> In the year 1492, on the second day of the month of January, Granada with all its kingdom was captured by the monarchs Don Fernando and Doña Isabel, the Most Reverend Don Pedro González de Mendoza, Cardinal of Spain, being archbishop. This same year, at the end of the month of July, all the Jews were expelled from all the kingdoms of Castilla, of Aragón and of Sicily. The following year 93 at the end of the month of January, this holy church was completed, Don Francisco Fernández de Cuenca, archdeacon of Calatrava, being in charge of the decoration, painting and tracery of the vaults.

I had not intended saying anything about 'The Burial of Count Orgaz,' the chief work of El Greco, for this has been so well and so repeatedly described that there seemed little I might add, but I passed the church of Santo Tomé so often on my way to the synagogue of Santa María la Blanca or to the damasquinado shop of Señor Simón that I thought it silly not to revisit the magisterial painting; however, I did not do so until one afternoon when a party of English tourists asked me the way to St. Ptomaine's and I accompanied them to the church, where I took a seat with them and decided simply to look at the painting as if I had never seen it before. Santo Tomé's makes it easy to see its stupendous El Greco: a section of the church is set aside for this purpose, with eight comfortable Renaissance armchairs facing the picture, plus benches for ten and folding chairs for an additional thirty-five. It was late afternoon and we were the only group in the church; soon the English travelers left and I was alone in my Renaissance chair with the marvelously fresh and well-lighted canvas before me.

Like most universal masterpieces, this one has many fine passages and others that are frankly bad. There are three glaring defects: the picture breaks into two unrelated halves, an upper and a lower; the yellow-robed angel that is supposed to unite them is one of the sorriest figures El Greco ever drew and fails completely in his mission (in Spain all angels must be male); and the clouds of little bodiless angels consisting only of head and wings are ridiculous and, unlike the similar putti of Raphael and the other Italians who used the convention with charm, accomplish nothing. The unresolved breaking into two halves is caused by that much-vaunted line of heads which is one of the glories of the work but which in its excellence creates a problem that El Greco could not surmount. The faulty angel is poorly designed, poorly placed and poorly executed, which is curious, since El Greco used the same device with success in other paintings. As for the clouds of bodiless angels, I am not one to discuss El Greco's success or failure with this device because to me the convention has always seemed stupid, but I do know that in this great work it clutters up the heavens with ugly or even repulsive forms, whereas in certain Italian works it seems to add a sense of mysterious unearthliness. What I object to most, however, is that the putti are badly painted, and as one looks at the canvas with a fresh eye unimpeded by what others have seen, they merely add to the general clutter of a work that was poorly organized to begin with.

On the other hand, as I slowly studied the canvas I found hidden beauties which had escaped me on previous visits. In the lower left-hand corner of the painting, the right-hand panel of St. Stephen's cloak contains a small inserted depiction of the stoning of St. Stephen, which would have constituted one of the world's principal art treasures had it been painted as a full-scale canvas of its own. The naked figures throwing rocks would have anticipated Cézanne's 'Bathers' by three hundred years. In fact, this little excerpt is so good that it alone would establish El Greco as a major painter. I was similarly struck by the group of three heavenly musicians in the cloud to the Virgin's right, that is, at the extreme left-hand margin of the painting. These three in their powerfully sculpted robes are drawn and painted about as well as figures could be when seen from below, and I wondered that I had not noticed them before. Again, if they had formed the subject matter for a full-sized canvas they would now be famous. The marvelous figure of St. Peter, robed in saffron, with two giant keys dangling from his limp right hand, proves once more the affinity El Greco felt

Sunlight through the window of the synagogue
where the friends of El Greco once worshiped.

for this particular saint; he never painted Peter better than here, and in doing so, achieved one of his most successful religious portraits. But when one looks at the painting for a long time, three or four hours perhaps, one is struck mostly, I think, by that host of paradise that fills the upper right-hand corner. Here are the tormented figures from the streets of Toledo, the half-idiots that El Greco loved to paint, the aimless ones, the God-driven. They crowd in upon the scene, beseeching the Virgin to receive the soul of the Conde de Orgaz and present it to Christ, robed in white, who waits above. They are a remarkable assembly, more compelling and more Spanish, I think, than the notables lined up below, even though El Greco himself stands among the latter. For me the painting repeats the dichotomy of Spain that we saw earlier in the two paintings by El Greco and Goya: the sober, secure and well-groomed nobles who now keep and have always kept Spain under rigid control, and the wonderfully human peasant types whose fiery passions have provided the torment and vision of the land, but as I look at the latter crowding heaven I ask, 'If this is paradise, what must hell be like?'

The Conde de Orgaz, a citizen of Toledo and lord of the town of Orgaz, some twenty miles south of the city, died in 1323, and El Greco painted the legendary miracle of his burial in 1586. The conde had assumed responsibility for enlarging and rebuilding this church of St. Thomas the Apostle at the turn of the century, thus assuring his ultimate burial in the church. In 1312 the conde increased his fund of heavenly gratitude by obtaining from the queen a grant of property in Toledo so that a community of Augustinian friars, formerly located in unhealthful surroundings on the banks of the Tajo, could move within the walls, and by insisting that the new church should be dedicated to St. Stephen, the same as the old one had been. 'When the priests were preparing to bury him,' as the tablet below the picture explains, 'an admirable and unusual thing, St. Stephen and St. Augustine came down from heaven and buried him here with their own hands. Since it would take long to explain what might have motivated these saints, ask about it of the Augustinian friars, who are not far from here, if you have the time. The way is short.' The plaque then continues with a fascinating bit of local history: 'You have heard the gratitude of heavenly beings; hear now the inconstancy of mortal men. The same Orgaz bequeathed to the curate and ministers of this church, as well as to the poor of the parish, two sheep, sixteen hens, two wineskins full of wine, two loads of firewood and eight hundred of the coins that we call maravedis, which they were to receive annually from the residents of Orgaz. Since these people refused for two years to pay the pious tribute, in the belief that with the passage of time the matter would be forgotten, they have been forced to pay it by order of the Chancery of Valladolid in the year 1570, the case having been prosecuted energetically by Andrés Núñez de Madrid, curate of this church, and Pedro Ruiz Durón, the administrator.' It was undoubtedly this successful lawsuit that led to the commissioning a few years later of the painting. I should add that the above inscription is in Latin.

Two of the finest portraits in the standing file belong to this curate Núñez (the golden-robed, iron-faced prelate holding a book at extreme right) and to the administrator Ruiz (the ecstatic figure clothed in white surplice standing nearest the spectator). Among the worthies one finds the grave and bitter-faced old Covarrubias brothers, El Greco's son and others who may have been well known in Toledo when the painting was done.

The line of standing figures has always bothered me, so I was pleased to come upon the facts relating to its inception, because I believe the sequence of events helps explain how great works of art are sometimes evolved. There had been talk in Toledo of applying to Rome for the sanctification of the Conde de Orgaz, seeing that heaven itself had sent messengers to supervise his burial, but the movement had got nowhere, so Father Núñez proposed that at least the body of the conde be moved to a finer tomb, but his archbishop said, 'No, it is not proper that sinful hands should move the body that saints themselves have buried.' Father Núñez thereupon came up with a third proposal: 'Mark Orgaz's humble grave with a painting which will retell the glories of the conde,' and to this the authorities agreed. So a contract, which still exists, was drawn up between Father Núñez and El Greco, perhaps with Administrator Ruiz looking on, in which the artist outlines his understanding of what he is being required to do:

> On the canvas will be painted a procession, showing how the curate and other clergymen were performing the offices for the burial of Don Gonzalo Ruiz de Toledo, lord of the town of Orgaz, and St. Augustine and St. Stephen descended to bury the body of this caballero, one holding him by the head and the other by the feet, depositing him in the sepulcher, and presenting round about many people looking on, and above all this will be depicted a sky filled with a heavenly scene.

As in many cases of Renaissance masterpieces, it was the client who determined much of the basic design, and El Greco saw to it that the two men who were footing the bill, Núñez and Ruiz, occupied prominent positions when the job was done.

Two sayings sum up all we require to know about this monumental work. One of the Spanish critics responsible for generating world interest in El Greco said of him and of this painting in particular, 'When he's good there's none better and when he's bad there's none worse.' One Englishman, as his group left that day, said of the painting, 'This is the best thing in Spain and the cheapest.' To spend an hour or two before this superbly presented picture, lounging in a Renaissance chair, costs eight cents.

On one of my casual wanderings through Toledo, I came to the quiet Plaza de Carmelites, on whose wall appeared this notice:

GLORY TO THE CARMELITE MARTYRS
FOR GOD AND FOR SPAIN
THERE WERE ASSASSINATED IN THIS STREET
IN JULY 1936 BY THE MARXISTS
THE FOLLOWING RELIGIOUS

The names of seventeen friars were listed, and I was once more brought face to face with the Civil War; no city knew worse atrocities than Toledo. In the beginning days it looked as if the Republic were going to win, and since Toledo had always been conservative and the seat of Catholic power—for the Bishop of Toledo is the primate of Spain—men who felt they had old scores to settle with the Church killed wantonly, as this sign testified. Later, when the war in Toledo had settled into a siege-type operation, Republican hotheads imported from Madrid coursed through the streets rounding up all conservatives, whom they herded in large groups to that very precipice from which the Jews had been flung in 1405, and there they slaughtered the prisoners in obscene brutality, sometimes throwing their bodies over the cliff as had been done 531 years before; history in Spain has an ominous way of repeating itself. As might be expected, when the Franco forces triumphed a savage retaliation was launched by the victors, who applied one simple rule: if the man has fought on the Republican side, kill him. And how was the best way to tell if he had fought? Look at the right shoulder of his coat. If it is worn it means that he has been using a gun, so shoot him.

How many conservatives the Republicans killed in Toledo cannot be calculated, but it was in the thousands; how many liberals the Franco forces slaughtered is not known, but the number was at least as large.

In this vengeful killing and counter-killing occurred one act of incandescent heroism which has come to summarize the Civil War as seen from the Franco side, and the visitor to Toledo can explore the history of this event. On a hill overlooking the Río Tajo stands an old square fortress on a site originally selected for this purpose by the Romans and used by the Moors when they held Toledo as their northern capital. Rebuilt many times, destroyed repeatedly by mines and fire, it could never have been beautiful, but after the defeat of Napoleon, who burned it, an attempt was made to bring the various parts of its façade into some kind of harmony, and the result, while far from artistic, did have a certain heavy balance. It was a four-story building, very large, with four squat and brutal towers topped by dark metal spires of no quality whatever. It was called the Alcázar (Ahl-kah-thar, with a heavy accent on the second syllable) and

This massive door knocker reminds one that the Spanish home has usually been a fortress.

more prominently even than the cathedral it dominated the skyline of this old fortress city.

In the summer of 1936 its barracks were practically empty, because a short time before, the cadets living in the Alcázar had been involved in a fracas in the Zocodover, and so Republican leaders of the government, eager to find an excuse for disciplining the army, which they did not trust, had banished the young army men to another barracks some distance from Toledo. This meant that the senior official remaining in the military area was a fifty-eight-year-old colonel of infantry, José Moscardó e Iriarte, heavy of face and heavier of bottom. He then held a job he loved, director of the army's physical education program, for his passion was sports, especially soccer, and he was about to leave Spain to serve as national representative at the Berlin Olympic games.

When his superiors launched their rebellion in Africa against the Republicans, Colonel Moscardó summoned all military personnel in the Toledo district, plus elements of the Guardia Civil, into the Alcázar, and there, on July 21, assembled 1205 fighting men plus 555 noncombatants, among whom were 211 children. They had ammunition but little food; they did have some horses, and when night fell on that first day they must have felt that they would be in the Alcázar for a week at most. They were to stay, at the point of starvation, for ten weeks.

Outnumbered, outgunned and under constant attack, with only the determination of Colonel Moscardó to provide any kind of military leadership, the defenders of the Alcázar hung on. The Republicans made many sorties against the stout walls but quickly learned that they would not be able to take the fortress by direct assault. However, they had other devices and these were potent.

On July 23, the third day of the siege, according to the modern Spanish legend, a Republican leader called Colonel Moscardó on the telephone and told him he held his sixteen-year-old son prisoner. He threatened to have him shot if Moscardó did not surrender the Alcázar immediately.

Republican: Do you perhaps think my statement is untrue? You are now
　　going to speak with your son.
Luis: Papa!
Moscardó: What's happening, son?
Luis: They say they're going to shoot me if you don't surrender.
Moscardó: Then commend your soul to God, shout ¡Viva España! and
　　¡Viva Cristo Rey!, and die like a hero.
Luis: A very strong kiss, Papa.
Moscardó: Goodbye, my son, a very strong kiss.

The Alcázar was not surrendered and later the boy was shot. One who underwent the siege reported that it was this event that steeled them to an acceptance of starvation and death, 'Because who could go to the colonel and complain about what the siege was costing him when the colonel had given his son?' Today on the wall of the room where Moscardó held this phone conversation hang translations of it in all important languages; the English is a botch job and very un-Spanish, because someone felt that Anglo-Saxons would not understand a father's sending his sixteen-year-old son a kiss. The English comes out like this:

Moscardó: Then turn your thoughts to God, cry out, 'Long Live Spain,' and
　　die as a patriot.
Luis: All my fondest love, father.
Moscardó: All of mine to you.

(Facts concerning the Alcázar are so confused and open to challenge that I have relied upon one principal source, *The Siege of the Alcázar* by Cecil D. Eby [1965], which is in the main pro-Franco. Many important data used by Eby have been controverted by anti-Franco sources, often with good reason, as in Herbert Rutledge Southworth's *The Myth of the Crusade of Franco* [1964], which cites many sources to prove that the famous telephone conversation was either apocryphal or—if it did happen—without the inflated significance it has been accorded. The Moscardó son, who was sixteen at the time, is now living happily in Madrid at Calle Castelló, 48. There was an older son who was shot, but under much different circumstances.)

When the Republicans could not take the Alcázar either by frontal assault or by pressure on Moscardó, they wheeled up heavy artillery which fired point-blank into the fort, and when this failed they summoned airplanes which dumped tons of bombs to knock the old walls apart. The walls did collapse, but the men inside did not, so the attackers resorted to a sensible device: they brought miners down from the Asturias coal fields to dig a tunnel under one of the towers. There they piled a vast charge of high explosive and warned Moscardó that they were going to blow the Alcázar to bits. They even summoned newsmen from Madrid to watch the end of the siege. The explosion came at 0631 in the morning of September 18, the sixtieth day, and true to prediction, it annihilated the southwest tower in a blast that could be heard forty miles away in Madrid. The Alcázar had fallen, and the news was sent around the world.

But inside the building the stubborn old colonel recoiled from the shock, assembled his assistants and through the smoke inspected the damage. The tower was gone, the wall was breached, but for the Republicans to take advantage of the blast they would still have to climb the hill, cross the rubble and take the building at bayonet point. Moscardó doubted that they were willing to pay the price.

He was right. In the days that followed, the siege degenerated into a bloody, ruthless struggle of many Republicans trying to overcome a few Franco men holed up in the ruins. Day by day artillery shells and airplane bombs proceeded with the destruction of the walls until the Alcázar seemed a good two-thirds gone. The patio was filled with rubble and the upper rooms were no more. How the ruins, which appeared to offer no hiding places, could hold out was a mystery.

Many of the defenders were killed in the fighting; others died of causes relating to starvation. Among the greatest heroes were the women, who not only helped the men but looked after the children as well. And day after day Colonel Moscardó sent out the radio report which would become the catchword of the siege, 'Sin novedad en el Alcázar' (Nothing new in the Alcázar, or, as some translate it: All quiet in the Alcázar).

When it seemed that one more push from the Republicans must wipe out the defenders, word came that a column of General Franco's troops had reached Talavera de la Reina and would shortly arrive to lift the siege. A race between Franco's oncoming troops and the Republican besiegers then developed, with odds in favor of the latter, but the iron-willed men in the Alcázar held out against all pressures, and on September 28, the seventieth day of the siege, when the defenders had become matchsticks through hunger, General Franco's troops arrived. The first contingent to enter the Alcázar was a unit of black Moors from Africa. Their ancestors had been thrown out of this city in 1085. Now, 851 years later, they were returning. It was then that the dreadful reprisals began.

The newsmen who accompanied Franco's forces into the city were eager to make of Colonel Moscardó, now a general, the hero of new Spain, but they found him a stolid, unimaginative old man whose main concern was still soccer. The awful realization dawned on them that when Moscardó had said, 'nothing new in the Alcázar,' he had not been uttering a heroic statement but the simple truth as he saw it. His job, as senior officer present, had been to hold the command he found himself with, and he had done so.

The somewhat doddering old fellow was a source of embarrassment to the Franco government, for he was unquestionably the salient hero of the war, but when he was assigned to a military command commensurate with his fame, he fumbled it and continued to send in reports: 'Nothing new at the front.' Finally, with the coming of world peace, the perfect job was found for him: he put on his general's uniform and as Conde del Alcázar de Toledo, represented Spain at the London Olympic Games of 1948 and the Helsinki ones of 1952. That he enjoyed.

I wanted to see what the Alcázar was like, so on a warm September day I left the Zocodover and walked down into the valley where the Republicans had had the command post for shelling the fort. Above me loomed the Alcázar, newly rebuilt but as brutal and ugly as ever, and I shuddered at the thought of being a soldier required to scramble up that hill and assault that fort. Later, when I had climbed to the plaza at the east end of the building, I saw the grandiloquent monument erected to the men of the Alcázar, and for a strange moment I thought I was in another century. Victory, whose garments flowed behind her wings, held aloft a golden sword while two women knelt in grieving position. Behind Victory stood two well-carved friezes in white marble featuring workers and women mourners. On the front of the monument was carved the word Faith, represented by a man with shield and sword; on the right Valor, a blindfolded woman holding a cross; and on the left Sacrifice, a man offering a lamb. On the back I saw a good pietà in which a shrouded woman bent over a fallen man, while far away on either end rose three tall metal shafts topped by the fasces, the eagle and a third symbol I could not decipher: it looked like a large cross with studded edges.

Leading up to the monument were flights of stairs, balustrades, promenades and landscaped areas much like Hadrian's villa at Tivoli, but juvenile delinquents or cryptic Republicans, as the case might be, had gone about toppling the ornaments which graced the approach, so that the whole had a sense of a crumbling Roman forum. All was noble; all was very nineteenth century; all yearned for the past.

Statue of the Commander Villamartín, machine-gunned daily by the Reds during their siege of the Alcázar.

Inside the Alcázar, I caught many glimpses of the Spanish army at work, for set into the walls were tablets whose words evoked past glories:

THE XXI GRADUATING CLASS OF INFANTRY

1914–1917

ON ITS GOLDEN ANNIVERSARY

TO THE DEFENDERS OF THE ALCAZAR

1964

In one corner a white plaque read: 'Here on September 11, 1936, was celebrated the only Holy Mass of the Siege. Catholics! This corner is land sanctified by the visit of the Divine King. To our heroes.' Another shield read: 'To those who endured the siege by the Communist hordes and converted this Alcázar into a symbol of the unity and independence of the nation.' But the most telling item was something I had seen on my earliest visit, when the gaunt old fortress was still in ruins. It was a magazine and a most unlikely one, *The Illustrated London News* for January 24, 1914. Colonel Moscardó had found it in the Alcázar library and had used it to help barricade his windows from Republican bullets. It was opened to a complicated story: 'Sold by Rumour. A Fine and Famous Holbein Portrait.' The painting was shown in a small photograph, 'Thomas Cromwell, Earl of Essex,' owned by the Earl of Caledon and rumored to have been sold by him for $150,000, a charge which he denied. A bullet had passed through the earl's head and nine others had splattered the page.

The best thing about the Alcázar has always been the cloistered central courtyard, not because the cloisters are attractive, for they are heavy and lack gracia, but because the area was spacious and did contain a famous statue of Carlos V in military uniform. The base carried two quotations uttered by the emperor on the eve of a crucial invasion of Africa, and these had become the slogans of the Franco forces who defended the building: 'I shall enter Tunis as conqueror or remain dead in Africa.' And: 'If in the battle you see me and my flag go down, rescue first the flag.'

As I stood in the Alcázar with this statue of Carlos, I reflected upon the years I have spent studying this emperor and his works. For me he has always been a central fact of Spain and one of the figures of world history who best repay study. When I was a young professor I used to daydream about what I would do if placed in charge of a college whose only responsibility was to provide a selected group of students the best possible education without regard to outside pressures from alumni, large contributors, the sports editors of the nearby metropolis or the general damn-foolishness of American life. Like any sensible man I would naturally sponsor only a general humanities program, reserving training courses like law, medicine, engineering or business for university specialization which would come later. My students would direct themselves to language, literature, science, philosophy, the fine arts and history, secure in the knowledge that if they mastered those subjects they would later be in a position to control such social functions as medicine, manufacturing, constructing, teaching and governing. In other words, I would stress with my students the widest possible exploration plus the most intensive analysis of two or three specific unities.

The latter, which would be the heart of my system, would be attacked in a radical way. Twice in the student's four years—once at the beginning and once at the end, so that he could see in himself his deepening capacity—I would ask him to spend the year or most of the year in studying one brief segment of history. During that time he would take no traditional courses whatever, no mathematics, no chemistry, no Literature IV. Instead he would immerse himself in the world culture operating at that period in time, and to do so he would study the art forms, the music, the contemporary understanding of geography, the philosophy, the religious convictions, the economics, the travel, the architecture, the writing and the daily life of the peasant. And he would be obliged to explore in depth the half-dozen nations or principalities which best illustrated the significant meanings of the age being studied.

I have often speculated on what periods would be most fruitful for such an approach and have felt inclined toward A.D. 70 and the fall of Jerusalem, and 1832 and the passage of reform in Great Britain, plus some one date to be agreed upon when Greece and Rome were in confrontation and another in the Middle Ages before dissolution of old patterns had begun. Any two of these, properly investigated, would provide a young man with enough insights to illuminate the rest of his life, but there has always been one period which has stood preeminent. If I were now forced to educate myself anew, it would be to this period that I would direct myself, the period when more notable men were in power and more ideas in conflict than at any other in world history.

It would be sometime in the 1530s, when Catholic Spain and France, Protestant England and Muslim Turkey were contesting the leadership of Europe and when Hindu India was preparing itself for the advent of Akbar the Great, and Orthodox Russia was beginning its consolidation under Ivan the Terrible. To understand this period would be to understand the movements that formed modern history. Observe the dates, the right-hand one representing more or less when the man in question came into power:

Francis I of France	(1494–1547)	1515
Henry VIII of England	(1491–1547)	1509
Carlos I and V of Spain	(1500–1558)	1519
Suleiman I of Turkey	(1495?–1566)	1520
Martin Luther	(1483–1546)	1519
Ivan IV of Russia	(1530–1584)	1547
Akbar of India	(1542–1605)	1556

These men were titans and they tore the preconceptions of their narrow worlds to shreds. They were builders, and when they died they left their nations a legacy of accomplishment. They were warriors who defended their realms and extended them. They were patrons of the arts and left their cities richer and their universities improved. Some were good administrators and set patterns which determined the future conduct of their lands, and all were men who wrestled with great forces.

Of the seven Luther was the most intelligent, Suleiman the most glorious, Akbar the finest human being, Francis the most cunning, Henry the most determined, and Ivan the most violent. Carlos V excelled in nothing, but it was he who commanded most of the world and who left the most lasting impression.

Americans are apt to ignore the tremendous power of Carlos and Spain in these critical years toward the middle of the sixteenth century. There was no nation which came close to rivaling Spain. Because of its ownership of the Low Countries and certain provinces which are now part of France, it exercised a pincers movement on that country and kept it frustrated. England, not yet a major power, was neutralized by marriage compacts. In the Mediterranean, Spain held control of the north coast of Africa and kept the Muslim power of Turkey at least at arm's length. Through its ownership of Sardinia, Sicily, Naples and some of the smaller Italian states, Spain exerted great pressure on the Papacy and exacted favorable decisions when it was not engaged in outright war against the Pope. And in Mexico and Peru it owned mines from which floods of wealth reached Spain, rarely to stay there.

The Spanish fleet, brought into being by Cisneros, was the best operating. The Spanish army was the terror of Europe. Spanish universities were without superiors. To Spain were attracted the foremost painters of Europe, and the merit of Spanish letters was acknowledged. It was truly an age of gold, when all nations lay in fee, as it were, to Spanish leadership and power.

All that was required, in those crucial years when the future of the world was being determined, was that Spain evolve some kind of government and economic system which would enable her to retain what she had and to build on it at a rate of growth comparable to that at which England, France and Germany would build. If Spain had maintained only that normal rate of progress, she would have remained the world's dominant power for two or three more centuries and we might now be speaking Spanish. The central problem of Spanish history is why Carlos V and Felipe II failed to discover the system of government and the patterns of growth required to sustain their nation.

At the foot of the hill on which the Alcázar stands is a fine museum which not many Toledo visitors see, and that is a pity, because it is a memorial to the greatness of Carlos V. It is housed in the old hospital of

Santa Cruz, built from funds left by Cardinal Mendoza, and the doorway is another flamboyant memorial showing Mendoza assisting the Empress Helena, mother of Constantine the Great, as she finds the true cross. The interior of the museum is of a type which I do not usually like, a conglomeration of tapestry, furniture, etching, carpeting, sculpture, bric-a-brac and mementos, with here and there a notable painting. But this museum is different, because it has been assembled with excellent taste. I have introduced half a dozen connoisseurs to it—ordinary travel literature does not stress it, perhaps because the custodians don't want too many visitors—and they have been enchanted.

I shall not speak of the paintings; the museum has only twenty-three El Grecos, including the 'Assumption of the Virgin,' one of his latest and greatest works. But I should like to comment briefly on the many objects relating to Carlos V. Here is the well-known bronze statue of Carlos, with jutting jaw, suspicious little eyes and hair coming down to a sharp V above his eyes. He seems a compact, determined man, visibly apprehensive about the tasks confronting him, for he was called to transform a peninsular mentality into one with a world outlook; he tried to avoid but could not the religious challenges thrown at him by that damned monk, Martin Luther; professors at the University of Salamanca were warning him that if a nation brought in so much gold from Mexico and Peru it might go bankrupt because of the ensuing rise in the cost of living, but that made no sense at all; and the various popes in Rome kept passing edicts which caused confusion.

Along this wall, strung out for some forty-five feet, is the printed scroll depicting his coronation as Holy Roman Emperor. In the procession we see hundreds of figures—kings, scribes, musicians, heralds, cardinals, along with Pope Clement VII and a display of war machines. Oxen are being roasted and stewards are throwing out free bread to the peasants.

In this corner is a handsome little carving showing Carlos and his younger and more gifted brother Fernando, who excelled him in so many ways. Fernando looks larger, seems intelligent, is better-looking, but Carlos by holding on far outdistanced Fernando. It was he, not Fernando, who was elected Holy Roman Emperor, although at the end of his life he passed the job on to his brother.

At the far end of the museum, in a gallery two stories high, hang the blue battle pennants flown by Carlos' illegitimate son, Don Juan de Austria, at the Battle of Lepanto, where the Turks were contained in 1571. The largest of the flags is about sixty feet long, emblazoned not with nationalistic slogans but with I.N.R.I. and Jesus on the cross. Spanish galleons really did go into battle with the goal of saving Christianity.

Below the blue pennants rests a portrait of Don Juan, the preserver of Spain, for had he lost at Lepanto, Islam would have controlled the Mediterranean and Spain might once more have become Moorish. Don Juan is shown as a young man in ruffs and battle armor, with a bright-red scarf over his right shoulder; he was a man of such charismatic power that when he died in the Low Countries his body was cut into four parts, pickled in brine and smuggled home so that the French might not know so great an adversary was dead. Of course, as soon as the barrels had crossed the Pyrenees the body was sewn together again.

In another room I see the tall, brooding figure of Carlos' legitimate son Felipe II, husband of Mary Tudor and Spain's most typical king, and off to one side, in a place of honor, I see again that marvelous bronze statue of Isabel, the Portuguese princess whom Carlos married. Look at her, standing in a stiffly brocaded dress, bejeweled, confident, half smiling. She is regal and self-assured, and her statue is one of the most pleasing in Spain. Carlos loved her and was a good husband. If she was as charming as her statue, one can understand why.

On the walls of the upper cloister appear two gold-encrusted maps which summarize Carlos. The first depicts his numerous battle campaigns: 'Tunis 1535; Algiers 1529; Zaragoza 1518; Naples 1528; Brussels 1521; and chief of all, Mühlberg 1547.' The second map shows his travels and is a jungle of crossing lines which wander off to strange locations. It carries the well-known passage from his abdication speech: 'I have been nine times in Germany, six in Spain, seven in Italy, ten in Flanders. In peace and war I have been four times in France, two in England and two in Africa for a total of forty expeditions, without counting the voyages to my kingdoms. Eight times I have crossed the Mediterranean and three times the Ocean [to England]. I am at peace with all and from all ask pardon if I have offended anyone.'

These maps help explain a cardinal fact about Carlos: although King of Spain he was rarely in the country. His preoccupation was always with the other parts of his empire and he allowed the internal government of Spain to drift. At the beginning of his reign he set the pattern for much that was to follow. Faced by civil war throughout Spain, he summoned his nobles to distant Santiago de Compostela and told them, 'This nation is faced by a crisis which could destroy it. Do something. I'll be back in three years.' At a later period he was absent for fourteen years.

Carlos was never a congenial man, but in the last two years of his life he performed an unexpected act which captivated the imagination of his people and continues to do so today. While still possessed of full powers, he voluntarily resigned as emperor and turned his scepter over to his son Felipe. To appreciate fully what he did next I had to take a long expedition westward into the mountains of the Sierra de Gredos.

I drove north out of Toledo to the Madrid–Badajoz road, which carries traffic heading for Portugal. There I turned left for Talavera de la Reina, the ugly commercial town, center of Spain's ceramic industry and forever remembered as the place where Joselito, prince of bullfighters, was gored to death on May 16, 1920. West of Talavera, I headed north toward the

Gredos mountains, but before entering them turned west and drove along the foothills for about fifty miles through bleak and desolate scenery. How empty most of Spain is.

At last I came to a sign which indicated that a short distance off the road to the north lay the monastery of Yuste. I followed the dusty road which seemed to lead nowhere, when suddenly I turned a corner and saw a low, mean building of no attractiveness whatever but the goal of all travelers who want to pay their respects to Carlos V, for it was to this remote monastery, isolated, forlorn and with nothing to commend it, that the great emperor retired.

I had the good fortune to reach Yuste at the same time that two French priests drove up in their Renault. 'What a road,' they said, eager to compare experiences. The driver was tall and taciturn, but he had the facts. His passenger was on the chubby side and he had the enthusiasm.

'You must imagine Carlos in Brussels at the height of his powers,' the round priest said. 'Sixty years old, maybe sixty-five, and the most powerful man in the world.'

'Fifty-five,' the thin one said. 'Born 1500. Abdicated the Netherlands throne 1555. Abdicated the Spanish throne 1556. You can figure it out for yourself.'

'It was to this spot he came. Look. Not a house. Not even a church. Think how lonely it must have been for him, the great man, to end his days in such surroundings.' He shook his head sadly, then turning to his comrade, asked, 'How many years was he here?'

'Came in early 1557. Died in late 1558.'

'Two years of this desolate hell. Why?'

'Because he wanted to make his peace with God, that's why.'

We walked through the cold, dark monastery and imagined Carlos alone here and praying. 'He brought only one friend with him,' the fat priest said. 'What was his name?'

'An Italian engineer, Juanelo of Cremona. Remember, Carlos was emperor of much of Italy too.'

'It was what's-his-name from Cremona who invented a special pump for lifting water from the Río Tajo into Toledo. Carlos loved him and the two spent what amounted to an exile here.'

We left the forbidding monastery and walked through the unkempt grounds. To the north were the Gredos mountains, in all other directions the lonely emptiness of Extremadura. 'What a place for a great man to die,' the fat priest lamented. Apparently he was imagining how many of the good things he appreciated would not have been available had he accompanied the emperor.

'I believe he really came here to get closer to God,' the tall priest said. 'He prayed a good deal. He used to write to his son. "Above everything else hold fast to the Catholic Church. Support the Inquisition. Stamp out heresy." He really believed in God.'

The chubby priest, who was the more sentimental of the two, insisted that we go back into the monastery, although his friend and I were ready to push on. He led us to a bare room, of which he said, 'Here Carlos died. What age did you say?'

'Fifty-eight.'

'His body was kept here in this chapel for . . . How many years did you say?'

'Many years.'

'It was then translated to El Escorial and buried beneath that pile of granite.' He fell silent for a moment, then added, 'But here is where his soul will always rest.'

We three paid our respects to Carlos, ruler of much of the known world, determiner of Spain's history, defender of the faith. The two priests prayed and we shook hands. The fat one said, 'Amusing. An American who had no contacts with him. Two Frenchmen who fought him all his life. We meet here to pay him homage. What a miserable place.'

It was not till four years later that I came upon a modern biography of Carlos V which took the edge off our prayers and philosophizing at Yuste. Researchers have found documents that spell out what happened at Yuste and it was somewhat different from what the French priests and I had imagined. When Carlos sat in cold Brussels, contemplating retirement, his thoughts kept going back to a monastery he had once seen in the blazing summer heat of Extremadura and it was this that encouraged him to give up the crown and have some relaxation and pleasure in his last years. He drew up a list of those who were to share his lonely exile at Yuste and it totaled seven hundred and sixty-two people, but when it was suggested that so many might crowd the place he trimmed it down to a hundred and fifty, of whom two-thirds actually accompanied him to the monastery, where he was visited by a constant stream of nobles and members of the royal family. At first he calculated that he could get by on a yearly allowance of sixteen thousand ducats but soon found that he would need at least twenty, with another thirty thousand to serve as a contingency fund.

Inventories have come down to us of what Carlos lugged out to Yuste: magnificent tapestries, choice furnishings, paintings by Titian and jeweled bric-a-brac. The cells of the monastery were for his entourage; for him a special house was built with a man-made lake under his window so that he could fish for trout from his living room. His kitchens were supervised by a Portuguese who had been with him for years, a cook much addicted to heavy German sauces which, when accompanied by gigantic quantities of alcohol, inflamed his gout. When an attack came, Carlos retreated for a few days to a salubrious diet, then gorged himself on slabs of red beef and fish, both bad for gout. He insisted upon hors d'oeuvres of jellied eel and stewed partridge and loved desserts of the richest and heaviest sort. Such a diet alone would have insured the return of his gout, but he was also insanely fond of anchovies; his staff saw to it that little kegs of them were sent ahead whenever he took a trip. Naturally, when he had eaten his quota of salted anchovies he generated a huge thirst, which he slaked with large bottles of beer kept in buckets of snow brought down from the mountains.

When I read these new researches on Carlos the ascetic recluse of Yuste, I felt very close to him, for I too suffer from gout and I too crave anchovies above any other food; in this matter Spain has been a temptation to me, a kind of self-inflicted purgatory in which those marvelous little fish stare at me from every bar, in every salad, and I had real tears in my eyes when I read of how one day Carlos, after a long trip across the countryside, came to an inn where his keg of anchovies waited, only to find that they had been so jostled by horses coming across the mountains, they were reduced to a formless pulp. Today, thank heaven, Swedish research men have developed a simple pill which controls gout, and when I read the letters of Carlos and Felipe, for the latter inherited the disease in even more virulent form, and see how they hobbled about much of their time and developed the evil tempers which they vented on their under-lings, I reflect that the history of Spain might have been much modified had the two kings been given not buckets of anchovies but a supply of Swedish pills.

The strangest fact about Carlos was not his retirement, nor his lust for anchovies, nor his extended absence from Spain, but that he ruled the country from 1517 to 1555 without being legally king, for during these years his mother, Juana la Loca, lived hidden away in a filthy room that we shall visit later. She was unquestionably Queen of Spain, and legal documents during the period bear her name first, followed by that of Carlos as her executor. She died on April 11, 1555, and Carlos abdicated the Spanish part of his holdings on January 16, 1556, so that he did finally acquire the kingship—but for only nine months. Scholars in increasing numbers are turning up evidence which suggests that Juana was not really mad but that it was to her son's advantage to keep her penned up, which he did.

Carlos V, this little man called upon to wage vast struggles, this least of the quadrumvirate—Henry of England, Francis of France, Suleiman of Turkey, Carlos of Spain—seemed at the time to be victor by virtue of his obstinacy and his dedication to one religious principle. It required the passage of two centuries to prove how wrong his decisions had been, how hollow his victories. The ideas of Francis and Henry blossomed into great kingdoms and empires, whereas those of Carlos withered into national disaster. It is such thoughts that torment one at the monastery of Yuste.

FOLLOWING PAGE: *Mosque.*

IV

CORDOBA

OCEANO
ATLANTICO

MAR MEDITERRANEO

Barcelona

Madrid

Lisboa

San Calixto
Hornachuelos
Córdoba
Sevilla
Granada
Guadix

MILES
0   100

The traveler wishing to observe Islamic Spain has his choice of two cities, Granada with its Alhambra or Córdoba with its Great Mosque (in Spanish, Mezquita). Of the two the former is by a considerable degree the more exciting and also the easier to absorb, for its buildings, gardens and geographic setting are immediately recognizable as significant. It would take a dull man to miss the point of Granada, for its Alhambra is a museum of Islamic memories.

But for three personal reasons I chose Córdoba. It was more prosaic and therefore showed its Islamic heritage with less hyperbole. It had been the intellectual center of Islam, so that its influence lasted long after the expulsion of the last Moors from Granada. And in Córdoba had lived four of the Spaniards who were most important to me and I wanted to see where these excellent men had lived and why they had been born here and not in some more congenial place. It is interesting but accidental that each gained his greatest fame after he had left Spain.

Córdoba is a fine city laid out along the right bank of a bend in the Río Guadalquivir, and to reach the site of my first pilgrimage I had to walk down a pleasant avenue named after Generalísimo Franco and through a shady park, at the end of which I came to the limits of the old Jewish quarter, evacuated in 1492 but since occupied by working-class families. I followed an ancient Roman wall which had outlined the Jewish quarter and came to a Roman gate where a plaza had been built, providing a rustic vista marked by three reflecting pools lined with roses, cypresses and willows. At the end nearest the gate a series of low stone walls, handsomely proportioned, created a small plateau, in the middle of which rose a column of cream-colored granite on which stood the statue of a shortish, baldheaded man in a toga, bearing in his right hand a manuscript scroll of some sort, perhaps a tragedy in verse. His face was what I would have expected, that of a grave gentleman utterly unafraid of adversity or death or the persecution that might be visited upon him by the tyrant Nero. He stood looking away from the wall, away from Rome, and over the distant hills of Andalucía, his homeland.

He was Lucius Annaeus Seneca (c. 4 B.C.–A.D. 65), whom many consider to have been the foremost Spaniard who ever lived; more consider him the representative Spaniard. Philosopher, orator, essayist, playwright and poet, he not only had a distinguished literary career that marked him as the leading intelligence of his time, but he also became a political leader, serving as consul of Rome. He had been appointed tutor to the boy Nero, whose counselor he later became and whose excesses he modified. He was a Stoic by nature, a city man by preference and a manipulator of political forces by design. In all that he tried he succeeded and he was both a perfect Roman and the ideal Spaniard. In the end his flexible principles proved not elastic enough to keep up with Nero, and the emperor commanded him to commit suicide, which he performed with the noble stoicism he had recommended to others.

Most Spanish intellectuals, especially those with a mordant cast of mind, consider themselves the children of Seneca; his ideas are as vital today as they were when he first propounded them, and I have known one politician, one novelist and one bullfighter who have assured me that the principles by which they live and practice their art derive from Seneca. His capacity to see the world cynically but with wit endears him to the Spaniard; his exaggerated sense of pundonor was one of the foundations of that philosophy; and his skillful use of words served as a prototype for Spanish verbosity. I suppose that the best single thing I did to prepare myself for intercourse with Spaniards was to read Seneca again; he seemed as contemporary as a man lounging in a café, as thoroughly Spanish as anyone I was to meet. The more I reread his prosaic and often pedantic works, the more Spanish they have seemed, and I imagine that the two pole stars of Spanish thought are Seneca and Cervantes; at least they are the Spaniards who speak most directly to me.

To catch the flavor of Seneca's message it is necessary to hear him speaking at some banquet in Rome, where he was often in the company of the empire leaders. One recurring principle was stoicism and to this he constantly returned:

> Anyone may take life from man, but no one death: a thousand gates stand open to it.

> Behold a spectacle to which God may worthily turn his attention; behold a match worthy of God, a brave man hand-in-hand with adverse fortune.

> Fire tries gold; misery tries brave men.

It is not because things are difficult that we do not dare to attempt them, but they are difficult because we do not dare to do so.

The fear of war is worse than war itself.

Life, if you know how to use it, is long enough.

Seneca was constantly concerned with the application of philosophy to daily life, and some of his best writings are his sententious prose essays on the virtues and limitations of moral judgment. His plays, which deal with the same problem, are apt to be pompous if not ridiculous, for in them he sounds as if he were orating old-fashioned opinions to which he himself did not subscribe (a common fault of Spanish writing), but elsewhere some of his conclusions carry a striking sense of modernity:

> As wool imbibes at once certain colors and others it does not, unless it has been frequently soaked and doubly-dyed: so there are certain kinds of learning which, on being acquired, are thoroughly mastered; but philosophy, unless she sinks deeply into the soul and has long dwelt there, and has not given a mere coloring but a deep dye, performs none of the things which she had promised.

> Human affairs are not so happily arranged that the best things please the most men. It is the proof of a bad cause when it is applauded by the mob.

> A large library is apt to distract rather than to instruct the learner; it is much better to confine yourself to a few authors than to wander at random over many.

> Truth will never be tedious to him that travels through the nature of things; it is falsehood that gluts us.

> From the time that money began to be regarded with honor, the real value of things was forgotten.

A recurring theme of Spanish history is the failure of Spaniards, no matter in what part of the world they find themselves, to develop a workable system of self-government. It is strange, therefore, that the first great Spanish thinker directed himself repeatedly to this problem. I suppose Seneca said more on this topic than on any other, and to call him primarily a Stoic is misleading; primarily he was a speculator on what the role and forms of government should be:

> He who dreads hatred too much, knows not how to reign. Terror is the proper guard of a kingdom.

> That government is ill conducted, when the mob rules its leaders.

> Life is like a school of gladiators, where men live and fight with each other.

> He who has committed a fault is to be corrected both by advice and by force, kindly and harshly, and to be made better for himself as well as for another, not without chastisement, but without passion.

> Man is a social animal, and born to live together so as to regard the world as one house.

> The society of man is like a vault of stones, which would fall if the stones did not rest on one another; in this way it is sustained.

In view of the fact that Spain was to become the champion of religion and today considers herself the nation most deeply committed to the defense of Catholicism, it was appropriate that her premier philosopher should have concerned himself with this matter. Spaniards are proud of the fact that certain of Seneca's writings are sufficiently ambiguous to permit him to be called the first important classical figure to have embraced Christianity, but whether he did so remains a subject of controversy. The following quotations echo with curious overtones:

> Live with men as if God saw you; converse with God as if men heard you.

> God is nigh to you, he is with you, he is in you: I tell you, Lucilius, a holy spirit resides within us, an observer and guardian of our good and our bad doings, who, as he has been dealt with by us, so he deals with us; no man is good without God.

> A great sacred spirit talks indeed within us, but cleaves to its divine original.

> God is not to be worshiped with sacrifices and blood: for what pleasure can He have in the slaughter of the innocent? But with a pure mind, a good and honest purpose. Temples are not to be built for Him with stones piled on high: God is to be consecrated in the breast of each.

> The same being whom we call Jupiter, the wisest men regard as the keeper and protector of the universe, a spirit and a mind, the Lord and Maker of this lower world, to whom all names are suitable. Will you call him Destiny? You will not err. On him depend all things, and all the causes of causes are from him. Will you call him Providence? You will say well. For it is his wisdom that provides for this world that it be without confusion and proceed on its course without change. Will you call him Nature? You will not commit a mistake. For all things have had their beginning from him, in whom we live and move and have our being. Will you call him the World? You will not be deceived. For he is all that you see wholly infused into his parts and sustaining himself by his own power.

As in many Spanish cities the central plaza, serving as a kind of huge open-air bus terminal, is named after José Antonio, and not far away is the statue of my second favorite Córdoban, Bishop Hosius (in Spanish Osio, c. 255–c. 358), whom I first met in Nicaea in Asia Minor when I was studying the Church council at which the Nicene Creed was promulgated as the normative theological guide for all Christians. Hosius was a man of enormous conviction who battled to establish the trinitarian definition of God under which Christianity would prosper; his archenemy was Arius of Constantinople, father of the Arian heresy subscribed to by the German tribes, including the Visigoths who ruled Spain, which taught that Jesus could not logically be coexistent with God but must be of lesser nature. Even before I knew that Hosius was a Spaniard, I was much attracted to him; he was a furious man, a terrible warrior for his interpretation of God and a fearsome enemy of those who did not agree with him. He ranged from Córdoba to Rome to Asia Minor to Constantinople, and wherever he went he brought reason and devotion. Repeatedly he was anathematized, abused, arrested and persecuted, but he continued to wage his war against Arianism, even offering his life to prove the rightness of his beliefs. He was a very human prelate, for when nearly a century old he lost his old fire and succumbed to pressures, publicly turning his back on all he had previously believed, accepting Arianism and paving the way for a conciliation that helped make Spain temporarily Arian. At a hundred and two the old renegade died—and I find something quite Spanish in his behavior, both his stern advocacy of an idea and his ultimate betrayal of it when conditions changed. Hosius is a complex and fascinating figure, one of the greatest churchmen and probably Spain's principal contribution to Church history.

Today in the quiet square facing the church of the Capuchins in Córdoba the old bishop stands tall and baldheaded in marble toga and sandals. In his left hand he carries a staff ending in a gilded bronze eagle perched on a cross which rises from a globe. Not even in death is he serene, for he seems eager to leap forward to the next brawl. At the base appear three good bas-reliefs showing the old man bared to the waist being flogged by Roman soldiers; defending the Trinity before one of the Holy Roman emperors; supported by three other churchmen wearing crosses as he expels a figure who must be Arius, author of the heresy. On the back stands the plaque: 'To Hosius, Bishop Confessor of Christ in Torment. Counselor of Constantine the Great. On the sixteenth centennial of the Council of Nicaea over which he presided, the citizens of Córdoba dedicated this monument, under the initiative of their prelate. December 31, 1925.'

In a corner of the Jewish section, opposite to the one where Seneca presides, appears one of the gentlest and most attractive statues in Europe. The courtyard which it dominates is paved in small pebbles set in cement; the walls are whitewashed and plain; brick archways form beautiful short vistas, and flowers bloom about the base of the statue and in the nearby windowboxes. The base consists of a series of random-sized brown rocks fitted into an attractive cube on which rests a plain marble bench containing the sitting figure of a man wearing the robes and twisted turban of the desert. In his lap he holds a book kept open by his right thumb; his face and bearing are those of a philosopher who is resting here in the quiet prior to meeting with his students.

It is Córdoba's memorial to a brilliant man whom the city treated shabbily, the Jew Moses Maimonides (in Spanish Moisés de Maimón, 1135–1204), a worthy partner to Seneca and Hosius. I suppose that intellectually he is the most brilliant man that Spain produced, a medical doctor of wide reputation who wrote basic treatises on such subjects as asthma, living healthily without medicine, and the principles of sexual intercourse. In fact, his medical knowledge was so comprehensive and his skill so highly regarded that he spent the last years of his life as personal doctor to Saladin in Cairo.

His chief fame, however, was as a religious philosopher, in which capacity he helped establish the norms of Judaism. He wrote brilliantly, argued persuasively, and laid down a body of principles which had much effect on non-Jews like Thomas Aquinas, Herbert Spencer and Gottfried von Leibniz. If one wants to savor medieval thought at its best, I recommend Maimonides' *Guide to the Perplexed,* in which he takes a bewildered applicant step by step through the religious process, providing rational explanations for the existence of God and for lesser theological problems. It is a beautifully composed work and explains why Jews consider him the foremost Jewish intelligence since the time of Moses: 'Between Moses and Moses, there was no one like unto Moses.'

Maimonides was born in Córdoba and lived not far from where his statue now stands, but shortly after his bar mitzvah the Muslims controlling the city launched a series of persecutions from which he fled. It was while wandering from one inhospitable city along the Mediterranean littoral to another that he became a notable scholar. We catch glimpses of him in Algeria, in Tunis, in Turkey perhaps, in Palestine definitely and finally in Egypt, where his medical proficiency earned him a livelihood. He was a prodigious worker, and one of the most attractive letters surviving from this age was written by him, explaining how he spent his days; he found time in his schedule for medical duties, contemplation, meeting with Jews seeking religious opinion, leadership of the synagogue and service as advisor to the sultan. His hours fitted together like the pieces of a mosaic and he reported that he had no time for even one additional obligation. His collected works, which are voluminous, are currently being edited and published uniformly by Yale University, which is appropriate, for he is one of the fathers of modern intelligence.

It was surprising for me to learn that Córdoba, so long the center of Islamic culture in Spain, contained no statue of the principal adornment of that culture, the philosopher Averroës (1126–1198), who played a major role in codifying Islamic thought and in bringing Aristotle to the attention of the west. It is quite possible that he knew Maimonides, whose life his own parallels, for he too was a medical doctor of note, and he too was expelled from Córdoba by the reactionary fanaticism of Moors, who despised books. He too ended his life as doctor-in-residence to a ruler in North Africa, in this case Morocco, and he was, in his field, at least as

Seneca.

brilliant as Seneca, Hosius and Maimonides in theirs. It is extraordinary that Córdoba contains no memorial to so famous a son, but if there was one I failed to find it. It would be pleasant, on my next trip, to discover that the city had remembered Averroës, for then I could make an intellectual pilgrimage to the four statues and thus pay homage in turn to the finest pagan of Spanish history, the finest churchman, the outstanding Jew and the most brilliant Muslim. No one can explain why it was Córdoba that produced these four excellent men from four different religions.

Today the city betrays few signs that it was for so long the center of Islamic rule in Spain. The Moors crossed over from Africa on April 27, 711, and before the end of that year had captured Córdoba, where they remained till June 29, 1236. They thus occupied the city for half a millennium, making it their resplendent capital, but except for the Great Mosque and a fortress called the Alcázar, it is easier to find Roman ruins than Islamic, and this is true throughout Spain; Moors were in the peninsula from 711 to 1492, but in city after city, like Toledo and Salamanca, one finds little to remind him that these centers were once Islamic; and when a building has been preserved, it has usually been so well masked by later architects that it goes undetected.

A word as to nomenclature. The warrior tribes that invaded Spain from North Africa were united in only one thing: they were followers of Muhammad and his religion Islam. Insofar as their beliefs were concerned, it is proper to describe these men as Islamic. Unfortunately, the adjective derived from Islam has never come into popular use for identifying an individual follower; we rarely say, 'He is an Islamite.' Instead we use the word Muslim, philologically derived from the same root as Islam (one who submits), so that the adjective Muslim is identical with Islamic. The noun Muslim identifies a follower of Islam, and it is proper to describe the invaders as Muslims. Tribally, they were composed from such varied sources as Berbers of the Atlas Mountains, who comprised the vast majority of the early invaders, and men from former Roman colonies reaching from Morocco to Egypt. They were a mixed lot. The designation Moor is an imprecise word of no scientific meaning; its derivation is not religious, nor geographic, nor ethnic. Some experts claim that it comes from the Greek word for black or dark; others say it is derived from some African word meaning black, but few of the original Moors were Negroes. Historically it has come to mean 'any member of the North African groups who invaded Spain, including the Arabs.' I shall be using the word in that sense.

Who were the Arabs? Technically they were members of that incandescent and superior group which spread out from the Arabian desert and with matchless speed overran surrounding cultures. Muhammad's Hegira took place in 622; he died in 632; the flood tide of the faithful did not reach Spain till 711, a delay of nearly eighty years. In that time the Arab leadership had been thinly dispersed, and it is unlikely that many pure Arabs crossed over into Spain, although it has always been popular to assume that they did. Spaniards prefer to speak of this experience as 'the Arab occupation,' as if the Muslims who surged across the Straits of Gibraltar had been mainly Arabs, but we know that in the first foraging party, which captured most of southern Spain within a few weeks and got all the way to Toledo, there were no Arabs at all. There were, however, small Arab cadres in most of the succeeding armies and Arab leadership in the government, but to extend this to 'the triumph of Arab culture' is meaningless, for there were few Arabs and less culture; the salient innovations in architecture, art, literature and philosophy were imported mainly from long-established cultural centers to the north of Arabia. It is, however, accurate to speak of an Islamic culture and to speak of it with a certain amount of awe, for at its heyday in Spain it must have been impressive. It reached Spain in later waves, after the Berbers and the other mountain folk had conquered the peninsula.

Finally, we know that when the fanatical fundamentalists of Islam, the Almoravids, conquered southern Spain in 1086, only to be supplanted in 1146 by the even more fanatical Almohads, there were no Arabs whatever in their ranks. Both groups were composed principally of mountain wild men recently converted to Islam and of the opinion that Arab leadership, what there was of it, had gone soft and was ignoring the true teaching of Muhammad. Of any thousand Islamic invaders chosen at random through the centuries, I suppose not more than three or four could have been Arabs, but Spanish writers have felt that in surrendering to Arab superiority there was honor, but in losing to Berber inferiority there was ignominy.

To be accurate we should content ourselves with saying, 'The Muslims brought Islam to Spain,' but that begs the question of who the Muslims were and where they came from. It has therefore become the custom to say, 'The Moors occupied Spain,' and this locution applies to everyone, whether from Morocco on the west or the Balkans on the east, and includes people from three continents, Africa, Asia, Europe, and all complexions of skin. The word blackamoor was invented to describe Negroes; the great bulk of the Moors must have been white men tanned by the sun, like Arabs.

The impact of Islamic culture on Spain is well exemplified by Córdoba, for during several centuries this city was among the most scintillating of the world and comparable to Damascus as a center of Islamic culture. It was rich in palaces, gardens, libraries and university buildings. Its ordinary homes were probably the finest in Europe; for their amenities they could draw not only from goods produced in the east but also those brought down from Germany and the north. Muslim chroniclers claim, no doubt with eastern exaggeration, that in those days Córdoba had a population of about one million (today 190,000) and more than three thousand mosques, public baths and palaces. It was supposed to have had 260,000 buildings in all, including 80,000 shops. Its principal library had 400,000 volumes, and its poets and philosophers made it the peer of Baghdad or Cairo.

It is important to realize that Córdoba was self-contained. Under a series of cruel but capable military leaders it served as capital for most of

FOLLOWING FACING PAGES: *Film makers from all parts of the world shoot motion pictures with Muslim backgrounds in Spain because the inhabitants recall the Moorish occupation.*

Spain and no longer felt itself subservient in any way to Damascus. It conducted its own affairs and enjoyed a reputation throughout the Muslim world as a center of learning and medicine. Córdoba had its own publishing houses in which scores of women were employed to make copies of the Koran for distribution to mosques throughout Spain, and love poems written in this city were circulated to all parts of the Muslim world. In the eyes of Córdobans, the North African tribes from which they had originally sprung were little more than savages to be imported now and then for military service. Córdoba was a mighty metropolis when Granada was a provincial headquarters, and it was not until Spanish Christians captured the city and ended the empire that Granada, protected by a rim of mountains, came into its own as the last great Muslim city in Spain. Córdoba was lost to Islam as early as 1236; Granada hung on till 1492, and that accounts for the predominance of the latter during the concluding centuries of Muslim rule.

To appreciate what Córdoba must have been like in its days of grandeur, you must make an expedition out into the country west of the city to the ruins of Medînat az-Zahrâ, but do it only if you are possessed of a vivid imagination, for otherwise the trip will be disappointing and even misleading. You depart from the park at whose edge I found the statue of Seneca, cross the railroad tracks and follow an interesting country road till a branch cuts off to the right and twists up a steep hill. At the top you find yourself facing an old fence and a barred door. Here there is certainly no grandeur of Islam, and when the door is opened by a woman in bedroom slippers you find nothing startling: the merest outlines of walls that once ran down the slope up which you have just driven, a few stones here and there indicating where important buildings might have stood, and well down the side of the mountain the only ruin that still has a roof. You would be justified in asking, 'Is this the glory of Islam? This barren hillside with its unimpressive ruins?'

Then the guide begins to speak, and if you are able to credit the greatness that once characterized Córdoba, you begin to visualize what Medînat az-Zahrâ must have been like in the year 960. 'We are five miles from Córdoba,' the guide says, 'and one day when a foreign ambassador came to see the caliph who was residing here, he found that a matting had been laid for him all the way from Córdoba. It was lined by soldiers and eunuchs and musicians who played music for him as he walked the five miles. Along the whole route umbrellas kept him protected from the sun and dancing girls accompanied him. When he reached this place he found a palace that covered the entire hillside. The sultan's rooms alone numbered four hundred. The roof was supported by 4,313 marble columns. The fountains were without number, for merely to feed the fish required eight hundred loaves to be baked each day. It wasn't a palace, really, but a sultan's city, all under one roof. More than twenty-five thousand people worked here. Slavonian eunuchs, three thousand seven hundred. Other male servants, ten thousand. Female servants, six thousand. Pages, at least a thousand. Musicians, many score. To feed only the people living under this roof required seven tons of meat each day, not to count the chickens, partridges and fish. It was the most luxurious palace that Spain has ever seen, or the world either, perhaps.'

To perceive in these desolate ruins the wizardry that was once Medînat az-Zahrâ requires faith, and certain critics have recently begun to question whether it was ever much more than the normal-type summer retreat favored by all Moors. They point out that such floor plans as can be extrapolated from the ruins do not begin to provide space for twenty-five thousand people, nor for a caliph's quarters of four hundred rooms. And if anyone did feed eight hundred loaves of bread daily to the fish, they must have thrown it in the Guadalquivir, because there was no space here for ponds of that magnitude. I found myself unable to accept the grandeur that my guide reported, yet I was aware that she had not invented these figures; they came from well-documented contemporary sources, so that if what has come down to us is mere invention, it was contemporary invention and not afterthought. It is possible that those marble waiting rooms in which ambassadors prepared themselves to face the caliph once existed, but they have vanished as if made of paper. In doing so they anticipated the disappearance of all Muslim culture from Spain. On this hillside men may have governed for a while and kept their thousand concubines, but their reality has evaporated and even the buildings in which they luxuriated are known no more.

Although I could not accept the figures given for Medînat az-Zahrâ, I was hesitant to dismiss the legend because only a few miles to the east stood the very real Great Mosque, and if a gigantic thing like that was possible, Medînat az-Zahrâ was not impossible. I first saw the mosque from the tower at the southern end of the Roman bridge which crosses the Guadalquivir, and from there it looked like an ordinary Christian church, ugly rather than otherwise, set behind old brown walls, some of which were crumbling, others of which bore false arches that led to nowhere and pillars which should have supported huge gateways but whose openings were bricked up. I spent a long time walking completely around the mosque and failed to detect any façade, or any part of a façade, which impressed me as worthy of what I had been told lay inside. In fact, the outer walls were grubby and what entrances there were consisted of uninspired square pillars between which had been set short and stubby doorways capped by Moorish half-moon arches whose tiles had fallen away in various spots. Few of the world's great buildings can be so disappointing from the outside.

Loath to believe that this was the building I sought, I withdrew some distance to study it afresh, and it appeared as before: a dumpy Christian church hidden by a wholly undistinguished wall, except that now I could see the bell tower, and a sorrier bit of architecture I had rarely come upon. It looked as if a tower twice as high had been built, with no style whatever, and then squashed down to half its height, so that all parts became sort of ridiculous. They were too fat, too compressed, too formless. Horizontal lines dominated the vertical, resulting in something that was neither a satisfactory Gothic tower to accompany a church nor a poetic minaret to grace a mosque, and I was ready to dismiss the Great Mosque as a fraud.

When I passed through the dingy walls to enter the Patio de los Naranjos (Courtyard of the Oranges) my disappointment was increased, for here I saw a rather large area of no distinction in which trees grew at random and around which walls ran, all in bad need of a washing. Especially drab were the walls of the mosque itself, a compromise between Moorish arches and Christian brick but having the dignity of neither. I was really perplexed as to why this building was so highly regarded, because so far I had seen nothing.

I then entered the mosque by an unprepossessing door and decided to look with unprejudiced eye at this so-called miracle; and as I stood in the darkness and began slowly to adjust to the shadows, I found myself in an architectural fairy tale, surrounded by so many pillars and arches that I could not believe they were real. I suppose that from where I stood I was seeing something like four hundred separate marble columns, each hand-somely polished and with its own capital of Corinthian foliage. The arches that rose above these columns formed a maze which attracted the eye this way and that, for they were striped with alternate bands of yellow and red, and they were extra impressive in that in certain parts of the mosque they were double, that is, from the top of a capital one arch was slung across to the facing capital, and then three feet above that a second arch was thrown across in the same plane, producing a wild confusion of line and weight.

My first impression was of this wilderness of columns and arches; my second was expressed in an involuntary cry: 'It's so big!' I think no words could prepare one for the magnitude of this immense building. Its columns stretch away to darkness in all directions, so vast are the distances, and the fact that light enters at unexpected places adds to the bewilderment. Also, those vibrating bands of yellow and red increase the confusion, so that one cannot focus on a specific spot in the distance, for his eye is constantly drawn to another. The men who built this mosque, over the remains of a Visigothic church, had a vision of permanence and magni-tude that still stuns the imagination.

My eyes never became adjusted to it, but when they had ceased darting this way and that, I started a slow circuit and after some minutes came to a section where the columns were of special beauty, a kind of creamy white and dark brown, and where the sets of double arches drew

Islamic tracery.

the eye to a focus on the far wall, where carving of the most exquisite sort graced a series of intricate arches. A group of French tourists went past, and I heard the guide saying, 'Now we approach the mihrab.' This is the niche set into the wall of every mosque, indicating the kiblah, that point which one faces when praying if he wishes to kneel in the direction of Mecca. The mihrab in Córdoba was the finest I had ever seen, and I am familiar with all the great mosques of the east except those in Mecca and Medina. It was a niche large enough to stand in, covered with delicate tracery in blue and bronze, with passages from the Koran written in gold against a blue ground. It was ornate beyond description, yet it hung together to create a sensation of Asiatic splendor as alien to the continent of Europe as the cry of the muezzin. I was overcome by the beauty of this spot, by the tragedy of its vanished significance. The psychological distance between this alcove and the cathedral in Toledo is at least as great as the distance between the moon and the earth. Perhaps it is greater, for one day, apparently, the moon and earth will be united by human contact but it seems unlikely that the mihrab and the cathedral ever will be.

Christian and Muslim were further alienated by a relic preserved in the Great Mosque, the verified arm of Muhammad. It was the holiest item in Muslim Spain and was invoked by generals when going into battle against the Christians. It seems to have had magical properties capable of inspiring Muslim armies and terrifying their opponents, and for the better part of a century this arm had a clear field in Spain, without losing one battle; then in desperation the Christians came up with a surprising countermeasure which bestowed invincibility on them, but we shall not meet this new force until the last chapter.

I had been wandering about the mosque for the better part of an hour, keeping to the outer walls because I wanted to savor the immensity of the place, when I became aware that a structure of some size rose in the middle of the eight hundred and fifty pillars, and I walked casually in that direction to find that my earliest impression of the mosque, the one I had gained from the tower at the Roman bridge, was correct. Here, lost in this wilderness of columns, hid a full-sized Catholic cathedral, and one of colossal ugliness. When the Christians captured Córdoba in 1236 and expelled the Moors, it was understandable that they should wish to convert the now useless mosque into a cathedral, for the Moors had done the converse in 711 when they captured the city. I think no one can complain of such conversion; it is one of the logical consequences of war, and if the truth were known, Sancta Sophia in Constantinople, which started life as a cathedral, did not suffer much by being sanctified as a mosque. In Córdoba, the Christians did little to damage the mosque; they merely ripped out a few rows of pillars so that the interior would look like a church with a central nave plus two aisles on each side, and thus it stood from 1236 to about 1520; I suppose the untrained eye entering the building in those centuries could not have detected that changes had been made, because the visual difference between a thousand columns and eight hundred and fifty cannot be significant.

However, when Carlos ascended the throne, the Christian hierarchy of Córdoba saw a chance to do something they had long wanted to do but which Fernando and Isabel, sensitive to the Moorish architecture of the south, would never have permitted. They wanted to erect across the inconspicuous nave a transept, which when properly covered and cut off from the rest of the mosque, would constitute a proper cathedral. They therefore petitioned Carlos for permission to do this, and he, knowing nothing of the problem, for he did not appreciate the south, carelessly granted it. Speedily Christian stonemasons went to work and built, right in the heart of the mosque, their monstrous structure. When Carlos finally visited Córdoba in 1526 and saw what had been done under his aegis he was ashamed, saying, 'If I had known what you were up to, you would not have done it. For what you have made here may be found in many other places, but what you have destroyed is to be found nowhere else in the world.'

I do not share the emperor's lament. As my own experience proved, one can visit the mosque without at first being aware that the gigantic church is there. It certainly did not spoil my visits, and while I know that without the cathedral I would have seen vistas that must have been profound, I could still see so far along the outer walls that my eye got lost in the arches. That the Christians had a right to use the mosque as a cathedral, there can be no question; that they found it necessary to build a transept, and such a gross one, is regrettable.

I spent many hours inside the church, for I found the choir a comfortable place to rest. I grew to like the intricate vaulting, and particularly the pink marble ox that held up the black pulpit; his carved entrails had burst loose in conformity to the local legend, which said that the Córdoban ox which bore the pillars for constructing the cathedral burst his insides with joy to think that the building was once more to be a church. The white eagle that served as a lectern also attracted my attention and I did much of my reading in its shadow. I rather liked the idea that what had once been a pagan temple of the Romans, then a Christian church of the Visigoths, next a mosque of the Muslims, was now a church for Catholics; it was proper and in the order of things, but in spite of the hours I spent there reading and thinking, I never felt it to be a consecrated place. It was more like an ornate museum, as if the contamination of having been a mosque had not been properly cleansed. This feeling did not arise from the fact that the cathedral was an ugly building, for in a sense that was appropriate; much of what Christians introduced when they expelled the Muslims was uglier than what it replaced, but on balance the change was inescapable; it was necessary for the development of Spain.

I was less generous in my judgment of that endless chain of second-rate chapels that usurp the outer walls of the mosque; once these walls had stood open so that worshipers might enter the mosque from any direction, and then when one was inside he looked through this maze of columns out to the free sky of Andalucía, and the impact must have been tremendous; but since the building was now a cathedral it required chapels, so the once-open walls were bricked shut, and as mournful a bunch of cubicles as I have ever seen was strung along them. How many are there, unused, undusted and unsung? One morning I walked past the locked gates of each one, not slowly, but pausing now and then to look at the moldering statues and the bad painting, and it took me twenty-nine minutes to make the circuit, for there must have been more than fifty. A few had touches of real charm, and I could see that others had historic validity in that they related to important figures in Córdoba's history, but for the main part they were a dismal, unattended group of structures which came off poorly when compared with the mosque they had helped deface.

One must be careful not to generalize about this matter, for a distinguished French critic whom we shall meet later in another context points out that it would be fallacious to condemn the Christians for defacing a Muslim masterwork, because Muslims had very little to do with the building of this mosque! The design came from the Christian basilica around which the original mosque was built. Most of the marble columns and their capitals were appropriated from existing Christian monuments in Spain or Africa. The workmen who built the mosque were Christians; even the glorious mihrab which I had liked so much was built by Christian workmen loaned to Córdoba by the Christian emperor at Constantinople, who also sent as a gift three hundred and twenty quintals of glass pieces for the mosaics (about thirty-five tons). 'Accordingly, in this great sanctuary of Islam, the first after that of Mecca, everything, or nearly everything, is Christian: the plan of the edifice, the material employed, and even the workmanship.'

Much confused, I left the Great Mosque. In many respects it was unsatisfying; its Christian and Muslim halves were uneasy with each other and failed to attain that harmony one finds in Sancta Sophia. There is here a sense of imbalance and restlessness, as if the Muslim component of Spanish life had accepted its role of submission and were trying to escape; or as if the Christian component were not content with its conquest and were endeavoring to suppress even further the Moorish. In such circumstances the Muslim explodes to the surface through weakened fissures. There is in much of Spain this contradiction: it is a Christian country but one with suppressed Muslim influences that crop out at unforeseen points; it is a victorious country that expelled the defeated Muslims from all places except the human heart; it is a land which tried to extirpate all memory of the Muslims but which lived on to mourn their passing; and it is a civilization which believed that it triumphed when it won the last battle but which knows that it lost in fields like poetry, dancing, philosophy, architecture and agriculture. To me Córdoba's mosque was the most mournful building in Spain, and on the evening after my first visit I went into the old Jewish quarter, where memories of the Moors still linger, to see if I could banish my unease.

If I had been disappointed by the mosque, I was enchanted by the little courtyards of the Jewish quarter, for I suppose they represent one of the perfect sights that a stranger can come upon in Europe, like the Spanish Steps in Rome or the island museums of Oslo. They are a series of small, informal patios strung out by accident along unimportant back streets, and they number perhaps a hundred. You see them casually through doorways as you walk along, and occasionally one acquires a greater importance than the others because it stands behind formal arches and has had professional attention. Mostly, however, they are family gardens, but unlike any you have seen before.

By luck, the first one I happened upon as I was looking for the restaurant to which I had been directed by a friend, was one of the best. I saw it through an open doorway, an ordinary patio surrounded on three sides by a low two-story house whose walls were whitewashed. The floor of the patio was paved with pebbles set on end, so that it had a pleasing design. A flight of stairs led to a second-floor balcony, over whose edge hung nineteen potted flowers with tendrils covering the wall of the balcony. The top of the balcony was lined with twenty-seven flowerpots which also dropped flowers in abundance, while the six posts supporting the roof each held three beautiful flowering plants. The two side walls could scarcely be seen. In one corner of the patio stood a well with a masonry rim, whitewashed and containing a dozen larger pots of roses and dahlias, while around the line where the walls met the patio floor scores of pots were ranged, each with some flowering plant. To the right of the entrance a low wall had been erected in previous centuries, perhaps when Jews still occupied the house, and it must originally have been intended for visitors to sit on like a bench, but now it too was crowded with flowerpots, all of whose plants were in bloom. The little patio was thus a theater offering a ballet of color against the stark whiteness of the walls. The flowers danced up and down the stairway, pirouetted across the balcony, around the well, up and down the posts, and in a kind of majestic march moved about the lower walls. How many separate plants were there? Well over a hundred, I suppose. How many colors? More than I could count. How many different kind of flowers? I'm not good at identifying them, but there were at least a dozen.

There was one patio which quite captivated me, for I had not heard of such a way of using flowers. In a whitewashed area of rough walls and arcades, some sixty flowerpots were hung from wire loops, and all were painted Muslim blue. This is a dark blue often seen in the Middle East, where it is

popular as a charm guaranteed to keep away evil spirits; on the road from Tel Aviv to Haifa, in the heart of Israel, there is an Arab village named Faradis (Paradise) that used to be painted blue. In Córdoba the concentration of blue pots against white walls was most charming, and when varied flowers crept down from the pots to hang in a hundred festoons, the effect was unlike anything I had seen before.

These two patios were in no way exceptional; I must have seen about sixty that evening as I wandered down the street of the Good Shepherd in the general direction of the Maimonides statue, but finally I found my restaurant and much to my satisfaction saw that a flamenco concert was scheduled for that night. I had dinner in a delightful room which duplicated something of the charm of the patios, and while waiting for the program to begin I wondered whether the spectacular display of flowers I had seen was an inheritance from the Moors, who were reported to have been excellent gardeners. I suppose I could have found comparable gardens elsewhere in Spain, but as a matter of record I didn't, so I concluded that these Córdoban patios were a Moorish carry-over.

About flamenco there is much debate. The easy explanation of this unique art form, which combines guitar playing, singing, chanting, dancing and staccato handclapping, is that it is a very old inheritance from Moorish days, in which the distinctive wail is an echo of the muezzin's cry with Jewish overtones; but if, as some think, it was derived from gypsy patterns imported from Asia rather than from Africa, it must be a fairly recent importation, for the gypsies did not reach Spain till 1435. We know that the name dates only from 1520, when the Flemish courtiers of Carlos V burst on the drab Spanish scene with slashed doublets showing flashes of brilliant color and gave their name to anything conspicuous or garish, like the flamingo bird and the flamenco dance.

I had been introduced to flamenco under appropriate conditions in that café in Valencia, because there I heard some first-class guitar playing and that important flamenco song 'Petenera.' In intervening years I had bought most of the good flamenco records reaching America, but they were not many, for much junk was then purveyed as flamenco, a custom which has not been broken. In Mexico I attended several flamenco parties, and they were awful, though the versions offered in New York were worse. The fact was that after that first superb evening I had heard no acceptable flamenco and it was gratifying to find myself now in the heart of the flamenco country, where I could catch up.

The room in which the dance was to be held could hardly have been more suitable, a cellar-type place with old iron-studded doors, a beamed ceiling, intricate trellises up which vines crept, and what looked like authentic Roman pillars except that they were topped by rude, country-

the blazing heat of Andalucía how pleasant it is
be inside a darkened room protected from the sun
thick walls and growing plants.

Although to the practiced Spanish eye this gesticulating flamenco dancer would be spotted as an amateur, because his fingers are distorted in grotesque rather than poetic fashion, he is properly caught up in the spirit of the dance and is experiencing catharsis in the Aristotelian sense of the word.

style capitals that seemed just right for this room. The furniture was rough, and as the people near me talked I was pleased to find that the room had a fine resonance, for the brick walls absorbed sound. It promised to be an exciting evening.

Then the troupe appeared, five people dressed a little too finely for the work at hand. The three men (guitarist, singer, dancer) wore suits that were too professional in their tightness and cut. The two girl dancers wore dresses strongly modified by French ideas and their heels were of an exaggerated height. What was most disturbing, the girls were too young and too beautiful; when this is the case the dancer is tempted to say, 'Look at me, how lovely I am,' and not to do much honest dancing. The sleazy guitarist struck a few dramatic chords, ran a series of notes and went into the kind of sequence burlesque orchestras use to announce the impending appearance of their chief stripper. One of the girls rushed forth, assumed a fatalistic pose, stamped her feet a couple of times and grunted, '¡Ole!' I thought, Oh boy! All the duende of a boiler factory.

What a horrible evening it was. I had been trapped in a tourist show of the worst sort: the dancing was strictly Hollywood, with much heel banging and head gesture; the guitarist was nimble rather than profound and his playing tended toward the staccato chord; the singing done by the pomaded man in the tight suit was closer to the Beatles than to either Moors or gypsies. All this I could have borne, but the girls were arch and danced so as to display their legs up to their navels and one even wore a rose between her teeth; when I thought I had seen the worst, and that can be pretty bad, for in this country when taste abdicates, the results are unpredictable, the girls called onto the stage two German sailors, wrapped mantones (shawls) about the bottoms of the two men and proceeded to burlesque one of the few authentic entertainments Spain has to offer its guests. It was shocking, as vulgar as the scenes in Hawaiian night clubs when hula girls lure men onstage to make asses of themselves. The two Germans were good sports and one had a bawdy sense of humor: he grabbed at the skirts of the flamenco girls; they stumbled and he fell on his face. The audience roared approval and the guitarist played a version of 'Anchors Aweigh.'

The performance was so dismal that all I could do was sit there and recall the jokes I'd seen on television about flamenco. A dancer does the foot-stamping bit and the comedian says, 'He's mad at the floor.' The dancer looks back over his shoulder: 'He's very proud of his bottom. Wants to be sure it's still there.' The dancer looks under his left shoulder: 'He wants to see if he needs a deodorant.' The dancer stamps again: 'He wants the janitor to send up more heat.' It was on that level.

When the miserable night was over I walked back to the Maimonides statue and in that peaceful place contemplated the mockery that Spain was making of certain of its treasures, simply to collect a few tourist kroner or francs. I was in a rather bitter mood, when the musicians from the show came out and one asked me, 'How did you like it?' I did not know enough Spanish to tell him, so I said, 'I had rather hoped to hear something like a petenera.' The men stopped, for it was obvious that the name of that song was a rebuke. The guitar which they had abused grew heavy and the pomaded heads became ridiculous. 'Qué lástima! (What a pity!)' the guitarist said. 'Here we get few people who know peteneras.'

Spain runs a considerable risk of cheapening the very things that have made her attractive to tourists. She has enjoyed an enviable reputation in reports of men like Mérimée, Havelock Ellis, Somerset Maugham, Henry de Montherlant and the others who have been captivated by an authentic Spanish culture displayed with fierce honesty. If this culture is to be made a mockery of, and by Spain itself, then there will be little reason for anyone of good taste to bother with it. I cannot believe that the notable visitors of the past, men like George Borrow, Richard Ford, Sacheverell Sitwell and especially the keen French and German travelers, would have tolerated a scene like the one that was forced on me in the Córdoba restaurant; and had they been required, as I was, to sit through it they could have described it later only in words of scorn. It was cheap, and vulgar, and an insult to the visitor; but even worse, it was an abuse of the cultural heritage and it was this more than my own deprivation which infuriated me.

I am not going to bore the reader, city by city, with an account of my attempts to see in Spain a good flamenco; in each place I was abused about as badly as I was in Córdoba. It was all junk, save for a few nights when I happened upon a near-blind old man whose voice was gone but who had the pundonor of his trade and the gracia to communicate it to others. If on some subsequent trip to Spain I were to be told of a bar where one could occasionally hear real flamenco, I would travel a considerable distance to hear it; but if, as I suppose, it has all been corrupted by the quick tourist dollar, and if enough of the rest of Spanish culture goes the same way, I would be better off turning flamenco and Spain over to others, for it would no longer have much to say to me.

As for Córdoba the city, my days there were delightful. I had nothing much to do and spent long hours lounging in the sun at one outdoor bar or another in the Plaza José Antonio. Occasionally I would wander over to talk with old Bishop Hosius, but for the most part I rested and caught up with a lot of reading I wanted to do in the field of the Spanish novel.

My stay was made extra pleasant by the fact that I had a room in the local parador, which stands some miles out in the country on a fine hillside from which I could overlook the Guadalquivir as if I were a caliph at Medînat az-Zahrâ, which lay not far away on roughly the same spur of hills. For some reason which no one explained in advance, this parador has developed the best restaurant in Spain, better, I thought, than even the ultra-posh ones in Madrid because its cuisine was more honest, and people traveled long distances to dine here. The menu was not exceptional in its variety, but each dish was properly prepared. For example, I would not have expected to find in Córdoba the best sole à la Colbert I have ever tasted, but there it was, delicately flavored with butter and crisp along the edges.

Each day for a week my waitress warned me, 'You're missing the best thing we do if you don't take the rabo de toro.' Now those words had to mean *tail of bull* and I have never been a big partisan of braised oxtail, which is what I supposed it was. 'No, thank you,' I said.

Her other suggestions had worked out so satisfactorily that I was not easy in rejecting this one. For example, one day she said, 'No matter what you think you want, take the stewed partridge.' I recalled my unpleasant

Like flamenco dancers they stomp the stage on which they perform. They spread their fans, they move in graceful rhythms and cry out in rasping voices.

experiences with this delicacy in Toledo and started to say no, but she whisked under my nose a serving which she was delivering to a nearby table, and it was so enticing that I allowed her to bring me a portion, and thereafter whenever it appeared on the menu I took it, a truly fine dish. But the tail of bull I avoided.

One day I had as my guests a pair of archaeologists who had been digging in the Old Testament copper mines at Río Tinto, northwest of Sevilla (they said there was a wealth of digging to be done there in a civilization three thousand years old), and they were delighted when they saw rabo de toro on the menu. 'Famous throughout southern Spain,' they said, so I went along with them and tried it. By itself it would have made the parador famous, so after the archaeologists had left I went into the kitchen to ask the chef how he made this dish, and even a quick glance at the place told me all I needed to know about why this parador was so well regarded for its food. The kitchen was both old-fashioned with handsome clay pots and modern with stainless steel; immaculately clean, it was also properly cluttered with vegetables and shellfish, and the people working in it were a robust crew who had fun in handling food and dishes. My waitress whispered that the excellence of the place could be traced to the unmarried daughter of a leading Andalusian family who had surprised her friends by volunteering to work in the parador and who had ended by being its chatelaine.

Her chief cook was hardly what I had expected, a bull-like man who spoke in a confused rush with few verbs, but since he was using Andalusian, a much truncated dialect, I may have missed the verbs. He avoided all *s* sounds and most *d*'s and invariably used *er* for *el*.

Castilian	Andalusian
mismo	meemo
madre	mare
bueno	wayno
Jaime Ostos	Aim O-o
el matador	er matao
los amigos	lo jarmigo
cuidado	cuiao

The last word, pronounced in drawling whine *kwee-ow,* in which the last syllable rhymes with *now,* means "take care" and is much used in the region; it is practically the shibboleth of the true Andalusian.

The chunky cook was pleased that someone wanted to know how he made his rabo de toro: 'So it's a good bull's tail, fat, much gristle in the joints. Taste from the gristle. Cut, cut, pieces not too big. Roll in flour, much salt, braise in fat. Cuiao! Don't burn, but cook well. Must have juice left for sauce. Everything is the sauce. Cuiao! No spices. No pepper. Onions well fried for flavor. Olive oil, but cuiao! Not too much. Garlic, celery, carrots, mushrooms, but not one water. Cuiao! No water, or you make soup. Bake one hour and half in hot oven. To serve put three joints bull's tail in ramekin, sauce, vegetables, two fresh onions, bake few minutes to turn brown. Cuiao! No water, no wine.'

As I sat on my hillside looking down on Córdoba, I became so preoccupied with Muslim Spain that I decided to take the journey over the mountain to Granada, where my driving companion had an excellent idea. He wanted me to approach Granada by a special route, so short of the city he turned to the south and took me a good twenty miles away. He turned into a narrow twisting side road that led into the mountains of the Sierra Nevada, where we came upon a remote village perched on the edge of a cliff, a most frightening but beautiful spot. 'Here we'll have our picnic!' he said, and as we unpacked the car and sat beside a stream which tumbled into a valley far below, he pointed to the encircling mountains and said, 'Tourists spend a lot of time oohing and aahing over the Alhambra, but it teaches them nothing about Islam. It's this that explains why Granada was able to hold on for so long. The Christians couldn't root the Muslims out of fastnesses like this. For more than three centuries they tried, but with no luck. This is Granada. Not the city back there.'

It was an ideal spot in which to contemplate the fortunes of Islam; the combination of mountain and valley refreshed the eye and the sight of people moving about the landlocked village at the edge of the cliff gave one a sense of historical continuity. Under Muslim rule their ancestors had lived in those homes and after the collapse of the Muslim kingdom they had probably reverted to Christianity. Royal lines had come and gone but these farmers and smugglers had bothered little, and now, when their country perched on the edge of a precipice of uncertainty as to what might happen when Generalísimo Franco left, they were as unconcerned as ever. This was really timeless Spain, even more remote than the parched villages of Extremadura, for here movement in or out was much more difficult.

'The wonder of the Christian Conquest of Granada,' my friend said, 'was not that it came when it did but that it came so very late. For nearly eight hundred years the Christians of Spain conducted what they describe as a permanent crusade. That's why no Spanish knights appear in what we call the Crusades. They were occupied at home. But they rarely fought all-out battles. It was mostly a "you let me hold Toledo and I'll let you hold Córdoba" business. Muslim armies served Christian kings and Christian knights worked for Muslim caliphs, and a kind of happy-go-lucky truce operated most of the time. By 1242 the Christians had maneuvered themselves into such a favorable position that one final push would have kicked the Moors out, but they dawdled for another two and a half centuries. I suppose when Spanish generals pictured themselves leading their armies over terrain like this they lost heart.'

On the rocky earth by our picnic ground I traced out a series of maps showing Spain in various periods, insofar as I could remember them, and my friend was right. In 711 the Muslims had conquered a defunct Spain with indecent ease. Had there ever before been a nation so large that had collapsed so swiftly to an invader with so few men? In one battle, the chroniclers tell us, more than one hundred thousand well-armed Christians evaporated before twelve thousand partially armed Berbers, and the conquest of most cities was more like a procession than an invasion; even Toledo fell with shocking speed. In contrast, when the time came for the

Christians to reconquer Spain, their advance was slow. The final stage began in 1482, when Fernando and Isabel, with a more or less united Spain behind them, were at last able to bring the weight of the nation to bear on Granada.

On our way back to inspect the city we reached the mournful point on the road known as El Ultimo Suspiro del Moro (The Last Sigh of the

This Spanish horse, so thick-necked and muscular that it seems to have been sculptured from bronze, exhibits its Arab ancestry.

Moor), where Boabdil is supposed to have paused, as he abandoned Granada to the Christians, for one last look at his noble city. Here he lamented his loss, whereupon his mother remarked, 'You do well, my son, to weep as a woman for the loss of what you could not defend as a man.' From this spot the towers of Granada, set down among mountains, were exciting enough to evoke a sigh.

We did not stop there, however, nor in the city itself, but went to that hill east of the city on the road to Guadix where one can look down upon Granada and perceive its structure. Two rivers join, and instead of plunging through the mountains eastward to the Mediterranean, start west across Andalucía to enter the Guadalquivir near Córdoba. At their confluence a town grew up prior to the Romans, under whom it flourished. It provided a starting point for the Muslims when they sought a mountain capital safe from Mediterranean pirates and Christian land armies. The main body of the city crouched in valleys but the gypsy quarter perched on a hill. 'It's the other hill you should study,' my guide said, and it was from this favorable position that I looked down onto the most famous hill in Spain. Its crest consisted of a long, narrow wooded area completely enclosed by a turreted wall inside which were many gardens, pools and rambling buildings, the whole creating a sense of beauty and repose.

'Which building is the Alhambra?' I asked.

'Everything within the walls. The whole complex of woodland, water, gardens and buildings. It all goes together to make the Alhambra.' Seeing it thus from a mountainside, I was able to appreciate the inventiveness of the Muslim architects in converting a considerable hilltop into a natural palace in which gardens and fountains were as important as buildings.

I can still recall my first experience within the walls of the Alhambra. My friend had gone to confirm our reservations at the parador, which stands within the Alhambra and is a part of it, and I went off into one of the gardens, and there an old man, clad much as he would have been five hundred years ago, was gathering figs, pulling the branches down with a crook and examining each fruit to see if it was ripe. He gave me one, black as night and filled with seeds. From all parts of the garden I smelled the heavy scent of boxwood, and in the valley below, where the city stood, I could see mists covering the roofs. In the trees at the edge of the garden, birds sang and beyond them rose the somber wall and the turrets that protected it. This was the Alhambra; the buildings would come later.

If I had been disappointed in Córdoba's Great Mosque, the contrary was true in Granada, for the Alhambra was much lovelier and much more Muslim than I had anticipated. I think what pleased me most in the buildings was the subtle manner in which one memorable room or hall led quietly into the next, as if an intricate musical composition were unfolding with always the right notes appearing where they were needed. One moves through this extensive collection of architectural highlights as if he were in a dream, in which one gentle surprise lures him on to the next.

It is not my intention to describe the buildings of the Alhambra, since it has already been well done. I was amused, however, to discover in an alcove of the Courtyard of the Myrtles, with its large reflecting pool, the shell of Santiago used as an ornamental device. There it was: the symbol of the force that would drive Islam from Spain built into the final palace, as if

719
AT THE HEIGHT OF THE MUSLIM OCCUPATION

Pamplona
Barcelona
Toledo
Lisboa
Córdoba
Sevilla
ENCLAVE TILL 741

Christian lands
Muslim lands

950
RECONQUEST LAUNCHED BY LEON AND ARAGON

NAVARRA
ARAGON
LEON
Salamanca
Toledo
Córdoba
Sevilla
Granada

1035
CONSOLIDATION ACHIEVED BY SANCHO DE NAVARRA

NAVARRA
ARAGON
LEON
Toledo
Córdoba
Granada

1214
AT THE DEATH OF ALFONSO VIII DE CASTILLA

LEON
NAVARRA
Barcelona
ARAGON
PORTUGAL
CASTILLA
Toledo
Córdoba
Granada

1242
CONSOLIDATION OF FERNANDO III DE CASTILLA

Pamplona
NAVARRA
Barcelona
ARAGON
PORTUGAL
CASTILLA
Toledo
Córdoba
Granada

1482
ON THE EVE OF THE FINAL CONQUEST OF GRANADA

NAVARRA
ARAGON
CASTILLA
PORTUGAL
Toledo
Córdoba
Granada

the Muslims had foreseen their own expulsion. And in a room off the Courtyard of the Lions, I found the Star of David, because as I said before, in Spain one finds old memories at unexpected places.

I think the most beautiful thing I saw among the buildings was the passageway leading from the Courtyard of the Myrtles to the Courtyard of the Lions, because here the architect was faced with a universal problem: how to relate two unrelated spaces? He solved it by placing two doorways of radically different widths side by side, then uniting them with one lintel, whose ends dropped down around the sides of the doors, and covering the entire with handsome carving. When I looked at the two doors everything about them seemed wrong; a child could have designed them better, but only a great artist could have juxtaposed them so as to achieve an effect so right and good. I studied them for a long time, because in my own work I have often tried to attain a similar result. It seems to me that any writer should be able to produce 'a well-constructed English novel'; it takes someone like the Alhambra architect to slap together disparate items and make them sing, and if I have not always been successful in my own efforts, I know success when someone else achieves it.

I was surprised at the flimsy construction of the buildings. Is there another structure of comparable importance put together with such contempt for permanence? The ceilings, whose stalactite traceries are so exquisite, are nothing but stucco whose points one could knock off with a knuckle, and the walls of delicate geometric pattern are built up of plaster exactly as one would build up the decoration of a wedding cake and of not much greater permanence. That the palaces of the Alhambra have survived for seven hundred years is astonishing; when one sees how fragile they are, one better understands how vast areas like Medînat az-Zahrâ and caliphate Córdoba have vanished. The surprising thing is that any Muslim remains have survived.

The Courtyard of the Lions was as pure a work of art as I had been told, for here the inventive architects had converted a collection of slim marble columns and filigreed arches into a garden of stone which includes that handsome twelve-sided fountain protected by a pride of granite lions who look more like friendly puppy dogs than jungle beasts.

Turning a corner on one of the upper floors, I came upon the plain notice: 'In these quarters Washington Irving wrote his *Tales of the Alhambra* in the year 1829.' It was easy to visualize the bachelor lawyer, embassy official and future ambassador to Spain ensconced in these rooms with their cloistered balcony of marble columns overlooking the hills and caves of Granada. The workroom looked onto a patio with tall cypresses and a chattering fountain built up from a square inscribed with a circle, and it must have been a romantic place for a man with Irving's imagination; one can understand the flowery visions he entertained here. *Tales of the Alhambra*, composed in a few weeks' time, swept the English-speaking world and made its author famous. Irving was partial to the Muslims as contrasted to the Christians, and his slight tales, often no more than mood pieces, had considerable effect upon subsequent historical judgment; one could not read Irving, especially his more substantial *Conquest of Granada*, without becoming an advocate of Islam and a mourner over its expulsion.

There is no place better, I think, than Irving's rooms in the Alhambra for weighing the moral significance of the Muslim occupation of Spain, and here I tried to reach a judgment. I had always been much disposed toward the Muslims, both in Spain and elsewhere, and I had once written an essay on Muhammad that had gained approval in various countries of the Muslim world. I had lived in six different Islamic countries—Turkey, Afghanistan, Iran, Pakistan, Malaya and Indonesia—and had visited half a dozen others. I had schooled myself in at least the outlines of Islamic philosophy, poetry and art and found myself sympathetic to the Muslim view of life.

I was therefore susceptible to the Washington Irving point of view that Spain had called down upon herself a sad retribution when she expelled the Moors; special damage had been done to her intellectual and agricultural life, and from this she had not recovered. Certainly, post hoc ergo propter hoc reasoning substantiated this: as long as the Muslims were in Spain and making their contribution to Spanish life, Spain stood at the head of nations, but coincident with the expulsion of the Moors, starting in 1492 and ending in 1609, began that long decline which the country has not yet reversed.

In an out-of-the-way inn in a different part of Spain, I had come upon a three-volume book of travels published in 1829, entitled *A Year in Spain* and attributed to 'A Young American.' Who he was I did not know, but whatever college he attended had taught him fine writing; his sentences were some of the longest and most polished I had read and his reflections on the Conquest of Granada were typical of the attitudes which I had inherited:

> Though this victory of Ferdinand and Isabella was a Christian triumph, in name at least, it was not a triumph of humanity; and if the philanthropist or the colder economist, speculating with a view to utility alone, were to inquire what use Christian Spain had made of her dear-bought conquest, and how far the aggregate happiness of mankind and the interests of civilization had been promoted by the extermination of an heroic, ingenious, and industrious people, a picture of fraud, cruelty, and oppression would be presented, as frightful as the world has ever witnessed, and followed by consequences equally ruinous to the oppressors and the oppressed.

(Upon my return to America, I learned through the kindness of the librarian at The Hispanic Society of America that the author of this book was Alexander Slidell [1803–1848], the younger brother of that famous John Slidell of New York City who, after graduating from Columbia College in that city, wound up as United States senator from Louisiana, a post he surrendered when Louisiana withdrew from the Union at the start of the Civil War. As a diplomatic representative of the Confederacy, the older Slidell earned a place in history when the northern navy lifted him from a British ship in which he was traveling to Europe, thus precipitating an incident which nearly brought Great Britain into the war on the side of the Confederacy. Alexander Slidell published his book on Spain at the age of twenty-six; three years later, on August 20, 1832, the Spanish King Fernando VII issued a royal decree banning him from Spain because of intemperate remarks he had made against the country. In 1838 Slidell added the name Mackenzie and was henceforth known as Slidell Mackenzie. In 1842, after three of his sailors were detected in a mutiny, Mackenzie hung the trio from the yardarm of his ship, thus involving himself in a scandal, since one of the hanged men was the son of the Secretary of War. Seven years after the publication of his first book on Spain, he issued a second, *Spain Revisited,* which would indicate that the ban against him had been lifted after the death of King Fernando.)

By training and inclination I was disposed to agree with Slidell Mackenzie's attitude on the Muslim expulsion, but recently I had come upon Bertrand and Petrie's refreshing history, and Bertrand's austere judgments on Muslim Spain derived from his experience and study in the Muslim colonies of French North Africa. Bertrand knew Muslim culture and history in a way that Washington Irving and the anonymous 'Young American' never did, and his acerb views are a corrective to their romanticizing. One of Bertrand's repeated cautions is that we must be suspicious of pro-Muslim writing because its real intention is anti-Catholic; Protestant writers had found in the banished Muslims a convenient club for beating Spaniards: 'To judge Islamic civilization reasonably, it is important not to let ourselves be carried away by the hyperbolical admiration, the preconceptions, and the prejudices of those who exalt Arab-Spanish culture to an exaggerated extent only in order to degrade Catholic Spain in proportion.'

I recommend especially Bertrand's four-page chapter 'The Balance-Sheet of the Arab Conquest,' in which he summarizes his conclusions: Spain owed three positive debts to the Muslims. The concept of the university was Muslim, even though the teaching was 'terrible in its verbalism and almost entirely theological.' Muslim art also exerted a strong influence, as did Muslim poetry. More important, however, were the negative influences upon Spanish character, and these manifested themselves in various ways. The excessive individualism of the Spaniard, his tendency toward anarchy, is a Muslim inheritance 'to such a point that half a dozen Spaniards could not find themselves together in a fort or a caravel without at once forming two or three parties bent upon destroying one another.' Especially destructive to the Spanish character was 'the sinuosity of these Africans and Asiatics,' for from this developed the Spaniard's tendency toward bad faith and the breaking of his word. The bloodthirsty rapacity of the Spaniard and his lust for gold are directly attributable to his contact with the Muslim, as is the custom of keeping women behind bars. The worst of the borrowed characteristics was the parasitism of the nomads whereby living off one's neighbor became an acceptable practice, but almost as bad was the habit of putting the conquered to fire and sword, which the Muslims introduced into the peninsula. Bertrand concludes his dismal summary by citing two influences that were particularly destructive and persistent: the cruelty of the Muslim warrior, which became the cruelty of the Spaniard, and the incapacity of the Muslim to organize a government or to run it methodically. 'The traveler through the mournful solitudes of La Mancha feels only too intensely that the Berbers of Africa have passed that way.'

Elsewhere he makes an additional point of great importance. Conceding that agriculture declined when the Moors were expelled, he warns against interpreting this as proof of Muslim accomplishment, because wherever the Moors went they destroyed agriculture; they did not promote it. The secret was that the good agriculture of the Moorish period was attributable to Spanish farmers using Spanish methods. They had converted to Islam, but when the Moors left, they left too, out of loyalty to their new religion. Bertrand's final comment is unqualified: 'On balance, it can fairly be said that the Muslim domination was a great misfortune for Spain.'

If I were forced to choose between the sentimentalities of Washington Irving and the hard analysis of Louis Bertrand, I would be inclined toward the latter, but I suspect that Bertrand's strictures are somewhat more harsh than truth would dictate, for I detect in his argument more a defense of France's contemporary policy vis-à-vis the difficult Muslims of North Africa than a concern for Spain's historic problems with those same people. It seems to me that Bertrand underemphasizes the artistic accomplishments of the Muslims while overstressing their cruelty; but on one point he is eminently sound and it is one that has not been stressed before: that Spain's proven incapacity to govern herself in the responsible French-English-American pattern is due primarily to her extended experience with Muslims, who fragmented their own holdings into a score of petty principalities and who prevented Spain from doing otherwise until the habit became so ingrained that regional economic separatism became the curse of Spanish life, whether in the homeland or in the Americas. It is this dreadful heritage of anarchy that keeps the Spanish republics of our hemisphere in confusion.

I was restrained from accepting all of Bertrand's conclusions by a curious experience I was having in the Alhambra. Whenever I was tempted to agree that the Moors were as bad as Bertrand said, I would close my books and walk out into the gardens, and there I would find myself face to face with that hideous stone palace which Carlos V had caused to be built in the middle of the grounds and juxtaposed to the loveliest of the Alhambra palaces. One sight of that monstrous edifice, better suited to a cliff along the Rhine than to Granada, satisfied me that although the Moor may have had faults, he also had taste; this castle was so alien to the spirit of the Alhambra that no reconciliation of Spanish ideals and Moorish was possible.

The castle boasts a façade that is grotesquely ugly, as if someone had set out to burlesque the worst taste of the time. Its lower ranges consist of massive stones cut in that style which leaves the central area six or eight inches higher than the edges, producing an effect of brute strength, while the upper portions consist of some of the heaviest and most overly ornamented windows I had ever seen. Since the sides of the building form a square, what one has is an undigested cube of rock, and whoever designed it failed to realize that when plumped down beside the delicate Moorish palaces upon which it encroaches, it could only look ridiculous. There were reasons to forgive the intrusion of the cathedral in the middle of Córdoba's Great Mosque, but the Carlos V castle in the Alhambra can have no justification.

For several days I refused to enter the place, but finally a Spanish friend took me inside and I saw that the interior was a bleak two-tiered circular cloister, unfinished and gapingly open to the sky. This meant that the brutal cube had rooms only around the four sides and these I did not care to see, but my friend insisted, and on the second floor I did find something that made the visit rewarding. I was standing in a royal dining hall, one end of which was decorated by a marble fireplace featuring a medallion bas-relief showing Leda being raped in the most explicit way by Jupiter in the form of a swan, and I said to my guide, "I'll bet a lot of Spaniards spilled their soup in this room,' but he was already leading me to another hall that contained a painting which years ago I had seen reproduced. It was titled 'The Expulsion of the Jews' and was by Emilio Sala (1850–1910), who won a prize with it at the Berlin Exposition of 1891. The guide said, with much enthusiasm, 'It shows us a historic event which occurred in this very city in January, 1492. You see King Fernando on his throne and beside him Queen Isabel. Look at their banner which united Spain with its motto, Tanto Monta. It means that he and she are equal in dignity. Now, who are those two churchmen who seem so excited? The one in crimson, under better control, is Cardinal Mendoza, who served as a general during our Christian victory at Granada. The one in black is the great Cardinal Cisneros. Look at him point with his forefinger as he shouts, "The Jews must go!" You can see that Fernando and Isabel don't want to throw their Jews out, but Cisneros insists.' I was fascinated by the canvas, vast in size, for it was the only one I knew showing the four figures whose histories had become so important to me: Fernando, Isabel, Mendoza and Cisneros, and to see it was worth a trip even through the gloomy palace of Carlos V.

Alas, my enthusiasm was misguided. Long after I had left Granada, I discovered that the agitated figure in black was not my hero Cisneros but rather his predecessor as head of the Inquisition, Tomás de Torquemada, and the scene represented was the famous incident in which King Fernando announced that he had decided not to expel the Jews because they had offered him a bribe of thirty thousand ducats not to do so. Then Torquemada stormed into the room where the sovereigns were listening to the Jews plead for their freedom and he waved on high a crucifix, shouting at the same time, 'Judas Iscariot betrayed our Lord for thirty pieces of silver. The kings of Spain would sell him a second time for thirty thousand. Well, here he is.' With this he threw the crucifix onto the table and disappeared, crying as he went, 'Take him and barter him for thirty thousand pieces of silver.' And the decision to expel was decided upon that day.

In Granada one has conflicting thoughts about Cisneros, for it was as late as 1499, when passions aroused by the Conquest should have subsided, that he ordered the collecting of all Muslim manuscripts in the area and supervised their burning in what has often subsequently been lamented as a major crime against both history and scholarship.

It is appropriate, I suppose, that Fernando and Isabel rest permanently in Granada, the city which had attracted them like a magnet and whose capture became the principal jewel in their crown. In the center of the city, in a royal chapel of florid but pleasing design, lying adjacent to the cathedral, of which it is a part, rest the tombs of the Catholic Kings. The plain leaden caskets lie below ground in a crypt, which can be visited so as to satisfy oneself that the wishes of the kings were respected; they preferred to be buried simply and without undue panoply. But above them, on ground level, a magnificent wrought-iron grille subtends an area which is further enclosed by a plain but handsome iron fence, inside which stand four splendid catafalques, the first pair carved in Genoa of Carrara marble, the second pair in Spain. They represent four royal persons who concern us repeatedly in this book. As you face them, King Fernando V lies to your left in premier position, hands on chest and very regal. Beside him, in second position, lies Queen Isabel I, hands folded and, for some reason I have not been able to discern, looking away from her husband. As we shall see later, he gave her ample reason for dismissing him in this manner, but it was not within her character to do so and I find the tombs disturbing. Beside the great kings, and elevated above them, which seems quite improper, rest two of the unhappiest rulers who ever held a throne in Europe. The young king, who again lies to the left in the premier position, is Philip of Burgundy and Austria, known in Spain as Felipe I of Castilla, recognized in his lifetime as the most elegant of princes and known through Europe as Philip the Handsome. He was a miserable, mean human being, and it is shameful to have him sleeping where he does, for he served Spain poorly, abused the faith Isabel placed in him, fought openly against Fernando and crucified his unfortunate wife, their daughter Juana, who lies beside him. This time it is understandable that the thin-faced, demented woman looks the other way. Hers is a tragic figure, excellently portrayed by the Spanish sculptor, who may have worked from a death mask but also from reports of how the mad queen behaved.

The fact that young Felipe's body is here at all is a compelling story, for the path to this sepulcher was a grim one, but of that we shall hear later. For the present we must fix in our minds the noble panoply of the four kings: Fernando, Isabel, Felipe and Juana la Loca. No kings of Europe enjoy a more gracious mausoleum.

In the sacristy next to the chapel appear two wooden statues which bring the Catholic Kings to life, for here are Fernando and Isabel kneeling on purple pillows as they pray. The wood is polychromed, so that the cheeks of the rulers look as if they had been rouged this morning, and each strand of hair is carved and painted a Spanish black. The statues are delightful and show two pudgy-jowled monarchs in the early years of their reign, with none of the heavy seriousness that characterized them later. They are so appealing that they must be quite popular with Spanish visitors, but I had never heard of them; one look satisfied me that this was the way they appeared to their subjects, and now whenever I think of the Catholic sovereigns, I think of them as these polychromed statues kneeling in prayer. Had they been shown sweating over the problems of government, or leading armies, or haggling with cardinals, or writing snippy letters to the Pope, or deciding what to do with Fernando's regular procession of illegitimate children, the statues would be closer to the truth. These two had but little time for prayer, yet that is how they come down to us.

One day as I was walking through the gardens adjacent to the Alhambra, I came upon a kiosk selling a postcard titled 'Carmen de Manuel de Falla,' a carmen being a rustic house and garden, and it showed an attractive patio with a winding iron-railed staircase leading to the second floor. I knew that Falla (1876–1946) was of Catalan descent but did not know that he had been born in Cádiz and had lived in Andalucía, even though some of his themes appeared to be of that derivation. 'Yes!' the kiosk keeper said. 'Don Manuel had his carmen along that road that climbs the hillside. In the shadow of the Alhambra, you might say.'

I walked along a beautiful road that clung to the hill and provided a fine view of the valley, but soon I came to a fork, and the left path was so narrow that cars could not enter. I hesitated, but a woman cried, 'Is it for Falla's carmen? Along, along.' This trail was even more pleasant than the other and finally I came to an unpretentious house with a garden that climbed up the hill to three different levels, each of which had its unique natural quality. I had not at this point determined whether this was the carmen of Spain's foremost modern musician, but I was satisfied that it was the house of one who loved nature, and it required no imagination to visualize Falla sitting in this exquisite spot as he traced out in his mind the piano passages for his delicate orchestral suite *Noches en los jardines de España* (Nights in the Gardens of Spain, 1916).

Once inside the house one knew that it had belonged to Falla, for it was crowded with mementos of a life to which fame had come abundantly, not only in Spain but also in France. In the bedroom hung the English card commemorating his first communion: 'His death our life. His life our death. June 26, 1886.' For his first confession on June 20, 1884, the card had been in French. Here also were the works of art he had enjoyed: a Goya etching showing the torero Joaquín Rodriguez, called Costillares; a fine Hiroshige print showing two geese, one white, one colored, flying against a full moon with three reeds below. Teófilo Gautier had lived in this street and there was a memento giving his Spanish name. Here Federico García Lorca had attended a testimonial dinner to Falla on February 9, 1927, and farther on was a recollection of Pío Baroja. In these rooms I felt close to Falla, but it was in the wandering gardens that his music came alive.

Standing beside the bamboo trees and looking out across the dry fields and mountains of Andalucía, I could begin to hear those extraordinary rhythms he had used in his four chief works, *Noches*, *El amor brujo* (Love the Magician, 1915), *El sombrero de tres picos* (The Three-Cornered Hat, 1919) and the little-known *El retablo de Maese Pedro* (The Puppet Show of Master Peter, 1920). Here, too, I could understand better how he caught those dark and precise chords so representative of Spanish thought.

To Falla, Spain was important, and the part of Spain he understood best was this hot, impassioned Andalusian section. Contrary to what most believe and many write, he did not introduce folk themes directly into his music, for in his work only two or three instances of such use occur, but he did allow the intention of folk music to infect him, and his re-creation of its purposes is what makes his music so superior to that of colleagues like Albéniz, Granados and Turina. The more I hear Falla the more convinced I am that he was a true original. He is a very clean and honest composer; he speaks with a compact vocabulary and his message is no less profound because it is so brief. I once had the interesting experience of hearing Igor Markevich directing a conductors' school in a baroque church in northern Spain, and for two days I listened to the Radio Madrid Orchestra playing dances from *El sombrero*, over and over again, and two things impressed me: the music never grew stale, for on each repetition I heard some brilliant bit of orchestration or juxtaposition that I had missed before, so rich was Falla's construction; but when the would-be conductors were German or English or Russian, they seemed to fight the rhythms, whereas

The type of gypsy family
Falla remembered when composing
for El amor brujo in Paris.

when the conductor was a Spaniard he fell with ease into what Falla intended. Conversely, of course, the other Europeans found Mozart rather easy to handle, whereas the Spaniards treated him too heavily.

Falla is the most important composer Spain has produced since the closing years of the sixteenth century. It is Falla's solid authenticity that appeals to me, the high specific gravity of all he does. His themes are inventive and speak of the Spanish soil; his rhythms are unexpected and although they do not copy the handclapping of flamenco, they derive from it, as in that series of twenty-one staccato chords that closes the 'Ritual Fire Dance' in *El amor brujo* and the seven strange chords that intrude in the Miller's farruca in *El sombrero;* but it is principally his orchestration, as precise as Bizet's, that accounts for the high quality of his work.

That he did not compose much, when compared to contemporaries like Debussy and Richard Strauss, and that he did not attempt large pieces in the great tradition followed by Sibelius are characteristics common to all the Spanish artists of his day. When I was in Granada, wasting lovely hours in Falla's carmen, I had not yet tried to rationalize why the Spanish composers produced so little and I did not yet see this as part of a general cultural malaise; that would come later. For the present I was pleased to have seen the workshop of this notable artist and to have heard again in memory those unanticipated dark notes which García Lorca praised.

Then, as I was driving out of Granada on my way back to Córdoba, I saw on the road map a name which evoked a whole cascade of sound, trivial, to be sure, but sound which I have long enjoyed. The map had a small red arrow pointing to a cul-de-sac and the words Torre Bermeja. I had not known that the Torre Bermeja actually existed, nor had I realized that if it did exist it was in Granada, for this was the title of an unimportant orchestral piece by Isaac Albéniz, another Catalan who chose to write about Andalucía. I had first heard 'Torre Bermeja' (Bright Reddish Tower) as a student attending a concert in London, and even then I had enough knowledge to know that this was not a major piece of music, but it had a captivating lilt and one lambent theme, which Albéniz overworked. But what made the piece important to me was the program note which said that the Torre Bermeja was a Moorish tower, and that was enough to send me daydreaming of a Spain I had not yet seen. I supposed the tower to be some magnificent thing which bespoke its Moorishness to all who saw, and through the years I kept looking for a photograph of what I was sure must be a considerable structure; since I did not know what part of Spain it was in, I never saw it, but whenever I accidentally heard the slow sweet music on the radio I visualized a brooding Moorish tower and felt a strange identification with Spain.

I left the main exit road and headed for the cul-de-sac, which turned out to be a miserable track leading down a hill, the last part of which I had to negotiate on foot. The Torre Bermeja might be a fine structure but it was clear that the people of Granada thought little of it. Then it was before me, this soaring tower of my imagination, and it turned out to be a pair of square, dumpy things with undistinguished lines and little to commend them. 'Is this the Torre Bermeja?' I asked a workman who was hauling out rubble from a nearby cellar and he said, 'La misma' (the same); in Spanish the phrase 'Lo mismo' can have a fine sense of contempt, as if to say, 'Believe it or not, this is it.' An improvised wooden runway led up the side of the nearest tower to a gaping hole, and through this I peered into the interior, but it was even more drab than the outside.

'It used to be a jail,' the workman said. If so, it must have been a dismal one even by Spanish standards, which were never high. I scrambled down the hill to catch the other face of the tower, hoping that there was some point from which the old semi-fortress would look romantic enough to have justified Albéniz's composition, but there was none. I had before me a squat tower built of ugly brick in the worst possible proportions, as far removed in spirit from the music of Albéniz as one could imagine; yet there was about it a fine heaviness, a kind of brutality that was Andalusian. I was glad I had seen it, and had compared it to its music, for although I was not aware of the fact at the time, the experience prepared me for the intellectual adventure I was about to undergo when I got back to Córdoba.

I describe it as an adventure, although I doubt if others would, because it related to the nature of romanticism, and it was my concern with this out-of-date literary style that had first awakened my interest in

Spain. I was about to visit one of the fountainheads of Europe's romantic movement, and this side trip to the Torre Bermeja would serve as a relevant preamble; for what had happened in the relationship between Isaac Albéniz (1860–1909) and this tower was what happened whenever an artist became entangled in the romantic fallacy: a man of creative mind saw something in nature or history with an echo of the past, and around it he constructed an inflated fantasy, often bearing no relation to fact. Much of what had been written about Spain suffered from this fallacy; people looked at old Moorish structures and evoked from them a civilization that simply did not exist except in the imagination. Few things I did in Spain were more instructive than this visit to the Torre Bermeja, for it placed in proper perspective the romantic interpretation from which Spain suffers.

In the preceding sentence, and also in the opening of this book where I refer to the romantic cast of mind and its relationship to Spain, I use the word in its literary sense, referring to the Gothic novel, the tragedies of Victor Hugo, and that artistic movement common to all Europe in which imagination, emotion and introspection were stressed in contrast to classical understatement, and in which extravagant natural settings were chosen instead of arid Greek landscapes. When I returned to Córdoba I was thrown by accident into the heart of this literary romanticism, for as I was sitting one day at a café in the Plaza José Antonio, studying a road map and trying to decide how to get to the marshes lying south of Sevilla, I saw a name which had played a major role in the Romantic Movement: Hornachuelos.

I was surprised to find it a real place, a village of apparently trivial importance off the main road and situated on the bank of the Río Bembézar, which according to the markings on the map ran at this point through a defile. With some excitement I asked whether one could drive to Hornachuelos, and two Spaniards at a nearby table said, 'Fine road. Because farther along is San Calixto, where King Baudouin of Belgium and his Queen Fabiola, who is a Spanish girl, as you know . . .' The men gave a rambling account of how Baudouin had married the beautiful daughter of a Zaragoza family and how their honeymoon at the monastery of San Calixto had been interrupted by a revolution of some sort, '. . . in Belgium, that was, because here in Spain we don't have revolutions any more, thank God,' and how Baudouin had left his bride at dead of night and had sped down the very road I was studying. 'I think the Spanish government built the new road especially for Baudouin and his queen,' one of the men said.

'At any rate,' I interrupted, 'I can use it?'

'Best road in the district,' he said. Then he had an afterthought: 'While you're there, don't miss the Convento de los Angeles.' As he said the words I could hear an opera chorus led by Ezio Pinza chanting the great prayer of the monks as they worship in the Convento de los Angeles.

'You mean there's a real convent by that name?'

'Boys' school now. But it's perched on a site you'll never forget.'

I returned to my map and saw once more that magic name, Hornachuelos. For generations it has captivated operagoers because Giuseppe Verdi's *La Forza del Destino* takes place in and around 'The Inn at Hornachuelos.' I left the café, sought a bookstore, where I purchased a copy of the Spanish classic from which Verdi had borrowed his libretto, *Don Alvaro, o la fuerza del sino* (Don Alvaro, or The Force of Destiny, 1835) by the Duque de Rivas (1791–1865), then went back to the parador and packed my bags.

The road to Hornachuelos led down the right bank of the Guadalquivir and followed the old royal highway to Sevilla, now superseded by a new superhighway on the left bank. After a few miles I saw straight ahead and perched on a cliff overlooking the river one of Spain's most dramatic castles, that of Almodóvar del Río, all crenelations and towers in good repair and as usual abandoned. Some miles farther on, the Río Bembézar entered the Guadalquivir, and this was my sign to turn north along the new road built for the King of Belgium. In a few minutes I saw, off to the right, a bare, whitewashed village nestling on the edge of a cliff at whose feet ran the river. This was Hornachuelos, the epitome of Andalusian villages, as clean and hard as the skeleton of an ox whitening in the sun. At the oak table of an inn that could have been the one in the opera, I took out the play which had served as the Spanish counterpart to Victor Hugo and the German romanticists.

The author was as romantic as his creation, a duque of great inheritance whose liberal convictions had led him to speak out against the royal tyranny of Fernando VII. Surrendering his seat as liberal deputy in the Cortes, in 1822 he suffered banishment and entered upon that long exile in Gibraltar, London, Italy, France and particularly Malta, where he wrote exalted poetry and cultivated his addiction to romanticism. Recalled to Spain when the tyranny of Fernando ended, Rivas entered the government as a minister, and when his tendencies had become less liberal, found himself in charge of putting down a liberal revolution, which when it succeeded threw him once more into exile, this time because he was a reactionary. Again he wandered and again he intensified his commitment to romanticism. In the end he had acquired most of the honors to which he was eligible and was recognized as one of the grand old men of Spain and of European letters.

His masterwork, *Don Alvaro,* is practically a textbook of the high romantic style. A play in five acts, it tells the story of a mysterious young man of unknown antecedents who woos the daughter of an impoverished noble family of Sevilla. The introduction of Don Alvaro is classic and the despair of playwrights who followed. At the end of the Triana bridge in Sevilla a group of townspeople are discussing yesterday's bullfight, and here begins the description of the hero, whom we have not yet seen.

Seventeen-year-old gypsy mother.

SECOND TOWNSMAN: The fight wasn't as good as the previous one.

PRECIOSILLA: Because Don Alvaro, the rich fellow from Peru, wasn't there. And either on horseback or on foot, he's the best torero in Spain.

GALLANT: It's true, he's a real man.

Why wasn't he at the fight? Because he was beweeping the termination of his suit for Doña Leonor's hand; she still loved him but her proud father forbade the wedding: 'My friend, the noble Marqués de Calatrava, is too haughty and vain to permit an immigrant nobody to be his son-in-law.'

Bystanders say of Don Alvaro that he 'is worthy to be married to an empress.' He is generous and tips well. He is valiant. 'In the Old Park the other night seven of the toughest thugs in Sevilla jumped him, but he backed them like sheep against the mud wall of the riding school.' Another recalls that 'in his conflict with the captain of artillery he carried himself like a true gentleman.'

OFFICIAL: Then why doesn't the marqués accept Don Alvaro? Because he wasn't born in Sevilla? Gentlemen can also be born outside Sevilla.

PRIEST: Yes, but is Don Alvaro a gentleman? All we know is that he came here from the Indies two months ago bringing with him two Negroes and much money. But who is he?

FIRST CITIZEN: They say a great many things about him.

SECOND CITIZEN: He's a most mysterious fellow.

UNCLE PACO: The other evening there were some gentlemen here discussing the matter, and one of them said that this Don Alvaro made his money from being a pirate . . .

GALLANT: Jesucristo!

UNCLE PACO: But the other held that Don Alvaro was the bastard son of a grandee of Spain and a Moorish queen.

The priest says that it was proper for the marqués to reject such a suitor, and the official asks what must Don Alvaro do, and for the first time a forewarning of tragedy is struck, the fate that will doom the young man.

PRIEST: He ought to find a different sweetheart, because if he persists in his rash pretensions, he will expose himself to the sons of the marqués when they return to break the skull of anyone who has trifled with their sister.

Because this is a romance, the two brothers are formidable, one a soldier dedicated to defending his honor, the other a hell-raising student at the university. Their sister, meanwhile, has been sequestered at the family hacienda to protect her from Don Alvaro. The stage is set for the entrance of the hero, and this direction indicates how he arrives:

Night begins to fall and shadows obscure the theater. Don Alvaro enters, muffled in a silken cloak and wearing a great white sombrero, half-boots and spurs. Very slowly he crosses the stage, gazing with dignity and melancholy this way and that, and exits by the bridge. All observe him in deep silence.

Where is he going? The observers guess that it must be to try to see Doña Leonor, whereupon the priest whispers in a broad aside to the audience, 'I would be delinquent to my friendship with the marqués if I did not advise him this instant that Don Alvaro has been prowling about the hacienda. In this way perhaps we can avoid a misfortune.' Don Alvaro does go to Leonor's room, where the alerted marqués upbraids him. In one of the best inventions of the romantic theater, Don Alvaro, in a gesture of submission, throws his revolver at the feet of the marqués, but the shock of striking the floor discharges the weapon and its bullet kills the marqués, who, as he dies with Doña Leonor looking on in horror, utters the fatal malediction, 'I curse you.'

The second act takes place at the inn of Hornachuelos, where we hear reports of how the brothers returned to Sevilla, seeking vengeance. The scene shifts to the Convento de los Angeles, then serving as a monastery, and at this point I closed my book and started north to see where the tragedy had culminated. After a few miles a narrow trail branched off from King Baudouin's road and led through a recently harvested cork forest, which in turn led to the edge of a rather steep cliff. After one or two miles of this rather frightening road, I reached the canyon of the Río Bembézar, which lay far below. The road threatened to peter out but finally turned sharp left and ended at the entrance to the ancient convent, wedged in between a mountain to the left and the precipice to the right.

As I studied the site a taxi drove up behind me and a father and mother, he obviously a farmer, descended with a frightened boy of eleven. 'This is your school,' the mother said reassuringly, but the boy drew back and bit his lip to keep from crying. The father tugged on a bell rope exactly like the one that must have hung in that spot centuries ago, and the solemn bell began tolling, perhaps the same bell that under similar circumstances had set aflame the imagination of the Duque de Rivas one day around the opening of the nineteenth century. A friar, such as the duque might have seen, came to the gate and swung it slowly open to admit the small family. He allowed me to enter too, and while he processed the new student I was permitted to wander through the school, and I noticed on three different floors series of posters imploring boys to consider the priesthood as their vocation. The drawings were modern, as if they had been done in some first-rate industrial-arts shop in Milan or Rome; they had humor and color and made the profession of the Church seem a desirable vocation, with problems, defeats, triumphs and great spiritual satisfaction. The fact that three separate series of about a dozen posters each were displayed led me to think that the Church must be having a difficult time filling its seminaries, and it required no imagination to see the young boy who arrived with me electing the priesthood in such surroundings.

I left the old convent and sat on a wall along the edge of the cliff to read the famous stage direction of the third scene of the second act; it had inflamed the readers of its period, including Verdi in Italy, and is still remembered as one of the classic bits of the romantic age:

> The theater represents a piece of level ground wedged into the declivity of a rude mountain. To the left, precipices and craggy steeps. Facing, a profound valley traversed by a rivulet on whose bank can be seen in the distance the village of Hornachuelos, terminating at the foot of high mountains. To the right, the façade of the Convento de los Angeles, of poor and humble architecture. The great door of the church is closed, but workable, and over it a semicircular window of medium size through which can be seen the shimmering lights from within; closer to the proscenium, the door of the porter's lodge, also workable but closed, in the middle of which a peephole which can be opened or closed and at the side a bell cord. In the middle of the stage there will be a large cross of rough stone corroded by weather, rising from four steps which can serve as seats. All will be illuminated by a brilliant moon. From within the church will be heard the pealing of the organ and the choir of monks singing their matins, while from the left, very fatigued and dressed like a man in a hooded coat with sleeves, a sombrero with drooping brim and boots, staggers Doña Leonor.

The simple plot is now prepared. Doña Leonor, burdened with the guilt attached to her father's death, will have nothing to do with ill-fated Don Alvaro, who has joined the Spanish army in Italy to seek an honorable death. She is allowed to inhabit a grotto near the convent, disguised as a monk, and plans to spend the rest of her life in a remote cell. Her soldier brother, seeking Don Alvaro, also goes to Italy and unwittingly finds himself in the same regiment as the Peruvian, who saves his life. In spite of this, the brother is determined to kill Alvaro and goads him to a duel. Alvaro kills this brother, whereupon the university student intensifies his efforts to track down the Inca who has betrayed his sister and killed his father and brother, but he has a hard time finding Don Alvaro, because the latter has grown weary of a life so stalked by doom and has decided to enter this same convent as a monk, not realizing that Doña Leonor is living nearby. To this rocky defile the student finally comes and in a scene of wild passion duels with Alvaro and receives a mortal wound, but when he calls for extreme unction he uncovers the fact that his sister and Don Alvaro have been staying in the same holy place. Assuming them to be sharing their guilty love and revolted by the profanation, he stabs his sister to death and himself dies. What happens to Don Alvaro we shall see in a moment.

The play introduced certain conventions of the romantic theater. When the plot reaches an impasse at which the masquerade of the soldier brother must be disclosed if he gives his right name, and when there was no reason for him not to do so, he turns to the audience and delivers these inventive lines:

DON CARLOS: (*Aside*) I think I won't tell the truth. I am Don Félix de Avendaña.

At another point the hero uses for the first time on any stage a gesture which will become traditional furniture on the romantic stage:

> DON ALVARO: Woe is me! Woe is me!
> (*He presses the back of his hand against his forehead and remains in great agitation.*)

Romantic excess reaches its climax in the closing scene, which became notorious. I have never seen *Don Alvaro* on stage, but I've read several contemporary reports of its reception and this last scene was apparently a shocker. I wish the Spanish department of some American university would stage the play if only that I might see this final scene:

> *There is a long moment of silence; thunder sounds stronger than ever, and lightning increases as we hear in the distance the chanting of the Miserere by the holy community, whose members come slowly closer.*
>
> VOICE: (*From within*) Here, here what horror!
> (DON ALVARO *recovers from his fainting spell, then flees toward the mountain. Enter the* GUARDIAN FATHER *and the holy fraternity.*)
> GUARDIAN FATHER: My God! Blood spilled everywhere. Cadavers. The penitent woman.
> THE FRIARS: A woman! Heavens!
> GUARDIAN FATHER: And you, Father Rafael!
> DON ALVARO: (*From a crag, completely convulsed in a diabolical smile*) Seek, fool, for Father Rafael. I am the ambassador from hell. I am the fiendish exterminator. Fly, miserable ones . . .
> ALL: Jesús! Jesús!
> DON ALVARO: Hell, open your mouth and swallow me. Let the heavens crash. Perish the human race. Extermination . . . destruction . . .
> (*He climbs to the highest point on the mountain and leaps off.*)
> GUARDIAN FATHER and FRIARS: (*Kneeling in diverse attitudes*) Misericordia, Father! Misericordia!

Little can be said in defense of such an ending; in its way it is as bad as the fake classicism it supplanted. Exess in either direction was regrettable, but the grotesqueries of romanticism had the added weakness of being open to burlesque, so when the duke's play had been on the boards for some years a cartoonist offered this spoof: a demented poet, ranting his verses on a night when the moon scuttled between clouds, stands tiptoe on a precipitous cliff, with a rope around his neck, a dagger at his throat, a lion at his rear and a crocodile waiting for him below. The whole extravagance of romanticism is lampooned, and especially the extravagance of *Don Alvaro*. Yet the play was not a waste. It paved the way for realism and for a while provided much pleasure and excitement. It also questioned the nonsense of exaggerated family pride, but I suppose that during the years of its greatest success this parody of pundonor was not so recognized; the landed families of Spain must have seen the play and said among them-

selves, 'By God, that's the way brothers should act when an upstart med-
dles with their sister.' In fact, if the play were given in Sevilla tomorrow, I
would expect the great families to applaud.

After similar plays of the Romantic Movement had circulated for
some time, accompanied by novels and music of like vein, the adjective
romantic acquired a new definition which stressed not a literary tradition
emphasizing nature but a sentimental mélange of sex and adventure
summed up in the advertising phrase which has come to characterize
Spain: 'Visit Romantic Spain.' This tag is both the damnation and the
salvation of Spain and she had better be careful what she does with it. By
damnation I mean that it encourages the country to engage in certain
abuses solely because tourists from abroad will pay money to witness
them. Thus, in recent years in tourist cities like Palma, the bullfight has
been burlesqued into a vaudeville show because tourists and uneducated
Spaniards prefer it that way. Flamenco, as I have pointed out, has degenerated into a flabby night-club act, because such debasement is profitable. In
Spain generally stress is laid on the past rather than the future, because it
is the past that is marketable. Romantic carry-overs like the imprisonment
of women, the excesses of pundonor and the backward look in the arts are
supported. Enough wrong judgments of this kind can destroy a country,
and thus Spain's official adoption of romanticism as her international
badge is damning.

By salvation I mean that whether one likes it or not, this is the
concept available to Spain for peddling to the world at large, and if she
does her job well, she can earn needed income from it without corrupting
her soul. The enormous building developments which we shall later see
along the Mediterranean coast of Spain are there because northern European capital considers Spain romantic; financially, Spain would be ill-
advised to alter the image of herself which she circulates abroad. I can
best explain what I mean by reference to Hawaii, which is something like
five-percent Polynesian, fifty-five-percent Oriental. Some years ago the
Caucasian and Oriental businessmen who were putting up most of the
money for advertising the islands said in effect, 'It's silly to keep on
publishing those photographs of hula girls and ukuleles and grass shacks.
We're a modern society with fascinating Oriental customs, a great art
museum, a fine university and forward-looking industries. These are the
facets we should be stressing.' So they took the hula girls off the advertising and put on the alternatives, and incoming travelers diminished by
some startling percent. The rest of the world had decided that Hawaii was
the land of the hula girls, and if facts proved otherwise, then to hell with
Hawaii. Who would want to spend the time and money to visit islands
simply because they had a good university, an art museum and challenging confrontations between the Orient and the Occident? The tourists of
the world knew what Hawaii was better than the business leaders, and

after a disastrous hiatus, the posters reappeared with hula girls, and everyone has been happy ever since.

Spain, I am afraid, is stuck with the romantic legend portrayed in *Don Alvaro;* people shivering in Sweden and Germany want sun and romance, and Spain has no alternative but to provide them. The neat trick, as the people of Hawaii have learned, is to peddle this romantic illusion to outsiders but not to oneself. For the present, Spain has not yet mastered this trick; however, a few leaders of the country are becoming aware of the facts and they will probably adopt the policy of Hawaii's canny leaders: 'For the tourists hula girls. For the natives IBM computers!'

But even as I was formulating these judgments in the rocky defile of the Convento de los Angeles, I was false to my own conclusions, because when I approached King Baudouin's road I decided to turn right toward San Calixto rather than left toward the highway that would take me to Sevilla; I wanted to see the refurbished monastery where Baudouin and Fabiola had stayed and to compare it with the convent I had just seen. The monastery was nothing, but as I reached it I found that the hunt clubs of this part of Spain had convened for a trial of their packs, and some four or five hundred of the best hunting dogs, lashed two-by-two for safety in transportation, were preparing for a dash across the desolate emptiness of these hills. It was a brilliant moment, with rural costumes, the sound of horns, the yapping of the dogs and on some distant hill the waiting stag. Five hundred years ago men and women exactly like this, with dogs like this, had come here attended by servants no whit dissimilar to hunt over these barren reaches. A thousand years ago, when Moors held the land, these were, of course, cultivated fields supporting hundreds of families, but with the expulsion of the Moors the lands had fallen idle and would long remain so. My companion, listening to the confusion of sound and looking at the huntsmen as they saddled up to chase across the distant hills, asked, 'Isn't it romantic?' It was . . . in both senses of the word.

FOLLOWING PAGE:
From the swamps.

LAS MARISMAS

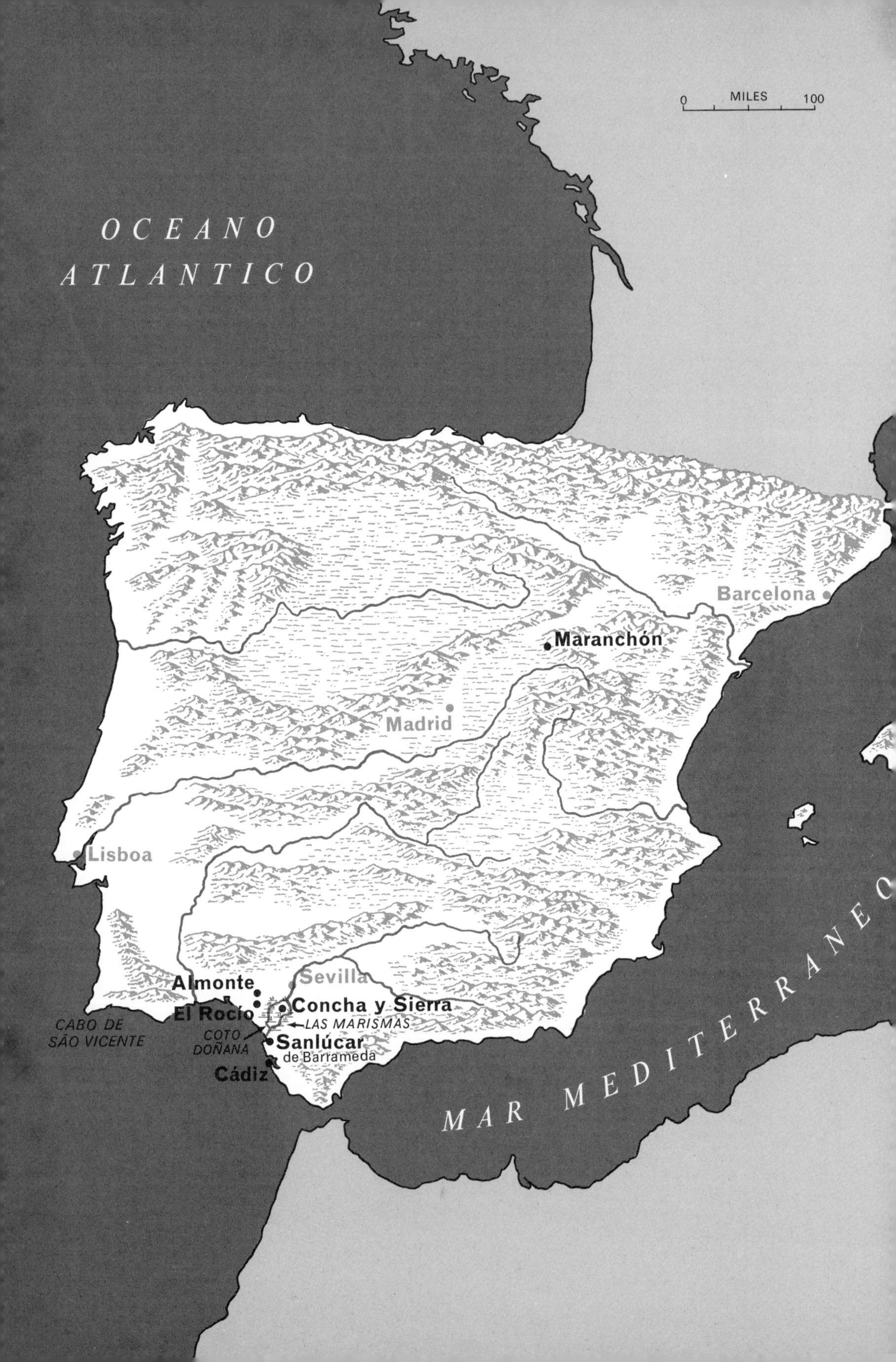

OCEANO
ATLANTICO

MILES
0   100

Barcelona

Maranchón

Madrid

Lisboa

Sevilla

Almonte
El Rocío   Concha y Sierra

CABO DE   ←LAS MARISMAS
SÃO VICENTE   COTO
                   DOÑANA   Sanlúcar
                              de Barrameda
              Cádiz

MAR MEDITERRANEO

One wintry day when storm clouds hung low over Sevilla, I set out on a journey to the south to complete a task I had set for myself some years earlier. I had been planning a novel with a Mexican setting, and because of the Spanish background of one of my characters I required to know something of life on a Spanish ranch given over to the rearing of fighting bulls. I had selected as my prototype the historic and honored ranch of Concha y Sierra (Shell and Mountain Range) and a matador living in Sevilla had agreed to show it to me. He respected the Concha bulls because of their heroic performance during the past eighty years.

'The ranch lies in the swamps,' he warned me as we set forth, and this seemed an unlikely statement, since one visualizes a bull ranch as occupying hard, rough soil which strengthens the bull's legs. 'A common misunderstanding,' the matador assured me. 'It's the nature of the grass, the minerals in the water . . . something in the essence of the land and not its hardness. That's what makes a good bull. Anyway, the Concha y Sierras live in the swamps.'

We drove south to the end of the road. Parking our car in the rain, we set out on foot along a narrow earthen path that might have been passable in the dry season but which was now so muddy that going was difficult; if we stepped off the path on either side we were in swampland, not the green-covered stagnant swamp of fiction but an interminable area extending for miles in all directions, consisting of completely flat land covered with grass and two or three inches of water. 'These are the swamps of the Guadalquivir,' the matador said, and for the first time I looked out upon the infinite desolation which was to attract me so strongly and in so many ways.

Lean matador, chunky author trudging home after a day studying the bulls.

The storm clouds swept rain squalls ahead of us which beat down upon the brackish waters to bounce back in tiny droplets, so that it seemed as if there were no horizon, as if sky and earth alike were made of mist and grayness. For two reasons that first day persists in memory. The immensity of the swamps astounded me; I had not realized that Spain included so large an area of primitive land, a retreat given over primarily to wildlife, where birds from all parts of Europe and Africa came in stupendous numbers to breed; this swamp, lying so close to Sevilla, was as wild as the seacoast of Iceland, as lonely as the steppes of Russia.

What I remember most vividly, however, is that on this introductory day, for reasons which no one has been able to explain, as the matador and I walked a flock of swallows stayed with us, perhaps a hundred in all, and

when we took a step they swooped down to the tips of our shoes, then off into the sky, one after another, so that we moved in a kind of living mandorla such as encloses the saints in Italian religious painting. At times the swallows came within inches of our faces, swooping down with an exquisite grace past our fingertips and to our toes, flicking the swamp water with their wings. This continued for about half an hour, during which we seemed to be members of this agitated flock, participants in their spatial ballet, which moved with us wherever we went. It was one of the most charming experiences I have ever had in nature, comparable I suppose only to the day when I first skin-dived to the bottom of the coral beds off Hawaii; there was the same sense of kinesthetic beauty, of nature in motion, with me in the center and participating in the motion.

Why the swallows stayed with us for so long, I cannot guess; once during the walk I wondered if our feet, to which they seemed to be paying most attention, might be kicking up insects too small for us to see but inviting to the birds; but I had to dismiss this when I saw no evidence that the swallows were catching anything. There was also the possibility that our steps were throwing up droplets of water which the birds were taking in the air, but again there was no evidence that we were doing so, and I concluded that they were simply playing a game. This was not unreasonable, for obviously they were enjoying our walk as much as we were. At any rate, they served to remind me that these swamps existed as a realm for birds and that in entering it I was trespassing on their terrain.

The area is called Las Marismas (The Tidelands, in this instance a twofold tide, one coming in from the Atlantic Ocean direct and a more important one creeping up the Río Guadalquivir to spread out over an immense area). Las Marismas is roughly forty miles from north to south, thirty-five miles from east to west, but it is not square and has an area of less than a thousand square miles, or about six hundred thousand acres, of which only about three hundred thousand could be called swampland proper, the rest being equally flat and bleak but free of water most of the year.

I was fortunate in visiting Las Marismas for the first time in winter, for this was the rainy season and I was thus able to see the bull ranch in maximum swamp condition; it seemed to me that about seventy percent of its land was either under water or was so water-logged that if I stepped on what appeared to be a solid tussock, it collapsed beneath me with a soft squish, so that my feet were again in water. It was on such land that the Concha y Sierra bulls flourished, but it was not until the matador led me to the dry area on which the ranch buildings stood, and I saw the famous brand of an S inside a C scrawled on the side of a corral, that I was ready to believe that this was the territory of the bulls about which I had read so much.

The Concha y Sierra bulls had a brave history, and many a noble head had gone from the bullring to the taxidermist's and from there to the wall of some museum, with a plaque beneath to inform the visitor as to what this bull had accomplished before he died.

On June 1, 1857, the Concha bull Barrabás participated in what the books describe as 'one of the most famous accidents in the history of bullfighting' in that, with a deft horn, it caught the full matador Manuel Domínguez under the chin and then in the right eye, gouging it out. It was assumed that Domínguez would die, for his face was laid open, but with a valor that had characterized his performance in the ring he survived, and three months later was fighting again as Spain's only one-eyed matador, having stipulated that for his return the bulls must again be from Concha y Sierra. For another seventeen years he fought with only one eye and

Concha y Sierra brand painted in whitewash on a wooden shield in the testing ring. The horn scratches remind the visitor that the bulls of this ranch have given tremendous glory to some bullfighters and have taken the lives of others.

enjoyed some of his best afternoons with Concha bulls. He is known in taurine history as Desperdicios (Cast-off Scraps, from the contemptuous manner in which he tossed aside his gouged-out eyeball).

On August 3, 1934, the Concha bull Hormigón (Concrete) verified his name by killing the beginning bullfighter Juan Jiménez in Valencia, and on May 18, 1941, in Madrid the gray Farolero (Lamplighter) killed the full matador Pascual Márquez, thus ending the career of a young fellow of great promise. On August 18, 1946, the Concha bull Jaranero (Carouser) killed young Eduardo Liceaga, brother of one of Mexico's best matadors. And so the story goes, with the great gray bulls of Concha y Sierra defending themselves valiantly in all plazas.

The matador and I left the ranch buildings and on horseback set off across the marshes to see if we could find any of the bulls in pasture, and after we had ridden for some time in the direction of the Guadalquivir, that meandering, desultory river of such force and quietness, the matador suddenly cried, 'Look!' and off to our left, rising from the reeds and thistles like an apparition, loomed a gray bull, his horns uptilted, his ears alert. We stopped the horses. He stopped. We stared at each other for several minutes, and then we saw, gradually appearing from the mists behind him, the shapes of fifteen or twenty other bulls, and slowly they moved toward us, not in anger but rather to see what we were doing. They came fairly close, much too close for me, but the matador said, 'They won't charge as long as they're together and we stay on the horses,' and so we stayed, among the bulls who had materialized from the swamps, and after a while they gradually drifted away and the mists enveloped them.

It was while wandering in this fashion in Las Marismas that I became aware of the Spanish seasons—the rain and the drought, the cold and the heat, the flowering and the harvest—and I decided that if I ever wrote about Spain, I would endeavor to cover each of the seasons. I have never spent all of any one calendar year in Spain, but I have visited each major area except Barcelona during at least two different seasons so as to see the effect of the passing year upon it; so far as I can remember, the only month I have missed is February, and it is possible that one of my Easter visits started in late February, but if so, it could have involved only a few days, and I do not remember it. I have seen Las Marismas in all seasons, never as much as I would have liked but enough to teach me a few facts about the land of Spain.

Spain! It hangs like a drying ox hide outside the southern door of Europe proper. Some have seen in its outlines the head of a knight encased in armor, the top of his casque in the Pyrenees, the tip of his chin at Portugal's Cabo de São Vicente, his nose at Lisboa, his iron-girt eyes looking westward across the Atlantic. I see Spain as a kaleidoscope of high, sun-baked plateaus, snow-crowned mountains and swamps of the Guadalquivir. No one of these images takes precedence over the other, for I have known fine days in each of these three contrasting terrains. That snow should be a permanent part of my image may surprise some, but Spain has very high mountains and even in the hottest part of July and August, when the plains literally crack open from the heat and when the blazing skies described in Spanish fiction hang everywhere, snow lies on the hills less than thirty miles north of Madrid. In the middle of August not long ago I drove across the mountains that separate the Bay of Biscay from the city of León and saw snow about me for mile after mile; at another time, when I had come to Spain in midsummer for my health, doctors in Philadelphia asked, 'Is it wise to visit Spain in July? Won't you suffocate?' But my plans took me to the high north, where during much of the summer I needed a topcoat at night.

But now we are speaking of Las Marismas, in the heart of the

The ancestors of this fighting bull, standing along the banks of the Guadalquivir, were brought up the river by Romans more than two thousand years ago.

southland, and to appreciate it, and the land of Spain in general, we must watch it through one whole year, and if in doing so I seem to be speaking primarily of birds, that is appropriate, for here is one of the great bird sanctuaries of the world, as if nature, realizing how difficult it was going to be for birds to exist in a constantly encroaching world, had set aside this random swamp for their protection.

WINTER

The Guadalquivir itself never freezes, of course, but occasionally areas of shallow water with low salt content will freeze to a thickness that would support a bird but not an animal. In winter the tides run full, and even if no additional rain fell they would be sufficient to fill the streams that crisscross the swamps; but rains do fall, most abundantly week after week, and the tides are reinforced, so that water stands on the land. The sky is mostly gray, but when storms have moved away, it becomes a royal blue set off by towering cumulus clouds moving in from the Atlantic; Las Marismas is a product of the ocean; it is not a somnolent offspring of the Mediterranean Sea.

Maximum flooding occurs in January, and then one can move by boat across large segments of the land, and in this boggy, completely flat wilderness life undergoes conspicuous modification. Animals like the deer and lynx have taken refuge by moving to preselected higher ground, and in their place come several million birds from northern Europe to prepare for breeding. Three hundred thousand game ducks have moved in to winter, ten thousand large geese. In January untold numbers of coots arrive to breed. Through a hundred centuries they have found in Las Marismas a plentiful food supply, for the marsh grasses provide seeds and roots and the shallow waters teem with swimming insects.

Toward the end of winter the birds begin to settle upon specific clumps of grass, testing them for strength and protection, and in March they begin weaving nests which will house them for the important work ahead in spring. Where do they get the material for the million or more nests they must build? From all imaginable sources but particularly from the weeds themselves. However, in the nests I have seen feathers, bits of mouse fur and even strands of hair from cattle.

In the winter men leave Las Marismas pretty much alone. Along its edges, of course, towns have grown up and in them live skilled hunters who know all the footpaths that cross the swamps. Here also are herdsmen who pasture their cattle on the grassy portions in the summer, and fishermen who work the Guadalquivir. And there are, I am glad to say, a handful of men who simply love the bleakness of the swamps and study it year after year, as they would a book, but in winter even they stay mostly at home.

Río Guadalquivir.

Over the vast area one sees mostly the movement of birds, thousands upon thousands of them, birds that have known Siberia and the most remote fjords of Norway, that will spend their summers on the moors of Scotland and in the forests of Germany. They live in tremendous families, each associating with its own kind, but a single area of marshland may contain fifty different species, waiting through the long winter till their summer feeding places in the north have thawed.

On the thirteenth day of January each year, in obedience to one of those unfathomable rules that govern birds, storks fly north from Africa to their chimneys of Holland and Germany and continue to do so for some weeks, so that the Spanish have a saying which could be translated as:

> At the day of St. Blas
> The storks do pass.

Why they go north in midwinter has never been explained, but in midsummer they will go south, as if their calendar were askew.

But there are also, in these months, the birds that live permanently in the Spanish swamps, and in some ways these are the most interesting because they are the ones that we shall see in all seasons, like old friends. There is no more beautiful small bird in Europe than the goldfinch of Las Marismas, a tiny gem of color and design. I have watched a group of goldfinches for an entire morning and have never tired of their display, the flash of their color against the brown swamp, the chattering of their family life. Large numbers are trapped here and sold throughout Europe, for they make fine pets, and whenever I saw them caged in other parts of Spain, I thought of Las Marismas, for they seemed to take the swamps with them.

At the opposite end, so far as size is concerned, was quite another bird. I remember one day, when I was on the Atlantic Ocean edge of the swamps, seeing a huge creature fly into the crown of a tree. It was slightly smaller than a griffon vulture, which are common throughout Las Marismas, and of a different character. Since it remained motionless in the tree, I was able to study it at leisure, but it was not a bird with which I was familiar; later I learned that I had seen an imperial eagle, the noblest inhabitant of the swamps. There are partridge, too, and magpies, and crested coots, and purple gallinules, and a species of owl.

The resident bird which dominates the scene in winter is the cattle egret, a snowy-white bird with yellow legs, a long yellowish bill and a silhouette much like a heron's or a small stork's. They get their name from their habit of feeding not only with cattle but on them, so that if you are wandering through Las Marismas it is not unlikely that you will see a sleek and coiffured little egret riding like a debutante between the horns of some massive fighting bull as he grazes in the swampland, and I have often watched a herd of bulls and a flock of egrets as they blended together in such harmony that one would have thought they had been created as halves of a symbiosis. Certainly they form one of the most attractive features of the year. Regardless of where one sees them, the egrets are winsome birds, delicate in motion on the land and unforgettable in their broad-winged flight. They range far from the swamps and can often be seen in the fields near Sevilla, looking for insects, but no matter where they spend their days, at night they return to the swamps in flocks that number in the hundreds. They can be seen in all seasons but are most appreciated in winter, when they have least competition, as the total bird population is then at its smallest.

Primarily, winter in Las Marismas is a resting time, for the birds, for the animals, for the seed plants and for the men; but to see the swamps in this season is an intellectual challenge. Can you imagine what they will look like in summer? I failed the test, for I was unable to visualize this watery world, this endless waste of tussock and salt, becoming other than what it then was. I could not imagine the transformation it was to undergo.

SPRING

The rains cease. Evaporation begins, and with each inch that the water falls, grass springs up to take its place. What had seemed, only a few weeks ago, seventy-percent water, now seems ninety-percent grassy meadowland, but if one steps off established paths, he sinks in up to his knees, for the underlying water will remain until well into June. As the waters recede, the swamps cease being attractive to ducks and geese, who fly north in huge flocks to the thawing lakes of Russia; but as seed grasses appear, with their assurance of food, large numbers of terns and coots arrive to set up housekeeping, and the men of Sanlúcar de Barrameda, the town at the mouth of the Guadalquivir, prepare their boats for one of the strangest harvests in Europe.

It begins when grass has fairly well covered the swamps, so that horses and cows can be let in to forage. They eat such grass as shows above the water, in which they stand up to their knees, but as they feed they leave behind shreds of grass that float on the surface and these the terns and coots collect for their nests, which they build on circular flat constructions that float on water and stretch in all directions for miles.

Now comes the harvest. In these semi-floating nests the birds lay large quantities of eggs, and for as long as men have lived along Las Marismas they have poled their flat-bottomed boats into the marsh in spring, collecting these birds' eggs. They work in teams of six or seven men to a large boat, from which small skiffs, each bearing a single man, set out to explore tiny rivulets, gathering eggs which will later be sold for food. Year after year they rob the nests of hundreds of thousands of eggs, but the bird population seems not to suffer, for enough eggs are overlooked to ensure the perpetuation of the species.

Only once did I see a team of egg collectors in action. They came, as

usual, from Sanlúcar, one of my favorite towns in Spain, a sun-baked, miserable dump of a place that looks much as it did in the days of Columbus and Magellan, who knew it well, a most authentic remnant of old Spain. Five men entered the area in a large boat painted blue and boasting an outboard motor. In the boat they carried a small skiff which they launched in the marshes. The man who poled it through the shallow waters was indefatigable, for he moved swiftly from one floating nest to the next, scooping up enormous numbers of eggs. How many did he gather in the short time I saw him? Probably five or six hundred, and he had touched only a small portion of those available to him. The men in the blue boat were drinking wine and encouraging him, and I never understood what the division of labor was supposed to be. Perhaps the man in the skiff was the only worker; the others may have come from Sanlúcar for the ride.

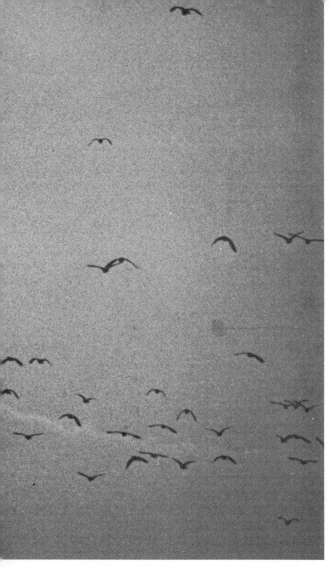

A flight of cattle egrets returning to roost in Las Marismas at end of day.

As the grasses grow and the land begins to solidify, small land birds begin to crowd Las Marismas in flocks of such magnitude that most Americans have no experience with which to compare them. Many arrive from Africa and the Holy Land, and I shall never forget my astonishment, one spring day when I had arranged a picnic in Las Marismas for a group of friends, at seeing, near the clearing in which we ate, two of my favorite birds from Israel, the long-billed, inquisitive hoopoe and the brightly colored bee-eater. 'Are they native here?' I asked an expert who was sharing our picnic. 'No, they migrate from Africa but they arrive so regularly each year that we think of them as native.'

Even in spring, when the swamps have begun to look like land, it is the water birds that one remembers best, for now the avocets arrive, those delicate, long-legged birds with the upturned bills; I had not known the avocet until I spent some time in Colorado, where they were common, but the Spanish ones seem larger and more colorful. The stilts come now, too, and the slender-billed terns, so that what lakes remain are crowded with fascinating life, even though the spectacular ducks and geese have gone.

SUMMER

Summer is something to see in Las Marismas! Even though storm clouds occasionally hang over the Atlantic, the sky over the land becomes an incandescent arc producing temperatures that go well above a hundred degrees in the shade, if any can be found. Day after day the sky hangs there, motionless, relentless, drying up the waters and bringing the grasses to seed. What few streams remain are covered with golden pollen, and even their banks are barren for yards on each side. Young birds are everywhere, feeding on fallen seeds and slapping their awkward feet on the baked earth as they look for water. Jack rabbits appear in large numbers; they attract fox and lynx, who hunt them constantly, but it is from an unexpected source that the food supply becomes abundant.

As the accidental streams that crisscross Las Marismas dry up, multitudes of fat carp search frantically for the permanent rivers which will sustain them through the summer, and in great numbers they move in obedience to faulty instinct from one evaporating fragment of water to the next, until at last they perish in vast numbers on dry earth. At times their glistening bodies completely cover what had lately been a lake, but before they have a chance to rot and thus contaminate Las Marismas, flocks of kites and vultures, sensing the impending tragedy while flying over North Africa, swoop in and help the local birds clean up the carcasses.

The bird that seems to represent summer at its best is the heron. The large white ones appear in flocks of up to six thousand at one time, the smaller in flocks of twenty thousand, ranging over the entire area in white dignity. How can so many birds find food? They eat fish when they find them, and frogs, lizards and the larger insects. They scour the dried earth for remnants of the carp and uncover so much food that they prosper where other birds would fail.

A bizarre ·tragedy now occurs and one that I would have thought improbable had I not seen it. Among the hordes of aquatic birds that resided here in the spring, and I am speaking not of hundreds but of hundreds of thousands, most have left, but there are some who nested here, and they seem unable to believe that these watery lands are going to dry up, so in spite of mounting evidence in late June and early July, they linger on. Now the remorseless drought of late summer catches up with them and for some weeks the three-month-old ducklings search frantically for ponds which they knew existed in a given spot only a month before, but they find only sun-baked earth. Sometimes they march on webbed feet,

Man of Las Marismas.

three or four thousand in a small area, searching vainly for water, and one by one they perish.

Now the raptores move in on silent wings to kill off the survivors. The sharp-eared lynx darts out from his hiding place to catch his supper, while the fox and the rat keep watch. The mournful pilgrimage continues for the better part of a week, this noisy march of hopeless ducks trying to find water, and then Las Marismas is silent once more.

The extraordinary thing about this season is that in drying, the once-muddy areas of land become a perfect highway for automobiles—flat, even, undisturbed and so hard that cars throw no dust. I have several times driven far out into the summer swamps at thirty miles an hour, and when something interesting loomed ahead, at forty or even forty-five, and in this way have covered twenty or thirty miles with no inconvenience but with a sense of flying low in an airplane over a placid bay. Of course, the driver must have some general knowledge of where the permanent water-ways are, for even if the water has evaporated, as is sometimes the case, the vanished rivulet leaves such a depression that the car could not cross it. Except for this limitation one can ride for hours across Las Marismas and see the skeletons of carp.

223

If one were to see Las Marismas for the first time in midsummer he would find it difficult to believe that the place should be called a swampland, for there is certainly no evidence to justify such a name. Perhaps *marshland* would be a better translation of the Spanish, or even the Scottish *moorland,* because when dry, Las Marismas has many characteristics of the latter; but considering the area as it exists throughout four seasons, swampland is not an inappropriate description.

In summer many men come into Las Marismas, some to tend cattle, others to hunt and still others to wander through the wilderness as their ancestors have done for generations. The immense expanse of sky and the weirdness of the absolutely flat landscape exert a powerful appeal to these men, and one of their delights is to shoot a rabbit, skin it and then spread-eagle it on a structure made of three sticks tied together in the form of a Cross of Lorraine. The upright member of the cross is left long, so that it can be used as a handle for holding the rabbit over a fire of hot coals until the meat is hard and crisp. Salt is rubbed on the finished meat, which is cut into thin strips and mixed with raw tomatoes, peppers, much onion, garlic, olive oil and vinegar. 'Maybe the best salad a man can eat,' those who live along Las Marismas claim. For as long as men can remember, huntsmen who prowl the swamps have been entitled to shoot all the rabbits they need for food; the most recent estimate is that about eight thousand are taken each year.

But as the knowing men cross the hard-baked swamp they are careful to watch out for a menace which through the years has taken the lives of many animals and occasionally even of men. This is the ever-present ojo (eye), which stands invitingly here and there in attractive spots, a kind of minute oasis with a central eye of water, perhaps a swampy spring or well, and surrounding green grass and shrubs and sometimes even small trees. On the great arid swamp these ojos are most tempting, for they promise both water and shade, but they are treacherous because they also contain quicksand of a most virulent sort, and once it grabs hold of a leg it rarely lets go. Domestic animals wander into the ojo alone, get stuck and never break loose. If they die, they do so beside the carcass of some boar or deer that got stuck in exactly the same way a week before. Within a few hours the bones are white; vultures keep watch on the ojos.

No matter how well one knows Las Marismas he occasionally meets with surprises. One day as I was riding past a section of the swamp I saw long rows of what looked to be human beings, each bent forward from the waist as if gleaning a field for some lost object. I stopped and crossed the intervening land to see what they were doing; much of the land was under water but ridges had been left as footpaths, and after I had walked along these for a few hundred yards I saw that the bent-over people were women,

On the banks of the Guadalquivir
rice planters work at one of the relatively
high-paying occupations of Las Marismas.

Apparition in Las Marismas.

with heavy nets over their heads and faces, and that they were engaged in transplanting rice, digging handfuls of young rice plants from the seed bed, where they grew in close profusion, and carrying them to the larger fields where they would be transplanted, one stalk at a time in the mud. The women were thus required to stand in water and bend over the soggy fields for eight and ten hours at a time, exactly as other women were doing in Asia.

The nets over the face served two purposes. If a woman bent close to the water on a sunny day for extended periods, the reflected rays of the sun would bounce up at her face and produce a sunburn that might in time cause cancer. More immediately, the nets kept away the hordes of mosquitoes that infested Las Marismas in summer, making it at times almost unbearable. 'If you're going into the swamps,' Spaniards told me repeatedly, 'take along some 612.' This was a potent insect-repellent that worked.

And occasionally as one penetrates the swamps he sees on the horizon a strange brown animal larger than a bull and thinks for the moment that his eyes are deceiving him. Then the animal moves, in an undulating manner, stops, twists his long neck and raises his long-nosed face. It's a camel. His ancestors were brought over from Africa in the latter part of the eighteenth century for use among the sand dunes around Sanlúcar; they adapted well to Spain, but peasants protested that they frightened them and that if God had wanted such ungainly beasts on Spanish soil He would have seen to the matter. Men interested in working the area tried to explain that the camels were harmless, but to no avail. In 1828 all those in the Sanlúcar area were rounded up, transported across the Guadalquivir and set free. There cannot be many left, and I suppose that within another decade they will have disappeared.

The kangaroos that were introduced somewhat later than the camels have already vanished, as have the monkeys which were brought to Sanlúcar from nearby Gibraltar. So far as climate and food are concerned, there

is no reason why monkeys should not have prospered in Las Marismas, but
once more the peasants of Sanlúcar, who must have been an unusually
suspicious lot, protested that the almost-human faces of the monkeys
scared them at night, and that if God had wanted such beasts . . . The last
monkeys were killed off about fifty years ago.

More rewarding than the camels that one occasionally sees are the
melons, which are among Spain's best. They grow luxuriantly wherever
sandy soil remains soft enough during the early summer to permit the
vines to mature; most often the blazing sun absorbs all moisture and the
plants wither, but if they survive, the fruit they yield is delicious. Apart
from the rice, it is the only edible thing grown here commercially.

But whatever the season, Las Marismas is primarily the residence of
birds, and what happens to men or camels or melons is a secondary
concern, and so as summer ends one looks again to the sky and sees aloft
the great bustards, accompanied by their cousins the little bustards, coming in to glean the hard ground for seeds and bees and insects. They fly in
splendid circles and land in two or three hops. Their quick eyes scan an
area in seconds to determine where the good feeding will be, and they pick
the land clean, quarreling among themselves as to who saw which first.
When they take their short hops and rise again into the air they see below
them only a parched earth, blazing in heat as great as that of a desert, with
the somnolent Guadalquivir wandering southward through the middle of
Las Marismas, and at its mouth the sunburnt adobe of Sanlúcar de
Barrameda, blistering in the sun as it did in the days when Columbus
stopped there.

AUTUMN

The best time of year, for me, in Las Marismas is autumn, because three
things happen to make it both bearable and exciting: the dreadful heat
diminishes, so that temperatures become quite pleasing; the first rains

come and with them a new color in all living things; and the movement of birds is captivating. As for the heat, Las Marismas, which in midsummer seems as hot as tropical Africa, stands at about the same latitude as San Francisco (Sevilla 37°, 27′N; San Francisco 37°, 40′; Richmond 37°, 30′, Wichita 37°, 48′). Therefore, when autumn comes and the baleful effect of winds blowing in from Africa and the Mediterranean has gone, the temperature is delightful; one wears loose clothing during the day, a substantial jacket of some kind after dark, and if one wishes to ride over Las Marismas at midnight to spot wildlife, a sturdy coat. I would suppose that anyone who loved the outdoors, and especially the tracking of birds in their larger migratory movements, would find Las Marismas in autumn almost irresistible, for then nature changes its aspect daily, and what has been a barren wasteland marked by whitened carcasses becomes a meadow which will sustain millions of birds in their migrations.

The change begins with the first rain. Year after year it arrives sometime between the twentieth and twenty-fifth of September, as if it had been waiting for summer officially to end. This is only a slight rain, not even enough to heal the cracks that mar the land, but it is followed in desultory fashion by one or two others. On Columbus Day, October 12, celebrated throughout the Spanish world as El día de la raza (The Day of the Race), the people who live along the edges of Las Marismas enjoy their last guaranteed clear day and their picnics are apt to be gay, for with strange regularity, on October 13, comes the first drenching rain of sufficient duration to soak the ground, but even though enormous quantities of water fall in this and subsequent storms, there is still not enough for any to collect. No lakes re-form and the permanent rivers are no higher than they were before; this water seeps into the dried earth. In doing so it reactivates plants, and even before the swamps re-form they look as they did when water was plentiful.

Now a few courageous ducks and geese begin to arrive from Scandinavia, and they must be sorely frustrated by what they find, for there are no lakes and food is bitterly scarce, for seeds of autumn have not yet fallen and the water plants on whose roots the birds exist have not matured. There is even trouble in finding a lake on which to rest; most are dried basins, their cracks just beginning to heal. And even when some accidental lake is found, its water is extremely brackish and unable to provide the swimming life which ducks and geese use to supplant the seeds and roots. But these first arrivals struggle with their problems and no living thing in Las Marismas must welcome subsequent rains with more excitement. One day I watched as a group of land-bound geese wiggled and cried with delight as rain came down upon them; it was the promise of a fruitful autumn.

These newcomers face an additional problem, for when they are kept from their normal feeding and hiding grounds, they lay themselves open to attacks by the imperial eagles, who now move in for easy kills. Perhaps easy is the wrong word, because the eagles have to exercise real skill if they want to catch a graylag goose who has protected itself in the north for the last six months. No eagle flying alone has ever been seen to take a goose except by sheer accident, for although the eagle is stronger and has powerful talons, he cannot overtake a goose in full flight; pursuit is useless. Therefore, the eagle finds himself a partner and as a pair they become formidable. One flies rather high, in the fly-space of the goose, and somewhat awkwardly, so that the target gets the idea that he can outfly this enemy. The other eagle flies low and well behind the first, and as the awkward eagle maintains altitude on the goose and makes a series of futile passes at him, the big bird takes the easy way out and with adept spirals evades the eagle by dropping to a lower altitude, where the second eagle sweeps in with terrifying talons.

There is other death in Las Marismas now. The cattle who have been browsing all summer on the safe flat lands begin to withdraw to higher ground as the rains start to engulf them, and by following paths long established, they retreat, but often one stumbles into an ojo, now camouflaged by growing grass and shrubs, or he waits too long and is trapped on an islet, where he dies, or the long trek weakens him. In any case, he is carefully watched by the vultures who scout the vast expanses day after day. In Las Marismas nothing rots.

For human beings in the region the autumn is as exciting as it is for the birds and animals, because this is the season of the vendimia (vintage) when the first fruit of the vine is pressed to the accompaniment of week-long celebrations. If one wanted a single painting of Spain to remind him of the best of the country, he could do worse than choose Goya's exquisite painting of the vendimia, now hanging in the Prado in Madrid, in which idealized peasants bring in the grapes while a nobleman, his pretty wife and their little boy, dressed in green velvet and red sash, taste them. Spaniards love this unpretentious work, for it speaks to them of the land, the rich, hard land of southern Spain when the harvest is under way.

In Sanlúcar the vendimia is celebrated with the same rustic vigor that it has been for the last thousand years, but at nearby Jerez de la Frontera, from which sherry takes its name, occurs the most renowned vendimia. Then the world-famous families who make and sell sherry—Domecq González, Byass, Osborne—set up kiosks where wine is served. Countrymen arrive to promenade in carriages drawn by six horses. There are bullfights and celebrations that last through the night. All around the rim of Las Marismas there is festivity in which Catholic Spain remembers pagan rituals and combines the old religion and the new in fascinating juxtapositions.

Now, too, is the time when huntsmen concentrate on the swamps, for the latter contain two enormous herds of deer, an indigenous red deer with

No. 608, whose deep horn wound on the right flank proves he is a horse that works the bulls at Concha y Sierra, comes out of the Guadalquivir after his bath in the late afternoon.

pointed horns, which is held to be an honorable target for the huntsman, and the grosser-formed fallow deer with palmated horns imported from Asia in the early 1900s, and not allowable as quarry for a gentleman. One autumn I was in a car filled with huntsmen speeding over the macadam-hard swampland, scouting for deer, and because I wear rather strong glasses I could see farther than my companions. 'Buck!' I shouted with some excitement as I spotted a handsome animal with large horns off in the distance. The car slowed down; the men looked; and there was silence as we drove on. I concluded that I had mistaken a doe for a buck, but shortly thereafter I spotted what could only be a buck. To my eyes he was majestic, with a spread of antler exceeding any I had seen before. 'Buck!' I

230

cried, this time with firmness. The car stopped; the men looked; and in embarrassed silence drove on. On the third spotting, for I was still seeing animals before the others, I cried, 'Goddamn it, that's a buck.' This time the car did not even bother to slow down, but one of the Spanish gentlemen did whisper, 'Michener, look at the horns! No gentleman would shoot a beast like that.' I had been spotting fallow deer, and they didn't count. After a long silence I saw a herd of perhaps sixty deer, and they were different, red instead of spotted brown, pointed horns instead of palmate. 'Buck!' I shouted for the fourth time, and there stood a series of noble beasts with proper horns. My alarm caused some excitement, and the gentleman at my side whispered, 'Well done. Those are deer.'

I am not a huntsman, except with camera, so to me the deer-stalking of autumn was less exciting than the subtle transformation of the land. I have never seen Las Marismas in late autumn when the water system of winter is fairly well formed, but I have seen it twice in early autumn when the rains have begun to take effect, and to see lakes quietly come into being, to watch dead rivers creep back to life and above all to see the surface of the land begin to collect its water and soften itself from concrete into mud, with grasses and flowers gently appearing, is a profound experience. I wouldn't be able to say when the swamps had fully reestablished themselves, perhaps by the first weeks in December, but at any stage in the process they afford an insight into nature that one cannot obtain elsewhere. How beautiful this transformation is, how simple: the land was barren and a raceway for the wind; it is now a meadow and a home for birds.

As always, it is the birds that inspire. A cold wind comes down from Madrid and next day all the migrants from Africa have taken flight. Remember, it is hardly five hundred miles from Las Marismas to the first deserts of Africa, and beyond them it is a couple of days' flying time to the warmer regions in which the birds are accustomed to spend their winters. The bee-eaters, the hoopoe birds and some of the egrets depart, and in their place come the robin and woodcock and widgeon. For a short period the swampland seems relatively depopulated, for the birds that have fled were conspicuous in size and color whereas the newcomers are markedly less brilliant, but after a few weeks of emptiness the damage is repaired, for now the real flocks of ducks begin to appear, so that a lake that was empty one day may have a thousand birds the next, and as the waters replenish themselves, the birds do likewise, and the poetic year of Las Marismas draws to a close.

It would be difficult to say where the capital of Las Marismas was, because the Guadalquivir cuts the area into two parts, the larger lying on the right bank, the more productive on the left. The right bank contains no major settlement, although, as we shall see, it does have the two major features, a shrine and a palace; the left bank contains one of the most memorable towns in Spain, and so far as I am concerned, it is the capital.

Sanlúcar de Barrameda is a dirty, low-lying settlement located at the mouth of the Guadalquivir, a seaport partaking of the nature of both the ocean and the river. When I first saw it, only one street was paved, and it poorly. The bullring was built in the ancient Moorish style, with onion-bulb gates and crescent windows. On the small hill that rises in the center of the town a ruined castle perches; it houses a tribe of gypsies and four families of peregrine falcons that fly out each morning to hunt the swamps. In its alleys, incredibly dirty in comparison with the rest of Spain, I saw many more horses than automobiles, and the only industry I could spot besides fishing was the lonely salt bed in which overflow from the ocean was trapped and allowed to evaporate, leaving behind a brownish deposit, half mud, half salt. In one of the bars a man said, 'You're in the best town in Spain. Real spirit here. This is where we make manzanilla.' If this was true, Sanlúcar deserves more fame than it has received, for manzanilla is one of Spain's noblest wines, a sherry so pale and dry that it seems hardly to be a liquid but rather a delicate spirit. I had not imagined it as having come from a miserable spot like Sanlúcar.

But the more I came to know the town, the more attractive it grew. In the old days every treasure boat from the New World was required to drop anchor in these roads so that government officials could go aboard and check the bullion. 'The men in Sanlúcar you could trust,' a Spaniard explained, 'but if the gold once slipped through to Sevilla unweighed, there wasn't an official who was honest.' It was from this dreary little port that Christopher Columbus set sail on his third voyage to the New World. He had a difficult time in Sanlúcar, for reasons unconnected with the town, as we shall see shortly. It was also from here that Magellan set sail to circumnavigate the globe, and it was to Sanlúcar that one of his ships returned three years later, but without him.

Noble families distinguished in Spanish history had their seats in Sanlúcar, though why, I shall never know, and in the middle of the last century the sun-baked little town became rather prominent; Queen Isabel II's younger sister married a son of the King of France, and when apprehension arose lest he try to gain the Spanish throne, he and his bride were banished to Sanlúcar where they could do no harm. Only a few years ago another noble, with vague claims to the throne, died here in Sanlúcar, and as I wandered through the streets I tried to visualize what royal exiles did to occupy their time in this backwater. In their letters they usually spoke of Sanlúcar with affection; in recent years adventurous American naval officers who work at the submarine base not far away have rented fifteenth-century homes on the hill and have lived there without electricity or running water. 'The best town in Spain,' they report unanimously. 'It has character.' If I were to live in the south for any period, I think I would elect Sanlúcar. It has quality and lies near Las Marismas.

In the heart of the swampland there was a building which I scarcely expected to find in such a place, a stone church which served as a shrine for a dramatic cult centering upon a wooden statue of the Virgin, known formally as Nuestra Señora del Rocío and popularly as la Paloma Blanca (the White Dove). Around the church has grown up an extraordinary village of some six or eight tree-lined streets with cottages on each side, so that the place looks almost as much English as it does Spanish. The village is unusual in that it is empty for fifty-one weeks each year; it is the fifty-second week that counts.

To appreciate the significance of El Rocío one must go far back in history to a time prior to 711, when the Visigoths still ruled Spain after having converted it to Christianity. There must have been in those days many churches in Sevilla and other settlements along the edges of Las Marismas and each contained a stone or wooden statue of the Virgin, who even then was popular in Spain. In 711 the Muslims invaded from Africa and within a few months overran the southern areas of the country and threatened the others. Then Christians, terrified by this unknown enemy who crushed any army that confronted him, grabbed the statues from their churches and buried them in remote spots to protect them from profanation by the infidel. As it turned out, their apprehensions were unjustified because Islam, even though it sought converts, preferred that conquered peoples remain Christian, for if they did extra taxes could be levied. Thus churches were not only permitted to continue but were encouraged to do so.

When the relatively benevolent nature of the new order was discovered, many of the buried statues were dug up and returned to their niches, but others remained where they were and were forgotten. Perhaps the man who had buried a given statue was the one who embraced the new religion when he saw that it was economically profitable to do so; if he had converted, it was unlikely that he would dig up a statue relating to his old faith. At any rate, when four or five centuries of Muslim occupation had passed and Christians began regaining their lost territories, it became fairly common for shepherds, who lived under the open sky year after year with little to occupy them, to uncover by accident in some remote spot one of these long-buried Virgins. Word of his discovery would flash across the countryside and before long would reach the bishop in the capital. Investigations would be launched, but by this time the simple act of uncovering the statue would have been clothed in heroic or spiritual garb. 'For three nights running Juan the Shepherd saw a light hovering above a rock.' Or 'While Tomás was tending his sheep he heard a voice speaking to him.' Thus a miracle was born.

In my travels through Spain, I was to come upon at least eight of these miraculous appearances of the Virgin, but none with a more appealing history than the finding of the El Rocío statue in Las Marismas. More than a century had passed since the area had passed from Muslim control to Christian, and one day a hunter from the town of Almonte was looking for game when his dogs assumed a point before a thicket. He verified that there was no game in the brush, but the dogs continued their point, so he investigated and found hidden in the hollow of a tree a statue of the Virgin. He abandoned his hunt, took the image in his arms and set out for Almonte, but with his burden he became weary and fell asleep, only to awaken and discover that the image had disappeared. He returned to the tree and was overjoyed to find that the statue had returned there and was once more in the hollow, where he left her to report the miracle in Almonte. A group of villagers, doubting his story, walked the long distance to the tree to see for themselves, and when they entered the thicket they found the statue hiding in the tree. Again they tried to carry her to Almonte and again she insisted upon returning to the tree, whereupon the men ran back to the village and informed their priest, who explained that by this gesture she meant to tell them that it was there that she wished to be worshiped. Accordingly, they raised a hermitage on that spot, which accounts for the remote location of so famous a shrine. She was at first called, after the place of the apparition, Nuestra Señora de la Rocina, a name which was later altered by the villagers, no one knows exactly when or how, to the simple and poetic Nuestra Señora del Rocío (Our Lady of the Dew).

As for the village that has grown up about it, a full-scale settlement with many cottages wholly furnished for one week's occupancy a year, the fame of the Virgin of El Rocío became so widespread that each spring an enormous pilgrimage is organized throughout southern Spain, when families in traditional two-wheeled carts decorated with banners and flowers and drawn by oxen similarly decorated take the long trek to El Rocío to pay homage to the stubborn Virgin who knew where she wanted her home to be. In special years as many as eighty thousand pilgrims ride over dusty roads to enjoy as wild a weekend as Spain has to offer.

Unfortunately, I never saw El Rocío in fiesta, but friends introduced me to Don Luis Ybarra González, the forty-year-old son of a distinguished Sevilla family that specialized in all things relating to olives. Their commercial empire became so extensive that they were required to put together their own shipping company, and this in turn encouraged them to enter collateral fields. Señor Ybarra was a well-known amateur naturalist with whom it was a pleasure to roam Las Marismas, except that he entertained so many foreign visitors, each speaking a different language, that in self-defense he referred to birds and animals only by their Latin names. 'The only sensible way,' he told me. 'Birds are the same everywhere. It's the countries they visit that change.'

He was cousin to the Conde de Ybarra and knew well the history of the region, especially that of El Rocío. 'It's a great pity you couldn't have seen it during celebrations,' he said. 'You won't get much seeing it this way.' And I must admit that as he drove me across the swamps to a large grove of eucalyptus trees I could not visualize eighty thousand pilgrims converging on this lonely spot, for there was nothing to commend it, neither natural beauty nor buildings of interest. When we reached the village itself I was astonished by its emptiness; we were like characters in a romance who had come upon a sleeping town. Here were the houses, street after street of them, and the stores, and a church and all the appurtenances of a village except people. It was uncanny, and I asked, 'It's empty like this all year?' He nodded and pointed to one of the larger cottages. 'My family's. We've come here one week a year for as long as I can remember. Beneath those eucalypts there will be tents for ten thousand. Farther along many refreshment bars. No roof, no walls. They will serve thousands of snacks. Over here beer stands. More than you could count.'

As he spoke, I wished that we were in one of those movies in which, as the hero begins to explain something, the scene he is describing begins to take form. I should have enjoyed seeing this deserted village spring to life for its one wild week, and I was lucky to find, in a small town on the other side of the Guadalquivir, an unusual Englishman who had settled there years ago as the Volkswagen representative for southern Spain, and he turned out to be both an El Rocío enthusiast and a spirited raconteur and it was through his account of adventures on the pilgrimage that I gained some sense of what it must be like.

He was John Culverwell, a handsome bull-necked fellow with a petite wife from the English Midlands who was fluent in Spanish and a fine horsewoman. Without repeating the questions I asked to keep their commentary flowing, I should like to report on their experiences in undertaking a Spanish pilgrimage.

'Cecilia and I had been so often that three years ago our community came to us and said, "Señor Culverwell, you and your wife are as good Spaniards as any of us, so when the grand parade is formed to ride past the Virgin next week, we want your wife to ride at the head of our column and carry the flag of our village. You are to ride at the end of the parade and carry the standard of the Virgin of El Rocío." You can imagine that this struck us as something of an honor, because I can't recall another instance when a foreigner was invited to carry the flag of his community at El Rocío.

'The pilgrimage occurs each year at Whitsunday, which if you were a Catholic you'd call Pentecost, the seventh Sunday after Easter, that's the fiftieth day, when something or other important happened. From our side of the Guadalquivir you can get to El Rocío only on horseback, so early in the week we arrange for our horses and at sunup on Friday we leave home and ride to Sanlúcar, where we meet with hundreds of horsemen who have collected from towns around here. We ride down to the river's edge, where barges wait to ferry our horses across to the other side, and after delivering them we walk to a different pier, from which we are taken across in small boats. On the opposite bank we recover our horses, saddle up and head for an adventure you'd never believe if you hadn't seen it.

'Did you know that on the other side of the Guadalquivir there are first pine forests, then sand dunes for eight or ten miles? Yes, big, flowing, beautifully sculptured sand dunes with hardly a tree or shrub. During the trek to El Rocío horsemen frequently get lost in these dunes. I don't know whether any have died in recent years, but I do know that a couple of years ago I got separated from Cecilia and the others and it was rather touch-and-go before I got back. A wilderness of white sand with desert birds you won't spot elsewhere.

'Well, we ride for many hours through the dunes and it's difficult to believe that we're in Spain, but toward evening we come in sight of the palace . . . Yes, there's a full-scale palace hidden away in the loneliest part of Las Marismas, off beyond the dunes. I'll explain some day why it's there. Anyway, we ride up to this palace and there we spend the first night among so many birds you'd not credit the number. My chief delight these days is studying birds, and I doubt if there is a better place in the world to do this than at the palace, for there you get land birds, sea birds, swamp birds, dune birds . . . everything a man could want to see. Whether you ever get to El Rocío or not, you really should try to see the palace.

'On Saturday morning we rise early, saddle our horses and cut off along the edge of Las Marismas, past the famous heronries and into the eucalyptus groves and to El Rocío itself. It's about a seven-hour ride as we take it, because we stop to check on how many birds are nesting. You can see, I would suppose, several thousand nests without much searching, but toward midafternoon we come in sight of El Rocío. You can tell where it is because of the enormous cloud of dust that rises over it. Thousands of oxcarts converging on the shrine. We spur our horses, dash into the village, go straight to the chapel and from outside salute the Virgin, then make a couple of circuits to inform the world that our contingent has arrived.

'El Rocío! If you haven't been there I can scarcely describe it, but imagine a convocation of thousands of people, hundreds of gypsies, and drums and flutes, guitars, hand-clapping and a world of two-wheeled carts from the last century, and no sleep.

'No sleep! You arrive Saturday afternoon and until late Monday there's no sleep. If a man begins to nod, somebody wakes him up. He couldn't sleep anyway. The noise is too tremendous. Bang, bang, bang! A clatter such as you've never heard before. Naturally, tempers get a little short. In fact, the game is to make the other fellow's temper explode. You kiss his girl or steal his wine. But if he makes one move to hit you, everybody shouts, "¡Viva la Paloma Blanca!" As soon as this is said he has to laugh, shake hands and share a drink with you. One year I watched them badger a chap beyond endurance. He was about to clout his chief tormentor when we all shouted, "¡Paloma Blanca!" He went ahead and busted his enemy in the eye and shouted, "¡Paloma Blanca! ¡Ojo negro!" (White dove! Black eye!)

'Each community in this part of Spain owns one of the cottages which it dresses up for Whitsuntide and it serves as your headquarters. Here you get free drinks, meet your friends, leave your wife when you want to raise hell somewhere else. But late Saturday evening you must report back, for now the formal parade of horsemen in honor of the Virgin is about to begin. As I told you, our group, which contains some of the best horsemen in the south, was to be led by Cecilia.

'About nine o'clock at night there's one hell of a noise. Flamenco music and shouting and general brawling. And then on all sides of the central plaza, the Real del Rocío, the parade forms, and for more than three hours we ride past the chapel of the Virgin and pay our respects. It's something to see, a recollection of old Spain, but the best part comes after the formal parade breaks up, because then gangs of riders rip and roar through the village all night. When I am in England and try to recall why I love Spain so much, I think of two things. The birds at the palace and the night-riding at El Rocío.

'On Sunday morning at ten o'clock something happens you wouldn't believe. The Real is crowded with people who have come to celebrate a field Mass in which a portable altar is set up. Riders attend on horses, as they did in cavalry days, and when they dismount to kneel, it's something to see.

'Sunday night is a sort of bleary time, a sentimental wandering from one community house to the next. Men you wouldn't bother with in normal business suddenly become good friends, because they took the trouble to visit El Rocío. The singing continues all night, and if there is someone who simply can't take the noise any longer, he sneaks out into Las Marismas and sleeps under the stars.

'Monday is the day! Early in the morning the Virgin, the original statue about which all this fuss is being made, is brought out of the church atop a rather large wooden structure like a float in order to make a paseo so that she can bless the pilgrims who have come to do her honor. Honor! That's the word. By tradition her float is carried only by the men from Almonte, because it was they who first did so when they took her from the tree. But the rest of us are free to volunteer, but if we do the men from Almonte push us away.

'So how does a man win the honor of helping to carry the float? By gouging, kicking, pulling and clubbing whichever men have her at the moment. A shirt lasts about three minutes. I have seen fights in the shadow of this Virgin that make one of your sales at Macy's look puny. I've seen men so eager to touch the float that they rear back, take six running steps and torpedo themselves headfirst into the face of the man who was holding the float. You'd think the man who was hit wouldn't have a tooth left in his head. He'd stagger back and want to fight, but someone would shout, "¡Viva la Paloma Blanca!" and he'd wipe his mouth and grin.

'How long does the brawling last? Four or five hours. Maybe more. The Virgin moves a few yards at a time, trembles, teeters, almost falls in the dust, but hands always catch her at the last minute and keep her erect. The fighting continues at fever pitch because as soon as anyone is exhausted and has to withdraw, someone fresh plunges in determined to capture the float.

'By late afternoon Monday the two-wheeled carts begin to drive back along the roads to sanity. The battered Virgin is restored to her quiet niche in the shrine and the community houses are slowly boarded up for another year. The stores that have been opened to serve the pilgrims are shut down. The gypsy bands move on to another fiesta and everywhere you look you see tired men and women sleeping on porches or under trees. Horses that have not rested for days sleep standing or graze along the edges of the swamp.

'On Monday, Cecilia and I ride back to the palace, and believe me the birds are a welcome change from the madness we've been sharing. On Tuesday we return through the dunes and come to the edge of the river. On the other side we see the low roofs of Sanlúcar and wonder if the ferry will ever spot us and come to fetch our horses.'

In the spring of 1498, when Christopher Columbus proposed to sail from Sanlúcar on his third voyage of exploration to the New World, he was forced to delay the departure of his six ships until the thirtieth of May, 'because his sailors had gone off to El Rocío and would not return.' When the five ships of Magellan assembled at Sanlúcar in 1519, prior to setting out for their circumnavigation of the globe, the season of El Rocío was well past, for it was mid-August, but most of his sailors from the Sanlúcar district would have made the pilgrimage earlier, for the Virgin looked after her devotees.

'She's a wonderful Virgin,' Señor Ybarra assured me as we stood under the eucalypts in her deserted town, 'and she'll forgive me if I say that the best single thing about El Rocío is the honey. Until you've tasted our honey, you can't know what Las Marismas is.' I asked him why he spoke of 'our honey,' and he said, 'Each Whitsuntide my father drives here in a carriage and opens the cottage as his father did before him. We send ships all over the world, but El Rocío is our spiritual home. Taste the honey.'

We had stopped at the only store which keeps open throughout the year, a thoroughly beat-up shack with earthy peasant proprietors who looked after the cottages during the silent months, and the wife brought us a kilo of dark honey in a glass jar that had once housed peanut butter made in California. How it had reached El Rocío, I could not guess, but the honey, when I tasted it on a piece of hard bread, was all that Señor Ybarra had predicted. I've sampled honey in most of the areas where it is made and have had some very fine brands, especially in Japan and India, but the heavy, dark El Rocío honey gathered from flowering weeds in Las Marismas was finer than any I had previously tasted. Señor Ybarra summarized its quality precisely when he said, 'Tastes like Spain, doesn't it?' If Spain has a taste, it would be either that of El Rocío honey, or a dark red wine from Rioja, or a fish zarzuela from Badajoz or the anchovies of Barcelona or perhaps the incredibly good bread of Arévalo, which we shall meet later. Certainly this excellent honey would be one of the components.

Like the honey, Señor Ybarra was a heavy, dark man with a graying mustache who spoke rapidly with both a lisp and a marked southern accent, but the subjects with which he dealt were so interesting that I found myself understanding him better than I did most Spaniards. 'The unique flavor of El Rocío honey comes from the rosemary and eucalyptus on which the bees feed, and also from the swamp flowers.

'One thing you must see while you're here is the new chapel we're building for the Virgin. Look! She'll have a throne of pure silver. What a change from the tree trunk in which she used to rest. You ought to take a set of the El Rocío tiles home with you.' He showed me the nine orange, blue and yellow tiles which when cemented side by side in a wall would create an image of the Virgin enthroned and surrounded by a grand halo of sixteen gold disks. 'Our legend says that the statue was carved in Italy and sent to North Africa to help convert the heathen. She wound up in Morocco, and after converting that land, was brought to Spain to save us. When the Moroccans changed to Islam they wanted to take her back lest she bring us good luck, and that's why Spain was invaded.' In bemused silence she sits in her old shrine waiting for the new one to be finished, as profoundly loved as any Virgin in Spain, in a strange, wild way.

The more I was with Señor Ybarra the more impressed I was with his affection for the land; again and again he returned to this topic. 'My father had a great love for the Guadalquivir, probably because he saw it in such majesty here in Las Marismas. Anyway, he said, "There's nothing another river can do that our river can't." Somebody said that the Volga could produce caviar, and my father took this as a challenge. He remembered that even in Roman times the Guadalquivir was famous for its sturgeon. There was an old Roman coin found at Coria del Río which showed the sturgeon. So he searched through Europe to find Russian émigrés who knew how to make caviar and finally found an expert living in Cape Town. Brought him here in 1929 and within a year my father was producing all the caviar sold in Spain. You go into a fine hotel and ask for caviar . . . Well, a lot of people do. You get Guadalquivir caviar and even the experts can't tell the difference.'

It was unusual to find a Spaniard who spoke with such love of rivers and meadows and mountains, for Spain more than any other European nation has abused its land. It is in this respect that Spain is guilty of the charge that Frenchmen so often make against her, that she is not a European nation but an African: 'Africa begins at the Pyrenees.' Demographically this is not so; in the abuse of natural resources it is.

The nearly eight centuries during which Spain waged intermittent war against African invaders, 711–1492, created a type of gentleman to whom the maximum good in life was knightly behavior in war, which was not in itself destructive, because for different reasons similar values were respected in all European countries, but in Spain a contempt developed for anyone who worked with his hands, especially farmers. It became an actual disgrace, from which a family could not cleanse itself, for a member to work at agriculture; inevitably, the land suffered.

What was worse, a system grew up whereby gentlemen who were not allowed to farm were allowed to herd the highly profitable Merino sheep, so long as the animals grazed at will over vast territories rather than on a single farm owned by one man. A gigantic cooperative developed, the Mesta (The Group of Proprietors of Sheep), and because only gentlemen were allowed to join, it won special privileges from the Spanish kings and flourished as a major economic agency in Spain from about 1300 through the first quarter of the 1800s.

Its flocks were so huge that in one poor year the census showed 1,673,551 sheep, ceaselessly in motion, like a great pendulum of destruction oscillating between the northern limit of the central plateau and the southern. In this heartland of Spain where a rational agriculture should have been developing, fencing off was not permitted; fields had to be kept open for the passage of sheep, and any settled farmer who tried to protect his crops from the vagrant sheep was hauled not before a magistrate but before an officer of the Mesta who traveled with the sheep, dispensing a harsh and arbitrary justice. Before 1585 there was no appeal from a decision of the Mesta judges.

Many books have been written about the terror that possessed Christian settlements in Spain when the Muslims came up from the south; others have dealt with the fear engendered by the Inquisition when it was probing into private lives, but I suppose the best book that could be written, the one that would tell more about day-to-day Spanish life than any other, would be the story of some village whose farmers watched in dismay as the outriders of the Mesta crossed their fields, warning them that the sheep would soon follow. Then the farmers had to retire, remove obstacles, make no effort to protect their crops and wait in their huts until the all-powerful sheep had passed.

Why did this extraordinary condition prevail? Partly because sheep-herding had become recognized as an occupation for gentlemen but mainly because the kings of Spain had discovered that in the wool from their Merinos, which under pain of death could not be smuggled out to other lands which did not have them, they possessed a commodity which other nations would pay for at a price that Spain would determine. Merino wool was recognized as the best available and the Spanish economy was geared to produce Merino and to protect the men who tended the sheep that grew it. The Mesta existed as a mobile feudal kingdom, ravaging the best land and inhibiting its proper utilization. By the time the Mesta declined, an irreparable damage of two kinds had been done: the land was depleted and the ordinary agricultural processes which English, French and German farmers had mastered through the centuries were not known.

The capricious nature of this division between acceptable sheep growers and unacceptable farmers should not disturb the reader, for many other societies have made similar distinctions, equally impossible to justify. Thus in the American west it was the cattleman who was acceptable and the sheep man who stood outside the pale; I have been present when a self-respecting Coloradan entered a restaurant, took one sniff of the cooking odors, turned on his heel and stalked out, growling, 'They're serving lamb in there.' It was in Hong Kong, however, that I observed arbitrary categories at their best. A long-time English resident, having volunteered to help me buy a watch, took me to a shop called something like Ledyard's, and when a satisfactory deal had been concluded, he said, 'Good fellow, Ledyard.' In the street he reprimanded me for having said, 'Mr. Ledyard.' 'The man's in trade,' he pointed out. 'Should never be addressed as Mister. Couldn't possibly be a gentleman.' When I asked why, my friend said, 'Ledyard could buy and sell me seven times over, but by God, in nineteen years I've never called him Mister.' While I was in Hong Kong a convivial chap who ran a bar was finally admitted to one of the exclusive clubs, to which he had sought admission fruitlessly during many years; the club had not changed its rules excluding men who were in trade, but the saloon owner had that week sold his bar and gone into wholesale distribution of beer and whiskey, and that, according to British tradition, was not trade.

But if all nations have similar peculiarities, few have suffered from theirs as much as Spain has from hers. Hundreds of perplexed travelers during the last three hundred years have commented on the fact that the country was filled with virtual paupers who maintained their classification as gentlemen by refusing to work; they starved but they remained gentlemen. Although such a system had deleterious effects on farming and manufacturing, it had the virtues of not being based exclusively on money or big houses; a man with one room and one suit, if he carried himself properly, could be just as much a gentleman as a man with a palace, and this universal eligibility has permitted a friendship between economic classes which has not existed in other European countries. The impoverished Don Quixote, and many of them exist today across Spain, feels no sense of embarrassment in addressing as an equal the duque or conde or

It was the inherent surrealism of Spain that produced a painter like Salvador Dali.

marqués with whom he comes in contact, while to the recent millionaire he feels superior.

The effect of all this upon the land has been tragic, and I remember one hot summer day riding through the heart of the Mesta territory, northeast of Madrid, and coming upon the village of Maranchón, so typical that it could represent all that had grown up in the sheep country. How beautiful and quiet this place was, with majestic old houses crowding each side of the somnolent main street. How enticing were the views I caught of the narrow streets that led off to right and left as I passed. Here was the inevitable sign, 'Correos,' plus an arrow, indicating that down this alley there was a house serving as post office. Another sign, common to all villages, read 'Telégrafo' and a third said 'Teléfono.'

In Maranchón I saw one shepherd, but he had no sheep. I caught sight of a woman ducking into a doorway and then I was in the outskirts of the village, but when I came to the little bullring, 'Erected 1915,' I had an overpowering desire to know more about this town, so I wheeled my car about and parked on the main street. I walked up the grass-grown Calle Generalísimo Franco, to where it met Calle Calvo Sotelo, and I stayed there for some time just looking. Almost no one moved, for Maranchón was largely deserted. The fine houses were shuttered and the doors over which family shields had been carved were locked.

Where had the men gone? 'To Germany, señor. They have all gone to Germany.'

But these houses held women, too. Where are they? 'They've gone to Barcelona, señor. The lucky ones are in Barcelona.'

But your fields are rich. Why aren't they tilled? 'The men have gone to Germany, señor. There they can make a living.'

Maranchón lives in my memory as a permanent symbol of Spain, even more lasting than the depopulated villages of Extremadura, because it was more beautiful and in its day had known a more complete life. How really lovely that main street was! If it could be transported bodily to California it would be one of the treasures of the United States and artists would fight for the privilege of renting the rooms that stand behind its plain, perfect façades. Where have all the people gone? If Maranchón itself could speak, it would say, 'For five centuries my people were abused by the Mesta, whose courts used to sit in that hall over there, sentencing farmers unjustly. Any man who had a good idea about caring for his land was muzzled. The fields that could have been so productive have gone to waste and the boys who once ran in these streets have gone to Germany and Barcelona.'

It seems uncanny that a nation which made the miserable mistake of chasing after Mexican and Peruvian gold instead of developing manufactures should in the field of agriculture have made an equally destructive wrong choice, electing the quick money of the Mesta rather than the sustained productivity of an orderly system of farms. Just as the gold damaged the country instead of helping it, so the Mesta destroyed the land instead of making it productive. As I say, it is unusual to meet a Spaniard like Don Luis Ybarra, who understands the land, especially when he is a distinguished gentleman.

'At the palace,' he said one day, 'we're taking steps to correct our indifference.'

'What is the palace? Culverwell mentioned it too.'

'I'd like to show it to you.'

The prospect of seeing a fresh section of Las Marismas under Señor Ybarra's guidance was so inviting that we made plans to visit the secluded place. We left El Rocío and drove south toward the Atlantic Ocean west of Sanlúcar and soon were in the kind of sand-dune country that Culverwell had described. When we had about reached the seashore we turned back north on a miserable track and for the better part of an hour crawled along, trying to keep out of the watery ditches on either side. When we escaped them we found ourselves stuck up to our hubcaps in drifting sand, and if bushes had not been plentiful, so that we could tear off their tops to throw under our spinning wheels, I doubt that we would have made it. At last, however, we broke through and found ourselves in a wild and barren land with a chain of small lakes off to our right.

'Look!' Ybarra cried. 'Eagles!' We stopped to watch two imperial eagles chasing a goose who must have had experience with them, for he not only dodged the upper eagle but did it in such a way as to stay well clear of the one waiting below. We cheered the clever goose and with this appropriate introduction I entered one of the rare spots of Europe, or the world either for that matter, the Coto Doñana (Wildlife Preserve of Doña Ana). We turned a corner in the road and saw a lake on which there must have been a thousand ducks. Ybarra said, 'They're back! Early, but they're back.' When we had passed this check point I saw ahead of me a compact, very old three-story stone building rising mysteriously out of the swamp-land, a true fifteenth-century palace set down here God knows how, a refuge inhabited in times past by kings who sat for Velázquez, by the Duquesa de Alba, who is said to have posed here for Francisco de Goya, and by the man whose spirit seems to haunt the place, King Alfonso XIII, who came here in his impeccable hunting suits and was driven over the swamps and dunes in a 1922 Citroën fitted with tank tracks. This was the palace of Coto Doñana, and in the past fifty years almost every leading naturalist in the world, if his specialty was birds, has caught his breath with excitement as he came upon this unbelievable building in the marshes.

The Coto Doñana is a large area of wilderness consisting of part marisma, part sand dune and much water in the form of semi-connected lakes strung together like the beads of a rosary. On the north it reaches almost to El Rocío, on the south and west almost to the shoreline of the Atlantic and on the east almost to the Guadalquivir. It has many oak trees, not huddled together in a forest but standing each one by itself, with gaunt branches suitable for supporting nests. It also has a copious supply of shrubs and low grasses which produce seeds. It is thus an almost perfect haven for birds of every sort, from the eagle that needs a tall tree to the widgeon and coot that require water and grass. Since sometime around the year 1500 it has been known as a hunter's paradise, because in addition to a bird life of unimaginable fecundity, it has also contained very large herds of red deer, and, since their introduction in the early 1900s, of fallow deer as well. When I say large I mean that in an average walk across six or eight miles of the Coto one may see forty different herds of deer, each containing fifty or sixty animals.

For several centuries the Coto was set aside as a hunting preserve where bears and wolves and wild boars were protected from poachers, hence its name, and where the elite of Spain came on quite primitive safaris, as much to enjoy the wilderness as to hunt game. Kings and dukes, famous bullfighters and actors, visiting nobility and merchant princes made it to the Coto and stacked their guns in the racks of the palace. The area was owned by noble families living in the Cádiz region and was held by them for the enjoyment of their guests.

Very early in the Coto's history its owners realized that some kind of permanent building was going to be necessary, not only for the yearly guests but also for the gamekeepers, so the palace was built. How were these stones brought over land with no roads? How could a building of this excellent quality have been erected in such a wilderness? The records of its construction are lost, but it is known to have existed in the sixteenth century. Hundreds of peasants must have labored a long time, hauling materials on their backs from dumping grounds at the edge of the Guadalquivir. Or perhaps the stone and timber came by boat to the open beach along the Atlantic, from which they were hauled in two-wheeled carts over the sand dunes. At any rate, the old palace was finally completed, centuries ago.

It is not, as Señor Ybarra warned me, 'a palace palace.' It's more like the fortress palace one finds in rural Italy, a large rectangular block resembling more an oversized farmhouse than an urban palace; but when one comes upon it after a trek over the dunes or the swamps it has a palatial grandeur, so that the name is not amiss.

Among the noble hunters who occupied it in the last years of the nineteenth century and the early years of this were some who forgot the herds of deer and the lynx and fox and began to look at the bird life, and through them the fame of the Coto as a bird sanctuary began to spread. Throughout Europe naturalists who wanted to study the birds of England or Denmark or Russia found that to complete their information they must come to where their birds came, the Coto Doñana in southern Spain, and as so often happened in such matters, it was a group of public-spirited Englishmen who brought the Coto to the attention of the world at large and formulated plans for its acquisition by an international body that would protect it permanently as a wildlife preserve.

Under the leadership of the Duke of Edinburgh, Lord Alanbrooke (of World War II fame) and Prince Bernhard of The Netherlands, aided by Frenchmen and Germans and perhaps an American or two, including Roger Tory Peterson, the bird expert, the World Wildlife Fund was established to preserve areas where birds and animals take refuge, and one of its first acts was the purchase of the Coto, which was saved just in time from the inroads of modernization. The Fund has offices throughout the world, but its spiritual home is the palace. One of its principal assets in Spain is the talented man chosen as director of the Coto, the ornithologist Dr. José Antonio Valverde, who keeps an office in Sevilla. He is a learned and very amusing man, and anyone wanting to visit or support the Coto should seek him out.

'Ah!' Señor Ybarra cried as our car came to a halt under the eucalypts which surrounded the palace. 'Our welcoming committee.' A bedraggled nanny goat appeared to greet us, followed by a tame red deer with only one horn who made straight for me. Since it is not often that I get a chance to play with deer, I stepped forward to scratch my friend's nose, but Ybarra grabbed me and drew me back. 'Watch out for Bartolo! He was suckled by that goat and now thinks he's one. That horn can raise hell.' As he spoke, Bartolo took a leap at me, lowered his head and came right at my stomach with his one sharp horn. Ybarra kicked him away just in time, and he stood off to one side, his head cocked. Later he came at me more properly and we had the first of many fine visits. Ybarra was right. He thought he was a goat and even ate odd things the way his foster mother did.

On my first night at the palace I met a widely informed Spaniard who was to serve as my principal mentor in Spain, although neither he nor I was aware of this fact at the moment; it was not until I had come upon him again in Madrid and in the various cities of the north that I appreciated what an unusual fellow he was, how wise and well-intentioned. He was an ardent patriot, had a keen appreciation of what was happening in Spain and would discuss it frankly. Had he known of any adverse comment on Spain that I intended including in this book, he would have stayed up all night trying to argue me out of it; if on the other hand I report upon certain aspects of Spanish life with affection, often it is because he instructed me about them.

He was introduced as Don Luis Morenés y Areces, an avid huntsman from Madrid. He was about my height, somewhat on the heavy side but surprisingly light on his feet. He had a head much larger than that of the average Spaniard and heavy dark hair with slight streaks of gray, even though he could not have been more than thirty-five. His features were large: broad-set eyes, a substantial nose, a large, mobile mouth, a heavy neck running into shoulders that sloped like an athlete's. He loved the outdoors and had a keen eye for all natural phenomena. He was a born huntsman and loved guns, which I do not, but in all else his interests and mine coincided; particularly, he had a boisterous sense of humor, a really rollicking Sancho Panza type of Spanish laughter, and as in the case of most good storytellers, a fair share of the yarns he told were at his expense, for he was in no way pompous. He spoke English and French with little accent and had what I especially appreciated, an almost total recall of places we had seen together or conversations we had held, often years before.

The first question I asked him was typical. 'Who was the Doña Ana after whom the Coto was named?' and his meticulous reply was representative of thousands that I would receive in subsequent conversations: 'There are three theories on that. Some say it was Ana, the Duquesa de Medina Sidonia. The family that produced the admiral who led the Great Armada against England in 1588. They come from down here and had an important seat at Sanlúcar. But Señor Ybarra believes it was Ana, the Condesa de Denia y Tarifa. The big family over by Gibraltar. They owned the place for a while. I'm of the personal opinion that it must have been named after Ana de Austria. Ah, but which Ana of Austria? The fourth wife of Felipe Segundo and mother of Felipe Tercero? I don't think so. More probably the second wife of Felipe Quarto. She was his niece, you know, and the mother of Carlos Segundo. This Ana loved the hunt and often came to the Coto, which in honor of her visits was named Coto de la Reina Doña Mariana de Austria, to give her full name. This was contracted to Coto de la Reina Doña Ana, and then to Coto de Doña Ana, and finally to Coto Doñana. You would be interested to know that it was this queen who gave her name to the Marianas Islands in the Pacific Ocean.'

He told me something else that seemed logical though surprising. 'The Coto played an important role in the history of India. Some British officers stationed at Gibraltar during the years when Spain and England were allies against Napoleon were invited here as guests of the Spanish king, and while staying at the palace they saw him hunt boar with a lance from horseback, and when they were transferred to India they introduced the sport there. So Errol Flynn and all the other Bengal Lancers got their start here.'

Don Luis then solved a problem for me. 'You asked how the stones for this palace reached here? You wouldn't believe it. They came from quarries north of London. When the English discovered our sherry wine and started to import huge quantities of it, their ships could think of nothing to carry back to Spain on the return trips. So for ballast they loaded up with granite blocks, but no one in Cádiz or Jerez wanted the stone, so they dumped it on the shore and men hauled it in handcarts to build this palace.'

In the pause that followed, Señor Ybarra queried Don Luis concerning a girl who had made herself a depositada, and Don Luis said, 'She's doing as well as you'd expect.' He then turned to me and explained. 'In our country, getting a girl of good family married sometimes involves a lot of problems. Suppose that José, age twenty, wants to marry Rosita, age seventeen. In the eyes of the law and the Church they were old enough to do so when he was fourteen and she twelve, but until Rosita reaches the age of twenty-one she must have her parents' permission. If they approve, okay. If they object, Rosita must wait till she's twenty-one. Then she can marry José whether her parents like it or not.'

I pointed out that many countries had similar rules. 'Ah, yes!' Don Luis agreed. 'But what they don't have is our depositada process. The girl is free at twenty to marry only if she leaves her parents' home. If for any reason—and when good families are involved this is usually the case—she continues to live with her parents in order to win from them a dowry, she cannot marry without their consent until she is twenty-five, but a recent law has dropped that age to twenty-one. Nor can she become a nun without their permission. It is in the interest of family continuance that this law exists, and we observe it. But it is also in the interest of Church and state that girls marry young and bear children while they are able. So a compromise is necessary, and here it is. A girl who cannot get her parents' permission to marry can throw herself upon the mercy of the court, which will deposit her, hence depositada, in the home of a relative or friend so that others can inspect the young man and supervise the courtship for a period of somewhat less than six months. At the end of this cooling-off period, as we call it, if she still insists upon marrying her young man, the family into which she has been deposited acts as her parents.

'Now, if young José fails to win permission from his parents, he can't marry either, but what he can do is send his father, through the offices of a judge, a registered letter setting forth the reasons why he intends to marry, and at the end of a reasonable time if he proves to the judge that his father did not respond to the letter, the court will grant him permission to marry. Again there's been the cooling-off period.

'There's one more way out. If at any time young José and Rosita, regardless of their age, can steal away and find some priest to marry them, they're legally wed—except that neither has a right to a share of the other's inherited property—and their parents can't do a damned thing about it except to organize a hunting party and go out and shoot the priest. It's rather impressive how many priests are willing to run this risk. The Church tends to favor early marriage, and if a couple are truly in love the priest can usually detect it, but on the other hand, they don't abuse the practice because they know that if the people of the countryside felt that they were going too far, the Church would suffer. Besides, the new law of April 24, 1958, has liberalized the system. It's still complicated, like much in Spain, but it works.'

Señor Ybarra asked if it was working in the case we had been discussing, and Don Luis said no.

Don Luis had come to the Coto by special invitation and for a particular purpose. The herds of deer about the Coto had grown so numerous that they were endangering the sanctuary's food supply, so a few huntsmen like Don Luis had been called in to kill off some of the bucks. 'Would you like to join me?' he asked, and we set off in a Land Rover at thirty miles an hour over the parched marismas. We passed about a hundred and fifty fallow deer but by now I had learned not to comment on them. However, Ybarra asked, 'Are you going to thin out the fallow deer?' but Don Luis said, 'I'd prefer not to bother with them.' Later I spotted a herd of at least a hundred red deer, but they were much too far away. Apparently they knew this, for they grazed quietly and took little notice of us except to look up now and then to stare across the cracked earth.

The sun was beginning to set and Don Luis said he was afraid we'd not be able to approach any of the herds in the time remaining, but very far in the distance I spotted a group of about forty red deer in good position, and we drove to within a quarter of a mile of them, then descended to try to creep up on them. When we had reached a point from which I could not yet be sure that the herd contained bucks, Don Luis said, 'This is about right.' I asked if he intended shooting from there, for the deer seemed to me to be almost two football fields away, and he said, 'Why not? Anyway, they won't let us get much closer.' As a matter of fact, the outlying watchers had already detected us and were alerting the herd, but as one handsome large buck stopped to sniff the air, Don Luis took careful aim and with one shot dropped him. Unable to believe that a hunter could be so accurate from such a distance, I stepped off the measurement, a yard a step, and it came to one hundred and seventy yards. The bullet had struck the deer in the head and death had been immediate.

I felt uneasy about sharing in the killing of an animal on a game preserve, even though I could see from the size of the herds that it was necessary, so I was gratified when we turned from deer to the inspection of the lakes to which the aquatic birds of the north were beginning to arrive. This brought me into the activity of the Coto and I saw the useful role it played in European conservancy.

The significance of the Coto is best expressed in what one of its directors told a Danish hunting club which had been solicited for funds and had been hesitant: 'Gentlemen, if the lakes of the Coto are allowed to disappear, within five years there will be no ducks in Denmark.' The money was forthcoming, and the same appeal had proved effective elsewhere in northern Europe. Consider merely the birds I watched while I was there.

From Denmark came the graylag goose; from England the robin; from Scotland the woodcock; from Sweden the mallard; from Siberia the widgeon; from Germany the starling; from Holland the avocet; and from France the stilt. From Africa and Asia, too, the traffic was considerable. From Ethiopia came the bee-eater; from north Africa the hoopoe; from south Africa the stork; from west Africa the egret; from central Africa the kite; from various parts the spoonbill; from the Sahara the ruddy shell duck; from the Congo the purple heron. Destroy the Coto, and the life patterns of these birds and hundreds of others which I did not personally see would be altered, perhaps with serious consequences.

To cross this apparently barren and remote area at night, with flashlights probing the low cover to spot the lynx or the fox or the silent herds of deer, is to see nature in one of its most impressive forms, because wherever you look you see evidence of wild things living in a precarious balance of water and grass and dune and tree. By some extraordinary accident these components are preserved here, in an area that man has not spoiled.

In a quiet pool in Las Marismas a European pochard rests on his flight north from Africa.

Next morning Señor Ybarra started introducing me to the nesting areas of the Coto, explaining the wildlife in Latin phrases which he later interpreted into English by means of Roger Tory Peterson's handbook. In his infectious lisp, highlighted by fascinating stories of bird behavior, he introduced me to several birds I had not known before and two for whom I developed a considerable affection. Before speaking of them I should like to relate some of the surprises Ybarra showed me.

Along the ground at the edges of the swamps, in trees and higher shrubs, we frequently saw a gray-brown bird with a camouflage that could only have been developed as a mask for the bird as it perched among leaves. The disguise was well-nigh perfect, and sometimes I would stare at a branch for some moments without realizing that the leaves I thought I saw consisted mainly of this bird. 'Observe its huge mouth,' Ybarra said. '*Caprimulgus europaeus*. Flies almost blind, with its big mouth open like a seine for trapping insects.' It was the nightjar, a bird peculiar to Europe and known popularly as the goatsucker because of the widespread belief that that is how it feeds.

He also showed me a splendid bird of the *Circus* family, a hen harrier we later decided it was, which flew like our hawks in graceful sweeps, its black wing tips and white under-feathers making it a fine sight in the sky. I grew fond of watching its swift movements and concluded, perhaps incorrectly, that it attained higher speeds than the hawks with which I was familiar.

I asked if the Coto had any peregrine falcons and after this was translated into Latin, *Falco peregrinus*, Ybarra said, 'One pair! Would you believe that on land which used to nest dozens of pairs, only one remains? The reason? Too many chemical poisons spread on the grounds where they used to feed. Also, the old castles in which they nested are being torn down or renovated. This rare bird is almost gone from this part of Spain.' I told him of seeing four pairs in the ruined castle at Sanlúcar, and he said, 'Yes, in a few of the old ruins you can still find them.'

In happier vein he told me of the bird-banding experiments carried on in the Coto. 'We banded thousands of little egrets. And what do you suppose? Two of them wound up in the Caribbean. One in Trinidad. One in Martinique. If we understand correctly, this is the first time in history that we can prove birds to have emigrated naturally from the Old World to the New over the full width of the open ocean. And do you know what those clever birds did? They followed the same course as Columbus. Who taught whom?'

At the lakes we had an exciting time watching hundreds of coots and purple gallinules; the latter were the more beautiful, with subdued colors that shone in the sun, but the coots were the more fun. They were a heavy, blackish, ducklike bird with snow-white beaks and white foreheads, and they obviously enjoyed the water, diving and splashing like a bunch of children. They were aware of our presence, and if we made an unexpected move, they would take off in large numbers, tiptoeing across the waves as if in secrecy but making a huge clatter with their wings; I was surprised at the distance they required to get airborne, some thirty times their length. After they had been aloft for a while and were satisfied that we were not going to harm them, they returned to the lake and landed like reluctant auks, their feet acting as brakes amid a noisy screeching. 'The best water birds we have,' Ybarra said. He preferred them to the showier ducks that would arrive later from Siberia.

The first of the two birds that captured my affection was the kestrel. '*Falco tinnunculus*,' Ybarra said. 'A true falcon but smaller than the ones you've seen in America.' It was a bird that was handsome in any posture. When perched on a tree at the edge of the marsh, it was a compact, medium-sized bird about a foot long with a fine reddish speckled body and a bluish head and tail. For some reason which I could not explain, it carried itself with a sense of confidence and was so common throughout the Coto that I had adequate opportunity to study it. All things considered, it was the most enticing bird I saw in Spain. In flight the kestrel is magnificent, swooping in large arcs through the sky or hovering almost motionless above some suspected quarry. Seen from below, its wing tips are delicately speckled, so that they reflect light coming up from the lakes, and its tail has a sharp, clean bar near the tip. It looks much like the land of Spain, but Señor Ybarra told me that it is equally at home in England, where it is highly regarded.

It was not surprising that I should have liked the kestrel, for it resembled the hawks which nested near my home in Pennsylvania, so that I was in a sense prepared for it, but if anyone had predicted that I would find my second choice in Las Marismas so appealing, I would have laughed at him. When I first saw this creature, for it was only with difficulty that I could accept it as a bird, it was standing in a meadow across which we had been riding in the Land Rover. It was enormous, with a wingspread when it waddled over the ground of about eight feet. From its clawlike feet to the top of its apparently bald head it would have measured another three feet. 'In English it's the griffon vulture,' Ybarra said. 'It flies up here from Africa, and without it Las Marismas couldn't exist. It's the scavenger that keeps us cleaned up.' When we moved in on the first griffon I had ever seen, we found that it was hacking away at a dead rabbit. Later we found a dead calf at which some thirty or forty were feeding. Ybarra said that sometimes as many as a hundred and fifty descend on the carcass of a steer, but I never saw that.

The griffons were so common in the Coto that I came to know them as friends, and the more I learned about them the more respect I had for them. They are a sandy brown, with a head that is always described as bald but which is covered with a silky down that wraps around to protect their face and neck as well. A circle of white feathers about the neck creates the impression of some drunken Velázquez noble in ruffs, for when they move on land, which they do constantly, they lurch and roll as if intoxicated. They are a noisy lot, quarreling, gouging at each other with hawklike beaks and pushing for the best position at the feast. Since their heads are much too small for their bodies, they look grotesque; they are awkward in all they do but possess a quality of stubborn endurance which makes them as interesting as any bird in the Coto and more useful than most. They serve an essential purpose, and if one dismisses them because they are ugly, as I used to do, he misses a major point of nature. They too are much like the land of Spain: awkward, formidable, sometimes repellent but always fascinating.

While Señor Ybarra was instructing me on birds, Don Luis was setting me right on a famous fable attached to the Coto. From various books on Goya, I had gleaned the information that he often visited the estate at Sanlúcar de Barrameda owned by the Duque de Alba and that while there had fallen in love with the duquesa, with whom he had gone to

Griffon vulture.

the Coto. Certainly in the Hispanic Society of New York there is a portrait of the duquesa standing near a lagoon which has been identified as one in the Coto, but it was two other supposed portraits that gave rise to legend, the notorious 'Maja desnuda' and the 'Maja vestida' (Flashy Woman Nude, and Dressed).

'Not a word of truth to the legend,' Don Luis protested. 'Both the previous Duque de Alba, who was ambassador to London, and his successor have presided over conferences of savants who have totally demolished that libel. Spanish historians have proved that the supposed love affair could not have taken place and art experts have demonstrated beyond question that the 'Maja' could not have been the duquesa. Three distinguished medical men, Blanco Soler, Piga Pascual and Pérez de Patinto, have proved in their book that she did not die from poisoning, as the legend claims. Please do what you can to silence this silly tale which has brought so much offense to one of Spain's noblest families.'

One afternoon Don Luis took me to the second floor, where a row of windows looked out upon the flat lands of Las Marismas, and said, 'At these windows King Felipe IV stood with his arquebus . . . Like the one his son carries in the painting by Velázquez . . . And while he stood here the peasants down below drove a herd of deer past the window and he blazed away. After several tries he bagged one.'

What interested me most among the many things Don Luis showed me was a long row of carefully framed photographs covering the years from about 1890 to 1931. Judging from the excellence of these shots, it was customary for hunting parties to bring along professional photographers, so that today the gallery of the palace contains an enviable visual record of those last days of monarchy. Duques, condes, famous bullfighters and occasionally some burgeoning industrial magnate fill the photographs, dressed in costly hunting clothes from London and driving even more expensive automobiles from Paris, but the unquestioned hero of the series is a tall, slim, impeccably dressed man with aquiline nose, long mustaches and imperial bearing. He is King Alfonso XIII, last of the Borbón rulers and probably the most regal and handsome king of this century.

He was a vapid young man interested only in hunting. It is doubtful if he ever read a whole book, and when he was required by custom to visit a university it was understood that no professors or students with serious interests would bother him; a few noble youths experienced in hunting were to surround him so that he could speak of things he understood. The handsome photographs at the palace prove that in the hunt, at least, he was expert and that his love for the outdoors was both sincere and inexhaustible.

One of the pictures I liked best showed him in a suit which only a king would be brave enough to wear: the background cloth was a quiet gray, beautifully cut to fit his austere build, but into it was woven a series of huge brown diamonds five inches tall, their points standing vertically. At first sight the king looks like an advertisement, but as one sees him in various poses and in the company of others, one realizes that he selected this suit on purpose, for when it appeared in a crowd, its wearer stood out as majesty.

After I had seen a score of the Alfonso photographs—he must have been a frequent visitor to the Coto—I began to realize that my guide, Don Luis, must have come from a family that knew the king personally, for he spoke of details which otherwise he could not have known: 'It is these three portraits which have the deepest meaning. Here is Alfonso in the last days of his reign. He's more serious now. His troubles have begun and it's sad to think that soon after this was taken he deemed it prudent to leave Spain, to which he never returned. He loved the Coto and during his exile he must have longed for it. Here's a fine photograph of his family taken in Madrid a few years before his departure. His English queen . . . She was a granddaughter of Queen Victoria . . . A splendid woman and very loyal to him. This is the oldest son, Don Jaime, who would have made a fine king except that he was removed from the succession because he was a deaf-mute. This is Don Alfonso, the unfortunate son who married a Cuban commoner and died in an automobile crash in Miami in 1938. This is Don Gonzalo, the youngest son, who also died in an auto crash.' He pointed out the children one by one, ending with a handsome young man. 'And this is Don Juan de Borbón, who now lives in Estoril, near Lisboa in Portugal.' He said no more and I was unable to ascertain his opinion of Juan; it would have been improper for him to express one, because Juan, as the legal heir of Alfonso XIII, who died in 1941, ought to become King of Spain when Generalísimo Franco goes, except that powerful forces, including Franco, prefer that Juan's son, Prince Juan Carlos, take the throne. There could be trouble between father and son, and prudent Spaniards are reluctant to tell foreigners whose side they support. Pointing to the last of the three photographs, Don Luis said, 'And this is Don Juan by himself . . . photographed in Portugal, where he lives in exile.' He was an attractive fellow and others in Spain told me that he would make a fine king, but what Don Luis thought of the matter, I was not to discover.

Wherever I turned among the photographs I found some aspect of Spanish history which attracted my interest. Here was the dictator Primo de Rivera standing over a wild boar which he had just killed with a lance. Over here was the Conde de Tarifa, who once owned the Coto, at the wheel of the Citroën swamp wagon he had bought for the use of Alfonso. This handsome woman was the Duquesa de Medinaceli, from one of the noblest families in Spain, standing with the man she had invited to the Coto, the famous matador Rafael Guerra, called Guerrita; the photograph must have been taken around 1910, when Guerrita was in retirement. This solemn-looking man was the Duque de Cádiz as he appeared in 1908; of his home city in that year it was said, 'It has three hundred and sixty-six churches and no library.' In 1966 a resident told me, 'Today things are better. We have three hundred and sixty-five churches and one library. But mostly it's closed.' In this corner is Alfonso, clean-shaven and just as good-looking that way as with his Kaiser-like mustaches; but the photograph which lives in my mind showed him ready for the hunt, a dashing king with enormous mustaches and a rifle cradled in his arm. He wore heavy peasant trousers with pronounced vertical stripes, English leather boots, and over all zahones, which formed a heavy leather apron divided down the middle and tied securely about each leg. He was an archaic figure, best suited to the seventeenth century; how admirable a subject he would have been for the brush of Velázquez. The camera barely does him justice.

I am constantly fascinated by this empty-headed, charming fellow, because there is a strong possibility that he was a part-American whose name should have been Alfonso McKeon. Clearly he was the son of King Alfonso XII and Queen María Cristina of Austria; no one questioned that, but who Alfonso XII might have been was another matter. He was the son of Spain's notorious Queen Isabel II, probably the most lecherous crowned head ever to rule in Europe, man or woman; if she is in second place it is only to Catherine the Great of Russia, and this I doubt. Obligated by dynastic reasons to marry her cousin, impotent and a homosexual, she said of him, 'What can I report of a man who on his wedding night wore more lace than I?'

Since she and her impotent consort had numerous children, of whom five lived to become fine persons, each birth became the occasion for a good deal of open speculation as to who the father might have been, and since Isabel took a bewildering series of lovers in rapid succession, the guessing sometimes became confused. The father of her first child could have been any one of four: a general, an opera singer (tenor), a marqués or a young colonel in the army. This child died. Who the father of her second baby was no one cared to state, for this time there were six putative fathers, but the little girl, who lived to become one of Spain's gentlest and noblest ladies, beloved by everyone, was generally known as Arañuela, after her mother's prominent lover at the time, an ordinary soldier named Araña.

The next child, who also died, was attributed to either Obregón the singer, Arrieta the composer, Puig-Moltó the soldier or an unspecified marqués. Regarding the parentage of her later children the guesses were fantastic, for preceding their births Isabel had what might be termed a catch-as-catch-can series of lovers from all ranks of society, although she always maintained a preference for musicians and soldiers. What concerns history is the parentage of her first surviving male child, the boy who later became King Alfonso XII. Prior to his birth the queen's favorite had been the soldier Puig-Moltó, who enjoyed a longer stay at the palace than most, but there is reason to believe that he could not have been in attendance when the child was conceived; he was absent on maneuvers. The honor of siring the future king probably went to an itinerant American dentist named McKeon, who, the gossips said, 'did a lot more at the palace than fill teeth.' For more than a year he was the royal favorite and this during the time when the future king was conceived. The extraordinary fact about Isabel's children is that regardless of who their fathers were, each looked a true Borbón, while Alfonso XII and his son Alfonso XIII actually had Habsburg chins!

When Don Luis and I finished our tour of the portrait galleries, Señor Ybarra suggested that we go out to see a remarkable oak tree. I replied that in America we had oaks of all kinds and there were further photographs on another floor that I wished to see, but Ybarra said, 'Oak trees you may have, but none like this.' So I went with him to a part of the Coto I had not seen before, and in the distance I saw a large oak whose branches and trunk were almost completely white. As we approached, I saw that it contained many nests, each about the size of a small table, built of hundreds of fairly good-sized sticks laid crossways like the nest of an eagle.

'How many nests would you say?' Ybarra asked.

There were clearly more than a score, and when I started to count only those on one branch I saw that the total must be over a hundred. 'About three hundred and fifty,' he said.

'Eagles?'

'No. One of the most beautiful birds to nest in Europe. The *Platalea leucorodia*, spoonbill.' In fact, so many spoonbills nested in this particular oak that their droppings, made acid by the fish they ate, had not only colored the tree white but were also causing its death. The one thing that might operate against the Coto's continuance as a sanctuary, for certain kinds of birds at least, was the constant killing off of the bigger trees by the birds themselves.

'We don't know what to do about it,' Ybarra said. 'We're especially concerned about the spoonbills, because they began to come here only in 1959. Two pair appeared that year and apparently enjoyed their experience, because just as a satisfied customer at a summer resort spreads the news, they told their friends and next year we counted two hundred and fifty-five pairs. I wouldn't like to guess how many we have now. Twenty or thirty large oaks like this one, each with hundreds of nests. They're about the loveliest bird we get, spectacularly beautiful.'

The spoonbill reminded me of another bird, and I asked whether the Coto attracted any flamingos, who have been known to breed in Europe, and a knowing smile came over Ybarra's lips. 'Do you really like birds?' he asked; and when I nodded, he said, 'It's not generally known even yet, but some years ago in a series of pools leading off from the Rhone in southern France a large colony of flamingos bred for about twenty years. Of course, naturalists heard about it right away. A sensation in bird circles. But we kept it a secret among ourselves. Perhaps two hundred men in eight or ten different countries. Because if the general public knew, they would swarm to watch the birds, and inevitably some damn fool would shoot them. He wouldn't be able to help himself. So we kept it a secret and in due course the flamingos left their French lagoons.'

He hesitated for a moment, and I suggested, 'And they came down here to the Coto?'

'Yes, but not to breed. However, they do come to ————,' and he mentioned an area not far from the Coto where a substantial colony of perhaps the world's loveliest bird, certainly its most dramatic, had been breeding for several years with an apparent prospect of continuing for many more. Experts in London and Paris and Stockholm know about this phenomenon and it is watched with care, because many of the flamingos' normal breeding places in Africa are being destroyed, so that within a hundred years perhaps the African flamingo may cease to exist, as may other rare species that now use the Coto as a breeding ground.

'All sensible men, who cherish the world as it has been,' said Ybarra, 'are engaged, whether they wish to be or not, in a crusade to keep whole species from being exterminated. If our human population continues to explode at its present rate, and I see no reason to suspect that the rate will diminish, the pressure on open land like the Coto will become unbearable. In our lifetime we'll see it.'

'It's begun,' Don Luis told us at dinner one evening. 'In Madrid there is much agitation, even among men who love the outdoors, to dam off the overflow waters of the Guadalquivir and drain the swamps of Las Marismas. It could be done with relatively little effort, and all the land Michener has seen north of here could be converted into rice fields and wheat.'

'Why do that?' I asked. 'Spain's got ample food.'

'The phrase is "social necessity." Spain wants entrance to the European Common Market, but as long as we must be classified as a backward country economically, it is not attractive to the other countries to admit us as an equal partner. If we reclaim our marshes and increase our food supply, then we stand in quite a different light and the other nations may want us. We may have to drain the marshes.'

Don Luis was speaking as if he were attached to the government, and I started to ask what job he held in Madrid, but talk turned to other matters and Ybarra said, 'The irony of the situation, and its danger, is that the Coto Doñana is viable as a truly great sanctuary only so long as Las Marismas exists out there. Because then our birds have a substantial feeding area and the millions of birds that live off Las Marismas form a kind of biological unit with the ones in the Coto. Destroy Las Marismas, and you destroy at least half our effectiveness.'

'But doesn't the Coto already control a good deal of Las Marismas?'

'A common misunderstanding. We own so little that you'd hardly believe it. Considering our entire area . . . dunes, lakes, dry land . . . we have only seventeen thousand acres altogether. And of that, only about five hundred acres are marismas . . . and not the best. You see, in the old days Las Marismas was so enormous, so useless, that everyone said, "It'll always be there. For the Coto we'll buy only the good land." So now we have good land and almost no marismas. And suddenly, with the prospect of draining the swamps, Las Marismas has become very valuable, far beyond our means to acquire it. Within five years, if men worked energetically with bulldozers and dams, they could make Las Marismas disappear.'

I left this gloomy talk and walked out beneath the eucalyptus trees. Bartolo, the tame deer, ran up to nuzzle me, accompanied by his nanny goat, and in the shadowy distance I could see the forms of fifty or sixty wild deer that always moved in close at night. Beyond lay the flat lands of Las Marismas in whose depths the camels wandered still free and birds nested without number. As far as I could see there was only flatness and the slowly returning waters that would soon make of the area an enormous lake a few millimeters deep in which substantial rivers would mysteriously form and islands where the fighting bulls would congregate and rabbits and foxes and the endless herds of deer. It was an area that I had seen in all seasons, whose dreamlike transmutations I had followed from north and east and south. In its heart and along its perimeter I had organized a dozen picnics so that I might know it more intimately; I had seen it from Sevilla and from across the river at Sanlúcar, that grubby little town I loved so well. Instructed by Las Marismas, I had come to know birds that I would otherwise have missed, the gape-mouth nightjar winging past to trap insects, the clean and fiery kestrel, the spoonbill and the vulture, that handsome and repulsive thing. Was it possible that within my lifetime this concentration of natural wonder was doomed? I could not believe it, and yet on the previous day while roaring across the hard-baked marismas I had seen a ridge of earth, a rather simple one about six feet high that a bulldozer had thrown up with no great effort, and after we had followed it for some miles I asked, 'What's the ridge?'

'It's an experiment,' Ybarra said. 'To see how difficult it would be to prevent water from coming into Las Marismas.'

'Does it work?'

'When they seal off the other end, over by El Rocío, they'll have dried out about twenty thousand acres.'

The land of Spain! For the last three thousand years it has been a challenge and on its relentless bosom men have made one ghastly mistake after another, as the moribund village of Maranchón demonstrates, but within the last decade there have been signs of hope. In the barren reaches of Extremadura, where flood waters used to rage three years in ten, and in many other parts of the country, large earthen dams are being constructed which will irrigate once-useless fields and bring them into productivity. In the mountains hydroelectric systems are proliferating at a surprising rate. Perhaps Las Marismas will have to be drained, out of deference to opinions in Paris and Berlin, but there is a possibility that it can be done leaving strips or areas where the old conditions can continue. Knowing the greediness of men, and especially the greediness of Spaniards, I doubt that any of Las Marismas can be saved and I would expect it to have vanished by 1985. The Coto Doñana, because it has fallen into careful hands, has a chance to continue, but only if its custodians are vigorously supported by those who love nature and appreciate its subtle influence on man. However, if Las Marismas vanishes, many of the birds who now use the Coto will no longer have reason to do so; perhaps even the vultures will stop coming when animals no longer die on the flat lands, but I suppose the Coto lakes, filled with rich animalcules, will still attract the ducks.

To have seen Las Marismas and the Coto while they were still at their peak was to have seen the best that Spain can offer the naturalist. For the immediate future these areas will continue to be available for those to whom ecology is at least as sacred as eschatology.

FOLLOWING PAGE:
Sculptor's studio in Sevilla.

VI

SEVILLA

OCEANO
ATLANTICO

MILES
0   100

Barcelona •

Madrid •

Lisboa •

• Almendralejo

• Córdoba

• Jaén

Huelva •

• Sevilla

• Granada

Jerez de la
Frontera

Almería •

• Málaga

• Cádiz

MAR MEDITERRANEO

One of the top experiences a traveler can have in Spain is to visit Sevilla for Holy Week, which ends at Easter, and the feria that follows. I suppose there is nothing in the world to surpass this, not Mardi Gras at New Orleans nor the Palio in Siena when the exuberance of the Renaissance is re-created. Carnival in Rio de Janeiro is an epic of noise and color, and for sheer celebration it would be hard to equal Bastille Day in Tahiti, when the island goes mad for two weeks; but these events lack spiritual depth.

In Sevilla each spring one finds combined within the span of a few weeks six major diversions: the world's most profound religious spectacle plus a rustic fair recalling those of a thousand years ago, plus a congregation of circuses drawn from all parts of Europe, plus a bizarre open-air carnival, plus a daily program of social events and stunning promenades on horseback, plus a series of first-rate bullfights conducted in Spain's most beautiful plaza. And these six features are encapsulated, as it were, within the confines of an ancient city studded with handsome buildings, narrow streets where only pedestrians are allowed and exquisite vistas along riverbanks. At any time of year Sevilla is a distinguished city, but during Holy Week and the days that follow, it is without peer.

I have attended several of Sevilla's spring celebrations, and when I try to recall the essence of what I saw I picture myself standing at four o'clock in the morning at the entrance to the tobacco factory where Carmen spun her smoky web to entangle a soldier. I am in a very old city and it is dark, for winter has only just ended and the early rising sun has not yet returned, but along the horizon to the south a dull glow is visible, as if fields were being burned off before the planting.

No prudent farmer accounts for those fires. In a tree-lined park on the edge of the city, Sevilla is holding revelry and the lights will continue until dawn and for half a dozen dawns to follow, and if one listens closely he can hear, coming to him over the intervening space, the muffled sound of carnival and circus, of promenade and castanets.

But it is neither this beautiful glow on the horizon that I remember as the characteristic of Sevilla when I am away from the city nor the sound of the revelry. It is the shadowy approach of figures looming out of the dusk as they wander past the tobacco factory on their way home from the festival. They come like ghosts of ancient Spain, from Roman times or Visigothic or Arabic or medieval Christian, moving in stately silence until some member of the group begins softly to clap his hands. And it is then that the sound of Sevilla, the sweet memorable sound of this most dramatic of the Spanish cities, overtakes me.

The hands I hear do not clap as they would at a football game nor even at a flamenco party. They tap in a seductive night rhythm, with variations which a person reared in Massachusetts or Stockholm could not devise. They tap out the beat of some old song, well known to all in the crowd, and before long a woman walking through the night adds her staccato. Others follow, and soon one has along the broad street before Carmen's tobacco factory a dozen or so persons clapping out this strange rhythm.

No one sings. No one chants the words of the mute song. There is only the soft clapping of some dozen pairs of unseen hands, but I get the impression that the participants are softly repeating the words to themselves as they pass me by. No one speaks, and when the group has gone the sound of clapping hangs in the night air for a long time as the revelers proceed to some point near the cathedral, or in back of the bullring, or at the beginning of the narrow street called Sierpes (serpents), where they break apart, each member going to his own home to sleep for a few hours before the next day begins.

But before the first group has reached the point of separation, other groups have come along the lovely dark street, which in the growing twilight looks much as it did in the days of Carmen, and they too clap softly in the night. And for more than a week, for almost twenty-four hours each day, the visitor to Sevilla will hear this compelling tattoo. It is the sound of Sevilla in spring, one of the most persuasive sounds I have ever heard.

To savor the six-part spectacle you must set aside several weeks and plan to arrive before Palm Sunday. Depending upon the date of Easter, the six parts can cover from three to five weeks. Some travelers skip the first three and arrive only in time for the final crescendo, but this is a miscalculation which robs them of the spiritual preparation necessary for the full enjoyment of the spectacle. It is like listening to only the fourth movement of Beethoven's Ninth Symphony, since that is where the human voices appear, and missing the preparation which Beethoven has laid out in the preceding three movements, when only the orchestra is playing.

For the heart of Sevilla's spring celebration is a religious experience, and it throbs through the city for an entire week. Beginning with Palm Sunday an atmosphere of sanctity settles over the towers and the alleys of Sevilla, permeating every crevice of the city, and so it will continue for the seven days which recall the passion and death of Jesus. Bells start tolling from dozens of steeples scattered through the city. Even across the river, in the gypsy quarter of Triana, ordinary noises stop. Citizens dress in their best black clothes, men and women alike, and at selected parishes scattered through Sevilla two radically different types of men begin to assemble at church doors: the religious men and the laboring men. Spectators, who may number in the thousands, gather in the streets outside the churches to watch these men, for they are about to become the most important in Sevilla. Let us follow one man from each group.

Don Francisco Mendoza Ruiz is a cautious man who works in a bank and lives with his wife and three children in a fine little house in the old Jewish quarter, where no automobiles are allowed. After church on Palm Sunday he invites us to accompany him home, where he takes down from a closet a set of boxes from which he unpacks a costume that looks as if it had come from the Middle Ages.

'Heretics condemned by the Inquisition used to wear costumes like this,' he says. After stripping down to shirt and trousers he massages his feet prior to putting on a pair of heavy-soled black shoes. 'I shall be walking, walking,' he says. Then he puts on a tunic which covers everything from neck to shoe tip. Each parish church will have for its members a distinctive color. Don Francisco's is purple, and over it he throws a white cape which reaches to his knees. About his waist he ties a sash eight inches wide made of an expensive damask and allows its ends to fall free.

'Now comes the good part,' he says as he takes from a long, thin box a stiffened purple hood about three feet tall with a tip at one end and a broad cape at the other. There are two very small slits for his eyes, and when Don Francisco puts on the hood, pulling the cape end far down over his shoulders, he transforms himself into a mysterious figure with only his eyes showing.

'To you norteamericanos,' he says apologetically, 'I must look like a member of your Ku Klux Klan.' He is right. During Holy Week whenever members of the confraternity (in Spanish cofradía) assemble they will look like a bunch of Kluxers on the rampage through some bayou village. 'Thus do rascals appropriate the robes of the just and contaminate them,' Don Francisco says, and again he is right, for the Ku Klux Klan did borrow its costume from the religious procession of Sevilla. Señor Mendoza next takes a six-foot candle, which he bought a few days ago, and stands with it at an angle to his hip. 'I am now a member of the confraternity, ready to march.' There are fifty-two confraternities in Sevilla, each connected with a parish church. Like a lodge or brotherhood they meet throughout the year to collect funds for their church and particularly to arrange for the processions of Holy Week.

As the sun sets, Don Francisco says, 'It's time for the church,' and as we pick our way through the crowd we recognize other men dressed in his colors: purple tunic, white cape, purple hood; but we also see a few who wear different colors, and they are on their way to join up with some other confraternity. At the church there is much confusion. Outside, a huge crowd has gathered to watch the beginning of this first procession, which will be followed by others for each of the next seven days; inside, the two floats sponsored by this church are being given their final inspection. They are strange and wonderful things, each twenty feet long by nine feet wide by fifteen feet tall, and the route they will follow through the city streets was laid out more than a century ago and will require twelve hours to complete. The float to the left shows Christ at the Crucifixion surrounded by Roman guards, and it will go out first. The float to the right, and much the more important of the two, contains the Virgin Mary in glory. She is life-size and every effort has been taken to make her seem alive. Her eyebrows are made of real hair; her cheeks are delicately rouged; six glass tears run down her cheek; her hands are manicured; she wears a wealth of jewelry.

'Oh, darling Virgin!' people cry when she appears.

'Sweetest Virgin, if you're real, toss me some of those jewels.'

'My Virgin! My Virgin! You make the other Virgins of Sevilla look like a bunch of putas [whores].'

She is greeted as a living person, a blend of queen and popular singer. 'I throw you a kiss, lovely one,' a man shouts.

Don Francisco, beneath his mask, does not participate in this frivolity, for he takes religion gravely. It is, he says, the most important aspect of his life. 'I serve in the confraternity,' he explains, 'because I am convinced that a good Spaniard must give part of his life to the Church and all of his devotion to the Virgin. For me the year comes to a head with Holy Week, and this year is special.' In a few moments we shall see why, but as the day ends let us move to an old river-front warehouse to meet our second man.

He is José (Pepe) Gómez, a tattooed stevedore, twenty-nine years old, and he too is about to march in the procession, but the religious ideas expressed by Don Francisco Mendoza are alien to him. 'I leave church to the priests. My father was a Communist and during the Civil War he was shot.' We ask him why then is he marching in the procession, and he says, 'Because I get paid. And because my Virgin is the best damned Virgin in Sevilla.' His actual words are more profane than that, but they reinforce a

Holy Week.

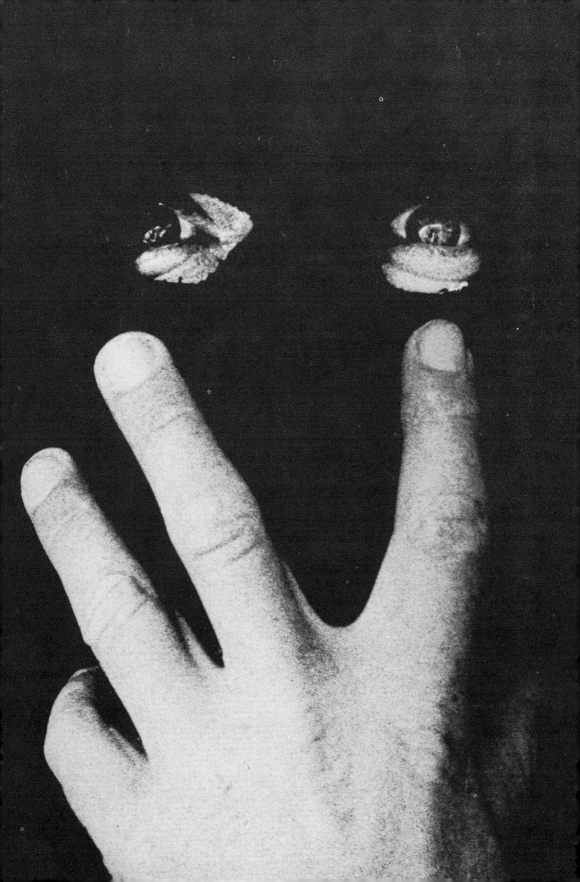

basic fact about the Holy Week processions. To many of the marchers the carved Virgins and Christs are real people: the Virgin of this parish who has looked out for her people for the past century, the particular Christ who loves the children of this parish.

Pepe Gómez dresses in the only suit he owns, a pair of white trousers and a torn shirt. He wears no socks but does have a pair of new rope sandals, supplied by Don Francisco's confraternity. He also has a canvas bag about the size of a pillowcase, and this he partly fills with a mixture of sand and sawdust, placing it on his head in such a way that the sand falls to the end of the bag that is over his shoulders. A fellow stevedore hammers the bag to see whether it is taking up the shock, and Pepe says, 'Good. Let's go.'

We leave the waterfront and walk through the narrow streets to the church where Don Francisco and his confraternity have assembled about the float of the Virgin. When Gómez appears, along with thirty-five other laborers similarly dressed and with bags of sand and sawdust resting on their heads, the treasurer of the confraternity pays each worker one dollar and ten cents, whereupon the stevedores prepare to crawl under the float, which has been built upon a large table with legs that keep it about four feet off the ground when it is rested. The space between the float and the ground is masked by a heavy brocade skirt which will hide the feet of thirty-six stevedores below. Thus, when the workmen march, the float will seem to move by itself and the men inside will do their work in sweaty darkness, turning the float only as a captain directs from outside.

A float may weigh as much as half a ton, so that the task of bearing it through the streets for twelve hours is not a light one. A few extra stevedores go along to provide occasional relief; also, during the twelve-hour march the float may be stopped by a traffic jam or by reaching an intersection when another float is passing in a different direction. When such things happen the stevedores lower the float and scramble out for air, and one of the amusing sights of Holy Week is that of a beautiful Virgin Mary temporarily deserted by her bearers, who have ducked into a bar where someone is standing drinks.

When they do move, the floats sway gently from side to side, giving the wooden figures a kind of poetic life. A float never seems static. Along the course, which winds in and out through all parts of the city, each float having its own route, which does not necessarily follow that of any other, citizens note with approval any new statues or repainting introduced during the past twelve months. I once heard a man remark to his wife as the float of his church went by, 'I think our new head of Jesus is the best in Sevilla.'

Pepe Gómez and his fellow stevedores now pull up the brocaded skirt and crawl into position beneath the float. Adjusting their bags over their heads and about their shoulders, they test the weight and try to find

269

Pepe Gómez.

positions which will be comfortable. Outside, the captain waits for a signal from the priest, then slaps the corner smartly.

'One.' The unseen stevedores brace their heads and shoulders against the floor of the float.

'Two.' They rise to a standing position, and the Virgin seems to ascend of her own accord.

'Three.' The stevedores move slowly forward and the first float for the Holy Week parade is under way. From balconies people cry ecstatically, 'Oh, sweet Virgin. Come back to us, you little beauty.'

It is incredible with what skill the stevedores move this huge float. At the doorway there is a clearance of about four inches, and as the Virgin moves through narrow streets there will be many points where encroaching buildings seem to make progress impossible, but through obedience to signals the men move their burden an inch at a time and rarely scrape a doorjamb or a wall.

The hooded members of the confraternity, their long tapers held at an angle from their hips, fall in line before the float as if to give it protection, but Don Francisco is not among them. He told us earlier that for him this year was to be special, and now he sits on a chair in his church and takes off his shoes. From beneath his hood he says, 'In February I faced a crisis at the bank. It could have been disastrous. But I prayed to the Virgin and she rescued me. I told her, "Save me and I will do penance." It was a promise.' When he is barefooted he lashes chains about his ankles and the heavy links drag behind him for six or eight feet. He lays aside his candle to take up a heavy, full-sized wooden cross. Then he rises and steps into the street, where his chains jangle on the cobblestones. He is prepared to drag his cross through the streets of Sevilla as Jesus dragged his through the alleys of Jerusalem. 'Blessed Virgin,' he mutters with intense devotion, 'accept my penance.' For twelve hours he will march barefoot with half a dozen others who have made similar vows to this Virgin. The confraternity does not appoint these men to their task; they are volunteers who feel that some aspect of their lives requires atonement, and the punishment to which they submit themselves is not light.

I followed Don Francisco most of the twelve hours, and it was morning before the Virgin returned to her church, where at least two thousand people waited to watch her come home. As long as the Virgin was in the plaza before the church their cries of welcome were such as a man might give his betrothed on her return home, but when she entered the portals, inch by inch, the greetings were those of children to their mother. Thus the Spanish Virgins fill a dual role.

'Jesucristo, that was a hard night,' Pope Gómez admits as he crawls out from under. Tomorrow he will carry a float from another church, and so on throughout the seven days.

Don Francisco's words are quite different. As he lays aside his cross and unbinds his chains, he says with his mask off, 'I feel that the Virgin was very close to Sevilla this day. I could sense her nodding as she accepted my penance.'

Each day from Palm Sunday through the Saturday before Easter this procession will be duplicated, but Don Francisco's confraternity will not march again, for Sevilla has many parish churches and the days must be parceled out among them. In 1967 the processions were as follows:

Day	Confra- ternities	Mary Floats	Jesus Floats	Mary and Jesus Floats
Sunday	7	7	8	1
Monday	8	6	6	1
Tuesday	7	6	8	0
Wednesday	7	6	4	3
Thursday	7	6	7	1
Friday morning	6	6	6	0
Friday evening	7	5	4	3
Saturday	3	3	2	1
Total	52	45	45	10

Some of these hundred floats leave their little churches at one in the morning to march all night and stagger home at noon. Others go out at dawn and wander through the streets till sunset, but on Good Friday two sets of confraternities go out, one early and one late, and it was to one of these that Don Francisco took us at four in the afternoon to watch the departure of a float showing Jesus and the Roman soldiers whose parade would mark those solemn evening hours when Christ died of his Crucifixion.

'Marching barefoot with the Virgin is an honor that no man . . .' Don Francisco says as he watches the Friday parade. He stops. He is in his late forties and is an important businessman in the city, hefty, dark-haired, amiable. He wants to explain what Holy Week means to him but is afraid a Protestant would not understand. 'It's an honor,' he says quietly, 'but to march with one of the Jesus floats on Good Friday . . . You'll understand when you hear the tremendous silence. Señor Michener, when this float comes through Sierpes, Jesus Christ himself is in that street.'

The Jesus float is much different from the one that Don Francisco attended, for in the latter the Virgin sat in awe-inspiring splendor with a hundred and fifty tall candles as the major piece of decoration. The Jesus float, on the other hand, is a tableau centering upon a life-sized figure of Christ on the cross, each element of his agony depicted in minute detail. Beads of sweat stand on his forehead. Ruby drops of blood run down his side where the spear has pierced him. His feet are turning blue from the nail, and his crown of thorns brings blood. This particular statue was carved some ninety years ago to replace one that came originally from The Netherlands. It is accompanied at the four corners of the float by life-sized imperial Roman guards in resplendent uniform. Each carries one of the implements of the Crucifixion and they form a terrifying and brutal group. Similar Roman soldiers will appear on many of the floats and one of the greatest Virgins will be preceded by a marching company of live men dressed as Roman legionnaires. If the rest of the world has sometimes been perplexed as to who was responsible for the death of Jesus, some blaming Jews, others Romans, the confraternities of Sevilla are not confused. Their statues show Romans in the act of villainy.

In addition to Jesus and the four soldiers, our float contains about a dozen additional figures, some large, some small, and over the years whenever a given statue has worn out or been damaged, it has been replaced by a new one. Or if a tradesman of the parish prospered he might one day announce, 'I will give a new Roman soldier to the confraternity.' Thus, of the figures on our float, all might be of different age, yet all combine to present a harmonious picture of Christ in his last hours.

The oldest figures on the hundred floats date back to the seventeenth century. In the intervening years well-known sculptors carved figures which gradually supplanted originals, and in the nineteenth century there was a general refurbishing, at which time the emphasis was on strict fidelity to the living figure. It was then that the glass teardrops and the specks of ruby blood became common. The twentieth century has been the age of adornment and most of the ultra-luxurious costumes date from this period.

The most extraordinary, and by far the best loved, are those like the one we saw first which simply present the Virgin Mary throned in glory, dressed in gorgeous robes and with a crown of silver and gold encrusted with hundreds of precious stones. Of the forty-five floats presenting Virgins alone, two are preeminent and the subject of such veneration that even the most casual observer must reflect on the fact that Holy Week, which commemorates Christ's passion and death, has become in Spain a celebration in which he plays a secondary role, with his mother becoming the central figure. The first is La Esperanza, the Virgin of Hope, from the gypsy quarter of Triana across the river. She became famous as the patron Virgin of the bullfighter Juan Belmonte and remains the focus of much popular affection. The second is La Macarena, named after an Arabian princess, and she was preferred by another great matador, Joselito, and to see her leave her parish church of San Gil at one in the morning of Good Friday or return later in the day is held by many Sevillanos to be the most important thing that can happen during Holy Week.

Late at night one Holy Thursday I went to watch La Macarena leave her small white church, and an hour before the time of her departure all

Roman soldiers preparing
for the execution of Christ.

streets were jammed. Not far from the church, devotees of this Virgin have built a permanent arch of triumph, a delightful little stucco affair with seven Moorish towers, the only one of its kind in Sevilla. I was standing in a throng near this arch when the float left the church, and it seemed miraculous that the stevedores behind the curtain could maneuver this immense structure so delicately through the doors.

The float was in some ways the most ornate I had seen, with a baldacchino of gold and an edging of silver; but it was also the simplest, for it contained only the Virgin clad in white dress, green and gold cape and red sash, and wearing a corona featuring sixteen silver stars and a diamond cross. She was a majestic figure, with tears on her cheeks and a pearl necklace wrapped about her left hand. In place of the subsidiary figures that accompanied most floats stood several score of tall wax tapers, and she was preceded by a confraternity dressed in white satin robes and emerald hoods. Like the other great Virgins of Sevilla, she carried no child.

When she appeared the crowd reacted with joy, bestowing upon her a love which has no counterpart in other countries. It required about forty minutes for her to inch her way from the church and through the arch, even though they stood only a few yards apart. The crowd would not give way; everyone wanted to stand as close to the wonderful Virgin as possible, and we were behind schedule when we finally set out through the darkened streets for the traditional passage of La Macarena.

After proceeding by herself for some hours, La Macarena, like all the other floats that were out at this time, began heading for the center of the city, and by the time the sun rose, they had coalesced into a long official procession that would pass before the town hall and end at the cathedral. At no time during this preliminary activity was any float unattended. Its approach was heralded by two or three men carrying wooden staves from which dangled iron rings. When the staves were pounded down against the paving of the street, a harsh jangling sound warned beholders to draw back. Some sort of band accompanied the float, beating out a somber half-step which had the effect of a funeral march. Then came the confraternity followed by the float, which during the night was illuminated by flares. Finally there were the penitents, marching barefoot over the stones with their burdens of chain and cross. It is this whole unit that creates the noble impression, forcing the observer to reconsider any prior judgments of religion.

In reviewing mine I was confused by three extraneous elements that helped make up the parade. First, each float was escorted by a company of soldiers in full military regalia including loaded rifles, and they marched with such solemn ferocity and proprietary interest that no one could ignore the fact that in Spain the principal job of the army was to defend the Church; this had been its preoccupation from the time of its war against the Moors and apparently it would always be. That is why on the left wall of the shrine of La Macarena stands the tombstone of General Gonzalo Queipo de Llano y Sierra (1875–1951) with the ominous date '18 July 1936,' which was when he exercised the brutalities that earned him the title among Republicans of 'The Butcher of Andalucía,' and among Franco men of 'The Savior of Sevilla.' I spoke to a Spaniard about this and was told, 'Why not? Queipo de Llano saved the Church in Andalucía. In the old days we'd have made him a saint. Now we have to be content with his tomb beside our Virgin.' If the parades of Holy Week were religious processions, they were also military ones, and one day Don Francisco said to me, 'We Spaniards cannot understand that strange thing that happened in the United States army. One of your artillery colonels devised a banner and a slogan for his gunners, "For God, for country and for Santa Bárbara." But atheists protested and your government made him stop. Everyone knows that Santa Bárbara is the patron saint of bombardiers.' I tried to explain that in the United States we subscribed to a separation of Church and state and to us it was offensive to confuse an artillery unit and a female saint, to which he replied, 'You must indeed be confused. If Santa Bárbara watches over your gunners in battle, why not admit it?'

Second, at frequent intervals units of the Guardia Civil appeared in full uniform and heavily armed. They stared with what I thought at the time was a menacing gaze, but which I suppose was only an impassivity, at the spectators, as if daring them to make any move against the Church. If the Holy Week procession was partly a military manifestation, it was also a police function, for the two elements were never far separated.

Third, when the parade had formed and it was time to march through the center of the city, political leaders of the community slipped into position, some as penitents lugging crosses, some as members of the confraternity but with their faces exposed, and some as honored marchers in morning coats and top hats; it was clear that no politician could hold office in Sevilla who did not conform to the observances of the Church. The presence of these officials was made conspicuous; they were preceded by bishops and soldiers and bands and guardia; they were accompanied by hushed and approving whispers from the crowd; they were clothed in a kind of extraterrestrial glory and formed as significant a part of the parade as any of the floats, the capstone, as it were, of the religious-military-police-political edifice that was Spain.

Of course, some years later I witnessed exactly the same kind of exhibitionism in New York City when I watched the St. Patrick's Day parade along Fifth Avenue and saw that any Jewish politician who hoped for favor with the Irish electorate had better put in an appearance on that day. A few years after that, when I was myself running for Congress in a different part of America, my advisors warned me, 'There is one thing a politician must do. March in the St. Patrick's Day parade or else.' I was as warmly received in my community as were the Sevilla politicians during their obligatory parade. In Sevilla it was only the appearances that were different. As a matter of fact, one year when Adlai Stevenson was in Sevilla for Holy Week he was invited to march with a confraternity, and as a wise politician he did so.

When I had watched the floats, supervising their exits and returns, I felt that I understood something of the spiritual quality of Holy Week, but it was two unplanned experiences which brought me close to the heart of the matter. The first had occurred on Palm Sunday, when I had been following Don Francisco's float for more than ten hours. We stopped for some unknown reason in a small plaza, and the stevedores came out from under their boards and lounged about with beer bottles in their hands, for it was now daylight and the sun was growing hot. The soldiers, the guardia and the politicians had left us, for we were in the backwaters of the city far from the formal parade route; we were in a sense on our own and some members of the confraternity removed their hoods, and it was then that I came face to face with Don Francisco Mendoza Ruiz, so exhausted and beat down by the weight of his self-assumed cargo that I thought him close to fainting.

For a long, long moment we stood facing each other, and the mark of pain was so visible in his face that I had to acknowledge that here was a man who had truly assumed the burden of Jesus Christ in the moments of the passion. This was neither the play-acting of the men who carried the iron-ringed staves, beating them about as if they were marshals, nor the parade heroics of the armed soldiers looking as if they were about to enter battle, nor the posturings of the politicians as they exhibited their public spirituality. This was the face of an ordinary man who had assumed a burden that was almost more than he could bear; he was undergoing a religious experience that I had not ever come close to, and when I gave him a drink from my bottle he thanked me with an expression of ecstatic gratitude. I have never forgotten his face; he was not of the procession; he was the procession, standing at its very heart, and he was accepting as much of the passion of Jesus as any man could comprehend.

The whistles blew. The captain shouted at the workmen. The lines re-formed. And the staves thundered against the roadway. 'One, two, three,' came the signals, and slowly the Virgin rose into the sunlight, wavered unsteadily for a moment, then resumed her soft undulation as the huge structure moved forward once more. And behind the Virgin, so richly dressed and so wooden with her face staring straight ahead, struggled this weary barefooted man bearing his cross.

My second insight occurred on a street far removed from the little plaza. In the center of Sevilla, running from the commercial headquarters to the government buildings, is a narrow pathway which in ordinary circumstances would be an alley but which in Sevilla has become a major pedestrian thoroughfare. Its shops are the richest in the city. The big plate-glass windows behind which lounge the principal men of Sevilla, like a coterie of lesser gods on a lower Olympus, here seem more formidable than elsewhere. The pretty girls who throng the street are more relaxed. The corner restaurants are busier and the quiet bustle of the little pathway is more exciting.

Because of the manner in which this slim, beautiful street lies stretched out in the sunlight, it has for many centuries been known simply as Sierpes and has been termed by many 'the loveliest street in Europe.' To justify this, one must accept certain special definitions, for Sierpes cannot compare with a boulevard in Paris or with one of London's wide streets. How little it is! I once measured its width at the Restaurante Calvillo and it was exactly fifteen shoe lengths across. To see Sierpes at its best is to understand the saying: 'The three finest pleasures a man can know are to be young, to be in Sevilla, and to stand in Sierpes at dusk when the girls are passing.' I would add a fourth: 'And to stand in Sierpes during Holy Week when La Macarena is passing.'

The first evening I ever spent in Sierpes was when the floats of Holy Week were going by and even then I sensed that this must be the high point of the parade, for it was in their passage down this brilliant street that all participants tried to do their best. The rope-sandaled men stifling under the boards moved cautiously so as not to scrape the walls. The cries of the captains became whispers. The bands played in better rhythm and the professional soldiers marched with increased precision. At the entrance to Sierpes additional politicians slipped into line, so that they could be observed during the march past the city hall, which stands beyond the exit from Sierpes, and those penitents who were uncovered straightened up so that their faces might be seen. In those moments Sierpes became the focal point of Spain, for although similar processions were under way in Madrid and other cities, this was the famous one.

I now understood what had determined the width of the floats, because there were several tight spots in Sierpes where the tableaux of Jesus and Mary had to be borne just so in order for them to slip between projecting walls. Not many spectators could crowd into Sierpes; on the other hand, since it was the culminating point of the procession, as many as possible jammed in, chairs being sold at a premium. Directed by a group of young Spaniards, I had slipped in and wedged myself against a wall, where the floats passed me by at a distance of inches rather than feet. It was exciting to be so close to the carved figures and to see the nuances of their expressions; there was also a kind of animal pleasure in seeing now and then beneath the protecting curtains the softly moving feet of those who bore the floats and to hear their whispers, as if the spirits of the statues were speaking.

But as an insight into religious experience it did not compare with my earlier confrontation with the penitent; that had been a true revelation and this spectacle in Sierpes could be no more than a well-conceived parade. However, on Good Friday evening, as I was watching in Sierpes, I heard from a balcony projecting over the street the high, piercing scream of a woman. '¡O Dios!' she cried, and all movement along the pathway stopped. '¡O Dios!' she repeated, and when the throng was silent she launched into the most strange and impassioned song I had ever heard. She had a deep effect upon the emotions of those who listened, for her voice alternated between throaty cries of pain and soaring evocations of ecstasy. She continued thus for some four or five minutes, pouring forth a personal song of devotion to Jesus Christ, and her performance was so powerful that all in Sierpes, marchers and witnesses alike, paid her the homage of silence, so that her voice rang out like a bell, floating over the massive crowds. She paused. No one moved. Then she entered the passionate coda of her song, with her voice ascending in spirals and fury until at the end she was possessed. Then silence, as if the crowd wanted to consider her song, then the sounds of the soldiers and the police and the clanking chains and the rustle of the float, as all resumed their march toward the city hall.

The woman had been chanting a saeta (arrow; in plural, ecstatic religious outcries), which would be heard throughout the city on this day. My Spanish friends tried to tell me that such songs were spontaneous outbursts of persons overcome by religious experience, but I found it hard to believe that this woman was an average person overcome by her identification with the passion; she was a professional singer if ever I heard one, and I thought that I was fortunate to have had her as my first saeta performer because she introduced the form in such a flawless setting that I have ever since been a devotee. A great saeta, well sung, is something one can never forget. But I felt sure she had been planted on that balcony with instructions as to when and how to sing for maximum effect.

Some hours later, on Good Friday night, when I had wormed my way to a different segment of Sierpes, across from a corner bar which had closed in honor of the procession, I watched as an ordinary man pressed in against the wall shook himself free when one of the great Virgins approached. Staring as if transfixed by the statue, this man threw back his head and poured forth a simple, unadorned song in praise of this Mother. It was an extraordinary song, more moving than the first, for it was uttered rather than sung professionally. It was an offering from this man to this intercessor and it was volunteered in humility and deep feeling. Its authenticity impressed the marchers and they stood at solemn attention as the singer's voice grew stronger and his cry more fervent. Then suddenly he stopped and returned as if in embarrassment to his former position against the wall. The wooden staves with their iron rings beat against the pavement of Sierpes and the procession continued.

At the far end of Sierpes the floats exit to a large square along whose side stands the city hall, and it is here that the procession reaches its temporal climax, for on the wooden grandstands are seated the official families of the political leaders who have been marching down Sierpes. Now the various bands explode into a roar and additional soldiers and police slip into the parade. Very bright searchlights illuminate the scene and there is no place here for the singers of saetas.

From the city hall to the cathedral is a short distance along Sevilla's main street, and here large areas of chairs have been rented out by the city government. Here also the parade prepares itself for the spiritual culmination of the procession, the entrance to the cathedral. This is much more impressive than it sounds, for Sevilla's cathedral is one of the most enormous in Europe. Its aisles are so broad that the floats are able to pass through more easily than through Sierpes. I suppose all the Holy Week floats could fit into the cathedral with ease. As one astonished Frenchman wrote home: 'I am sorry to tell you that Notre Dame could fit inside this cathedral without causing much stir.'

It stands in the center of the city and can be seen from miles out in the countryside. It is a barnlike structure and only in size does it compare with Toledo's Gothic masterpiece, but it does have two features which make it unique. At one corner rises a graceful Moorish tower which once belonged to a mosque that was torn down to make way for the cathedral. This tower is called La Giralda (Weathervane), after the female figure representing faith which tops it, and it has become the symbol of the city. I have often seen it from points many miles away as the driver of my car would call, 'Ah, La Giralda. Home at last.' The second feature is less conspicuous but perhaps even more lovely, a large walled-in garden with cathedral cloisters at one end and long rows of orange trees which spread their fragrance through the area. It is called the Patio de los Naranjos (Court of the Orange Trees) and at any time of the year is worth visiting.

It is to this massive cathedral that the floats finally move. They leave the street, pass through the cathedral door and stop for ecclesiastical blessing. The hooded confraternity kneel and the penitents drag their chains before the altar, some with ankles bleeding from the irons. In silence the float leaves the cathedral and the politicians duck away. The stevedores wait for the first stopping point, then crawl out and head for the nearest bar to refresh themselves before the long march back to their home church.

One would miss the spirit of Holy Week if he saw only the solemnity. In the silent crowds are groups of young girls who would otherwise not be allowed on the streets, and boys follow them. There is much pinching and bumping and hushed giggling, and for many girls their first fumbling introductions to sex come at this time. As Pepe Gómez told me, 'We don't always crawl out from under the boards to get a drink or listen to a saeta. It's fun to look up the girls' dresses as they stand on the balcony.' The excitement is keenest in those moments when some popular Virgin passes, for then the boys and girls press together without supervision and give meaning to the cry that will later be shouted to the Virgin as she returns to her church: 'Oh, dearest Virgin! How I remember you!'

On Sunday two significant things happen. The faithful gather in the cathedral to celebrate the resurrection of Jesus, but not much is made of the matter, for Sevilla in spring is concerned mainly with the Crucifixion. And promptly at five in the afternoon Holy Week ends in the blare of a brass band whose lively tempos herald the beginning of the Easter bull-fight, first of the season.

In the weeks that follow, depending upon the year's timetable, activity begins in two widely separated quarters of the city. The first is the more important historically; the second is the more significant today. Many centuries ago a channel was dredged connecting Sevilla with the Río Guadalquivir, which flows some distance to the west, and this enabled Sevilla to function as the major port of the south, even though it lay many miles from the ocean. On the flat land that lies between the channel and the river, gypsies now begin to gather and are in the process of erecting a tent city with restaurants, bars, trading points and other appurtenances. They appear to be preparing a traditional gypsy fair, with spiced foods, crooked horse races and beautiful fortunetellers.

That is not their intention. For as one studies the strange town he sees an uncommonly large number of horses, mules and donkeys. From outlying rural areas come peasants who would normally have little associa-tion with gypsies; the processions of Holy Week were not attractive enough to lure these peasants, but the gypsies do. Experts from France and Portugal also arrive, and the last time I was there three tall gentlemen from Texas appeared in spurs and sombreros.

For this is the famous horse fair of Sevilla, dating back two thousand years to the days when Romans came here to buy horses for their generals. Some think that it was this primitive trading that later called forth the processions of Holy Week; certainly it formed the vital nucleus around which the rest of the present complex fair was built.

When I was in Las Marismas, watching birds with Don Luis Ybarra González, we had discussed Sevilla's horse fair, and at that time he had explained, 'The fair probably goes back to Roman days, but sometime in the eighteenth century it was discontinued. In 1847 my great-grandfather, the Conde de Ybarra, was serving as mayor of Sevilla. He loved horses, had a bull ranch of his own and one day got the idea of having an old-style fair. So in its present form it dates only from 1847.' To it come horse traders from all parts of southern Spain, eager to test their trading skill against the practiced gypsies. There is much bargaining, much riding of horses back and forth across the dusty plains, much noise.

If a man likes horses, this rough-and-ready market with no rules and little order would delight him. It is conducted under a blazing sun and has

At the great horse fair a young man studies a possible purchase.

about it a strange and ancient quality. I have attended at three different times and found it difficult to believe that I was in the twentieth century; always I have thought it regrettable that most visitors to Sevilla miss the horse fair, because in many ways it is one of the most authentically Spanish parts of the spring celebration.

Last time I was there a gypsy boy of eleven was showing a donkey to a suspicious farmer from a vineyard north of Cádiz. Boy and man studied the donkey for more than an hour, and if they found anything unusual in the beast, I did not. The boy kept stressing the good points of the animal while the man parried with his suspicions about the wind, the hooves, the obviously weak back, the splayed foot and the visible sore near the tail.

Hoping by some dramatic gesture to conclude the sale, the boy took the donkey's halter and cried, 'But observe how he runs.' The beast would not move. Repeatedly the boy urged the animal to show his unusual skills, but apparently the donkey had none. All this time the farmer stood aside in contemptuous silence until finally the child screamed at him, 'Sir, you have bewitched him!'

Two hours later I observed the same boy with the same donkey arguing patiently with the same farmer. During the whole of the horse fair one can see such bargaining taking place along the banks of the Guadalquivir.

I once spent the better part of a morning with a tall gypsy named Antonio Suero Varga from the Extremaduran town of Almendralejo. He was broad-shouldered, had dark hair and very dark eyes and carried the badge of the gypsy horse trader, a rattan cane with which he conducted most of his business. 'Look at that horse. Have you ever seen finer legs for heavy work?' With his cane he would point out the special features of the animal he was trying to sell, but after I had been with him for a while I heard him say, as he jabbed at a mule with a weak back, 'You expect an honest man . . . Let's say a farmer who has to earn his living . . . You want him to buy a mule like that?'

I asked, 'Are you buying or selling?'

'Either.'

'Where are your horses?'

'Mine?' he laughed. 'I have no horses. I'm a comprador [purchaser].' He went on to explain that he made his living by attending fairs and bringing suspicious farmers who wanted to buy into contact with other suspicious farmers who wanted to sell. 'The Spanish farmer is a suspicious creature. He'll never trust himself or another farmer, so he has to trust a gypsy. He hires me to do his bargaining for him.'

I had been with Antonio Suero for some time when he was approached by two fine-looking young farmers from a village near Almendralejo. José Gallardo and his brother Juan farmed a profitable wine and olive plantation of a thousand acres. 'We already have three tractors,' José told me, 'but we'd like to buy a good mule to do the close-up work.'

'Why don't you just buy the mule?'

The Gallardos looked at me as if I were insane. 'Us? Buy a mule?' I judged I had offended their pundonor and wondered if I should apologize, but José said, 'A Spaniard can't go to another Spaniard and argue with him about the price of a mule. Well, it just couldn't be done. Nor would the man with a mule to sell want to haggle with me. It would be beneath his dignity. So we hire Señor Suero here to do it for us.'

At this point José and the gypsy withdrew to discuss terms, and I asked Juan, 'Do you trust him?'

'Suero? He's famous for being the best bargainer in these parts. We have to trust him. Watch.'

The gypsy, having learned what the Gallardo brothers wanted and what they would pay, left them and ran like a young boy from one group of men to another, waving his rattan cane and cursing. Once I heard him bellow, 'For that mule? My friend, I have two gentlemen who know mules. I'd be ashamed to take that animal before them.' Before long he came running back, waving his cane in the air. 'My God!' he cried. 'I've found the finest mule ever to reach Sevilla.'

He brought with him an old, suspicious, mean-tempered farmer in a broad hat and chaps who was leading what I took to be a very average mule, but as I watched, Suero put on one of the finest bits of acting I was to see in Spain. He laughed, he wept, he cursed, he pleaded, he cajoled and he swore as heaven was his witness that this was a good mule and that the price was just, but apparently he had not yet received a firm price from the seller, for as the bargaining proceeded the latter changed his price, where-upon Suero began reviling him as a thief for trying to sell this spavined beast to a decent man. Then, as soon as a firm price was determined, he became the seller again. Taking José Gallardo's hands in his he became a wise and understanding father. 'Believe me, Don José, I knew your father, I knew your uncle, and fine men they were. How many animals did I find for them, tell me. And did I ever recommend one that was faulty? Take my word for it, Don José, you'll search this feria on your knees before you find a mule as good as this one.'

According to the tradition of the feria the gypsy's job was to make the Gallardo brothers produce a hundred-peseta note, which he would then hand as a token to the seller, and the deal would be closed on the word of the two men. Suero, therefore, took José's hand in his right hand, the dealer's in his left and brought the two together, pleading with José to produce a hundred pesetas as a token. Tears came to his eyes; his voice broke; he could only mumble; then be began to speak like a machine gun and it seemed to me that about ninety percent of what he said was irrelevant. Slowly Gallardo produced a note and placed it among the four clasped hands, at which Antonio Suero gave a deep sigh.

'You have bought yourself a great mule,' he said, and with this he turned his attention to a farmer who had been tugging at his sleeve. To my surprise, it was the suspicious wine grower from Cádiz who had been haggling with the boy over the donkey. Apparently the two had remained locked in an impasse and now sought adjudication from Antonio Suero Varga. 'Coming, coming!' the gypsy cried as he ran off, waving his rattan cane, to solve this new problem. Later he would return to collect his commission on the Gallardo purchase.

It was during the horse fair some years ago that I stumbled upon a rewarding acquaintance. I had ridden a bus out to the Guadalquivir to spend the day with the gypsies and had eaten, at one of their kiosks, a mixture of grain, chopped meat and gravy, and now I returned on foot to the heart of the city. I rested for some time in the Court of the Orange Trees, using the stone slabs provided there, and then went into that fine street along which the Holy Week procession ends.

Spanish police are notoriously abrupt with pedestrians who try to cross other than at traffic lights, so I waited in line for the green to show,

The white dove of Spanish poetry rests easily on the shoulder of the arrogant gypsy.

because I wanted to spend the rest of the day wandering in the area by the bullring. I happened to look across the street at the people waiting on the other side and saw there two handsome young men whom I judged to be in their late twenties. One of them, a tall slim fellow with unusually fine features, I was sure I had seen somewhere before; these were the days when Hollywood was beginning to produce many films in Spain and I supposed he was an actor. Then it came to me. I had seen his picture in an American paper. And his name, for some curious reason, leaped to mind. He was John Fulton Short. And he came from Philadelphia. And he was a bullfighter.

We met in the middle of the street and I said, 'Aren't you John Fulton?' which was the name he fought under. He nodded and I introduced myself. He nodded again in much the manner that a Spanish grandee nods to the baker peddling bread from a barrow. 'Good luck, Matador,' I said, using the traditional Spanish phrase, and we crossed over, each headed his own way.

I learned later that the young man with him that day was Jerry Boyd, an aspirant writer from America who happened to be married to the daughter of one of my favorite artists, the fine Jewish Shakespearean actor from Budapest and London, Abraham Sofaer. It was Boyd, I later learned, who told Fulton, 'My God! If that's who he said he was, he's from Philadelphia too. Maybe we better see if he'd be interested.' John Fulton, in the manner of matadors, knew nothing of books and had no special desire right then to meet anyone from Philadelphia, for he was conspicuously down on his luck, but he allowed Boyd to double him back, and after a short walk, for I was moving slowly, they overtook me near the bullring.

'Are you from Philadelphia?' Fulton asked. I replied that I was and he gave me his card: 'John Fulton, Matador de Novillos, Hernando Colón, 30, Sevilla, España.' He smiled and said, 'Why don't you drop around?' But Jerry Boyd intercepted the card before I could take it and asked, 'You did say your name was Michener, didn't you?' When I nodded, he asked, 'And you do write books?' I nodded again and he let me have the card, and it was through this chance meeting that I embarked upon those adventures of the spirit which led to the writing of this book.

John Fulton, art student and would-be matador from Philadelphia, had a small second-floor apartment on a side street which debouched into the Court of the Orange Trees, and here, during a period of some six or seven years, came most of the Americans who got as far south as Sevilla. Maharajas stopped here and dozens of actors making movies in the area and writers and newspapermen and artists from England. The hospitality that John Fulton extended during the years was astronomical and he offered it while being stone-broke and trying to make his way in one of the toughest professions in the world. To be a bullfighter in Spain requires from even the Spanish youth an endurance that most men cannot visualize; but to be an American trying to crack that vicious and closed society demands absolute courage.

How Fulton supported himself during those bleak and wonderful years, I do not know. Most of us who trespassed on his hospitality managed in some way or other to leave behind donations: one brought the wine, another the anchovies, another the cheese. Hemingway made his contribution by check; a delightful woman from Cleveland made hers by throwing memorable flamenco parties at which she gave John a fee for his professional help; I made mine by commissioning Fulton to paint me a picture, for I judged that he had more chance to succeed as an artist than as a matador.

I was right. He was an excellent artist and subsequently made a name for himself as an illustrator of children's books; for his paintings he also acquired a distinguished list of patrons, including Adlai Stevenson and the Baroness von Trapp. But whenever I talked with him about the desirability

FOLLOWING FACING PAGES: *John Fulton and Antonio Ordóñez*
at the entrance to a small-town bullring.
They wear the traditional Andalusian cowboy costume
used in non-formal fights.

of his attending art school somewhere and applying himself to that profession, he replied, 'I am going to be a matador.' His dedication never faltered, in spite of doubters like me, and I watched with sorrow as he beat his head in futile rage against the indifference of Spanish promoters. This handsome young fellow from Philadelphia might want to be a bullfighter, but the impresarios of Spain did not intend to help.

Those were marvelous days in Sevilla. In the afternoon we ate at a small restaurant called El Mesón (The Inn), where substantial food was served at reasonable prices in an atmosphere of bullfight posters and butchered pigs hanging from the ceiling. Food in Sevilla during the spring festival is apt to be dismal; some meals served in the major hotels are shocking, but at El Mesón we ate well. It was there I first tasted three fine Spanish items which together made a meal. First we had a tall pitcher of sangría, a drink made of harsh red wine, cognac, seltzer water, quartered oranges, lemon juice, some pineapple squares and red cherries, sweetened with not too much sugar and served with lots of cracked ice and cinnamon. It was delicious, and travelers who learn to like its different taste prefer it to other Spanish drinks.

For our second course we had gazpacho, an ice-cold soup which can be compared to nothing. If you ever travel in Spain and come upon a restaurant that serves gazpacho, take it, because no other dish in the country will you remember with such affection. Once when I had been out of Spain for some years, a neighbor found in a gourmet shop in Princeton a shelf of canned gazpacho, but since she could not be sure whether it was any good or not, she bought only one can, plopped it in her refrigerator and when it was ice-cold, called us over. When she served it with some chopped onion, cubes of cucumber and bits of tomato, tears of joy came to my eyes, something she had not been able to achieve with flamenco records or colored slides of Spain, and next day I drove all the way to Princeton to buy up the remaining cans. For gazpacho is Spain. The cook at the Mesón told me how to make it.

Take two stale rolls and reduce them to crumbs. Soak in water until they form a thick paste and set aside. Into your blender put two pounds of tomatoes, one large pared cucumber, two large green peppers, a quarter-cup of pimientos and two small sweet onions. Season with pinches of salt and pepper. Now comes the tricky part. To this mixture you must add olive oil and vinegar, which are the heart of the soup. A Spaniard will use one cup of the former, a tablespoon of the latter. Americans, of whom I am certainly one, prefer not more than a quarter-cup of oil and four tablespoons of vinegar. At any rate, reduce all ingredients except the bread to a liquid, then mix in the bread by hand and put the result in a covered wooden bowl and place in the refrigerator for six hours. Serve ice-cold and pass a serving tray containing separate dishes of chopped tomatoes, cucumbers, onions and small cubes of bread. No part of this strange recipe sounds very good, but taken together and properly blended, these ingredients produce a soup which is as distinctive as vichyssoise.

For dessert we had membrillo and Manchego cheese. The latter is the only good cheese Spain produces, a salty, coarse-grained product from the Don Quixote country. When eaten along with membrillo it makes a spicy dish, for membrillo is a grainy gelatin-like dessert made of quince. It is both sweet and acid and has a delicious chewy quality. Burnt orange in color, it is served in generous slabs as if it were a cheese, and at the Mesón was extra good, brought in from a small town near Córdoba which specializes in its manufacture; I believe that it too can sometimes be bought in the United States, but I haven't tasted it yet. However, the waiter warned me, 'Be careful where you buy your membrillo. Some of those other restaurants make theirs of sweet potato.'

At night in this in-between period we would rout out a near-blind flamenco singer, Gafas (Spectacles) they called him, and in the old days he could chant flamenco with as great an artistry as anyone in Spain, but now his voice was gone. We used to rent an attic in the medieval part of town, import a set of dancers and drag in a keg of wine, some bread, cheese and anchovies, and dance till morning. It was with Gafas singing in his cracked, wine-heavy voice, which no one could call beautiful, that I learned his version of that haunting song whose music I had first heard in Valencia years before, 'Petenera,' about the forbidden Jewess who brought disaster to her village and herself:

> Where are you going, beautiful Jewess,
> All dressed up and at such an hour?
> I am going to meet Rebeco,
> Who is now in the synagogue.

> Whoever named you Petenera
> Didn't know how to name you.
> You should have been named
> The perdition of men.

> If you hear the bells,
> Don't ask who has died,
> Because you will be told
> By your own remorse.

One would like to know the origin of that last verse. Is it an authentic Spanish statement anticipating John Donne? I suspect it's a late addition reflecting the popularity of Ernest Hemingway.

Whenever Gafas sang 'Petenera' to the rather banal music that accompanies it, I felt that I was in medieval Spain, as I do today when I hear it. In time this unimportant little song, to which each singer had his own dozen verses, including usually the three given above, came to represent for me the best of flamenco, and even though it is not one of the great songs, I would rather hear it sung well by a peasant voice like that of Gafas, tired and world-weary at the end of the day, with the guitar flying in mournful accents, than the finest formal chanting I have so far heard. It is in a very real sense my particular song of Spain; in the years when I worked submerged in Jewish materials I would often recall its phrases, and they came to me not in the syllables of the various recordings I had purchased, nor in the poetry, which is of good quality, but rather in the cracked and reedy voice of Gafas as he sang in the attics of Sevilla in those good days. Shortly after I heard him for the last time he died, leaving behind no recording of his 'Petenera.'

At John Fulton's there was much talk of art, but as I have said, I got nowhere trying to convince him that he should apply himself to painting. In his apartment when I knew it, one found Mexican matadors, Chilean painters, Minnesota architects and Vassar philosophy majors in Spain for their junior year. The visitor who gave me the most trouble was a Danish schoolteacher from Copenhagen; she was in her late twenties and no beauty, but she had a wonderfully soft quality about her and obviously loved children, to whom she imparted her strong sense of values. She taught, if I remember correctly, chemistry, which seemed an odd subject for a quiet girl like her, but she explained, 'There's an unusual need for chemists today. Especially in Denmark. And those of us who have any skill in the field are kept busy.' I judged that her pupils received good instruction.

But one meets many schoolteachers in Spain. What set this admirable young lady apart was the fact that on a previous vacation she had conceived a grand passion for a young Welshman who, like John Fulton, was determined to become a bullfighter. The fellow had no prospects whatever, insofar as I could determine, yet he hung on, year after year. At the beginning of each summer his Copenhagen schoolteacher appeared on the scene, with her savings from the term before, and together they moved from one fair to the next, she blond and he swarthy, clinging to the fiction that one day he would become a great fighter, one day they would marry. The illusion kept them going, and I was with them at the end of one season when the little Welshman actually got an invitation to fight in the fair being put together by an impoverished village.

It would be more accurate to say that he had been invited to participate in the fair, because it wasn't going to be a formal bullfight; the Welshman would be welcomed if he paid for his suit, for his assistants, for a horse to be ridden by his picador and for part of the bullring expenses. In return he would receive no wages at all but would be allowed to test himself against an overage, overweight, wily old bull who had already in previous fights sent two men to the hospital.

This offer presented a serious dilemma to the schoolteacher. Obviously the funds required of the Welshman could be provided only by her, and if she laid out this substantial amount she felt that she ought at least to attend, especially since there was a strong likelihood that her matador would be wounded, if not killed. But to attend the fracas, for that's what it shaped up to be, would require her to miss the opening of her school in Copenhagen. She asked me what I thought she ought to do, and I, as a conservative who used to teach school myself, taking it very seriously, said without hesitation, 'You take the next plane to Denmark.'

Apparently I brought her to her senses, for she put down the money for the fight, canceled her flight to Denmark and accompanied her hero to the village festival. On the way she explained, 'They can't fire me. Chemistry teachers are hard to come by.' I asked if her school board knew that she was spending her vacations in Spain, living with a bullfighter. She replied, 'I suppose they know. At least the children do. They think it's rather sporting.'

We got to the village, a Welsh bullfighter with a Danish manager, a Portuguese assistant, a Mexican picador and an American cheerleader. As so often happens, there was no fight; the local impresario had collected funds to buy the two bulls and had then absconded.

It was in this world of broken promises, venal arrangements and utter corruption of all principle that John Fulton struggled. How he maintained his good humor I will never know, for he was humiliated by the numbers. One, promise him a fight. Two, wheedle him into designing the handbills. Three, make him agree to fight overage bulls. Four, make him employ my brother-in-law as his picador. Five, postpone everything. Six, abandon everything. Year after year this continued; year after year he either told me or wrote me: 'I will be a matador.'

Gradually, as I visited him more often, I became aware of a quiet young man who seemed to be sharing the apartment and to be decorating it with photographs of high quality. For long periods, when the talk was on subjects in which I had little interest, I would study the photographs, excellent works in very dark blacks and pure whites, and I became convinced that the man who had taken them understood Spain.

The quiet young fellow with well-fitted suits and conservative haircut was Robert Vavra, from California, a nature photographer. He had been working for some years on a book of text and pictures describing in detail the life and death of the fighting bull, and from the first moment I saw his work in sequence I was convinced that here was a man who could photograph the movement and sense of animals; but I was equally impressed by his shots of people. He seemed to catch the spirit of things in repose; there was little artiness about him and I began to look forward to my visits to the apartment: I wanted to see what Vavra had done recently.

There followed a chain of unforgettable days in Las Marismas, tracking bulls, watching wildlife and marking the migration of birds to Africa. It was on such trips that I renewed my acquaintance with the bee-eater, that spectacular bird which was to become so important to me when I worked in Israel. Here, too, I saw my first hoopoe bird, which would be even more important.

Then one day, as I studied a batch of Vavra's photographs and listened to his plans for a series of children's books in color, a project which has happily come to fulfillment, I happened to see a chance arrangement of some twenty or thirty fine photographs depicting the people and life of Spain: they were not the usual body of material, for there were no cathedrals, no medieval houses and no flamenco dancers. There was simply the look of Spain, static and yet persuasively alive, and in that moment not far from the Court of the Orange Trees this book was born.

Because I was burdened with a heavy schedule that would keep me busy for some years, I could not then speak to Vavra of my incipient plans; but when my work was completed I went back to Sevilla, and in that same quiet and delightful period between Holy Week and carnival, when the gypsies were again preparing to trade horses on the riverbank, I proposed that we do this book together.

I remember the commission we agreed upon: 'Vavra will go over Spain guided only by his own eye, completely indifferent as to what Michener may write or think or prefer. Shoot a hundred of the very finest pictures he can find and make them his interpretation of Spain. If he can succeed in this, the pictures will fit properly into any text. But Vavra must avoid trying to guess what someone else wants. Make others see what he has seen.'

For the capacity to see a foreign country is extremely rare; hardly one person in a thousand can do this, so that all the vast sums of money spent by Pan American and Air France in their enticing advertisements—'See Lebanon. See Egypt. See Brazil'—are largely wasted, because the people who fly forth to see these places rarely do. Vavra can see.

When the religious parades have ended, when the horse fair on which the spring activity originally centered has started to convene, and when old friends have had a chance to renew acquaintances during the time of relative rest, the real Sevilla fair, as most people think of it today, convenes. Now the night clapping begins to echo through the city.

In a spacious park lying at the southern edge of Sevilla, and within easy walking distance from the center of town, three separate but connected areas have been staked out, each the size of a small pueblo. For the next week these three areas will become the heart of Sevilla to charm the visitor as few other fairs in Europe can.

In the first area, improbable as it seems, five different circuses, each complete in itself, have gathered from various parts of the continent. There's a Swiss circus, with famous clowns, an Italian one, a brilliant Chinese one featuring acrobats and Oriental girls, a Spanish one and, best of all, a large German circus with four different wild-animal acts.

To one who loves circuses, the Sevilla fair is unique: one can spend three days moving from one tent to the next and even then he will not be able to see all the acts. There is something quaint and even nineteenth century about these European circuses; occasionally a family will work in one for forty or fifty years, and no effort is made, as in America, to keep all the women beautiful. In these tents one sees whole families growing old surrounded by events they love. For example, I have never seen another animal act so utterly delightful as the one in the German circus in which a hefty woman in her late fifties, dressed in bespangled tights, put a cageful of tigers through their paces. It was charming in the way sadistic old fairy tales are charming.

In the area adjoining the circuses noise is king. Here you will find more noise than the human ear can absorb or the sane man imagine, because this is the carnival space, filled with rides, games, shooting galleries, half a hundred outdoor restaurants, loop-the-loops, trips to Mars and a near-score of other rides. Apparently it is obligatory for each business to own a microphone and five or six of the loudest loudspeakers. 'Come here!' bellow the shills. 'Mothers, take your children through the mysteries of outer space!' The call of '¡Churros!' is popular, for these greasy fritters served laden with sugar, are the delicacy of the fair. But no one cry predominates, for wherever you stand you are assailed by at least twenty loudspeakers relatively close to your ears.

One night I took a friend from America to the middle of the carnival area, and he stood in admiration at the frenzy around him. 'The Spaniards are to be congratulated,' he said. 'They've discovered noise incarnate.'

Yet the area is not vulgar. It too has a controlled Spanish charm and a much wider variety of booths at which to spend money than I have been able to indicate. Merely to stroll through the lanes and sample food at each of the booths would require, I suppose, a couple of days, and to ride on each of the wheels and whips would take another two. The section is clean, brightly lighted and constitutes a little fair by itself, a swirling concentration of revelry.

It operates, of course, twenty-four hours a day. At four one morning I wandered among the tents, checking to see how many features I had missed on previous visits, and I came upon a large field jammed with nothing but trucks and wheeled caravans that had hauled this weird collection of rides and restaurants to Sevilla. Painted red and green and gold and blue, the trucks huddled together like a collection of bizarre animals assembled from all parts of Europe, and in almost every cab some man or woman was sleeping. Now when I think of the carnival part of Sevilla's fair I remember not the noise but rather that silent, slumbering collection of gaudy vehicles.

In spite of the richness of the circuses and the flamboyance of the carnival, it is the third section of the park that captivates most people, and

This mother-and-daughter fruit-selling team expresses the gracia of Sevilla.

it is true that of a hundred foreigners visiting Sevilla for the spring festivities, a good ninety see only the area I am about to describe. They miss the Holy Week, the horse fair, the circuses, the carnival and even the bullfights, but what they do see makes the trip worthwhile.

This part of the fair has been laid out along a grid of unusually wide streets, the main ones forming a massive capital H with top and bottom closed. Along the sides of the streets forming this enormous H, and along lesser contributory streets as well, the citizens of Sevilla have been accustomed for the past half-century to build each spring small wooden structures whose walls and roofs consist of brightly striped canvas. They are called casetas (little houses), and each has a wooden floor, electric lights, running water, perhaps a refrigerator, a table and at least two dozen chairs. Each caseta stands jammed against its neighbors, and to see a quarter of a mile of such little houses, each with its distinctive and gaudy color system, is delightful to the eye.

It is in these casetas that the well-to-do people of Sevilla will spend most of their time during the fair, returning to their homes only in time to catch a few hours' sleep between five and eleven in the morning.

What happens in the casetas? When the front canvas wall has been rolled up so that passers-by can see within, specially invited guests stop by for refreshments, drinks and light conversation. Entertainment is provided by amateurs and by troupes of noisy flamenco dancers imported from across the river in Triana. With music and dancing, with sherry wine and churros, with laughter and flirtation the long nights drift by. Young couples sometimes wander away from the caseta to the carnival area or even to the circus, but by one in the morning most are back where they belong. A special feature of the casetas is the presence of children between the ages of four and twelve, beautifully dressed in folk costumes and dancing flamenco patterns until two or three in the morning. It is incredible how much music there is in these lines of gaily colored casetas: one night at two o'clock I made a casual count and came up with sixty-five different orchestras.

And the songs! In one tour of the casetas I heard amateur performances covering the complete range of flamenco, from the so-called deep songs to the little songs. One jazzy folk song intermixed with the flamenco had a standard opening verse and a rather startling conclusion:

> If a brunette is worth a duro
> Any blonde is worth two.
> But I go to the low-priced love,
> The love of my heart.
>
> My Virgin of Macarena is brunette,
> Oh, she's a real brunette!
> She comes from Sevilla
> And is sweeter than the morning star.

When the real morning star appears the father of the family rolls down the canvas wall facing the street. A son runs off to summon a horse-drawn carriage. The gypsies are paid off and the refrigerator is locked. The tired family piles into the carriage and drives off through the morning twilight. From the carnival area nearby come volumes of sound, for the rides and restaurants are still busy, and as the family rides homeward through the darkened streets they hear the sound of muffled clapping coming from other groups who are walking home. At dusk next evening the family will return to its caseta, and for a whole week this procedure will be repeated. During the fair Sevilla gets little sleep.

In addition to the small family casetas, at which no stranger is welcomed unless specifically invited, so that many Americans spend an entire week at the fair without ever being inside one, most companies doing business in Sevilla operate their own large casetas, and some of these are public. By paying a small fee one can sit at a table, listen to professional flamenco and drink beer or champagne.

Among these large casetas stands one with special importance. It belongs to the Aero Club and its membership is so highly restricted that it constitutes, during the season of the fair, the focus of Spanish society. Here congregate those especially handsome people who form the apex of Spanish life: the duques, the condes, the grandees of Spain. And they are a forbidding, impressive lot, perhaps the most conspicuous nobility operating today.

In daylight hours the side curtains of the Aero Club are rolled up, so that passers-by can observe the great figures taking a light lunch or drinking their Tío Pepe along with a handful of roasted nuts. Condesas, accompanied by leading bankers, sit at tables looking out into the street; duquesas share their tables with famous bullfighters; at one table it's all pretty women and racing-car drivers. At night the curtains are lowered and two different bands alternate from six in the evening till four in the morning. During two fairs I held honorary tickets to the Aero Club, and I would judge the Spanish leaders I met to be among the most carefully groomed people I have ever seen. It is difficult, as one observes their old-fashioned gentility, to believe that they are part of this century.

To observe this manifestation of Spanish society one does not require a ticket to the Aero Club, entrance to that establishment costing some forty dollars. Each day at noon an informal parade starts through the wide streets of the H and in it participate most of the leaders of Sevilla society. As twelve o'clock approaches, in all parts of Sevilla horses are saddled up and handsome young men appear dressed in formal riding habit. They wear fine jackets with five buttons on the sleeve, dark riding trousers covered by large hand-tooled leather chaps, white ruffled shirts with lace at the throat and front, and flat, wide-brimmed hats. When they have mounted they adjust a pillion behind them, from whose rear projects a small leather handle which passes under the horse's tail. It is on this pillion that the gentleman's girl companion will ride, perched sideways across the rear of the horse, one hand passing about the man's waist, the other gripping the leather handle. Since the girls are dressed in resplendent gypsy costume, gold and blue and red predominating, the couples form attractive images as they ride forth. When three or four hundred begin to converge in bright sunlight on the caseta area, a parade of lovely dimensions is under way. For some three hours they ride back and forth along the tree-lined streets, halting now and then to chat with fellow riders, dismounting occasionally to visit with friends in the casetas and displaying to good effect both their fine costumes and their well-trained horses. The girls resemble a convocation of butterflies, they are so colorful.

At the same time other couples are about to join the parade, and these are much different. The men's suits are more subdued. The horses' garnishings are more expensive, as are the horses themselves. And the

*In her palace stands
the Duquesa de Medinaceli,
most betitled woman in Spain.*

women, who this time will ride alone, each on her own animal, are stunning beyond compare. They are the gentry, the social leaders from the Aero Club, and all are dressed in formal black or charcoal gray or very dark brown. The women's suits are of whipcord; their hats are slimmer and flatter than the men's; their heavy leather chaps are apt to be trimmer than those we saw before. They ride with the reins lightly held in the fingers of the left hand, their right hand turned in against the waist, and invariably their hair is done with austere plainness. With little or no make-up they ride forth, as handsome a group of women as one can find. In some strange way, in their somber mien, they make the pillion riders, despite their rainbow colors, seem drab.

But even these beautiful women are overshadowed by a phenomenon of this fair: ornate carriages pulled by two or four beribboned horses, driven by two coachmen in antique costume and bearing four or six girls in colorful dress, accompanied sometimes by gentlemen. These delightful carriages, looking like some procession that had driven into Sevilla from the eighteenth century, ease themselves into the files of horsemen, and around the streets of the H they go, back and forth for three or four hours. Sometimes as many as a hundred carriages, each of different size and quality, move along under the trees, the occupants laughing and visiting with their friends; half the parade moves clockwise, the other half counter-clockwise, so that on any one tour, if that is the proper word, one meets half the paraders, and since it is permissible to reverse one's direction after having made a couple of circuits, by the time the huge promenade has ended, one has met up with most of the participants.

I cannot describe how lovely and quiet and satisfying this parade under the broad trees and along the casetas is. Even if one has no horse and saddle of his own, nor access to the expensive carriages, he can still join the parade, for at any corner he can hire a kind of horse-drawn taxicab and for surprisingly little money ride back and forth along the majestic streets of the H. Where do they come from, these hundreds of carriages for hire? How can a modest city like Sevilla find so many horses?

Whenever a horseman reins up before a caseta owned by his friends, courtesy requires that both he and his lady be handed small glasses of sherry. Without dismounting, the riders drink, return the glasses and thank their hosts. Once I was left in care of a caseta while the family joined the riders in a carriage, and not then knowing the custom of the sherry I stood by while a particularly vivacious couple reined up before me. They waited. I waited. Then, in disgust, the man snapped in Spanish, 'At this damned caseta the hospitality flows like lead.' I understood enough to catch his meaning and in my broken Spanish asked what had gone wrong. When he realized that I was a stranger he jumped from his horse, showed me where the sherry was and flagged down all his friends. That night he took me on a tour of his favorite casetas, and we hired our own band of Triana gypsies, and the boisterous flamenco we provided with our company of fifty is still spoken of.

A feature of the parade is that select band of carriages which are pulled by eight horses, the postillions being dressed in robber costumes from the eighteenth century. Not only are the carriages worthy of respect and the horses a delight because of their matched appearance, but a ninth horse in front seems not to be attached to the carriage in any way, nor to the other horses. He moves by himself, guided by invisible wires attached to his bit and by words called by the driver, who rides a considerable distance behind. It is something to see such a carriage coming down the avenue, surrounded by a hundred riders and meeting dozens of other carriages, with the lead horse quietly picking his way without apparent assistance.

Thus the great fair of Sevilla continues, day after day. Toward dawn on the last night I stood at the entrance to the Aero Club as members of the nobility departed for the last time, and in the street stood an old man leading a donkey. He was not the kind who would own a caseta, nor a horse to ride in the daily procession, nor even a job in one of the carnivals. He was a rural peasant come in with his donkey to see the sights, and as he watched the ending of the fair he sang:

> 'Yo soy un ánima infeliz,
> Perdida en este mundo atormentado.'

(I am a miserable spirit lost in this tormented world.) And as he wandered off, singing to himself, the tents of the five circuses were coming down, the parking lot where the carnival trucks waited came back to life and electricians were disconnecting their wires from the multitude of little casetas, which would soon vanish.

As I stood in the darkness that night I reflected upon the strange development of Spanish history which permitted the nobles to play so important a role without suffering the limitations to their power that overcame their fellows in England, France, Italy, Germany and Russia. In Spain a conde is still somebody and a duque is a near-god. In the year 1400 the arrogant nobles of the major European countries were about equal in the power they exercised, but one by one the other European nations, in the order named, underwent revolutions of fact and spirit which cut back the absolute power of their nobles and transferred that power to a new and educated middle class, from which would come the political and industrial leaders of the future. In Spain this did not happen; on the contrary, the nobles arrogated more and more power to themselves, so that as late as the nineteenth century they dominated Spanish life, especially in the countryside. They told priests what they might and might not preach; they terrorized schoolteachers; they put newspapermen out of business; they exercised control over the cabinet, the army, the Church hierarchy and agriculture. Even today, as we shall see later when discussing a typical business operation in Madrid, they dominate Spanish life. No other nobility in the world compares in power and wealth with Spain's, and as one watches it in operation the only parallel he can find is the operation of the Hungarian nobility in the late 1700s.

If the Spanish nobility had exercised a leadership commensurate with its privilege, as was frequently the case in England and France, Spain would have prospered, but that did not happen. When Spain needed industrialization, the nobles said no. When Spain required a first-class army and navy to defend its empire, the nobles insisted upon using these services as their private playthings, with one general for every ten or fifteen men, and so abused the army that it fell from being the best in Europe to the worst. When the Church should have been doing what it did in all other major countries, adjusting religion to a changing world, the nobles, through their occupancy of high positions, refused to allow speculation. No nation in Europe, except possibly Hungary and Rumania, has been so badly served by its upper classes as Spain. With the intellectual and moral capacity to govern, they refused to do so; instead of seeking the common good they sought their own preferment, and the gap between them and the people became tragically wide.

I think the best light one can throw on the problem of the Spanish nobility is an oblique one shining from Peru, Chile, Paraguay, Venezuela and other Spanish countries of America. In the capitals of Europe one of the standard figures is the exile bearing a name like Juan Jiménez López. He was born in one of the Latin countries of South or Central America and was either elected or appointed to office, which he held for about five years, during which time he stole every peso or bolivar he could and sent it to a numbered account in Switzerland. Señor Jiménez caught the last plane out, said goodbye forever to his homeland and now lives happily and with a certain flair in Europe. Never in his upbringing did he catch a glimpse of what public service meant. Reared on a mixture of pundonor and Viva yo, he had no option but to do what he did, for he felt no obligation to his homeland other than to use it as his milk cow. The defect lay not in Jiménez but in the fact that the Spanish upper classes, from which he at least spiritually sprang, have never undergone indoctrination in the principle of noblesse oblige.

There was another contributing factor. During the critical years, say 1500–1815, when the nobility of England and France were being either educated or eliminated, Spain was governed in a spirit of absolutism not known in the other major countries save Russia by a series of kings who were not Spanish, and under their system of rule most of the best administrative jobs went to foreigners. Forget the fact that these foreigners stole the country blind, one after another retiring to his homeland with a fortune; forget the savage mismanagement and forget the subversion of law; the important fact was that the Spanish upper classes were thus deprived of the schooling in government which might have modified their insularity, arrogance and general incompetence. Other nations have suffered foreign kings. If Flemish not Spanish was spoken at the court in Toledo, so German not English was spoken in London; but the English upper classes would not permit their German kings to import outside ministers; indeed, it was sometimes the presence of the German king that spurred the English upper classes to greater energy and a more resolute defense of national prerogatives. Therefore, in the period when new lessons were to be learned, the English upper classes were in a position to learn them and the Spanish were not. Later, when it was necessary to make crucial decisions on which the fate of the social order as well as the empire rested, the English had been trained to make those decisions; the Spanish had not and the series of disastrous wrong choices followed.

The choices were wrong only for the nation and the general welfare. The upper classes looked out for themselves, so that each year the chasm between the very rich and the very poor became greater, until it seemed that all Spain was divided between these two extremes. No region of Spain is better equipped to exhibit this differential than Andalucía, which includes both Córdoba and Sevilla, for here the extremes are even greater than in Extremadura. The poor of the two regions are equally poor, but the rich in Andalucía are much richer; Extremadura has produced few noble families and those not of top power. When one speaks of a 'grandee of Spain' he visualizes primarily the great families of Andalucía: aloof, arrogant, powerful, indifferent.

This was illustrated one hot afternoon as I was driving from Sevilla to Córdoba and was accosted by a workman who said he must get to the latter city. He said, with no reluctance before a stranger, 'It's dreadful for a poor man to live in Andalucía. We starve. The rich ones don't live out here, you can be sure of that.' When I asked where they did live, he pointed contemptuously over his shoulder at La Giralda. 'Huddled together in the city where the police and the army and the Guardia Civil can protect them.' When I asked him why, he said, 'Because if they lived out here they'd be killed in their sleep. That's why.' It is this legacy of bitterness which one sometimes glimpses during the spring feria that otherwise seems so gay. It recalls the perceptive statement made by a Frenchman: 'Spain has had many revolutions but it has always missed the revolution.'

In recent years the feria has acquired an international cast which it did not formerly have. So many famous people arrive and so many motion pictures are shot in the surrounding area that the Alfonso XIII, a grand hotel situated not far from the cathedral, the casetas and the bullring, becomes during this period the jet-set capital of Europe. Orson Welles holds court here and American visitors are impressed by the reverence in

301

which he is held by Europeans; he is judged to be one of the six or seven most significant Americans. Audrey Hepburn lends gracia to the old hotel, while Rita Hayworth and Juliette Greco add piquancy. In 1966 the two American princesses, Jacqueline Kennedy and Grace Kelly, stole the show as they paraded their crystal beauty at the various exhibitions. Spaniards were especially pleased when Jackie Kennedy rode through the park dressed in a faultless costume of Andalucía topped by a flat-brimmed hat. They were surprised at her fine horsemanship, and several members of the noble families expressed the hope that she might want to settle permanently in Spain. 'She is one of us,' they said. 'She'd find our way of life congenial.'

The daily schedule during feria is a demanding one:

11:00 A.M.	Get up. Breakfast on hard roll and coffee.
12:00 NOON	Dress in riding habit and join the parade.
4:00 P.M.	Leisurely lunch.
5:00 P.M.	Walk to the bullfight.
8:00 P.M.	Visit with friends and talk.
11:30 P.M.	Leisurely dinner.
2:00 A.M.	Drive to the Aero Club for dancing.
5:00 A.M.	Nightcap with friends, then off to bed.

The above is of course the schedule of a cautious man who prefers to take things easy. If at dawn there is excitement on one of the bull ranches or if Don Angel Peralta is giving an exhibition of horsemanship at his ranch near Sevilla, the true devotee skips the sleep.

As to the bullfights, one evening I dined with Orson Welles, that scowling giant who in his youth had trained to be a matador, and he said in his rumbling voice, 'What it comes down to is simple. Either you respect the integrity of the drama the bullring provides or you don't. If you do respect it, you demand only the catharsis which it is uniquely constructed to give. And once you make this commitment you are no longer interested in the vaudeville of the ring. You don't give a damn for fancy passes and men kneeling on their knees. There used to be this fraud who bit the tip of the bull's horn. Very brave and very useless, because it played no part in the essential drama of man against bull. Such tricks cheapen the bull and therefore lessen the tragedy. What you are interested in is the art whereby a man using no tricks reduces a raging bull to his dimensions, and this means that the relationship between the two must always be maintained and even highlighted. The only way this can be achieved is with art. And what is the essence of this art? That the man carry himself with grace and that he move the bull slowly and with a certain majesty. That is, he must allow the inherent quality of the bull to manifest itself. Today in Spain we

Grand entrance of the bullfighters
at Sevilla's Maestranza,
the La Scala of bullfighting.

have many vaudevillians and you won't waste your time completely if you watch them. We also have men of bravery and it's always rewarding to observe this rare commodity in action. But of the true artists who comprehend the fruitful relationship that ought to exist between man and bull there is only one, Curro Romero. And until you have seen him, my friend, you have seen nothing. For this young man, handsome of face but round of body, can launch passes which are the essence of bullfighting. He is really so good that it's difficult to believe that this age produced him, for he has the style of the past, when vaudevillians had little place in the arena. Some day you'll see this boy at his greatest, and I'll be there, and we shall nod to one another across the intervening people, and you will thank me for having insisted that you go to see him.' Unfortunately, Curro Romero did not fight when I had tickets, so I had no chance to see him.

If Córdoba is the apex of the Romantic Movement because of *Don Alvaro, or The Force of Destiny,* Sevilla is the popular capital because of the works which have used this city as their locale. The story of *Carmen* takes place in Sevilla and one needs no imagination to see the gypsy lounging in the doorway of the old tobacco factory, second largest building in Spain and now used as part of the university. Spaniards profess to be irritated by the attention given *Carmen* throughout the rest of the world and claim that it damages the image of Spain, but I have noticed that whenever a Spanish impresario needs a full house, he puts on *Carmen.* One of the greatest performances came in the bullring at Sevilla; when the brigands filtered onto the stage they came with lanterns from all parts of the ring, and in the gala scenes carriages with prancing horses and three hundred extras filled the ring. Say the Spanish intellectuals with resignation, '*Carmen* is the cross each Spaniard has to bear.' But others confess, 'We're just bitter that it took two Frenchmen to invent her.'

Naturally, it was here that *The Barber of Seville* plied his trade and went forth to conquer the theaters of the world. Many other works of a romantic turn have centered on this city, but the most seminal was a curious play which appeared in print, without fanfare, for the first time in 1630, although it may have been on the boards for as long as fifteen to twenty years. Since then many people have wished that they could have been in the audience on opening night, whenever it was, to see the birth of what has become the most ubiquitous legend in world drama, yet one whose significance has never been adequately explained.

This fateful play was *El burlador de Sevilla y convidado de piedra,* and I have left the title in Spanish because of the difficulty English translators have faced with the second word. Obviously we are speaking of the standard hero of the play, and he was a burlador, or one who engages in burlas. Any standard Spanish-English dictionary shows that a burla is a joke, a jest, a trick, a sneer, a gibe, a mockery, a taunt, a scoff, so we are here dealing with what we might call a prankster, and this accounts, I think, for the erroneous titles which English-speaking translators have used: *The Rogue of Seville*, or Mocker, or Rake. Actually, in Spanish daily life a burlador is a seducer of women and the title should only be *The Seducer of Seville*, which is not only alliterative but also pertinent to the action. Why English translators have shied away from this simple word, I do not know.

Who is this seducer? We meet him at the medieval court of the King of Naples, where his uncle serves as Spanish ambassador. He is leaving the bedroom of a duquesa whom he has seduced in the royal palace by posing as her future husband. This incurs royal displeasure, so he flees to Spain, where he is shipwrecked on the Catalan coast and saved by a lovely fishergirl who nurses him back to health and whom he seduces with promises of marriage. He moves on to the court of the Castilian king at Sevilla, where his father is chancellor and where his servant announces that for the good of all maidens a public crier should precede his master with the proclamation, 'Let all beware of a man who deceives women and is the seducer of Spain.' The king has learned of the Naples escapade but forgives him, with the stipulation that he marry the duquesa, but before this can be arranged he enters by trickery the house of a noble lady loved by a friend of his and attempts to seduce her. When her father, the Comendador de Calatrava, rushes in to protect her honor, the seducer kills him. He now flees to a nearby town, where he thrusts himself into the midst of a local wedding and, with a violent promise of marriage, seduces the intended bride. As the duquesa and the fishergirl appear at court to complain to the king, the seducer returns to Sevilla, and chancing upon the tomb of the Comendador, with a show of bravado seizes the stone statue by the beard and invites it to dine with him that night, which explains the second part of the play's title: convidado de piedra (guest of stone). To his astonishment, even though he has had a table set as his part of the bargain, the statue appears, eats, then invites the seducer to dine the following night in its chapel, on which they shake hands. Although the seducer notes a certain unearthly quality in the handshake, his pundonor obligates him to keep the appointment. At the conclusion of the meal, which has consisted of scorpions, vipers and wine of bile and vinegar, the statue extends its hand, which is taken, whereupon host and guest sink down amid sound and fury into the fires of hell.

Thus appears for the first time in the theater Don Juan Tenorio, hero-villain of demonic proportions. Imagine the reincarnations he is to have. In France, Molière (1665) and Corneille (1677) will produce plays on his life, while at a later date Mérimée, Dumas and De Musset will base stories on his legend. In Italy there will be several versions, the best being Goldoni's (1730). In England, Shadwell (1676) will construct a play on the subject, which Purcell (1676) will use as the basis for an opera, and Byron (1819) will borrow the theme for his major poem. In Germany three distinguished musical versions will appear: Gluck (1760), Mozart (1787) and Richard Strauss (1889). In Spain the recensions will be numerous, until in 1844 a dramatist of whom we shall speak later will construct of the legend a play which will become Spain's national drama, a kind of *Hamlet* and *Faust* combined.

I cannot recommend too highly the original version of this legend. It was written by an ingratiating friar, Tirso de Molina, nom de plume of Gabriel Téllez (1571?–1648), thought to be the illegitimate son of some noble family and the author of four hundred plays, of which nearly ninety are extant. In many ways Friar Tirso's account of Don Juan excels anything that followed, even Mozart's *Don Giovanni*, because it is a hard, clean, unsentimental play with terrific impact. It is realism ahead of its time; ironically, it was to serve as the source of much romanticism. The scenes move rapidly and with a grand fatality; the character of the seducer develops properly and those about him are well differentiated; and the device of the marble statue is used with stunning effectiveness. The style of writing is most attractive, a lean statement not overburdened with simile but filled with salty observation. One matter is of particular importance: although this original version was written by a friar, it does not, like some of the later accounts, end in an orgy of religious reconciliation. Don Juan dies a cynical, tough rogue. At the final banquet with his stone host he dares retribution to overtake him:

> 'What do you call this dish, Sir?'
> 'Scorpions and vipers. These are our foods. Aren't you eating?'
> 'I'd eat it if it were all the asps in hell.'

His only concession comes in his next to last speech, and it was on this that the later versions built their scenes of redemption: 'Then let me call someone to confess and absolve me.' To which the statue replies, 'You have thought of it too late.'

Tirso's version has a classic dignity. It was apparently written about the time of Shakespeare's death (1616) and shows Tirso to have been rather less inventive and poetic than his English contemporary, but in the use of characters from everyday life he is as good. Actually, the form of the play and its development remind one of Racine and Corneille, who followed him. It makes a strong impression on stage, the flow of scenery and costume being particularly attractive, but it requires a strong actor to carry the role of Don Juan. He cannot burlesque it or play it as a dandy; he must be more like the resolute hero of a western movie than a fancy gentleman in lace and ruffles. He is, indeed, the archetype of the hero-villain and should be played as such.

Excellent as the Tirso original was, so far as Spain was concerned it remained merely one more good play among the hundreds produced in this period and it appeared in the theater no more often than any of the minor

Actor as Don Juan Tenorio.

works of Lope de Vega, who died just about the time when Tirso's play was published. But in 1844 something happened, of itself of no significance but of great accidental importance. A romantic playwright named José Zorrilla y Moral (1817–1893), the darling of the theater at that time, produced *Don Juan Tenorio,* a metrical version in full-blown romantic style. It was a sloppy play filled with so many improbabilities that any critic could tear it apart, as many did. The author himself termed it 'the greatest nonsense ever written' and listed the dozen or so points at which it violated dramatic canons and psychological reason. And yet it was touched with flashes of true poetry that tugged at the sentiments; it was flamboyantly staged and excited the imagination, and in some curious way that has never been explained, it evoked a sense of Spain, and in its bombast people of all degrees could see themselves. It leaped into prominence and has ever since retained a hold on the Spanish imagination, both in Spain and in the New World.

Zorrilla's Don Juan is an astonishing man to have become the hero of a nation. Before attempting to guess why this has happened let me assert briefly that it has; intellectuals today in Spain will try to pooh-pooh the idea and say, 'Don Juan Tenorio? No one takes him seriously any more,' but I have talked with too many Spaniards to accept that easy dismissal. Toward the end of October, for reasons which I will describe later, newspapers across Spain carry full-page analyses of Don Juan and find a surprising number of public figures to admit that he is their hero. 'Tenorio lives the way a hero should, not giving a damn for anyone, and when it comes time to die he dies like a man.' 'Tenorio is Spain. I feel very much like Tenorio. I hope I can stand up to adversity the way he did.' 'Estupendo! I vote for Don Juan.' 'What I like about Tenorio is the way he was willing to fight anybody for any reason. The bit about the girls? Well, a man couldn't get away with that today. At least not so much, but men are fundamentally like that. He's my hero.' The statements go on and on. I have more than fifty before me as I write, and some are much more revealing than the commonly heard ones which I have quoted. Today Zorrilla's Don Juan has practically the same power over the imagination of the Spanish male, at least certain males, that he did when he first appeared in 1844.

What changes did Zorrilla introduce to account for the popularity of his hero? Well, the setting remains much the same but the time has been advanced from the indiscriminate fourteenth century to the heroic 1550s, when Carlos V was king and Spain was on the move. In the play there is a sense of Spain's new greatness and some of this rubs off on Don Juan.

This time the curtain rises on an inn in Sevilla, where Don Juan sits writing a letter to his intended bride, Doña Inés, on whom he has not set eyes, since according to custom she has been hidden away as a novice in a convent. He is masked, for it is carnival, and is awaiting the arrival of his friend Don Luis Mejía, with whom he made a wager a year ago 'as to which could commit in a year more evil.' This is the night for casting up accounts. Unexpectedly Don Juan's father and the Comendador de Cala-trava, father of Doña Inés, arrive separately, also masked, and take chairs in a side room so as to overhear what this disreputable young man is up to. Don Luis appears; the bettors unmask; and they proceed to report on their behavior. Don Juan says that he chose Italy as his theater of operations and in Rome fixed the following notice to his door:

> Here is Don Juan Tenorio,
> For anyone who seeks anything of him.

When forced to flee from Rome because of his evil reputation, he repaired to Naples, where he posted another sign:

> Here is Don Juan Tenorio
> And there is no man his equal.
> From the haughty princess
> to the lowly fisherwoman
> all women are fair prey;
> and he will undertake anything
> if it involves gold or valor.
> Let troublemakers seek him out;
> let gamblers crowd around him;
> let anyone who dares come forth
> to see if anyone can best him
> in gaming, dueling or making love.

When his extended list of accomplishments is compared with that of Don Luis, it is seen that Don Juan has won, with thirty-two men murdered in duels and seventy-two women seduced. Don Luis admits himself the loser but points out that Don Juan's list lacks one type of seduction to make it strictly first-class, that of a novice about to take vows as a nun. Don Juan leaps at the challenge and says that for good measure he'll add an addi-tional category, the intended bride of some good friend. Don Luis proposes a time limit of twenty days, but Don Juan says that six will be sufficient, because he does not require much time per woman:

> One to make love to them,
> another to enjoy them,
> another to get rid of them,
> two to replace them,
> and an hour to forget them.

With supreme arrogance he climaxes his boast with the announcement that the bride whom he will ravish shall be none other than Doña Ana, Don Luis' betrothed. At this dreadful statement the two men in the side room have heard enough. The comendador, convinced that his intended son-in-law is a monster, announces that Don Juan's engagement to Doña

Inés is ended, whereupon Don Juan says that the novice he must seduce shall be Doña Inés. At this blasphemy his father disowns him with the words, 'You were never my son.'

Don Juan succeeds both in seducing the novice, Doña Inés, and the bride, Doña Ana, but at his country house, to which he has taken the former, he discovers that she is madly in love with him, in spite of his treatment of her; overcome by her pure innocence, he awakens to the fact that he loves her. His change of heart comes to nothing because at this moment the comendador and Don Luis Mejía break in, seeking satisfaction for their injured honor. Don Juan kneels before the comendador, begs his forgivenness, and tries to convince him that he is a new man, but to no avail. When the comendador seeks to engage Don Juan in an honorable duel, the latter whips out a pistol unexpectedly and shoots the old man dead. He then kills Don Luis, too, and escapes to continue his rampage of destruction. He has proved false to his love, whom he has seduced and abandoned, to his father, whom he ridicules, to his religion, which he has debased, and to every generous impulse save bravery alone.

What can a foreigner make of a nation which elects such a man its national hero? Before trying to explain we must look at the surprising conclusion of Zorrilla's play. Years later Don Juan returns to Sevilla to visit his family home but finds it converted into a cemetery, one corner of which is a mausoleum in which a sculptor is at work putting finishing touches to a group of life-sized statues representing the victims of Don Juan. To the latter's surprise, he notices among the dead a beautiful standing statue of Doña Inés and he learns that she died of a broken heart. When the sculptor has left, the don addresses the effigy of his lost love and confesses that he did truly love her. Overcome with grief, he leans weeping upon her tomb, and when he opens his eyes he finds that her statue has disappeared from its pedestal. In a dream sequence the ghost of Doña Inés appears and tells him that since she has chosen to remain faithful to her satanic lover, God has condemned her to the purgatory of her tomb to await the return of Don Juan, both of them to be saved or lost together. Don Juan dismisses her appearance as an illusion and his old bravado reasserts itself. As in the Tirso play, he invites the statue of the comendador to dine with him; subsequently he dines with the statue in the cemetery. Again the statue offers its hand, and Don Juan feels himself pulled down toward hell. 'Lord, have mercy on me,' he cries, but the statue replies stonily, 'It is too late.' But now Doña Inés takes a hand in the proceedings, and the stage directions for the final scenes explain better than the dialogue what is happening:

> *Don Juan falls on his knees, stretching toward heaven the hand that the statue leaves free. Shades and skeletons are about to throw themselves upon him, but at this moment the tomb of Doña Inés opens and she appears, taking the hand which the don stretches upward.*

Flowers open and little angels issue forth, surrounding Doña Inés and Don Juan, scattering over them petals and perfume, and to the sound of a sweet and distant music the scene is diffused with the light of dawn. Doña Inés falls on a bed of flowers instead of in her tomb, which disappears.

Don Juan falls at the feet of Doña Inés and both die, but from their mouths issue their souls, in the form of two bright flames, which disappear in space as music plays and the curtain falls.

This Mercy of God and the Apotheosis of Love, as the last act is subtitled, can be quite moving if well staged and if no one laughs; it has made the play acceptable to believing churchgoers in spite of Don Juan's execrable list of crimes in the first two-thirds of the play. *Tenorio* thus becomes a sardonic morality play, demonstrating the doctrine that even the most flagrant advocate of Viva yo can attain salvation. In fact, God seems to approve of Don Juan and, through him, of Spain as well. Also, the engaging figure of Doña Inés—and she can be one of the most appealing heroines in drama—as she saves the rakehell through the purity of her love, is attractive to women. I have seen the play four times in Spain, twice in Mexico and twice on television, and each time as it ended the women around me were crying. A friend once explained, 'Every Spanish woman sees herself in Doña Inés. By her love alone is her husband saved.'

One of the reasons why *Don Juan Tenorio* is so popular is accidental and relates to cemeteries. Because Zorrilla introduced in his concluding scenes a mausoleum containing marble statues of the don's victims, a tradition was established for Spanish cities to offer *Don Juan Tenorio* in the week of November 1, the eve of All Souls' Day, which is the Spanish Memorial Day, when families traditionally visit cemeteries. This aspect of the play's acceptance is of course irrelevant and childish.

But Zorrilla's *Don Juan* is much more than an accidental cemetery prank. To understand the strange grip it has on the Spanish audience one must remember what was happening in Spain when it appeared. It was 1844, a time of chaos, when knowing men already suspected that Spain was in permanent eclipse. The empire was falling apart; the internal government was inept; the economy had failed; the storms of liberalism and conservatism were beginning to rip the country; and here came a figure who recalled the days of glory when Spain ruled Europe. (Remember that numerically most of Don Juan's adventures took place in Italy, not Spain, and those of Don Luis in Flanders, along with Germany and France.) He was a kind of challenge to the rest of the world, the brave, arrogant man who would surrender to no adversary. He was Spain entrapped; he was Spain fighting against great odds; and in the end he was saved, partly because of his tremendous intransigence.

Don Juan is also the exemplification of male values in Spanish life. From what I have said of his career one might suspect that Spanish women would hold him in contempt, but that is far from the case. He is their hero as much as he is the hero of their husbands and sons. His love scenes are never gross; he woos with tremendous passion and with a poetry that explodes in symbols and verbal fancies; he is no cruel Bluebeard but a devoted lover; that is, during those two days that he can allot a woman. He is also manly in a general sense, quick with the sword, swift to resent insult and brave beyond challenge. On stage he is enormously attractive; Enrique Guitart, one of the actors who specialize in portraying him, wears a large variety of brocaded capes, which he has learned to flourish in beautiful sculptured circles much as a matador does when fighting a bull, although better because the stage capes are bigger and their flourishes more unexpected, cutting wide swaths of astonishment.

Finally, say the critics, Don Juan is more than a man, more than a hero. He is all humanity, and like humanity he seeks ideal solutions. He is not chasing women; he is seeking the perfect woman. He is not a cowardly murderer; he is mankind faced with the inescapable responsibility to kill in warfare. And in the culminating scenes of apotheosis he becomes all guilty men throwing themselves on the benevolence of God and finding themselves saved because of their submission to the female principle of love. All these things Spain believes of herself; redemption is possible. I spoke a few paragraphs ago of how I have seen women weep during the scene in which Doña Inés rescues Don Juan; I have seen just as many men weep in an earlier scene in which Tenorio, learning for the first time that Doña Inés died after he stole her from the convent and abandoned her, utters a heartbreaking sob and acknowledges that he did truly love this girl. 'At this moment,' a friend explained, 'each man in the audience remembers all the pretty girls he kissed years ago and didn't marry, and the passage of time and the closeness of death become very real.' My friend had tears in his eyes as he spoke. Without question, this strange and poorly written play evokes in the Spaniard a memory of Spain and of lost opportunities.

My own interpretation of Zorrilla's play is that it epitomizes the union of pundonor and Viva yo. At a dozen places Don Juan affirms the principle of pundonor. In defense of his peculiar definition of honor he would die, kill his best friend, duel his closest associates, challenge the marble statue or oppose God. He is almost a burlesque of pundonor, but not quite, because both he and the audience take his challenges seriously. At the same time he is the epitome of Viva yo. No other national hero is so self-centered as Tenorio. Faust is concerned about human values and is hesitant about ignoring the rights of others until Mephistopheles goads him to do so. Hamlet constantly weighs the good and evil which his actions might impose on others: the king praying, the queen's right to remarry, Ophelia's future. Don Juan Tenorio indulges in no such soul-searching, not even when it is forced upon him by his father, whom he spurns abusively.

And this makes him attractive to the Spaniard, who feels the same way about his country. The visitor to Spain is often shocked by the fact that what he holds to be a cause for condemnation is judged by the Spaniard to be a cause for congratulation. Later when I speak of Queen Isabel the Catholic, I shall make it clear that I find her one of the notable women rulers of all time, probably greater even than Elizabeth of England, but I have always regretted two acts which tarnish her reputation: her sponsorship of the Spanish Inquisition and her expulsion of the Jews. I was surprised to find that Spaniards are apt to love her *because* of those reasons: 'She showed the rest of the world that she was boss and that Spain was Spain.'

Before ending this adventure in romanticism run wild I must point out that among young Spaniards the cult of Don Juan is being subjected to analysis and sometimes to ridicule. One newspaper in 1966 asked its readers whether Don Juan still existed in Spain: 'Yes, and in today's world he's contemptible.' 'Sure, in the cinemas. He's masquerading as James Bond.' 'Of course, in the Spanish gallants who swarm the beach at Torremolinos, trying to seduce Swedish girls.' 'Yes, the gamberros [hoodlums] and the ye-ye crowd [rock-and-rollers].' It was generally agreed that Don Juan was hanging on, especially in small towns, where men took seriously their obligation to be lady killers. 'He exists in every real Spanish man. We all dream we are brave, honorable and death to ladies.' But one young woman warned, 'I've got news for Don Juan. He may exist but girls like Doña Inés are no more. I don't know any girl who's going to swoon because some man looks at her.' Another girl said, 'Doña Inés is still around but today she's comical.'

If one were preparing for a visit to Spain it would be profitable to learn the language; it would be more so to see a performance of *Don Juan Tenorio,* for with mere words one can go only so far, but with the vocabulary of this play one can speak of central matters. To prowl the streets of Sevilla with Don Juan in cloak and poignard is to explore permanent Spain.

Even if Sevilla had no Don Juan and no feria, it would still throw down a unique challenge. Outwardly it strikes the visitor as a congenial place, but inwardly it permits no stranger to penetrate its secrets. It is not a city of contrasts; it is a city of contradictions, enticing but withdrawn, alluring but arrogant, modern in appearance but eighteenth century in attitude. In Madrid or Barcelona the stranger has some hope of forming friendships which will uncover something of the workings of Spanish life, but in Sevilla this happens so infrequently as to constitute a miracle when it does. The symbol of Sevilla is the caseta, brightly illuminated and with its front wall removed so that the passer-by can observe the festivity of a

FOLLOWING FACING PAGES: *During feria the young women of Sevilla appear at their most seductive. And always in the background, iron bars of tradition.*

closely knit family group. If he is lucky enough to own a horse, he can even rely on a traditional sherry if he stops outside. But to enter the caseta and to participate in the mystery that surrounds the family of southern Spain seems almost impossible.

Sevilla is a feminine city, as compared to masculine Madrid and Barcelona, but if one finds here the ingratiating femininity of grillwork on balconies and grace in small public squares, one finds also the forbidding femininity of a testy old dowager set in her preferences and self-satisfied in her behavior. It is not by accident that Sevilla has always been most loyal to movements that in the rest of Spain are in decline.

For example, at repeated points in history Sevilla has been faithful to the crown when other cities have not; the symbol of Sevilla is the rubric NO-8-DO, in which what looks to be an 8 is really a skein (madeja), so that the whole reads: 'No madejado' (She has not abandoned me), referring to a time when a king in trouble appealed to Sevilla for help. The city also adheres to an older interpretation of religion and to feudalism. As we have seen, in the countryside surrounding Sevilla the relation of noble to peasant is much the same as it was in England in 1400. Laws of course proclaim otherwise, but custom prevails.

Sevilla is ancient and as a city of importance nearly two thousand years older than Madrid. It was an important Roman center, and near its present site stand the excavated ruins of a considerable city named Itálica. But Roman occupation of the area left little imprint on Sevilla, although Sevilla made considerable impression on Rome, having contributed two of the principal Caesars, Hadrian and Trajan. Sevilla was also a major capital of the Moors, having been occupied by them in one capacity or another for 536 years, yet today one finds in the city even fewer of the Muslim memories that make Córdoba and Granada such noble testaments to the Moorish influence in Spanish history. Even the graceful Giralda has had its Moorish origin submerged in Christian additions, while in the nave of the massive cathedral the Moorish pillars are lost in heavy Gothic shadows. Whenever a conqueror departed, Sevilla quickly reestablished itself as a Spanish city, jealous of its prerogatives and marvelously insular in its attitudes. If one seeks a whole body of people who have refused to acknowledge the advent of change, few can compare with the citizens of Sevilla.

Of all the cities involved in the Spanish Civil War, Sevilla was modified least by the experience; the governors required only a few hours to make up their minds as to which side they were on, and after an initial slaughter of six thousand, took over the place for General Franco and his troops. Avoiding the agonizing indecision that paralyzed and even doomed other cities, the people of Sevilla almost avoided the war. Little of moment happened here and the return to peace was accomplished more quickly than in any other city of comparable size. To Americans, whether from north or south, Sevilla is of special interest because although the colonies of Spain were conquered by Extremadura, they were governed from Sevilla; the cargoes of gold from Peru and Mexico were brought up the Guadalquivir to the docks where the bullring now stands, and the nobles who were to rule the distant lands either well or poorly sailed with their commissions from this port. Scholars have long believed that one day the inexhaustible depositories of Sevilla will produce hitherto unknown documents relating to the early history of the Americas, and they expect maps to be uncovered which will alter our present understandings, for to Sevilla came reports from all parts of the world. Here also centered the branches of the Church dealing with America and the administrative cadres, both civil and military, responsible for the actual governing. Sevilla might properly be termed the historic capital of the Americas; during some three centuries it was the nerve center which controlled all.

If a stranger could inspect but one city in Spain and if he wished to acquire therefrom a reasonable comprehension of what the nation as a whole was like, I think he would be well advised to spend his time in Sevilla, for this city, even though it is too individualistic to be called a microcosm of the whole, is nevertheless a good introduction to classical Spanish life. I was familiar with the rest of Spain before I saw Sevilla, but nothing I had learned elsewhere taught me so much about Spanish behavior. Others have reported a similar experience, for Sevilla does not have ambiente; it is ambiente, and nowhere has this been better expressed than in a lyric by Manuel Machado, written in this century, which is quoted constantly throughout Spain. It is a litany of Andalusian names, each described with its most typical appositives except one, for which no adjectives or nouns suffice:

> Cádiz, salada claridad,
> Granada, agua oculta que llora.
> Romana y mora, Córdoba callada,
> Málaga, cantaora,
> Almería, dorada.
> Plateado Jaén.
> Huelva, la orilla de las tres caravelas.
> Y Sevilla.

(Cádiz, salt-laden brilliance/ Granada, hidden waters that weep/ Roman and Moorish, silent Córdoba/ Málaga, flamenco singer/ Almería the golden/ Silvery Jaén/ Huelva, the shore of the three caravels [of Columbus]/ And Sevilla.)

No part of the spring feria was more enchanting to me than the way it ended. As dawn breaks following the last night of the fair, or perhaps at six or even at seven o'clock, when there is no longer any hope of encountering late revelers, and when the sound of clapping has finally died out in

Time and tradition pass very slowly. It is the people who age rapidly.

the streets, drivers of horse-drawn cabs assemble informally at the southern edge of the city. There, from whatever bottles **of** wine they have reserved for this moment, they drink together and stare back at the outlines of Sevilla as it becomes visible in the morning twilight. Then they climb onto their seats, whip their horses gently and begin a single-file trek to the south.

Here comes a carriage with arms blazoned across the door. Behind it moves a pair of white horses pulling a cab which today bears no paying

318

passengers but only the driver, his wife and their three children, all five sleeping as the horses jog slowly homeward. Here come two more cabs with their drivers asleep, for many of the cabbies have not been to bed for more than a week; during the fair cabs are busy twenty-four hours a day. In quick succession three businesslike cabs pull out of line and overtake the others, for their drivers hope to gain additional fares by reaching home before nightfall. And at intervals one sees highly polished carriages being driven by boys not much older than ten or eleven; the rightful drivers have gone south by bus so as to get in a full day's work at some regular job, leaving the cabs to be brought home by their sons.

For fifty miles this extraordinary parade stretches out, a hundred carriages or more, so that if you travel this day along the eastern edge of Las Marismas you will see fine vehicles all the way to Jerez de la Frontera and even on toward Cádiz. For these are shrewd men whose ancestors learned more than a hundred years ago that if a driver can somehow get his carriage to Sevilla during the fair he can pick up a good deal of money from the excess of strangers who crowd the city at that time. It is worth making a drive of sixty miles or more each way to qualify for a chance at this money, and now the cabs are heading home.

If any reader should want to see the feria for himself, he'd better hurry. On my last day in Sevilla I asked Señor Ybarra, whose ancestor had revived the fair in 1847, if there was any truth in the rumor that the fair grounds had been sold for industrial buildings, which would mean the end of the circuses, the carnival and the casetas, and he said, 'We've been told that the land has been sold. It's economically impossible to keep so much land near the center of the city lying idle eleven and a half months a year so that people can ride horseback for one week. But don't worry. Plans are under way to move the whole thing out to the river lands where the horse fair is now held.'

I cannot imagine Sevilla in the spring with a fair so far away that I could not easily walk to it. I cannot imagine the nights without groups of people passing beneath my window on their way home. I am sure the new fair will be approved by many, but not by me.

FOLLOWING PAGE:

La zarzuela.

VII

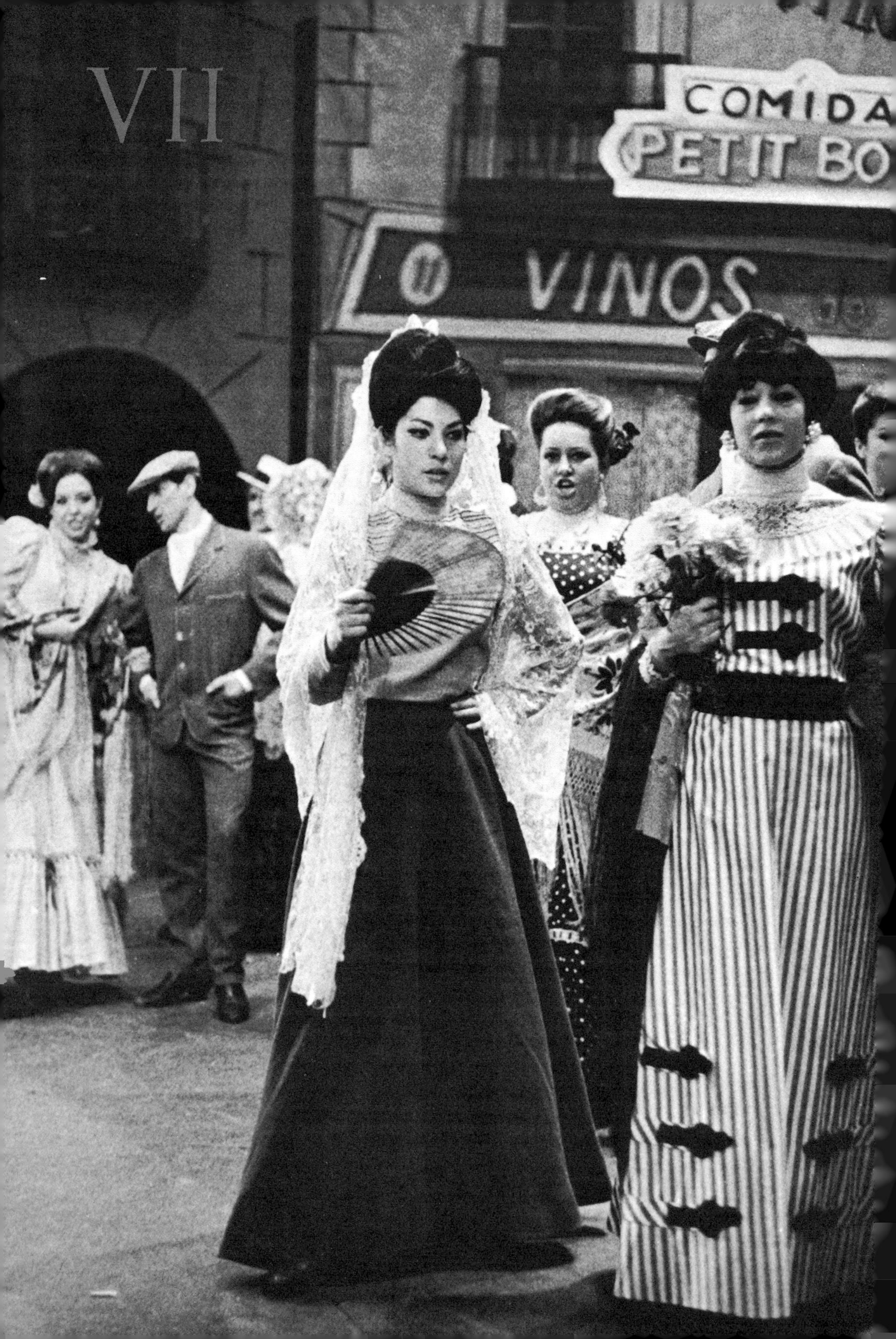

MADRID

OCEANO
ATLANTICO

MILES
0   100

Barcelona

El Escorial
Alcalá de Henares
Madrid
Cuenca

Lisboa

Alicante

Sevilla
Ronda
Torremolinos

MAR MEDITERRANEO

From the first moment when as a boy I read of Spain, and in high school when I studied my first Spanish short stories, and even in college when reading simplified novels, one corner of Spain always preempted my affection, as during recent centuries it preempted the affection of Spaniards. Poets wrote verses about this part of Madrid; novelists laid some of their most powerful scenes within sight of its buildings; painters depicted it at various times of day; and on frequent occasions the ordinary people of Spain erupted into its confines to launch either protest or revolution. Scenes of the most dreadful savagery had occurred here, but scenes of compassion and love were not uncommon.

It was appropriate that the first literary work I read in Spanish was *El capitán Veneno* (Captain Poison, 1881) by Pedro Antonio de Alarcón (1833–1891), in which a gruff and surly captain is wounded in one of the frequent uprisings of the time and thereafter takes refuge in the house of an impoverished woman and daughter who live in the vicinity of the Puerta del Sol.

Gate of the Sun! Eastern Gate of Madrid, from which road distances in Spain are measured. Beloved of Madrileños for centuries and focus of their life in a way that the popular squares of other European capitals could not equal. I was a young man filled with unrealistic visions of Spain when I first saw it, and from an inconsequential hotel which stood nearby I began those quiet explorations and investigations which brought my preconceptions of Spain into some kind of harmony with the facts. I could have wished little better for myself than the experience of seeing the Puerta del Sol as I did in the days before its significance began to decline as sharply as it has done in the past thirty years. Then it was a summary of the Spanish history of the nineteenth century, preserved like a museum into the twentieth, and to wander in its surroundings was to walk intimately in the alleys, if not the grand halls, of Spanish memory.

What was the Puerta del Sol? In my day there was no portal or gate as such, although in earlier centuries there must have been. There was, however, an intimate plaza shaped somewhat like a half-circle, around whose curved side stood a collection of sturdy, symmetrical beige buildings of almost classical charm. Along the flat side stood government buildings of some sort, but these never attracted my attention. A total of ten streets debouched into the plaza, which explained how, in time of riot, it could so swiftly fill with people. The Puerta itself contained no shops that interested me, but in the warren of streets and twisting alleys which fanned out from it were some of the most enticing businesses in Spain. Here one could find almost anything he desired and, as we shall see later, almost any kind of restaurant.

How utterly lovely the Puerta del Sol was in those days, how exciting for a foreign tourist! This word has come into ill repute in recent years, because so many tourists have gone abroad with no preparation which would enable them to appreciate what they were about to see and no humility to make them approach the country on its own terms. In Spain I have always been a tourist and have been rather proud of that fact. This is the book of a tourist and the experiences described herein are those which are open to any intelligent traveler. If, as I once heard an Englishman say, 'to be a tourist is to stand gape-eyed with love,' I have been one, and never more so than in my first days in the Puerta del Sol.

Because I wanted to stay as close to the heart of Madrid as possible, I took a room in the old Hotel París on the Calle de Alcalá, a room as dark and confined as any I have ever stayed in. There was no reason why a sensible young man would remain in such a room a minute longer than necessary, for my lone window looked into a ventilation chute and the bathroom was so far down the hall that I could not luxuriate in the tub. It was rather like the bunk on a submarine, a place which one uses only when in a state of utter exhaustion. Thus I was thrown into the Puerta del Sol for as long as I could walk and then into the public rooms of the Hotel París when I had to rest.

In the plaza I met wonderful people who enjoyed talking with a norteamericano. In the hotel I met considerate men and women who wanted to be sure that I saw the best in Madrid. 'Have you been to the military museum?' they would ask, or, 'Have you tried the seafood restaurant in the Calle de los Cuchilleros [Cutlers]?' And they talked with me, abiding my poor Spanish but recognizing my enthusiasm. It was with strangers from this hotel lounging room that I first saw the Prado Museum and stood 'gape-eyed' at the plethora of greatness it contained. It was with a family that was bored with its room as small as mine that I went to the Teatro de la Zarzuela to resume my study of what I had liked so much at the theater in Castellón de la Plana. With these congenial strangers I saw the parks, the boulevards, the bars of the grand hotels and the music halls, but always we came back to the Puerta del Sol, that magic plaza along whose edge the trolley cars ran to all parts of the city. In my travels I have sometimes been disappointed in sights which publicity has built up; at other times I have been surprised by the excellence of things I had not previously heard about; but I believe the most pleasant experience is to find something like the Puerta del Sol which is exactly the way the poets, historians, novelists and musical composers have said it was. Now, of course, it is much diminished; the burgeoning growth of Madrid has dragged the center of the city to other quarters and the tourist will no longer find in the Puerta what I found there. I went down the other day and it looked much like an open square in New York or Mexico City and it was difficult to believe that this was the spot which had had so strong an effect upon me years ago. The Hotel París still stands and in its rooms travelers with small funds still stare at ventilation shafts, but the glory of the Puerta del Sol is dimmed.

The same can be said, I think, of that really noble area that stands just off the Puerta del Sol, the Plaza Mayor, a huge thing rimmed with classical buildings and massive stone arcades. A rather fine equestrian statue in the middle of the plaza carries a plaque which summarizes the history of the place:

QUEEN ISABEL II, AT THE REQUEST

OF THE GOVERNMENT OF MADRID, ORDERED

TO BE PLACED ON THIS SITE THIS STATUE OF

KING FELIPE III

SON OF THIS TOWN, WHO RETURNED THE COURT

TO IT IN 1606 AND IN 1619 CONSTRUCTED THIS

PLAZA MAYOR

1848

An eighteenth-century engraving shows the great plaza prepared for a bullfight in which four mounted noblemen were to participate, and the caption, written at the time, states that 'the Plaza Mayor on this day showed seven hundred balconies and contained fifty-two thousand spectators.'

The plaza is linked, in the minds of those who read Spanish history, with Spain's most unfortunate king, Carlos II (1661–1700), known as El Hechizado (The Bewitched) because of his twisted and incompetent body and mind to match. He was the last of the Spanish Habsburgs and the inheritor of all their weaknesses; a substantial case could be made that he was insane, but he reigned from the age of three, and it was his childless death that brought the Borbón rulers to the Spanish throne and the war of the Spanish succession to Europe.

When Carlos was eighteen he caused much excitement at court by finally expressing an interest in something. Overhearing that the Inquisition's jails in outlying districts were crowded with heretics whom the judges had found guilty but had not yet burned, he announced that it was his pleasure to hold in the Plaza Mayor a sumptuous auto-da-fé at which a hundred and twenty condemned would be brought forth for sentencing. With real excitement the slack-jawed monarch organized a spectacle of which the English historian John Langdon-Davies has said, 'There can be no denying that the show staged on June 30th, 1680, in the Plaza Mayor of Madrid, must have been one of the most dramatic, the most moving, conceived by the mind of man since the days when Christians and wild beasts fought one another for the amusement of decadent Rome.' Carlos spent a month formulating the complex ritual for the exhibition and running through a series of dress rehearsals. On the day itself fourteen uninterrupted hours were spent preaching at the heretics and reading their sentences, after which one hundred and one were dismissed with lesser sentences, like flogging or a term in the galleys, while the remaining nineteen were prepared for the stake.

It is not my intention to recite the details of this grisly day; anyone wishing to know what was entailed in an auto-da-fé—for some curious reason this particularly Spanish institution has always been known in English in its Portuguese spelling, instead of the Spanish auto de fé (act of faith)—should consult Langdon-Davies' *Carlos, The King Who Would Not Die* (1962). I am more interested in that author's researches as to how the king who had organized this spectacle for his personal edification had become the way he was, and what Langdon-Davies has to say on this subject throws much light both on Spanish history and on the decline of the Habsburgs.

Spain had had two crazy queens. The second we have already met, lying in state in the mausoleum in Granada, Juana la Loca (1479–1555). The first was her grandmother, Isabel of Portugal (c. 1430–1496), whom we shall meet more fully in the next chapter. It was through these two unfortunate women that the madness of the Spanish Habsburgs was transmitted; had their offspring married outside the family it is highly probable that the faulty strain would have been submerged. Instead, look at what happened to produce a near-idiot like Carlos II:

> A man's ancestors in the third, fourth and fifth generations comprise eight, sixteen and thirty-two relationships respectively. Thus Carlos' parents, like everyone else, each had fifty-six such relationships in their family trees, or one hundred and twelve between them.
>
> These one hundred and twelve relationships in their case were shared between only thirty-eight individuals. Of Carlos' mother's fifty-six ancestors,

The Rastro, Sunday morning.

forty-eight were also ancestors of his father. Of the thirty-two women in the fifth generation, that is the sixteen of one parent and sixteen of the other, twelve were descendants of mad Isabel of Portugal.

In the two family trees the name of Juana la Loca occurs eight times, the names of her two sons nineteen times. Seven out of the eight great-grandparents of Carlos II descended from Juana la Loca. No wonder he was bewitched.

Today the Plaza Mayor is a vast empty area in which little happens. The many balconies still lend the place an architectural charm, but even when I first knew it the predominant echoes were tragic, for history has passed it by and it is only in the lesser streets surrounding it that the life of Madrid moves with its old vigor. I first became aware of this one Sunday morning when I saw large numbers of people leaving the Puerta del Sol and heading for what I supposed was the Plaza Mayor, but I was wrong, for they passed right by this empty square and sought another set of streets leading to a narrow plaza watched over by a heroic statue of Eloy Gonzalo, a bearded soldier who had conducted himself with glory in the Spanish-American war in Cuba. What stretched out at the foot of the statue was something that was difficult to believe. Thousands upon thousands of people had convened, as they did each Sunday, to see what bargains they could pick up in the junk stalls of the Rastro (Slaughter-house), and I was later to discover that no traveler can feel like a real Madrileño unless he can announce at dinner or when entertaining friends, 'You must see the wonderful purchase I made in the Rastro last Sunday.' Some of my friends have furnished their whole apartments from handsome odds and ends acquired in this way; one man bought in June six bronze candlesticks, each seven feet high, for three hundred dollars and sold them in August to a New York antique dealer for three thousand. Renaissance pictures, empty Coca-Cola bottles, antique needlepoint, Chevrolet carburetors, Roman coins, damaged Goya etchings and positively anything a human being could want or which in normal circumstances he would throw away can be found in this amazing market. It operates in diminished size the rest of the week, of course, but the Sunday outpouring is something to see.

And so in my early visits to Madrid I stayed at the Puerta del Sol, wandered in the Plaza Mayor, absorbing history, and refreshed myself with the mobs in the Rastro. When I had saved a few pesetas I followed the advice of a gentleman I had met at the Hotel París and took my meals in either of those two fine restaurants that lie just off the Plaza Mayor, Botín's dating back to 1725 and The Caves of Luis Candelas, a rambling affair named in honor of Spain's Robin Hood, who was a great favorite in Madrid. When I first encountered them these restaurants were well known; now they are world-famous and worthy of their reputation.

In 1966, as I approached Madrid once again as a tourist, intending a long stay during which I hoped to clarify my ideas about Spanish politics, I began to reflect upon the changes whose development I had observed during the last fifteen years, and I think the city will be more meaningful if I describe it in terms of those changes, which any tourist could have noticed.

In a sense no visitor can ever be adequately prepared to judge a foreign city, let alone an entire nation; the best he can do is to observe with sympathy. But certain recent experiences had qualified me to look upon Spanish life with better than average understanding. Spain was a theocracy, and I had lived in Israel and Pakistan, which were also theocracies, and the problems of such governments tend to be the same, whether the theocracy is Jewish, Muslim or Catholic. Spain was also a dictatorship, and I had recently come from the Soviet Union and could compare what happened in Spain's relatively relaxed tyranny with what happened in a hard dictatorship like Russia's. 'We no longer have a dictadura, a dictatorship,' a Spaniard told me, 'but rather a dictablanda, a bland dictatorship.' And what was most instructive, I had known Japan, and it, like Spain, was feudal, ritualistic, devoted to honor and committed to maintaining a closed society. In fact, I found Spain to be the Japan of Europe, and at many points I was able to fathom the incomprehensibility of Spain only because I had first met the similar incomprehensibility of Japan.

In 1950 Madrid was one of the most delightful world capitals to visit, for then I could debark at the airport, ride quietly along beautiful streets to the center of town and choose at will from some twenty good hotels, where I would be welcomed; *now* Madrid is grotesquely overcrowded so far as tourists are concerned and I have learned to steer clear unless I have confirmed reservations. In 1963 I could not find hotel space, but that was understandable because I had come in May, when the fair of San Isidro was under way. In October of 1964, when nothing was under way, I was absolutely unable to find a room in any hotel and had to scrounge around among my friends. In May of 1965 I invited an American to stay with me in Madrid, and all the services of the air line, the police and my friends could not find him accommodation. He had to sleep on a cot in a hallway. And in September of 1966, in the real off-season, I could find not one hotel room, and it was only when Don Ignacio Herguete, whom we met in Trujillo, interceded that something was provided.

Then Madrid had one of the most charming trolley-car systems in Europe, and on it I wandered through the various sections of the city, watching as people of various types clambered aboard to argue with the conductor. Getting about the city was not only easy but positively pleasant, for Madrid had the characteristics of an overgrown country town, with unexpected nooks at the end of each trolley ride; *now* the trolleys have largely vanished and I have to go by subway or cab, and no other city has so miserable a taxi system. There are not enough cabs; they do not serve the proper centers; and they will not respond to phone calls. After the theater, or a bullfight, or a football game or dining out one must wait forty or fifty minutes to catch a cab, and even then he must walk eight or ten blocks to reach a point where cabs will stop. At least five times on each trip to Madrid I swear, 'I'll never come back to this city . . . the humiliation is too great.' The government is aware of the problem but can do nothing about it, for reasons which have been explained to me but which I cannot understand.

Then Madrid was a compact city of one million, six hundred thousand; *now* it is a sprawling metropolis of more than two and a quarter million.

Then its buildings looked as if they were at least two centuries old; *now* the new growth startles me whenever I have been away as long as six months.

Then Madrid was a city of little traffic, for cars were few; *now* it is a perpetual traffic jam, not yet as bad as Florence or Nice but bound to get worse because within ten years the number of cars will double.

Then Madrid was a puritan city, with police watching for any display of modern life such as short dresses on women, or hand-holding between lovers or flashy dress on men, and the crackdown could be embarrassing. I saw English women thrown out of churches because their bare elbows showed, and German men visiting the Mediterranean beaches were arrested for not wearing tops with their swimming trunks; *now* the city is like a delightful garden in which young people in love kiss openly, girls wear pretty much what they want, and the only women who bother about covering their heads when visiting churches are self-conscious American Protestants. It is difficult to believe the transformation that has occurred in less than a decade.

Then if an American woman traveling alone wished to eat in a restaurant at night, even inside her own hotel, the head waiter would place before her a small American flag to warn the Spanish dandies that this one was not a prostitute, even though she was eating alone in public; *now* women frequent cafés alone, a thing quite impossible even five years ago. I was in one of the famous bars when unattended women began to appear, and one would have thought the roof had suddenly collapsed, but in late 1966 it was not uncommon for business girls to meet in threes and fours after work to drink beer.

Then on church doors across Spain appeared notices, which were taken seriously, warning females against wearing anything but skirts, and these of a dignified length; *now* minifaldas (miniskirts) and slacks are popular.

Then young people had few places to go; *now* it is quite different. On

*This modern mother and daughter
run a fashionable boutique.*

my last trip I stopped for dinner in what had once been a fairly good Chinese restaurant and was shocked to find in every booth a young couple locked in a public embrace. The owner no longer ran the place as a restaurant because he could earn more with less work running it as a cock-tail bar for young people who worked. When I asked about this, a friend told me, 'But all those girls still have to be home by nine o'clock. A lot of Spanish families are discovering to their amazement that girls can become pregnant between seven and nine in the evening, as well as between one and three in the morning.'

Then Madrid was a dark city with few street lights; *now* it is a lovely place in the early evening, brimming with light. The Avenida José Antonio is one of the most pleasant I know and its fountains are a joy. I have lived at one time or another in about six different parts of the city and they were not only varied but also charming. This is a city of much beauty.

Then prices for things like men's suits, women's gloves, leather goods and Spanish-style jewelry were low and represented the best buys in Europe; *now* there are no bargains, but quality is good and what you pay for you get.

Then there were few elevators, and if you wanted to do business with the average Spanish company, you had to climb, climb, climb; *now* each new building has its elevator, and sometimes it works.

Then the newspapers of Madrid were the worst one could read in any major capital, so fantastically bad that it would be painful to describe them. I happened to be in Spain during three different international crises and from the available newspapers I could obtain no logical or sequential news. Imagine how impossible it was to discover anything about Spain itself. Once I brought home with me three sample Madrid dailies to prove to my unbelieving friends how awful they were. The front page usually had a bombastic picture of Generalísimo Franco dedicating a dam. The second page carried a sentimental essay by some hack professor about how Cervantes represented the soul of Spain. The third contained an article on Bishop So-and-So and his belief that Spanish women, when they attend church regularly, are the noblest in the world. On the fourth page appeared a selection of news items ingenious in their ability to say nothing. I remember two complete items. 'Today General Eisenhower made a startling change in his cabinet.' 'General de Gaulle announced today that from here on the French government will pursue a different policy regarding Algeria. The general said that the old policy has not succeeded.' On the following days there was no development of the story and no attempt was made to explain why Eisenhower had shifted his cabinet or what France's new policy was to be. The last three pages provided as good sports coverage as I could have found in London or New York. *Now* the Madrid newspapers have escaped somewhat from the heavy hand that held them down, and from them I can get a sensible idea of what is happening in the world.

During one American election there were extensive analyses of the senatorial race in Illinois, the influence of Robert McNamara on national policy and the shifting popularity of President Johnson as the Viet Nam war intensified. I could find out almost anything I wanted to know except what was happening in Spain. Although censorship of Spanish news had not been relaxed, a salient difference between the Spain of two decades ago and now is the improvement of the newspapers.

Then television was nonexistent; *now* it dominates Spanish life and most of the Madrid homes I visited had a set. Since American shows are popular, magazines regularly offer articles such as 'What Was the Real Eliot Ness Like?'

Then Madrid was a fairy-tale city in which one rarely dined before eleven at night and could go to the theater for the second show at one . . . in the morning, not the afternoon. There was an infectious charm about long afternoons in which luncheon was served at four if anyone was in a hurry, at five if not, and no one acquainted with Madrid in those indolent days will ever forget the gracious city; *now*, although the eleven o'clock dinner is still popular, one can eat at nine or even earlier, and the theater begins at ten.

Then wine was the drink; *now* beer is popular.

Then anything like a cafeteria would have been an insult to the Spanish way of life. A few were attempted but they were derided as American abominations; *now* grab-and-run restaurants are not only popular but essential, because the noontime break in offices is being shortened from three hours to two or even one. The most popular medium-priced restaurants in Madrid today are chrome-brightened places with names like California, Nebraska, Iowa and Samoa, the American name having become an asset rather than a liability. 'You can trust such places to serve good food, clean food and quick food,' a Spanish secretary told me as she, had a hot dog while I had gazpacho.

The biggest social differences between then and now is the radical change effected by what a Spanish man called 'the revolution of the Sueca.' I had better let a Madrid businessman explain: 'I'm not joking when I say that the Sueca has had an effect in Spain somewhat greater than the atomic bomb on those atolls in the Pacific. We had been taught for centuries that any woman who allowed a man to touch her before marriage, and I mean touch literally and not as a euphemism for sexual intercourse, was damned. Society was rigid and allowed no deviations from the central rule. Life was hard and anyone who transgressed was doomed. It was what you call in the United States puritanism, but much stronger than yours because our whole society supported it. Then came the Swedish girls, Suecas we call them, young, blond, laughing, the most beautiful girls in motion anywhere. Of course, there were also Finns and Norwegians and Danes and Germans, but we link them all together as the

333

Suecas. They discovered Spain and flocked down here by the planeload. Their first impact was on the beaches, and once they stripped down to their bikinis and we saw what the human body could be, the old laws simply could not be enforced. You couldn't tell a Spanish man he had to wear a top with his trunks when those damned Suecas were on the beach. He wanted them to see his pectorals.

'Well, the first result of the Sueca invasion was cataclysmic. I can't tell you what a thrill swept over the manhood of Spain when they discovered that such girls were on our beaches looking for sun . . . and romance. In the old days the proudest boast of a Madrid dandy used to be "I know a bullfighter" or "I'm having an affair with an actress." Now it's "I have a Sueca down at Torremolinos." To have a Sueca as your mistress, tall and leggy and blond, is the best thing that can happen to a man these days. I know half a dozen of my friends who have Suecas, and their lives have blossomed like lilac bushes in spring.

'Take this fellow Agapito. A very conservative vice-president of a bank here in Madrid. When I visited Torremolinos, here comes Agapito dressed in old blue dungarees, with a tattoo on his arm, a ring in his ear and a beard. I say, "Agapito! What the hell has happened?" and he says, "Ssssssh! I dress this way every vacation and tell the Suecas I'm a sailor from Alicante. They think it's romantic and I'm doing better than ever." I asked him, "But, Agapito, what do you do when your vacation ends?" and he said, "I throw a party at a restaurant and tell everyone sadly that my ship is sailing from Alicante and I must be off. They cry. I cry. Then I drive to the next town and shave my beard and come back to Madrid." You know what I think, Michener? I think that one of these days some Sueca is going to go into his bank to cash a traveler's check and there's going to be hell to pay.'

This gentleman also told me that the Sueca invasion has yielded two unexpected results. 'It's been rather hard on the traditional Spanish gallant to whom courtship is a series of set positions, as it were. In church he stares at the girl. At the grille he sighs deeply. In the cinema he is allowed to hold her hand for three minutes . . . each show. He has his set speeches, arranged in order of passion, and these he delivers on schedule over a six-month period. It's all been set out for him by custom and if he omits even one step the girl feels he isn't properly ardent. Imagine what happens when such a system runs up against a Sueca who has paid a lot of money to get to Torremolinos, has a limited vacation and doesn't have much time to waste. When our Spanish gallant starts to go into his set act she's liable to say, "Sure, where?" I've seen a lot of Spanish men completely thrown over by such a response. They don't know what to do. They're unnerved and they run away.

Although Madrid is the youngest city we shall visit,
its Retiro Park, with its stone royalty,
has a classic beauty.

'But a more lasting effect has been the psychological. As I said, we've been taught that if a girl allowed a man to touch her, she was proscribed, but we see the Suecas come down, live with men, have a marvelous time and go home as good as they were when they arrived. In my group the enlightenment came when we saw in a newspaper that Birgit So-and-So, whom we had all known at Torremolinos, had married a Swedish official. One of my friends yelled, "But I used to sleep with her!" What he meant was that if a girl had slept with a man she was condemned. But here was this Sueca marrying an important man. It didn't seem fair. But slowly the Suecas have revolutionized our thinking. Not all the world needs to live the way we do in Spain. I cannot begin to tell you how profound this revolution has become. Its effects will be greater, in the long run, than those of the labor unions.'

He then added an interesting afterthought. 'It has many ramifications. Especially regarding you norteamericanos. We see your beautiful girls at our university here, or visiting the military bases. And we see that they are as free sexually as the Suecas. It's fun for us and we have some great times. But then the nagging question comes up. "Should we respect the norteamericano for his manufacturing, his successful democracy, his rich way of life . . . if he can't even protect the honor of his own daughters?" ' I asked him if he thought the Spanish way was better, and he said, 'In the long run, yes. Women should not appear in bikinis at Torremolinos. Or stay out at night the way your girls do in Madrid. Women should be kept closely guarded at home.' Then he looked wistfully across the avenue and said, 'But the Suecas have ruined all that. Because our women have begun to study the Suecas too.'

One aspect of Madrid remains unchanged, then or now, the Prado. This collection of paintings has such a plethora of riches that I know travelers who plan any trip to Europe in such a way as to have a couple of days in Madrid, not to see the city but to stroll once more through this forest of masterpieces. If I want to see eight top paintings, I go to Venice. If I want to see eighty, I come to the Prado.

I was therefore excited as I walked down the avenue one morning in 1965 and saw this stalwart, unimaginative building waiting. The miniskirts, the traffic, the restaurants might change, but the Prado remained permanent and unique. It is a family museum, most of its paintings having been acquired because some specific king or queen loved art and bought a specific painting. Here there was no buying of already assembled collections formed in Paris or London, the way the Romanovs gathered the paintings in Leningrad's Hermitage. Here there was no robbing of museums in cities defeated in war, the way Napoleon robbed to fill the Louvre in Paris. The Prado began as a private collection formed for the most part by the people of one continuous family, at first Spanish, then Habsburg, finally Borbón, and it was never enriched by theft or expropriation. From 1492, when Queen Isabel I the Catholic was making her first cautious purchases, to 1868, when Isabel II of Borbón ended her reign, the pictures were bought one by one, and what we see today are the family heirlooms of this extraordinary sequence of rulers.

Of course, when the Prado was opened as a public museum other Spaniards contributed pictures, and some were very good, but essentially the museum reflects the taste of Habsburg and Borbón.

Among the royal donors, three kings stand out. Carlos V regarded Titian (1477–1576) as the best painter in Europe and commissioned several portraits. In the best of these the emperor appears in full armor astride a black horse caparisoned in purple. In a stormy landscape the setting sun illuminates the small, bearded king as he appeared during the notable victory of Spanish forces over German at the battle of Mühlberg in 1547.

The second of the great collectors was Carlos' son, Felipe II, whose portrait by Titian shows him as a young, intense and capable man. Felipe was known as an ascetic, yet if one segregates the paintings he brought into Spain one finds that he was responsible for the glowing nudes of Titian and Rubens (1577–1640); he also added the wonderful sex-filled paintings by Hieronymus Bosch (c. 1450–1516) to the collection and other lush canvases from Venice and Brussels.

The third of the master collectors is as familiar to us in appearance as one of our own family, for Felipe IV, grandson of Felipe II, was painted numerous times by Velázquez (1599–1660) on horseback, or standing in lace ruffles, or half-length in austere black, or even as seen in a mirror while having his portrait painted. This king stares back at us with heavy-lidded eyes, huge curling mustache and that enormous chin which characterized the Habsburgs. His family is also known to us through many Velázquez portraits: his two wives, his handsome son and above all his adorable little daughter.

The relationship between Felipe and Velázquez was one of the most rewarding in art history, for not only did the royal family provide the artist with some of his finest subjects, but Felipe also commissioned Velázquez to travel in Europe and buy paintings on his behalf. Twice he toured the continent, and many of the choice works in the Prado are there because in riding back and forth between Italian cities he came upon canvases which he thought the king might like.

Today the royal collections are housed in a dark and handsome building located in the center of Madrid. The Prado was originally built in 1787 as a natural history museum but in 1814 was converted for its present use. I had hoped that I might see it in company with Señor Don Francisco Javier Sánchez Cantón, who has been associated with it for many decades and has been responsible for its catalogue. Museum people in other countries hold him in high regard, but each time I reported to his office he was engaged elsewhere, so I missed meeting him, but his secretary provided me with a guide who in many ways was even better, because with Sánchez Cantón, I would have seen merely paintings; with José María Muguruza, I saw everything else.

He was a tall, scholarly Spaniard in his mid-sixties, outspoken and enthusiastic. In the circular tower room which he used for his office he said, 'Everybody knows me because of my brother. A really great architect. He did lots of the buildings Spain is proud of and I suppose I got my job because of him. He died young, you know. I'm an architect in charge of the Prado and you might like to see some of the crazy things we've been doing.'

I said, 'I'm familiar with the changes. The new wings, the way you've converted empty courtyards into new exhibition rooms.'

'Those things are nothing!' Muguruza said. 'Are you game for some real excitement?' I said I was, and he grabbed a cane which he would use for pointing out details of what had taken place. 'From the outside does the museum look any different from when you first saw it?' I shook my head. 'But from the inside! That's a different story!'

I did not know what he was talking about, for as I had said, the inside changes had been no different from what take place in any good museum, but what I was about to see was unique. Dr. Muguruza led me up a steep flight of stairs, then another and another, until we stood on the roof of the old building. There, in Madrid sunlight, he said, 'In the building below us,' and he kicked on the roof, 'we have a collection of paintings which are beyond value. What would they bring? Supposing they could be sold? A billion dollars, two billion? And if they were lost, the damage to the human spirit would be incalculable. So we couldn't risk keeping them in an old building put up a hundred and seventy years ago.'

'That's where they still are,' I said.

'That's where you think they are. Come inside and see.' He led me to a crawl space under the roof and showed me how the vaulted ceiling of the old museum had been left intact, as had the roof on which we had been standing, but between them had been inserted a steel-and-concrete shell nearly a foot thick and invisible from either within or without. The old vertical walls had also been left as they were, and the exhibition walls on which the pictures were hung, but between them new walls of steel and concrete had been inserted.

'We never closed the museum one day,' Muguruza said. 'Working quietly, where no one could see us, we built a concrete cocoon which encloses every area. We have made the museum as fireproof and as burglarproof as possible, because you can't get into it without penetrating this cocoon.'

I could scarcely believe that this transformation had taken place during the years that I had known the Prado. How had the massive girders and the tons of concrete been slipped into position? 'We were satisfied to work slowly,' Muguruza said. He jumped up and down on one of the mammoth concrete vaults and asked, 'What do you suppose is below us right now?' I didn't know, and he said, 'Room XII,' and I visualized that finest single room of the world's museums, a room whose twenty-six paintings represented one of the chief treasures of history.

'Jump up and down on it,' Dr. Muguruza cried, and I did so. The concrete shell did not even reverberate, but I felt uncomfortable jumping on top of Room XII of the Prado.

When I climbed down from the roof and studied the museum from street level I could find no mark that betrayed its renovation, and I reflected that much of modern Spain was like this, heavily reconstructed but with few external marks showing, because the comfortable old appearances had been retained.

How good is the Prado collection? Because of the personal manner in which it was assembled, it has to be uneven. Since the kings of Spain considered Dutch painting plebeian because it portrayed scenes of everyday life, the Prado has practically no Dutch school, and since they cared little for English painting, none were there until a few years ago when a New Yorker who had grown to love the museum unexpectedly gave a Gainsborough and a Lawrence, which look quite out of place. The French school is poorly represented, with no moderns at all, and several of the major Italian schools are ignored. In comprehensiveness the Prado does not begin to compare with great collections like those in the national galleries of London and Washington.

But where it is strong, it has no equal. Thanks to Carlos and Felipe it has the world's top collection of Titians. One room alone contains sixteen prime works by the Venetian, a staggering collection of portraits, religious subjects and nudes. As if that were not enough, in the next room hang eleven more, each good enough to be a major item in an ordinary museum, and in the storeroom hide an additional dozen!

Equally rich is the Rubens collection. In room after room the visitor finds those choice canvases crowded with nudes with which he has been familiar for years without realizing that they were all in Madrid.

That we can still enjoy these nudes of Titian and Rubens is something of a miracle, for although they were among the favorites of the early kings, by the later they were judged scandalous, and toward the end of the eighteenth century were condemned to be burned. Plans were made to destroy every nude in the collection, but in 1792 a group of men, at considerable risk to themselves, hid the offending pictures in a back room of a lesser museum, where they stayed unseen for more than thirty years until it was safe to bring them forth again.

The museum contains many Italian masterpieces. Raphael's (1483–1570) 'Portrait of an Unidentified Cardinal' is here, staring at us coldly from beneath his red hat; scholars have suggested seven different churchmen as the possible sitter, but he remains a mystery. Here also is Paolo Veronese's (1528–1588) radiant little jewel, 'The Finding of Moses,' probably the best painting this polished artist ever did.

My favorite among the Italians is Correggio's (1494–1534) exquisite 'Noli Me Tangere' (Touch Me Not), about as fine a work as the late Italian school produced, for the figure of Christ with arms extended has the quality of supreme religious painting, while the Magdalene in her rich brocade represents humanity at its most enchanting. The landscape, showing as it does the hour of dawn, is faultlessly done and all parts combine to make a most gratifying work.

One of the surprises of the Prado is a series of small rooms on the second floor, so unpretentious that many visitors miss them. Here are displayed the Flemish and German paintings collected by Felipe II and his contemporaries, and to understand the work of these schools one simply must visit the Prado. Two works easiest to grasp are the powerful self-portrait by Albrecht Dürer (1471–1528) and the exquisite little blue painting by Gerard David (c. 1450–1523) showing the Holy Family resting on its way to Egypt. It is one of the purest of paintings, a jewel perfect in all parts.

The picture here that no one should miss is, of course, Hieronymus Bosch's 'Garden of Delights,' in which the precursor of surrealism presents a teeming canvas flanked by two wings in which the delights of sensuality are portrayed with heavy but not offensive emphasis on sex. The central panel is divided into three parts: at the top a lake on which fantastic pleasure boats appear and over whose rivers nightmare bridges rise; in the middle a pool in which lovers swim and around which ecstatic couples parade on all kinds of beasts, including unicorns, griffins and camels; at the bottom a bewildering maze of persons engaged in various delights, such as lovers entrapped in a giant clamshell, dancers whose heads unite to form an owl and a pair surrounded by an evanescent soap bubble.

The curious thing about the 'Garden of Delights' is that it was a favorite picture of Felipe II, and we know that it occupied a place of honor in his palace, but this particular Bosch is only one of several in the Prado, for the more the men of Felipe's time brooded over religious matters, the more they appreciated these lusty pictures from the north.

The most important picture in the Flemish section, however, is of quite a different kind. Many critics have held it to be one of the four or five most significant paintings in the world, and I know two experts who deem it the best canvas ever painted. It is of particular interest to anyone visiting the Prado, for it illustrates better than words can explain the peculiar quality of this collection.

Early in his life Felipe II heard that in a small chapel in Louvain, dedicated to the Confraternity of Crossbowmen, there stood an altarpiece by Roger van der Weyden (1400?–1464) depicting the body of Christ being lowered from the cross. Visitors familiar with the marvelous painting reported to Felipe, 'It is the greatest of the north.' In vain the king tried to buy it, and when this proved impossible he sent a court painter to copy it, and with the copy he was content for several decades. Later his aunt, the Queen of Hungary, succeeded in acquiring the painting for her collection, and remembering how much her nephew desired it, gave it to him as a present.

In the depiction of the ten differentiated figures, in their placement, in the use of color, design and space, and above all in the symbolization of religious emotion, this marvelous stark painting is one of the major accomplishments of western culture. The best painting in the world? That is too strong. One of the four or five best? Without question.

The lasting glory of the Prado lies, however, not in these importations from foreign lands but in paintings from the Spanish school. In this field the Prado has no equal or even any close competitor.

Leave the Flemish rooms and walk down the long corridor housing the works of the Spanish school, and see for yourself the incredible richness of this collection. To take only one example, near the rotunda you will find not one elegant Murillo (1617–1682), 'Immaculate Conception,' with Mary, surrounded by angels, standing on the defeated crescent of Islam, but three separate versions. The third and finest has a strange history: when Napoleon conquered Spain in 1808 to place his brother Joseph on the throne, his general in command of the invasion, Marshal Soult, packed up this Murillo and hauled it back to Paris with him, where it found a home in the Louvre. More than a hundred years later, in 1941, the Franco government in Spain arranged a deal with the Vichy government in France whereby the Soult Murillo was returned to Madrid in exchange for a Velázquez which went to the Louvre, whereupon certain Spanish art critics said, 'To trade a Velázquez for a third copy of a Murillo! We Spaniards must be crazy!' A kinder judgment would be that the Soult Madonna is superior to the other two versions, and to have three such Murillos together in one spot, while other museums have none, demonstrates how lucky the Prado is where Spanish painting is concerned.

Leading off from the Murillos is the long, specially lighted room on whose ceiling I had been jumping. It is known simply as Room XII and has no equal in other museums. Many travelers who schedule their trips so as to see the Prado come only to see this room.

It contains twenty-six paintings by Velázquez, works so varied and magnificent that of themselves they comprise a museum. One Spanish guidebook says bluntly, 'In this room and those nearby hang all the best Velázquez paintings in existence.' Certainly, if one wants to understand this master he must come to Room XII.

I have spent so many hours here that they must add up to days or even weeks, and even yet I don't know how to view it properly. First, of course, one looks at the huge 'Lancers' on the end wall, a painting, like Rembrandt's 'Night Watch' in Amsterdam, so complete that one either perceives its majesty at once or misses it. Words cannot help. There it is, a mammoth canvas overflowing with vitality and perfection, and some people are content to spend their time with it, ignoring the other paintings.

I prefer, however, that series of three powerful canvases in which Velázquez portrays ordinary Spanish life: the weavers, the blacksmiths, the winebibbers. Any one of these paintings, given a room to itself in some museum in London or New York, would be the gem of the collection, but in Room XII it is merely one among twenty-six.

Most visitors to the Velázquez room stand a long time before the two portraits of a young prince named Baltasar Carlos, for these are two of the most engaging and tragic child portraits ever painted. They are engaging because in the first we see him at the age of four or five, dressed as a knight astride a pudgy brown pony set in an idealized landscape. In the second we see him at the age of six—the canvas tells us that was his age—posing as a hunter, cap awry, attended by two brilliantly painted dogs.

The pictures are tragic because of what happened to Baltasar Carlos. The son of Felipe IV, he was a handsome child, apparently intelligent, and Spain was relieved to know that the throne one day would pass into his hands. As he matured he became even more attractive, and Velázquez painted him at various ages, showing him finally as a young fellow of sober bearing with a conspicuous Habsburg chin. But from fifteen on, the young heir fell into debauchery, from which at seventeen he died. The throne passed into the hands of his near-idiot half brother, whom we saw at the auto-da-fé of 1680, Carlos the Bewitched, and the Spanish Habsburgs were doomed.

Women visitors to Room XII linger before the graceful portrait of a little girl, Velázquez's personal favorite, the Princess Margarita, who would grow up to marry the Emperor of Austria. Velázquez painted her many times; several European museums contain versions showing her standing in extremely wide dresses made of lace and satin, and in a moment we shall see that his masterwork also focused on her. By all accounts the little princess was a charmer who matured into a responsible empress, but like her brother Baltasar Carlos, she died prematurely, at the age of twenty-two. That Velázquez loved her strange mixture of imperial dignity and childish charm there can be no doubt.

Some years ago a group of art experts in Florence became irritated by the publicity given the fact that Rembrandt's 'Aristotle Contemplating the Bust of Homer' had sold for $2,300,000, and they issued a statement estimating that the famous first room of the Uffizi, with its three versions of the Virgin enthroned by Cimabue, Duccio and Giotto, would bring $25,000,000 if offered at auction. What would the contents of the Prado

Room XII bring? For the 'Lancers' I suppose a bid of $5,000,000 would be only an opener. For any one of the three genre scenes the price would have to be around four or five million. For the great portraits? I suppose the final figure for the room would be well above $80,000,000, which was one reason why I was somewhat apprehensive about jumping on it.

In an isolated room not far from Room XII hangs in solitary majesty a Velázquez which has attracted attention since the day it was finished. On a special plaque set into the wall nearby, the curators of the Prado describe it as 'The culminating work of universal painting.' It is 'Las Meninas' (The Maids of Honor) and it unfolds on many planes, one behind the other. Six conspicuous ones are, first, a lifelike dog; second, little Princess Margarita attended by her maids of honor and a well-known dwarf; third, Velázquez standing back from his easel on which he is painting a picture which we cannot see; fourth, a man and woman observing the scene; fifth, a wall containing a mirror in which we see that Velázquez is painting the portrait of Margarita's father and mother, Felipe IV and Queen Mariana; sixth, seen through a doorway, a flight of stairs up which a chamberlain is walking.

The picture is unbelievably complex, a kind of exercise in dexterity that only an established painter would attempt in order to prove that he could do it. The various planes are indicated by perspective, the interplay of light and dark, and a clever use of colors. The figures are well done and breathe vitality, but the essential mystery of this work lies outside such considerations. It is a moment of family life caught in suspension, and the groups represented are as real today as when Velázquez painted them.

For visitors interested in modern painting, that is to say the work of artists like Cézanne, Manet and Van Gogh, two small pictures in one of the lesser Velázquez rooms attract most attention. These two unimportant landscapes show the gardens of the Villa de' Medici in Rome and were done on one of Velázquez's scouting expeditions to Italy. The first landscape appears finished and shows simply the façade of a wall of some kind, tall cypresses, a hedge and two male figures. The second, and more important, shows a comparable scene except that the wall is replaced by an archway beyond which rocks and landscape can be seen. Three male figures populate this picture, which might seem unfinished except that this was the way Velázquez intended it.

It is an extraordinary work. It could have been done by any of the modern artists mentioned above, or by Renoir or Pissarro. The subtle brushwork, the spare use of color, the impressionistic drawing and the manner in which space and planes are indicated combine to make this small canvas one of the gems of the collection. It speaks directly from the age of Velázquez to the present, reminding us that all artists face similar problems.

As one would expect, the Prado contains superior works by a host of other important Spanish artists like Ribera (1588–1652), Zurbarán (1598–1664) and El Greco (1541–1614), but it is the paintings by Goya (1746–1828) that astonish. So rich is the museum in works by this artist that a major room on the second floor is given over to them, plus a series of rooms on the first. In the former is found that intriguing pair of portraits which we discussed when visiting the Coto Donaña, 'Maja desnuda' and 'Maja vestida.'

It is in the downstairs rooms that Goya's work seems most impressive, for only here can one see this virile, tough artist at his best: his etchings on the horrors of war, the bullfight series, the famous black paintings. Here also are those exquisite scenes of picnics and parties in the outskirts of Madrid, and the little landscapes that seem to be from another artist, so delicate and poetic are they.

The most famous of the Goyas are those showing the brutality of life, and none excels 'The Third of May,' in which soldiers are shooting down unarmed citizens against a leaden sky showing the spires of a nearby town. This powerful work might almost be termed a summary of Goya's social philosophy, but it is also a masterful work of art.

Concerning the black Goyas, I am embarrassed. On my first visit to the Prado, years ago, I was repelled by this series of fourteen gloomy works in which dark paint predominates. I had not heard of them before and was unprepared for their power. On my second and third visits I also failed to appreciate them, but then I read an essay by Dr. Sánchez Cantón (this was one of the things I had wanted to speak with him about) and I began to understand why experts praised these works so highly; today a painting in comparable style, 'El Coloso o El Pánico,' has become one of my favorite Goyas. It shows a brooding landscape with turbulent sky, a low mountain range flecked by purple clouds, and a valley down which cattle and covered wagons and people are fleeing in obvious panic, driven onward by a terrifying apparition. At the head of the valley, his legs hidden behind the mountains, rises a colossal nude figure, bearded and with enormous arms which he brandishes boxer-style. He is thousands of feet high and is obviously infuriated by some unseen thing which has attacked him. With one hand he could crush all the fleeing people. The total scene is so bizarre and the flight so headlong that the picture remains a masterpiece of terror, as psychologically bewildering as it is artistically exciting.

There are many such Goyas in the Prado, some so revolting as to repel the average viewer, but when one is surfeited with them he finds a small painting, perhaps the last that Goya did, a beautiful work in grays and blues depicting the young French woman who used to deliver milk to his home when he was living at Bordeaux. It was painted, the signature states, when Goya was eighty-one, and like the 'Medici Gardens' of Velázquez seems as modern as any work by Cézanne or Renoir. It is a marvelous thing, a true portrait of one real milkmaid, yet an evocation of all the women Goya loved throughout his life.

Whenever I visit the Prado I am tantalized by the fact that in 1870, during a troubled period, some dozen top-quality Goyas were stolen from the museum. They have never been recovered, but Spanish experts believe they are in existence somewhere. So at any time some lucky seeker, rummaging through old stacks of paintings, may discover one of the missing Goyas and find himself half a million dollars richer.

I end each visit to the Prado by going to a remote room on the ground floor which houses a mysterious statue. It shows a young woman, handsome rather than beautiful, wearing a curious headdress, and was found in 1897 buried on a farm near Elche in eastern Spain. In some way that has not been explained to me it reached the Louvre, where it was recognized as a major work of art, probably the best statue ever carved in Spain, but remained unidentified. When was it carved? Not a clue, but it seems unquestionably old. Who carved it? Not a clue, but guesses have oscillated between a pre-Roman artist and a pre-Renaissance. Who is the woman? Not a clue, but she must have been a person of rank, for the headdress is extraordinary. The statue found its way back to Spain as part of that deal in which the Louvre traded its Soult Murillo for a Velázquez, and as the significance of this statue becomes recognized, critics begin to modify their earlier objections: 'It's still true that to swap a Velázquez for a Murillo is insanity, but if you get the Dama de Elche thrown in, it's not so bad.'

Present judgment inclines toward a theory that this enigmatic statue was carved by Iberians either a few centuries before Christ or a few after, and I have inclined toward the former, but I was startled by the most recent speculation: 'Probably not a woman at all. More likely a young king dressed in ritual battle gear.' When you're next in the Prado, judge for yourself. It will be worth the effort, for this is one of the world's most compelling statues.

In my wanderings about Madrid I kept running into a gentleman who intrigued me. I did not know who he was, but at the bullfights there he would be. In the cafés, at the theater, strolling along the promenades he appeared, always grave, bald, handsome. He looked like a Spanish Charles Boyer and conducted himself in the same courtly manner. He never seemed to make noise but he did exert an authority which was acknowledged by those who came within his circle. I often wondered who he was, for in his combination of studied dress and casual manner he seemed to me Madrid's essential man-about-town, and I knew I would enjoy meeting him.

I did so in a curious way. Front-row tickets for the special series of bullfights held in May were impossible to get, but a Spanish friend showed me how to butter up one of the attendants—fifty pesetas a day, whether anything happened or not—and this fellow would keep an eye on the front row and slip me into any seat left vacant. Some days it worked; some days it didn't; but at one important fight there were two seats vacant and I was summoned to one of them. The man who got the other was this gentleman I'd been seeing about the city.

'I am Manolo Torres,' he said quietly. So this was he, Madrid's legendary bon vivant, a man with a most unusual reputation. Everyone knew him. I'd read three or four long newspaper stories telling how he was held in affection by different strata of Madrid's society, but the thing that all remembered best was that he made flan (egg custard).

'I read about your flan,' I said.

He smiled with genteel embarrassment. 'I do most things poorly,' he said, 'but flan I make as only the angels do.'

It had become a custom in Madrid for Don Manolo to make up a large batch of his special flan each noontime, and there were many important figures who had developed the superstition of never making a significant decision before having had a good-luck flan with Don Manolo. Was a bullfighter flying to Mexico for six fights? Better share a flan with Don Manolo. Was the impresario opening a new musical comedy? Better ensure good reviews by taking a cup of Don Manolo's flan. Cartoonists, politicians, athletes and especially those in the theater relied on Don Manolo's magic to bring them luck.

'How do you make it?' I asked between fights.

Don Manolo's face became ecstatic, one of the few times I was ever to see him betray enthusiasm. 'If when you return to América del Norte you wish to make true Spanish flan, proceed in this manner. In each of six molds put a spoonful of sugar and melt it over the fire until it covers the bottom and almost reaches the point of caramel. Take it off the fire. In a bowl beat three whole eggs and the yolks of three more. Grate some lemon rind. Mix one soup spoon of sugar, not too full, for each of the egg yolks, in this case six. Add milk sufficient to fill the molds, which you now put in the Mary's bath.'

'The what?'

'Baño de María. It means you don't put the molds directly against the heat but with their feet in water. And the flame mustn't be too strong. It should be low. When the mixture seems to have become like gelatin, that is, after about an hour, put the molds in the oven or even better in a little electric stove so you can brown the crust. Then move them to the refrigerator, but don't eat them until you have a guest who has a delicate palate. Estupendo!'

It was a strange thing. I came to know Don Manolo and also read a lot about him but never discovered what he did for a living. It was known that from the age of twenty-four he had gone to the theater every night save when kept in bed by illness. 'Cinema, opera, comedies, tragedies,' he said. 'It's been all the same to me. I am afflicted with the theater. But especially zarzuela.'

I caught my breath. Ever since that first night in Castellón de la Plana, when the man working the barges had taken me to the theater during feria and I had seen my first zarzuela, I had wanted to talk with

El gran flanero.

some expert who knew something of this unique musical form, but in all the years of casual inquiry in both Mexico and Spain, Don Manolo was the first I had met. It was not possible that day to speak with him as much as I would have wished, but later I was able to do so, and I will share his comments in a moment.

The Spanish zarzuela was one of four distinct yet comparable theatrical forms which grew up spontaneously during the last half of the nineteenth century, only to subside in the twentieth, and each seems to have arisen in response to a similar need, even though the four audiences voicing the need were dissimilar.

In England it was the evening of music-hall acts which developed, with its broad mixture of comedy, dance and song. In Vienna the same impulse gave birth to the operetta, which utilized the above three ingredients but added a story. In the United States the best we could do with these ingredients was the sui generis minstrel show. It was in Madrid that this type of popular art found its artistic apex in the zarzuela, which was a playlet, half spoken, half sung, with dancing, comedy and delightful music.

I have often tried to find the name of that first zarzuela I saw in Castellón, but with no luck. All I know is that it had a lasting effect. When the curtain opened and a costumed chorus sang about how pleasant it was to live in Madrid, I settled back for a typical evening of Viennese operetta, but soon a soprano sang an aria of startling dimension, and she was followed shortly by a contralto and a tenor who sang a duet that could have been written by Verdi. But just as quickly the chorus took over to chant something about taking a walk in the park, and I heard no more opera. In other words, in each of the best zarzuelas two or three operatic numbers will explode through the theater for several minutes, after which things subside to routine comedy or folk tragedy.

Most Americans who enjoy good music remain ignorant of the zarzuela, and that is a pity, because Spain today offers more than eighty different zarzuelas in recordings, including some in stereo if preferred. There are also a few records of high quality offering anthologies of choral numbers, the best duets or the best solos for various voices, and these are excellent. For example, if one heard fifteen or twenty of the best duets he would be confused as to their origin; they are equal in intensity, drama and vocalization to the best of Italian or French opera. It is difficult to convince Americans of this, but two summers ago when André Kostelanetz wanted to introduce some sparkle into his series with the New York Philharmonic he offered a soprano singing selections from *La revoltosa*, and the New York audience was delighted. The singers of zarzuela are also of top operatic quality. One year I heard Pilar Lorengar doing zarzuela in Madrid, the next year *Don Giovanni* in Tel Aviv. The tenor Alfredo Kraus has made a similar jump. Not long ago in a zarzuela in Toledo, I heard a soprano who was eligible for work in any opera house in Italy or Germany.

It is in the lack of scope and sustained musical narration that zarzuela suffers when compared to opera, and this deficiency takes some explaining. The composers demonstrated that they could write as good music as their competitors in other nations; the librettists often wrote better; and the performers were as good. I suppose it was the public that was defective, preferring the brief and incidental to the sustained and generic. There is also a noticeable lack of mature dramatic themes—all Donizetti and no Wagner—so that today the typical zarzuela seems as old-fashioned as an antimacassar.

'I like it that way!' Don Manolo says. 'I don't want some clever hack to update the jokes or to place the action in modern Barcelona. The zarzuela is nineteenth-century Madrid and its charm lies in its authenticity. Leave it alone.'

I asked him if he enjoyed zarzuela as much today as when he first saw it. 'Of course! It's engrained in my life. It's me and I respond to it.'

When I asked him what had arisen to take its place, since it was so dated, he became angry and said flatly, 'The zarzuela will never be replaced by anything. In its day it was Spain, and Spain is not replaceable.'

I pointed out that since zarzuela is not presented much any more, something must have taken over the theaters which it used to occupy. What did Don Manolo think of the modern revue? 'Please don't ask me even to attempt such a comparison. The real zarzuela was music, book, setting, a bite of real life. The revue? Beautiful girls and snappy jokes.'

I asked what it had been in the zarzuela that had pleased him most, the dramatic action or the music, and he said, 'There you have the secret. Zarzuela was a perfect blend of each, and any that were deficient in either have died out. I would, however, grant that even if they alter the words too much you can still enjoy the music.'

Then came the two questions which I had been wanting to ask someone for so long: What zarzuelas had he liked as a boy? And which of the old classics still had most life in them? Of those he had seen when he was beginning to attend the theater two stood out, *Molinos de viento* (Windmills) and *Los cadetes de la reina* (The Cadets of the Queen). I had not seen either, but judged from the titles that they had played in Don Manolo's growing up the role that *The Student Prince* had in mine, except that the music was better.

Of the classics, Don Manolo mentioned four which among them cover the main aspects of zarzuela. *La viejecita* (The Little Old Lady, 1897) represents about two-thirds of the plays in that it is merely a frothy entertainment which cannot be taken seriously except for the lilt of its music. In this case it is Brandon Thomas' *Charley's Aunt* (1892) set to music, and is a frolic because it calls for the hero, an infantry officer, to be played by a beautiful soprano so that later on she can masquerade as the old lady. Spanish theater has many roles in which actresses appear as men, to the delight of the audience; since Spain is so essentially a man's country and since the honor of manhood is so stressed, audiences find it refreshing to witness scenes in which mere girls can be better men than the pompous males. I am sure there must be something darkly Freudian about this, but when set to music it is fun.

La revoltosa (The Rebel, 1897) is typical of those zarzuelas which offer a cross section of life in the Madrid streets; of the dozen best zarzuelas, I suppose eight or nine deal with such subject matter, so that the zarzuela could properly be said to be a product of Madrid. This version deals with a high-spirited girl growing up in a Madrid semi-slum and with how she defends herself from the older men who bear down upon her while she tries to decide what to do with the young man who wants to marry her. Some of the music, especially the duet between Mari-Pepa and Felipe, is of high quality.

Gigantes y cabezudos (Giants and Big-headed Dwarfs, 1898) represents the zarzuelas which were not content to mimic Madrid life but which went afield to report on the local color of Spain's various regions. There are those who feel that when the zarzuela does so wander it loses quality, but this one is something quite special and lovely. A good translation of the title, since it refers to figures who appear during festival, might be something like *Halloween*. The action occurs in the northeastern city of Zaragoza, where an illiterate girl who works among the vendors in a marketplace receives letters from her soldier-lover in Cuba. A rascally sergeant from Andalucía makes believe that he too has received letters from her soldier and reads them to her, inventing a series of outrageous lies about the young man—he has married a girl overseas, he has been killed in battle—intending to win the girl for himself. The whole thing works out, of course, but what endeared this zarzuela to the Spanish public was the time and circumstance of its birth. It was the tragic year of 1898, when Spain's military, shot through with corruption, came face to face with a well-disciplined opponent at Manila Bay and Cuba. Suddenly the façade of Spanish life broke away to show the crumbling structure beneath, and the shock would never be forgotten. Symbolic of the trauma that jolted Spain was the fate that overtook the hero of the Cuban war, Eloy Gonzalo, whose statue we saw at the Rastro. After defying Yankee guns with rare bravado he died senselessly of malaria. In that doleful year the theatergoers of Madrid trooped out to see one more new zarzuela, *Gigantes y cabezudos*, and the first scene was the light comedy to which they were accustomed, but then came a brief entr'acte. The stage was empty save for a painted backdrop depicting the Río Ebro, behind which could be seen the outline of La Seo, Zaragoza's unique Moorish-looking cathedral. Onto a bridge came a group of soldiers straggling back from defeat in the New World. They stopped, looked at their beloved cathedral and sang.

Their words tore at the hearts of the befuddled audience, for they spoke of patriotism, love of home, fidelity to old beliefs. The zarzuela swept over Spain, and choruses everywhere sang this chant of the repatriated ones. I have seen it only twice, but when that entr'acte curtain falls, now old and dusty, and when the defeated soldiers reiterate their faith, something happens.

> At last I look upon you, famous Ebro—
> today you are wider and more beautiful.
> How I wondered if I would ever see you.
> After long absence, how happily I look upon you;
> only on your banks can I really breathe again.
> Once more I tread the soil of Zaragoza;
> there is the Seo and there the Pilar.
> For the fatherland I left you, woe is me,
> and with longing I always thought of you there.
> And today, mad with joy, ay madre mía, I am here.
> Very bitter waters are those of the sea;
> I learned the reason when I went away.
> So many sorrows sail over the sea that
> they make it bitter from so much weeping.
> Ay, my Aragonese maid, I have not forgotten you.
> I return to your side, full of faith,
> and I shall nevermore leave you.

The strange thing about this chorus is that the music, which falls into three parts, is as inventive as the words are moving. One naturally compares it with Gounod's 'Soldiers' Chorus,' from which it was probably copied, but the zarzuela is better. One feels that Gounod and his librettist said, 'Let's have a good chorus as the wooden soldiers come back.' In the Spanish version a group of defeated real men have come back to a specific city and the difference is tremendous.

By common consent, the masterpiece of zarzuela is a work bearing the curious three-part title *La verbena de la Paloma, o El boticario y las chulapas y celos mal reprimidos* (The Fiesta of the Virgin of the Dove, or The Apothecary and the Flashy Dames and Jealousy Ill-repressed, 1894). I do not find the word *chulapa* in any of my dictionaries; it is Madrid slang for tarts, hot numbers or, as I indicate, flashy dames. The genesis of this satisfying work helps explain why it is so loved by Madrileños.

There was a poet in Madrid who had such bad handwriting that when he wrote his zarzuelas the print shop sent him, by means of a young man who worked as typesetter, an extra set of galleys for his corrections, and on the Eve of the Virgin of the Dove this young man arrived at the poet's home in foul humor. When the latter asked what was wrong, the boy gave a distraught account of his love affair with a girl who was 'as precious as an ounce of gold,' except that she kept playing around with a dirty old apothecary who gave her such presents as a lace shawl and a silk dress. When the poet asked the young man what he proposed doing about it, the latter said, 'For one thing, I'm going to tear the verbena apart in a way they'll remember forever.'

The poet said later that on this clue alone he visualized a complete zarzuela, which he dashed off in the space of a few days, having the additional good luck to find a composer who inclined toward grand opera. At the first performance the audience realized that they were seeing the kind of work which comes along once in a generation. Curtain calls lasted for half an hour, and both the poet and the musician were carried through the streets till dawn. The excitement has not even now subsided, for *La verbena* is accidental perfection.

It is hardly what you might expect. The scene opens with a city character discussing aimlessly with a lecherous apothecary the merits of various laxatives: 'Castor oil isn't bad if you take it in capsules, but purgative lemonade isn't worth a damn.' Slowly, speaking a wonderful Madrileño argot, the various actors wander in, an untidy lot, some of whom appear only briefly. There is a haunting moment as a young singer advises the crowd that since she has no mother, do not look for her at home; her home is in the streets. Briefly a night watchman appears, almost too drunk to negotiate but willing to explain to two policemen the government's attitude on the social question. From within a building a disembodied voice summons the watchman with the name 'Francisco!' to which the latter reacts in a variety of ways, all to the most delicate night music. Belatedly the main action is set in motion by the apothecary, who is over seventy but who finds pleasure in keeping two girls simultaneously, one blonde, one brunette, and in scandalous song explains the advantages of doing so. The two girls appear and also Julián, the young man who loves the brunette. The girls' aunt is a bawdy old witch with a voice like a bullfrog which she exercises frequently. In desultory but enchanting action the zarzuela develops, broken frequently by songs bordering on opera, until the emotional climax is reached in an unexpected and natural way. Susana, the brunette, and Casta, the blonde, are on stage with their apothecary, and Julián, without looking at Susana, begins to sing softly:

JULIAN: Where are you going with Manila shawl?
Where are you going with Chinese dress?

SUSANA: To show myself off, to see the fiesta,
and afterwards home to bed.

JULIAN: And why didn't you come with me
when I begged you to so much?

SUSANA: Because I'm going to assuage in the drug store
all that you've made me suffer.

JULIAN: And who is this lad so handsome
you're going to carouse around with later?

SUSANA: A fellow who has vergüenza, pundonor,
and all a fellow needs to have.

JULIAN: And what if I just took a notion
that you shouldn't go arm in arm with him?

SUSANA: Why, I'd go with him to the fiesta anyway
          and then to the bulls at Carabanchel.
JULIAN: Oh, yeah?
SUSANA: Yeah.
JULIAN: Well, we'll see about that right now.

The words are sung to the hesitating music of youth; Julián becomes all young men bewildered by love, Susana is the timeless flirt, yet there is something typically Madrid about the duet. It is one of the highlights of the zarzuela, not pyrotechnical in its music but perfect in its style.

What happens? Nothing much you could put your finger on. Julián wrecks the verbena, is arrested, released on the pleas of his neighbors and wrecks the verbena all over again. The closing words of the zarzuela are uttered by a policeman: 'Ladies and gentlemen, please don't cause any further scenes at the Fiesta of the Dove.'

If one were to arrange in order of artistic merit the four popular forms that appeared at the end of the last century, it would be zarzuela, operetta, music hall and minstrel show, with little constructive to be said for the American entry. It is strange, therefore, that in spite of the zarzuela's excellence it has not traveled well to other countries. It has been too specifically Spanish, and sometimes too Madrileño, to be appreciated abroad, except of course in the Spanish countries of Latin America, where it still evokes a powerful nostalgia. It is not presented much in Spain any more, although most large cities will offer a short season now and then, but modern young Spaniards would no more think of bothering with zarzuela than American university students would with a minstrel show. On the other hand, zarzuela seems to have a vital life on records; from time to time on the good-music radio stations in America zarzuelas are played late at night, and if *La verbena* is offered it is worth staying up to hear.

In the years when zarzuela flourished, an attractive custom grew up in Madrid, which is still observed. In the narrow streets and alleys clustered throughout the district of the Teatro de la Zarzuela were small bars specializing in tapas (hors d'oeuvres) set before the public on long rows of dishes from which one more or less helped himself. Today on the Calle Echegaray, named after the dramatist who won the Nobel Prize in 1904 and whose brother wrote zarzuelas, a taxi can barely pass because of the crowds who come and go from the dozens of tapa bars.

There is a long bar behind which two men in traditional aprons serve cold beer and other drinks. Upon the bar have been arranged some two dozen open dishes crammed with a wild variety of tidbits tastefully arranged and accompanied by glasses of toothpicks, which are used to spear the goodies. The tapa place that I have frequented for many years offers dishes in four categories: first comes the seafood—the anchovies, eel, squid, octopus, herring, shrimp, salmon, five kinds of sardines, five kinds of fish; next come the boiled eggs, deviled eggs, egg salad, potato omelets cut in strips, vegetables, onions, salads; third are the cold meats in great variety, including meat balls, York ham, Serrano ham, tripe, brains, liver in a variety of styles, beef, pork and veal; and finally the hot dishes, which can be delicious. Shish kebab in hot sauce is good but I prefer mussels in a sauce of burned onions and clam broth, but there are five or six other kinds of shellfish which are about as good.

Tapa bars, so far as I am concerned, are divided into two groups, those that serve cocido Madrileño (Madrid stew) and those that don't. This is a heavy peasant concoction made of beans, flank beef, salted ham, sausage, onions, carrots, potatoes, kohlrabi and garlic, allowed to cook for days, with new ingredients thrown in from time to time. A good cocido, with hard bread and red wine, is a real Spanish dish.

The traditional way to enjoy the tapa bar, however, is not to sit down for a dish as formal as a cocido but to gather a group of friends and wander leisurely from one bar to the next, taking from each the one dish for which it is famous. In this area there is one bar that serves nothing but octopus and squid, prepared in various ways, and another that specializes in shellfish. One of the best known is a very small corner place called La Gaditana (The Girl from Cádiz), which advertises 'The largest restaurant in the world. You enter at Cádiz and leave at Barcelona,' those being the names of the streets which form the corner.

One aspect of the tapa bar frightened me. About half the dishes are bathed in a heavy, bright yellow mayonnaise that shimmies like gelatin when you put the spoon in. The finest shrimp, the best eggs, the fresh vegetable salad are drowned in this rich, inedible goo, but with care one can avoid it. However, if you dine with a Spaniard and he sees that your plate contains nothing but wholesome octopus, mussels and anchovies, he will insist upon slapping on a final gob of mayonnaise. Otherwise it wouldn't be a respectable tapa.

At my favorite bar one night a Spaniard who had learned to speak English while working the Venezuela oil fields suggested that I take in the jai alai at the frontón (court) where professional teams of Basques played this swift and exacting game. He was a nut, himself, and an ideal cicerone. 'Don't bother to come,' he warned, 'unless you enjoy gambling,' for the major purpose of jai alai is betting, and to see gambling run wild, one must attend a Madrid frontón.

'It starts with an act of sheer insanity,' my oil man explained. 'At the beginning six players appear on the court but the game is going to be two against two. So how to decide which two will play which two?' He took me to a large board containing the names of the six players and their numbers, from one to six. Bookmakers were taking a flurry of bets which I couldn't understand. 'Simple,' the oil man said. 'At this board we bet on what the composition of the teams is going to be. Suppose you buy that ticket for Team 4–6. It means that you are betting that one of the teams will be made up of Player 4 as captain and Player 6 as his mate. If it works out that 6 is captain and 4 is mate, you lose. As you can see, there are thirty possible teams, so the odds against guessing right are thirty to one, about the same as in roulette.'

'How do they determine what the teams are going to be?' I asked.

'Don't worry about that. Just pick three or four tickets here for the fun of it.' I chose Team 1–2 and Team 3–4 and Team 6–5. 'They're as good as anybody else's,' my oil man said, and we went inside to watch the six players warming up and I was amazed at their skill. Soon they began a round robin, with Player 1 taking the floor against 2 and holding it for as long as he continued to win, after which he gave way to player 3 or 4 or 5. A large scoreboard showed the names, which were part of the fun, long Basque words like Azurmendi, Urtasun, Azcarate and Yrigoyen, and whenever one of the players approached a score of five, excitement grew. Finally Player 2 accumulated five points, and a red star was placed against his name, signifying that he would be captain of the red team. Soon Player 4 scored five, and he was designated captain of the blue team.

At this point the round robin halted and we all trooped back to the gambling board. It was now known that the two teams would be 2 plus somebody and 4 plus somebody, but who their partners were to be would not be known till later. So bets were placed on the eight possible combinations, and since my first tickets had been proved worthless I switched to Teams 2–6 and 4–5. We went back to the arena, where the same six players went at it again. The scores made by 2 and 4 did not count, for they were assured of positions, but soon the excitement grew as the other four players approached scores of five. Finally the teams were decided, 2–5 red, 4–6 blue. I'd picked the right players but on the wrong teams, so once more my tickets were no good.

Now the game proper started and such bedlam I had not heard for years. Inside the screen and facing the audience stood nine husky men in official coats. Each carried a stock of tennis balls with one side cut away leaving a hollow, and as they brandished these balls they bellowed at the crowd, offering bets on the game between Teams 2–5 and 4–6. 'We better bet,' my guide said. He held up his hand, indicating by some signal that he wanted two bets on 2–5. One of the gamblers caught his eye, then looked about for someone who wanted to bet on 4–6. Pointing quickly to the two locations, he confirmed the bet, then wrote two receipts on government forms, stuffed them into two tennis balls, and with lightning accuracy pitched them long distances to the two bettors. The unit in this frontón was $6.40, of which the government took eighteen percent.

I now had my money riding on Team 2–5, but as play progressed toward the game point of 45, my team fell behind. Then the screaming of the gamblers increased, for they offered me a chance to copper my bet at attractive odds, and this I did, but my partner was contemptuous of hedging, so the further our team fell behind, the more vigorously he backed it at generous odds and soon was in a position to make some real money if Team 2–5 pulled itself together. Sure enough, our boys drew the score to 40–38 in favor of the other team and the excitement in our part of the frontón, at least, grew intense, but in the end Team 4–6 steadied and pulled away to a 45–41 victory.

At one o'clock in the morning the frontón was echoing with shouts, but then the games ended. 'Damn you norteamericanos,' my oil man growled. 'In the old days we used to play till three or four, but you've ruined it.'

'How can you blame us?'

'You've preached, "All Spaniards are lazy. They take a siesta." So the damned government wants to look modern. It's outlawed the siesta and everything has to shut down at one o'clock. Hardly worth living in Madrid any more.'

Soccer, known in Spain and the rest of the world as football, appears to be the kind of sport the Spanish government prefers to sponsor; it's international, it's modern, it's out-of-doors, and it's good for children, in that it can be played without expensive equipment. For a series of exciting years, Real Madrid proved itself to be the best football team in the world and Spaniards turned in large numbers to this frenzied sport.

I have often lived in countries that played soccer, but I have never become involved; however, during my last visit to Madrid the World Cup was being contested in London and no one who read a paper or listened to radio could escape being caught up in the frenzy. Spain beat Switzerland in one of the early rounds, and there was joy throughout the city, which closed down to watch on television, but she lost to Argentina and West Germany, and there was gloom. Shortly after, the local papers featured an incident which had occurred in Mogadiscio, the capital of Somalia, where the referee, one Salak Mobarek, made a wrong call against the Public Works team, which proceeded to kick him to death. The report said that because of this action, the Public Works team had to forfeit the game, a penalty which some of my football-playing friends considered vengeful. The Madrid papers went on to recall the number of times in recent years that referees had been killed, and since no plea was added to halt the violence, I concluded that the list was meant as a warning to the local men to watch their calls.

One beautiful moonlit night I went out to Madrid's Estadio Bernabéu to see what this madness was about, and long before I reached the approaches to the stadium I could see that a fair portion of Madrid's population was converging on that spot, for I was trapped in traffic that no longer moved. I finally had to leave my cab and walk about one mile, but it was worth it, because the stadium was one of those new affairs which one enters at street level to find himself halfway up the side of a long graceful

356

bowl set deep into the earth. The playing field was thus three flights below street level and the topmost seats about three flights above. It was huge, with something like a hundred and ten thousand seats. During the pre-game period it was illuminated by the moon and a group of soft lights, which converted the grassy area into a kind of silver, but as game time approached, four rows of lights around the stadium flashed on, and day-light enveloped the field and the grass turned green. It was the most beautiful stadium I had ever seen.

Barcelona was playing Madrid and the excitement was intense as the players ran onto the field, but as play progressed it grew. At some times all hundred and ten thousand spectators screamed at the referee, and armed police moved into position to repel those who might want to run onto the field. 'We behave better than they do in Brazil,' a Madrid fan assured me. 'There they've had to dig a moat between the stands and the playing field, so that the wild men can't rush the referee, even if they want to.'

Madrid was favored to win, but at the half the score stood Barcelona 1–Madrid 0. The crowd was disconsolate, but the man next to me said, 'Don't worry. Madrid is bound to win. This is the team that used to be world's champion. They have pundonor.'

Their vaunted pondonor did them no good when the second half opened, for Barcelona made a great sally at the goal and scored again, and the men around me groaned as if such a thing were indecent or unlawful. A moment later they were cheering wildly because the referee had disal-lowed the Barcelona goal on some technicality which no one could explain. I thought the decision was fishy and that it had come suspiciously late, and the next day the papers said the same thing. A statistical study had recently been made of Spanish football, proving what everyone had sus-pected, that a disgracefully high proportion of games was won by the home team, the theory being 'If the home team wins, nobody riots.' Tonight the referees seemed determined to prevent riots.

Soon thereafter, Madrid tied the score, then quickly made a second goal, but the referee was so embarrassed at having robbed Barcelona that now he did the same to Madrid. The man next to me really wanted to kill the swine, but a friend reminded him, 'They're supposed to even things out,' and the game ended Madrid 1–Barcelona 1.

Some time later I was in Córdoba when Madrid visited there, and in the days before the game one of the executives of the Córdoba team said in the local paper, 'The reason Córdoba has lost its last two games is that our fans have not been terrorizing the referees the way they do in Palma and Sevilla. Loyal fans are the twelfth man on the field. If you want us to beat Madrid, you must come out and scare the referee.' I attended that game, and the fans did their part. From the opening whistle to the last they created a bedlam, and although they may not have scared the referee, they did me. In the second half, when a bad call was made, a young man leaped from the stands, grabbed a camera from a newsman, rushed onto the field, and swinging the strap in a full circle, cracked the referee on the head with the camera and laid him out on the turf. The crowd applauded and apparently the official got the message, because Córdoba won.

The miracle of soccer as compared to American-style football is that the men who invented it came up with a game in which, because of the low scoring, ties are frequent. This means that if you bet on a game you must take into consideration three, not two, possibilities. Your team may win, or lose, or draw, and it would require a good man to predict accurately all the results of the fourteen games that appear each week on the betting list. The obvious wins and losses are easy, but what about those possible ties?

It is this unpredictable aspect of football that has made it such an ideal gambling game. Today all over Spain you see grubby little bare-window shops with the magic sign 1 X 2. It is to these shops that the people of Spain flock to mark their ballots for the slate of games to be played on the coming Sunday. Each ballot lists the fourteen games, eight from the first division, three from the northern section of the second division, three from the southern section, plus two reserve games to replace any of the scheduled ones that might be rained out or otherwise suspended. Alongside each game are the fascinating figures 1 X 2. If you circle the 1 it means you predict that the home team will win. Circle the 2 and you're betting on the visiting team. But circle X and you back a tie.

If you guess all fourteen correctly, and are the only one to do so, that week, you stand to win a fortune. The twenty-first Sunday in the 1964–65 season saw many upsets and only one man guessed them all, winning 15,364,075 pesetas (about $256,000), but that was exceptional. More typical were the results last year. There were thirty-nine betting days and 808,916,155 bets, of which only 19,129 gained top position, or one in every 42,000. On five of the days no one guessed all fourteen results, so naturally those who hit thirteen won. On one day of many upsets only two people won, and they got about $130,000 each, but on another day 3,836 did and won only $112 each.

Football betting is a mania in Spain and few are the homes with no addicts. Each year the newspapers carry agonized stories about some man who has studied the teams, made form sheets for the players, kept a record of which referees favor which teams and then gotten weather reports on the various playing fields before making out his list. With infinite care he has checked it, tried to anticipate where ties might fall and then decided on his fourteen outcomes. Where games are extra chancy he has bet a second and a third time, or even a twelfth, trying to cover all contingencies. He wins nothing. But his wife gets a first prize with fourteen correct. When asked what her system was she says, 'I took my list to the butcher's. He was cutting up bones, and every time he raised the cleaver I asked, "One, two or tie?" and he would whack the cleaver down and say, "One," or whatever came into his head. Fourteen times in a row his cleaver was right.' An amusing debate runs in the papers, 'Does It Help to Know Anything about Football?' and the consensus seems to be that too much knowledge inhibits freedom in spotting the ties. It is apparently better to wake up some morning and say, 'You know, I wouldn't be surprised if Barcelona ties Madrid.' Few Americans who have lived in Spain for any time have escaped infection: 'Let's throw a hundred pesetas in the pool to see if we come up with something.' Spoken like a Spaniard.

One fact about the pools astonished me. On those rare Sundays when no games are scheduled in Spain, the pool is based on some league in Italy that no one ever heard of and about which he can learn little. The betting is just as active as on a normal weekend and everyone seems to have about the same amount of fun.

I was able to resist the betting until I stumbled into the zany world of books written on the higher mathematics of the subject; then I became a sucker for each new theory and came home with half a dozen intricate systems based on permutations and combinations. I found there was a Norwegian system which would protect me against ties and an Italian system based on identifying a few sure wins, eliminating them and covering myself three ways on tricky games. Like thousands of Spaniards, I became fascinated by the pure mathematics of the thing; for example, supposing you are morally certain of the outcome of twelve games but have no clue as to how the other two will go. To cover yourself, you'd have to bet nine columns with the two dubious games marked thus:

| Game A: | 1 1 1 | X X X | 2 2 2 |
| Game B: | 1 X 2 | 1 X 2 | 1 X 2 |

If you did that, you couldn't lose. (If you are interested in either mathematics or gambling, draw up a table showing that to ensure yourself against all contingencies when eleven games are certain and three uncertain, you will have to bet twenty-seven columns.) Tables have been prepared whereby you can ensure yourself mathematically against any contingency, but the insurance is costly. For example, suppose you know the outcome of seven games, are completely confused about five and reasonably certain about the remaining two, you would bet the seven games in one column, the five confused games in three columns and the two chancy games in two columns, but to do this properly would cost you the betting fee for 972 columns, and one unexpected tie in the supposedly sure games would ruin everything. I favored the wild system worked out by Alejandro Abad, who gave personal consultations like a psychologist. He sold a large book of tables showing how to bet on one hundred and forty-four different columns properly arranged and get a sure win . . . unless something unforeseen happened. Other counselors, whose books sold for as much as ten dollars a copy, advocated other systems, but in spite of them a disconcerting number of top prizes still went to the women who sought advice from their butchers.

My visits to Madrid were made pleasant by the fact that I had been invited to attend a well-regarded tertulia which met at four-thirty each afternoon in the Café León (on the signs, Lion, from the French Lion d'Or), across from the post office. Here, around old tables kept scrubbed by the courtly waiter Mariano, a group of men convened, as their counterparts had in Badajoz, to discuss everything except religion and politics. They saw no reason to discuss the former because all were Catholics and had nothing to argue about; they avoided the latter because they had found it wise in Spain to do so.

The membership was distinguished. José María de Cossío, of the Royal Spanish Academy, attended, and one who knew anything about bullfighting recognized him as the authority, his four-volume *Los toros* being the ultimate reference in argument; I was surprised to find that a man whose reputation I had known for so long was still very much alive. Camilo José Cela, another Academician, whose *The Family of Pascual Duarte* and other novels were respected in all Spanish-speaking countries, was there. The Conde de Canilleros, a historian from Extremadura, had strong opinions, as did Gerardo Diego, poet and member of the Spanish Academy.

The tertulia was held together by the strong personality of its founder, Antonio Rodríguez Moñino, Spanish bibliographer of world-wide fame and now a professor at the University of California at Berkeley, who spends his academic leaves in Madrid. In addition to the Spanish members, the tertulia also attracted a goodly number of the Spanish professors from the United States and other countries who came to Spain on scholarships or sabbaticals. My favorite was a valiant debater named Ramón Martínez López, a Spanish professor at the University of Texas, for he had strong and hilarious prejudices on everything, which made him a delightful conversationalist.

If I had wanted to explain to a stranger how a tertulia operated, I could have contrived no better experience than what happened accidentally one October afternoon in 1966. The group was seated in the leather-upholstered chairs about the marble-topped tables and I had asked them, 'What percentage of Spaniards use the Castilian pronunciation I learned in college as opposed to the Andalusian or South American pronunciation?' The question was good for about an hour of discussion as the men recalled their experiences and the opinions of their friends.

'Figure it out this way. Years ago somebody convinced the intellectual community in the United States that gentlemen speak only Castilian. The word veces must be pronounced *vay-thayce* with a th and not *vay-sayces* with an ese. Well, in Spain itself we divide this way. In Cataluña nobody uses the th. In Galicia, maybe one-third of the people. In the islands, one half. The Basques, one half. Andalucía, none. Valencia, half. So you see, it's restricted mainly to the Castillas and León.'

'Percentages? Perhaps one-third of Spain uses Castilian.'

'In Spanish America no one uses it except immigrants from Spain who want to lord it over the locals.'

'And actors.'

'That's right. Because of some curious tradition, you must speak Castilian on stage. The way in Minnesota you try to speak Oxford English on stage.'

'They were making this movie about Jesus Christ in Mexico City and the big hassle was, how should Jesus speak? They took the problem all the way to the cardinal, and he said, "It would sound sacrilegious if our Lord spoke anything but Castilian. But it would be pompous for a mere tax-

Two immortals. The tertulia has seven participants who are also members of the Spanish Royal Academy. Here famed critic Guillermo Díaz-Plaja explains a point as José María de Cossío listens.

collector like Matthew to do so." That's how they made the picture—Jesus Castilian, the disciples Mexican. And everyone said, "Sounded just right." '

'I knew García Lorca and he never spoke Castilian. He said you couldn't write poetry in it.'

'He was right. I speak only Castilian. But the th sound was a late development. Probably not known before the sixteenth century.'

'There was this university in the United States. Had on its faculty the best student who ever graduated from Texas, and they wrote me asking if I could provide them with a head for their department of Spanish. I wrote back and asked, "What's the matter with López? There's nobody around better than he." And they wrote back and said that López didn't speak Castilian and they'd feel uncomfortable with him.'

'When Fernando de los Ríos from the Ronda region was elected to the Royal Academy he announced to the members, "Now that I'm an Academician I promise to speak respectable Spanish, and I've tried to say *civilización* the way you do, *the-vee-lee-tha-thyóhn*. But I'll be damned if I can get that third th out. So you'll have to be satisfied with *thee-vee-lee-tha-syóhn*.'

And so the discussion went, as it did day after day, but this time there was to be something different. By sheer accident an American professor visiting the tertulia dropped a bombshell by identifying a date as the year in which Magellan circumnavigated the globe.

'What did you just say?' Dr. Martínez López of Texas snapped.

'I said it was when Magellan circumnavigated the globe.'

'Magallanes!' one of the professors cried, using the Spanish version of the great explorer's name. 'My God, man, are you out of your mind?'

'In 1521. When he circumnavigated the globe.'

'My dear man! There is no reputable scholar in the world today who thinks that Magallanes was the first to circumnavigate the globe.'

'I do.'

'Apparently. But no one else I've heard of in the last hundred years has had such an idea. Does anyone in this tertulia think for a moment that Magallanes was first around the world?'

With some temerity I raised my hand, and the Spaniards turned to look at me with the compassion they would have directed to an idiot. 'Have you never heard of Juan Sebastián Elcano [in English del Cano]?' they asked.

'No.'

'My God! He was the first around the world. And he was Spanish.'

'Wait a minute!' the American professor cried. 'Magellan . . .'

'My good man,' Dr. Martínez López said, 'King Carlos himself gave Elcano a coat of arms showing a globe inscribed with those glorious words, Primus circumdedisti me (You were the first to circumnavigate me).'

The other Spaniards confirmed this, but the American was not overawed.

'Merely because a king made an error . . .'

'Carlos Quinto did not make errors.'

And so the debate went on. On succeeding days the Spaniards lugged books and citations to the tertulia, including an Italian encyclopedia, proving that whereas Magellan (in Portuguese Magalhães) had started the voyage around the world, he had died in the Philippines, leaving its completion to his Spanish assistant, Juan Sebastián Elcano. The evidence was impressive and I began to think that here was a corner of history about which I was uninformed, but then the American lugged in his evidence, which was hard to ignore.

'If in your insularity,' he said, 'you wish to maintain that a man could circumnavigate the globe only if he started from Spain and ended in Spain, then Elcano is your man. But if going around the globe means going around the globe, or, in effect, proving that the earth was a globe that could be gone around, then Magellan, who had already traveled to and from the Philippines by the eastern route and then had returned to the same point by the western route, was the first around.'

'My good man,' the Spaniards argued, 'one day a group of ships set sail from Sanlúcar de Barrameda and one of those ships, the *Victoria*, went in an unbroken journey around the world, and when it had completed its journey Magellan was not aboard. Juan Sebastián Elcano was. What, in all decency, can you conclude from that?'

The American replied, 'Merely that the *Victoria* was the first ship, and Elcano the second man, to circumnavigate the globe.'

The debate extended over a full week, and by the time it ended, with no satisfactory resolution of the point, everyone participating understood the facts and their implications. No one in the tertulia would admit then that he had changed his mind, but I would suppose that in their subsequent writing and teaching they would at least allude to the position contrary to their own.

In the winter of 1967 the tertulia came into momentary prominence when one of its members held a press conference in Boston which reverberated around the world. When Dr. Jules Piccus joined the tertulia he appeared to be merely one more visiting American professor, this time from the University of Massachusetts at Amherst. He was a young man, bearded, prematurely gray, lively in manner and quick in argument. Members of the tertulia knew him mainly as a scholar searching the archives of the Biblioteca Nacional, and there had been many like him in the past, but on February 13, 1967, Dr. Piccus announced that one day while looking for a medieval manuscript he had found instead two manuscripts by Leonardo da Vinci which had been catalogued in 1866 by B. J. Gallardo but which had subsequently been misplaced. One was a notebook, the other a set of sketches obviously intended for publication. They should have been filed at numbers AA-119 and AA-120, but a century ago someone had carelessly tucked them away at numbers AA-19 and AA-20, and there they had remained. The announcement of their recovery launched a storm. 'Why should treasures of a Madrid library be introduced to the world at a Boston press conference?' was merely the most temperate of the Spanish headlines. 'If you speak of this matter,' Dr. Piccus told me one day at the tertulia, 'please be sure to state clearly that I recovered the manuscripts. I did not discover them. The Spaniards had always known they were in existence. I happened to find out where.' Not everyone took the misadventure of the Leonardo so seriously. Mingote used the subject for one of his finest cartoons. Against a wall which was adorned by the 'Mona Lisa,' freshly painted, sat Leonardo in his traditional cap, beard and long robe.

Angus Macnab.

He was writing the last page of a manuscript and saying these words: 'Well, I've written it backwards so they can't read it. Now if I could only think of some place to hide it.'

My life in the tertulia, which was one of the most instructive things that happened to me in Spain, was marred by envy, because although this was the most prestigious tertulia then operating in Madrid, there was another which met in an opposite corner of the café which fascinated me and I longed to join it, but that would have been impossible. It was composed of six or eight elderly men, caricatures of Spanish gentlemen, in tweed trousers, hunting jackets, mustaches and with low rumbling voices. 'It's a huntsmen's tertulia,' one of my group explained. When I asked what they talked about, he said, 'Horses, dogs and things they've shot.' What impressed me most about this tertulia was that for long periods the members would sit just looking straight ahead and saying nothing. Occasionally one would mumble something about wild boars or stags and the others would nod. I was assured that it was a most exclusive tertulia and that its members looked on our group as young radicals who read books, something which none of them did.

366

In Madrid I met an unusual man whose friendship was to mean much, the dour and salty Scotsman, Angus Macnab, who wrote about Spain with such insight that I wondered how an outsider had managed to penetrate so acutely the Spanish mentality. 'Simple,' he said, drawing on his pipe and speaking out of the corner of his mouth, 'I'm a Spanish citizen.' After knocking about in various countries, he had found Spain the most congenial and had decided to make it his home.

'I like the cautious form of government, the rocklike stability of the people. Mind you, there are many things wrong, but none that hard work won't mend. And it's a marvelous place to bring up children.'

Through visiting Macnab, I came to know the new suburbs whose spectacular proliferation had allowed Madrid to increase its population so sharply. 'Is there another city in Europe which has built so high a percentage of new homes in the last decade?' he asked, and I could think of none. Scattered about in all directions, eight-story apartment buildings had spread over the countryside, not a dozen here and there, but hundreds in clusters. Architecturally they were bleak, and some were beginning to crack after only six years of life, but they were homes. Macnab, his lively wife and children lived in such a colony out beyond the bullring, and as I visited him through the years I could watch the sudden manner in which sixty or seventy great buildings appeared during a ten-month absence.

'Last time I was here you were on the edge of the country,' I said. 'Now it's a new city!'

Macnab said, 'You must keep this in mind when you ask why so many Spaniards support the government. It has built homes and it's given them to us at reasonable rates. You were complaining about the fact you can never find a taxi when you want to come here. Why can't you? Because the rates are kept so low that any workman in Madrid can afford a taxi. Here the good things are not restricted to the rich.'

Macnab's apartment in one of the new buildings was comfortable and well arranged. 'A home for a workman,' he said proudly. 'That's what I am. I work in the foreign office.' He did not tell me what kind of work he did, but he was such a skilled linguist that I assumed it had to do with international documents.

'Didn't you go to Oxford?' I asked one day.

'Indeed yes. Some of my chums from those days would be surprised to see me here, spending my years as a Spaniard. But this is a good country . . . a good country.' He spoke with such conviction that I felt certain he had found in Spain a depth which other Anglo-Saxons missed.

'Mind you,' he said, 'out in the suburbs like this we have our young hoodlums, just as you do in America. But our police don't coddle them.' Macnab showed me many aspects of modern Spain that I would otherwise have missed, but the point he made repeatedly was that it was an excellent place to raise a family. 'Here the emphasis has always been on the family. It's the fundamental fact about Spain, and if you miss that you miss

everything.' On picnics he would point out the families; when we discussed
education he would stress what it meant to family life; and often when we
were just wasting time gossiping about things Spanish he would revert to
this matter of stability. It was obvious that he loved Spain and felt it deep
in his bones. One day I accompanied him to Toledo, where he had lived for
some years following his arrival in the country, and I remember how,
when we reached the church he had attended, people of all ages ran out to
greet him as if he were a member of their extended family. I thought it
strange that a Scotsman with an Oxford education should have been
adopted so easily into Spanish life; perhaps it was through the Macnab

Even the most modern buildings in Spain are apt to be enclosed by traditional fences whose beautiful geometry sets the pattern for the cities.

children that this acceptance came, for they were Spaniards and indistinguishable from the others.

'There is a profound permanence in Spain,' Macnab told me one day, 'and if you're lucky enough to identify with it, you have found yourself a very stable home.' He knew the regions of Spain, and certain of the cities I chose for my tour, those that might not attract others, were chosen because of his recommendation. 'You'll like that city,' he would say. 'It has an honest quality.' Talking with him convinced me that he had chosen Spain as his permanent home because of this honesty.

Twenty-eight miles northwest of Madrid lies a vast and gloomy building off to itself, El Escorial (The Slag Heap), a strange pile of gray-black stone set among foothills and the subject of much debate. I find it not only impressive in an overpowering sort of way, but also representative, in its heaviness and simplicity, of the essential Spanish characteristics. El Escorial is Extremadura carved in rock, the barren plains of Castilla set in order by an architect.

Others who know Spanish architecture better than I condemn the building as an alien monstrosity. Where, they ask, is the beautiful ornamentation of plateresque? Where is the echo of Romanesque or Gothic, two styles that made themselves at home in Spain? And where in this enormous rectangle is there even a hint of the fact that Spain was for seven hundred years Moorish? These critics charge that the mausoleum, for that is what El Escorial is now principally restricted to, is a poor rendition of an Italian idea and about as appropriate to Spain as a replica of King Victor Emmanuel's wedding-cake monument would be if it were translated from Rome to the plains of Castilla.

The traveler must make up his own mind in reference to his own experiences, and since most foreigners visiting Spain see the Gothic, the Romanesque and the Moorish and come to think of them as representing Spanish values, El Escorial must be a disappointment. Those like myself who have identified with Extremadura, and Las Marismas and the lonely plains of Castilla, have developed different visions of the country, and to these El Escorial conforms.

What is it? Four things, interrelated and enclosed within common walls: a palace from which kings ruled Spain; a grandiose mausoleum holding the sarcophagi of many kings; a monastery; and an enormous church. It came about because the death of Carlos V at Yuste in 1558 followed closely upon a signal victory of Spanish troops at St. Quentin on the tenth of August, 1557, which day happens to be the feast day of St. Lawrence (in Spanish San Lorenzo). During his last illness Carlos had directed his son to assume responsibility for burying him wherever Felipe thought appropriate, and the latter had the happy idea of building a monastery of unprecedented dimensions which would serve as a mausoleum for the Habsburgs. He scouted the countryside and found this hill onto which mining scoria had once been dumped, whence the name El Escorial, and there he caused work to begin. St. Lawrence had been martyred by being roasted alive on a gridiron, and whether by conscious design or not, when El Escorial was finished, it resembled a rectangular gridiron, complete with handle.

The building has four severe façades whose rather pleasing lines derive from the multitude of windows set into the otherwise bleak walls. The main façade has an entrance marked by twelve Grecian columns and two bronze doors to which the dead kings of Spain were brought for sepulture.

'Who seeks entrance?' the monks asked.

'The Emperor of the Spanish empire.'

'Who seeks entrance?'

'The King of Spain.'

'Who seeks entrance?'

'The man Carlos.' Only then did the gates swing open to admit the dead man to his mausoleum.

Today it is one of the most provocative spots in Spain, an octagonal room deep in the lower reaches of the building. In tiers of four sarcophagi each, the kings of Spain lie as if on file in a library, waiting to be lifted down. At the top of one group lies Carlos V, below him Felipe II, then III, then IV. In other tiers the queens rest, but since some of the kings had three and four wives, only those who gave birth to children who inherited the throne are interred here. Associated with the main mausoleum are others reserved for the royal heirs who died in infancy and for the royal bastards, of whom there was a plentiful supply. In this last room lie the reassembled remains of Don Juan of Austria, who even today has the power to attract more visitors than the legitimate rulers.

El Escorial contains much more: galleries of art, tapestries by Goya, long halls covered with pictorial maps, a fine library and the living quarters of the ancient rulers. It is so immense that when one has seen all this, the complex of the monastery remains to be explored, for this is a town set within walls.

I am embarrassed to report that it was not until my third visit that I discovered El Escorial contained, hidden away in its capacious interior, a church much bigger than many cathedrals. I had wandered through the halls for two days, vaguely aware that off to one side stood a chapel of some sort, but I was preoccupied with other areas and so missed a building of mammoth dimension. How could such a thing happen? When I travel I am wary of guides, preferring always to look at things for myself. I find that if I do not see an object fresh, on my own terms as it were, I often never see it except through a haze of verbalism. Guides, I find, are trained to reduce all things to a common level, and their flow of words weaves a net over the whole, so that one sees only through the interstices and never clean. Furthermore, the things they point out that I might otherwise have missed I would often have been well advised to miss. When I visit a site I want to see three or four things at most and am never loath to ignore others that might have little interest for me. Sometimes my plan causes me to miss something I should have seen, as at El Escorial; I must be the only visitor ever to have missed so large a church.

As if to rub it in, it was a professional guide who finally pointed it out to me, and I was surprised at how clean and beautiful it was. The Patio de los Reyes, the enclosed area before the entrance to the church, was big enough for army maneuvers, while the interior vistas, all severely neo-classical, were much more spacious than I would have guessed. When imprisoned inside the church and unable to see the expanse of the surrounding building, I felt it to be totally un-Spanish, and even when I came to the two groups of statuary for which the church is famous, I found them also alien, which was not surprising, since they were cast in Italy by Pompeo Leoni.

They are delightful and were described to me by an Englishman as 'poor art but pure heart.' Facing the high altar on the gospel side is a group of five life-size figures, three kneeling in prayer, two standing in the rear. They are Carlos V, accompanied by his faithful wife Isabel of Portugal—not to be confused with the earlier Isabel of Portugal, who went mad—his two queenly sisters, María of Hungary and Leonor of France, and his daughter María, who married Maximilian II. The group is ranged behind a beautifully draped table carved in bronze and topped by a pillow whose tassels are so real they seem ready to flutter should a breeze come unexpectedly through the church. I liked especially the bronze robe worn by Carlos and decorated with the Habsburg eagle and panels from the lives of saints. The whole group is sized so as to fit comfortably in the towering spaces of the church and placed so high that it is not dwarfed, a delightful Italian version of a Spanish royal family.

Poised opposite, on the epistle side, is a matching set, also of five figures, also ranged behind a draped table and a pillow, but this shows Felipe II, brooding spirit of El Escorial, and it has a certain quality of arrogance befitting that prince. Where the eyes of Carlos are downcast in prayer, those of Felipe stare straight forward, as if daring God to touch him. He is surrounded by three of his four wives—Maria of Portugal, Elizabeth of Valois and Ana of Austria, with his second wife, Mary of England, appropriately absent, for she had always been difficult for him to handle—and by his heir, Don Carlos who is shown as a thin-faced, intelligent young man of sixteen or seventeen.

If I had missed the hidden church, I wouldn't have lost much, but if I had missed these two sculpture groups I would have missed a view of Spain that I could have acquired in no other way. I had always felt kindly toward Carlos, but the austerity of Felipe repelled me, proving that I was guilty of the grave error which Spanish critics charge against most Anglo-Saxon writers, that I had been contaminated by the Black Legend, that body of charges assembled by non-Spanish scholars, especially Protestants, to discredit Spain and Catholicism.

In recent years much has been written about the Black Legend and its genesis. A personal enemy of Felipe's fled Spain and supported himself for the rest of his life by peddling lurid rumors involving the Spanish court. William the Silent, of the rebellious Low Countries, saw a chance to unite his fractious countrymen by creating in Felipe an object of terror and scorn, so he added to the rumors and gave them circulation. Protestant apologists saw in the charges a chance to defame Catholicism, so they added their inventions, but the worst damage was done by fellow Catholics, the Italians, who wanted to create a political counterbalance to Spanish influence in Italy and did so by spreading existing rumor and creating new. As I read these new studies deflating the Black Legend, I found that they were directed at people like me, for I was almost the archetype of the person corrupted by the legend. It consisted of these postulates: 1. Catholicism captured Spain and adopted a policy of keeping the country in darkness. 2. Using Spain as a base, Catholicism intended to enslave the world. 3. In order to police its conquests, Spanish Catholicism invented the Inquisition, which it proposed to install in subdued territories. 4. The archpriest of these evil designs was King Felipe II. 5. He was personally evil and committed many crimes in furtherance of his aims.

A special emphasis in Spain's refutation of the Black Legend has been the charge that it was promulgated in the first place by a conspiracy among Protestant scholars who had consciously engineered a campaign to defame Spain and had manipulated histoɪical facts to do so. Phrases like these were common in Spanish writing on the subject: 'una fobia contra España' (a phobia against Spain) and 'un complot contra España' (a plot against Spain). Certainly my initial experiences with the legend supported these Spanish charges, for I became aware not only of manipulation of fact but also of a phobia against Spain. I did not come to believe the legend by accident; I was taught it by professors. I remember how my sixth-grade teacher created in me a long-lasting ambivalence toward Spain by first teaching us that western civilization owed Spain much, in that she had saved Europe by preventing Islam from moving north of the Pyrenees, and that if she had not done so, we would all now be Muslims. We then analyzed how horrible life would be in our little town if we had mosques instead of churches, and it was fifteen years before I lost my fear of Islam. Shortly, however, this same teacher showed us how Europe was saved in 1588 by the English fleet that drove off the Armada. This time we were told, 'If the English had not defeated the Spaniards, we would now all be Catholics,' and we analyzed what our town would be like under those conditions, and it was equally bad.

My problem was simple: 'How could Spain have been civilization's savior in the fight against Islam and only a few centuries later the villain in the fight against England?' The answer was also simple: 'Felipe II was an evil man.' Thus the Black Legend was promulgated.

I was so fascinated by the ominous character of Felipe that I read all I could find about him, and when the normal histories were exhausted, a librarian dug up the only book in my life that I wish I had not read. I once heard a spellbinding gospel preacher in Colorado shout that as a young man he had read a filthy book which had so contaminated him, he would gladly cut off his right hand if he could erase having read the book; I was amused at his ranting, because I'd read such books and they hadn't hurt me much. But I have often wished that I had not as a boy read Rider Haggard's *Lysbeth, A Tale of the Dutch* (1901), because it imprinted on my mind so evil a picture of Spain in the age of Felipe and the Duque de

Alva, who represented him in The Netherlands, that it was fifteen years before I was able to counteract it. No other book had so baleful an influence on me, nor one so permanent, partly because it confirmed what my teacher had said about Spain, partly because it carried a series of prejudicial pictures. Two remained with me, as vivid now as when I first saw them. Two Dutch Protestants were reading the Bible furtively at night while a spy from the Inquisition peered from behind a door, and such an air of terror was engendered that I required to know no more about Spain than that. The second picture was more direct. One of the leaders of the Protestants was captured by the Spaniards, and when he refused to betray his fellow Bible readers, he was locked in a room containing a small barred window and there starved to death . . . but not just any room. This one overlooked the kitchen, whose sights and odors came to him as he starved. This was so diabolic, so typically Spanish, it was not until years later that I realized Rider Haggard was merely a storyteller in need of detail who had invented the room and the kitchen.

I had read *Lysbeth* fifty years ago and wanted to check whether it was as virulently anti-Spanish as I remembered, but I was unable to find a copy of the book; in its day it had been widely read but was no longer in print or on library shelves. However, my town librarian located a copy in Minneapolis and borrowed it for me, and in the introduction I came upon the first phrase I remembered: 'By an example of the trials, adventures, and victories of a burgher family of the generation of Philip II and William the Silent, the author strives to set before readers of to-day something of the life of those who lived through perhaps the most fearful tyranny that the western world has known.' I found the book as intemperate now as it had been terrifying half a century ago; the Spanish were real villains, especially the clergy: 'Before he answered the priest threw off his dripping hooded cape . . . revealing a coarse, wicked face, red and blear-eyed from intemperance.' The Dutch were invariably heroic: 'This was William of Orange, called the Silent, one of the greatest and most noble of human beings who ever lived in any age; the man called forth by God to whom Holland owes its liberties, and who forever broke the hideous yoke of religious fanaticism . . .'

The story was well plotted and contained two figures whom I still remembered with fascination, a hideous witch called Martha the Mare and a giant red-bearded Frisian named Red Martin. The purpose of the plot was to provide opportunities for Spaniards to demonstrate how cruel they were. The sin of the Dutch stemmed from their Bible reading:

'What has he done?' asked Lysbeth in a low voice.

'Done? My dear lady, it is almost too dreadful to tell you. This misguided and unfortunate young man, with another person whom the witnesses have not been able to identify, was seen at midnight reading the Bible.'

'The Bible! Why should that be wrong?'

'Hush! Are you also a heretic?'

One of the highlights of the yarn came when the hideous Mare climbed into a pulpit and disclosed the infamy of the man who had made her look the way she now did:

'You call me the Mare,' she went on. 'Do you know how I got that name? They gave it me after they had shrivelled up my lips and marred the beauty of my face with irons. And do you know what they made me do? They made me carry my husband to the stake upon my back because they said that a horse must be ridden. And do you know who said this? THAT PRIEST WHO STANDS BEFORE YOU.'

As the mob surged toward the culprit she reminded the cowering priest who she was: 'I was once called the Lily of Brussels. Look at him now. He remembers the Lily of Brussels. He remembers her husband and her son also, for he burned them.' The crime so infuriated the Dutchmen that they hanged the priest, preparing the way for the central paragraph of the book:

Thus ended the life of the Abbé Dominic at the hands of avenging men. Without a doubt they were fierce and bloody-minded, for the reader must not suppose that all the wickedness of those days lies on the heads of the Inquisition and the Spaniards. The adherents of the New Religion did evil things also, things that sound dreadful in our ears. In excuse of them, however, this can be urged, that, compared to those of their oppressors, they were as single trees to a forest full; also that they who worked them had been maddened by their sufferings. If our fathers, husbands and brothers had been burned at the stake, or done to death under the name of Jesus in the dens of the Inquisition, or slaughtered by thousands in the sack of towns; if our wives and daughters had been shamed, if our houses had been burned, our goods taken, our liberties trampled upon, and our homes made a desolation, then, my reader, is it not possible that even in these different days you and I might have been cruel when our hour came? God knows alone, and God be thanked that so far as we can foresee, except under the pressure, perhaps, of invasion by semi-barbarian hordes, or of dreadful and sudden social revolutions, civilized human nature will never be put to such a test again.

As I approached the climax of the story, where the Spanish villain was about to condemn the Dutch hero to death by starvation, the horror that I had experienced at first reading came back to me:

'Now might I trouble you so far as to look out of this little window? What do you see in front of you? A kitchen? Quite so; always a homely and pleasant sight in the eyes of an excellent housewife like yourself. And —do you mind bending forward a little? What do you see up there? A small barred window? Well, let us suppose, for the sake of argument, that a hungry man, a man who grows hungrier and hungrier, sat behind that window, watching the cooks at their work and seeing the meat carried into this kitchen, to come out an hour or two later as hot, steaming, savory joints, while he wasted, wasted, wasted, and starved, starved, starved. Don't you think, my dear lady, that this would be a very unpleasant experience for that man?'

'Are you a devil?' gasped Lysbeth.

But as I finished the passage a strange thing happened. I looked for the illustration, so indelible in my mind, and it was not there. It had never been there. The verbal description of Spanish perfidy had been so real to me that I had imagined the illustration; I can see it yet in perfect detail, yet it never existed. Nothing could better exemplify the persistence of the Black Legend and its deleterious effect on the rest of the world's relations with Spain. If the average educated American wanted to approach Spain afresh, he would have to cleanse his mind of many illustrations imbedded there without reason.

Felipe II has suffered much from the embroidery of the Black Legend, and not all the wrong can be charged to aliens. One nineteenth-century Spanish dramatist summarized Felipe thus: 'Cowardly where his father was brave, cruel where the other was generous, and fanatical where Carlos was religious, no crime frightened Felipe when it was a matter of his security, his revenge, or the misunderstood interests of his religion.' His reputation was especially damaged by Friedrich Schiller's poetic drama *Don Carlos* (1785), which portrays him as an insanely jealous king who orders the murder of his own son because he thinks the boy not only is turning Protestant but also is involved in an incestuous relationship with his stepmother, Felipe's third wife, Elizabeth of Valois. Felipe comes out of this play poorly, and no better from Verdi's operatic version, *Don Carlos* (1867), in which he again orders the murder of his son and a bloody auto-da-fé to celebrate the death. But bit by bit the truth regarding Felipe is coming to the fore. He did not launch the Inquisition, nor was his version of it as harsh as that of his predecessors. He was a good husband to Queen Mary of England, who was eleven years older than he and his full cousin, and he did not adopt covert or immoral strategies to trick England into becoming part of Spain. He was a devout Catholic and naturally he tried to convert the people of the Low Countries to his religion in accordance with the principle of *cuius regio, eius religio* (whose country, his religion), and if the Armada had been victorious he would surely have tried to bring England back to the religion from which under Henry VIII and Elizabeth I it had strayed. There is now grave doubt that Felipe murdered his son out of sexual jealousy or suspicion of the boy's incipient Protestantism. Nor is there any proof that he ordered the poisoning of his half brother, Don Juan of Austria, for fear of dynastic rivalry; on the contrary, it was Felipe who generously rescued his much younger brother from obscurity and gave him positions of command. The other murders charged against him do not withstand investigation, and he seems on balance to have been a pedestrian but capable administrator, a just ruler and a king who sought peace more often than war.

The one charge that can truly be laid against him is one which the Black Legend did not make. Felipe ruined Spain. When he was through with it the once-great kingdom was finished, and over the sprawling empire lay the seal of death. The trouble started with Carlos V and his siphoning off of Spain's wealth into bottomless European adventures, though if one had told the old man this when he was pottering about the monastery at Yuste, he would not have understood. 'Look at the territory I have brought Spain,' he would have said, and the new map of Europe would have borne him out; but what he should have been looking at was manufacturing in Spain, agriculture, the decline of the army, the encrustation of incompetence. That balance sheet was dreadfully against him. He knew that something had gone wrong, but he blamed the wrong forces. From Yuste he wrote: 'Of all the goods that arrive from the Americas at the port of Sevilla, ninety percent goes into contraband that does the nation no good.' Smugglers had not stolen Spain into poverty; Carlos himself had done the job.

He left Spain bankrupt, so that many of the failures which finally engulfed Felipe were not of his making and were, by that time, inescapable. But he could have avoided others had he comprehended the changes overtaking Europe. Again and again, in his bitter and narrow way, he turned his back on the present and tried to maintain in Spain a type of life and government that should have been allowed to vanish. Industry, the prerogatives of a middle class, a rationalized army, a Church responsive to modern trends and an educational system based on merit he ignored, and in doing so, sealed the ruin of his country. Solely because of the headstrong policies pursued by Carlos and Felipe, the cost-of-living index rose as follows: 1500—100; 1521—150; 1550—200; 1590—315, reflecting the fact that supplies of foodstuffs and manufactures were declining. If ever the principle of divine right of kings aborted, it was in the case of Felipe II, for he may have had the divine right to rule Spain, but he did not have the right to ruin it.

It is for this reason that I find El Escorial so moving; it is a fitting monument to Felipe, a vast, dark building to commemorate his monolithic soul. He caused it to be built. He selected the architect and approved the design. In the hills back of the building you can still see the seat carved in rock where he used to sit and watch the progress of the construction, and it was he who conceived the happy idea for the two groups of bronze statuary in the church. There is a small room in El Escorial where Felipe used to sit, his foot propped up to relieve the unbroken agony of his gout, and here he spent his last days surrounded by deepening woe. He had survived the death of his insane grandmother Juana, his father, his mother, his first three wives, his heir Don Carlos, his half brother Don Juan and many of the advisors who had been close to him. From the

loneliness of this room he could peer down into the church through a little window and eavesdrop on the progress of the Mass. Here also he met his couriers and studied by candlelight the reports they brought him from all parts of the world. I suppose no other king in history applied himself so diligently to his paper work as Felipe, for the margins of his documents are cluttered with his minute and often pertinent observations: 'He should be hung.' 'The ships should be sent south.' 'The governor must be changed.' Energy, dedication, devotion, constancy and courage Felipe had, but sympathetic intelligence he did not, and in the end it was this lack that undid him.

From El Escorial I traveled over the mountains to Alcalá de Henares, the ancient city known to the Romans as Complutum, where Cardinal Cisneros had built his famous university. It had long since been abandoned, for reasons we shall inspect in the next chapter, but I wanted to see what buildings remained, and I was directed by a policeman to a former residence hall now converted to a public hostel. The doorman said, 'You are welcome to see the ruins of the university,' but this was hardly what I was looking for. The guard understood. 'You want to see the building of Cisneros! Ah, it's on the other side of the square.'

There, shaded by trees and set back from the road, I found the stately building which had formed the core of the university. From the outside it was dignified, with a façade of carefully balanced items; from the inside it offered as noble a cloister as I was to see in Spain, three-tiered and marked off by thirty-two half-columns. In the park facing the building stood a statue of Cisneros, showing his intense, small face, his high cheekbones and his penetrating eyes. His military adventures behind him, the burning of Islamic treasures forgotten, he stands as a churchman with a book and stave in his left hand, a heavily knotted cord in his right. Nearby, in an old chapel, rests his modest tomb, so different from the bombastic one of Cardinal Mendoza in the cathedral at Toledo.

In Cisneros' university great things had been accomplished. The cardinal had insisted that his students be trained in the most advanced theories of their day, and Alcalá became a center of liberalism. In one stroke Cisneros established thirty-three full professorships, 'according to the number of years of Our Lord,' including some in subjects new to Spain, such as recondite ancient languages, new concepts of philosophy and a chair for that abstruse intellect, Pedro Ciruelo, who claimed that theology could be understood only if studied in conjunction with mathematics. Three of the professors personally selected by Cisneros had been born Jews, even though he was at the time head of the Inquisition; when suspicious Catholics protested, Cisneros defended his nominations and said the men were needed for a major task which only they could fulfill.

In 1513, when King Fernando inspected the university to see if there was truth in the condemnatory rumors which had reached him, Cisneros said calmly, 'Sire, it is your job to gain kingdoms and make generals. It is mine to build those men who will honor Spain and serve the Church.' The roster of great men who acquired their education here has seldom been equaled: Lope de Vega and Calderón, to name two of the writers; Tomás de Villanueva and Ignacio Loyola, to name two who attained sainthood.

As we saw earlier, Alcalá was famed internationally for its *Biblia Poliglota Complutense*, a particular brainchild of Cisneros. It provided the first printing of the Hebrew text ever to have been compiled by Christians and the first Greek text to have been printed anywhere. Both remained standard till well into the nineteenth century; the compilation as a whole has been termed 'the first scientific work of the modern world.' Books were being printed in Spain at least three years and probably nine before William Caxton published his first work in England, but the *Poliglota* was long delayed because Cisneros had to encourage his Spanish paper makers to produce pages of the size and thickness he required and his imported French and German type founders to cast Hebrew, Aramaic and Greek type faces. In an edition of six hundred copies, Volume Six appeared first, in May of 1514, followed by Volume Five a month later. The first four volumes appeared at intervals, the last on July, 10, 1517, four months before the death of Cisneros. The completed volumes were not put on sale till 1520, for the Spanish government was apprehensive about distributing them prior to their having been approved by the Pope. In the interim the university generously allowed scholars from other countries to consult the finished volumes, and in this way much of the original work was published elsewhere before it appeared in Spain. Cisneros would not have minded, for his memorial existed not in printed books but in ideas.

Forty-five years after his death an event occurred in his university which has ever since preoccupied historians. To Alcalá for their education had been sent three young men: Don Carlos, son of King Felipe II; Don Juan, the bastard brother of the king and therefore half uncle to Don Carlos; and Alexander Farnese, nephew of the king and thereby cousin to Don Carlos. They were not regular students at the university, for they had private tutors, but they did attend classes and participate in university life.

Their regimen, as laid down by King Felipe, was strict, but on the night of April 19, 1562, young Carlos slipped out of his room to visit the attractive daughter of a porter, and in creeping down the darkened stairs he failed to see that the fifth step was broken and pitched headlong downward, so that his forehead struck a closed door. He was found stretched out unconscious and the matter was reported to the king.

Fortunately, young Carlos made an easy recovery and the escapade was forgiven, but on the tenth day alarming symptoms suddenly appeared and it looked as if he were going to die, presumably from pressure on the brain. Nine specialists were summoned, among them the Fleming Andreas Vesalius, skilled in performing trepanations of the skull. Fifty separate consultations were held, for the stricken boy was heir to the crown, and while the doctors were trying to decide what to do, help came from two unexpected quarters. From Valencia a quack arrived, a Moor bearing two jars of ointment. 'The black one,' he explained, 'has a repercussive action, but the white one is a strong unguent to attenuate it. Black, white. Black, white. It is the warring of the ointments that saves the life.' At the same time a strange troupe appeared from a nearby community, a group of peasants attending several Franciscan friars who bore the cadaver of one Diego (1400–1463), a Franciscan who had died a century before but whose body had not been contaminated by the grave. Standing before the doctors, they pulled back a cloth and displayed Fray Diego's face, and the sunken eyes seemed to be alive. The peasants explained that the cadaver had already worked miracles in their community and they believed it could save Don Carlos.

So three alternatives were laid before the doctors and the king's representatives: Dr. Vesalius could trepan the skull and thus let out the diseased blood that was pressing on the brain and causing the damage; or the Moor could apply his alternating unguents; or the cadaver of Fray Diego could be placed in bed with the unconscious prince in hopes that it might work one more miracle.

What happened that day has since been the subject of much speculation. Don Carlos' two principal physicians each left behind his own report; they agree in the main but are contradictory on important points; foreign ambassadors then resident in Spain collected rumors, which they sent home; and other participants left diaries. From certain reports it seems clear that Dr. Vesalius and his team prepared to do a trepanation and laid back the scalp so that the white skull was well exposed, but when they had done this they satisfied themselves that the blood oozing through the bone of the skull was normal and that a complete trepanation was not called for, so they sewed the scalp back together; other reports indicate that the trepanation was completed and that it saved the boy's life.

We know that the Moor was allowed to apply his unguents, first black, then white, but they seem to have been so powerful, especially the black or repercussive one, that the dying youth grew noticeably worse. The doctors grew frightened and packed the Moor out of Alcalá; he went to Madrid with his jars and there offered to cure the knight Hernando de Vega, but after a few applications of the powerful stuff Hernando died.

We also know that when hope was almost gone, the century-old cadaver of Fray Diego was placed in bed with Don Carlos while the Franciscans prayed, and in the morning Don Carlos awakened, with clear mind, and said that in the night he had seen a vision of a friar in Franciscan habit lying beside him, and this had cured him. At any rate, both he and his father petitioned Rome to declare Fray Diego a saint, for this was but the latest of the miracles this obscure friar had worked; three separate popes delayed action on the matter, but King Felipe was so insistent that a fourth pope, Sixtus V, speeded up the investigation and took pleasure in announcing in 1588 the entry of San Diego into the saintly brotherhood. His day was identified as November 13, and in honor of his having saved the intended King of Spain, a pueblo in the colony of California was some years later named after him.

The saving of Carlos' life was a mixed blessing. In the six years that followed, the young man degenerated pathetically; crippled, hunchbacked, of wandering mind and evil habits, he became a kind of incubus, and it was even rumored that he might have been toying with the idea of becoming a Protestant. What seems more likely is that he had initiated or had been caught up in some kind of intrigue against his father, King Felipe. At any rate, there can be no question about the fact that Felipe believed his son was plotting treason and that the pathetic and even repulsive young man was a danger to Spain. Therefore, at midnight on January 18, 1568, Felipe, accompanied by advisors, marched into the room of Don Carlos, who looked at his father and asked, 'Are you planning to kill me?' Felipe told him to calm himself and in this manner placed him under arrest, without ever giving Carlos or the world any substantive reason for having done so. 'I have reasons,' Felipe said.

Almost immediately the young prisoner, twenty-three years old, began to decline, and this time there was no Dr. Vesalius, no Moor with repercussive unguent and certainly no cadaver of a saint to cure him. What was his malady? No one knew. Was there any specific or even probable cause? No one could say. It was a general illness without a seeming focus and on the evening of July 24 he died. King Felipe refused to give an explanation even to the Pope, and when rumors of the most evil sort circulated, he did not dignify them with notice, let alone an explanation. He spoke of the matter only once, eighteen years after the event, when a book appeared in France claiming that Don Carlos had been killed because he was a secret Protestant. Then Felipe said to the ambassador who reported this, 'You are right in becoming indignant over the false testimony that he was not a good Catholic. It is not wise to allow such a great lie to run current.' Ten years after the death of Don Carlos, Felipe had a second son, by his fourth wife, Ana of Austria, and it was this boy who grew up to be Felipe III, never a great king, never approaching the quality of his father Felipe II or his grandfather Carlos V, but certainly not a degenerate like Don Carlos, who would have inherited the throne had he not died so mysteriously.

In July, 1966, events occurred which were to make the city of Cuenca an almost obligatory excursion from Madrid, and I had the good fortune to make mine in the company of a talented Filipino who had been centrally involved in those events, Don Enrique Francisco Fernando Zóbel de Ayala y Montojo Torrontegui Zambrano, Harvard 1949, sometime bibliographical expert in rare books at the Houghton Library in Cambridge, etcher extraordinary and one of Spain's major abstract artists.

Don Fernando drove me ninety miles east and a little south of Madrid through virtually empty land; a few white-walled villages appeared here and there, clean and inviting in their harsh simplicity, and I was once more impressed with how swiftly in Spain one passes from the heart of a major metropolis like Madrid into empty countryside. On this street a fourteen-story apartment building; fifty yards farther on, open land. In Spain prudent people have long learned to live within the safety of city walls. When we did come upon a village I again noted something that I had often reflected on before: that the rural children of Spain all look as if they had been fifty-six years old at birth. How ancient their faces are.

Our route to Cuenca took us through several types of land that could have been a summary of Spanish history. Here the flat lands of Castilla reminded one of how the clever kings of this region had built a nucleus around which to unite the country. Don Fernando suspected that at one point we were close to the upper edge of La Mancha, and when I saw how bleak and empty it was, without a house to be seen in any direction, I appreciated why Cervantes, wishing to poke fun at the pretensions of would-be nobility, had set his knight down in such prosaic terrain. Next we came to the pine forests of Cuenca province, mile after mile of tilted and rocky land, and I could understand how the Muslims, once they had captured such a fastness, were so difficult to dislodge.

'In some ways a most uninteresting drive,' Zóbel said, 'but if you can imagine the ebb and flow of forces, the movement of kings and peasants, one of the best.'

We passed through two tunnels that served somewhat as the gates to Cuenca and in a short time saw the distant hilltop city perched above the gorges of two rivers that meet here for a run down to Valencia on the coast. Don Fernando was eager that I see Cuenca at its best, so we stopped the car for me to look up at the remarkable collection of houses perched along the edges of some very high cliffs; they seemed about to fall into the rivers but were kept aloft by sturdy cantilevers set into place some five hundred years ago. Porches and balconies projected well out into space and even from below induced vertigo.

'Cuenca is like the prow of a ship sailing into space,' Zóbel suggested, and his image was appropriate. 'When they first proposed Cuenca to me I couldn't visualize locating here, but once I spotted these fantastic houses, these cliffs, winding streets and the tremendous views one gets from everywhere, I knew that this was what I'd been seeking.'

As he spoke, we were in the lower town, which dates from relatively modern times, say four hundred years ago, but we left this by a steep and twisting road which carried us upward at a good rate, and in a few minutes we came upon a medieval square and a very old cathedral with a new face. I entered because I had long ago heard of the four remarkable jacent tombs of Church dignitaries dating from the sixteenth century, and these I wanted to see. They were as lovely as I had been told, four high-relief slabs of stone carved with figures of dead prelates, each highlighted by the addition of a few streaks of color which made them seem almost alive. The tombs were delightful and set the stage for what I was about to see.

Don Fernando led me down a side street which ran along one wall of the cathedral, then took me on a cobbled street which ended in a cul-de-sac marked by several medieval doors of handsome design. 'This is it,' he said as he unlocked one of the huge doors and swung it slowly open.

I entered upon a wonderland, something so unanticipated in a remote city like Cuenca that it has become world-famous in less than a year, for it is a museum of Spanish abstract painting set down in three of the cliff houses, so cleverly interrelated with flights of stairs, balconies, strange corners and large exhibition areas that it is a delight to the eye and a challenge to the mind. From the windows one looks off into miles of empty space, with the Río Huécar six hundred feet below in the gorge. Inside, one sees a series of varying rooms filled with handsome paintings by young artists whose reputations have been made not in Spain but in Paris, London and especially New York. One sees the finest work of men whose names are well known in all art circles: Antoni Tápies, whose earthlike canvases speak so strongly of Spain; Antonio Saura, whose works are in most modern museums; José Guerrero, better known in New York than he is in Madrid; Luis Feito, whose work is as modern and colorful as any being done in the world; Eduardo Chillida, whose heavy, powerful sculpture is much appreciated in foreign exhibitions; and Rafael Canogar, whose reputation is the most recent of the Spanish internationalists.

'This is some of the best painting being done today,' Zóbel says enthusiastically as he points to one after another of the fine canvases. 'Only New York excels in concentration of talent. I believe we have more superbly gifted young painters in Spain today than they have in either Paris or London and certainly more than Berlin or Rome. This group of men is going to create the art history of the next quarter-century. Tell your friends who may be interested that these men are as good as Picasso and Miró were when they began.'

As we wandered through what must be one of the world's loveliest museums, Zóbel estimated that there were more than thirty young Spaniards who had a chance to build major international reputations. 'That's what makes this museum so fascinating,' he said. 'The culture of a nation coming into focus in a way it has not done since the early 1600s.' We found chairs from which, if we looked to the right, we saw the spectacular valley or, to the left, a series of brilliant canvases by painters I had not previously heard of. It was a visual feast, but what interested me as much was the conversation.

Zóbel: For the first time in many years Spain is taking its contemporary artists seriously. This is good for the country. Good for the artists.
Michener: But is it not true that at least eighty out of every hundred

canvases these men paint leave the country? In Pittsburgh we Americans appreciate this art. In Sevilla you Spaniards don't.

Zóbel: Up to now that's been true. This museum may change the percentages. Spaniards may begin to buy Spanish art, other than Sorolla-like scenes in which colorful fisherwomen sell baskets of clams.

Michener: The other day I had lunch with José Ramón Alonso, the editor, and he said the typical Spanish attitude toward art was that of a friend of his who asked, 'Pictures? We have three pictures. Why would we want more?' Alonso asked him what three he had, and he replied, 'One Velázquez, one El Greco, one Goya.'

Zóbel: He was right on both counts. Families like that won't buy paintings. And you'd be amazed at how many El Grecos and Goyas remain in private hands. Spain has always liked paintings, but only the ones they liked, if you understand the contradiction.

Michener: I see less evidence of connoisseurship in Spanish private homes than I would in similar homes in Israel, Japan or Germany.

Zóbel: The basic fact you must accept is the joyous provincialism of Spanish thought. Have you discovered that the Prado is really the most provincial great museum in the world? Only Spanish painting.

Michener: Wait a minute! What about those great Flemish and Italian paintings?

Zóbel: That's what I mean. As long as Flanders and Italy were Spanish colonies we accepted their painting. That's why we have Bosch and Titian. Because we thought of them as Spaniards. Once the colonies broke away, to hell with them and their painting.

Michener: You believe then that this group of artists will be able to make a living by painting in Spain? And selling to Spaniards?

Zóbel: They already are. Every painter you see on these walls makes a good living right now. And they don't have to teach in art schools or colleges the way your painters have to do in the States.

Michener: They make a good living, but doesn't it come from sales abroad? Do Spaniards buy?

Zóbel: Yes, they do. In the old days all you could sell was the kind of romantic subject matter done by Zuloaga and Sorolla. You're right that Picasso and Miró never sold in Spain. And Spanish families would have found it inconceivable to buy something like a Cézanne or a Paul Klee, because those men were not Spanish. Even today no one would buy a Francis Bacon or a Willem De Kooning or even a Morando. But they are beginning to buy Spanish works. And I am proud that this museum has had something to do with that change!

Zóbel had a right to be proud. That morning the Spanish government had convened a gathering of notables at which he was made a member of the Order of Isabel la Católica in gratitude for what he had accomplished in Cuenca, for not only had he personally paid for the heavy expense of converting the cliff houses into a museum, with splendid marblelike floors and much clean and freshly painted wall space, but all the canvases in the museum were also from his private collection. 'Fifteen years ago I did a simple thing,' he said as we finished our conversation. 'I looked about me and saw that Spanish painting was good . . . very good. So I began to collect it. And now the world confirms my judgment.'

The paintings which I had been admiring, by artists I did not know, seemed to support his argument. There was a fine, swinging op art construction by Eusebio Sempere, only forty-three years old; a clean and hard collage by Gustavo Torner, forty-two; a most imaginative portrait of a group of men by the Equipo Crónica (Chronicle Team), a pair of twenty-five-year-old Valencians who collaborate on such excellent work that they must become internationally popular; and what pleased me most, a wonderfully poetic white canvas by Manuel Mompó, forty and also from Valencia. It was so good that I asked to see more of his work, and each thing I saw showed a lyrical quality that was enchanting. Mompó paints somewhat in the style of Miró, but with his own fairyland interpretation, and I suppose he will become well known throughout the world.

Part of the museum structure is leased out to an excellent restaurant, and as we finished our dessert of coffee ice cream garnished with roasted and delicately flavored walnuts, a friend said of Zóbel, 'He and his group are the avowed enemies of corsi.'

I thought, from the way the word was used, that Corsi must have been a competing painter. 'No,' my informant explained, 'it's the most in-word in Spanish society today. You can kill a man with it by saying at a cocktail party, "Cayetano tries hard but he's painfully corsi." ' It means cheap but pretentious, kitsch but heavily pompous. Cuenca is the battleground of the Spanish mind in its war against everything that is corsi.

Some dozen major painters have taken up residence in the cliff houses of Cuenca. Travelers come from all over Spain to the museum. In summer students flock to the exquisite valleys that surround the town, camp out and work during the daytime in the fine museum library. In autumn artists and townspeople alike climb down from their cliff to work in the fields, gathering, by means of delicate brushes, the golden pollen of a lavender flower on which the economy of Cuenca partially depends, for this is the saffron capital of the world. And each day the message of this unusual museum reverberates through Spain.

The pleasure of my visits to Madrid was enhanced when I met one day in the Ritz Hotel my hunting companion from Las Marismas, Don Luis Morenés y Areces. If he had been instructive in the marshes, he was more so in Madrid, for this was his city and he delighted in showing me aspects of it that I would otherwise have missed. I was surprised some time later, as we were walking down the Avenida José Antonio, when a gentleman

Don Luis Morenés,
Marqués de Bassecourt.

stopped us and addressed Don Luis as 'Marqués de Bassecourt.' When he had gone I asked Don Luis about this and he invited me to join him at one of the sidewalk cafés. What he said, often under insistent questioning by me, was a surprise.

'Yes, my father happens to be a grandee of Spain. My family goes back in one straight line to the early eighth century when Pedro Duque de Cantabria fought the Muslims, but to make the line straight a few kinks have to be kicked out here and there. My father's titles happen to be fifteenth Conde de Villada, eighteenth Marqués de Argüeso. In 1491 los Reyes Católicos confirmed our family titles as those of grandees immemorial. Duque de Infantado, Marqués de Argüeso and Marqués de Campoo. The present Infantado and the Campoo are uncles of mine. But I work in government offices, as you see. I'm a clerk who hopes one day to become a chief clerk.'

I asked him to what other families of Spanish history he was related, and he said, 'My own title is eighth Marqués de Bassecourt. It sounds French and this is why. The Bassecourts were knights of the Artois and in the Peace of the Pyrenees in 1659 Felipe IV ceded to Louis XIV the territories in which my ancestors lived, but they refused to take up French citizenship and remained faithful to Spain; so in 1736 Carlos III made Don Francisco de Bassecourt a general of his army and then, because of his heroism in the Two Sicilies, created him a marqués. Alvaro de Luna, whose mobile statue you saw in Toledo, married into our family, which has always been associated with the Medinacelis, the Medina Sidonias and the Osunas. But like most young men from such families I have to work.'

I knew the nobles Don Luis was speaking about, for they passed like golden threads through the history of Spain, people of enormous power whose deficiencies had perturbed me in Sevilla. I asked Don Luis about this and he thought I was wrong. He believed that it had been the permanence of these families that had given Spain its solidity in duress. 'Anyway,' he said, 'the old charge of doing nothing no longer applies. Look at the leaders in government now being provided by these families.'

One of the recurring jokes in Madrid concerned just this matter. There was this management consultant who was explaining to a group of businessmen how he operated in selecting candidates for top jobs in Spain. 'This morning, for example, three contestants for a major job. All equally well groomed, equally educated. So I asked each one privately how much is two and two. The first said instantly, "Four." Solid man, quick, stable, conventional. Second man thought a moment, saw a trap and said "Twenty-two." Imaginative, willing to take a chance, best type of man to head a project entering new fields. Third man thought a long time, looked at me suspiciously and asked, "What do you want to know for?" Finest type of scientific mind, probing, not easily satisfied with snap decisions, can be trusted to get at the heart of things. And that's how we judge men in this business.'

'But which one did you hire?'

'Oh, the Duque de Plaza Toro, of course. We've got to have a title.'

I myself had been vaguely involved when a major American automotive company sought Spanish management for its Iberian branch. They had settled upon a most promising young man with training in London's equivalent of the Harvard Business School and several years' experience with a German motor company in France. To me he seemed an inevitable choice, but Spanish advisors warned the Americans, 'We think you'd do better with the Duque de Plaza Toro.' So the Detroit experts had an interview with Plaza Toro, who arrived in a chauffeur-driven Mercedes, dressed flawlessly, ten pounds underweight and with manners that could have charmed Artaxerxes. When questioned about his qualifications for the job, the duque said, 'I'd want a hundred and twenty thousand dollars a year. And for this I'd let you use my apartment.'

'But what exactly would you do?'

'Do? I'd represent you . . . introduce your people to the right circles.'

'Have you had any business experience?'

'Me! Of course not.'

Understandably, the Detroit people chose the trained young man, and their business went promptly to hell. He had been great in an interview, but he couldn't seem to get anything done. The leases that Detroit needed were not forthcoming; import agreements were stalled and remained so. In despair the Americans sought private counsel as to what had gone wrong, and were told, 'Nothing. Everything's about the way it ought to be at this stage, and the young man is doing a fine job . . . inside. But what you need now is somebody like the Duque de Plaza Toro . . . outside.'

Against their better judgment, the American firm hired the duque for $52,000, and within a few weeks everything was moving smoothly and continues to do so. The duque appears now and then in his Mercedes, hands over his apartment for business negotiations with men of equal breeding who represent other firms, and everyone is happy, especially the young expert who is left free to run the business.

The Marqués de Bassecourt was no figurehead. He worked long hours at his ministry, specializing in tourism, and through watching him I learned something of the new spirit that animates Spain. 'We literally work seven days a week to ensure that you tourists get an even break,' Don Luis said. 'Inspectors, loans to small businesses, new hotels, new roads. For example, how many minutes did it take you this time to get through customs at the airport?'

'I noticed that. From the time the plane landed till I was free to go, nine minutes.'

'It's one of the shortest waiting periods in Europe and we'd like to make it even shorter.'

'How many tourists last year?'

In his methodical way he took a piece of paper, ruled it into columns and wrote down these startling figures:

Number of Tourists Entering España

Year	World	United States
1951	1,263,197	44,677
1954	1,952,266	203,029
1965	14,251,428	687,106
1966	17,251,796	733,109

I told him that my dismal experiences in Toledo had more than instructed me about the sudden flood, and he said, 'All problems like that we're going to clean up. We're going to build a first-class hotel there. We're very excited about the future.'

I asked him if he thought Spain could continue to give the foreign tourist good value, quoting a recent study which gave the following index figures for tourist costs: New York 100, London 94, Paris 90, Rome 79, Madrid 39. 'We're aware of the problem,' he said. 'We can't control all prices. Wouldn't want to if we could. But we can police services, and that we'll do, because tourism is too valuable to us to be abused.'

'How about taxis in Madrid?'

He threw up his hands. 'What city is handling its taxi problem sensibly? Is Madrid as bad as New York, where you simply cannot get a taxi in the evening?'

'I think it's worse,' I said. He shrugged his shoulders, as if he were the mayor of New York, and asked, 'Who can tell taxis what to do?'

Through Don Luis I met a series of minor government officials who introduced me to other Spaniards, and slowly I began to overhear a type of discussion which earlier I had rarely heard: 'What is going to happen to Spain when Franco goes?' In what follows I will not attribute opinions to specific persons, for to do so might cause embarrassment, but they do not come from Don Luis unless I so specify. It was a man from Badajoz who established the theme.

'You must start, Michener, with the fact that Spaniards are utter bastards to govern. We are Texans cubed.'

Once the marqués said, 'In the hundred years prior to the generalísimo we had one hundred and nine changes of government, twenty-six revolutions and three major civil wars. Would you agree that an attitude toward government which produces such results needs overhauling?'

'We lie awake at night wondering what's going to happen when Franco goes. We say little in the newspapers, but that doesn't mean we don't discuss it among ourselves. It is topic one.'

'Forget the trappings about monarchy this or monarchy that. The fundamental fact is this. We will never go back to the United States pattern of a two-party system. It works for you. It doesn't work for us. Through some miracle you are able to divide your country into two parts from September to November, then unite it again the morning after election. Believe me, this is a bigger miracle than you imagine. In Spain we also used to divide into various parties and in the campaign we'd say such dreadful things about each other . . . well, the matter of pundonor comes in. Anyway, on the morning after the election the only thing an honorable man could do was shoot the son-of-a-whore who won. I think that if you were to ask a hundred average Spaniards, a good eighty would say, "Let's have no more party fighting."

'What will take its place? Here we get to the second fundamental. You must view Spain as a nation resting on a three-legged stool. Church, army, landed families. If any one of the three topples they all go down. We have what you might call an ipso facto oligarchy to which the only alternative is anarchy. Therefore, the three legs of the oligarchic stool must support one another. And this they do, not always happily, so that what we will have when Franco goes is something roughly like the present form of government.

'What the Protestant norteamericano sees as the Spanish Church is really two churches, and in his mind he must keep them separated, as they are separated in Spanish life. First there is the hierarchy, meaning the cardinals and bishops. With not more than two or three exceptions these men are the creatures of the regime. They were put in office by the oligarchy, were supported by it and will be loyal to it until death. They oppose all liberalism and have been badly shaken in recent years by the winds of reform that have been sweeping through Rome. At the Vatican councils they voted against every proposed change, and when they lost to the liberal wing of the Church, they returned to Spain more determined than ever to save Spain from the liberal errors of their own Church. Opposed to them are the young Spanish clergy who foresee that if Catholicism does not liberalize, it may be eliminated when Franco goes. So a kind of second Church has grown up consisting of educated Jesuits, priests from worker families, seminarians who take the conclusions of the Vatican councils seriously, and all who vaguely want the Church to sponsor social justice in a tired land. The differences between these two arms of the Church are much greater than the differences between Republicans and Democrats in the United States.'

Another said, 'In your country the Catholic Church argues over matters of liturgy, celibacy of priests, birth control and similar points of procedure. In Spain we are riven apart by fundamental matters like Pope John's two encyclicals, *Mater et Magistra* and *Pacem in Terris*, and especially the Council Schema XIII, with their startling statements on freedom of speech, freedom of belief, freedom of assembly, separation of Church and state, the right of labor and so on. These documents constitute a refutation of everything the Spanish hierarchy stands for, and the young liberal priests know it. If the plan goes through to make Pope John XXIII a saint, his day will not be celebrated in Spain . . . unless the young priests win the current battle.'

On the other hand, a defender of the Church insisted, 'If you look at the three elements of our oligarchy, Church, army, landed families, it has got to be the Church which will lead us to liberal revisionism. Watch! In the years ahead you'll see the conservative army called in to discipline the liberal young leaders of the new Church.'

'The army is much more the key to Spain than outsiders imagine. I include the Guardia Civil as part of the army. In the press you can say things against the Church and maybe you'll get away with it, because everyone wants to slow down the Church a little bit. But you are absolutely forbidden to say anything against the army. They rule. You asked me the other day why individual issues of newspapers are sometimes confiscated. You wondered if the editor had said something against the Church or Franco. It's almost always because they said something against the army. That cannot be tolerated. You also asked which of the three claimants to the throne will finally be installed as king, supposing we have one. That the army will decide.'

I asked, 'Then why doesn't the army rule outright?'

'Because if it did there would be rebellion, and the army knows it. Like the German army the Spanish army has rarely been sagacious. If it were able to rule, we'd probably have a military dictatorship right now. But, of course, if it were a sagacious dictatorship, it would confirm most of the freedoms we now enjoy, so in the long run things would be about the same.'

Another informant challenged these statements about the army. 'Because the army is conspicuous don't overestimate its importance. Of fifteen recent cases when editions of newspapers were confiscated by the censors, only one involved the army. Fourteen involved the hierarchic Church, which is heavily protected by the regime. Jesuit papers were closed down because they supported young priests against police brutality. Two were shut down for criticizing the reactionary attitudes of the hierarchy. Several were disciplined for publishing articles on the succession. And five saw their editions confiscated because they were too enthusiastic in defense of freedom. One suffered because of its editorial, "Protest is not always morally wrong." The censor held that it was.

'The landed families, the third leg to the stool, play a powerful role in Franco's Spain because he can trust them. They're conservative. They're smart. They're self-disciplined. Whether they can drag themselves into the

Spanish soldier waiting
for the parade to start.

twentieth century I sometimes doubt. A fellow like your friend, the Marqués de Bassecourt, knows what the score is. So do hundreds like him, but they aren't the ruling families, which are at least three hundred paces farther to the right than chaps like Bassecourt. I see the families continuing as a kind of unelected senate, tough, conservative, determined. A hundred years from now life in rural Andalucía will be about what it is right now, if the families have the say. But the Church and the army will bring pressure on them to liberalize things a bit.'

'The hope of Spain lies in a group you haven't mentioned—the new industrialists . . . the fellows who are building the apartment houses along the Mediterranean . . . the big printing plants in Bilbao . . . the factories in Barcelona. They know. They travel to Germany and Poland. They have suppliers in Rome and New York. They don't fill any of the government positions yet, but do something more important. They supply the taxes and they insist upon modernization of social patterns, education, military service; I have great hopes for this new class of Spaniards.'

I asked why they didn't exercise more control in government, and my informant said, 'Because this is Spain and control will always rest in traditional hands, like that of the Church, the army and the landed families. If the industrialists made one false move they would be wiped out overnight and their businesses expropriated.'

I suggested that if this were done, Spain would be bankrupt again. 'That has never bothered a Spaniard. If he feels the industrialists are modernizing Spain too fast, he'll eliminate them, even though it means economic chaos for another fifty years. But the question you pose is academic. The industrialist knows he must move forward slowly with the rest of us. That's why I place so much hope in his accomplishments. Within the Spanish pattern he's going to create wonders.'

I asked what technical form the government would take after Franco's departure, but the man to whom I spoke was not interested in so specific a question. 'The Damoclean question is quite different,' he said. 'What is labor going to do? The other night I watched you in the hotel lobby when that disgraceful television program came on. The one where the government reporter asked fifty day laborers what they thought about Spain's system of controlling labor unions. And each of the fifty came to the microphone and said, like a parrot, "I think the syndicates are wonderful because they protect the working man." You were embarrassed and looked at me to see if I was too. I didn't want to express myself in public, so I kept staring at the television and that preposterous parade. I felt humiliated. Because you knew and I knew that at the slightest spark those fifty workmen would ignite and blast that damned-fool government man right into oblivion. I wouldn't like to guess right now what role labor will play. If the army, backed up by the Church and the landed families, tries to imprison all labor in the national syndicate much longer, there's got to be trouble. But the liberal wing of the Church knows this, and if it attains power it will press for a freer labor law. When this happens Spain will move to a position similar to Italy's or Germany's.'

In a different part of Spain I asked a group of workmen what they thought on this question. 'You're going to see strikes all over Spain. We've been told for the past twenty-five years that the loss of some of our freedom wasn't too high a price to pay for national solidarity and peace. So we paid it, and all we got was solidarity and peace. The good things went to the rich, and the Church and the army. We got damned little. Now we have to adjust the balance.'

After this discussion of five fields—the controlling trio of Church, army, landed families plus industrial leadership and labor—I returned to my original question: 'What will happen when Franco goes?' and a government official said something that should be remembered: 'You speak as if you thought Generalísimo Franco sat in his office and personally passed all laws. How do you suppose Spain has been governed for the last fifteen years? By a committee, of whom Franco is the most powerful. Much of our government moves forward without involving Franco. He's invaluable as the symbol around which we coalesce. And he can both initiate and veto. But Spain without Franco would still exist. It would have to. So after he's gone I personally suppose that things will continue pretty much as they have in the past. Our great loss will be in a symbol around which to rally. That poses a real problem, but the government per se will go right on.'

'Without trouble?' I asked.

'Without revolution, if that's what you mean.'

A dozen times, a hundred times I heard reassurances like this and always I pressed to the logical consequences, asking, 'Then you think the transition at Franco's death will be peaceful?' Almost without exception the Spaniards replied, 'Once before, we had civil war and we know what that means. Almost any price we might have to pay to avoid rebellion would be worth it.' When I pressed further to identify what 'any price' would include, the typical answer was, 'We don't insist on free elections . . . or the two-party system . . . or this king or that . . . or who actually takes Franco's place in the palace. But a better social justice than we have now . . . that we do insist on.' I asked what would happen if it were denied, and the answer of a man in Pamplona can stand as typical: 'If the army and the Church tried to deny us social justice I suppose we'd have to fight.'

Back in Madrid, I returned to my earlier question: 'What kind of government?'

'It's got to be a continuation of the oligarchy. Once Spain is agreed on that, and I think we are so agreed, then the precise form doesn't matter too much. But to the outside world it's pretty important. The choice is between a dictatorship of some kind or other or a restoration of the monarchy. I believe it will be the monarchy. After all, our constitution states that we are a monarchy and Franco has openly announced that he serves merely as caretaker for that monarchy. There would be an advantage to us in having a king again, because it would make us popular in England and the United States, both of whom love royalty. I suppose nothing we could do would make us more acceptable in the States.'

I asked which of the two claimants, whose conflicting chances I had become acquainted with in the picture gallery at the Coto Donaña, would probably be appointed the next king. 'Ah, but there are three pretenders! We must choose among three.' I said that I knew about Don Juan, the legitimate heir living in exile in Portugal and very unpopular with Franco. And I had met his son Don Juan Carlos, living in Spain and popular with Franco. Who was the third? 'A carry-over from the Carlist Wars of the last century. The Carlist pretender . . . Don Hugo Carlos, who married that pretty Dutch princess who changed from Lutheran to Catholic. I think they live in Paris, and sometimes you see his name as Carlos Hugo, because he only added the name Carlos for effect and we aren't sure whether it goes in front or back. He's a poor third in the running but he does claim the throne and many support him.' When I asked which of the three would win, my informant bit his lip for some moments and said, 'Some time ago Franco authorized Vice-President Muñoz Grandes to conduct a secret poll among the military leaders and to everyone's surprise they favored bringing back Don Juan from Portugal . . . even though Franco had said he didn't want him. I understand the generalísimo was irritated by the vote, but in my judgment it was right. I know young Juan Carlos quite well and he's a weak sort. Maybe when he's fifty he'll be strong enough to govern. So I say give the throne to his father now and give the boy time to grow up. I was in Sevilla when he was presented to the aristocracy of Andalucía and he cut a poor figure.' (Since the taking of this poll Muñoz Grandes has been succeeded in the vice-presidency by Admiral Luis Carrero Blanco, a sixty-four-year-old conservative.)

However, an American businessman who had participated in an extended series of negotiations in which Juan Carlos took part gave this report: 'A most attractive young man with everything he needs in order to reign. By that I mean good looks, a beautiful wife and fine children. He has the manners required for public functions and more than enough intelligence to discharge the duties of a constitutional monarch. Spain will be lucky if he's the one chosen.'

I asked if having a king once more would mean much to Spaniards. 'The fact that the extreme right is so strongly in favor of it makes me have doubts. But Spain is a very difficult country to govern, and I think that having a continuing symbol which remains above politics might give us help. You read our papers. You see how we play up the successes of nations with royalty. Denmark, Greece, Norway, especially England. We are told year after year, "Countries with kings are happy. Those without are miserable." Believe me, since the Estados Unidos installed Jacqueline Kennedy as a kind of queen, your popularity in Spain has risen considerably.'

To the outsider it is perplexing that so many elements in Spain should remain so loyal to an institution that has served her so poorly. For a monarchy to produce a superior form of government, it must discharge certain technical functions, and the British and Danish monarchies, which Spaniards so often cite in defense of the system, have done so, but not the Spanish. Monarchy should provide an unbroken sequence of leadership; but twice in Spain the royal family died out, subjecting the country to the perils of a contested inheritance in which foreign powers became involved. It should provide for an orderly transfer of power at the death of a ruler; but in Spain numerous wars of succession have resulted when the inheritance was questionable, as in 1475, 1520, 1700, 1835 and 1875, to name only a few. It should unite the population behind a symbol; but in Spain it has had the opposite effect, as in the savage divisions of the Carlist period. And it should provide competent if not brilliant leadership; but in Spain it has thrice propelled mental defectives to the throne, as in the case of Juana la Loca, Don Carlos, son of Felipe II, and Carlos the Bewitched, and on numerous occasions it has installed protracted regencies, as in the case of Isabel II and Alfonso XIII. In spite of such a delinquent record, Spain today looks sanguinely to the reestablishment of her monarchy, even though the new trial will begin with three different men contending for the throne. To prophesy success for such a shaky venture requires hope rather than logic.

One Spaniard spoke for the many who had doubts: 'It's one thing to keep a royal family installed in a country like Denmark, which already has it. Quite another to introduce a king into a nation which doesn't. If Spain brings back a nonentity like Juan Carlos he'll rule for about twelve years. He'll side with the landed families, meddle in government and be disciplined by the army, which will then establish a dictatorship in the Primo de Rivera mold. I see no merit whatever in reviving the monarchy.' I asked him what alternative he saw, and he said, 'A one-party state, with liberal safeguards. Power in the hands of a cabinet, pretty much as we have now. More and more, the leaders are coming from the new industrialists. What I'm saying is, a continuation of what we have now with logical improvements.'

Another man explained the prevalence of articles favorable to the monarchy: 'A whole lot of Spaniards visualize the return of the monarchy as a chance for them to shine in an archaic court life. They see the peasants kowtowing to them, carriages drawing up with footmen, titles and prerogatives, castles and sweeping gowns, as if that was what Spain needed today. So they support the concept with articles and books in hopes that when the restoration comes they'll have a part in the court life, no matter how trivial.'

Three different men in three scattered parts of Spain pointed out something I had not formulated for myself. To lead into the generalization they reiterated a truth which I already knew. 'It's a sad fact that during the nineteenth century no Spanish-speaking country on earth learned how to govern itself effectively by a system of ballots. We're a people of such mercurial temperament that the two-party system is quite beyond our capacity to handle. Spanish countries require a one-party state, something perhaps like Mexico's, although I deplore her attitude toward religion.' Then came the surprise. 'You norteamericanos haven't liked Franco, but have you noticed how many travelers to South America report that they were told in Argentina or Uruguay or Bolivia, "What we need here is a Generalísimo Franco"? Believe me, when people from South America see how we achieved balance and peace for more than a quarter of a century, they yearn for the kind of stable government we have.' In succeeding months I watched the Spanish newspapers, which carried numerous stories of this type; many were suspect, because Spanish newspapers subservient to the Franco regime had sponsored the reporters who had dug up the quotes, but others appeared to be authentic. A good many South Americans, lost in the political confusion that seems to be the Spanish heritage, hungered for the hard, tight kind of rule Franco had provided the mother country.

In Barcelona I heard a cautionary report. 'This country is a boiling pot with the lid wired down. Coal continues to be thrown on the stove. Heat continues to generate. And the pressure of steam does not diminish. The army and the Church are going to try to keep the lid clamped down, but they're not going to succeed. I do not think we can avoid major trouble when Franco goes.'

Earlier I reported that whenever I asked the question 'What will happen when Franco goes?' almost without exception my Spanish friends replied that the transition would be both uneventful and peaceful; but when I got to know these people better, sometimes at night or after a long ride, it was they who raised the permanent question that hung over Spain: 'Do you suppose there will be some kind of civil war?' Apparently the problem was much discussed in private. I shall specify the types of persons whose answers I summarize:

A top intellectual from Cádiz: 'We've had twenty-five years of peace. It's been a boon only an idiot would destroy. There will be no war.'

A seminary student from Valencia: 'The Church is so advanced in its social thinking that you wouldn't believe what we discuss among ourselves. There is no need for war against the Church and there will be none.'

Spokesman for a group of students in Barcelona: 'I am worried. I see no sign that the government appreciates how determined the young people of Spain are to have more freedom. If we are refused it, there can be only one result. War is a possibility, but I pray that the government will see reason and take the simple steps necessary to avert it.'

A rancher in Extremadura: 'Let the Communists try. We learned how to handle them last time.'

Guardia Civil.

A strong anti-Communist in Córdoba: 'I am frankly afraid. If there were serious trouble, or even war, I wouldn't be surprised. Our government hasn't done enough to win the working people over to our side. I see many signs that worry me.'

A government official in Madrid: 'War would be impossible . . . impossible. Can you imagine what the last one was like? No one would plunge this country into a repetition of that.'

A literary man in Madrid: 'Spanish history has an aggravating way of repeating itself. In 1833 when King Fernando VII lay dying without a successor who had been agreed upon by the nation, he could foresee the Carlist wars that would follow. He said, "Spain is a bottle of beer and I am the cork. When the cork pops out, all the liquid inside will escape, God knows in what direction." Does the idea seem familiar?'

A housewife in Jerez de la Fontera: 'I come from an educated, liberal family who opposed General Franco in 1936. Today I would kiss his hands, for he has brought us twenty-five years of peace. When I hear students who can't even add two and two trying to tell me what Franco should do, I want to spank them. What can they know of how Spain was during the war? There will be no repetition of that, I can assure you.'

An industrialist in Sevilla: 'I fear there's got to be trouble. When I walk through our plant I can feel the workmen staring at me with hatred, ticking off the days. It will not be pleasant here in southern Spain if trouble breaks out. We can always pray that the transition will be placid, and I must say that the closer we get to it, the more moves we are making to avoid trouble. They're not dumb in Madrid. Slow, but not dumb.'

A diplomat: 'You forget how stable we are economically. There's no cause for war simply over this king or that, this form or that. Now, if the United States hadn't poured in money to help us out ten years ago, and if our tourism hadn't brought us in billions of pesetas in the last five years, there would be cause for upheaval. But now? No.'

In 1967 I found the mood of my informants a little less sanguine. Student riots in Madrid, widespread strikes in the north and the arrest of more young priests in Barcelona were disturbing signs that all could read. There was still no fear of open trouble, for all believed that the oligarchy was strong enough to maintain control and, indeed, there was no desire on anyone's part to have trouble. 'We must keep our heads,' a Madrid businessman said, 'because to do otherwise would be insanity. Let the college students blow off a little steam. The police know how to handle them. Let the young priests agitate. The cardinals know how to bring them back into line. Labor? We may have to give a little here and there, but the future is reasonably secure.'

A leading intellectual from Andalucía startled me by saying, 'The forces we've been discussing—Church, army, labor—don't touch upon the problem which looms largest to me. And to a lot of men like me. What should I do about Opus Dei?' I had first come upon this mysterious organization of Catholic laymen in Mexico in 1959, when some feared that it was destined to take over that country, and I had long been interested in it, having read everything I could about its manner of operation. Those favorable to the movement maintained that it was a beneficial, voluntary organization of Catholics who were dedicated to the job of building better men and women and hence a better society. Those opposed said that it was either the agency for clerical fascism or Catholicism's answer to Free Masonry, but all agreed that it represented a canny preparation for taking over Spain when Franco departed. 'My problem is more difficult than you might imagine,' my Andalusian friend explained. 'On the one hand I am opposed to secret societies of any kind, and when they are led by priests I am terrified. Four times I've been approached to join Opus Dei and the invitations have been subtle. "We are the force of the future. We are the men who will count. Join us and help make the vital decisions." I have never wanted to be a political leader and that sort of reasoning repels me. But now I begin to see that not only are three of the most powerful cabinet ministers Opus Dei, and some of the strongest generals and businessmen, but also the editors of the journals in which I want to publish and the intellectuals with whom I want to associate. And I also see that unless I join Opus Dei, I am going to be slowly excluded from the really important things I want to do.' He was perplexed and I asked him about the politics of the society, which had been launched in 1928 by a devout Spanish priest who saw it as a means to regenerate the world. It had spread to most Catholic countries, and I pointed out that whereas in 1959 it had seemed destined to control Mexico it had subsequently lost its power. 'In Spain it will grow,' he insisted. 'The men in Opus Dei are dedicated. Have you ever met an Opus Dei face to face? He'd surprise you. The typical one is a layman not a priest, but he's taken vows of celibacy and poverty. He lives in a communal hall and gives his salary to the movement. He dresses in an ordinary dark business suit and works in one of the economics branches of the government. Most of Spain's finest economists are Opus Dei. And they're dedicated to public service. Tough-minded, well-behaved, moderate, attractive. Such men enable the Opus Dei to prove its claim . . . that it's the best force in Spain. In the decades to come you may hear a great deal more about Opus Dei.' When I left him I had the feeling that he had about decided to become a member, and that when decisions were reached as to what direction the new Spain should take, he and his fellow members of Opus Dei would do much of the deciding.

But it was a businessman from Barcelona who came closest to my own guess as to what would happen: 'I think that when news of Franco's death flashes through the countryside . . . As a matter of fact, if they're smart they'll not announce his death for two or three days while they move troops into position . . . Well, hotheads in the cities will think, "Now's the time!" and for six or seven days there'll be sporadic trouble, which the army will suppress. Then a dictatorship from the military until things are stabilized . . . six months, maybe . . . then a general relaxation to the same thing we've had for the past fifteen years. I suppose they'll choose young Juan Carlos to be king and throw him out about ten years later. Ultimately a gradual relaxation until we're something like Italy.'

An American expert on Spanish affairs spoke for many foreign observers: 'At the change-over no visible trouble. But six months to two years later a substantial redistribution of power, probably without fighting . . . possibly with.'

Don Luis Morenés: 'The men I watch above me in the government are smart enough to make the adjustments necessary to keep this country stable. We have everything on our side and I can think of no one who would profit by a civil war. I think the transition can be made quite peacefully.'

FOLLOWING PAGE:
*The hand of Salamanca
has always extended a welcome.*

VIII

SALAMANCA

OCEANO
ATLANTICO

MAR MEDITERRANEO

0   MILES   100

La Coruña

Burgos

Valladolid

Toro
Tordesillas
Medina del Campo
Madrigal de las Altas Torres
Porto
Arévalo
Salamanca
Avila
Madrid

Barcelona

Guadalupe

Lisboa

Sevilla

Salamanca's Plaza Mayor is the finest in Spain and one of the four best in the world. St. Mark's in Venice has a richer variety of architecture; the Zócalo in Mexico City is larger in expanse; and the barbaric Asian splendor of the Registan in Samarkand is without equal. But the Plaza Mayor is unique in that its spacious area is bordered on all four sides by what amounts to one continuous building, four stories high and graced with an unending arcade of great architectural beauty. It is the most harmonious plaza extant, with its repetitious balconies and windows providing just enough accent and its blending colors creating a vision of amber loveliness. On a sunny afternoon, with the sidewalk cafés filled and the parade of charming girls in progress, it has a human warmth that the other great plazas lack, and it is worth a considerable trip to see.

To sit lazily in the plaza and study the minor variations in the vast building which curls about you is delightful. On the north side and the west the balconies are continuous, but on the south and east they are broken in interesting patterns. Both the north and south façades are interrupted by two large gateways, but the east and west have only one. The plaza isn't quite a perfect square. One afternoon when I had nothing better to do I stepped it off in all directions, but I forget the results. And on the north face the continuous building elevates itself slightly to become a palace serving as the town hall.

The outstanding feature is the endless arcade; in heat of day café chairs are moved off the plaza and under the arcade, but at other times it forms a graceful promenade lined with fine stores. Between the arches of the arcade, medallions have been prepared for bas-reliefs showing the prominent figures of Spanish history; medallions along the north and west have remained empty, but the first in line along the east contains Generalísimo Franco, well sculpted and imperial of mien, followed by imposing figures like Alfonso XI, Fernando and Isabel, she most stalwart, and Juana la Loca and her collar-ad husband Felipe I, the tragic couple whom we met at Granada. A curious feature of the medallions, and one which must have been accidental, is the fact that the carving of Carlos the Bewitched has begun to crumble, so that his features have fallen away to leave a sense of idiocy. The once-proud Habsburg chin has vanished in the rain.

Along the south there are generals, too. El Cid looking like a knight of medieval Germany, and el Gran Capitán who conquered Italy, Pizarro from the plains of Extremadura, and a strange fellow with German mustaches labeled Don Xptova Colón, the one who discovered America. The permanent impression of the plaza is one of complete unity rigorously enforced and quiet beauty where human beings can rest. Day or night, it is a magnificent setting.

Salamanca is a very old city and the town fathers must have had courage to decide, as late as 1729, to build a new plaza whose four sides would be kept harmonious. The work of renovation took seven decades, and not one façade was left untouched. In recent years the city fathers have been less courageous; they have surrendered to the automobile. Salamanca is so laid out that the easiest solution to its traffic problem is to allow several main arteries to flow into the Plaza Mayor, which thus becomes a huge traffic circle, and one can no longer dawdle across the beautiful pavement for fear of being run down. Furthermore, as in most European cities, the politicians have been unable to withstand demands for parking space and have allowed this once-glorious spot to degenerate into a vast parking lot, while from its rooftops gleams a forest of television aerials.

When I sat in the plaza I was accompanied by a ghost from my childhood days, a man whose trail I was to follow through many different parts of Spain, a man of the most contradictory and perplexing character but one who had been important to me for half a century. I could close my eyes and visualize him in this plaza he had frequented and recall the first time I had met him. It was in the sixth grade in a small Pennsylvania school and our teacher, a tall, rather thin woman whom we liked, had finally found a subject she could get her teeth in, and she spoke with an intensity that I can still remember.

'Especially the boys in class should listen to what I'm going to say.' No one moved. 'In your life you must have some great man to whom you look up.' We looked up to the basketball captain, who was in high school. 'Not many are worthy of such respect, but the hero of our next poem was.' We slumped. Another sales talk on memorizing poetry. 'He was one of the bravest men in history and he did something I don't believe any boy in this class could have done.' We sat up again. 'Any of you could be brave in

A street lamp in the Plaza Mayor.

victory. When your side's ahead I've seen how brave you can be. But this man was brave in defeat. And that requires a real man.' This was new and we listened. 'Against odds so great that other men would have crumbled, he fought on. When his companions failed, he didn't. He was more heroic than the heroes of fairy tales. He was a man you must remember.' I often recalled this sentence. 'But what do you suppose happened to him? At the very moment of victory, when he had done all he set out to do, what happened?' I wanted to slump, because I was pretty sure this was where the girl came in. He married her no doubt. It always happened in poems, but something in the teacher's voice caused me to hesitate. 'At the moment for which all boys long, the moment when he had won, a cannonball killed him.' No previous poem had ended this way, and we sat silent. 'In a strange city, on a battlefield overlooking the ships he had been fighting to reach, he was killed.' Moved by her own eloquence and feeling kinship with the boys of her class, she sat down, opened her book and began to read those lines which, unknown to me at the time, she was engraving on my mind:

'Not a drum was heard, not a funeral note,
As his corse to the ramparts we hurried.'

Books were then distributed, bearing not only the poem but the famous painting by Smith, and we read the history of Sir John Moore, the English general who in 1808 and 1809 led an invasion into Spain against Napoleon and without fighting one engagement turned around and retreated to the northern port of La Coruña, where at the moment of having brought his army into sight of the rescue flotilla, he was killed by a cannonball.

Whenever our class memorized a poem, we held a competitive recitation, and in the case of 'The Burial of Sir John Moore,' I won handily, which was not entirely fair because I *was* John Moore. I had read everything I could find on him, and traced his route from Lisboa into Spain and out again, and knew La Coruña rather better than I did my home town. It was the first time in my learning that a subject had completely overwhelmed me and I it.

Therefore, it was with a sense of acquaintanceship that I sat in Salamanca and reflected that a hundred and fifty-eight years earlier, on November 13, 1808, General Moore had arrived in this plaza to hear reports of a concentration of English defeats and Spanish confusion. Suddenly, what had begun as an invasion to consolidate English and Spanish forces against Napoleon had become a trap in which Moore's entire army, the best in the field, was about to be swallowed up. If Moore had lived he would have hated the memory of Salamanca, for here he heard nothing but news of the most disheartening sort. The allies were in a state of collapse and Napoleon was triumphant.

As a boy I had not yet learned about my hero certain facts which were probably not in the books at that time, namely, that from Salamanca he had sent off a most puzzling series of letters in which he showed no hesitancy in predicting his defeat. To his quasi-sweetheart, Lady Hester Stanhope, who imagined that she was engaged to him and survived him to become one of England's outstanding eccentrics, he wrote that her little brother James, for whom she sought a commission, 'must get the Commander-in-Chief's leave to come to Spain. He may join me then. He will, however, come too late; I shall already be beaten.' In his diary he wrote: 'We have no business being here.' In his dispatches, either to England or to his fellow commanders in Spain, he wrote constantly of the probable need for retreat rather than attack, and a palpable sense of gloom possessed him. In Salamanca, General Moore had hardly been the hero whose exploits I had memorized; in fact, he was something of a fuddy-duddy and the disasters he foresaw were brought on partly by his own indecision and fatalism.

On December 11 he evacuated Salamanca and headed for the north, uncertain whether he was advancing to battle or taking the first steps in what would degenerate into a forced retreat. Rarely has a more confused and undecided leader led his troops into unknown territory, and we shall leave him as he marches out of the city but we shall meet him again in the north.

If you quit the Plaza Mayor by its southwest exit and wander through a series of attractive narrow streets you will come eventually to an austere little plaza presided over by the statue of a professor in robes, Fray Luis de León, whose spirit guards this place, and enclosed on four sides by old brown walls on which students have used a mixture of hog fat and bull's blood to scrawl the dates of their doctor's degrees, for this is the noble University of Salamanca, once the world's preeminent center of learning.

In the academic year 1567–1568 its rolls showed seven thousand eight hundred students taking courses ranging from mathematics to medicine and another five thousand hanging around the city to audit lectures. Carlos V spoke the truth when he said, 'This university is the treasury from which I furnish justice and government to my people of Spain,' for the cachet of a Salamanca degree could not be equaled. Throughout Europe foreign kings and cardinals submitted disputes to this faculty for adjudication, and if a professor from this university approved a debatable point, that practically established it.

The scholars teaching here investigated all matters. It was a Salamanca economist who first pointed out the national danger involved in bringing so much gold into the country without increasing at the same time the production of consumer goods; he saw that ruinous inflation must

FOLLOWING FACING PAGES:
Shields at the University of Salamanca.
Observe the busts set within the cockleshell
of Santiago de Compostela.

follow. Far more than half the intelligence of Spain centered in this school, and the roster of graduates who attained fame is a roll call of Spanish power. The most daring intellects, I suppose, attended Cardinal Cisneros' university at Alcalá de Henares, but it had a relatively brief life, whereas Salamanca continued through the centuries as the heart and core of Spanish culture.

Bologna, Paris and Oxford, all founded in the twelfth century, were the only schools that could compete with it, and during its early life—it was founded about 1230–1243—it tended to be more liberal and introspective than the others. It was powerful in theology and often provided

*In the cloisters of the university
some of the foremost scholars
of the world assembled,
but there have also been periods
of darkness.*

opinions on which the Spanish kings based their defiance of the Roman popes, but its greater fame lay in mathematics and science, in which it was a beacon light far ahead of its competitors.

Not all students who came here prospered, and in fiction 'the student from Salamanca' became a stock figure. In the Duque de Rivas' tragedy, *Don Alvaro*, the younger son, who follows Alvaro's trail to Peru, is described in this way:

> My cousin, who has just arrived from Salamanca, has told me that Alfonso is the crazy man of the University, more swordsman than scholar, and that he has the student bullies flabbergasted.

In an earlier play by Lope de Vega the earthy dialogue catches the spirit of Salamanca as understood by the common people across Spain:

BARBILDO: How did you get on at Salamanca?

LEONELO: That's a long story.

BARDILDO: You must be a very learned man by now.

LEONELO: No, I'm not even a barber.

BARBILDO: At least you're a scholar.

LEONELO: Well, I've tried to learn things that are important.

BARBILDO: Anyone who's seen so many printed books is bound to think he's wise.

LEONELO: I admit that printing has saved many talented writers from oblivion. Printing circulates their books and makes them known. Gutenberg, a famous German from Mainz, is responsible. But many men who used to have a high reputation are no longer taken seriously, now that their works have been printed.

Today the old classrooms, the cloisters, the marvelous library and the chapels can be inspected in the dignified buildings that enclose the plaza, and here one can catch a sense of what it must have been like to attend a university in the late Renaissance when ideas were exploding at such a furious rate. Each component at Salamanca is perfect, as if time had frozen the old patterns.

As a matter of fact, that is precisely what happened. Under pressures which will be made clear in this chapter, this grand university, light of Europe, began to grope and fumble. First, any student suspected of Jewish blood was excluded. Then it became difficult for bright boys from untitled families to gain entrance; vacancies were reserved for the nobility, who used the university as a kind of gentlemen's finishing school. At the end of the sixteenth century Salamanca no longer taught mathematics in any form and fifty years later enrolled not a single student in medicine. The fine interchange of ideas that used to be carried on with Oxford and Bologna was halted, and the sharp debate that once characterized the intellectual life of the university was silenced. Registrations dropped from seven thousand eight hundred to a mere three hundred in 1824.

I know of no other educational institution in the world that started so high as Salamanca to fall so low. Its eclipse was one of the severest blows Spain ever suffered, for with its castration the spark of national vitality ebbed, and any nation today that wishes to attain similar results should start by closing down its equivalent of Salamanca. Of course, the university did not physically disappear; except for years of revolution and crisis it kept its doors open and admitted a few hundred students who mouthed cautious doctrine taught by frightened professors. During the heyday of the Spanish empire students from Mexico and South America came to

A feature of university life in Spain is the tuna,
a group of students dressed as medieval troubadours
who roam the streets playing guitars and tambourines
in which they collect contributions.

Salamanca so as to be able, when they returned to their colonial cities, to boast as scholars had for five hundred years, 'I am from Salamanca.' There was also an Irish College attached to the university, and here young Catholics who could not obtain an education at home studied for five or six years, a large proportion of them finally becoming priests, so that much of Ireland's intelligence over long periods of time was trained in Salamanca.

Today the university functions normally. It is neither the superior center it once was nor the fraud that followed. It is known within Spain as the school for lesser intellectuals of good family, and few enterprising businesses would hire a Salamanca man when they might get a sharp young fellow trained either at Madrid or Barcelona.

Halfway between the university and the Plaza Mayor, at the northeast corner of two narrow streets, stands a stalwart brown Renaissance building four stories high, built in the early 1500s in the shape of a fortress. In Salamanca one can find many such buildings but this one has captured the imagination of all, because its main façade is studded with sixteen rows of beautifully carved conch shells, with varying numbers of shells to the row; some contain as many as twenty-three, others only fourteen, but they mark the building with elegance. This is the famous Casa de las Conchas (House of Shells), whose owner was a member of the Order of Santiago, and it illustrates how a capricious artistic invention can sometimes convert an ordinary structure into something enchanting.

When I am in Salamanca, I like to go to La Casa de las Conchas at noon as the sun creeps into the Calle de Meléndez and begins to throw the shells into lovely patterns of light and shade. I sit for about an hour on the stoop of a shoemaker's shop cater-cornered to the shells and enjoy the sensation of seeing the tip of one shell after another emerge from shadow into sunlight until finally the whole shell glows. The carved shields that top the windows burst into sunlight; the eagle pecks at the rays as they slide past and soon his wings are golden.

From the nearby cathedral, a curious affair in which a very old cathedral about to fall down was propped up by building a new one alongside it, bells begin to toll the quarter-hour and enough sun reaches the wall so that the protruding shells cast long diagonal shadows. At half past twelve the shoemaker suggests we have a cold drink; the whole façade is now in sunlight and will stay so for some hours. I see that the stone wall is not entirely flat, for the building is old, and here and there its stones have bulged, but now the house can be seen at its best, glowing in sunlight, and I wonder at myself for finding so much pleasure in watching the metamorphosis of a building notable only because some crazy architect slapped a couple of hundred conch shells across its face. Still, if I returned to Salamanca tomorrow I'd perch myself once more on the shoemaker's stoop to watch this bewitching ballet of sun and stone.

The ways of tourists are strange, and one afternoon as I sat in the Plaza Mayor I heard some Frenchmen at the next table tearing America apart. To the first barrage of criticism I could not logically protest: Americans were uncultured, lacked historical sense, were concerned only with business, had no sensitivity and ought to stay home. The second echelon of abuse I did want to interrupt, because I felt that some of it was wide of the mark: Americans were all loud, had no manners, no education, no sense of proportion, and were offensively vulgar in dress, speech, eating habits and general comportment, but I restrained myself because, after all, this was the litany one heard throughout Europe, here expressed rather more succinctly than elsewhere. But when these Frenchmen added a third charge I had to intervene: Americans menace the world because they refuse to face reality.

I happened to have in my hand at that moment the official card distributed by the French government honoring the twentieth anniversary of the Allied landings at Normandy on June 6, 1944. It was a well-presented design, as such things are apt to be in France, and showed a heroic General de Gaulle leading ashore an army of French soldiers and being greeted by stalwart members of the underground who had already vanquished the Germans occupying France. Far in the distance and bringing up the rear were one American foot soldier and one English officer. I passed the card along to one of my French neighbors and asked, 'Is this reality?'

He took the card, looked at it, smiled and said, 'History is what wise men say it is.'

'Do you really believe it happened that way?'

He tapped the card, neither in approbation nor rejection, and said, 'This is what has been agreed upon.'

'Have the charges you've been making about Americans also been agreed upon?'

'Yes.'

'So they are now the truth?'

'In Europe, yes.'

'Very interesting,' I said, turning away from the noisy Frenchmen to ponder the curious fate of Americans in the world today. I was at the moment especially depressed by some English books I had been reading, in which sensible writers with university degrees said the most extraordinary things about American travelers whom they had met in Europe. The Americans were all stupid and objectionable and loud and uneducated; and I sat at my table and made a list of the Americans I had met in recent travels: three Nobel Prize winners; two of the world's finest playwrights; three good novelists much read in England and France; four nationally famous bankers who in their spare time serve on the boards of universities, opera houses and museums; a score of quiet-spoken professors; a woman who helps run the Cleveland art museum; the director of one of our great symphonies; and two very well behaved painters. These people were, by any standard, among the leaders of the world and certainly

*Along the Sierpes in Sevilla,
along the promenade in Badajoz
and even in the smallest Spanish city,
you will find the glass-fronted club
where old men sit lost in reflection.
This one happens to be in the
Plaza Mayor at Salamanca.*

among the best educated and most gently cultured. Not one spoke in a loud voice; in fact, I had had to lean forward to catch what Tennessee Williams said, and the Ashcrafts, whom we shall meet in Pamplona, speak so softly they practically whisper.

'Why does no European ever meet this kind of American?' I asked myself. In the three latest English travel books on Spain there was a constant procession of American boors and boobs, but the authors were well-versed men and must surely have come into contact somewhere with the kinds of Americans I knew. I concluded that English writers could not be charged with animosity, for this they did not intend; they were merely accepting blindly a kind of American Black Legend and compounding it monotonously. I cannot charge them with planned falsehood, but I can query their powers of observation and their fairness in recording what they see.

In my travels I have encountered some pretty horrible English men and women. There was the chinless wonder in Singapore who for business reasons wanted to take me into the exclusive Raffles Club and spent some forty minutes coaching me on how I must behave, forgetting that I had

spent two years at one of Britain's best universities. He was so asinine he was funny. At the Sevilla airport I watched two formidable English women, the type who seem to be in constant supply, demand in piercing voices where their luggage was. In clear Spanish the porter replied, 'Enter the building, turn left, ten minutes.' The women, irritated by now, shouted their question again at the poor man, both speaking at once, and he with gestures explained once more, 'Enter the building, turn left, ten minutes.' The women looked at him with contempt, brushed him aside, and one said to the other in a loud voice. 'Poor beast. He doesn't understand a word we're saying.'

And so on. The point is that although I have seen such behavior ad infinitum I have refrained from writing about it as if it were standard English deportment overseas, because I know it isn't. I have met too many English gentlemen to allow myself such error. I do not refrain from lampooning the English because I love them but because I have regard for fact.

Sitting as quietly as my French companions would permit, I tried to discover what my true feelings were in this matter of honest description.

In my travels I have never met any single American as noisy and crude as certain Germans, none so downright mean as one or two Frenchmen, none so ridiculous as an occasional Englishman, none so arrogant as some Swedes and certainly none so penurious as the Portuguese. For raw misbehavior no American could surpass a prime example from India or Egypt, and for the unfeeling, uncultured boob that I encounter so often in literature as representing the American, I suspect one would do better to look among the Russians.

But in each of the national examples cited I am speaking of only a few horrible specimens. If one compares all English tourists with all Americans, I would have to admit that taken in the large the American is worse. If some European wanted to argue that seventy percent of all American tourists are regrettable, I would agree. If he insisted on eighty percent, I'd go along. If he claimed ninety, I suppose I wouldn't argue too much. But when, like the Frenchmen to my left and the English writers under my arm, he states that one hundred percent are that way, then I must accuse him of being false to the facts.

Of all the countries in which to travel, I find that today the American is judged more honestly in Spain than elsewhere. He is not loved, but neither is he abused. The average Spaniard objects to having American military bases on Spanish soil, but he acknowledges the need for protection. He is suspicious of the large number of American Protestants who come to Spain and is sure they are up to no good. He is aggravated by the sight of American military personnel spending large and easy sums of money, but he is gratified that the Yanks behave as well as they do. Because Spain is a dictatorship it is obligated to decry democracy, and since America is a leader among the democracies, newspapers run a constant commentary on our failures, especially in handling the race problem. Reading Spanish newspapers, one would judge that the United States was about to collapse, but at the same time the impression is given that she is a resolute ally on whom Spain can depend. Because Spain is a Catholic country, her newspapers must decry American excesses in sex, education and family life, and a lurid picture is presented, but Americans are also presented as courageous, good sports and dependable.

Two points are amusing. Because Spain for many years was lacking in consumer goods, it was obligatory to prove that the United States had lost its soul in pursuit of such goods. Special contumely was heaped upon our system of time payments. 'Americans have the television set, but they never own it. It has been loaned to them on time payments, and to meet those payments they mortgage their souls.' The soul of Spain, these articles pointed out, was not corrupted by time payments. But with the arrival of television the initial cost of a set was so great that the average Spanish family could not advance the cash at one time. A system of time payments was obligatory and one was initiated, but if you ask a Spaniard about this he says, 'Yes, but the system we worked out doesn't corrupt the soul.'

If on almost every topic Spain is reasonably fair to America, on one it is not. Spain hates Yale University. I suppose that if the government called for volunteers tomorrow to invade Connecticut and raze Yale, it could have an expeditionary force by twilight; in a period of three months I read four assaults on Yale, some lamenting that a great university should have fallen so low, others threatening reprisals. The trouble stems from the announcement by a group of Yale professors in 1965 that they had found a map proving that Christopher Columbus was not the first to discover America in 1492 but that a Scandinavian had by 1118 and possibly as early as 1020. 'The lie was bad enough,' a Spanish scholar told me, 'but to have announced it on the eve of October 12, El día de la raza, when the world was preparing to honor our great Spanish explorer—that was too much. With that action Yale blackened its name.'

It is surprising to find that most Spaniards consider the Italian Columbus as one of them, just as they nationalize the Greek El Greco. At the same time they protest when the French government includes Pablo Picasso in a list of French painters. When I commented on this contradiction, a Spaniard pointed out, 'You Americans insist in your literature courses that Henry James and T.S. Eliot were Americans, even though they emigrated to England, but you also claim a painter like Lyonel Feininger and a scientist like Albert Einstein, even though they did most of their work in Germany.'

Apart from such natural chivvying, the American traveler meets a more congenial reception in Spain than in other European countries, but I suspect this will not be true much longer, for the signs are that with affluence Spain will go the way of France. In Salamanca I decided to take advantage of the favorable travel conditions and visit a cluster of five small towns to the northeast, for in them I would be able to trace out a network of lives that had helped make Spain what it is today.

Madrigal de las Altas Torres (Madrigal of the High Towers), could there be a more poetic name for a town, even though the derivation must have been from some prosaic word like madriguera (burrow or lair of animals)? And could any town so named be lovelier than this, nestling sun-baked within its circle of ruined towers? Today it looks almost as it must have in 1450, its walls forming a complete circle, not large in diameter, its narrow streets wandering beneath arches. The same notable buildings are there, and when the church bells ring they send their evening song out across the same fields of wheat.

Only the towers are not quite the same. They still stand, of course, but many have lost their tops through crumbling, and the once impregnable defenses are no longer so. In spite of all I had read about Madrigal, I had not visualized what an excellent monument it was, a gem of medieval life protected within its walls.

The town is very ancient, dating back perhaps to Roman times. When the Moors reached this far north Christians tried to halt them here, and the town was destroyed in a series of sieges and countersieges, but when the Moors triumphed it was rebuilt and given both the towers and the name it bears today. It was the walls that attracted the kings of Castilla, for once inside these battlements they were safe, and it was here that Juan II, the one who sponsored the Conde Alvaro de Luna, whose genuflecting statue we saw in Toledo, built a palace in the early 1400s. Later it was converted into an Augustinian convent where surplus females of the royal line were hidden away, and it was in this convent that I picked up the thread I was to follow through the five towns.

I first saw the convent from a distance, an ugly, low palace with miserly windows and little to commend it. Walls in the shape of a lozenge enclosed a large garden, and I judged the whole could accommodate about three hundred nuns, but their lives would presumably be rather hard, for the old convent seemed cold and forbidding. I went to what must have been the main entrance to the castle when kings lived here, but it was closed.

'You enter by the side,' a woman called from the street, and I walked along the bleak wall until I came to a corner, where I found the present entrance tucked away under three handsome stone arches that formed a small protected porch containing a device I had often read about but never seen. It was a torno (wheel), a large lazy Susan with sides about two feet tall and set into the wall in such a way that the nun inside the convent who turned it could not see the person who might have deposited a bundle on the other side. This was the way in which the unwed mothers of Spain had traditionally turned their unwanted babies over to a convent without being recognized. Many notable Spaniards had started life in the turning of some torno.

I rang the bell which hung beside the contraption, and after a moment the torno slowly revolved while a nun inside checked to see if I had abandoned a baby.

'What do you want?' an unseen voice asked.

'To see the cradle of Spanish history,' I said, repeating a phrase seen on posters advertising Madrigal.

'Wait.'

There was a long pause, then finally a door, far removed from the torno, opened and I was greeted by two of the shortest, oldest nuns I had ever seen. 'Come this way,' they said, leading me into the convent that had once been a palace.

It was a quiet spot, marked with rough dignity rather than formal beauty. The double-tiered cloisters were low and unadorned, but they stood in such stateliness around the enclosure that they seemed more attractive than ornate ones I had seen elsewhere. In the center stood a low octagonal well, again of deep simplicity, protected by a plain tiled roof.

The rooms followed the lead of the cloisters, for they too were square and unadorned. 'This is the old kitchen,' one of the Agustinas said, and when I commented on how large it was, she explained, 'Yes, for in those days we had hundreds here. Now we are but twenty. And they speak of closing us down.' I looked about me at the medieval spaciousness, and she said gloomily, 'I know. It is large and we are small.'

Whenever the two nuns led me to a new part of the convent they first rang a warning bell, and I could sometimes catch the flight of skirts as someone disappeared around a corner, but if I did meet a nun unexpectedly face to face, one who had not heard the warning, she was always very old. 'This is the hall where nobles were received on visits,' my guide said, and for the first time I saw that long chain of portraits, painted in heavy brown by some untalented artist centuries ago. They are not good art, but they awaken powerful memories and convey an excellent idea of why such royal convents were necessary in the old days.

This tall, thin-faced nun is Doña María, the illegitimate daughter of Fernando the Catholic. This pleasant round-faced nun holding a skull in her right hand is Doña María Esperanza, also an illegitimate daughter of Fernando. This curious portrait of a nun who looks half infant, half dowager portrays Doña Juana, illegitimate daughter of Carlos V, while this austere nun proudly holding a crown is Doña Ana María, illegitimate daughter of an illegitimate son of Felipe IV and the actress María Calderón. And here is the most memorable of all, a saucy-faced young woman whom we must remember, for we shall study her strange career in detail. She is a delightful-looking person with her coif awry; of all the royal nuns she alone shows a peek of hairdo. She also is alone in wearing jewelry and in her left arm she carries a cute little puppy, and her whole manner is so provocative that one could predict from seeing her that 'this one will come to no good.' As a matter of fact, she ended her life as Mother Superior of the most powerful convent in Spain, but her road to that eminence was rocky. She is Doña Ana, illegitimate daughter of Don Juan de Austria, the illegitimate son of Carlos V. He was the admiral whose blue battle flags from Lepanto we saw in the museum at Toledo.

There are other portraits in this powerful row, many of them the illegitimate daughters of royalty, and one begins to understand why the existence of these girls, if they were allowed to move freely in society, could have been a considerable embarrassment to the crown. Since they were illegitimate they could not be offered in marriage to other heads of state, which meant that any adventurer might pick them up, sire a few children and claim hereditary rights to the throne of Spain. Great care was taken to keep them safely locked up and their imprisonment began at age five or six. The legend attached to the portrait of Doña Juana, daughter of Carlos V, tells the whole story: 'Illegitimate daughter of the emperor, died a novice at the age of seven years.' A legend across the frame contains a rather neat play on words:

Date a Dios en tierna edad;
Vivirás eternidad.

(Give yourself to God at a tender age, you will live eternally.) Many of these little girls matured to become responsible leaders of their convents.

'And here is the chapel,' the old nun intoned, 'and the beautiful marble tomb of Doña María, natural daughter of Fernando, and here is the organ brought down from Germany to soothe the king with soft music.' She went to the keyboard while her partner pumped a huge bellows, and soft wheezing sounds came forth as they had done four centuries ago.

I was beginning to think that we would never come to the room which had lured me to Madrigal, but now we passed along the upper tier of the cloister while my guide rang her bell to disperse any nuns working there and we came to a window from which I could look down into the rather large garden of the convent, where four nuns were weeding. 'We eat what we grow,' my guide said, 'and we don't get fat.' And then there we were! A very ordinary anteroom containing two royal portraits, and an inner room with no window and only a big rough wooden door whose panels opened one by one so that servants outside could pass food into the room without being seen. 'This is it,' the nun said reverently.

And I was in the room where Isabel of Castilla was born, known to history as Isabel the Catholic, loyal wife of that Fernando who sired the impressive line of illegitimate offspring. The more one studies Spanish history, tracing out the actual sources and operations of power, the more highly he regards Isabel. In personality, devotion, intelligence, fortitude and above all in administrative power, she makes all other women of her age and most of the men seem puny. War, the presence of Muslims on her soil and the philosophical upheavals of the age confronted her, but one by one she triumphed over them, leaving when she died a kingdom on its way to solidity where before there had been only a hollow crown.

The representative fact about Isabel is that she bore five children, some of whom were to become notable in European history, and she gave birth to each in a different city, often after days and weeks in the saddle protecting her realm. She was a colossus of her age, a woman who supported Columbus in his discovery of a new world, and Anglo-Saxon scholars fail to do her justice. For example, one major encyclopedia allots her only sixty-four lines while giving her unimportant daughter Catalina two hundred and forty-five merely because she happened to be the first wife of Henry VIII. And Mary Queen of Scots, who accomplished nothing compared to Isabel, is accorded a staggering eleven hundred and eight. This is not only insular; it is ridiculous.

How did she happen to be born in Madrigal? When the Conde de Luna was running Castilla on behalf of the weak and widowed king Juan II, he engineered, if you remember, a marriage between Juan and Isabel of

LOS REYES CATOLICOS

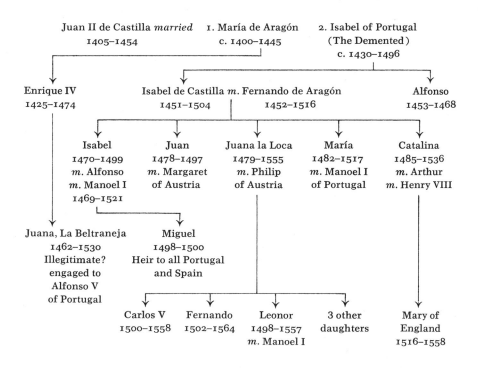

Juan II de Castilla *married* 1. María de Aragón 2. Isabel of Portugal
1405–1454   c. 1400–1445   (The Demented)
                                      c. 1430–1496

Enrique IV   Isabel de Castilla *m.* Fernando de Aragón   Alfonso
1425–1474   1451–1504   1452–1516   1453–1468

Isabel   Juan   Juana la Loca   María   Catalina
1470–1499   1478–1497   1479–1555   1482–1517   1485–1536
m. Alfonso   *m.* Margaret *m.* Philip   *m.* Manoel I   *m.* Arthur
m. Manoel I of Austria   of Austria   of Portugal   *m.* Henry VIII
1469–1521

Juana, La Beltraneja   Miguel
1462–1530   1498–1500
Illegitimate?   Heir to all Portugal
engaged to   and Spain
Alfonso V
of Portugal

Carlos V   Fernando   Leonor   3 other   Mary of
1500–1558   1502–1564   1498–1557   daughters   England
                          m. Manoel I   1516–1558

Portugal, the lady who shortly thereafter caused Luna's head to be struck off and who later became demented. Juan already had one son, Enrique, who was first in line for the crown, and this Enrique would have a daughter Juana, who would be second in line. Isabel of Portugal would also present the king with a son, Alfonso, who would be third in line. Therefore, when in 1450 the queen announced that she was pregnant it caused little stir, for the crown was already protected with heirs, so while her husband in his feeble way watched over the government she hied herself to the family palace at Madrigal, not yet a convent, and there gave birth to a daughter, Isabel.

In the bare anteroom there was a portrait of her, and she looked to be a stocky, heavy-faced, powerful woman with large eyelids and a stunning air of command. Whether or not the portrait was physically accurate I did not know, but psychologically it was. No one ever reported her to be beautiful but many commented on the fact that she was a tender mother, a wise ruler and a woman of merciless determination.

While I had Isabel's character in mind, I wanted to see Arévalo, which represented the next step in her development, so I left Madrigal by the southern gate, picked up a small road which led to the east and after some twenty miles I came to Arévalo and its brooding castle among the ruins. The town was strange in many ways; through the centuries an unusual number of churches had been built and the town found itself with a surfeit. Sensibly, some of the unnecessary buildings had been deconsecrated and converted into mental asylums, others into granaries.

Arévalo had a plaza, not the main one, which startled me, for it was unpaved and had the low monotonous buildings common five centuries ago, so that even when men in modern dress crossed it, I had the sense of being back in the time of Isabel. I stopped in a store facing the plaza and asked what accounted for this timelessness, and the woman explained, 'We keep it this way so that motion picture companies can shoot their films here. We've been in the movies many times. Look! To make this five hundred years old you simply take down those two electric light wires and that Coca-Cola sign.' She snapped her fingers and I made the imaginary transformation.

Today Arévalo is renowned for two accomplishments. It makes the best bread in Spain and the best roast pig. Of the bread I can say only that I ate it as if it were cake. Served in crusty small loaves, it seems to be made of honey, cream, rock salt and coarse grain which has lost none of its goodness through milling. Once I was in the area with a friend who at each meal ate three loaves, by himself. When I commented on this, he asked, 'Why eat meat when this is here?'

As for the pig, at the Figón de la Pinilla (Eating House of Mrs. Pinilla), an old restaurant on the main plaza decorated with scenes from plays and movies, the dish is served each Tuesday, on all feast days and during the June feria. It is so well regarded in the region that Arévalo's poet laureate, Marolo Perotas, has cast the recipe into heroic blank verse:

> Everything is golden,
> Everything is aromatic,
> Everything is glistening
> Because of the lard and garlic.

If the verses are reduced to prose, which hardly seems appropriate for such a dish, the directions become simple: 'Select a fat little suckling pig twenty-one days old and barely nine pounds in weight, because if it is larger the result will be greasy, tough and coarse. Remove all the hair and slit the pig open from head to tail. Then in a rough black earthen casserole bake it at a temperature of 185°, and in a little more than an hour and a half it is ready to eat.' The result was so good that I had to fault the poet for having kept to himself the basting secrets. Suspecting that a good

Dressed in traditional black,
the women of Spain can be the most delightful,
robust and amusing in Europe.

many herbs went into the dressing, I slipped into the kitchen of the figón to interrogate the cook. 'Of course! Butter, onion, salt, lots of paprika, bay leaves, garlic, lemon, parsley, thyme and white vinegar.' I complimented him, and he added, 'Don't go easy on the paprika.' As he cooked it, the roast pig of Arévalo was a rich, greasy, succulent feast which Spaniards enjoy and foreigners approach with caution.

It was not for roast pig that Isabel of Portugal and her daughter Isabel, who was to be known as the Catholic, came to Arévalo, nor for the bread either. They came here to live in the castle, a large gloomy place but one that could be defended, while the king spent his last days in confusion and died. Young Isabel, still far removed from the succession, was of little importance, so mother and daughter stayed in the forbidding castle and slowly Isabel of Portugal went mad. She used to scream at her attendants and alternately love and berate her daughter. She beat her head against the wall on occasion, but for the most part she receded to quiescence and sat for days staring at the walls of her self-made prison. Her daughter was allowed little freedom, and her long stay at Arévalo could just as well have been spent in any other of the nearby towns, for they were monotonously alike.

Isabel's half brother, the infamous Enrique IV, ascended the throne and debauched the Spanish court to an extent that made him the worst king Spain ever had. Morals degenerated, sexual abuses became open, and it is generally believed that the austerity which characterized Isabel stemmed from her revulsion at her brother's behavior. She became personally involved when Enrique discovered that in her he had a pawn of value and started those tedious negotiations whereby he offered her in marriage to this or that impossible French or German or Portuguese royal personage. At one point he proposed a most decrepit Spanish nobleman and at another he conducted serious discussions over a possible marriage to the hunchback who later became Richard III of England, but Isabel shied away. It was degrading, to waste one's time cooped up with a near-mad mother and to be bandied about by a degenerate half brother, but that was the way Isabel passed her days in Arévalo.

By the time I picked her story up again at the little town of Toro, perched on a cliff overlooking the Río Duero, which crosses northern Spain to enter the Atlantic at Porto, her luck had changed dramatically. She had taken matters into her own hands and had found a husband for herself, the dynamic and gifted Fernando de Aragón, two years younger than she but a handsome, daring fellow who was to prove so adroit in manipulating Spanish interests in Italy that Niccolò Machiavelli would use him as the archetype of the cynical ruler in *The Prince*. It was a love match, at least on Isabel's part, but also a miraculous union of equals; Fernando was probably the best man in Europe for Isabel to have married and together they made a formidable team.

Never did Fernando look better, either to history or to his young wife, than at Toro, for here by his gallantry he ensured her crown. Her incompetent father, Juan II, had died. Her half brother, King Enrique IV, had also died. Her full brother, who might have inherited the throne, had died earlier; but this did not leave Isabel next, because Enrique had left a daughter Juana, who if she were legitimate would become queen. Juana was born in wedlock, of that there was no question, but nobles who sought to place Isabel on the throne pointed out that during Enrique's life he had been known openly as The Impotent, and a credible rumor was started: 'Juana is the daughter of the queen but not of the king.' Matters were complicated when the King of Portugal, seeing a good chance to meddle in Spanish affairs and perhaps win the throne for himself, announced his betrothal to Juana and his intention of using the Portuguese army to put her on the throne. This the nobles supporting Isabel could not permit and war became inescapable. After much jockeying back and forth, the two armies finally faced each other here at Toro in the year 1475.

I was fortunate in Toro in finding as guide—impromptu friend might be the better word—an old man some five feet tall and weighing about two hundred and twenty pounds. He was remarkable both for his information and for his trousers, which had to be ample to cover his girth but which also came nearly to his chin. He was encased in wool and his fly was at least twenty inches long. He was in love with Toro and its distinguished old buildings but his field of specialization was the Battle of Toro. 'It determined the course of Spanish history,' he said. 'If Portugal had won, no Isabel the Catholic. No Carlos Quinto. And Portugal would have won except for two Spanish heroes. You ever hear of Cardinal Mendoza of Toledo? Our warrior cardinal? His bravery helped save the day. But our hero was Fernando. How lucky Isabel was to have chosen such a man. What he did here at Toro will always be remembered.'

What my roly-poly guide told me next was so improbable that I did not believe him, convinced that he was repeating a legend, but later when I looked it up in histories I found that he had been telling the truth. In 1475 Fernando made this proposal to the King of Portugal: 'Since our armies cannot seem to reach a conclusion, let you and me duel in the old manner, the lady of the winner to become Queen of Spain.' At first the Portuguese agreed and plans were made for what would have been the last time in history when two sovereigns met in single combat to decide the inheritance of their nations, but at the last moment the King of Portugal withdrew, not surprisingly, since he was forty-three while Fernando was only twenty-three. Later in 1476, when battle between the armies could no longer be avoided, Cardinal Mendoza's firmness and Fernando's fine generalship gave victory to the Spaniards, and Juana, whom many modern historians accept as the rightful heiress to the throne, was driven from Spain. Isabel, by right of conquest, was Queen of Castilla, and as soon as the Moors could be driven out of Granada, would be Queen of Spain as well.

Standing on the cliff at Toro, looking down at the Duero below me, I listened as my fat guide with the amazing pants said, 'To think that the history of an entire peninsula should have been decided here . . . in a little town like this,' but when I questioned him on details, he had to admit that the battle hadn't occurred exactly at Toro. 'Farther down the river . . . toward Portugal . . . and if the truth were known, Queen Isabel wasn't here during the battle. She was back in Tordesillas, waiting, waiting. King Fernando rode down that road over there to take her the news, and when he reached her and assured her that she was to be queen, she wept. It was a very good marriage, that one.'

I was much taken with Toro, for it was an excellent town, far enough from the main road to receive few tourists yet so filled with memories that those who did come could see shadows of kings as they prepared for hand-to-hand combat. At dusk one night I crossed the river to travel out to the scene of battle, and I understood then how Fernando had utilized the river to advantage, and when I turned back, there was Toro atop its eroding red cliff, magnificent in outline against the dark sky of evening, its turrets jagged, its crumbling walls still defiant. Next morning I went on to Medina del Campo, coming in sight of this once-great city not long after dawn.

I stopped on a slight rise to imagine what it must have been like, in the sixteenth century, to be a merchant coming to Medina del Campo from Flanders. The journey across France and the Pyrenees had been difficult, but the fair at Medina was so important that one dared not miss it, for here the commerce of Europe was largely determined. From a hill like this, one would have seen a dozen informal caravans converging on Medina: Italians on horseback, Germans on foot, Frenchmen in a brotherly union of merchants and churchmen, all on their way to the fair. Off to the left, down from the upland plains of Castilla, there would be herdsmen coming in with huge flocks of sheep and to the right other herdsmen from Extremadura bringing cattle. As many as fifty thousand traders converged on Medina each year in its days of greatness.

But when I reached the city I could find no evidence of that glory. No restaurants were open, no bars, but I did find a bridge that crossed the Río Zapardiel, a stream I had often read about: 'From Antwerp and London came the merchants to set up their booths along the banks of the Zapardiel.' I had imagined a broad, flowing river. It was four feet wide, six inches deep and its banks were lined with rubbish, but at one end of the bridge there was a churro shop, and even though I knew I would be sick the rest of the day, I entered.

'Señor! You're a norteamericano but you know what's good, eh?' The speaker was a robust woman barely visible through clouds of smoke coming from deep pots in which boiling oil was being used to fry churros.

The smell was overpowering but it did have a certain enticing quality, as if to say, 'You know damned well churros are inedible, but don't they smell good?'

At a chrome-plated machine the woman was cranking a handle which extruded a flour paste about the diameter of a quarter, but with fluted edges. This she cut off in ten-inch lengths, twisting their ends together and plopping them into the crackling fat, where they fried for a few minutes to emerge an appetizing brown. She sprinkled them with a coarse sugar and set two before me.

'Chocolate?' I nodded, and into a small cup she poured a chocolate thicker than most soups and as delicious as it was aromatic.

Churros and chocolate! I suppose if one searched the restaurants of the world one could not find a worse breakfast nor one that tasted better. The churros were so greasy that I needed three paper napkins per churro, but they tasted better than doughnuts. The chocolate was completely indigestible, but much better than coffee. And the great gobs of unrefined sugar were chewy. Any nation that can eat churros and chocolate for breakfast is not required to demonstrate its courage in other ways.

I remember Medina del Campo as fifty-percent churro indigestion, fifty-percent frustration, for when the town was awake I went into the plaza and began asking people, 'Where is the old palace in which Queen Isabel died?'

'She died in the castle up there on the hill,' they all said, pointing to one of Spain's better-preserved fortresses, and it was appropriate to think that a girl who had lived so long in a similar castle at Arévalo had died in this enormous pile of rock, but I knew that this was only legend. Records proved that Isabel had died in a small palace somewhere inside the gates of Medina del Campo and I wanted to see where.

'Wait till the stores open,' the policeman said, so I wandered in the plaza and came upon something I had not expected, four low pillars not more than two feet high, connected by heavy chains, inside which stood two large ruined pillars and a plaque which read:

DURING THE FIFTEENTH AND SIXTEENTH CENTURIES,
WHICH MARKED THE APOGEE OF THE CLASSICAL FAIRS
OF MEDINA DEL CAMPO, AT THIS POINT IN THE PLAZA
MAYOR THE MONEYCHANGERS AND BANKERS OF THAT
TIME INSTALLED THEIR BOOTHS OPEN TO ALL THE
WORLD. MEDINA WAS, DURING THESE CENTURIES,
COMMERCIALLY ECUMENICAL AND HERE THE LETTER OF
EXCHANGE WAS CRYSTALLIZED IN ITS DEFINITIVE FORM.

More important than the cattle fair or the assembly of merchants had been this yearly meeting in Medina of bankers from all over Europe for the purpose of determining the relative values of national currencies and the clearing of loans against one another. For example, a merchant in Antwerp could promise a customer, 'I will pay your banker in London three hundred pieces of gold at the fair of Medina del Campo.' Or a banker in Naples could say, 'Three hundred coins, their value to be determined by the price of gold at Medina.' Here also were developed, as the signs said, the sophisticated instruments of international banking, for just as the university at Salamanca had constituted a kind of clearing house for ideas, so Medina had set standards for commercial dealings. While I was in Medina a conference of international bankers was being held in Madrid, but they did not take a side trip to Medina, where their profession began, and I thought that a pity.

When the stores opened, so did my confusion. 'Isabel's palace was over there,' I was told, but that was wrong. 'It's over there,' another said, but that was wrong too. Finally a friend had the good idea of inquiring at a bank, and by luck we hit the nephew of Medina del Campo's cronista— that is, the town's historian, poet, bibliographer and publicist—and the young man said, 'You won't believe what I'm going to show you, but it will be the palace in which Isabel died.'

'How can you be sure?' I asked.

'My uncle is the cronista. He knows everything.' And he led us to a crumbling building at one corner of the plaza, and no one could have guessed that this had once been a palace fit for the death of Europe's noblest queen. Inside the creaking door a temporary wooden booth had been erected for the sale of tickets to a comic bullfight: 'The Fireman Bullfighter! Estupendo! 75¢!' A fine old wooden stairway led to a second floor littered with all kinds of filth, and the rooms which once had housed the queen and her attendants were now barred, for a century ago the palace had been converted into a jail. Men who had stolen sheep or murdered tailors had spent their last days in the room which Isabel had used for her dying. With the coming of indoor toilets one closet had been redesigned, but it had degenerated into a state of filth. And so it went through all this historic site. It was ironic, I thought as I left the palace, that even the nearby church, which Isabel had done so much to save, was the ugliest I was to see in Spain, a true masterpiece of junk.

But her monument is not a broken-down palace in Medina del Campo nor an ugly provincial church nearby. Spain is her monument, united and Catholic, as she had determined it should be. Her administration was the best the country would know, for she kept little books in which she listed the names of all the capable men she met, so that when a vacancy occurred in any department she had an immediate replacement, who rarely proved unworthy. Militarily, financially and spiritually she left Spain a bulwark among nations, and I judge her to have been twice the ruler that her grandson Carlos V was and also better than her great-grandson Felipe II.

It was an Italian humanist, Pedro Mártir de Anglería, servant at the Spanish court since 1487, who wrote in a private letter the eulogy which most Spaniards accept as the final word on Isabel:

> The pen falls from my hand and my strength fails through grief: the world has lost its most precious ornament, and the loss should be mourned not only by the Spaniards, whom she has so long led along the road to glory, but by all the nations of Christendom, because she was the mirror of all virtues, the refuge of the innocent, and the scourge of the evil; I doubt that there has lived in the world a heroine, either in ancient or in modern times, who merits comparison with this peerless woman.

One must note, however, that much of what is popularly taught about Isabel is not true. She did not unify Spain, for when she died the nation once more divided. Fernando kept for himself the Kingdom of Aragón, but the Kingdom of Castilla went to Isabel's daughter Juana. Fernando, treated miserably by the nobles of Castilla, sought revenge by marrying, within a few months of Isabel's death, nineteen-year-old Germaine de Foix, niece of the French king. He did this for two reasons, to spite the Castilians and to sire an heir who would inherit his half of Spain.

Promptly, Germaine gave him a son, and in this way Fernando, in an act of revenge, threatened to destroy all that Isabel had accomplished, but the boy died shortly after birth, whereupon Fernando and his child bride tried desperately to have another, but the old man was not equal to the task, so Germaine instructed her apothecaries to concoct a brew of blood, herbs, magic elements and bull testicles, which she fed Fernando in such quantities that she undermined his health. He died without further issue and it was due solely to this lucky accident that Spain had another chance to unite.

Isabel's life with Fernando had never been easy, for while living with the queen he had fathered four bastard children, each by a different mother. The two girls we have met, tucked away at Isabel's command in the convent at Madrigal de las Altas Torres. One of the boys became a soldier, the other, at the age of six, Archbishop of Zaragoza. When Cardinal Mendoza died Fernando insisted that this youth, then only twenty-four, be made Archbishop of Toledo and thus primate of all Spain, but here Isabel put her foot down. She preferred naming an archbishop of her own choice and it was the best decision she ever made, for her candidate was Cisneros, and had he not taken charge when Fernando finally died, twelve years after Isabel, the breach between Castilla and Aragón would probably have become irreparable.

I left Medina del Campo and drove a few miles north to another cliff on the Río Duero, where in the town of Tordesillas the tragedy of Isabel came to an end, years after her own death. I had known of Tordesillas in other contexts without realizing that it was one of the principal theaters of the Isabel story. In 1493 Pope Alexander VI, seeking to obviate colonial quarrels between Catholic countries, had established a Line of Demarcation between Spanish and Portuguese claims. It ran one hundred leagues west of the Azores but was not entirely satisfactory, so in 1494 envoys of Portugal and Spain, supervised by representatives of the Papacy, convened here in Tordesillas to sign the treaty defining a new line two hundred and seventy leagues farther west. It was as a result of this treaty that a country like Peru became Spanish, whereas Brazil was Portuguese. But for the student of Spanish internal history, events of much greater significance occurred in Tordesillas and it was these that I wished to track down.

As the genealogical chart shows, Fernando and Isabel were blessed with numerous progeny, and one of the queen's notable accomplishments was her manipulation of their marriages. She married her oldest daughter, Isabel, to Alfonso, heir to the throne of Portugal, but he died suddenly, so the young widow was passed along to Manoel, the next in line; but the young Isabel said she would not marry him unless he agreed to expel all Jews from Portugal the way her mother had from Spain. This curious wedding present was granted and the marriage took place to the wailing of many Jews. Then it was Isabel who died, so her mother quickly arranged for her third daughter, young María, to marry the widower Manoel (when María died in 1517, Manoel took a third wife from the family, Queen Isabel's granddaughter Leonor!). When Isabel's youngest child, Catalina, reached the age of four she was promised in marriage to Arthur, Prince of Wales to the English throne, who was three, and when the girl was eleven the betrothal was formalized. At sixteen the marriage took place but Arthur was sickly and soon died, whereupon shrewd Isabel, in defiance of the Church's decree against such incestuous marriages, passed Catalina along to the dead man's brother, the new Prince of Wales, who was to become Henry VIII. Life with him was hell, but Catalina did escape the ax which ended the reigns of two of her successors, and she did give birth to Mary, who succeeded in restoring England to Catholicism, as her grandmother would have wished, even though the restoration was reversed by her successor, the Protestant Queen Elizabeth. It was with her son Juan and second daughter Juana that Isabel had her outstanding success, because for them she arranged a double wedding with the daughter and son of Maximilian, ruler of all Germany, Holy Roman Emperor and head of the house of Habsburg.

In Spain, Margaret of Austria, Maximilian's daughter, married Juan, heir to the Spanish throne, while in Flanders, Archduke Philip of Austria, son of Maximilian and heir to vast estates in the Low Countries and elsewhere, known in Spain as Felipe I, married Juana. It was in this manner that Spain became involved not only with the Habsburgs, who ultimately inherited the throne, but also with the Low Countries, which were to be a permanent thorn in Spanish flesh. Young Felipe was probably the most attractive prince of the century, a lustful, vain and somewhat stupid young man who set out to humiliate his dowdy Spanish wife and who with his infidelities drove her mad. (John Langdon-Davies, in his study of Carlos the Bewitched previously cited, argues that it was the other way around and that it was Juana's encroaching madness that almost drove Felipe out of his mind; but one must remember that the thesis of his book is that Juana was genetically insane, because of her inheritance from the demented Isabel of Portugal.) When this happened it was of no great consequence, because Juana, like her mother a generation earlier, was originally well removed from the throne. First in line was her brother Juan, who had married Felipe's sister. Second was her own sister Isabel, now Queen of Portugal; if her brother died she stood to be queen of two countries. And third was Isabel's son, heir to the Portuguese throne and putative heir to that of Spain as well, in which case the Iberian peninsula would again be united as it had sometimes been in the past. So for the present no one bothered much about Juana's trouble with her handsome husband; it was no worse than what Catalina had to put up with from Henry VIII. But once again, as in the case of the famous Isabel, miracles began to happen. Juan died suddenly. Isabel did the same. And to the horror of Portugal and Spain alike, young Miguel died at the age of two. Suddenly Juana la Loca, as she was being called behind her back, found herself heiress to the throne of Spain. If she could somehow control her husband and her mind she might look forward to a reign equaling her mother's in brilliance. With these prospects Juana and Felipe came to Spain to claim their inheritance, and we shall see them next wandering about the open countryside north of Tordesillas under conditions so gruesome as to form one of the weirdest chapters of history.

Before I started to trace the story of Juana, I wanted to see what modern Tordesillas was like, so early one morning I perched myself in the Plaza del Generalísimo Franco, where grass grew in the corners. Forty-four awkward stone pillars supported an arcade which in places threatened to collapse, while many of the houses fronting on the plaza showed walls that had to be propped up with poles. Several had been patched with a cheap stucco painted to simulate concrete block, and all needed painting. Such women as appeared tended to be dressed in black; they worked while their men in patched pants lounged in the shade. I noticed especially six brightly painted heraldic shields of Tordesillas being used as decorations around the plaza; they bore a set of flashy symbols consisting of keys, mountains, a river and three saddles. The last, I was to discover, were debatable additions, for there was much confusion as to what they signified. A bartender said, 'There was a big battle over there. Very crucial. Everything depended on what the volunteers from this town did. But like always they messed things up. They were late in their saddles [tarde en sillas] and after the battle was lost we were stuck with the name.'

A customer said, 'Wrong again. One of the old kings was hunting here and he had a fine afternoon, so he named the town Tarde en sillas, which means Afternoon in the saddles.' Another said, 'The name of the town comes from a word. Tardecillo, a little late. Has nothing to do with saddles.' I said that must be wrong because three saddles appeared on the town shield, and he laughed. 'A friend of mine painted those shields last year. To please tourists'; whereupon a fourth man growled, 'They all don't know anything. This town was named by the Romans before Spanish was a language. The name has no meaning.'

The only things in the plaza that reminded me I was in this century were two signs splashed in dripping letters: 'Viva Franco' and 'Gibraltar Is Spanish.' The latter brought me back to Queen Isabel, for on her deathbed she had added a codicil to her will instructing her people never to surrender Gibraltar; with much effort she had won it back from a noble family that had usurped it for private use, and she foresaw its importance.

I doubt that she could have foreseen the important role that Tordesillas was to play in the history of her family. It began ominously. On September 25, 1506, Felipe I, who ruled jointly with Juana, died at Burgos in the north. The queen was understandably distraught over losing the man who had bewitched her, and unluckily at this moment she fell under the control of a Carthusian monk, who consoled her: 'With sufficient prayers your husband the king will revive. I know a case in which a king who had been dead for fourteen years rose to rule again.'

These words helped launch Juana on a course without parallel. Keeping her husband's casket beside her, she moved to various towns and monasteries in northern Spain, seeking some area which might inspire Felipe to return. On the night of November 1 in the monastery at Miraflores she commanded the casket to be opened to assure herself that the king was with her. Either on Christmas night or a few days prior, having moved to a new area, she opened the casket again, and one of her companions reported, 'All had calcified into a solid mass and it did not have the odor of perfume.'

In April, under the stars of an open sky, she inspected the remains once more, and this incident has formed the subject for several fine historical paintings. In July she was settled at Hornillos, where she gave birth to a posthumous child, and in the church she again tried to communicate with the sadly decomposed body, and for a fifth time in her room nearby. Finally, in February of 1509, after nearly three years of such wandering, she came to rest at Tordesillas, where she reluctantly consented to have her husband buried in the local monastery. Then, so as not to be parted from him lest he should, as the Carthusian promised, rise from the dead to resume his reign, she immured herself in a nearby palace, where she was to spend the next forty-six years of her life.

How did the body of Felipe find its way ultimately to the grandiose tomb in Granada? After Juana had been locked up for two years her mind wandered so badly that she forgot the casket which had haunted her, she forgot the handsome young husband who had treated her so poorly, where-upon officials quietly disinterred the body for the last time and shipped it off to the royal pantheon in Granada, which had been Felipe's choice in the first place.

She posed quite a problem for the Spanish government. She was clearly the Queen of Castilla with claims to Aragón as well, and if sane should be ruling in Madrid; but if she was, as seemed likely, insane, she should be kept locked up and her son Carlos V should rule on her behalf. When Carlos arrived to assume the crown he visited his mother; he could speak Flemish, French, German and Italian but no Spanish, and in his brief conversation with her satisfied himself that she was indeed insane. It was under his instructions, therefore, that she was kept locked up, to become a constant source of scandal in the other courts of Europe. Ambassadors paid large sums for rumors of the queen. One reported that she urinated almost constantly, another that she was more animal than human, another that he understood she was quite sane. When a revolution broke out against Carlos, the revolutionists naturally sped for Tordesillas, where after an interview with Juana they pronounced her sane. To this day debate continues. All we know is that for nearly half a century she was kept imprisoned in a ratty old building which no longer stands.

From its windows she could look below to see the Río Duero idling past the cliffs as if it were a lake. Trees filled the distance, and flat fields on which wheat and grapes had grown as long as men could remember. She could also see the road to Medina del Campo and must often have watched with vacant eyes as various messengers rode up that road with instructions from the king. When the sky was cloudless she could see the battlements of the castle at Medina, and on moonlit nights the scene must have been beautiful. In winter her palace was bitter cold, in summer stifling.

We know what life was like in the prison at Tordesillas because Carlos V kept close tabs on his mother lest she escape and embarrass him; a wealth of documents exists, none more interesting than the list of persons in attendance on the queen which Amarie Dennis found in the archives of the National Library when doing research for her biography of Isabel:

> The governing staff within the palace was composed of the Marqués of Denia and his wife; the Count of Lerma, Francisco de Rojas, and his wife; Fernando de Tovar and his wife; Luis de Cepeda, majordomo; Doctor Santa Cara; Ana Enríquez de Rojas, a nun; Magdalena de Rojas, Countess of Castro; Francisca de Rojas, Countess of Paredes; Margarita de Rojas; and Beatriz de Bobadilla, an elderly servant who had accompanied Juana to Flanders in 1496. The rest of the staff, whose names are all listed, was comprised of seven yeomen, two overseers, a food provisioner and seven assistants, a librarian, a bailiff, three cooks, three assistant cooks, a tailor and his helper, a cupbearer and his aide, an apothecary, a shoemaker, a

furrier, a man to attend the braziers, a watercarrier, a carpenter, a poulterer, a sweeper, a hunter of partridges, six servants to take care of the silver-ware, fourteen lackeys, six butlers, twelve chambermaids, one seamstress, four laundresses, five serving maids, one wardrobe keeper, one carver, two gate-keepers, three footmen, twenty-four *montero* [huntsman] guards, and five bodyguards. To serve in the royal chapel, there were fourteen chaplains, two altar boys and three sacristans. Aside from these, there were the wives and the children of a large proportion of the servants of the household.

In other words, a hundred and fifty-five people to look after one addle-brained old woman.

Juana la Loca constitutes one of the mysteries of Spanish history. I find it difficult to believe that she was sane, but on the other hand I find in European history several monarchs who ruled more or less successfully while no more.sane than she. I suppose that with a council to guide her she could have governed moderately well; however, her son Carlos V was doubtless far more capable, though I am far from satisfied the he was as good for Spain as she would have been. Juana, completely Spanish, would at least have focused on Spanish problems rather than dissipate her kingdom in an attempt to dominate Europe, and it is tantalizing to reflect that a sane son destroyed Spain whereas an insane mother might have saved it.

There is one spot in Spain that everyone should see, for it pertains to the character of the country yet is so inconvenient to visit that there is no rational point from which one can say, 'Let's visit the Shrine of Guadalupe now. We may never have a better opportunity.'

It hides in a remote corner of Extremadura and could be visited from Badajoz, but the road is poor. It stands not too far from Trujillo, but when I was in that city I was told the route was so inconvenient that I ought to by-pass the shrine. Religiously it is governed from Toledo, and once years ago I intended to set out from Toledo to see it, but friends refused to let me risk the miserable road. At the monastery of Yuste, I was almost due north of Guadalupe, but there was no direct communication. Now, from a totally ridiculous point of departure, I was determined to see the shrine, so one morning I set out from Salamanca, kept Yuste to the east and dropped down through Trujillo to try the ferocious road that appeared on the map with the proud title Route C-401. The scenery was exciting, with low mountains, long vistas and here and there small villages where life progressed much as it had four hundred years ago, but the road was so twisting, with eight or ten right-angle turns to the half-mile, that the couple riding in the back seat of our car got seasick and the driver complained that his arms were wearing out.

But even if one had no concern with religion, the drive to Guadalupe would be worth the effort, for just as it seemed that all of us had had enough, the road climbed a sharp hill and below us we saw one of the

She must also have seen the magpie flying to Medina del Campo.

choice sights in Spain: a compact monastery, so beautiful in all aspects that it is an architectural treasure, set down in a rustic small village surrounded by handsome olive groves that fill the valley. The road stops. There is no economic life, no transportation, no rich farming. In fact, if it were not for what happened here around 1325 there would be no reason for the village to exist.

One day a cowherd whose name is remembered, Gil Cordero (Giles of the Lamb), was looking for a strayed cow that had been grazing along the banks of a turbulent river which came out of these unpopulated mountains, and as he did so he saw projecting from the soil the brown and weathered statue of a Virgin, later to be known as the Virgin of Guadalupe (River of the Wolf, according to some; Hidden River to others). As her history was uncovered, it was seen that she was no ordinary Virgin.

The last work of art done by St. Luke, the painter-physician-evangelist, was this carving of the Virgin, for which she posed on the Greek island of Patmos just prior to her death in Turkey. The statue was buried at the city that later became Constantinople, whence it passed to Rome. Around A.D. 600 Pope Gregory the Great ordered that St. Luke's Virgin be paraded through Rome in an effort to end the plague, which she did. The statue was

439

then sent to Spain, but when the Muslims overran the country devout followers carried the Virgin to the banks of this remote hidden river and buried her, where she slept undisturbed for more than six hundred years, until Gil Cordero found her.

Her fame spread over Spain and was responsible for several victories over Muslim armies. As the Virgin of Extremadura she sponsored the settlement of the New World, where, after appearing personally to the Mexican peasant Juan Diego in 1531, she became even more popular than she was in Spain. From all parts of the world riches flowed into this remote shrine, until it became the wealthiest religious foundation in Christendom. The official historian of that period affirms that more than one hundred and twenty lamps of pure gold or silver burned at her shrine, that she had countless vestments heavy with jewels, and that the Hieronymite friars who tended the shrine had so much money that they ordered from Toledo cleaning buckets and broom handles of solid silver.

It became traditional for rulers of Spain to come to Guadalupe to pay homage to the Virgin, and large buildings had to be erected to lodge the royal visitors whose names form an index to Spanish history; therefore, it was not unexpected when in 1928 King Alfonso XIII came here to supervise the canonical coronation of the Virgin of Guadalupe; henceforth, she would be one of the official Virgin Queens of Spain.

There are three reasons why one should visit Guadalupe: to see the Virgin, to see her robes, and to see the Zurbaráns, and in the company of Don Pedro Rivas, the practical-minded mayor of the village, I proceeded to do so. Don Pedro was a different kind of mayor, a farmer with a rough-and-ready approach to his position and a manifest delight in the dark Virgin of Guadalupe. 'To approach her with due reverence,' he said, 'we must pause here in the anteroom. Look at those marvelous paintings! By Luca Giordano, who must have been an Italian. Aren't they glorious? And big? Look at that dear little angel with the bare bottom who leads Mary's donkey on the flight to Egypt. And the angels flying overhead with flowers. Isn't that a fine presentation of the Virgin protecting her child?'

I found the Giordanos (1632–1705) overpowering—nine huge canvases—but the eight polychromed statues of 'the strong women of the Old Testament' were delightful. They were carved in the fashion of eighteenth-century Versailles and showed shepherdesses with crucifixes, jewels, straw hats and those lovely flouncy skirts and aprons which milkmaids were supposed to wear at court revels. Ruth, Jael and Esther were especially charming, the first with wide black eyes and porcelain skin and under her arm a sheaf of gleanings from the fields of Boaz.

'But this is the room!' Don Pedro said with visible excitement as he led me to the shrine itself. How disappointed I was. There really wasn't much to see, just a wealth of gold and jewels and ornate carving. The Virgin, apparently, was not visible to ordinary eyes, and I must have

Even in the north, where one is not accustomed to the relics of the Moorish occupation, figures like this appear at the crèche to remind one that even cities like Salamanca were under Moorish rule for centuries.

shrugged my shoulders as if to say, 'Well, that's that,' when the mayor signaled two young friars, who slowly turned a revolving pedestal. As they did so, the Virgin came mysteriously into view, and she was so resplendent that no amount of previous reading could have prepared me for what I now saw. In a niche with wings, each inch of which was covered with either gold or enamel scenes from the Bible, stood a relatively small Virgin, an adorable figure, with dark mottled face and black right hand which held a scepter. She looked as if she had lain in earth for six hundred years, but her charm derived from the tradition of dressing her in a gown and cape made of luminous cloth of gold encrusted with jewels. Her robes flared out, hanging straight across at the bottom and tapering upward to her crown and halo of precious stones, forming a delicate, bejeweled triangle.

'¿Estupenda, eh?' the mayor asked. She was. It was the only word which applied, for visually she was one of the most appealing religious figures I have ever seen. I doubt if the leading prelates of Spain, sitting in conclave, could have come up with a more appropriate figure to epitomize their country's attitude toward religion.

'Do you like the Jesus?' Don Pedro asked. I looked about for a statue of Jesus and it was some moments before I discovered that in her left arm, which was of course invisible, the Virgin held a precious little doll-like figure of Jesus, also scarred in the face, also dressed in robes which duplicated the triangle formed by those of his mother. He too was crowned, but far less gloriously. As I looked at the two figures I reflected that it was at about the time when this series of buried Virgins was being uncovered in various parts of Spain that the country began to dedicate itself to Mary, long before the movement became common in other parts of the world, and I concluded that some two hundred years from now Spanish religion may well focus exclusively on the Virgin, with Christ having receded to a background position somewhat like that enjoyed by the Holy Ghost in Protestantism half a century ago. Already a Virgin like this adorable one of Guadalupe seems much closer to the heart of Spain than does a remote figure like Jesus.

I am not one to waste time marveling at the routine tapestries held in the usual monastery treasury, but at Guadalupe I was stunned when Don Pedro and the friars showed me where the robes for their Virgin were stored. One large shallow drawer after another was pulled out to display the many alternate sets of vestments. 'This one filled with flowers woven in silver,' explained the mayor, 'was sent here from the Netherlands in 1629. This one laden with diamonds and gold was made in the time of Carlos Quinto. And this one, well, who can describe it? The most costly piece of fabric in the world. A hundred and fifty thousand pearls, handfuls of diamonds, gold so heavy the cloth can scarcely be lifted. We have loved our Virgin and we have wanted her to dress well.'

'How many complete sets of robes has she?' I asked.

'These are just the precious ones,' and he indicated some thirty drawers. 'The lesser ones are over here. Peru, Chile, these three from Mexico with Mexican gold, Poland. She has many robes.' I had stopped looking at the robes, for I felt smothered in pearls and gold; instead I tried to imagine how a large meeting room nearby must have looked on that fateful first of January in 1577, when King Felipe II of Spain entered by this door and his nephew, King Sebastián of Portugal, entered by that to conduct the meeting which started the curious story that I shall be speaking of at the end of this chapter. It must have been an extraordinary scene and I wondered how kings could have covered the journey from Madrid and Lisboa to such a spot.

Finally, in the vestry of the monastery Don Pedro showed me that row of eight masterpieces painted by Francisco Zurbarán; if one does not see his work in this room one misses his talent. His commission was one of those ordinary jobs which have defeated so many good painters: 'Portraits of the leading friars in the history of this monastery.' The Hieronymites chosen were all of advanced age and position, mostly bald, and of monotonous history, but what Zurbarán accomplished with them is well-nigh miraculous, for the tall, powerful paintings unfold with a richness of style and imagination that one would never expect if he knew only Zurbarán's lesser work. The fine series impressed me as something that might have been done by Domenico Ghirlandaio, for though Zurbarán lived from 1598 to 1664, he painted with the style of an earlier age.

For me, the apex of the series was the third picture on the left-hand wall; it showed Zurbarán at his best. It was a portrait of Father Illescas, a political priest who ruled Guadalupe and later Córdoba. His cluttered desk provided an opportunity for one of Zurbarán's great still lifes; the figure of the Hieronymite became the occasion for a splendid hard-edge portrait of uncompromising intensity; the De Hooch-like scene beyond the pillars shows the entrance to the monastery with a friar at the door dispensing alms to beggars in a style recalling the best work of Giovanni Bellini. If this magnificent work were housed where large numbers of people visited, it would be an acknowledged masterpiece. It excels its seven companions only in the excellence of its parts and the variation shown therein. As a straight piece of painting I rather preferred the simpler picture of Father Yáñez, founder of the monastery, as he kneels before King Enrique III, who bestows upon him the biretta of Bishop of Toledo. It is uncluttered, direct and powerful. Spanish critics are amused by the fact that King Enrique, who ruled 1390–1406, is dressed in the costume of King Felipe III, who ruled 1598–1621. The courtier who looks out from the background is supposed to be a self-portrait of Zurbarán, and I wish this work were located in some capital city where I might see it more often.

One of the reasons why it is so rewarding to see the Zurbaráns in Guadalupe is that the vestry where they hang is a magnificent room well suited to the display of tall canvases. The walls are white and gold; the richly ornamented ceiling is studded with windows that admit good light; and the altarpiece of an attached chapel has a heavy ornateness that glistens. It is sometimes difficult for a foreigner to believe old accounts of how wealthy the religious buildings of Spain once were, but a visit to Guadalupe corrects that.

'But the thing to remember about this room,' says the mayor as we leave, 'is that lamp suspended from the ceiling.' He points to a huge bronze brazier of Oriental design, suspended on a fine chain. 'It was brought here,' the mayor explains, 'by Don Juan of Austria after the Virgin gave him victory at the Battle of Lepanto. Captured from a Turkish galleon. The point is, we Spaniards fought to attain buildings like this . . . rooms like this.'

From Guadalupe I went north over the Gredos Mountains to the walled city of Avila, judged by most people to be the finest medieval remnant in Spain. From any approach it is a handsome sight, perched on a hill with a river nearby and massive walls enclosing it. The gates of Avila look as if horsemen might clatter out through the portcullis, and I was fortunate on my first visit to enter the city along with a wedding party that had engaged a band. It was lunchtime and we were headed for the same restaurant near the walls of the city. It was very old, with low-ceilinged rooms and open rafters, and the food was heavy. The wedding party sang, and by the time everyone was half-drunk I could not tell what century this group belonged to. In 1300 they would have looked much the same, and in 1500, too. They were the perennial farmers of Spain come to town for a celebration, and it was a noisy, delightful day. I was invited to toast the bride in a harsh red wine that went well with the roast pig we were eating, and when I left I was given a boisterous farewell. Down in the streets of Avila the noise of the celebration followed me and I could imagine a watchman of some previous age clomping along and crying to the inn, 'Ho, there! Silence! Honest men want to sleep.' It was going to be some time before there was silence.

Most visitors who come to Avila do so to pay homage to a remarkable woman whose piety made the city famous; almost none come to seek out the musician whose genius I had discovered by accident and who now meant so much to me. The woman was Santa Teresa de Avila (1515–1582), foremost of the Spanish mystics and a writer of distinction. She was born of a good family and at the age of eighteen unexpectedly announced her intention of joining a convent, where she led a prosaic life marked mainly by a lively social life which she maintained with the leading families in the area, but at the age of forty she chanced to see a statue of Christ that had been left accidentally in her path and in a moment of divine inspiration she saw through to the reality of God. From that time on she became increasingly concerned with the mystical path to religious insight, retaining, however, the hard practicality of her upbringing. She sought Papal permission to reform the lax order of which she was a member and launched the Discalced (Shoeless; that is, they wore sandals) Carmelites as opposed to the traditional Calced Carmelites, who wore shoes. Her practical mind made her an excellent administrator, and before long she established branches of her reformed order in different parts of Spain, including two monasteries for men, but at the same time her spiritual life intensified, enabling her to write a series of books which constitute the classic statement of mysticism.

When she was fifty-two she met in Medina del Campo a young priest with whom her spiritual life would henceforth be linked, and their relationship forms one of the gentlest episodes of Spanish history. Juan de Yepis y Alvarez (1542–1591), twenty-seven years younger than Teresa, was the son of very poor parents. His father died early and his widowed mother took her brood to Arévalo and then to Medina, where Juan served as male nurse in a paupers' hospital. His close contact with misery bred two results: he took vows as a Carmelite and he entertained those first mystical visions which were to characterize his life. Like other great Spaniards he attended the University of Salamanca, where at the age of twenty-five he was ordained a priest. After brief service he met for the first time Teresa de Avila, whose fame filled the countryside. Judging from externals, no one could have predicted that this fashionable, witty nun from a fine family would find in Juan de Yepis, a retiring young priest from an underprivileged family, a bond of identity, but that is what happened. The English religious expert, F. Trueman Dicken, calls their friendship 'one of the most fecund of all Christian relationships since the time of the Apostles.' In Teresa's fight to defend her Discalced Carmelites, Juan became a bold champion, and as a result spent a long confinement in a Toledo jail, where his exceptional gift for poetry manifested itself. When he left the prison he was a major poet, a lyricist of the darker moods of the spirit; the title of one of his outcries has become almost a theme song of modern confusion, 'The Dark Night of the Soul':

> On a dark night,
> inflamed with love's desires,
> oh sweet happiness,
> I went forth unnoticed
> when my house was already asleep.

In the dark night Juan found the beginning of his mystical understanding, which drew him even closer to Teresa. During one five-year period he served as confessor to the convent in Avila, headed by Teresa, and for three of those years she was in residence, so that the two mystics were able to conduct long discussions which deepened the spiritual life of each. It was this period of shared ideas that led to the richest literary results; of her experience with Juan's sharp mind Teresa said, 'He is my little Seneca.'

Teresa lived to be sixty-seven; Juan died at forty-nine, as if he felt it unprofitable to continue without the presence of his mentor. Together they bore the moves made against them by the Church and the persecutions initiated by monasteries and convents that did not want to be reformed. Each suffered severe discipline and even the threat of investigation by the Inquisition, but when they were dead, persons who knew them began to realize that in Teresa of Avila and Juan de Yepis, now known as Juan de la Cruz, this wall-girt town had produced two saints whose miracles stemmed from their close acquaintanceship with God. Teresa attained sainthood first, in 1622, Juan in 1726, and they live today as the twin glories of Avila. In the fall of 1967 Pope Paul VI announced that henceforth Santa Teresa would be considered as one of the doctors of the Church. Prior to this, there had been no woman so honored.

To Spain mysticism is as natural as the olive tree, but here it avoids both the mysterious excess and the delirious rapture of eastern mysticism.

It is a practical, one might almost say realistic, method for attaining a realization of God. It requires no trauma, is far removed from catatonic trance and avoids special vocabularies and recondite ritual; it is a very special brand of mysticism and the principal theological gift of Spain to the world at large. No better exemplars could be found than this curiously assorted pair of Avila; they were hard-headed realists when it came to the management of religious societies and self-disciplined intellects when it came to rationalizing and reporting their religious experiences. They insisted, however, upon the reality of their approach to God and defended it in pure and simple prose, none better than these sentences from the opening of Teresa's *Interior Castle:*

> Few tasks which I have been ordered to undertake have been so difficult as this present one of writing about prayer because I do not feel that the Lord has given me the spirituality for it, and because for the last three months I have been suffering from such noises in the head that I find it difficult to write even about ordinary things. . . . But I began to think of the soul as a castle made of diamond or very clear crystal in which there are many rooms, just as in heaven there are many mansions. . . . For if we consider the matter, the soul of the righteous is but a paradise in which, as God tells us, He takes delight. . . . Let us then consider the many mansions of this castle, some up high, others lower down, still others along the sides, and in the very center of all the principal one, where takes place the most secret intercourse between God and the soul.

They are children bathed in sunlight, Teresa and Juan, and they illuminated Avila and all Spain.

It is obvious that to an organized Church the mysticism expressed in the above quotation from Teresa poses a threat, for it runs the risk of degenerating into the Quaker heresy of 'each man his own priest,' because if by the mystical process one can attain direct contact with God, the intercession of Church and prelate is no longer essential, although it may for social reasons continue to be convenient. It was this potentiality in the preaching of Teresa and Juan that kept them hovering between sainthood and heresy, and much of the opposition they encountered during their working lives originated in an honest fear on the part of the Church that they were encouraging in others, if not practicing themselves, a separatism which must end in apostasy.

After their deaths that is what happened. The Illuminati, those who found God for themselves through the mystical illumination of their own souls, became quite a plague to the Church in Spain; they were considered no better than Protestants and had to be eliminated. The Inquisition was especially harsh in dealing with them, and those who were not burned were exiled, so that one sees in Avila not only the glory of Teresa and Juan but also the degeneration of their ideas in the practices of the Illuminati.

I had not come to Avila, which I remember as a uniformly evocative town, to recall Santa Teresa; I came to pay homage to one of the finest artists Spain has produced, the equal in his field to Cervantes in the novel or Velázquez in painting. I had found him for myself in one of the tardiest discoveries on record. When I was a student the music of Palestrina struck me with force; it was exactly what I had been looking for and I have never since tired of listening to *The Mass of Pope Marcellus*, which must be one of the finest pieces of choral music. But once in Germany when I bought a Polydor record of some Palestrina music, I found that the second side had been filled out with a short composition by another Italian composer, Tommaso Lodovico da Vittoria, of whom I had not heard. It was an 'Ave Maria' of such exquisite construction that I found myself playing it eight times for every once that I played Palestrina. Of all the musical settings for this prayer, and I am not forgetting Bach and Schubert, I found Vittoria's the finest, and when I looked about for other compositions by this minor Italian, I found other pieces which seemed to me about as good as choral music could be, and I began to wonder why Palestrina was so well known and his countryman so little.

I am ashamed to say that ten or fifteen years passed before I discovered that my Tommaso Lodovico da Vittoria was not an Italian at all but a Spaniard from Avila named Tomás Luis de Victoria (1548–1611), who customarily added Abulensis (of Avila) to his name, and that he had written a dozen great works which stand with the best of his age, or of any age for that matter. In time I acquired recordings of his *Officium Defunctorum* (Mass for the Dead, 1603), which critics usually select as his masterpiece, his motets and especially his *Responsories for Tenebrae* (1585), those deeply moving evening prayers. The *Officium Defunctorum* has additional interest for anyone who has visited Avila; Victoria wrote it for the funeral of the Empress María, daughter of Carlos V and sister of Felipe II, and its first performance occurred in the convent where Victoria served as chaplain, that of the Descalzas Reales, first of the Teresan convents in Madrid.

As Victoria becomes better known, the grandeur of his production is increasingly recognized. He was the equal of Palestrina in all except homophony, and this he seems to have avoided consciously. The richness of his construction and the dramatic manner in which he interweaves as many as six threads of sound, uniting them occasionally in majestic chords, form one of the joys of sixteenth-century music and I would suppose that for many who know music generally, the discovery of Victoria will be one of the few remaining delights. There could be no better approach than a recording of his majestic Christmas responsory 'O Magnum Mysterium' (O Great Mystery, 1572), which is divided into three contrasting parts: the animals observe Christ lying in their manger; peo-

FOLLOWING FACING PAGES:
The demureness of the Spanish woman
and the arrogance of the Spanish man begin early.

ple voice their astonishment at a virgin birth; and all explode into one of the finest hallelujahs ever written. Because of its variety and power, the 'Mysterium' is a favorite of professional singers and numerous good recordings exist.

As I walked through the narrow streets of Avila, listening to the voices of Victoria's choirs as they sang the music I had come to know so well, I reflected on the curious fate that had overtaken Spanish music. Victoria died in 1611, on August 27, a day held in reverence by mystics throughout the world as the anniversary of Santa Teresa's vision of being struck in the heart by a lance of fire held by an angel. He left Spanish music the equal of any being composed in Europe; each basic building block required for future construction had been fashioned and there was no structural reason why Spanish music should not have matured as did Italian and German and every reason why it should have surpassed French and English, but in the decades that followed, it retreated slowly, step by step, from its capable beginnings until it foundered in trivia. Even its failures lacked reach; the inheritors of Victoria produced no great masses, no soaring affirmations of belief, no operas, no symphonies, no string quartets, so that one can only ask, 'What happened?'

I spent three nights in Avila wrestling with this problem, for although the focus of my question was music, it applied equally to drama, painting, poetry and to a lesser extent the novel, and if I could find a reasonable answer to the problem of music, I might discover what had happened to the other arts. After such favorable starts, why had there come decline?

I liked Spanish music. I had studied most of the work done by Falla, Albéniz, Granados (1867–1916) and Turina (1882–1949) and had an understanding of at least the first and last of that Big Four. I judged Falla's work to be as inspired thematically as any then produced in Europe; *El sombrero de tres picos* and *El amor brujo* are gold mines of invention and are equaled only by the best work of Richard Strauss. As for Turina, his *Sinfonía sevillana*, which one can hear only on records and then with difficulty, seems a fine lament for lost opportunities; it cannot be called a great symphony in the class of the best writing done by French and English composers, let alone the German, but it is a rich tapestry and one that I have always liked.

But the more I listened to Spanish music the more I began to suspect that it failed because it lacked inherent seriousness; it did not direct itself to the major themes of life and thereby condemned itself to a secondary accomplishment. It could produce zarzuelas but not operas or symphonies. The fault could not lie with the composers, for they give ample evidence of their competence; it must have lain with the society in which they worked. Something quite stifling happened to Spanish intellectual life following the death of Victoria and it is reflected in the decline of Spanish music, as it would have to be. The melodies remain, the rhythms, the technical competence and the brilliant orchestration, but the heart has gone dry.

I once asked an international conductor about this, and he said, 'I love to conduct Falla. So colorful, so inventive. But whenever I touch his music he reminds me that what Spain needed in his day was not Spanish themes but the full explosion of world ideas. Falla of course understood this, for he had worked in Paris, but his audiences did not, and they would not have supported a composer of international stature. When you cut a nation off from world intercourse dreadful things happen.' He had recently conducted in four Spanish cities and was disturbed to find that even in 1966 Spain did not import or know the work that was being done by contemporary composers. 'It's a closed society. Falla and Albéniz, Mozart and Beethoven.'

Why had silence replaced the song? It was not any aridity in Spain as such, for her daily life provided a lyricism used to good effect by alien composers as diverse as Mozart, Verdi, Bizet and Rossini. Of course, they wrote opera, which is a complex form that may or may not be congenial to a given group of composers, but even in simpler forms Spanish musicians had at their disposal thematic material much richer than that used by Brahms, Smetana and Bartók, but they did little with it, abandoning their subject matter to foreigners like Strauss, Rimski-Korsakov, Chabrier, Ravel and Lalo. Now, we know that Spanish composers had the training and the technique, so their failure to create must have been caused by some force outside themselves. And the more I contemplated this problem, the more I was driven to that central question of Spanish intellectual history: Was it the Inquisition that crushed Spain's creative life?

The Black Legend would have us think so. It says that the Inquisition so terrorized Spanish society that anyone with an inquiring mind was silenced, that science and invention were impeded and that the speculation which is necessary alike for progress and great works of art was impossible. Much evidence of philosophers imprisoned and theologians burned can be cited to support these charges, and years ago when I first studied the matter there was no adequate rebuttal.

In recent decades, however, Spanish intellectuals have begun to fight back and some of the arguments they have developed have been startling. For me the most representative came in a book where I did not expect them, César Silió Cortés' *Isabel the Catholic, Founder of Spain*, printed in 1954. Dr. Silió, a member of the Royal Academy of Moral and Political Sciences, finds in writing his biography that he must deal frontally with this matter of the Inquisition, since it was Queen Isabel who sponsored the institution. If the Inquisition were judged to be as bad as anti-Spanish writers have charged, its evil would reflect upon the patron Queen of Spain; but if it were seen to be otherwise, then whatever glory pertains to it would also pertain to Isabel.

Dr. Silió's arguments are unequivocal. 1. The Inquisition was not a Spanish invention but was of Italian origin, was centuries old and was introduced into Spain rather later than elsewhere. 2. It was not introduced by Isabel, for it had operated in Spain under her predecessors as early as 1232. 3. Compared to the earlier versions, the Isabel Inquisition was only one-fifth as harsh in the number of persons condemned to death. 4. It actually saved lives, for because of it the religious wars which seared the rest of Europe were avoided. 5. Far from inhibiting Spanish intellectual life, it in a sense encouraged it; on the Spanish Index one can find not a single book of philosophical merit, whether written by a foreigner or by a Spaniard. 6. Nor did it deter science, for it never proscribed a single line of Copernicus, Galileo or Newton. 7. The punishments it did administer were far less severe in kind and number than those exercised in other countries at the same time, a fact conspicuously true when one considers the large number of half-mad people who were burned as witches in Germany and England, a practice which the Inquisition did not tolerate, because only a brief questioning by the Inquisitors was needed to prove that the accused was mentally incompetent.

Silió makes three additional defenses which must be considered in further detail. 8. He points out that the period of Spain's greatest intellectual achievement coincided with the apex of Inquisition power, and no inhibition deterred the artists, writers and musicians. Cervantes wrote *Don Quixote* when the Inquisition was strongest. Calderón de la Barca wrote his soaring dramas in the same climate and so did Lope de Vega. Victoria composed his great music under the Inquisition. Poets, essayists and historians flourished in this period, and none seemed to suffer. Books were printed at a rate which exceeded that in other countries and philosophy and sciences prospered. This was the age of the university, when Salamanca and Alcalá de Henares were at their apex in both number of students and vitality of thought. If one wants to insist that the Inquisition hampered intellectual life, he has the Golden Age to contend with.

9. Furthermore, the Inquisition was necessary because Jews had infiltrated national life and had to be eradicated. In fact, the ordinary people of Spain were more insistent upon this than were the rulers, for as Silió says, 'The massacres of Jews were the work of popular wrath, of people faced by the infiltration of a tenacious race, astute and industrious, who, even though they suffered death and cruel exploitation, bent before the hurricanes in order to surge forth anew, like some evil weed, monopolizing the riches, exploiting usury and gathering together everything.' Silió also points out that it was impossible to accept Jews within the society because they stole little Christian children and crucified them, thus making a mockery of Good Friday. In proof of this charge he cites the case of Yucé Franco, who during the last days of June, 1490, assembled a group of Jews to perform just such a crucifixion. Franco, whose name was typically Jewish, was captured on July 1, 1490, and it was not until sixteen months later, after the most careful legal investigations by the Inquisition, that he was condemned. Even then all evidence was turned over to the university faculty at Salamanca for them to assure themselves that the trial had been

properly conducted, and when Salamanca approved, the dossier was forwarded to a jury of educated men here in Avila, and they too concurred. The public burning took place in this city on November 16, 1491, as a result of which wild popular riots broke out against all Jews, even though Fernando and Isabel had forbidden such outbursts. Silió contends that it was only this hideous Jewish crime, one of many, that forced the Spanish sovereigns to decree the general expulsion of Jews from Spain. Silió points out that the facts of the Yucé Franco case and the justice of the decision cannot be questioned, even though there was no visual proof of the crime, because the investigation was carried out under the personal supervision of a wise and just judge, Tomás de Torquemada, who is proved to have been a humble man, lacking ostentation, desiring only justice, and far from the 'new Nero' that popular writers have tried to make him. When the old lies against the inquisitor general are removed one by one, Torquemada stands forth as 'an agreeable, lovable, hard-working, able and modest man whose only ambition was to imitate Jesus Christ.' Such a man, Silió argues, would never have let the Inquisition get out of hand.

Silió's final point is brief and powerful: 'The Spanish Inquisition as established by the Catholic Kings was adequate to its time and necessary in that time.'

Some years ago I was obliged to read everything in print in the languages I could handle regarding the Spanish Inquisition, and I reached these conclusions, which in certain limited areas coincide with Silió's. 1. In the beginning Spain's Inquisition was no more cruel than similar inquisitorial bodies operating in other European countries. 2. The number of persons executed in Spain at the height of the European movement, say from 1492–1550, did not exceed records established in other countries. 3. The operation of the Spanish Index in proscribing books was more lenient than the Italian. 4. No one can deny that Spanish culture achieved its Golden Age coincident with the Inquisition. 5. So far as I was able to ascertain, no Jew was ever executed by the Inquisition. If a man under investigation could say simply, 'Yes, I'm a Jew and have never been otherwise,' his gold and silver were confiscated and he was banished from Spain, but he was in no way subject to the Inquisition and certainly he was never burned. 6. The Jews who did suffer, and in the thousands, were those who had at one time been baptized as Catholics, had been legal Catholics and had committed apostasy by reverting to Jewish practices. These were rooted out with great severity, but when they were burned, it was as Catholics, not as Jews. 7. Particularly sad were the cases of shipwrecked English sailors in the middle years of the sixteenth century, for if they swam to Spanish soil they were in real danger of being burned. The Inquisition maintained that any Englishman who was then a Protestant must have been born and baptized a Catholic and was ipso facto a heretic deserving death. The frequency with which such sailors were condemned on this theological technicality was appalling. 8. The persecution of Protestants in Spain, more especially the hated Lutherans, may have been more severe in numbers than the similar persecution of Catholics in Protestant countries, but it was not more vicious. The falsity of the Black Legend was obvious. 9. But the more I studied this problem the more apparent it became that something fundamental had happened in Spain that had not happened in the rest of Europe, and I began to think that the differential must be this: That whereas all European nations had originally sponsored some form of Inquisition, with Spain's less cruel than others, it was only in Spain that the institution lingered on, so that the last public burning occurred in 1781, when an old woman was hauled to the stake after witnesses had sworn that 'she had conducted carnal converse with the Devil, after which she laid eggs with prophecies written on them.' On February 22, 1813, the Cortes abolished the Inquisition by a vote of ninety to sixty, but on July 21 of the following year, King Fernando VII having regained the throne, it was restored. In 1820, when the nation turned more liberal, the king again had to order the abolishment of the Inquisition, but as soon as he felt himself strong enough to do so, he revoked his decree. It was not until July 15, 1834, that the tribunal was finally suppressed, its properties being applied to a reduction of the national debt, but even then strong movements arose throughout Spain demanding 'the restoration of our beloved Inquisition,' and for years the issue remained lively. The last public execution which could be charged against the spirit of the Inquisition took place on June 26, 1826, in Valencia, the victim being a schoolteacher whose crime was that in public prayer he used 'Praise be to God' rather than 'Ave Maria.' It was the terrible prolongation that constituted the difference, as if Spain had found in this bizarre social weapon a ritual that satisfied some deep national appetite. I therefore answered my rhetorical question affirmatively: The Inquisition, through its persistence, had been the cause of Spain's decline.

Then in 1965, when I had finished my study, a book called *The Spanish Inquisition* appeared and I discovered with a certain wryness that its author, Henry Kamen, who teaches history at the University of Edinburgh, had done my work for me, but about four years too late. He had summarized in unhysterical form our knowledge of the Inquisition, and I commend his book to anyone who wishes to pursue the matter. It is true that he relies on old standard works like Juan Antonio Llorente's *Historic Memoir Regarding Spanish National Opinion on the Inquisition* (circulated in manuscript in 1811; later developed into the four-volume *Histoire critique de l'Inquisition d'Espagne*, Paris, 1818) and Henry Charles Lea's *A History of the Inquisition of Spain* (1906–1908), but he also looks into collateral problems, and it is this aspect of his work that is most rewarding.

On basic facts about the Inquisition he differs little from Silió, except of course regarding the Yucé Franco ritual murder, which modern scholars know to have been an invention, and he also confirms my conclusions with an important exception, which I shall note in the next paragraph. The facts he cites are sometimes startling. 'The total number of so-called witches executed in the seventeenth century in Germany alone has been put as high as a hundred thousand, a figure which is probably four times as great as the number of people burned by the Spanish Inquisition in all its history.' The Bishop of Bamberg during the period 1622–1633 caused six hundred witches to be burned and in the same period the Bishop of Würzburg nine hundred.

Kamen reaches three main conclusions. The ordinary people of Spain applauded the Inquisition and did not think of it as oppressive. My argument, that the Inquisition caused Spain's decline, he holds to be inaccurate, in that he finds no substantial evidence to support it. He believes that the real tragedy of the Inquisition was that it helped create a closed society from which alien elements were expelled and into which no new ideas were allowed to enter. It is in the analysis of this third proposition that he provides much new material.

He contends that although the Inquisition may have begun as a solution to a religious problem, it quickly became an instrument for enforcing a pernicious theory regarding 'purity of blood,' which meant that any family whose ancestors had been either Moorish or Jewish was contaminated. Since Moors had married in Spain for seven hundred years and Jews for eleven hundred, and since there had been forced conversions of both, there had to be much impure blood in Spain, and its eradication provided a chance for informers to appropriate jobs, money and titles now belonging to the impure. Researchers who hoped to overthrow great families drew up a black list entitled *The Green Book of Aragón*, which identified families in that kingdom having impure blood, involving hundreds in catastrophe. It was so successful that in 1560 a disgruntled cardinal, irritated because two relatives had been refused admittance to a military order, compiled *Blot on the Nobility of Spain*, identifying by name those families with impure blood.

It is difficult to imagine what such a charge entailed. The family could have been practicing Christians for three hundred years and without blemish so far as their Catholicism was concerned, but merely because they had a touch of Moorish or Jewish blood they could not send their sons to a university, or work in certain jobs, or hold office in a cathedral, or become officers in the army, or dignitaries in the Church. Military orders like that of Santiago had strict requirements of racial purity and became instruments of reaction and oppression. All Spanish life was corrupted by this mania and thousands were drawn into the net of the Inquisition principally because friends reported that they had hidden their Jewishness. Before a man could apply for any important job he had to present a genealogy going back numerous generations, and the compiling of such records provided a fruitful source of bribery and blackmail. Incredible as it seems, laws policing purity of blood continued in force until January 31,

1835; in the army the application of the principle continued to 1859 and in the obtaining of marriage licenses to 1865.

It was this continuing battle for conformity that punished Spain so severely; although the role played by the Inquisition in religion could be matched in other countries, its part in eradicating those social variations which interact to build strong nations was here unique. Spain was driven by a mania for homogeneity, not realizing that no one group of people can generate all the concepts necessary for its survival. The country insisted upon a closed society and succeeded in getting it, but what it excluded was more significant than what it enclosed.

In 1770 the University of Salamanca forbade Descartes to be taught because he was dangerous to Catholic principles, Thomas Hobbes because he was too compendious and John Locke because he was obscure and must be read with extreme care. As late as 1645 a university professor in Logroño was sentenced to four years' imprisonment and perpetual deprivation of the right to teach because he had referred to the contents of a prohibited book. At one point the Inquisition of a northern city issued the blanket directive that no university should teach from any book that had been published within forty years. Even the great professors who had worked at Alcalá de Henares with Cardinal Cisneros building the *Poliglota* were intimidated and efforts were made to prohibit the study of Greek on grounds that devout men knew that the true Bible existed only in Latin. For me the insanity is best exemplified in the case of a man who was overheard wagering his word against God's nose. A learned gloss was issued proving that such a statement identified the blasphemer as a member of the Badian heresy, which treated God as a corporeal being with human attributes, and for believing this a man should be burned. Word crept across Spain that it was prudent to remain silent, and speculation ceased, but as Kamen points out, it was not the Inquisition that should be blamed but the total drift of society.

However, we must not explain away too much. There is today in Spain a strong spirit of revisionism in historical scholarship which says, 'Since the excesses charged against Spain by the Black Legend have been proved false, their contraries must be true. Thus Felipe II was a king without blemish. The Inquisition was good rather than bad. Tómas de Torquemada was a gentle Christian. And, as a matter of fact, Spain never suffered a decline.' A frontal attack is also mounted against any criticism of contemporary Spain, however mild, by charging that the author is once more purveying the errors of the Black Legend. In recent reading I have collected eighteen examples of newspaper articles attacking books, plays, paintings, motion pictures and general news stories as contaminated by the Black Legend. Honest and fair comment supported by historical re-

Born workers on a farm, Don Alipio Pérez-Tabernero Sanchón and his brother accumulated wealth and became masters of four of the greatest bull farms in Spain.

search on the one hand or by contemporary observation on the other is thus condemned, and it is even popular to deny that Spain ever suffered post-Golden Age reversals, but to refute this tempting thesis one needs only quote the experts. Sometime around 1640, when Spain ached from defeats in all fields, King Felipe IV said, 'These evil events have been caused by your sins and mine in particular . . . I believe that God our Lord is angry and irate with me and my realms on account of many sins and particularly on account of mine.' In 1957 Generalísimo Franco said of a later period, 'While other world powers were able to marshal their strength, Spain sank into a hundred-year sleep.'

The deǫline was real and I believe, in spite of Kamen's argument to the contrary, that the Inquisition was largely to blame. For almost four centuries it enforced an intellectual conformity and rejected all minorities. The Moors, the Jews, the Illuminati, the Jesuits and the Protestants were expelled and their ideas with them. Spain thus became the next nation in a tragic series who decided to fence out new ideas rather than welcome them and she suffered the inescapable penalty. An oyster can live to itself, but without grains of sand for agitation it cannot produce pearls.

Walking one night along the ramparts of Avila, I reasoned, 'If Spain had kept her Moors, her agriculture and manufacturing would have prospered. If she had kept her Jews, her commercial management would have kept pace with England's. If she had retained a few inquiring Protestant professors, her universities might have remained vital. And if she had held onto her Illuminati, her spiritual life would have been renewed.' But then I had to face the greater reality. 'If she had done these things, she'd now be a better Spain. But she wouldn't be Spain.'

After my wide excursions afield—to the fair at Medina del Campo, to the dark Virgin of Guadalupe, to the Avila of Victoria—I returned to Salamanca to visit for the last time those two rooms at the university, almost side by side, which were converted into shrines by the heroism of two philosopher-poets. The first was a stone-arched classroom left pretty much as it must have been on that day in December, 1578, when Fray Luis de León returned after an absence of some years. The rude benches without backs remain the same and the small windows in the outer walls. The lectern with its canopy is the same as the one at which the professor stood that eventful day. The room was crowded, not only because Fray Luis was the most famous of the Salamanca lecturers, a wise, gentle elderly man of sweet understanding and compassion, but because he had accomplished something that few men of his day could parallel.

In 1572, at the height of a brilliant career as Spain's leading theologian and humanist, he was attacked by jealous persons in the university, who whispered to the Inquisition, 'We all know that Fray Luis is half Jewish, so he's suspect to begin with. But he has now translated King Solomon's Song of Songs into the vernacular. He invites even the most ordinary man in Salamanca to read it. And that is heresy.' Especially serious was the additional charge that often, after studying the original Hebrew version of the Bible, he would question the accuracy of the Latin. Fray Luis was apprehended and for several months was under interrogation, after which he was thrown into jail at Valladolid, where he heard only silence. At the end of a year he pleaded to be told what the charges against him were and who his accusers, but he heard nothing. His trial was intermittent and clandestine; all he knew was that he had committed some serious crime bordering on heresy, but its definition he never knew. Finally, after nearly five years of this, he was set free and, what was the more miraculous, allowed to return to his post in Salamanca. Of his experience in jail he wrote:

> Here envy and lies   have kept me imprisoned.
> Happy the humble state   of the wise man who retires
> from this nefarious world,   and with meager table and house
> in the pleasant countryside   passes his life alone;
> he serves only God,   neither envied nor envious.

This was the morning of his reappearance, and notable persons came to the university to hear his reaction to his long persecution. As he made his way from his rooms, his gown slightly askew in his usual careless manner, the university plaza was crowded with silent students. Fray Luis walked with eyes straight forward, not daring to acknowledge the furtive glances of approbation which greeted him. As he entered the cloisters and elbowed his way through the crowd he came at last to the room in which he had taught for so many years, and when he saw its familiar outlines, with his friends perched on the narrow benches, and when he knew that among them must be those whose rumors had caused his imprisonment and who would surrender him again to the Inquisition within a few years (he was to die in disgrace at Madrigal de las Altas Torres), he must have wanted to lash out against the injustice he had suffered and would continue to suffer as a Jew and a humanist. Instead he stepped to the rostrum, took his place behind the lectern, grasped the lapels of his robe and smiled at the crowd with the compassion that marked all he did, and said in a low, clear voice, 'As we were saying yesterday . . .' And he resumed his lecture at the precise point of its interruption five years before.

Down the cloister from Fray Luis' austere classroom is another of much different character, the Lecture Hall, dating from the fifteenth century. Its principal adornment is a group of four handsome stone arches that support the ceiling and a grisaille of Fernando and Isabel done sometime in the eighteenth century. Lists of men who have brought honor to Salamanca appear, but one of the greatest is missing and will probably remain so until the passions of this age are past, after which he will occupy the place of honor. To understand why, we must see this hall as it was on October 12, 1936, the Day of the Race.

At one end of the hall rose a three-stepped dais, done in red carpeting.

It was lighted by two intricate chandeliers and ornamented with a large portrait of Francisco Franco. The dais contained ten long old-fashioned benches on which sat the dignitaries of the university and seven high-backed red-plush chairs occupied by the rector, the local bishop, generals from the victorious Franco army which had recently captured Salamanca and an extraordinary fire-eater type of man so common in Spanish history and so incomprehensible to outsiders. He was General José Millán Astray, leader of the Foreign Legion and the only hero to come out of Spain's disastrous military adventures in Africa. He was a psychotic man, preternaturally thin, blind in one eye, lacking one arm and scarred across his entire body with mementos of defeat in desert battles. A major reason why he was a popular hero was the battle cry he had sponsored, 'Long live Death!' What this meant no one understood, but it had a rich fifteenth-century ring, and Spain echoed Millán Astray's challenge, 'Long live Death!'

On this day the general had the pleasure of addressing a university gathering, and universities had long been his anathema because scholars were alien to his Legion and learning refuted his cry of 'Long live Death!' So with choice, sardonic words the mad general ripped into Salamancan life, excoriated people who bothered with books, cursed regional areas like Cataluña and the Basque country, and promised that when Fascism triumphed, all such aberrations would be cauterized with a flaming sword. Fascists planted in the audience cheered. Intelligence was condemned and students were summoned to an unending war of extermination. The cadaverous general sat down and the crowd roared its approval of the new world a-coming.

Then the rector of the university rose, the distinguished philosopher-poet Miguel de Unamuno (1864–1936), author of the widely read *The Tragic Sense of Life*, and, with José Ortega y Gasset (1883–1955), Spain's leading intellectual. He knew that he ought not let this nihilistic challenge go unanswered, but he was an old man; police forces of the new Spain surrounded him; and in the chair to his right sat Franco's wife. If ever silence could have been condoned, this was the time, but Unamuno adjusted his robes of office, like Fray Luis before him, and began speaking in a soft voice: 'I, as you know, am a Basque, born in Bilbao. And the bishop, whether he likes it or not, is a Catalan, born in Barcelona.' He said that to speak of liquidating such men was silly. He then turned his attention to General Millán Astray and said a few simple things that some, at least, in the audience had been thinking but which fear had kept muffled. He said that the emaciated general was a cripple, a heroic one to be sure, but a cripple in both body and mind, and that because of his own withered nature he was determined to enforce on healthy Spain his sickly philosophy. Specifically, Unamuno said, there could be no sense in a rallying cry such as 'Long live Death.' Exactly the opposite spirit was required.

General Millán Astray, accustomed to total obedience in his Legion, could not tolerate opposition and especially not from a college professor. He leaped to his feet, waved his one arm and screamed, 'Down with intelligence! Long live Death!'

At this moment the mad general and the poet stood facing each other and neither would give way. 'Long live Death!' the general bellowed. 'No,' the poet replied. 'Long live intelligence.' Like the permanent contrasting forces of Spain the two men stood, and because the hall was filled with blue-shirted Fascists, the general won. When Franco heard reports of the meeting and of how Spain's leading intellect had challenged the spirit of the new regime, he is reported to have ordered, 'If necessary, shoot him.'

It was not necessary. Unamuno was already stricken and died shortly thereafter, leaving behind one of the most glowing memories of contemporary Spain, that of the philosopher-poet who defended the permanent values of Spain at the risk of his own life.

(Just as the telephone conversation between Colonel Moscardó and his supposedly sixteen-year-old son has been proved to be largely apocryphal, thus destroying a legend favorable to Franco, so doubts have been cast on the authenticity of some of the details of the Millán Astray–Unamuno confrontation. The original account came from a journalist, Luis Portillo, and was accepted by Hugh Thomas and many other serious writers. José María Pemán, one of the scheduled speakers that day and member of the Royal Academy, has denied that it took place, but Emilio Salcedo, in his life of Unamuno [1964], says that during the formal addresses relating to Spain's role in the New World, Unamuno was inspired to take notes on a piece of paper which has come down to us. At the conclusion of the set speeches he rose to make a few observations based on his notes but was interrupted by the general, whereupon something like the scene I have described took place, though not in the highly dramatic form suggested by Portillo. I have discussed this matter with a fair cross section of Spaniards and they believe that an intellectual scuffle, pretty much as described by Salcedo, did occur.)

Today in the hall which his bravery consecrated there is no mention of Unamuno's name and surely no bust or portrait, but often visitors sit in silence, their eyes closed, thinking of this courageous man and of his poem to Salamanca, where so much of his creative life had been spent.

> Forest of stones that history tore
> from the bowels of mother earth,
> refuge of quietude, I bless thee,
> my Salamanca.

> In the depths of my heart I cherish
> thy robust spirit; when I shall die,
> cherish thou, my golden Salamanca,
> my memory.

THE DEMON PASTRY COOK

For some two hundred years the kings of Spain had been trying to trick Portugal into surrendering its independence and becoming a province of Spain. This was not unnatural, because under the Romans, Visigoths and Muslims, Portugal had been an undifferentiated part of Spain and all prudent Spaniards hoped for the day when that would be the case again.

In 1576, when Felipe II sat on the throne of Spain, prospects for union began to brighten, for Sebastián (in Portuguese Sebastião), the twenty-two-year-old King of Portugal, was a moody, headstrong ascetic who loved only horses and refused to marry, even though he realized that if he died childless his throne would pass, ridiculous as it seems, to his granduncle Henrique, a childless cardinal in his dotage, whose principal pleasure was supervising the Portuguese Inquisition. If the young king died childless and the old cardinal did the same, the crown of Portugal would then pass into the hands of Felipe, who was Sebastián's uncle, and the peninsula would once more be united.

Spies brought unbelievable news to Madrid. 'Sebastián refuses to marry. He has epileptic fits and is afraid he's impotent.' And 'His Jesuit advisors have convinced him that he has been chosen by God to lead a great crusade into Africa and rescue it from Islam.' And 'Poor Sebastián is so excited about his crusade that he can think of nothing else. Portugal is falling into ruin while he seeks only to make himself physically fit to captain his armies. Each day he trains, sleeps on the ground, rides horseback for miles and will speak to no one of government.' And 'He insists that every noble family in Portugal send at least one of its sons to fight in Africa against Islam.' And 'Portugal is bankrupt. King Sebastián constantly demands new taxes and no one can call him from his folly.' And 'The only persons who can gain the king's ear are his Jesuit advisors, and they keep telling him, "March to Africa." '

In December of that year Felipe II proved that he was a just and honorable king. He summoned his Portuguese nephew to the remote monastery of Guadalupe to caution him against the folly of such a crusade, and when they met there on January 1, 1577, Felipe pointed out how slim were the chances of success, how imprudent it would be to strip Portugal of her wealth, her army and her sons, and how important it was for Sebastián to raise up a strong line of future kings. In other words, Felipe argued against his own interests, for he had only to encourage Sebastián to make a fool of himself and die in battle, and the throne of Portugal would come to Felipe. 'Don't go to Africa,' he pleaded.

Sebastián, considering his Spanish uncle uninformed and cautious, said bluntly that he would go and he demanded Spanish help, reminding

Felipe that only eighty-four years ago this same enemy had occupied part of Spain. Such an appeal Felipe could not refuse. He promised Sebastián a fleet and an army. Then the two kings worshiped at the shrine of the Virgin of Guadalupe and prayed for a Christian victory.

Sebastián hurried back to Portugal. 'We shall save Africa!' he announced, but in assembling his reluctant army he was so tardy, and his plans changed so swiftly, that in the end Uncle Felipe had to say, 'You have wasted too much time. I have changed my mind and shall not send the fleet and army that I promised.' With this stroke he ensured the failure of the enterprise, and some of Sebastián's lay advisors tried to warn him of this fact, but his Jesuit counselors insisted that the crusade go forward.

How bombastic was the armada that sailed from Lisboa in June, 1578, eight hundred vessels under chaotic leadership. How ridiculous was the military adventure once Africa was reached, a young king who knew nothing of arms determined to seek out the enemy personally and destroy him. The adventure was a disaster, the worst item of which was the fact that when Sebastián finally died under an enemy onslaught, no one saw where he was killed or how. There was no witness to his death and his body was not then recovered, if indeed it ever was. He vanished from history as ineptly as he had appeared, a strange, quixotic youth who succeeded in nothing, not even in dying properly.

But he was dead and the precarious crown of Portugal passed into the hands of Cardinal Henrique, sixty-seven years old, childless, tubercular and even more bumbling than Sebastián had been. It seemed only a matter of time before Felipe II would inherit the throne and unite the two kingdoms. However, King Henrique showed unexpected spirit and decided to petition the Pope for special permission to marry the thirteen-year-old daughter of a duchess under the extravagant impression that he could sire a son before he died. Alas, the plan was tardy; the petition could not be acted upon by the Pope, and the old cardinal died without legal issue. Portugal became once more a part of Spain and would presumably remain that way forever.

That was in 1580. But as the years passed, Portuguese patriotism did not diminish and an understandable rumor began to circulate through the peninsula. 'Suppose King Sebastião did not really die in Africa! Suppose he was so ashamed of his defeat that he crept from the battlefield and took an assumed name! Suppose he should suddenly reappear! Why, he'd be the legal King of Portugal! The Spaniards would have to get out! And that would be the last we'd see of Felipe II!' It was an enticing possibility. In the year 1592, when the rumor began to gain its greatest credence, how old would King Sebastián, the one in hiding, be? Only thirty-eight. He'd be heavier now, of course, but he'd have the same general appearance. Tall, with a slight impairment in the left side of his body, a superb horseman, daring, hot-tempered, regal in manner, blond. Yes, he would be noticeably blond, with sharp blue eyes and fair skin. Where could he be hiding, this lost king who would save all?

Especially persuasive was the Portuguese explanation as to why Sebastián had gone into hiding. 'It's all very simple, if you think of it. Why did King Sebastião get into trouble in Africa in the first place? Because his uncle, King Felipe, offered him an army and navy and then took them away. Don't you see? Felipe wanted Sebastião to be killed by the Moors, and if they hadn't done the job he would have. Poor Sebastião had to hide. He's gathering another army in secret. And soon he'll reappear. Watch.' Supporters of this theory had to explain away one stubborn fact. Some years after the disaster in Africa, King Felipe, always studious to protect his claim to the throne of Portugal, dispatched envoys who discovered Sebastián's corpse, which they brought back to a well-publicized funeral in Lisboa. To this the Portuguese developed a persuasive argument: 'I grant that a funeral was held. I attended it myself. But when was it held? In 1582. And when does Felipe claim that Sebastião died? In 1578. How could anyone identify a body four years dead? Felipe tricked you with a false corpse. You listen to me. Our king never died. Right now he's wandering somewhere in Europe and I for one expect to see him any day.'

When these rumors reached Felipe in El Escorial he told his aides, 'We must keep an eye out for this make-believe Sebastián.' The absent king, if he returned, could cause much trouble. For one thing, he would tear Portugal away from the empire, and this King Felipe did not intend to permit. 'Watch for Sebastián,' was the command passed to the king's officials.

It is not surprising that the Iberian peninsula should have become preoccupied with such a bizarre problem as late as 1592, because in Russia at this time much the same thing was happening. There in 1591 the acknowledged heir to the throne, Prince Dmitri, had died, perhaps at the hand of Boris Godunov, who assumed the crown and whose reign was plagued by rumors that Prince Dmitri had not actually died but was merely hiding until it was safe for him to appear. At embarrassing moments a series of Dmitris did step forward, or persons claiming to be Dmitri, and Russia was threatened with civil war. If it could happen in Russia, it could happen in Spain, and the agents of King Felipe took extra precautions.

Madrigal de las Altas Torres! Could one find in all Spain a town more suited for swift intrigue and high romance? It lay in a gentle plain of considerable beauty and was completely surrounded by a high wall marked by many towers. Its small streets ran under poetic arches and its plazas were dignified by sturdy ancient buildings. It was particularly noted for its convent, because in one of its cells the great Queen of Spain, Isabel the Catholic, had been born, and here many fine ladies from renowned families lived as nuns, helping the poor and keeping out of the way of their richer relatives.

In 1594 the convent housed one beautiful nun who was to become famous in history, Doña Ana de Austria, twenty-six years old and the granddaughter of Carlos V. She took her name from her father, who had been the savior of Spain, Don Juan de Austria, half brother to Felipe, which made her niece to the king. This would be important.

Doña Ana was in the convent for a reason common to that age. She was without question the daughter of the great Don Juan, but her father had never bothered to marry her mother, so the child was put in the convent to expiate her father's sin. She was gracious, well educated and tender in spirit. She was also romantic and often wondered what her life might have been if she were not illegitimate. Finally, she was dreadfully uninformed about life in the world at large, for like all female bastards of the royal line she had been stuck away in the convent at the age of six and had known only uneducated country girls who were taking orders and who were required to address her as 'Your Excellency.' Oh yes, Doña Ana also had a collection of jewels, some of them so stamped as to indicate that they were part of the crown treasure, and this too would be important.

The only man whom Doña Ana saw regularly was her confessor, Fray Miguel de los Santos, an Augustinian monk who had once served as royal courier from the court of Portugal to Rome and twice as provincial of his order. He had an intensity of spirit that Doña Ana liked and a willingness to talk with her for extended periods following her confession. He told her that he supposed he was the most saintly of all living men in that he prayed most of each night, disciplined himself three times each week and gave all his money to the needy. Then he told her something which must have excited her profoundly. 'I believe God has selected me for some special task, because each day of my life, when I come to the most solemn part of the Mass, I see in the heavens a giant crucifix, and beside it dressed in kingly armor with a baton of gold and flag of green silk a blond young man whose face I cannot see.' 'Who might the young king be?' Doña Ana asked. 'I wouldn't know,' her confessor replied. 'When God wants us to know who he is, we'll see his face.' What no one in Madrigal seemed to know was that Fray Miguel had once been preacher to the royal family of Portugal.

In the spring of 1593, before any overt acts had occurred in Madrigal, Fray Miguel began having a new set of visions, and these, too, he communicated to Doña Ana, as was only natural since she appeared in them. 'I saw a vision of Jerusalem,' he told her, 'and it was groaning under the heel of Islam, but at the right side of the city I saw you standing to bring deliverance and on the left side the handsome young man who now wore the crown of a king.' When Doña Ana asked what this signified, her confessor replied, 'I suppose it means that you are destined to save Jerusalem.' And the young man? It was someone Fray Miguel had seen before but he could not remember exactly who he was.

He next had a vision of Jesus Christ being crucified, with Doña Ana on his right side and the same fair king on the left. This signified, he said, that Doña Ana and the king were to work together for Jesus, as man and wife.

Hard on this exciting vision came one which spelled out the future in specific terms. The young king was her cousin, Sebastián of Portugal. He was alive and God intended Doña Ana to be his wife and queen. For the rest of that year the monk continued to ensnare the nun with a kaleidoscope of visions in which she appeared as the bride of King Sebastián, and he hammered at how much more pleasant it would be to rule as queen with a handsome man at her side than to wither away as a nun in a cell. 'Where is the king?' she asked. 'We have only to wait,' Fray Miguel assured her. 'If it is God's intention that you marry the king, God will bring him to you.' So the beautiful nun waited.

Everything I have told you so far is a matter of history, well recorded in documents, because what happened in Madrigal beginning in June of 1594 shook Spain, and many self-serving reports were filed in the royal archives by participants in the drama. What happened in the next four months, however, cannot be accurately determined and has been the subject of much speculation. The best historical summary is found in *A King for Portugal*, published in 1964, by the student of Portuguese history, Mary Elizabeth Brooks. The best dramatic account appeared on the Madrid stage in 1849 and often thereafter, *Unconfessed Traitor and Martyr*, the work that José Zorrilla, who also wrote *Don Juan Tenorio*, considered his masterpiece. And recently, at a date I have not been able to determine, Alonso de Encinas, a native of Madrigal, published an enchanting little essay titled 'The Pastry Cook of Madrigal.' The Zorrilla play is pure invention and I shall not borrow from it. The Encinas essay purports to be fact but is at variance with Dr. Brooks, so I shall use it sparingly. I shall, however, rely for the next few pages upon fact and legend as I heard it in Madrigal.

A major point of difference between history and legend centers upon the person of Don Rodrigo de Santillán. Legend says that he was the leading citizen of Madrigal, and a man who took seriously his role of alcalde and confidential agent of King Felipe. A petty noble, pompous, suspicious and easily swayed by the merest whisper from the king, he kept an eye on all that happened in Madrigal and dispensed an honest justice in any matter that did not impinge upon the crown. That is, if two farmers quarreled over a pig, Don Rodrigo could be depended upon to ferret out the facts and render a just decision. But if the pig happened to belong to the king . . . well, that was quite another matter. That demanded looking into, and when Don Rodrigo looked into something where the king's interest was at stake, there was apt to be a hanging.

On this point history is clear-cut and firm. Don Rodrigo de Santillán was not the mayor of Madrigal; he was a senior and respected judge of the Chancillería de Valladolid (High Tribunal of Justice) and so far as can be ascertained had no personal connection with Madrigal. The Royal Archives

THE PORTUGUESE SUCCESSION

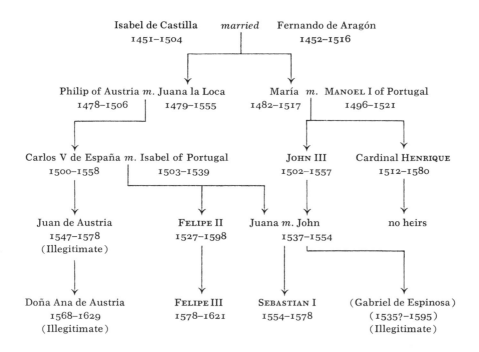

at Simancas contain literally a thousand pages of reports written by Judge Santillán and these show him to have been a perspicacious gentleman, jealous of his prerogatives and determined to do the king's will. Legend required him to be the alcalde of Madrigal so that his daughter María, a quiet girl, reserved and lovely, could play a major role in developments. When the events began to unfold she had not yet given signs of being interested in any of the young men in nearby towns who would normally have married her, and villagers began to wonder what was going to happen to her.

They liked her and their speculations were without rancor. They were therefore pleased when a tall stranger, who seemed to be about forty years old, accompanied by a fair-haired girl of two and a maidservant, appeared in town to open a pastry shop. He announced that his name was Gabriel de Espinosa and he posed only as an honest workman who baked good pastry and looked after his little girl, but his bearing was so noble, his speech so refined and his accidental references to past deeds in which he had participated so convincing, that the citizens of Madrigal were satisfied that he must be an important man in hiding.

'The younger son of some noble family,' was the general judgment. 'Got into trouble with the daughter of a duque or something. The mother died and he has their little girl. He's here in Madrigal only till it's safe to go back home and claim his inheritance. And his titles.'

Among those bedazzled by the handsome, taciturn pastry cook was María. She started frequenting his shop and soon made no secret of the fact that she was madly in love with him. Don Rodrigo had rather more exalted plans for his daughter than a pastry cook, and he interposed all sorts of objections, but María was firm. 'He's a great gentleman,' she insisted. 'One day you'll be proud of him.' Whenever her father was obliged to be in Valladolid, strong-willed María crept out of her house to visit with Gabriel.

On one such occasion Gabriel dropped certain hints about his past. When he had come to Venice . . . 'From where, Gabriel?' 'From Africa.' And in Venice he had had a series of wild adventures. He'd been married to a noble Italian lady, had fought duels, had been privy to many secrets of the Venetian government. 'Why?' 'Because they saw in me someone who . . .' Whenever pressed about his exact identity his voice trailed off. But it was clear that the Venetian state had devised plans whereby Gabriel de Espinosa could be of service to them in their war against Spain. 'I left Venice,' he said. 'Is the little girl the daughter of the Venetian noble lady?' He preferred not to speak of that.

The love affair of the alcalde's daughter and the pastry cook went forward at a steady rate, except that the more María spoke in behalf of her lover, the more the mayor objected. 'He's a tricky one,' Don Rodrigo said. Sometimes he would leave his office in one of the towers and stand looking at the pastry shop, and when he had about decided that this Espinosa was a fraud, the cook would greet a customer in such grandeur that even Don Rodrigo had to acknowledge that here was a most unusual man. Most unusual.

Don Rodrigo's problem was about to be resolved in a way he could not have anticipated. As soon as Gabriel de Espinosa arrived in Madrigal, Fray Miguel, still serving as confessor to Doña Ana, doubled his visits to her cell and warned her that the hour of decision was at hand. 'I had a vision. God appeared and told me that he was about to bring King Sebastián into our presence. Are you prepared?' She said she was ready for whatever God required of her, but how could she marry Sebastián, since she was already a nun? Her confessor reasoned, 'You were thrown into this convent at a tender age and against your will. When you took your vows to become a nun, did you do so willingly?' Doña Ana said she had never wanted to become a nun, and Fray Miguel cried, 'See! Your vows are void and you are free to marry.'

When this was settled, Fray Miguel had a further vision telling him that the long-absent king was about to arrive in Madrigal. 'How will we know him?' Doña Ana asked, and the friar said, 'When I was preacher to the kings of Portugal I knew Sebastián well. He was tall and gracious, bold and daring, a superb horseman and blond. I would know him.'

Finally, one day Fray Miguel arrived in a state of agitation. In his vision the night before he had seen God's finger pointing at a handsome man whom he had seen earlier standing with Doña Ana at Jerusalem and at the Crucifixion. 'He is King Sebastián and he lives,' said the voice of God. What was more, he was hiding right here in Madrigal until the day came to disclose himself. And what was best of all, he was now in the anteroom. Fray Miguel kept Doña Ana from fainting, and when she had composed herself he kicked open the door and there stood the king, waiting to claim her as his bride.

It was not long before the pastry cook was sleeping at the convent. (Many historians, especially those of the Church, deny that the affair reached this point; however, much evidence suggests that it did. At any rate, oral tradition in Madrigal insists that it did.) At the trial several nuns were convicted of having connived at slipping Gabriel into the convent, and the conspiracy was probably greater than the testimony admitted to public record showed. The whole convent seems to have been enchanted at the prospect that one of their members might become Queen of Portugal.

Espinosa had no trouble in convincing Doña Ana of his royal claims. He had indeed fled Africa in disguise, as Fray Miguel had guessed, and he had been wandering the earth looking for a queen exactly like Doña Ana. All auguries were now good for his recovery of the throne, and if she would stand by him in the months ahead . . . She wanted to know exactly what this meant, and he said there was the matter of expenses. 'I have these jewels,' she said, and he thought they would just about cover the cost of regaining the crown.

At the same time, however, he was not neglecting his duties with the alcalde's daughter, 'because,' as an old gentleman at Madrigal suggested, 'he wasn't at all sure he could get Doña Ana out of the convent.'

In October, 1594, events came to a climax and Fray Miguel prevailed upon Doña Ana, who was hopelessly in love with the pastry cook, whom she habitually called 'Your Majesty,' to give him her jewels to pay for a clandestine trip to France. 'There are in that country,' Fray Miguel said, 'thousands of loyal men waiting to rise on your husband's behalf.' The friar had fallen in the habit of speaking to Doña Ana as if she were already married to the king. 'It will be a simple matter,' he assured her, 'to explain to the Pope that you were made a nun against your will. He'll permit you to marry the king.' The passionately involved nun gave Espinosa her jewels, but at the last moment she either enclosed or mailed him two love letters as well, and in so doing condemned him to a dreadful death.

So much for the blend of legend and fact. From here on, each item of the story is historically founded and based on existing documents except as specifically noted. On October 7, 1594, Gabriel de Espinosa, on his way to consult with a group of supporters in France, left Madrigal and journeyed to Valladolid, where at an inn he fell in with a pretty country girl, whom he sought to impress by showing her the jewels he was carrying. He looked forward to spending a pleasant evening with the girl and offered her a drink from a cup carved from what he assured her was the horn of a unicorn. But she was no fool. She knew that unicorns were so rare that if a man of apparently modest means had such a cup he must have come by it evilly. She slipped out of the inn to inform upon him and by sheer coincidence came upon Judge Rodrigo de Santillán, making his nightly snooping rounds, for, as he later boasted in a letter to King Felipe,

> You have undoubtedly understood and noticed, sir, throughout my life, how lacking I have been in greed and how much more I esteem honor than wealth, and I seek this by patrolling by night and laboring by day as everyone knows.

Don Rodrigo listened to the girl's story and agreed with her that it sounded suspicious. He accompanied her to the inn and found there the mysterious pastry cook of Madrigal. Here was the chance he had been awaiting and he summoned the guard to arrest the man. When he searched Gabriel's belongings he found a cache of jewels, some of which were so marked as to make him think they belonged to Her Excellency Doña Ana de Austria, the nun at the convent in Madrigal.

'We have caught a thief,' Don Rodrigo announced, and after clapping Espinosa into jail, he returned to his quarters and at midnight wrote two letters which speak well for his sagacity in dealing with matters touching upon the royal family. The first was to Doña Ana and was couched in deferential terms, as befitted a letter addressed to the king's niece.

> Señora Doña Ana de Austria,
>
> Most Excellent Lady: Tonight I have personally arrested, at an inn of Valladolid, a certain Gabriel Espinosa, who claims to be a pastry-maker in the town of Madrigal, in whose possession I have found some valuable jewels which seem to belong to Your Excellency, and he says that he has been commissioned by Your Excellency to come to Valladolid to sell them. I humbly beg Your Excellency to inform me if what this Gabriel Espinosa has claimed is true, and, in the meantime, he remains in jail and the jewels in my possession, at the disposal of Your Excellency. May God keep Your Excellency many years as is the wish of this humble servant of Your Excellency, who kisses your hands. From Valladolid, September 28, 1594.
>
> The Judge, Don Rodrigo de Santillán

As soon as this was dispatched to Madrigal, Don Rodrigo sent a much different type of directive to Don Luis Portocarrero, Alcalde de la Real Chancillería de Valladolid.

My esteemed and respected friend:

Upon receipt of this letter, I ask you, the better to serve Our Lord the King, to go to the house of the pastry-maker Gabriel Espinosa in Madrigal and take possession of everything you find in it, and to arrest those who normally live in the house, except for any guests who might be there, whom you will order to find other lodgings unless they seem suspicious to you, for in that case you will arrest them also; search the house and, if you find documents, make a packet of them and send them to me as safely and rapidly as you can. This is all that I need to tell you, Don Luis, and I reiterate my friendship for you and bid you farewell. May God keep you. From Valladolid, September 28, 1594.

The Judge, Don Rodrigo de Santillán

The second of these two letters and the one that follows shortly are not reported in the archives but are of ancient tradition. For what happened next we have documentary evidence from Judge Santillán himself. Next morning, September 28, when Espinosa was already in jail as a thief, Don Rodrigo happened upon the two love letters from Doña Ana and in them found the words, several times repeated, 'Your Majesty.' On the evidence of these letters it was clear that the pastry cook had been passing himself off as the vanished King of Portugal, and this was quite a different matter. This was treason.

Don Rodrigo, recognizing that he had come upon something monstrous, immediately reported his conclusions to King Felipe at El Escorial. A full-scale investigation was launched, and then a trial, and in each, Judge Santillán conducted himself with dignity, if not impartiality. From the first he was determined to accomplish two ends: he would hang the pastry cook, and he would protect his own relationship with the king, to whom he wrote: 'Since, according to the indications given by the beginning of this affair, it seems that it might offer me some profit, I beg you not to let me be deprived of it now by those who used to sleep and wench while I was patrolling and working.' He was ambitious, but to accomplish his aims he did not pervert justice and at his hands the accused received fair trials. The daughter María, which legend gives him, does not appear in the official records as pleading for the life of her lover, but on this matter Madrigal tradition is unequivocal. She never wavered in her affection for the pastry cook nor in her belief in his innocence. She remained convinced that he was the younger son of a noble family and that he had behaved with pundonor.

In the lengthy investigation conducted by Don Rodrigo there were four principal witnesses: Gabriel Espinosa, the servant girl who had appeared with him in Madrigal, Fray Miguel and Doña Ana. A special ecclesiastical judge was brought in to try Fray Miguel and the nuns, and torture of the most severe sort was applied to all but the latter. One innocent bystander who was questioned was sentenced to four years in the galleys, but this was rescinded when the judge found that in his question-

ing, the man had been so severely tortured, he would never again be able
to use his arms.

The charge was treason. Fray Miguel and Gabriel de Espinosa,
whoever the latter might be, had cooked up a scheme whereby Portugal
would be detached from the throne of Spain, where it rightfully belonged.
In addition, a convent had been violated, a royal nun had been seduced
and jewels pertaining to the royal family had been stolen. The outcome of
the trial was known before it started. Don Rodrigo had found a way to
ingratiate himself with the king and nothing would prevent him from
pursuing his advantage. What the trial really came down to was a fourfold
mystery. Who was Espinosa? Was he widely supported in Portugal? And to
what extent was Doña Ana de Austria involved? In particular, King Felipe
insisted upon knowing whether the little girl was Doña Ana's daughter by
the pastry cook, for if so she was a member of the royal family and Felipe
felt that this changed everything.

The process against Gabriel continued for more than nine months:
questions, torture, compare the answers, questions again, torture again,
compare again and repeat the cycle. A particularly obnoxious aspect of the
trial, if it should be called such, was that on the surface it was an ordinary
trial for treason, conducted honorably, but at each step Don Rodrigo sent
King Felipe a summary of what was happening and sought from the king
advice as to what to do next. It was therefore the king who conducted the
trial, and always he wanted to know, 'Who is that little girl?' A good deal
of the torture was an attempt to find a satisfactory answer to that gnawing
question.

If Doña Ana was not put to the torture she received little consideration otherwise. Early in the process she felt herself so abused that she
wrote a strong letter of protest to her uncle, King Felipe, which we have,
and his response, better than anything else in the case, shows how Spain
was governed at the time.

> My dear niece:
>
> I have received with surprise your complaint against Don Rodrigo de
> Santillán and I regret that this judge has become involved in a dispute with
> you that I wish could have been entirely avoided. You are a person who,
> because of dedication and piety, lives withdrawn from the world and has
> no knowledge of administrators of justice, whose great severity must be
> tolerated and even applauded, first, because they act in Our name and
> know how to see that it is respected, and, second, because with their harsh
> severity they keep evil people cautious and fearful of punishment, thus
> preventing many crimes. For the common good it is better that they be
> harsh than lenient, because leniency is not understood by such people as
> mercy, but rather weakness, and they take advantage of it, multiplying
> their crimes and doing great injury to those who lead good and honest lives.
> Don Rodrigo de Santillán is perhaps more severe than he needs to be, but
> this is owing to the zeal with which he serves Us and has served Us all his

life. As for disrespect, if there should be any such as may be to the detriment of Our dignity (since you are so close a relative of Ours, the daughter of Our most dear brother), We should not hesitate to punish Don Rodrigo most severely if there were good reason for it; but if the disrespect is perhaps more apparent than real, it is wise of princes not to allow anyone to understand that it is even possible for a vassal to show them disrespect. It is better to leave well enough alone. The two persons whom you sent to me with your recommendation that the one be made a corregidor in the Indies and the other provisioner of Our armies in Flanders have been taken care of, but We beg you, Our dear child, not to be so soft-hearted with office-seekers, because they will eat Us out of house and home. I know that certain people are going to Madrigal to see you so that you may serve as intercessor with me in the affairs of Portugal. The Duque de Coimbra and two other important gentlemen of that kingdom, who have spent some days in the Capital, have told everyone that they would not seek an audience with me until they can present themselves with your letters of recommendation for me. This affair is very serious and I wish you to proceed with great prudence and slowly, and to inform me of everything secretly, to which end I have ordered relays of post-horses to be stationed along the highway, so that your letters can reach me within twenty-four hours. Receive these people, listen to them, communicate to me immediately what they say to you, and do not again receive them, under pretext of illness or with some other clever excuse, until I shall have written to you, counseling you as to what you should tell them, because in these affairs of Portugal it is necessary to proceed very alertly, and you can discover more than I could if I were seeing them, because with you they will not be so much on their guard. May God keep you many years, my very dear child, and do not forget in your prayers to plead with God for your uncle.

The King Don Felipe

Finally the judges handed down the sentences, first having received initialed authorizations from the king. Doña Ana was deprived of all privileges due her as a member of the royal family; for four years she would live in solitary confinement; she would be allowed to attend Mass only on feast days; on Fridays she could eat nothing but bread; and for the rest of her life she could have contacts only with the least-educated members of her order. The nuns who helped slip the pastry cook into her quarters were given harsher sentences.

Espinosa's serving girl, having confessed under torture that the child was hers and not the daughter of Doña Ana or some other noble lady, was given two hundred lashes, which must have nearly killed her, and was then banished.

Fray Miguel presented a special problem. As a friar he could not be condemned by lay authority, yet clearly he had been the manipulator of the whole plot. In Lisboa he had observed the Portuguese royal family at intimate quarters and had known how to find someone who looked like the king and then coach him in his role. He had done a great job. Many

Portuguese nobles were convinced that Espinosa was their lost king. Fray Miguel paid dearly for his fling but could not be hanged because as a priest his person was inviolate, even to the wrath of the king. However, Judge Santillán, after conducting scrupulous investigations into his background, developed the interesting theory that since Miguel's parents had come from Jerez de los Caballeros, where we found Balboa's birthplace, he must be a secret Jew because Jerez was known to contain many such, and as Santillán pointed out to the king, 'never has there been an evil of any importance or a crime of any seriousness where a converted Jew hasn't played a part.' At any rate, a weak-willed Spanish archbishop was finally found who was willing to strip the friar of his ecclesiastical privileges, whereupon the lay arm of the government grabbed him, led him through the streets of Madrid with chains about his neck, then dragged him back for public humiliation in Madrigal, after which he was hanged.

That left a problem. Who was this pastry cook? The strange thing is that no one ever knew. One fantastic rumor, which I both heard in Madrigal from people who swore it to be true and found in the Encinas book, is reflected in the genealogical chart on page 467, but kept within parentheses since it can only be legend. King Sebastián's father was John of Portugal, who failed to attain the throne because he died prematurely in 1554, eighteen days before Sebastián was born. When a mere youth he had married Princess Juana, daughter of Carlos V, and when the young couple were living in Valladolid, John of Portugal fell in love with the very beautiful daughter of a pastry cook who worked in Madrigal, and by her he had an illegitimate son who was given the name Gabriel de Espinosa. Later, by Carlos V's daughter, he had a legitimate son, Sebastián. Gabriel and Sebastián were thus half brothers, which accounted for the unquestioned similarity between them and also for the fact that when Gabriel returned to Madrigal he had a pastry shop waiting for him.

A second rumor was thoroughly explored during the trial and came to be the one generally accepted by members of the government. According to this, Gabriel was a child who had been abandoned in the torno of a Toledo convent and had grown up reckless and willing for any adventure. The turmoil in Portugal attendant on King Sebastián's crusade attracted him and he may or may not have gone to Africa with the king. On subsequent travels through Europe he learned German and French, but how he fell into the hands of Fray Miguel was not known. Furthermore, the very fact that he had been abandoned secretly in a torno added fuel to the suspicion that he was the offspring, legitimate or otherwise, of some noble family.

The third rumor was the one that Espinosa himself had used when wooing María, the alcalde's daughter. He was the acknowledged son of a noble family and for some reason wished to travel incognito for the time being.

And, finally, there were many in both Portugal and Spain who believed that he was indeed the lost King Sebastián, and that King Felipe knew it. Just as Felipe had tried in 1578 to cause his nephew's death by denying him the army and navy he needed, so he now in 1594 ordered his horrible execution.

At Felipe's direction Gabriel de Espinosa, whoever he might be, was taken back to Madrigal de las Altas Torres and was there paraded through the streets in a wicker basket. His tour ended at a gallows, where a discalced priest jammed a crucifix into his mouth every time he sought to address the crowd. He was hanged, cut down, beheaded and hacked into quarters, which were nailed to trees on four different roads leading out of Madrigal. The head was exhibited in an iron cage hung from the tip of a pike in the town itself as a deterrent to the next man who might want to challenge the right of Felipe II to rule Portugal.

Fray Miguel, when he faced death, recanted prior confessions made under torture and insisted that Espinosa was King Sebastián. On the gallows, Espinosa conducted himself like a true king and convinced many. It seems to me that the most damning evidence against him was twofold: when he was locked in his cell, without recourse to the dye pots of an apothecary, his hair grew in almost white, so that he looked more nearly sixty than the forty that Sebastián would have been; but as an old man in Madrigal pointed out to me, 'Think a minute! He was under such torture that his hair turned white.' And, as Judge Santillán skillfully brought out, he could not speak Portuguese.

Especially ironic was the fact that even if Espinosa had escaped hanging by Felipe, even if the plot had worked, he was doomed, because under torture Fray Miguel confessed that he intended using Espinosa only until Portugal gained its independence. Then Fray Miguel would have denounced Espinosa as an impostor. He would have been executed and a real member of the Portuguese royal family called to the throne. As for Doña Ana, she was a giddy nun and was expendable. As a matter of fact, such deviousness was not necessary, for in 1640, by what might be termed natural processes not requiring the existence of a King Sebastián, Portugal regained her independence from Spain.

Long after the executions of Fray Miguel and Espinosa, long after bitter Felipe II was dead, the dismal affair at Madrigal ended on a note of gracia. Felipe III, who had already reigned for twelve years, relented at the thought of his cousin Doña Ana de Austria's being immured in a cell and appointed her, when she was forty-two years old, abbess of the largest and most important convent in Spain, Las Huelgas, and there she ruled for many years, firm, able and disposed to listen sympathetically when young nuns came to her with emotional problems.

FOLLOWING PAGE:
Strings of garlic.

IX

PAMPLONA

OCEANO ATLANTICO

MILES
0   100

Santillana del Mar

Santiago de Compostela

Azpeitia   Roncesvalles

Pamplona

Tudela

Barcelona

Porto

Madrid

Sintra
Lisboa   Elvas

Sevilla

Faro

MAR MEDITERRANEO

Word had circulated through Europe and America that the mob was gathering in July for the feria of San Fermín at Pamplona. The two British bullfight experts Angus Macnab and Kenneth Tynan were to be there. The American aficionados Darryl Zanuck, Orson Welles, and Conrad Janis had reservations. Hemingway's mentor Juanito Quintana had assured us that he was coming, and although the queen of bullfight fans, the stately Tigre from London, couldn't make it, she was sending as deputy her son Oliver, a most attractive young man fresh out of Eton with a penchant for running a few inches in front of the largest bulls. The ineffable Matt Carney, whom I had not met, was coming down from his bizarre occupation in Paris, and I looked forward to making his acquaintance, and Bob Daley, who had just published a good book on the bulls, would be there, but what was most attractive to me, Robert Vavra, in charge of illustrations for this book, was to be on hand, as would be the American matador John Fulton, who was flying in from Mexico. I wanted to talk to both of them. So with a good deal of cabling for reservations and renting of cars, the mob set out for Pamplona.

My reasons for going were fourfold and none was connected with bullfighting, much as I enjoyed it. First I wanted to see the Navarrese city of Tudela; then I wanted to talk about music with Don Luis Morondo; next I wanted to study Pamplona's curious cathedral; and finally I wanted to picnic once more in the enchanted Pass of Roncesvalles. I would have traveled a considerable distance to do any one of these things, and the happy prospect of doing them all and in conjunction with the celebration of San Fermín was enticing.

Tudela is a small city on the right bank of the Río Ebro and has little to commend it except a public square with some fine arches and a few church buildings that might concern an architect but which had no interest for me. I was drawn to Tudela by a crowded district which huddled along the river's edge; eight hundred years ago this area had been a warren of narrow streets from which a great man had fled to adventures so preposterous as to make him one of the major travelers of history, and it was to him that I wanted to pay homage, for I was indebted to his work.

He was known simply as Benjamin of Tudela and probably he had no other name, for he was a poor Jew who lived in the local ghetto, but in 1165 he decided to see something of the world, and long before I had ever seen the city of Tudela, I had imagined him saying goodbye to the miserable Jewish quarter and sailing down the Ebro to some port city that gave him access to the Mediterranean and the known world of that time.

Now, seeing the Ebro as it passed Tudela, I doubted that he could have sailed it. He must have walked, perhaps to Zaragoza and then over to Barcelona, where he entered upon the Mediterranean. At any rate, in the years following 1165 Benjamin wandered through the Near East, trading and listening and making notes. He visited more than three hundred places, and wherever he went he asked about the condition of Jews in the region and compiled a census of all families known to be Jewish, so that today it is from Benjamin that we know about the Jewry of that time. He was especially careful to note conditions in the Holy Land, where the Crusades had pretty well eliminated Jews in 1099. But when he reached these supposedly destitute lands he discovered several enclaves in which Jewish families had persisted for a hundred generations.

Benjamin was an indefatigable traveler and apparently a man of courage, for he penetrated to areas that other Europeans had not seen, and if his report, existing only in manuscript till 1543, lacked the literary quality of Marco Polo's narrative, it surpassed the Venetian's account in factual matters and antedated it by more than a century. I owed Benjamin of Tudela much, for from his tight and cautious writing I learned things that I required to know in writing one of my novels, and now as I stood in his native city, looking at the narrow streets that he must have known and from which he had fled, I felt very close to him, for he had traveled the lands that I had traveled, and he had written of things I had written about, but he had done it when to do so required both imagination and courage. I wish I had known this doughty old Jew; I wish I could have sat with him on the shores of Lake Galilee when he noted in his journal that fourteen Jewish families had now crept back to this village or that, where all had been expelled or murdered half a century before. I found in Benjamin a great resilience of spirit and it was gratifying to walk the streets he had walked.

There was another reason why I wanted to see Tudela: here I would catch my first glimpse of the Río Ebro, to which the title of this book is related. In pre-Roman times this river was known as the Iberus and those who lived along it as Iberes. To the Greeks the eastern half of Spain was

Iberia, and thus the word entered classical history. The French writer Jean Descola in his *A History of Spain* (1962) offers quite a different derivation:

> At about this time the country acquired a name. The Hebrews called it Sepharad, 'border' or 'edge.' The Greeks christened it Hesperia, 'the Occident,' or He Spania, 'the sparse.' More significant, however, was the term 'Iberia,' which derived from the Celtic word *aber*, 'harbor' or 'river.' And indeed, the first known inhabitants of the peninsula were precisely the Iberians who came from the valley of the Ebro.

Since no authority I have consulted supports this theory, I do not know what to make of Descola's claim that the word *Iberian* is of Celtic origin.

To the Romans, of course, the name Iberia referred to that region of the Caucasus now known as Georgia, and it is surprising to find that a respected authority like William Smith in his *Classical Dictionary* (1881) limits his definition of Iberia to the Asian area, ending with the aside, 'No connection can be traced between the Iberians of Asia and those of Spain.' (Strictly speaking, therefore, the most notorious Iberian of history was Josef Stalin.) The more authoritative *Harper's Dictionary of Classical Literature and Antiquities* (1965) also defines Iberia as Georgia but does add a second definition: 'One of the ancient names of Spain, derived from the river Iberus.'

The Oxford English Dictionary cites Henry Cockeram's *The English Dictionary, or an Interpretation of Hard English Words* (1623) as reflecting general European usage in its simple definition of Iberians: 'Spaniards.' It was in this tradition, which I follow, that Isaac Albéniz in the years 1906–1909 composed his delightful suite *Iberia*, originally for the piano; six typical section titles are Sevilla, Ronda, Almería, Triana, Málaga and Jerez. For him and for all others who are mindful of the classical past, Iberia serves as a synonym for ancient Spain, and for the most evocative of modern Spain.

In general usage, of course, the word has come to indicate the entire peninsula, including both Spain and Portugal. The first recorded example of this usage in English came no earlier than 1611, but today *Lippincott's Gazetteer* (1952) says briefly: 'The Iberian peninsula comprises Spain and Portugal,' while *The Random House Dictionary of the English Language* (1966) relegates the traditional definition of Georgia to second place, defining the word primarily as 'a peninsula in SW Europe, comprising Spain and Portugal.'

Even though I am following the older definition, a chapter of this book could legitimately have dealt with Portugal, because in the years when I was visiting Spain, I grabbed at every opportunity to wander in Portugal; one of the most relaxed vacations I ever experienced came when a group of us rented a historic quinta (country seat) at Sintra, the exquisite hill town near Lisboa in which Lord Byron composed much of his heroic poem *Don*

Juan. For more than a month I tramped over the hills he had known and down those tight and twisted lanes that he had loved. The Portuguese spoke of him with enormous affection, as if he had been with them only a few tourist seasons ago; his demonic presence hovered about me as I worked at my typewriter, because at some earlier date someone had told the Englishman who owned our quinta that he looked exactly like Lord Byron, and this had had a bad effect upon the man. The study I was using was literally lined with volumes on the poet. Apparently my Englishman had a standing order with booksellers in London and New York: 'Send me anything printed about Lord Byron.' He also had copies of several of the more romantic portraits of the poet, which proved that Byron did resemble the owner of the quinta, or the other way around.

Wherever I wandered in Portugal, I discovered quiet Englishmen who had lived for decades in quiet crannies of this hospitable country. Portugal has always held a fascination for the English, who term it 'our oldest ally and one of the world's most civilized spots.' I often suspected that these Englishmen were engaged in a conspiracy of silence, and one afternoon a group of them begged me, 'For God's sake, Michener, don't tell anyone, and certainly not the rich Americans, how heavenly this place is.' It was Europe's most economical retirement spot; it had the best servants, the best wine, some of the best food, and a host of small localities from Porto in the north to Faro in the south to which an educated Englishman could retire in dignity.

I am often asked to compare Portugal and Spain, and the simple truth seems to be that whichever of these two countries one visits first continues as his preference. No one can be more energetic in defense of a new-found land than the Englishman, Frenchman or American who has visited Portugal first and then moved on to Spain: he loves the first and is never easy in the second. I discovered this when I traveled westward across Spain with an American couple who had worked for some years at our embassy in Lisboa, for it was touching to watch how apprehensive they were of all things Spanish and how their spirits revived the closer they got to their beloved Portugal. 'We wouldn't feel safe drinking Spanish water, thank you. We've been all through Portugal and we've never seen villages as dirty as those in Spain. Doesn't anyone have paint in this country? The fact is, we feel safe in Portugal but in Spain you never know. Our police are so much better.' As we approached the western border of Spain it became a question of whether we should take our lunch in Spanish Badajoz, which I preferred because of the great seafood zarzuela I knew was waiting, or press on to Portuguese Elvas, which lay just across the border. 'Oh,' my embassy friends said, 'we'd never want to eat in a Spanish restaurant if a clean Portuguese one were nearby.'

Well, the first of the two countries that I saw was Spain and my affection has always rested there. It was not until my trip with the Lisboa couple that I saw the peninsula through Portuguese eyes, and when I did this I had to admit that of the two countries Portugal was the cleaner, the better organized, the better controlled; it was not illogical that the knowing English had elected this small country as their choice of Europe. But I also found that it lacked the culture of Spain; there was no Portuguese Velázquez, no Victoria, no García Lorca, no Santa Teresa, and of course no Seneca. The genius of the Iberian peninsula seemed to have resided principally in the more easterly regions, and it was for this reason that I preferred Spain.

On two different occasions after long stays in Portugal, I crossed into Spain and each time those of us in the automobile felt a surge of joy, an expansion of the spirit and a sense of growing nobility as we entered Spain. Once the driver of our car dismounted, rubbed his hands in Spanish soil and exulted in being home again. My joining him irritated my wife, who like many women preferred Portugal. 'You're being silly and unfair,' she protested. 'Portugal is much finer than you admit it to be.' The driver, who had been disappointed in Portuguese girls, replied, 'There's one thing I'll admit. It's the only country in the world where a man's mistress is apt to be uglier than his wife.'

There was a final reason for choosing *Iberia* as a title for this book: the word is unusual in that it is just as beautiful in its English pronunciation (Eye-beer-ee-ya) as in its Spanish (Ee-bare-ya), a fact recognized by Matthew Arnold when he inserted the word in the closing lines of "The Scholar-Gipsy," one of the stateliest passages of English poetry:

> To where the Atlantic raves
> Outside the Western Straits, and unbent sails
> There, where down cloudy cliffs, through sheets of foam,
> Shy traffickers, the dark Iberians come;
> And on the beach undid his corded bales.

The short drive from Tudela to Pamplona ran due north through the handsome country of lower Navarra, climbing as it went, for I was approaching the Pyrenees, and although it was now early July, the air was brisk and I could sense the vigor that characterizes northern Spain. Then, as the car turned a corner, I saw before me the smokestacks and factory walls of a prosaic industrial city that might be termed the Youngstown of Spain, and I thought how disappointed must be those foreigners nurtured on Ernest Hemingway's vision of Pamplona as it existed in the late 1920s, when they saw this drab profile. Judging by first appearances, Pamplona was no romantic center for expatriates but rather a commercial hub more concerned about labor unions than fiestas.

My first explorations of the city through its southern gateway confirmed this judgment: I saw dozens of garages where knowledgeable young men were tearing down Ford and Citroën engines and rebuilding them. I saw glass factories and cordage shops and lumber yards and carpenters' benches. But when I entered the wide avenue leading to the central square I entered a new world, for now I found myself surrounded by a hornets' nest of small cars from all over Europe filled with some of the most attractive young people I had seen in years: blondes from Sweden, handsome dark-haired men from Italy, students in leather pants from Germany and a substantial quota of Americans under the age of twenty-five. There was noise and excitement. The heart of Pamplona was apparently going to be much different from the environs.

The first specific proof I had that a feria was about to begin came when I saw Spanish men parading with long strings of garlic about their necks, wearing them as women do pearls. I was to ask many times what these strands of garlic reaching down to the knees signified, but no one could tell me; doubtless it had something to do either with ancient fertility rites or with charms to banish ghosts during feria.

When I came to the public square it was as if I had entered another city, one belonging to the nineteenth century. In the center among scattered trees stood an old-style bandstand featuring iron grillwork; about the edges of the square sprawled a dozen cafés, their chairs and tables covering the pavement from door to gutter; above the cafés rose several ancient hotels with tall French windows that didn't close; and everywhere there were hordes of young people determined to have a good time.

I was supposed to meet Vavra at the Bar Txoco, but when I got there all tables were filled with students from South Africa, Germany, Sweden and Great Britain. They were a riotous lot, some with necklaces of garlic, most stone-drunk at five in the afternoon, with the feria not yet begun. Unable to find a chair, I was about to leave when I heard a loud, insinuating 'Psssst,' and I turned to face the man who would symbolize Pamplona for me.

He was in his late forties, a disreputable, baggy-kneed, bleary-eyed, gap-toothed, fumbling, stumbling waiter from a nearby café who made his living by luring customers away from the Bar Txoco to his flea-infested joint and exacting from them, for his pains, a shot or two of whiskey. He was the most debauched Spaniard I had ever seen, a disreputable Sancho Panza, and as he offered me a chair he whispered, 'You want to meet a refined Spanish girl? Speaks English.' When I ordered wine he made a new proposition: 'Can I pour a shot for myself?' The duplicity with which he dispatched his drink without being detected by the owner of the café was ingratiating, and as he placed my wine on the table he asked, 'You interested in marijuana?' I was to see a great deal of this one-man vice ring in the eight days ahead, for he seemed to work all hours without sleep, fortifying himself with cadged drinks and lurching about his corner of the plaza in a kind of Renaissance debauchery. 'Look!' he whispered admiringly as I sipped my wine. 'Ernest Hemingway. And our lousy newspapers tried to tell us he was dead.'

484

I looked to where he pointed, and my jaw dropped. There, entering the plaza behind the wheel of a small, trim Karmann-Ghia, came Ernest Hemingway, dead these five years. He wore his famous hunting cap with the short brim, and field jacket. His white beard looked exactly as it had during the last years of his life, and his portly figure was the same. Even the features of his expressive face were unchanged, and after he had parked his car in the space reverently saved for him by the police, he stepped into the plaza exactly as he had done forty years before when gathering the impressions that later served as the foundation for *The Sun Also Rises.*

'Adiós, Hemingway!' several Spaniards called, and a warm smile diffused the bloated face of my degenerate waiter as he cried, 'Don Ernesto! Welcome back to Pamplona.'

With much ceremony Hemingway was offered the table next to me, and two Spaniards asked for his autograph. Taking from an inner pocket of his field jacket a stack of printed calling cards, one face of which contained his photograph, he signed two and handed them graciously to the petitioners, who then withdrew.

'Are you Vanderford?' I asked across the tables.

'I am,' he said, and I was about to ask him for one of his famous cards when I was interrupted by two Pamplona newspapermen whom I had known some years before when making a pilgrimage to Santiago de Compostela. They wanted to know which bullfighter appearing in the feria had lured me back to San Fermín, or which parties at which café, and they were not prepared when I explained that I had come primarily in hope of meeting with Don Luis Morondo. The reporters hesitated a moment, as if they did not know the name of the man who is probably the most famous Pamplonan alive today. I thought it would be egregious of me to describe him any further, and I was pleased when one finally smiled and said, 'Oh, you mean Morondo the musician!'

I did indeed. For some years I had owned a fine phonograph record produced by Morondo and his chamber-music group from Pamplona, and I was so impressed by it—a collection of fifteenth- and sixteenth-century music sung a cappella—that I had made inquiries in musical circles in New York and London and found that among those who knew choral singing, Morondo's Pamplona group was considered one of the most polished ensembles. 'Can you arrange for me to meet him?' I asked the newspapermen.

'Perhaps,' they said, and I left them to attend a concert which Morondo was giving to honor the opening of San Fermín. On stage came sixteen singers, eight good-looking young women in evening dresses backed up by seven young men and one older man in tuxedos. Each man stood on a box of a different height, so that all seemed to be equally tall. Each singer wore the traditional red scarf of San Fermín. The group made a stunning appearance, but was its singing to be as good as I had heard on the record?

Then Morondo appeared, tall, slim, well groomed. He could have been a Spanish grandee in his fifties. With a minimum of gesture he launched his singers into a program which began with fifteenth-century church music and ended with 'Old Black Joe,' in honor of the Americans who had crowded into Pamplona. The Stephen Foster was sung in clear English and made an amusing effect, but the highlight of the performance was a work that fitted precisely the spirit of the feria, García Lorca's 'Lament for Ignacio Sánchez Mejías' arranged for choral group. At the repeated phrase, 'At five in the afternoon,' one could sense the beginning of the tragedy that would end in the death of this fine matador.

The group could sing. The individual pyrotechnics of the singers were less conspicuous than those of similar groups trained in London or Paris and there seemed to be less variation in attack and emphasis, but the ensemble singing, which is what such a group must master if it is to achieve a good reputation, was as good as any I had ever heard. There was less exhibitionism, less dramatic effect for effect's sake, than in a comparable American group, but a much nobler end result. If one demanded exciting solo work from either individual singers or the various choirs, he would not find it here, but if one sought a powerful and authentic total effect, here it was. The voices were wonderfully modulated, finely matched and superbly disciplined. It was obvious from the first note that Dr. Morondo had his group under control and that they sang pretty much as he wanted them to sing. I left the theater, thinking, It was worth the trip north to hear such music.

Next day I met Morondo, and close up he was even more impressive than he had been on the podium. He was taller than I had thought, had very blue eyes, a quiet voice and a most infectious smile. He wore an attractive jacket with no lapels and reminded me of a younger Toscanini. It was painful to discover that his life had been that of nearly every creative figure in Spain, an endless duplication of demanding jobs which taken together had barely paid enough wages for him to live and do the work of which he was capable. A pupil of a pupil of the Frenchman Dukas, Morondo had in recent years simplified his life: he now served as professor at the normal school, professor at the consistory, director of the orchestra, director of the choral group, lecturer at the university, plus teacher, advisor, consultant and friend to all young musicians in the area. In spite of this deluge he maintained a youthful appearance and a lively humor.

I began, 'Maestro, I've come to Pamplona to see you because in Avila I found myself perplexed about the problem of Spanish music.'

'I am too,' he replied.

'I've always heard of Felipe Pedrell [1841–1922] as the patron saint of modern Spanish music . . .'

I was not allowed to finish, for at the name of that great musicologist whose theories had inspired Albéniz, Granados, Turina and Falla, Morondo's face lit up and he cried, 'He was the master of us all.'

'But what actually did he accomplish?'

'He sent us back to Spanish themes, to the great work done by unknown Spanish song writers of the fifteenth and sixteenth centuries. You might say that all we've done has been built upon the bones of Pedrell.'

'Two problems confuse me.' I said. 'First, Pedrell in Spanish music seems to me like Squarcione in north Italian painting. Each was a notable teacher, but neither left much of his own work for us to hear or see. For twenty years I've been interested in Pedrell and I've yet to hear a note he wrote.'

'That can be corrected. I'll bring you his songbooks tomorrow.'

'Are there any recordings of his songs?'

'Actual recordings? No. But you hear Pedrell in all Spanish music. His songs live in all of us.' (During the rest of my stay in Spain I was not to hear a single note that Pedrell wrote, nor have I yet, but I sensed him to be a more important musician than many whose names and works I knew well.)

'Second problem. The individual themes that Pedrell brought to the attention of his group . . . Let's say the ones I hear in the four composers we named . . . They're some of the greatest themes in contemporary music. Better I'd say than similar national themes I find in Brahms, Dvořák, Smetana or Bartók.'

'I'd agree. They are supreme musical notations.' Morondo nodded. For eighteen years he had served as director of Spain's oldest symphony, the one Camille Saint-Saëns used to conduct, and he knew well the music I was speaking of.

'But Brahms and the others from the rest of Europe took poorer themes and made of them great symphonies and concertos and quartets. Why . . .'

Dr. Morondo interrupted me. 'You want to know why Spanish composers haven't done the same?'

'It seems to me they've abused the great material Pedrell handed them. They've utilized it on a lower level than was necessary.'

To this criticism Dr. Morondo preferred to make no comment, but some weeks later in Barcelona a more critical Spanish musician commented on the problems I had raised in Avila: 'When you demand that Falla and Albéniz take Spanish themes and build from them what Brahms and Dvořák built from theirs, you're out of your mind. Germany and Austria of that day had orchestras and opera companies and string ensembles that needed the music these men were writing. Spain did not. One small orchestra here, another there, a visiting opera company from Milan, and an audience who wanted to hear only *Carmen* and *La Bohème*. The

Spanish audience still doesn't want a symphony or an opera featuring a large ensemble and a complicated structure. It wants a short, individualized work and that's what the Spanish composer learned to supply. Zarzuela, not opera. Because symphonies and operas are not within our pattern. Besides, the material that Pedrell resurrected for these men was ideally suited to individual types of presentation. In criticizing Falla and Albéniz for not having produced in the grand manner, you are criticizing not the composers but the Spanish people, and you are betraying your own lack of understanding.'

'But do you agree,' I asked this Barcelona expert, 'that the themes themselves, those soaring, passionate Spanish groups of statements we find in Granados and Falla . . . They're better than what Brahms and Dvořák had to work with, aren't they?'

'Much better. But if you ask me next, "Then why didn't Spanish composers build better with those building blocks?" I'll have to repeat that your question makes no sense. It just doesn't relate to the facts in Spain.'

Back with Dr. Morondo, I changed the subject. 'The main reason I wanted to see you was to ask whether I'm correct in judging Victoria to be Spain's foremost composer?'

A look of joy suffused Morondo's agile face, and after nodding his dark head back and forth he said, 'There was the great one.'

'I'd hoped you'd have something of his on the concert yesterday.'

'A little too profound for opening a bullfight.'

I told him of my embarrassing experience in thinking for so many years that Victoria was an Italian, and he laughed. 'Many people still do. It's Italy's revenge for our stealing Colón.' I then explained how Victoria's 'Ave Maria' had come to mean so much to me, and Morondo began to hum the opening notes of this composition, those marvelous sequences broken in rhythm and emphasis. He conducted as he sang and I joined him in this haunting masterpiece, but when we came to the 'Ora pro nobis' with its majestic theme and timeless devotion he threw up his hands, halted his unseen choir and cried, 'What dramatic use of words and music. Victoria could do what none of us have been able to do since.' He then asked me if I knew Victoria's *Officium Hebdomadae Sanctae* (The Offices of Holy Week, 1585), and when I said no he promised to bring me a score to study, and this he did and to my pleasure I discovered that the nine *Responsories for Tenebrae* which I liked so much were part of this noble work. The *Officium* has not yet been recorded in its entirety, so I have not heard it, but from the fragments I have been able to acquire here and there I judge Morondo to have been correct in calling it Victoria's masterpiece.

Before I left America, André Kostelanetz had advised me, when in Pamplona, to visit the Pablo de Sarasate museum containing mementos of the violinist who began in Pamplona and startled the world with his virtuoso playing, and as I looked at the old programs with their florid fruit-flower embellishments, I recalled a dictum I had read years before: 'Spanish music has always been designed for the individual.' If this is true then some of the flamboyant compositions of Sarasate are closer to the essential spirit of Spain than the symphonic work of Turina, which I like. In praising Turina, I am perhaps being obstinate; but even though Spaniards insist that the symphony is not suited to their cast of mind, I prefer the reasoned symphony of Turina to the brilliant incidental pieces of Albéniz and Granados; in fact, I have begun to suspect that Pedrell was the evil genius of Spanish music. Had he not come along to draw his followers into the bypaths of antique themes, wonderful as they are, might not Spanish music have matured into major forms as did the music of Hungary, Austria and Czechoslovakia?

About the Pamplona cathedral I had no hesitation. It is the ugliest beautiful church in existence, and to study it carefully over repeated hours is an experience in art that proves invaluable to people like dress designers and poets. The beauty is provided by the cloisters, which cannot be equaled in northern Spain for graciousness and intricate Gothic poetry; critics have praised them in terms which I do not find excessive. The interior, with six fine arches running down each side of the nave, with spacious aisle and lovely chapels, is also a handsome creation, and when the especially strong transept is added, with soaring stone arches where it crosses the nave, one has a noble place of worship, not particularly spiritual, perhaps, but clean and hard as befits the north. I have always liked the beautifully carved tombs of King Carlos III of Navarra and his Queen Leonora as they stand exposed before the altar, for in them one sees carving of a high order, and they lend both royalty and somberness to the soaring interior.

It is the façade which provides the ugliness. Originally it seems to have been a perfectly good Gothic work suited to the cloister and the spacious interior, but at the end of the eighteenth century the architect Ventura Rodríguez, who had acquired a national reputation as the man who could be trusted to improve old churches, which he had done in other parts of Spain, was invited to try his luck on Pamplona. He proceeded to tear down the existing Gothic façade and to erect in its place a Greco-Roman horror that makes the once-gracious building look like the courthouse of Deaf Smith County, Texas. It is so bad it must be seen to be believed. I had very much hoped Robert Vavra would choose to photograph it for this book, but he said, 'It's so ugly that no film can do it justice.'

The tall Gothic towers have become blunt and squat, one a rigid duplicate of the other. Each is composed of many disparate elements that add up to miserable failure. Eight rather good Corinthian columns fail to convey any sense of loftiness because they are capped by a pediment totally lacking in inspiration. The main feature is a pair of horrible plaster angels in exaggerated poses between two senseless urns. Over the main door leading to the nave an Assumption of the Virgin of no discernible style whatever was added in 1956, while on the right tower a sundial has been placed, which because of the orientation of the church can tell time for only a few hours in the late afternoon. Finally, as if the twentieth century sought to help the eighteenth in the job of destroying a beautiful building, atop the whole is a huge and glaring neon cross.

I think a protracted study of the Pamplona cathedral should be obligatory for anyone who plans to revise the work of others who have gone before him. A composer who plans to update Victoria's 'Ave Maria' should see what happened when Rodríguez updated a Gothic cathedral. A film director about to improve on Molière should remind himself of the disaster that sometimes overtakes such ventures. If a whole work falls out of style, as can well happen, the fall will be mitigated by a certain inherent grace, whereas if one refurbishes a Gothic cathedral with a Greco-Roman façade, a couple of plaster angels and a neon cross, only confusion can result. I was reminded of something Ernest Hemingway said of motion pictures that had been made from his works: 'I attend each one with a trusted friend and a quart of gin and I haven't been able to last through any of them yet.'

There could be no locale more appropriate for recalling Hemingway than Pamplona during San Fermín and no year more suitable than this, for that morning in formal ceremony at the town hall the alcalde had conferred on Hemingway posthumously the distinction of the honorary red scarf of San Fermín, and the crowd had nostalgically approved; so in the evening I invited to the Caballo Blanco (White Horse), perched on the city walls, four devotees of Hemingway who had known him in the final years. I promised them mixed salad, a copious menestra and conversation, and I was gratified when they appeared: Juanito Quintana, who had served as prototype for Montoya in *The Sun Also Rises;* Kenneth Vanderford, that strange Ph.D. from Indiana whom I had met in the plaza; John Fulton, whom Hemingway had befriended in the last years; and Robert Vavra, to whom Hemingway had been especially kind.

When we took our seats in the handsome tavern—recently assembled on this spot, using stones and floor plans borrowed from various Renaissance ruins that were about to be torn down in other parts of Pamplona —the two women who ran the place brought bowls of mixed salad heavy with onion, olive oil and sharp vinegar, and we remarked how fortunate the timing of San Fermín was: it arrived just as the crisp lettuce, the red tomatoes and the strong onions ripen, so that all during feria one can eat this astringent dish. Tonight there would also be my favorite of northern Spain, menestra. In hot olive oil cloves of garlic are browned; vegetables of all kinds, including especially artichokes, are added until a soup is formed, then shellfish previously cooked, plus a boiled chicken. The whole is put in

Some handsome things of great age
should be left as they are.

the oven until properly blended, then served with onion bread and grated cheese.

When the menestra was finished and the flan was being served, cold and shimmering and golden, the conversation began, and I would like to report exactly what was said, retaining the contradictions and false starts as they occurred that night.

Michener: I've been reading Hotchner's book on Hemingway and I've asked you here to help on one point. Hotchner claims that in that last year when we saw Hemingway, he'd already begun to fall apart inside and was contemplating suicide. Did you catch any glimpse of that?

Quintana: I was close to him at that time. He never gave a hint that he might commit suicide.

Vavra: I certainly saw nothing. What impressed me was his willingness to help Fulton. At the Miramar Hotel in Málaga he took me aside and said, 'Fulton has guts and I know you kids are having it tough in this ambiente. I'd like to help.' Well, a lot of people said that in those days but nothing ever happened. And like all the rest, Hemingway left without doing anything. But about a week later, when I thought he had forgotten his promise, he very quietly slipped me a hundred-dollar traveler's check. For weeks we didn't cash it. Just sat looking at it.

Michener: You notice anything strange about him, John?

Fulton: One important thing. I'd read about his love for Maera, who was one of the great old bullfighters, a real man, and I simply couldn't comprehend his sudden affection for Ordóñez and Dominguín, they simply weren't in Maera's class as rugged men.

Vavra: At Málaga I heard Hemingway say, 'Poor boys, Ordóñez and Dominguín. They're really having it tough. Fight in the north one day, have to fly all the way to the south that night, then fight again next day.'

Fulton: Maera used to make such trips by car. And old cars, at that. And arrive shaken up and without sleep. And go out and fight Miuras. I never understood Hemingway's sudden debasement of his critical values.

Michener: Did he know much about bullfighting?

Vanderford: He knew a great deal. But the Spaniards love to put him down. They ridicule his knowledge of the bulls.

Vavra: But they ridiculed him only after his article criticizing Manolete, the article in which he put Manolete down for the very things that Spanish writers had been criticizing for years.

Vanderford: Yes, especially then, but I don't believe Spanish bullfight critics have ever taken Hemingway very seriously, or any Anglo-Saxon expert on the bulls. To show you how Spaniards reacted to Hemingway's remarks on Manolete, K-Hito, one of the best critics, wrote an indignant article which he concluded by stating that in the future, of the two Hemingways, I was to be known as 'Hemingway el Bueno,' meaning that the real one was a bum.

Vavra: Strange that he was so Madrid-oriented. Andalucía, the cradle of bullfighting, never much interested him, nor did Mexico.

Quintana: I met Ernesto when he first came to Spain. He stayed in my father's hotel. Hotel Quintana, on the square where the Bar Brasil now is. And he knew almost nothing about the bulls. Couldn't speak any Spanish either. I was a great admirer of Maera and I introduced Hemingway to him. I was amazed at how quickly this man could learn. He had a fantastic identification with the drama of the ring and caught on immediately. By the time he left Spain he knew bullfighting as well as any of us.

Michener: How did he treat you?

Quintana: Always a marvelous friend. Once he said, 'Juanito, you're never to worry about money. You've been my constant friend and I'm going to take care of you.'

Michener: Did he?

Quintana: No.

Michener: The Hotchner book says he kept you on his payroll. Sent you money regularly from the States.

Quintana: That book has done me much harm. If you want the facts, as a friend I can trust, here they are. Ernesto paid me faithfully every peseta he ever owed me, but only what he owed. Never sent me a penny from America. Only for services I performed in Spain. As a guide, that is. Since his death, people who were connected with him send me letters all the time asking for copies of this paper or that, so I get the photocopies made and send them to the States, but no one ever sends me expenses for the work. Nor even thank-you letters for my time and money.

Michener: The book says Hemingway was fed up with you. For having failed to get tickets for the bullfights in Pamplona.

Quintana: Señor Hotchner wasn't even with Hemingway when this was supposed to have happened. He hadn't asked me to get any tickets. In those days tickets were easy to come by. You could buy your own. I remember when I first met Hotchner. Little town called Aranda de Duero. Hemingway treated him with indifference. Certainly the great friendship Hotchner speaks of wasn't visible to me . . . or to any of the rest of us.

Michener: I take it you didn't like the book.

Quintana: Much was truthful and very sweet in its picture of Ernesto. But the bad things about me . . . I remember the day I introduced Hemingway to Ordóñez, here in Pamplona. It's not good to be made fun of.

Vanderford: You keep asking questions, Michener. What did you think about Hemingway?

Michener: One of the things I'm proudest of in my life is that when I was in the trenches in Korea, *Life* magazine sent me the galleys of Hemingway's *The Old Man and the Sea*. Wanted me to make a statement to sort of back them up in their venture of publishing the whole thing in one issue. So there I sat, absolutely cold turkey, knowing nothing about the book and remembering the debacle of *Across the River and into the Trees*, and how the critics had slaughtered him, and I was praying that this one would be good so that he could regain his reputation. So I read it by lantern light with the Chinese popping at us from across the valley, and a great lump came in my throat, and when I finished I wrote something about feeling good when the daddy of us all won back the heavyweight crown. I was the first to read it. And stick my neck out. It was used in full-page ads across the country. One of the best things I ever did.

Vavra: Did he ever say anything about it?

Michener: I met him only once. For about twenty minutes. I was working in New York, and Leonard Lyons, who was a close friend of Hemingway's, called at lunchtime and said, 'Papa's in town. He's having lunch at Toots Shor's. You want to meet him?' I did, very much, but couldn't get away. About four in the afternoon I was walking down Fifty-first Street to my hotel, and as I passed Shor's I thought, Hemingway may still be in there. So I went inside. Lyons was gone but Hemingway was in a corner surrounded by men I didn't know. Only one I knew was Toots Shor. After a while I introduced myself and Hemingway was embarrassed and I was embarrassed. He knew what I'd written about *The Old Man*, but we were both embarrassed. So he did all the talking, and I remember two things he said. That the time came when a man didn't want to be known locally as a distinguished Philadelphia novelist but wanted to put his work up against the best in the world. He had put his up against Pío Baroja and Flaubert, and any man who was satisfied to be idolized locally was a crapper. He also said he couldn't stand what the movies had done to his things.

Quintana: When he saw *The Sun Also Rises* he was very angry, and I asked, 'Where are you going?' and he said, 'To have a fistfight with Darryl Zanuck.' He asked me what I thought of the picture, and I said, 'Terrible. They made me short, with a ruddy face and very large cheeks. And they used a Mexican actor to play me . . . a Spaniard!' Ernesto laughed.

Fulton: He was always concerned with how he looked. You might even say

Quintana, friend of Ernest Hemingway;
Vanderford, the poor man's Hemingway;
and the Conde de la Corte, famous bull breeder.

495

he was vain. Arjona, the photographer from Sevilla, took a shot of him on a cold blustery day. Came out very bad. Reluctantly Hemingway signed a copy for me, 'To John Fulton, with best wishes from his paisano, Ernest Hemingway.'

Vavra: But when I pushed my copy of the same picture under his nose, he groaned, 'I'll be damned if I'll sign that one again,' so he drew a cartoonist's balloon out from his mouth and inside wrote the word 'Mierda,' and that's all he would do.

Fulton: Tell about the bullfight articles you'd written?

Vavra: I showed him some criticisms I'd written for a magazine in the States, and he read them carefully, put them down and said, 'It's easy for a critic to make wisecracks. It's easy to be clever. But its goddamned hard to be truthful. Now you sit down and write half a dozen more and I'll go over them with you. And we'll cut out the cheap cracks. Because a real critic is after the truth which the writer or the matador doesn't see for himself. Cheap cracks are the concern of vaudeville.'

Michener: In these last years what was he like as a man?

Vanderford: Class all the way. And with me he was a gentleman, too. He must have been irritated that I looked so much like him. Baseball cap and everything. But I'd had my beard long before I tangled with Hemingway. Anyway, he could have raised hell about me but he didn't. I remember when someone showed him one of his novels I had autographed: 'All that glitters is not gold nor is every man with a white beard named . . . Ernest Hemingway.' He looked at it, laughed and told reporters, 'I don't care what the sonofabitch signs so long as it isn't my checks or my contracts.' He showed class.

Fulton: He seemed anxious to help me and other Americans. Asked me, 'What can I do to help?' I said, 'For instance, you can ask Ordóñez to let me serve in one of his fights as sobresaliente [understudy].' He said, 'You're an American and I'm an American. If I can help I will.' Two days later he told me Ordóñez had said, 'Sobresaliente is for boys who are down and out.' But Hemingway said, 'This is a good fighter,' so Ordóñez agreed, 'I'll set it up for Ciudad Real.' I waited and the Ciudad Real date came and went. Then I had a letter from Hemingway's secretary telling me that Hotchner, who had never faced a bull, had got the job as sobresaliente. That fight was important to me . . . could have been very important in my career. It was disgusting to learn that such a mockery had been made of bullfighting.

Quintana: In the last year Ernesto was the prisoner of the people around him. But he still behaved with gracia. The people of Pamplona loved him.

Vanderford: But Hemingway could be ungracious too. Back in 1929 a little old lady . . . A retired schoolteacher, I'd guess. She approached him and said, 'Mr. Hemingway, I saw my first bullfight this afternoon and frankly I didn't like it as well as I thought I would from reading your description.' He could easily have replied, 'Well, there's no accounting for tastes,' or something neutral like that. But he asked, 'How much did you pay for your ticket?' She said, 'Three hundred pesetas.' He pulled some bills from his pocket, thrust them at her and said, 'Here's your money.' She wouldn't accept it.

Quintana: On the other hand, people who were jealous of him were always trying to make scenes. They didn't know him, so they said he was a drunk and a fighter.

Vavra: I found that out when I tried to track down the truth about the famous incident with Matt Carney. In a bar I heard some guy saying, 'Matt Carney tried to drink a toast with Hemingway, but the old man grabbed the bota, threw it a mile and cursed Matt vilely.' This didn't sound like the Hemingway I knew, so I asked around to get the true story. Seems Hemingway was giving a party and Matt tried to barge in. He was drunk and abusive, but Hemingway treated him gently and said, 'I can't drink with you now.' It was Carney who used the foul language, not Hemingway. Matter of fact, Hemingway tried to ease him away so the cops wouldn't arrest him. That's how they slander Hemingway in Spanish bars.

Vanderford: Michener still hasn't said what he thinks about the Hotchner book.

Michener: In our family it caused a brouhaha. Mari, as the wife of a writer, sided with Mary Hemingway. She thought the book was an unwarranted and inaccurate invasion of privacy and she wanted the courts to forbid its publication, even though it was our own publisher, Random House, who was defending the right to publish. Mari told Bennett Cerf, 'I side with the enemy.' I felt the opposite. Hemingway was a public figure and relevant facts about him should not be held from the public. I take my attitude on such matters from the Supreme Court decision in the case where some jerk called Senator Joe Clark a Communist. Clark sued for libel, and the Court held that when Clark entered the race for the Senate he offered himself as a public figure, which made him fair game for anything anyone wanted to say against him, so long as it wasn't part of a malicious conspiracy.

Vanderford: How does this apply to Hemingway?

Michener: Hemingway went to great lengths to constitute himself a public figure and Hotchner had every right to comment about the operation.

Vanderford: Even about the suicide?

Michener: Especially the suicide. Hemingway's whole public life was dedicated to the creation of a legend. And a legend with certain implications. Therefore, the suicide must not be seen as the act of a casual individual but as the culmination of a carefully prepared legend. Now, either the final act was in conformity with legend or it wasn't.

Vanderford: What do you think?

Michener: I've told you I wanted it printed.

Vavra: But when it was printed? What then? Because of its errors it's a betrayal of friendship. On the part of a guy who, it seems to me, had never really understood or known Hemingway. If you're going to do something like that you have to do it right. Tell the whole story and be honest about it.

Michener: Maybe that's why I liked it. It was a legend about a legend. As I read it I said, 'Hotchner gives me a picture of Hemingway the brawler, the boaster, the race-track tout, the Cuban exile. But he doesn't give me one glimpse of the man who wrote the great books.'

Vavra: How can you say that's good?

Michener: Because I think the lives of writers are like that. I think that now and then the public should see the terrifying contradictions. I can't get out of my mind an interview that *Time* magazine carried with Hemingway. They played it up like the word of God, and one part especially they carried in a box . . . for effect . . . Hemingway saying that as long as man's juices were running he was in good shape . . . and boasted to the world that his were still running. Very sexy. Very tough. But at the end of the Hotchner book we are shown a pitiful man who confesses that his juices have stopped running . . . nothing in life . . . no sex . . . no fun . . . so he blows his brains out. I've got to compare him with men like Verdi and Michelangelo and Hokusai, who never talked tough but who did their best work when they were old, old men. To them there was something superior to the running of juices.

Quintana: You're wrong when you say he committed suicide. I don't believe that. Not long before he died I had a wire from Ketchum, Idaho. From Ernesto, saying he wanted the best seats at Pamplona. He planned to be with us, that I know. Of course, he'd been drinking too much and had been told to stop. But not suicide. That wasn't in his mind.

Fulton: On the day the news came over the wire I went out to see Juan Belmonte and told him, 'Don Ernesto just committed suicide,' and Belmonte said, very slowly and very clearly, 'Well done.' In Belmonte's autobiography there's a long passage about how Belmonte had wavered about committing suicide in 1915. Had an obsession about it, and Hemingway knew this. Anyway, a little while later Belmonte, the greatest of them all . . . Well, he shot himself the same way. Right through the head.

Quintana: And you, Michener, what did you think?

Michener: I think he acted properly. He had built himself into a legend and when it showed signs of blowing up in his face he ended it with distinction. An act in harmony with the legend. He proved he was as tough as he had claimed to be.

Vavra: Then you knew it was suicide?

Michener: How could it have been anything else? Remember that time Hemingway came through Madrid incognito? Insisted he wanted no publicity. Big beard. Baseball cap. Hunting jacket. Wherever he went those six or eight bodyguards clearing the way for him. It was the most conspicuous literary disguise since Leo Tolstoy used to go around in his muzhik's costume. And you could see he loved every phony minute of it. But such performances run the risk of blowing up. And when his threatened to do so, he had the gracia to end the legend with a splendid gesture. The best thing about the suicide was that it was artistically right. And I'm damned sure he realized it.

I left the dinner party and wandered back to the square, where by purest chance someone said, 'That's Matt Carney over there. You want to get the straight dope about his fight with Hemingway?'

It was in this way that I met the legendary Carney, a forty-year-old California Irishman who, his friends are convinced, will become a first-rate novelist. Many years ago he came to Europe to finish a book but as he was knocking about Paris he was spotted by an agent whose job it was to find male models for advertising. Carney had the rugged New World look of a Mississippi gambler, and French advertisers flocked to him in such numbers that he earned a great deal of money. He was conned into posing for high-fashion ads and soon found himself the pin-up boy of Paris. For the past seven years he had been working on a novel, *Run Out of Time*, but had been somewhat sidetracked by the purchase of a bar in Torremolinos. He loved Spain and spoke like a drunken angel, with fiery Irish eloquence, and as he approached my table I saw that his handsome features were marked by a colossal black eye, which made him doubly Irish and doubly handsome.

'Who hung the mouse on you?' I asked.

'A Basque woodchopper with a right hand of phenomenal speed. But as I went down I had the presence of mind to kick him in the balls and when he doubled up I knocked out one of his front teeth. So now he's a Basque woodchopper with a phenomenal right and one missing tooth.'

A habitué of the bar ran up with a set of photographs from that morning's running of the bulls, and the photographers had caught Matt in regulation Pamplona costume of white shirt, white pants, red scarf and sash and rope-soled shoes, running about six inches in front of the horns of a massive bull. Later pictures in the sequence showed him flat on his face, with bulls, oxen and people running over him. A final shot showed him up and grinning, with his fantastic black eye.

'A very fine run,' he said as he studied the photographs, but in his opinion it did not equal the one which some photographer had caught four

years ago in color film. Matt had a copy of the postcard which was now sold in Pamplona souvenir shops. It showed him sprinting for life ahead of a bewildered bull whose left horn was about to toss him far and wide.

'He gave me a neat six-inch scratch which wasn't particularly dangerous, but could have been.' I suggested that judging from the photographs, he must carry quite a few horn wounds on his hungry-looking body. 'Nope. I've been lucky. But I do have this one to muzzle those clowns in Paris who sit around cafés explaining how to run the bulls at Pamplona.'

'How many years you been coming here?'

'This is my fourteenth. The running this morning was fine. Not great. Bulls couldn't catch up with the runners. But it would have to be graded fine.'

'Would you tell me what happened with Hemingway?'

'Will you treat it with respect?'

'In your words.'

He ordered a beer, sat back, fingered the edge of his eye and said, 'I revere Hemingway. And years ago I revered him even more. So this evening at San Fermín, I was sitting here, where you are, and he was over there, where Orson Welles is sitting now. He was with the elite of the feria, everyone important, and I looked like a real bum. Drunker than I am now. He had done some of the good writing of our generation. I'd done nothing more permanent than a popcorn fart in a typhoon. So I grabbed my bota, staggered over to his table and shouted, "Hemingway, you old bastard, have a drink with me." Mary Hemingway said, "Please don't. He's drunk." So I shouted, "Drunk or sober, Hemingway, have a drink with me," so he grabbed the bota, wound up and threw it as far as he could. It landed on a truck in the street, and I announced in a loud clear voice, "Mr. Ernest Hemingway, fuck you!" At this he brushed Mary away, leaped to his feet and began cursing me. He lunged at me and I was going to break him in half, fat old man that he was, but two Swedes dragged me away, and that night when I got back to my room I wrote a letter to him and said, "Mr. Hemingway, I revere you as one of the fine writers of my generation and I am overcome with remorse that I should have behaved in such a way. Please forgive me." I gave the letter to Peter Buckley, who did that great book on bulls in Spain, and he delivered it to Hemingway, but Big Dave, who was there at the time, told me that Hemingway took one look at the letter, sneered and tore it up. He was real big talking about brawls and that, but when he had one in his lap he didn't know what to do nor how to end it. To me Ernest Hemingway is a crock of shit.'

The one good eye that I could see was steely blue and the craggy face was resolute. The sandy hair, with a few streaks of gray, was tousled and the faded red scarf was pinned at the neck with the diagonal shields of San Fermín. At the edge of his shirt a jagged horn scar showed across his chest.

'The scar? How'd you get it?'

501

Matt Carney.

'I have this crazy thing. All year long, when I'm working in Paris, I keep thinking of Pamplona. San Fermín. To run, to touch, to feel the horn tips edging closer.'

'Is it something mystical?' I asked.

Matt looked at me as if I were out of my mind. 'Christ, you miss the whole flaming point. It's fun! It's joy!' He showed me a photograph from the morning paper and I suppose that in years to come this shot will often be seen in books, for there was Matt galloping a few inches ahead of the steers and bulls, alone and laughing his Irish head off. It was as lovely a portrait of man's inherent nonsense as I had ever seen. 'I run the bulls for joy, which is the chief ingredient in generosity. In this way I prove that I have the capacity to give myself whole hog to some activity.'

'Do you run to prove your bravery?' I asked, for in recent years the most courageous acts at Pamplona had been Matt's.

'To stand in the street before the run begins . . . to visualize the bulls coming at you . . . to sense what might happen . . . yes, that takes courage. But when those rockets go off and the black shapes come tumbling at you . . . Hell, you've already made your commitment and all it takes now is a sense of joy . . . to be part of the stampede.'

'Yet you think that Hemingway was a crock of crap?'

'I must. He glorified this sort of thing, but when it came to him, face to face with a bota of red wine, he didn't know how to handle it. No gracia. No understanding. A good writer. Not the greatest man. But a good writer.'

In this book I have tried to keep the focus on Spain and Spaniards rather than upon the experiences and opinions of foreign visitors. I have filed away those diverting accounts of what happened to a German in Córdoba or to an Englishman in Badajoz, but in this material on Pamplona during San Fermín, I must speak of foreigners, because the city is crammed with them and it is what happens to them that makes the festival intriguing. If three beautiful Swedish girls of nineteen can find no place to sleep but in the street, one cannot ignore them, nor can he close his eyes to a sports car filled with six handsome juniors from the University of California, three girls, three boys, who sleep sitting in their car near a main intersection.

I am not, however, going to deal with the young punks who have come here for a sexual holiday; what with the shortage of beds in Pamplona they could do better elsewhere. Nor am I concerned about the various groups who look at one running of the bulls, attend one bullfight and spend the rest of their time at LSD and marijuana parties. What I am involved with are those lineal descendants of Ernest Hemingway and his fictional characters who four decades ago discovered the high hilarity of San Fermín, which through the years has not diminished.

To understand the magic of Pamplona one must follow the passage of

Once a year, and once only, the citizens of Pamplona are not limited in the amount they drink or where they drink it or where they sleep it off.

a typical day. The feria, which regularly starts on July 7, San Fermín Day, is billed throughout Spain as the festival of the bulls, signifying that for once in the mean and ugly world of bullfighting the animal himself, known as the only element in the fight that has not been corrupted, is meant to be king. And in a sense he is.

Shortly before midnight, in the darkened streets of the lower part of town where barricades have been erected to form a runway, the bulls for the next day's fight are turned loose from the reception pens known as the Corrales de Gas, run across the river on a narrow bridge, then up the steep hill to the temporary corral at the bottom of the Calle Santo Domingo, where they will spend the rest of the night. It is an eerie thing to see the hurrying bulls loom through the darkness and rush past on almost silent hoofs. They are frightened by the dash across the bridge and uncertain about the rush up the hill, so they run with concentrated purpose, like ghosts who have little time for their night journey. A rush, the rattle of hoofs on paving stones, an echo of panting, the clean, lingering smell of animals on the night air and they are gone, mysteriously and with a sense of great drama.

From midnight, with the bulls now safely in their corral, until six o'clock in the morning, when the bands begin to play in all parts of town, Pamplona is a dream city. At the Bar Txoco on the square, customers from Scandinavia and Germany, delighted to be again where there is warmth, sit all night at small tables drinking beer. At the next bar my degenerate waiter whispers, 'Shift over to this table, and I can serve you.' With every order the Swedes give him, he pours one for himself, and for the whole eight days he will be drunk. In cars parked throughout the city, boys from Harvard and girls from Wellesley sleep on back seats, wrapped in blankets. Bank lobbies have been thrown open by the police, and college students from Oxford and the Sorbonne sleep on the marble, boy-girl, boy-girl, boy-girl, right up to the teller's cage. Others, not lucky enough to get into the banks, sleep on the sidewalks; and in the public square by the bandstand, hundreds lie on benches or on the grass. The town is a vast open-air dormitory, and each sleeper has about his throat the red scarf of San Fermín and in his hand a bota of red wine.

At a quarter to six bands playing the music of Navarra start circulating through all parts of the city, wakening both those who slept in beds and those who did not. If the sleeper is fortunate he is awakened not by a brass band but by one of the three-man groups consisting of two playing antique oboes and one beating a drum, for if there is sweeter music on earth I have not heard it. The sound that comes from these old oboes is like the whispering of a thousand birds at dawn; it is the fairy music that elves dance to; it is the Middle Ages captured in haunting notes; and long after all else in Pamplona has been forgotten, these delicious sounds will echo in the memories of men and women in small towns in Norway and Peru, those who were wakened at Pamplona by the oboes. I once had a record of them on their morning rounds, and at a house party in southern Spain I would occasionally play it on the gramophone, and those in the audience who had not known the music at San Fermín would ask, 'What's that wailing?' But those who had wakened to it during the feria would have tears in their eyes.

By six o'clock the streets of Pamplona are jammed with twenty or thirty thousand people, from boys of five to old couples of eighty, for to lie late abed during San Fermín would be insanity. Some fourteen thousand of these early risers are heading toward the bullring, and now one begins to understand why Pamplona is such an ideal spot for an all-out feria like this. The bullring is practically in the center of town, a couple of short blocks from the central square, so that life moves alternately from the ring to the square.

At the bullring, people pay sixty cents for entrance to what will become a major part of the feria. The real fun won't start till seven, but shortly after six a band, led by a zany conductor with a magisterial sense of comedy, entertains the crowd with songs of Navarra and nonsense of a high order. It's a bright, lovely part of the day and time passes swiftly.

Meanwhile, along a course nine hundred yards long and leading through the very heart of the city, temporary barricades have been erected in such manner that later on they can be dismantled in about ten minutes and stored along the sidewalk for use next morning. When in place, and it takes a goodly number of men to gear them properly, these barricades form a continuous runway from the Santo Domingo corrals, up to the colorful town hall, along Doña Blanca de Navarra (formerly known as Mercaderes), then up the historic Estafeta, an extremely narrow street, through an open square and into the tightly barricaded chute that will throw the stampeding animals into the bullring itself.

At half past six this narrow course has attracted young men from all parts of Europe, and some not so young. Matt Carney is running for the eighty-fourth morning. Tigre's tall son is running for his fourth; already he's been on the tips of the bulls' horns, but without incident. John Fulton and several Spanish matadors will run for the fun of it, and because they inherently love the bulls and enjoy being with them in any circumstances. Even Kenneth Vanderford, in his Hemingway cap, will be running, and he will by no means be the oldest participant, for yesterday a man of seventy-five was pegged by the bulls and is now in the hospital. It is a madness, this running with the bulls, and it never leaves a man's blood.

Promptly at seven a powerful rocket flies into the air and explodes aloft to signify that the gates to the corral have been opened. As soon as all the startled animals have dashed into the street, a second rocket explodes to warn everyone that they are on their way, six bulls and six large oxen pounding ahead at a full gallop up Santo Domingo, past the military hospital and into the square before the town hall. They run extremely fast, and as they go men run ahead of them, seeming to fly along the narrow streets. But since the bulls can run much faster than the men, the animals catch up with the speeding humans and sometimes knock them down or one man trips over another and there is a pile-up. When you first see a batch of runners stumble and fall into a heap, with enraged bulls bearing down upon them, you think, My God! They'll be killed.

But the forward motion of the bulls is such that they prefer to surge onward with the oxen rather than lag behind to fight with fallen men. I have seen incredible accumulations in which several dozen men have formed a mad pile in front of the flying animals, but the latter have plunged ahead, fighting to get over the human barricade, and whereas they have bruised some with their heavy hoofs they have not bothered any with their horns. If a man falls and can roll into the gutter and lie motionless, there's a good chance he will escape.

It is when a bull becomes detached from the herd and finds himself alone that he panics. Then he starts slashing out with his horns and darting with savage speed at whatever confuses him. It is then that young men, no matter how adept at dodging, go to the hospital. Over the years, of a hundred men wounded by horns at Pamplona, fully ninety-five have been

In the last century only butchers and those
who worked with cattle ran in the streets
before the bulls. Today any adventurer
from Vienna or Pasadena
is entitled to do so.

In ancient Greece and Rome and especially on the
island of Crete valor was proved by a man's
willingness to touch his fingers to the horns
of a wild bull. In Pamplona today the same ritual
persists unconsciously. Honor and virility are
believed to be bestowed by proximity to the bull.

wounded by solitary bulls who have been isolated as they rush toward the arena. But even if a man does get trapped by a lone bull, and even if the horns are two inches from his gut, there's always the likelihood that some other runner will attract the bull's attention at the last fragment of a second, and the horn will miss. When this happens people say, 'San Fermín came down to make the save.' San Fermín protects a lot of lives.

It takes the animals about two minutes to gallop the nine hundred yards, and now they thunder into the bullring, where some thousand runners have preceded them, and again the animals stay bunched and drive like lemmings for the exit that will take them to the corrals behind the stands. But again, if one bull gets detached he will drive and hook at anything that comes his way until he is lured by capes into the exit. One morning I had proof of this. Because I could not run with the bulls, the city authorities had granted me a pass permitting me to perch atop the barricade at the chute, and after the bulls were well past and safely in their pens I walked fat and happy into the arena in what I judged was complete safety, only to find that a huge red bull had become detached from the oxen and was running in a great circle about the arena on a course which brought him almost face to face with me as I stepped into the sunlight. I practically fainted with astonishment, to see that huge, horned face looming so close to mine, but he was intent on finding his mates and San Fermín led him on.

Rules for running with bulls are not haphazard. A local ordinance governs, and copies are widely distributed. The crucial rule, and one that could not be known intuitively, is that no runner may in any way attract the attention of the bulls by waving his arms or anything else. To do so might attract the bull not to himself but to someone farther on who is unaware of what is being done and is therefore unprotected. Also, once the bulls have caught up with a runner and passed him, he may not run at their heels, lest they sense him there and turn back into the crowd. Women may not run, nor drunks, nor men with unusual costumes that might attract the bulls in their direction. The governing concept is that once the bulls are started on their course, clearly marked by fences, they will keep going unless someone radically diverts their attention and lures them into masses of unsuspecting people. I have seen six bulls run right over a pile of twenty or thirty fallen bodies, so intent were they in plunging ahead. Had anyone at that moment sidetracked their herding instinct, someone would surely have been hurt.

When all the bulls are safely inside the bullring corrals a final rocket is fired to announce that all is well. If it goes off in less than three minutes, listeners know that the bulls made a good run without any having been detached from the herd, but if the final rocket is much delayed, apprehension grows. A bull may have become separated and young men from Norway and Holland may be pinned against the improvised barriers at the town hall or against some shop door in Estafeta.

Now that the bulls are out of the ring and it remains filled with young men in white trousers and red sashes, a different gate is thrown open and into the crowd catapults a heifer, the tips of her horns covered with leather. Year for year and pound for pound, the female of the fighting strain is as brave and rough as the male, a fact which she proceeds to demonstrate by slashing into the men and knocking them over as if they were tenpins. The audience roars its approval as the heifer sweeps the arena. She is like a charge of compressed dynamite, for her energy seems tireless and her aim unerring. She runs like this for eight or ten minutes, dispensing contusions as if they were kisses, but there is one group of men who bewilder her, and these she damages but does not disperse.

Among college students it is considered gallant to take up a position directly in front of the gate from which the vigorous heifer emerges into the arena. There they form a pile of some sixty or seventy students, several bodies high, and in this uncomfortable formation they wait the charge of the animal. I've seen heifers hit this pile of humanity like thunderbolts, bore into it with horns slashing and feet pumping, only to be defeated by the sheer bulk of the bodies. The students protect their heads, but their backs and bottoms sometimes take serious punishment. Yet there they are, piled up and waiting as each heifer emerges. They are the stars of the morning.

Each day some five or six heifers are thrown into the arena, occasionally two at the same time, and the havoc is hilarious. The band plays, people cheer, students limp off to the hospital, teeth are loosened, but the only real brawl I ever saw came when a bulldogger from Texas started to wrestle a heifer to the ground. Everyone in the arena who could lay a hand on the Texan beat the bejeezus out of him, knocking him flat and bruising him rather badly. It is forbidden to grab the heifer in any way or to strike her with anything but a rolled-up newspaper; she has all the privileges and that way the fun is better.

It is now eight o'clock, when the all-nighters drift off for a few hours' sleep. Others wander back to the central square, where the waiter whispers, 'Pssst, move over here!' Hot coffee and croissants are the order, and in many languages people discuss the events of the morning. At eleven, enterprising photographers appear with their postcards recording that day's excitement, and one shows Matt Carney, wild grin on his face, going down before a stray bull, while Tigre's son and John Fulton can be seen artfully dodging the pack as it sweeps by. A lot of astonished people in America and Scandinavia are going to receive these cards in a few days, showing their neighbors in extraordinary predicaments.

At high noon Don Luis Morondo will lead his a cappella group in a concert of sixteenth-century motets and at three a company of comedians from Madrid will perform in *La tía de Carlos* (*Charley's Aunt*), which is as funny in Spanish as it was in the Brandon Thomas original.

At four-thirty parades start to form in various parts of the city, the

best one originating at the town hall, where the morning's barriers have
been expertly removed and stacked. A brass band of about a dozen pieces,
all playing fortissimo, lines up behind the members of a drinking club
whose banners, brightly painted in comic-strip style, proclaim their faith
in Navarra, good wine and predilected bullfighters. Huge leather botas of
wine appear on many shoulders, plus bottles of beer and gin. At five a
group of picadors on their way to the bullring appear on horseback and the
parade sets forth, a noisy, raucous wonderful gang of men who won't be
sober for six days. They march through the streets at a leisurely pace,
shouting the songs of San Fermín and alerting the populace to the fact
that the bullfight is about to begin.

In 1966 the theme song was the first two lines of Verdi's splendid aria
from *Rigoletto*, in which Gilda realizes that she is in love with the duke
who masquerades as a student:

*Six Spanish women at a table
in the plaza during San Fermín.*

Caro nome che il mio cor,
Festi primo palpitar . . .

For eight days I was to hear this melody chanted twenty-four hours a day,
never more than the two first lines, never less. It became the haunting
leitmotiv of the feria, the half-mad cry of happiness. I am sure the
incessant repetition has permanently ruined *Rigoletto* for me and that if I
were tomorrow in an opera house where Joan Sutherland started 'Caro
nome che il mio cor,' I would rise and bellow, 'Viva San Fermín.' I am sure
that whenever I hear this theme again I shall smell Pamplona and taste
the flow of red wine from the botas. Never has a musical theme so
swamped a city.

Now from everywhere appear pairs of men lugging plastic buckets,
and even tubs, loaded with bottles. They converge on the Calle Estafeta,
where an ice company is ready to fill their buckets with ice, so that the

beer will remain cold during the fight. If Pamplona provides an excess of music, it also provides an abundance of beer and wine, and there is no bullring in Spain where so much is consumed during the fights. The result is that the public, especially the part occupying the cheaper seats in the sun, is always ready to protest violently the less fortunate performances in the ring, even to showering seat cushions and chunks of bread on the hapless bullfighters. This tense atmosphere means that the actual bull-fights at San Fermín are apt to be mediocre, and some of the best matadors prefer not to show themselves in this rowdy city. Others, because of the hostile ambiente, quickly lose whatever enthusiasm they may have brought to the fight. Many people blame the mediocrity of the fights on the early-morning running of the bulls, believing that the pounding of their hoofs on the hard stone paving blocks weakens their legs and that the presence of thousands of runners frays their nerves. Since Pamplona's is the only major fair in which the bulls are run through the streets, it is easy but perhaps not accurate to blame any deficiency in the condition of the bulls on this circumstance.

Take the fifth day of the feria in 1966, when everything went wrong. On July 11 three matadors of excellent reputation, Ordóñez, Murillo and Fuentes, were to face bulls from one of the better ranches, that of Don Alvaro Domecq. As the drinking clubs marched into their sunny-side seats, accompanied by their bands, they were excited, because this promised to be a great afternoon. It is difficult for one who has not been to Pamplona to imagine what that half-hour prior to the fight was like, because in the tightly packed stands seven different full-sized bands blared away, each attending to its own tunes, and the noise passed comprehension. From it there was no retreat, only surrender to the deafening salvos of raw sound.

Well, when the first bull appeared he looked wonderful, and since he was to be fought by Ordóñez, a recognized master, it looked as if the promise of the day might be fulfilled. The bands exploded with joy, but before Ordóñez had made even one pass, a peon had the misfortune of luring the bull against a post in such a way that it suffered a concussion and had to be destroyed in the arena. The crowd broke out in an angry demonstration, partly against Ordóñez and his unlucky peon, partly because this was the fourth such accident of the fair, and partly because it was not yet apparent whether the judge would allow a substitute bull. The substitute was granted, Ordóñez made a few passes, the bull fell down because of weak knees, and Ordóñez dispatched it with unseemly haste and with a sneaky, low-blow sword thrust, whereupon the crowd's protests were renewed.

The second animal proved difficult and Murillo could do little with it, so he killed it quickly to a chorus of protests. The third bull looked pretty good, but once more, as a peon was putting it through its first passes, it grazed a horn against the wall and snapped it off at the base. According to bullfight regulations, bulls injured after they are fairly in the arena are not to be replaced, but the judges frequently do allow such substitution, in part to avoid the public's wrath. A tremendous protest now broke out, which was increased when the judge, having ignored the regulations in the case of the first bull and having allowed a substitute, now decided to enforce them; he refused to grant a substitute. When a matador fights a bull that has lost one horn, honor requires that he never pass it on the side of the broken horn, but this afternoon the public was unwilling for Fuentes to pass this one on either side and insisted that he kill it forthwith, which he did.

As for the fourth bull, it remains in my memory as the worst-fought animal I have ever seen, for it was a fine-looking bull and brave with the horses. But Ordóñez, sick of the afternoon and the Pamplona mob, gave a few trial passes, noted that the bull had a slight tendency to hook to the right, and said the hell with it; and the audience had to sit in the stands and watch this fine bull wasted. To show his contempt for the crowd, Ordóñez deliberately killed in the most disgraceful manner, with a running, sideways swipe of the sword, a punctured lung, the breathing-out of the bull's blood through its nostrils. The protests began as soon as his intentions became apparent and finally became so clamorous that I feared a riot must ensue. It was a shame-filled conclusion to a shameful performance.

On the fifth bull it was clear that Murillo, a man noted for his pundonor, hoped for a triumph. He did a competent faena, during which the band played, but on the whole it was a lackluster performance that didn't get through to the public, with the result that he killed the bull perfunctorily, to a moderate chorus of protests. And this was a real pity, because some of us in the stands knew that Murillo, from the neighboring region of Aragón, had always been looked upon with a certain favor by the natives of Pamplona, and this was his farewell performance in the city, since he was to retire at the close of the season.

The sixth bull came weak to the fight, and poor Fuentes, a young matador who could not afford the luxury of a shameless performance like that of Ordóñez, tried his level best to make up for the disappointment of not having been able to fight his one-horned bull. And he did accomplish a few good passes, because the band played for his faena. But he tried so hard and so long that, running into unexpected difficulty on the kill, he heard the humiliating trumpets sound a warning. And so ended a representative, but nevertheless interesting, Pamplona bullfight.

Fights in this city have a unique feature, the singing of the audience.

'Navarra, Navarra, número uno!
Como Navarra no hay ninguno.'

(Navarra, number one. Like Navarra there is no other.) When a matador is doing poorly, through lack of pundonor, one row of chanting people starts swaying to the left, the ones above and below to the right, so that the whole plaza seems to be in motion, and if you look at the alternately

swaying figures you become dizzy, and all the while the swaying figures are bellowing a song whose shouted refrain consists of the phrase 'Todos queremos más.' (We all want something more.) At the fight when Antonio Ordóñez refused to try, the stands bellowed:

'Ordóñez, Ordóñez, sinvergüenza!
Ordóñez, Ordóñez, paga la prensa.'

(Ordóñez, shameless one. Ordóñez, pays the newspapers.)

The drabness of the Pamplona fights was underscored by the arrival that afternoon of Brewster Cross, an American architect, who during his years of work in Spain had learned to take such fine color photographs of bullfighting that they appeared on the covers of bullfight journals. For the past six years he had been seeing an average of ninety fights a year and during that time had turned down numerous promotions to work in other countries because, as he said, 'I've discovered an ambiente I love and I'd be nuts to lose it so long as I can make a living here.' He was delayed in coming to Pamplona, he told us, by a bullfight in Madrid. 'I've been waiting through more than two hundred fights to see that one special thing. That afternoon which the Spaniards describe as culminating. Each time you enter the gates you say, "I hope this is going to be it." But always you're disappointed. The other day, however, Curro Romero was on the program, and although I'd never seen him in top form, I knew he had the capability. If the right bull came along. On his first bull, nothing. But on his last animal, the greatest single performance in the world of art I've ever seen, and I've seen people like Horowitz and Menuhin. It was the most evocative, the most elegant, the most artistic. When he finished with that noble animal, my palms were wet with tension and Aristotelian catharsis.'

The fights had been bad that afternoon, but there are compensations. After the last bull the mob wandered slowly over to the square to drink beer and consume vast plates of expensive breaded shrimp. A gang of college kids from California, on marijuana and LSD, sprawled at a table served by the debauched waiter, who looked no worse than they, and Orson Welles, very handsome with slightly grayed hair, conducted an interview with Kenneth Tynan for the benefit of television cameras. Matt Carney surveyed the scene with bleary eyes and condemned it all as bad, while a group of Scandinavians, who had skimped to buy their tickets for the disastrous fight, sat glumly in a land from which the sun had vanished.

But by ten-thirty all had changed. From the public square a rocket ripped into the night air and exploded with a huge bang to initiate a half-hour of fireworks which festooned the sky with fiery banners. This night they were under the supervision of Pirotecnica Vicente Caballer of Valencia, the Vatican of fireworks, so they were bound to be good. There

Colonel Tom Nickalls, father of Oliver and one of England's top experts on horses, at the bullring in Pamplona.

were colored rockets and noisy ones and flowered ones, and at the end two powerful shots which signified that the display was over.

Now it was midnight again, and from the Corrales de Gas six more dark shapes emerged to run quietly across the bridge and up the hill to the temporary corrals, from which they would erupt next morning at seven to chase brave young men through the streets.

If I have not spoken in this account of orderly sleeping and eating it is because one does not worry much about such matters during San Fermín. The most gracious thing you can do for someone you meet in the plaza is to say, 'I have a bath at my place. You look as if you need one. Come along.' The invitee has been sleeping in a bank lobby for six nights and needs a wash. As for food, it is available if you can elbow your way to the counter.

The true heroes of San Fermín are not those who run with the bulls, nor the amateurs who dodge with the heifers, nor even the matadors who do the fighting, but the police of the city. With an unruly mob of many thousands on their hands, and most of them young people of high spirit from foreign lands, the quiet police steel themselves to show courtesy, tact, humor and a benevolent indulgence. To do so is not easy, for a young man who has just run before six Miura bulls is not apt to be frightened by a policeman, but at five o'clock one morning as I sat in the square I witnessed the following incidents, none of which unnerved the two stolid policemen who were keeping order. A sports car flying the flag of the American Confederacy roared past with two buglers playing their mangled version of the rebel yell. Three Swedish girls, who had slept in the streets, were playfully molested from four sides, to their delight. An impromptu band of six instruments played three different pieces of music, accompanied by revelers dancing in the streets and over the tables. An Englishman insulted two Spaniards, who quickly took care of him, but his place was taken by a Chinese student who came out flailing karate chops and elbow jabs; him the two policemen watched admiringly. Two drunken newspaper vendors sat in the middle of the street assuring each other in brotherhood, 'I'll sell your papers and you sell mine.' A French car banged through the square sideswiping two parked cars at different corners, then steamed off at top speed.

The imperturbable police did nothing, but what I didn't know until later was that at two that morning, when things had quietened down a bit, these same policemen had walked slowly through the sidewalk bars and had arbitrarily arrested the six or seven worst-looking hell-raisers, and these we would not see again for some days.

During San Fermín the government distributes thousands of copies of a pamphlet in Spanish, French and English warning against unacceptable behavior: 'Any act uncivil or offensive to common decency, such as a lack of respect to women, will be severely punished. All behavior that offends the moral sensibility of the people will be absolutely repressed.' This high-sounding dictum is enforced in a curious way. A French girl in our group nearly fainted when a Spanish man ran his hand so far inside her dress that he reached her navel. The police smiled. An English girl was astounded when another Spaniard slipped his hand deep inside her sweater. The police laughed. But at the bullring, when a deluge interrupted the fight one day, a Swedish boy happened to take off his shirt to wring it out, and the same policeman grabbed him, roughed him up and hauled him off to jail on grounds that his behavior had 'offended the moral sensibility of the public.'

I wander back to my hotel to read briefly in Pedrell's collection of old songs and to think how inappropriate to Pamplona is the famous one attributed to Juan del Encina (1469–1529). It is a mournful chant dating from around 1505 and probably referring to some royal death, perhaps that of Felipe I in 1506. In recent years certain pessimists have proposed it as an appropriate lament for the passing of Spain's age of greatness:

> Sad and hapless Spain,
> all should weep for thee,
> bereft of joy
> now and forevermore.

I have never felt that Spain deserved such a lament; her Golden Age vanished, to be sure, but there are many signs that she is capable of creating another, on altered terms. There is an enormous natural vitality in this country which, properly channeled, could produce a new age of literature, art, philosophy and even government.

Certainly the national sadness referred to in the chant is nowhere evident during San Fermín, so I turn to another of Pedrell's recoveries, a song which probably could not be sung publicly in Spain today. It is numbered 79 and the words were written about 1555 by some unknown poet and set to music by an irreverent troubadour named Juan Navarro (fl. 1540–1565) of Sevilla. Pedrell entitled it 'The Nun's Song' and in it are reflected the anti-religious feelings which are always cropping up in Spain at unexpected places:

> Alas for hapless me!
> What a hard life within these walls!
> What a close jail these bars make,
> Annoying, gloomy prison!
> Cruel convent, vexatious, avaricious, scornful:
> Would that I might see you burning in bright flame.
>
> Oh, what a harsh rule,
> Dismal and irksome choir!
> Why should one have beauty and grace
> If they cannot be seen or enjoyed?
> Life without hope!
> What a great injustice, what fate so hard,
> that only death should free us!

San Fermín provides a constant kaleidoscope of visual imagery. The parades vary; papier-mâché giants fifteen feet tall wander through the streets; sometimes additional bullfights are offered at eleven in the morning; and on Thursday morning the bullring is occupied by a weird exhibition of Basque sports featuring two events that defy reason. In the first, four huge men in rope sandals, white trousers and T-shirts march forth, each bearing two long-handled axes whose heads are protected by leather sheaths. The men divide into teams of two each and stand at attention before the wood they must chop: two rows of logs laid out on the ground, each row consisting of eight logs about eighteen inches in diameter.

Referee and timers appear and the contestants untie the leather sheaths; then you see how carefully the cutting edges have been honed. A whistle blows, and the lesser man on each team leaps onto the first log of his row and begins cutting a wide V into it, sending the chips flying as he swings the ax with fierce energy against the wood. When he has the V well defined and about half cut, he leaps down and his more skilled partner takes over, swinging with even greater force, and he completes the V halfway through the log, which is rather difficult, for as the cut grows deeper, wood grips the ax and lets go only when the man gives a powerful upward jerk.

At this point the first man takes over and starts the V on the opposite side, and when it is half cut, the second man jumps onto the log and hammers home a series of tremendous cuts until the log falls in two. Now the first man starts on the next log, and for some twenty minutes the two men alternate in chopping their way through the eight big logs, and remember that since they are standing on the log, to chop it they must bend forward so that the ax strikes below their feet, putting a severe strain on the stomach.

I was relieved when the leading team finally chopped its eighth log in two, for my stomach was hurting in sympathy, but to my surprise the two men ran from the row they had been chopping and across to those which their opponents had been cutting. It became apparent that both teams would chop through all sixteen logs with a combined thickness of at least twenty-four feet. Without pausing in the broiling sun, the superbly muscled men continued this extraordinary feat for some forty minutes and finished less than a minute apart. I could understand how the Basque in the bar had given Matt Carney the black eye.

What followed was for me even more memorable. Two Basque shepherds brought into the arena rams from the Pyrenees and allowed them to smell one another, whereupon the animals, each aware that a rival had come into its terrain, quietly withdrew to a distance of about twenty feet, dug their feet in and leaped forward, butting heads in the middle of the ring with shattering force. I expected them to have broken necks, but

This Basque woodchopper
has just won the national championship at San Fermín.
He is as great a local hero as any matador.

instead each blinked his eyes, shook himself and went back to his starting position, from which he leaped forward again, striking his opponent with unbelievable force, forehead to forehead. You could hear the impact a hundred yards away.

This continued, methodically but with deadly intent, for some twenty or thirty butts until you would think the horns must drop off. Occasionally one would feint cleverly and the other would fly over his head, to receive a sharp butt from below as he went past, but usually the two beasts met head-on, and the blows became sharper as the fight continued. What surprised me was that when at the start of a round the two rams considered themselves too close for maximum effect, they would back off so that the blows would be more shattering.

Finally the judge declared the contest a draw, and I asked a Basque sitting next to me what would have happened otherwise, and he said, 'They'd go right on till sundown. Or till one of them is killed.'

In view of the richness provided by San Fermín it seems captious to say that I arranged three excursions into the countryside, but there were places as important to me as Pamplona, so one morning, after no sleep, Vavra and Fulton and I set out for the little Basque town of Azpeitia, where I wished to pay my respects to a Basque who had played a significant role in history, Don Iñigo López de Recalde. The journey to Azpeitia was a delightful jaunt through the countryside of Navarra and Guipúzcoa. North of Irurzun we slipped through the Pass of the Two Sisters, a defile that reminded me much of the Iron Gates on the Danube but even more of the Cilician Gates in southern Turkey. From its northern exit it threw us into a fine hill country with alternate views across deep valleys and shrouds of fog which slowed us down to less than a walk. Finally, descending from a high plateau, we came upon Azpeitia, and it was exactly as I had imagined: a trivial place of no consequence, with an ordinary village church that one would not remember long and townspeople who greeted any stranger in French, for they stood close to the French border.

I got out of the car and started to walk to the small church, when a blacksmith at his forge, now converted into a garage, said, 'It's not here that you pay your respects but up the road a little farther.' I had expected little in the town to remind me of Don Iñigo and I found little, so I was willing to proceed in the direction the blacksmith had indicated, and after driving for a mile or two I received one of my major shocks in Spain.

For we came not to some small church memorializing a great man, but to a vast establishment centering upon a huge eighteenth-century basilica built of the finest marble. This was the memorial to Don Iñigo, better known as St. Ignatius of Loyola, the man who founded the Society of Jesus. His army was given Papal approval by Paul III on September 27, 1540, and the powerful work of the order stems from that date.

Before the basilica we found more than a hundred autobuses from all parts of Europe, for unexpectedly we had stumbled into a jubilee celebration of the order, and when we entered the basilica we found prostrate on the floor twenty-five young Jesuits about to be ordained as priests. Faces to the stone, dressed in white and gold, the candidates lay with their arms and heads covered by squares of gold cloth while a cardinal intoned a lengthy prayer over them while standing before a magnificent altar set among entwined Solomonic columns of gray-brown stone heavily ornamented in black and white and highly polished. Above the prostrate figures rose a statue of Ignatius Loyola, the young roustabout from Azpeitia who in 1521 at the age of thirty, while fighting for the king at Pamplona, had been severely wounded in the leg. During his convalescence, in a house that now stands encased as a shrine within the heart of the basilica, the young hellion had undergone conversion, and his years of travel and study had ensued, including a stay at Salamanca and a perilous brush with the Inquisition, which almost nipped his career at the start. He had persevered in his new-found devotion and had inspired others, Italians and Germans mostly, to an equal commitment, and with them had founded the order which was to shore up the Church at a time when it was beset by enemies from within and without. If Martin Luther was the scourge of the Catholic Church, then St. Ignatius was the scourge of Lutherans, and it was his movement in defense of Catholicism that helped establish a balance in Europe. He is my favorite Spanish saint, for I find Santo Domingo, founder of the Dominican order, too bloodthirsty for my liking—I cannot forget his persecution of the Albigenses—and Santa Teresa too nebulous. But Ignatius, the stubborn, worldly Basque who came to God late and then with such fury—him I can understand and him I regard with personal identification.

The history of the Jesuit Order in Spain has rarely been peaceful, but the lead in repressing the movement has usually come from neighboring countries. In 1759 Portugal decided that it must expel the Jesuits from both the mother country and the colonies. In 1764 France reached the same conclusion. So in 1767 King Carlos III of Spain announced the expulsion of the Jesuits from Spain and the New World alike, but later they crept back. In 1835, with the inauguration of reforms in government, they were expelled again, but again they returned; and in 1932, with the launching of the republic, they were ousted once more, but with Generalísimo Franco they reappeared. The loss involved in these expulsions was Spain's, for even though the Jesuits might be difficult to manage, it was they who were mainly responsible for what education Spain offered, and they were usually expelled at the precise time when the nation needed the international insights which they offered.

Now, as the twenty-five young Jesuits lie prostrate, the order seems secure in Spain, and as the priest prays he uses appropriately the Basque tongue:

'Ogi zerutik etorria
zu zera gure poz guztia
Bildots santua ara emen . . .

From the basilica of Loyola, whose magnificence had astonished us, we pushed on to Santillana del Mar, site of the Caves of Altamira, where in 1869 the world's first concentration of prehistoric art was discovered by accident. When first I heard John Fulton's reasons for wanting to visit Altamira, I must confess I could not express much enthusiasm for what he had in mind. He said, 'I want to see how cave men drew their bulls and how they colored them, because I have in mind to publish a book with a series of bull pictures done as these early men did them.'

'On rock?' I asked.

'No. With bull's blood and a mixture of oil and ochre.'

I said to myself, 'If that's what a young man wants to do, why should I argue?'

For more than a thousand years before that day in 1869 when the Caves of Altamira were discovered as a major glory of western art, the small town of Santillana had been well regarded as an exceptionally fine village. Here three or four country lanes intersect and each is lined with rare old houses and churches that date back at least to the year 870. In Santillana it was a custom for proud families to emblazon their homes with heraldic shields, so that today the town could well be set aside as a museum showing what happens when everyone tries 'to keep up with the Barredas,' for one house is finer than the next and this family shield larger than that, until finally the Villa family offers an escutcheon so tremendously big that the human figures on it are known locally as giants. The guidebook warns: 'This shield is so close to the spectator that the effect is perhaps a little pompous.' On the other hand, the Collegiate church is an unpretentious gem of Romanesque architecture, and even the emblazoned houses have an unusual charm in that their ground floors are given over to the stabling of cattle, whose aromas permeate the village, making it doubly attractive and homelike.

In other words, when the caves that lay below the village fields were about to be discovered, which would bring millions of visitors to Santillana, the town was already a poetic, pastoral museum; today it is a national treasure in which the Barreda palace has been converted to a handsome parador where one can obtain good meals and from which he can study the shields and explore the caves. There are few small towns in Europe more worth a visit than this.

The caves, at first sight, were merely a repetition of what I had come to know along tourist routes, whether in the Shenandoah Valley or along the rivers of Europe. Compared to the Carlsbad Caverns of New Mexico they are trivial in size, but they are clean and well lighted and their small rooms give a sense of underground living.

One area led to another of no conspicuous interest, but at the end of the trip I came to a low-ceilinged room about fifty feet long by thirty wide—as big as a motion picture house in a small village—and when my eyes had adjusted to the restrained light and when I looked upward I saw something so much grander than I had been led to expect that I can describe it only as one of the major surprises of my adventures in art. I had known the art was there. I could visualize what the wild bulls looked like. I knew what colors had been used to outline them, and I even knew how particular animals stood. But knowing all this, I knew nothing about the impact of this silent, hidden room upon the imagination.

For example, I had always believed that the great bulls of Altamira ranged along the walls of the cave. They are all on the ceiling. I had supposed I would find no more than a dozen good specimens. There are about thirty, each one a major work of art. I had supposed the colors to be faded, as they are in other prehistoric caves, and the bulls mere outlines which the mind fills in with pigment. Instead they are as bold and fresh in their color as if they had been painted last week. To stand at either the high end of the cave or the low and to look across the expanse of ceiling and see the animals rising and falling mysteriously along the rocky surface is to see not a prehistoric drawing but a field of bulls the way artists some seventeen thousand years ago must have seen them on the seacoast plains bordering the Bay of Biscay.

The thing that surprised me most, as I recall this amazing room, was the series of bulls constructed around rocky protuberances which jutted down from the ceiling. Mostly these extrusions are elliptical, but some are circular; they project eight or ten inches or perhaps even a foot, forming kinds of rocky hummocks standing forth from the rocky pasture lands. On these humps the ancient artists, using a trickery not surpassed by Salvador Dali, drew sleeping animals, wonderfully curled, with their feet tucked under them and their heads resting on their forelegs. The sense of reality thus created is magical; the bulls look as if at any moment they might rise from their slumber. One of the first French scholars to study Altamira summed it up in a phrase that has not been equaled: 'This cave is the Sistine Chapel of prehistoric art.'

John Fulton, studying the manner in which the pigment had been applied, pointed out something that I had not seen for myself: 'Nowhere in the cave is there a hunter, or any weapon used in hunting. The men who drew these animals must have loved them.' I've since seen a study which claims that the circular animals painted on the protruding rocks are wounded and about to die, but I saw no evidence of this and I suppose Fulton was closer to the truth. These are drawings done by men who studied animals and who loved them, the way the farmers of present-day Santillana love their beasts and share their houses with them, even though in the end they must live off them.

The cave was enhanced by a poetically enthusiastic guide four feet eight inches tall who spoke with swift impartiality a blend of French, Spanish and English, intermixing his words in such a way as to create the impression that he was speaking some ancient language that might have been used by the cave men: 'Regardez les animaux qui suivent el campo, comiendo, pensando, corriendo and lying down on their sides.' I found that if I could catch only a few words in each language I was able to build up a picture of the cave as it must have existed when men spoke with similarly fragmented thoughts.

One of the most interesting aspects of Altamira is a museum some distance from the entrance to the caves, for it contains a collection of the artifacts found on the site. The caves were discovered when a huntsman's dog fell into them one afternoon. The dog was pulled out and the incident forgotten until six years later, in 1875, when another in Spain's long line of amateur enthusiasts, this time Marcelino Sanz de Sautuola, heard of the cave and went exploring. It is interesting to note that it was only after four years of intensive work that the small cave containing the paintings was found by Don Marcelino's daughter María, who stumbled upon the scene where bulls wandered across the ceiling. In 1880 Don Marcelino published his findings, only to be branded a fraud. It was years before the authenticity and significance of the find were recognized.

In the building of which I speak, a small exhibition has been put together of the things Don Marcelino found and meticulously catalogued. Here are the stone axes, the wedges, the arrow points and the thin bones pierced to serve as needles, vestiges of a complex civilization. Especially attractive to anyone interested in art is a considerable group of sea shells, each containing the dried-out remnants of paint used by the prehistoric artists: red, black, gray, yellow, brown, white. Many of the pigments are the same as those employed by artists today, particularly a raw ochre which Fulton found in rock form on the beach nearby. If these dried colors were ground in a pestle and mixed with oil, they could be used now, and it is moving to think that in them we have the specific materials utilized in making the oldest surviving paintings in the history of art.

When I saw the shells I did not at first understand why they affected me as they did. Then I remembered. In the atelier of the American painter Karl Knaths at Provincetown on Cape Cod, I had seen exactly this type of shell, used precisely in this way and containing exactly these colors. In seventeen thousand years some of the ways of art had not changed, and at last I understood why Fulton wanted to paint his series of pictures using bull's blood, red ochre and native oils, for that was the way the whole exciting business had begun.

I was profoundly affected by Santillana: the houses with their arrogant shields, the good smell of cattle, the beautiful Romanesque church, the timeless bulls wandering across the roof-land meadows, and the seashell palette with its dried-up paints. I wanted time to think about this concentration of experience, so I walked slowly out of town and up the steep Camino Comillas to the fork where a secondary road branches off to Suances, and there sitting on a stone wall I had a splendid view of the region. Low mountains hemmed in the village and meandering stone fences outlined the fields. Red roofs marked the houses I had enjoyed and huge barns proved that the land was profitably farmed. This was northern Spain at its best, heavy with trees and richness, and I wondered if it were possible that the prehistoric men had lived above ground, reserving the caves as religious sites or refuges in time of war. If they lived on this particular bit of land they knew beauty at first hand, and it was this natural beauty that had characterized their art. I took a few steps backward, and I had crossed the watershed. Santillana had vanished and I was looking down at the Bay of Biscay, where rolling hills dropped to the sea, taking with them lonely, weather-beaten trees and a very old church that seemed about to plunge into the waves. Sunset was coming on and men were leaving the fields and heading for homes I could not see. They had been tending corn, which grows abundantly in these parts but is eaten only by animals.

It was night and I returned to Santillana, where the only argument that Vavra and Fulton and I were to have in five months of delightful travel ensued. There was a chirping sound, and Vavra said, 'Oh, it's owls.'

Without thinking that I was contradicting a professional naturalist, I blurted out, 'More likely frogs.'

'Couldn't be frogs up there.'

'Tree frogs.'

Vavra ridiculed this supposition and we agreed to lay our disagreement before Fulton, who said that to his uneducated ear it was neither frogs nor owls, so we turned to local experts. The first five farmers, who had lived all their lives in the presence of this sound, gave such radically different answers that I will merely repeat them.

'It comes from squeaking machinery.'

'It's a kind of fish that lives in the ditches.'

'An insect. Very bothersome.'

'It's made by the swallows going to bed.'

'Snails. It's the mating call of snails.'

Now, obviously the sound came from either an owl or a tree frog, and to have five local experts fail even to include these animals in their suggestions was unnerving, but Fulton came up with the first practical observation: 'Whatever it is, is singing down there in that sewer.'

Vavra refused to accept what seemed to me conclusive evidence that the singers were frogs; he claimed that what Fulton was hearing was an echo coming from the sewer, and we left Santillana not knowing what was responsible for the twilight serenade, but some days later Vavra, who takes these matters seriously, reflected, 'It would be extraordinary for an owl to live in a sewer.'

Excellent as Santillana was, it was our third excursion that remains most vivid in my mind. I have never bothered much about whether or not people will remember me when I am dead; but I am sure that as long as my generation lives, in various parts of the world someone will pause now and then to reflect, 'Wasn't that a great picnic we had that day with Michener?' I have lured my friends into some extraordinary picnics, for I hold with the French that to eat out of doors in congenial surroundings is sensible: in Afghanistan we ate high on a hill outside Kabul and watched as tribesmen moved in to attack the city; at Edfu along the Nile we spread our blankets inside that most serene of Egypt's temples; in Bali we picnicked on the terraces and in Tahiti by the waterfalls; and if tomorrow someone were to suggest that we picnic in a snowstorm, I'd go along, for of this world one never sees enough and to dine in harmony with nature is one of the gentlest and loveliest things we can do. Picnics are the apex of sensible living and the traveler who does not so explore the land through which he travels ought better to stay at home.

One of my happiest experiences in Spain was the discovery, many years ago, of a remarkable American woman who loved picnics almost as much as I did. Patter Ashcraft, in her late thirties, the descendant of a distinguished Cleveland family, had been early in life inoculated with bull fever. When I first knew her she had a monstrous Buick convertible, in which we drove like demented Spaniards, but now she had a more sedate Volkswagen, in which she followed the ferias up and down Spain, spreading hilarity wherever she struck. She was known to her friends as L'Incomparable, and she spoke in such a low whisper that her husband Edwin, a Princeton CIA type, had to be constantly reminding, 'Darling, turn up the volume control.'

It was during the Sevilla feria one year that we discovered our mutual interest in picnics; we organized repeated forays into Las Marismas, and in subsequent years we had cajoled our friends into the countryside at Salamanca, along the western rivers of Spain, in the rural areas near Madrid, and at the spot from which El Greco painted his famous view of Toledo.

Patter and I disagreed on only one detail: she thought a picnic should be composed only of items that could be bought in stores, like a round of cheese, a slab of ham, six bottles of wine, whereas the best picnic I had ever attended prior to Pamplona had consisted of ramekins of lima beans baked with traces of baked ham, garlic and blackstrap molasses, a green salad with a good dressing and ice-cold éclairs, three to a customer. In other words, Patter was of the American school; I of the French—and the latter is obviously superior.

On this day Patter's theory was to prevail, and her car was loaded with choice cans and bottles when we set out to a picnic ground which I had selected years before; I had spotted it on my pilgrimage to Santiago de Compostela. We were eight as we left Pamplona after the morning running of the bulls: Patter and her husband; Bob Daley, long-time European sportswriter for the *New York Times*, and his French wife, both with a good sense of what makes a picnic; Vavra and Fulton; the Hemingway double and I. We were headed north, toward the Pass of Roncesvalles, that historic and mystery-laden route through the Pyrenees which Charlemagne had used in 778 for his retreat through the mists and where he had failed to hear the battle horn of his dying Roland.

The success of our picnic was assured by the fine tins Patter had bought and by the rare site I had selected, but insurance was taken out when Bob Daley, fearing that we didn't have enough food, stopped in the town of Espinal, and while we seven studied the fine modernistic church, quite radical in its architecture, he bought an extra loaf of bread, and in doing so, acquired a culinary masterpiece: it was round and flat, about the size of a large chair cushion and not more than two inches thick, so that it was practically all crust, and better crust was never baked.

We drove to the statue of a pilgrim which marks the southern end of the pass, and thought with what relief the religious wanderers of the medieval period must have reached this spot and given thanks at the statue for having escaped the robbers that infested the dark woods of the area. Farther on, at the lonely monastery, the gates of which had rescued thousands and fed millions in the long years of its existence, the others studied the stalwart and well-carved church, but I wandered through the network of stables and barns from which the small fields in the pass had been farmed for twelve centuries. Everything was low and compact, to fight against the winter winds that tormented the area, and all things had a sense of past ages, so that one stood surrounded by history, whether in the barn or in the transept.

I had in mind a spot well beyond the monastery of Roncesvalles, a spot where a small stream came out of a woods, but Patter was by now in the lead car and she caught sight of a meadow far below the road where seven rivulets converged, their banks lined with moss-covered trees, and when I saw it I had to acknowledge that her choice was best. We lugged our tins and bottles and Bob Daley's marvelous chunk of bread down to the seven streams, and there in a glade so quiet, so softly green that it seemed as if defeated knights might have slept in it the evening before, we spread our blankets and prepared the meal.

It was not a picnic we had but a kind of dedication. We were in a pass where significant events had occurred, where the legend of Roland had been created to give meaning to Christianity's fight against Islam, and before we had been in the silent place for a dozen minutes it had possessed us and made us a part of history. 'If there ever were dryads,' Vanderford said, 'they must have lived here.'

For some hours we wandered along the rivulets and talked of the feria at Pamplona. One group of trees had strange knees that protruded to make

fine chairs, and in them we sat as we discussed the bullfighters, the disappointments they had caused and the near-tragedies that had occurred at the running of the bulls. As we ate, and relished the bread from Espinal, John Fulton told of the American military personnel in Spain who had planeloads of American bread, white, gooey, lacking in everything except chemicals, flown across the Atlantic to the PX's 'so that our children can grow up knowing what real bread is.' The idea was so fascinating that no one could think of any comment.

And then the mysterious thing happened that made of this picnic with Charlemagne a thing of haunting beauty, so strange and memorable that all who participated would afterward say, 'Remember that picnic in the Pass of Roncesvalles,' except that Peggy Daley, being French, would call it 'Roncevaux.' A fog rolled in and blotted out the sun. It was not a cold fog, but it was heavy, and soon we were immersed not in a woods cut by rivulets but in a dream through which strange figures moved and horns echoed. We could barely see from one to the other and the trees on which we had been sitting became vague shapes, but no one thought to leave, for a curious light pervaded and voices seemed unusually clear, though echoes were no more.

The voices said strange things. Bob Vavra surprised us by announcing that he was a gypsy, a real gypsy with roots in Bohemia in Czechoslovakia. 'You ought to see my father in California. In his seventies and as bronzed and lean as a hickory limb.' We recalled that unbelievable day, May 23, 1435, when through these passes came the Original Band of gypsies to burst upon an unsuspecting Spain. They were led by that engaging rascal, Thomas, self-proclaimed Earl of Little Egypt. The gypsies had learned that then as now Europeans were easy targets if one announced himself an earl or a duke or a count, so Earl Thomas brought along a couple of each. The gypsies had also learned that Christian Europe was much concerned about the advance of Islam, so Thomas explained that his band had been forced to flee from Little Egypt because they were Christians and their kingdom had been overrun by the infidel. Thomas said he could stay in Europe only a little while, collecting funds for the recapture of his native land. Then, at the head of a mighty crusade, he would lead his victorious Christians back to Little Egypt and win new laurels for the faith. Who had made him an earl? He was vague about that. Where was Little Egypt? He was vague about that, too. When would the crusade start? Any day now. In the meantime, money must be collected, and for a whole hilarious decade Earl Thomas and his brazen band hoodwinked Spain and gathered funds. 'Spaniards have ever since held gypsies in low regard,' Vavra reflected. 'Up to a few years ago they could have no passports, were not inducted into the army and suffered all sorts of restraint. You'd be surprised how many Spaniards stop cold dead when I say innocently, "But I'm a gypsy." ' What was at first held most strongly against them was the fact that after

529

The mists at Roncesvalles.

gathering all that money from Christian Spain, they made no effort to recapture Little Egypt, nor would they even divulge where it was.

Matador Fulton told an equally strange tale. He was born in Philadelphia, Fulton John Sciocchetti, to a conservative middle-class Italian-Hungarian family who changed their last name to Short, so his name was legally Fulton John Short, but in the ring he was known as John Fulton. As an art student at the Philadelphia Museum School he gained high marks, but reading Hemingway's *Death in the Afternoon* alerted him to the romance of the bullring, and when his military duty took him to camps along the Mexican border he began to train as a bullfighter, and once he did this, he was lost. He kept us chuckling in the mists as he recounted one after another of the misadventures which seem to overtake all bullfighters: 'I was fighting this time in Tijuana and there was this dippy dame from some society or other in southern California who conceived a passion for bullfighters, one after another, and this week it was "our heroic American matador, John Fulton." As the fight was about to begin she leaned down out of the stands, grabbed at my hand and told her husband, "I have fallen madly in love with this young man and I warn you that if the bull wounds him I shall leave you sitting here, because my place will be in the ring with the wounded hero." Her husband looked at her, looked at me, then put his hands to his mouth and bellowed, "Come on, bull!" '

Vanderford astonished me by having in his pocket the details of that first bullfight I had seen in Valencia so many years ago. Working in his patient way through the newspapers of the period on file in Madrid, he had found answers to my questions: The fight had occurred on the Sunday after Easter, April 3, 1932, in the plaza at Valencia. The bulls were from the ranch of Don Manuel Comacho of Sevilla, and the matadors appear to have been regular, no more. Marcial Lalanda, so-so. Domingo Ortega, details. El Estudiante, details. He continued with his deflating analysis of the fight which I had remembered as something rather more than regular. But there the record was: 'The bulls were mansotes y sosos' (cowardly and dull). Then he stunned me by saying, 'And the second fight, which you recall as having been held on Monday, actually took place on Tuesday, because on Monday there was a comic bullfight.' This I couldn't believe. I knew it was Monday, for I could recall every incident after the first fight and how I had got my ticket for the second and the conversations with the cuadrillas. If I was certain about anything in the past, it was the day on which this second memorable fight occurred, yet there the record was. Tuesday, bulls of no consequence, three novilleros of limited ability who never progressed to full matador. To me they had been good; the bulls had been brave; and the fight had taken place on Monday. I suppose much memory is like that.

Vavra coaxed Bob Daley to tell us how he had got married, and Daley said that as a fledgling foreign correspondent about to sail for Europe for the *New York Times* he had acquired from a chance acquaintance the name of a girl in Nice whom the acquaintance had seen once and had considered 'the most beautiful girl in Europe.' When his ship docked, Daley had headed straight for Nice, had searched for the girl and had married her on the spot. 'Everybody should be so lucky,' Vavra said, for all agreed that Daley had got himself a gem. In what spare minutes I could find during San Fermín, I was reading the manuscript of Daley's forthcoming novel, *The Whole Truth*, which dealt with a fledgling correspondent covering Europe for New York's major newspaper, not named, and at last I understood where Daley had got his idea for the central love story in which his young reporter goes to a setting like Nice to marry a girl like Peggy. I was finding Daley's account of newspaper life overseas faithful to what I had observed in Tokyo, Vienna and Paris but I feared that it would get an adverse review in the *New York Times* when it appeared, and it did.

Then someone asked why Roland had sounded his horn at this gloomy spot, and I explained that three events, one historical, two legendary, had been telescoped here, but that no one was required to believe either of the legendary versions. 'Young Charlemagne crossed the Pyrenees in 778 not to aid the Christians of Spain against the Moors but to subdue the fractious Basques. He failed, and on his return a rabble of Basques overtook his rearguard at Roncesvalles and killed some two dozen men, and Charlemagne was unable to do anything about it, for after their victory the Basques vanished. That much is history. Many years later a legend grew up, claiming that when Charlemagne invaded Spain he was an old man dedicated to helping Christians expel Moors. In his entourage rode his nephew Roland, the fairest knight who ever was, and Archbishop Turpin, as good a swordsman as he was a cleric. At Roncesvalles, when four hundred thousand Moors attacked, the archbishop slew four hundred but in the end was killed. Last of the defenders was Roland, who with his sword Durandal propped himself against the kind of tree we've been sitting on today and sounded his horn Olifant to summon his uncle back to the fight, but in vain. Turning his face to Spain, so that Charlemagne would know he had died confronting the enemy, Roland perished somewhere near here. That was the first legend. Centuries later another legend appeared, supposed to have been written by Archbishop Turpin, who did not die at the pass but escaped, and this account claims that the reason Charlemagné came into Spain was neither to punish Basques nor to brawl with Saracens but to go on pilgrimage to Santiago de Compostela. It was on his return that the Battle of Roncesvalles occurred, when Roland and his thousand knights perished at the hands of the infidel. I make no choice among the versions.'

The mists thickened and a kind of darkness covered the valley, up whose steep sides we could hear the whispering of birds; it took no imagination to believe that it was in such surroundings that Roland had sounded his horn Olifant, and one could understand how the notes had been absorbed, so that Charlemagne could not hear them. It was a pass, as we saw it then, where brave men had fought and where heroes had died. In the mists the members of our party looked like the ghosts of those heroes, looming now into view, retreating again into the mists, and we lingered on, barely making it back to Pamplona in time for the bullfight.

It was lucky for me that we were not delayed, for as we entered the patio de caballos, that part of the ring in which the picadors exercise their horses and where the cuadrillas meet to pray in the chapel before the fight, I recognized two figures whose presence in Pamplona could not have been more happily arranged. The first was one of the handsomest toreros, a lithe square-jawed man in his late fifties, with a heavy head of gray hair, who looked as if he might, with a little training, step forth to meet the bulls once more. Only a few years earlier he had appeared in that excellent motion picture *Tarde de toros* (Afternoon of Bulls), in which he had given a fine performance in the bullring. In the history of bullfighting he was an authentic master, Domingo Ortega, of whose fight in 1932 I had just been speaking with Vanderford.

Beside him was a taller man who might have been a few years younger, also handsomely preserved and with hair equally gray. He had the lean, aquiline face of a professor of philosophy at Madrid University and the clear eyes of a man who had served long as a matador. He leaned forward when he spoke, and his voice was soft, controlled. When he smiled it was with the inborn reserve that had characterized his fighting, for this was Luis Gómez, El Estudiante, the third fighter on the bill that day in 1932.

What happened next surprised me, even though I have often moved in the world of bullfighting and have known the idiosyncrasies of the professionals. I introduced myself to the matadors and they, accustomed to such interruptions whenever they wandered into the patio de caballos, nodded indifferently; but then I said, 'The first fight I ever saw was in Valencia early one spring when Marcial Lalanda and you and you fought, and I have never forgotten it.'

Ortega's deeply lined face broke into a wide smile. 'I remember exactly. It was in 1932. A great afternoon for me.'

'April 3, 1932.' El Estudiante nodded. 'One of my first fights as a full matador.'

Apparently the afternoon had meant as much to them as it had to me, for they recalled the scene and Lalanda's role and the fight the bulls gave; it was later that I learned how close Ortega had been to retiring from the ring before he got started.

In his first fights he had been desultory, 'Nada,' as the Spaniards say, and critics recommended that he quit. It was not until this fight in Valencia at the beginning of the 1932 season that he had demonstrated a classic quality which was to make him immortal: a dry, controlled, ascetic style which was the despair of those who loved flamboyance and the delight of those who respected art.

When Vavra suggested a photograph, Ortega was no longer indifferent. Smiling broadly, he looked at me and said, 'It's remarkable that you should remember.' It would have been remarkable had I forgot.

Any man who attends the feria of San Fermín must decide whether or not he will run with the bulls, and since thousands of men run each day for seven days and only a few go to the hospital, with not more than one fatality every eight or ten years, the chances are obviously favorable; yet there is that negative possibility, and on those days when I was not perched on the fence at the chute I had had the bad luck to be stationed opposite the military hospital on the Calle Santo Domingo, into which some of the damaged were hauled on stretchers, and seeing a rather lively trade, I decided not to run. There were also in 1966 special reasons which would excuse me from participating, in addition to which I was practically sixty years old, and runners of that age were not frequent.

However, on the next-to-last morning when the bulls were run I happened to be at a spot where few foreigners go, and as the dispatching rocket exploded at the corrals I happened to look down the street from which the bulls would appear, and there waiting for them was Hemingway's tutor, Juanito Quintana! He must have been in his seventies, yet there he was in the street, waiting for the bulls, with no friends around to applaud or no necessity to prove his manhood. The crazy idiot was there for the sheer hell of it, and as the bulls of the Conde de la Corte thundered up the hill, Quintana ran briefly before them, then ducked into a doorway. I think he would have been embarrassed had he known that I had seen him, for this was the action of a foolhardy man acting completely on his own.

It was also the action of a man who loved bulls, and the sight of him in the street haunted me all that day. I said to myself, 'You've loved the bulls as much as Quintana ever did. In Mexico and Spain you followed them as a young man. You may never be in Pamplona again, and tomorrow is the last running. You belong on the street.'

I scouted Santo Domingo, for if I were to be anywhere I wanted to be there where the bulls first meet the flying men, and since for extraneous reasons I was not able to run, I wanted to find some doorway in which I could take a relatively safe position. But when next morning I had taken my position, two unnerving things occurred at about two minutes of seven. A friend read me a passage from a recent book: ' "Sometimes, when a man knows the bulls are gaining on him, he falls flat on his face and lies still and the bulls go past; or he may do something that can be most perilous, he can step into a doorway and keep still; but there is a chance that a bull will stop and gore him." ' More disturbing was a wild-eyed man who took a position near me with a transistorized tape recorder strapped to his belly. The machine played church hymns nonstop and the man wore a doleful look as if he expected this to be his last morning with the bulls. But seven o'clock was at hand and I could not retreat.

The first rocket fired and the gates swung open. The second rocket fired, the oxen led the bulls galloping into the street and huge numbers of men began surging up Santo Domingo. Just as the main body reached where I was waiting, a young man fell in the street and others piled over him. One onrushing bull, distracted by the accident, lunged at the fallen man, missed, trampled him and came on toward my doorway. At the last moment the bull swerved back to join the herd and I vaguely remember a wild pounding of hooves as the animals raced past. It had all happened in a few seconds and somehow the fallen man at my feet had been uninjured, but as I lingered in the doorway talking with him, a stretcher came down Santo Domingo bearing a young man whose face had been crushed by the flat side of a horn; it looked as if he would lose his eye.

I have written favorably of two ferias, those of Sevilla and Pamplona, and the reader who finds himself with time to attend only one may wish a comparison.

Ambiente. The surroundings of the two are so radically different as to permit no comparison. Sevilla represents the soul of Andalucía; Pamplona is the heart of Navarra. If I were a first-time tourist and could see only one, I suppose I would learn more from seeing Andalucía; if I knew Spain reasonably well, I would want to see Navarra.

Setting. Sevilla is more interesting architecturally and culturally than Pamplona, but the physical accouterments of the Sevilla feria cannot compare with that charming proximity of bullring and central square in Pamplona. One can get swallowed up in Sevilla, and without money he can miss the feeling of the feria; but in Pamplona, if one can stagger he can find his way to the square, and there the action is.

Parades. The wild parades of Pamplona, lasting all day and night, with the giants, the big-headed dwarfs and the tipsy revelers, cannot be taken lightly; they are some of the best fun in Europe, and with a red scarf and a bota of wine anyone can participate in the street dancing. As a Frenchman told me in Pamplona: 'It's wrong to say there is dancing in the streets. It's the streets themselves that are dancing.' But the religious processions in Sevilla are incomparably greater. So, too, are the daily exhibitions of horsemanship in the park and along the casetas, for they are essentially Spanish and imbued with a grace that one does not often witness.

Music. The only folk instruments in the world that I have ever heard which approach the unearthly oboes of Pamplona are the rhythm drums of Afghanistan, and even against those wild instruments the oboes win by a mile. No matter how sorry the bullfight, when the oboes play during the

At dawn each year many foreigners dance in the streets,
reaching for a sun that once rose
but will not rise again.

placing of banderillas one finds three minutes of exquisite beauty. They stand without competition. Yet I cannot forget the soft midnight clapping of hands in Sevilla. Perhaps one should not make comparisons where pure beauty is concerned, as in the case of the oboes and the hands.

Food. During feria in Sevilla it is quite impossible to get a decent meal; even in fine hotels the food thrown at the customers is disgraceful. In Pamplona I had delicious plates at four places: mixed salad and menestra at the White Horse Tavern; bacalao at Marcelino's, where Hemingway used to eat; stewed veal at Casa Mauleón, near the bullring, where prices are reasonable; and delicious garlic snails at Olaverri's at the southern end of town. It is true that I spoke well of El Mesón in Sevilla, but that was only in comparison with the other restaurants in that city; compared with the best in Pamplona it was no more than average.

Bullring. A friend of mine partial to Sevilla once said, 'To compare the noble Maestranza of Sevilla with that dump in Pamplona is like comparing Yankee Stadium with the Little League park in Akron, Ohio.' So far as the interiors of the two rings are concerned, this is not an extravagant judgment, for the Maestranza is incomparable whereas the 1967 additions to the Pamplona ring, augmenting its seats by some six thousand, have only increased its lack of architectural beauty, but when one considers the whole setting, things are different. From the outside, the Sevilla ring cannot be seen; houses and stores encroach on every inch and the outer walls are actually not visible, so that the apparent ring, even though it sits beside a river, consists merely of a pair of undistinguished doors. But in Pamplona the ring sits within a lovely park of trees in one of the most congenial settings in Spain. Broad areas surround it, and fine walks. The architecture is pleasing and the ambiente is total. Inside the ring, during a fight, if one looks off to the southeast he sees high in the air the white marble tower of a neighboring church; the ramparts are filled with priests in black robes, taking in the fight with binoculars. In Pamplona this tower is known as 'the crow's nest.'

The bullfights. In Sevilla one has stately bullfights conducted in classic manner and with a noble restraint. In Pamplona one has lively exhibitions in which bulls play an honored role, but often a secondary one to the riotousness of the crowd.

The running with the bulls. Here Pamplona is so far ahead that it is embarrassing even to mention Sevilla. There is nothing in Europe, or America or Asia either, to equal these early-morning gallops with death, and if one is young and adventurous, even one morning running with the bulls might be worth two weeks of Sevilla.

Flamenco. Pamplona, on the other hand, has nothing to match the flamenco shows of the casetas in Sevilla, which is to be expected, since Pamplona lies outside the flamenco zone.

Circus. The circus area in Pamplona is scattered and ineffectual and the circuses that frequent it are small. The area in Sevilla is concentrated and the circuses are delightful. When the carnival area of Sevilla is added, the advantage is all Sevilla's.

Picnics. I have already spoken of the pass at Roncesvalles, but I am not forgetting the fine picnics in Las Marismas, and for the average visitor not concerned with Charlemagne and Roland, I suspect a picnic in the Sevilla area might be preferred.

Acceptance. This is a subtle point that might weigh heavily with younger people, although it is no longer of much importance to me. To be accepted in Pamplona one needs only a white shirt, tennis shoes, a red scarf, a red sash and a bota of wine. With this equipment the town and the square and the bullring are available, and the fellowship continues for eight long days. To be accepted in Sevilla . . . the phrase is a misnomer. One is never accepted in Sevilla. I have spent much time in that city, during feria and otherwise, and I have rarely received either hospitality or courtesy. I thought perhaps that this was because I didn't ride, but a distinguished horseman told me, 'If you ride you're treated even worse. If your jacket is an inch too short, the Sevillanos ask, "You hunting for frogs?" If your hat is not cocked at precisely the right angle, they say, "You boor." And if your horse is not obviously the most expensive, they jeer, "You cheapo." ' To wangle an invitation into a caseta is almost impossible, and I once sat for an entire feria in the Aero Club without once being spoken to, not even by waiters. Some of the loneliest and unhappiest people I have ever met have been Europeans, not Americans, trying to make a go of it in Sevilla. But I have reached the age at which I neither expect nor demand acceptance; all I require is that the local citizens not throw bottles at me, so my preference between the two ferias remains with Sevilla. The privilege of seeing the Holy Week procession before the feria starts, and the daily parade in the park, and the casetas, and the horse fair, plus the superb bullfights in the best of rings is an opportunity I would not surrender, not even when the people who organize these matters are so inhospitable.

All ferias end, but few so mournfully as Pamplona's. At nightfall after the last bullfight is over, the bands that were once so gay pass slowly through the plaza and the narrow streets playing dirges, and when they reach the mournful wail which concludes their requiem, those marching throw themselves prostrate in the street, and with their foreheads beating the stones, cry in the night,

> 'Poor me, poor me! How sad am I.
> Now the Feria of San Fermín
> Has ended. Woe is me.'

A city is in lamentation, and well it should be, for there are not many things like San Fermín.

FOLLOWING PAGE:
Intellectual Spain.

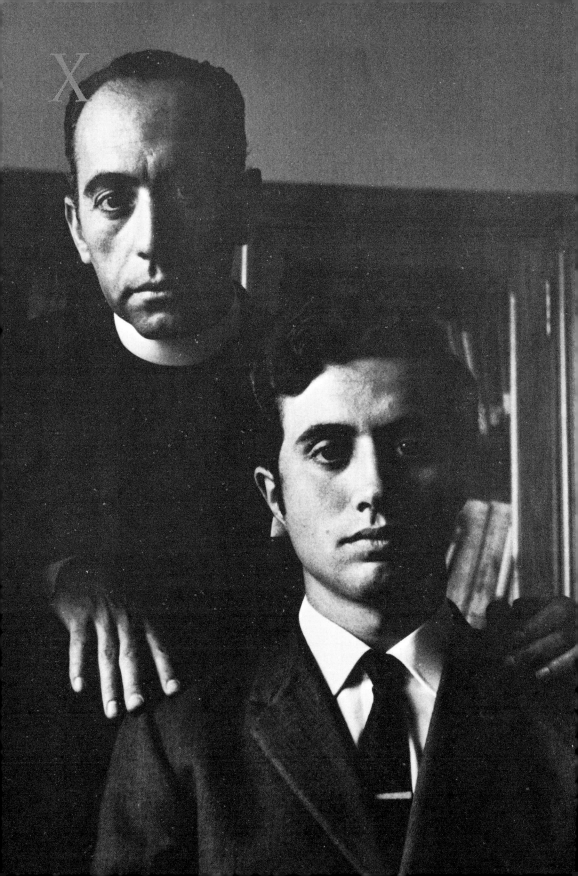

BARCELONA

OCEANO
ATLANTICO

MILES
0   100

Vich
Montserrat
Barcelona
Sitges

Teruel
Castellón de la Plana
Burriana
Valencia

Palma

Madrid

San Juan de Alicante
Benidorm
Elche

Lisboa

Guadix
Sevilla
Granada

Torremolinos
Gibraltar

MAR MEDITERRANEO

To travel across Spain and finally to reach Barcelona is like drinking a respectable red wine and finishing up with a bottle of champagne. For Barcelona is an exhilarating city, replete with challenging aspects. It is not only the political capital of the north, where one can best evaluate the problem of regional separatism in Spain, especially Catalan, but it is also the intellectual capital of the country, with a fascinating collection of museums. It is a world almost to itself, a unique metropolis bound more to the Mediterranean than to the mountains, more to France than to Africa.

I approached Barcelona in a leisurely and almost ideal way. One morning I awoke in the Parador de San Francisco inside Granada's Alhambra. This is generally held to be Spain's choicest parador if one is concerned with history and architecture, for it is very old and its cloistered patio is exceptional. After a farewell visit to the tinsel-and-stucco buildings of the Alhambra and a final look at Manuel de Falla's carmen, my wife and I drove out past the Torre Bermeja and up onto the plateau that would lead us eastward to the Mediterranean. At the last curve we looked back at the beautiful Muslim city and at the cathedral where my four kings lay, Fernando, Isabel, Felipe, Juana, and like the Moor we saw no more.

It was autumn as we drove north and harvesting was under way. Golden grain, russet fruits, red grapes and crimson peppers were being gathered and this part of Andalucía looked positively rich, so rich that I remembered the explanation as to why Granada produced poor wine: 'Her grapes have not suffered enough.' In the good fields we saw that morning there had been little suffering.

Before long I was surprised to come upon the famous village of Guadix, for I had supposed that it lay farther south. During the final siege of Granada in 1491 a crucial victory had been gained here by the Christians, but memory of it has pretty much been submerged by the fame of the town's cave dwellings, and these are something to see. Set in a lunar landscape of bleak hills and rocky pinnacles the houses of Guadix are dug into the faces of the hills, and when chimneys are piped up through the solid rock so that fires can be lit, are quite comfortable. This style of architecture has been adopted in many different countries, most notably in central Turkey, but at Guadix there is a difference, because the doorways into the caves have been handsomely plastered and decorated with red tiles, so that they look like the entrances to churches or villas of some importance. They have been rewhitewashed once or twice a year for six or seven centuries, so that like the house of Núñez de Balboa in Jerez de los Caballeros, they are now encrusted in a kind of man-made rock of soft and delicate outline. To see Guadix in the afternoon sun, with its pinnacles dark brown like burnished gold and its cave entrances stark white, is to see a dream village more appropriate for goblins and giants than for human beings.

The reason I wanted to see Guadix had nothing to do with its architecture, handsome though that was. This was the pueblo in which Alarcón had located his short novel *El sombrero de tres picos*, and as I looked at the miserable economic level at which the villagers lived, I could hear the music which Falla had composed for this work and I could visualize the four leading actors in the rustic comedy. This was the house of the hard-working miller and over there was the fly-stained office of the lecherous corregidor (one who corrects, hence magistrate) who had conceived an evil passion for the miller's wife. This grapevine could be the one from which she plucked the grapes used for bedeviling the corregidor, and that little stream is probably the one into which he tumbled while pursuing her. And the biggest of the houses, not attached to any cave, would pretty surely have been the corregidor's, where the miller went to enjoy himself with the corregidor's wife while the latter was having no luck with the miller's wife. Seeing the supposed setting of the ballet gave me a better understanding of Falla's music, for he caught the color and sound of a Spanish village. Two orchestral suites have been excerpted from the ballet. The first summarizes the dance of the miller's wife, the magistrate and the episode of the grapes, and is not outstanding; the second gives us the dance of the neighbors, the miller's farruca and the final dance, and is probably the best work Falla ever did. I have never been able to account for the discrepancy in the quality between the two suites, but I have come to prize the second as fit to stand beside Stravinsky's *Petrouchka* or Prokofiev's *Love for Three Oranges*.

Beyond Guadix we came to that series of Andalusian villages perched on the sides of hills where life is as bleak and unrewarding as anywhere in Europe. The bulk of the people are illiterate and are intended to be kept that way by their landed masters. Life is even more miserable than in the villages of Extremadura, because here there is less hope. The earthen floor, the solitary garment with patch upon patch upon patch, the early marriage and the early death, these are the marks of rural Andalucía. It is no wonder that whole villages have emigrated. Where do they go? Listen to the litany of rural Spain as I heard it from an Andalusian.

'A good many men from this village . . . Germany. When they go they promise, "We'll come back. I won't forget you, Prudencia." But we never see them again.'

'Do they find Catholic girls? In Germany?'

'They come back to Spain. But not to this dump.'

'Where do they go?'

'Where would any sensible man go? Barcelona.'

Whenever a man from Andalucía, fed up with his miserable lot, pronounced the word Barcelona it was as if he were uttering a benediction. 'That whole village beyond the hill, they all went to Barcelona. You can plow the main street and plant your grapes, because they won't be back.'

'Is life in Barcelona that good?' I asked.

'No. It's very hard. But it's a life.' Here the Andalusian made the gestures which I had seen before. He rubbed the cloth of his shirt to signify that in Barcelona men could afford clothing. And with his fingers he put imaginary food in his mouth, and this required no interpretation. Wherever I went in rural Andalucía, I encountered these signs.

I sought out an intellectual from the area, living of course in a different part of the country, and he said, 'My region is the heart and soul of Spain. Everything good comes from Andalucía, and believe me when I say that all of us who live in exile do so with a sigh. Just as our hard fields make great fighting bulls, so they make fighting men. If I thought I'd never again see Andalucía, I don't think I could live.'

'Then why do so many leave?'

'Two harsh reasons. The landed families own Andalucía and they've sworn that nothing down there will ever change. For them the system is good, and for them it will continue. The second reason, the Church. In this city you've met liberal priests. In Barcelona they have tremendous priests, willing to fight even the police on behalf of students and ordinary people. But in Andalucía the Church has one last stronghold of the old system, when peasants behaved and listened to their betters. So down there the Church is an agency of repression. It preaches a kind of life that flourished five hundred years ago . . . when things were supposed to be good.'

My informant paused and said, 'Actually, a thousand years ago when Moors occupied the region life was probably better than it is now. A thousand years and there's been no progress. Have you ever seen a true back-of-the-mountain Andalusian village?'

'I've seen Guadix.'

To residents of Andalucía who might have an adventurous or inquiring mind, Barcelona is as foreign and as exciting as France.

He laughed. 'That's a metropolis. They have buses and a cinema. They have no money but they do have spirit. No, I mean the really forlorn Andalucía. You haven't seen it and you can't know.'

I said, 'I went into the Sierra Nevada south of Granada. Well back. I've seen.'

He reflected on this for a moment and said, 'Even that's the good part. I'm speaking of the truly bleak areas over toward Murcia. Spend a week in one of those villages, as I have, and you'll understand why people from Andalucía flock to Barcelona.'

'Why not Madrid?'

'That's a subtle problem. In the minds of these people Madrid is merely an extension of what they already have. Landed power. The Church. Feudalism intensified. But Barcelona, with its nearness to France and its fronting on the Mediterranean, is a complete break. In Madrid there's not much hope for an Andalusian peasant. In Barcelona all things are possible. And when you get to Barcelona and see the tremendous number of Andalusians who have emigrated there, look at how poorly they live. Really, until they get established they live like swine. But not one ever leaves to return home. Because in Barcelona there is hope.'

I asked what would happen to Andalucía if the exodus continued, and he said, 'The landed families and the Church will win their battle. They'll keep it just as it was five hundred years ago. Unless . . . '

As so often happens in conversations with Spaniards, he hesitated, considered his words carefully, then plunged ahead. 'If at Franco's death there is trouble, everyone expects it to come in Madrid and Barcelona, especially the latter. It won't. Well, in a way it will. There'll be some rioting and temporary disturbances, but they'll be easily handled. But if the atheistic peasants of Andalucía rise, watch out. Because they will not be easily put down.'

He suggested that when the turnover came I forget Madrid and Barcelona, for they would provide only flashy headlines. 'Keep your eye on what happens in Andalucía, for that will be the powder keg. If it can be controlled, all will be controlled.'

I asked, 'But haven't the more durable spirits gone off to Germany and Barcelona?'

'They have. That's why the powers in control down there have never tried to halt emigration. They want the bolder men to get out. But conditions are so poor that even the not-so-bold may feel they have to do something. Watch Andalucía.'

At Guadix, I had faced two major decisions and with a lack of courage had in each case chosen the easier way out. Repeatedly I had been told, 'You cannot understand modern Spain unless you look into the Gibraltar Question. And you must see what's happening in Torremolinos.' Had I intended doing either, my last chance would have been to head south at Guadix, but I ignored the turnoff and continued due east. Concerning the Gibraltar Question, which monopolized Spanish newspapers during my last three visits, I did not feel qualified to judge. In 1704 the English had occupied the rock during a war in which Spain performed poorly. On July 13, 1713, a provision of the Treaty of Utrecht confirmed English possession. Since then the promontory had constituted a key link in the life line that bound England to Egypt, India and Australia. The Treaty of Utrecht contained many provisions, two of which England had apparently broken during the years when Spain was in no condition to challenge her: According to the treaty, England was allowed to occupy only the area immediately adjacent to the rock and was obligated to respect a demilitarized zone established between English and Spanish holdings, which was easy to comply with in an age of ships, but which could not be respected in an age of aviation when British forces stationed at Gibraltar required landing fields that could be built only in the demilitarized zone; in this respect the Treaty of Utrecht was unquestionably violated. Out of respect for Spanish sensibilities, England also undertook never to bring into Gibraltar any Jews or Muslims, but during the years of indolence she had allowed several Jews to take up residence and many Muslims, and had thus once more violated the treaty.

It was interesting to see how Spain enlisted support from jurists in all parts of the world, especially Latin America, to condemn England for having unilaterally abrogated a treaty 253 years old; but in addition to this legalistic approach there was the more persuasive one that colonialism as represented by England's holding on to Gibraltar when Spain wanted it back was outmoded. Again a storm of support was whipped up in the Latin countries, and barely a day went by without my reading in the papers some statement from a dignitary in Lima or Caracas condemning Great Britain as a colonial tyrant. This argument was somewhat blunted by the fact that Spain herself held tightly to a chain of colonies in Africa, and I was often amazed at the prospect of Spain's lambasting Great Britain for doing only what Spain was doing; but just before I left the peninsula for the last time, the Spanish government cut that moral Gordian knot: 'We will give all our colonies self-government as soon as they are ready for it.'

This question of self-government is a tricky one, because if a plebiscite were held in Gibraltar, which the Spanish often call El Peñon (the Large Rock), there is good reason to believe that at least seventy percent of the residents would elect to remain under some kind of British rule. To the Spanish this is an infuriating statistic, but I never felt that it was determinative. In the long run Gibraltar ought to be Spanish and to keep it in any other status is anachronistic. I suppose that most sensible Britons feel the same way and that in time some kind of modus vivendi will be worked out, perhaps fifteen or twenty years hence, when tempers have cooled a bit. In the meantime, two factors operate to keep Spain from pressing the matter as diligently as she seems entitled to. First, an open breach with Great Britain would necessitate an interruption of the profitable sherry trade with London, which would quickly throw Andalucía into bankruptcy. Second, Spain as a newly baptized tourist country could not afford a belligerency which would frighten away even one season's flow of tourist income. As a matter of fact, I thought that both Spain and Great Britain were behaving well. One day the Spanish press, in obedience to government orders, stirred up such a frenzy of attack against London that minor anti-British riots broke out in several cities, with the stoning of British automobiles and the menacing of British consulates. Later I learned that the Spanish government had been frightened by the implications, and during the next week the press carried no more inflammatory nonsense. Instead there was a warm article about England's queen, Isabel II, and a laudatory review of a London football team.

(When the plebiscite was held, on September 10, 1967, those living in Gibraltar voted as follows:

Citizens eligible to vote	12,672
Number who actually voted	12,247
Spoiled ballots	65
Number preferring to return to Spain	44
Number preferring staying with Great Britain	12,138
Percentage favoring Great Britain	99.6)

The Gibraltar Question has produced an accidental side effect that is unfortunate. Spain is one of the few nations in the world which has refused to recognize the State of Israel. Three reasons have been given: the government's reluctance to exacerbate Muslim feeling since Spain's colonies contain mostly Muslim inhabitants; the understandable desire of a Catholic country to have the holy city of Jerusalem governed by an international commission to which the Pope would appoint a large proportion of the representatives, rather than to have it as it long was, half in Muslim hands, half in Jewish; and the inconsistency that would result if Spain were to recognize a Jewish state while invoking against England the anti-Jewish terms of the Treaty of Utrecht. I suppose the last reason is the operative one. It is ironic that Spain should refuse this gesture to the Jews, because Generalísimo Franco is highly regarded by Jews; during the worst days of World War II, when pressures from Hitler were at their heaviest, Franco refused to issue anti-Jewish edicts and instead provided a sanctuary, never violated, for Jews who managed to make it to Spain. Many thousands of Jews owe their lives to Franco, and this is not forgotten.

On the other hand, it is not uncommon to find in unexpected quarters stubborn anti-Jewish propaganda. For example, Agustín Serrano de Haro's *Yo soy español* (I am a Spaniard), a text in primary history, was written by a government inspector of primary education, endorsed by Church and lay authorities, and widely used since publication in 1944. One of its chapters dealt with still another case of supposed ritual murder by Jews of a Christian child, this time seven-year-old Domingo del Val de Zaragoza, who in the thirteenth century was supposed to have been crucified, thus attaining local sainthood. Serrano's inflammatory text was accompanied by three horrendous illustrations, the last of which showed the hideous Jews catching the child's blood in goblets. When I first saw the book the chapter ended with this tag line, 'So now you know, children, what Jews are like.' After disenchantment with Nazi Germany set in, this line was dropped, and when in the spring of 1967 I saw the twenty-sixth edition of the text, I found that the whole chapter had been eliminated.

As for Torremolinos, I was visited in Pamplona by a delightful Californian who runs a bar in the beach town, and he said, 'Michener, you would be false to every canon of good reporting if you chickened out on

Torremolinos. It's the living most . . . the capital de gustibus . . . the new wave . . . the perpetual party. It's Sweden-on-the-Sand. It's the Lourdes of LSD. It's the only spot in Spain where the Guardia Civil doesn't run things, and you must see it.'

Several other advisors had recommended Torremolinos, in somewhat similar phrases; it had become the international capital of the Mediterranean, superior to Positano, more fun than Nice and less expensive than either. I heard some great stories about the goings-on in the marijuana belt, but I judged that here was a town that merited a younger man than I to record its frivolity, and with some regret I headed north.

Just before we hit the Mediterranean coast we came to Elche, where we saw a sign saying, 'See the Dama de Elche,' and I stopped quickly at a garage: 'Has the famous statue of Elche been brought down here from the Prado?'

'Yes. You can see it in town.'

I thought how fine it would be to see this famous work on the site of its discovery seventy years ago, but when I had parked near the building where it was on display, a policeman said, 'Never heard of it. What is it?' and I supposed that I was once more in an area where citizens were unacquainted with their town's principal treasure, but in a bookstore the clerk smiled warmly and said, 'Señor, what a pity! The great statue was here. For our two-thousandth birthday. But it's now back in Madrid.' I was disappointed, but she took a paper and drew a map. 'If you've already seen the statue, why not go out to the farm where it was discovered? You'd find it most interesting.'

So we sought a small country road and traveled through the once-great date plantations of Elche; in Muslim days there had been over a million date palms here and their fruit was famous as far as Egypt. Now the vast plantation has diminished to a mere fraction of its former size, and many have adduced this as proof of how Spain suffered when the Moors were expelled. I think a truer interpretation would be that tastes have changed and that non-Muslims simply do not eat as many dates; where the palms used to grow I found almond trees, one of the most poetic of the fruit family and as gracefully restrained as a solitary guitar playing at night. While I was marveling at the beauty of the almond trees, my wife pointed to a spot at which five fields came to a point, producing something I had not previously seen: growing side by side were dates, almonds, olives, oranges and pomegranates. As much as anything I saw in Spain, this curious juxtaposition demonstrated how rich the Mediterranean littoral had always been, whether under Roman, Visigoth, Muslim or Spanish rule; we were in a garden that stretched for hundreds of miles.

The farm where the Dama de Elche was found, if indeed she was a dama, had assembled a small, miserably arranged museum of artifacts found within its boundaries. In it we found griffons dating back to 400

B.C., lintels from Roman temples, Visigothic sherds and a wealth of urns, jewelry, lions and mosaic floors. The very helter-skelter of the place lent it a kind of historical integrity: this was how things were dug up at such a site; and when we explored the fields themselves we could see the roots of the buildings: this had been a temple which at some period had served as a synagogue and later as a mosque. Elche must have been enormously wealthy in its great days, for these buildings were rich; beyond them lay the field where the statue had been found and here I experienced the same sense of frustration that had overtaken the scholars who first studied the work. Judging from the site, the statue could have been lost there as late as Renaissance times, but if someone had told me, 'You can see that it might have been laid down long before the Romans came,' I would have had to agree to that too. I think it appropriate that this splendid work remain a mystery. Man or woman, Iberian or Roman, priest or warrior, the thing stands nobly by itself, a perpetual challenge to the imagination.

I had heard of Alicante, one of the big seaports on the coast, and I knew that like all the littoral it had experienced considerable growth in recent years, so I was not entirely surprised when I saw its dozens upon dozens of new high-rise apartment houses, occupied principally by new-comers from Scandinavia and Germany; but I had never heard of San Juan de Alicante, a trivial little seaside village four miles to the north. I suppose, looking back on it, that this was one of the biggest shocks I experienced in Spain for as we came around a bend in the road following the sea, I found myself facing a resort settlement which three years ago had been barren ground and which now sprouted some three dozen four-teen- and eighteen-story spanking-new apartment buildings done in the most advanced modern style. They looked like mushrooms that rise on a forest floor after a storm, and the storm that called them forth was a mighty one which has swept the entire Spanish seacoast. From the French border south to Gibraltar a score of San Juan de Alicantes have risen in the past five years, and for the remainder of our trip north to Barcelona we would never be out of sight of this forest of new apartment buildings . . . not clusters of two or three but literally hundreds at a time and many thousands in all. I doubt if there is another area in the world that even comes close to the explosion that has overtaken this coast.

Who built the apartment houses? Spanish gamblers who have put together a little capital, borrowed heavily from banks and sold off their product to tourists before the first floor was finished. Who owns them now? Mostly Germans, some Swedes, some Dutch, a good many French. Some entrepreneurs from those countries buy entire apartment houses, which they rent out by the season; more often the floors are sold off singly to individual families on a cooperative basis. In one area of San Juan de Alicante all signs were in German; in another, French. One has to travel this coast to appreciate how unimportant to modern Spain are the

English-speaking tourists, for I did not come upon any district in which the signs were in that language.

I suspect my description of San Juan has failed to convey to the reader what has actually happened; how can he picture that jungle of concrete that has risen so swiftly from bare land? How can he visualize these very tall apartments, with no gardens, no ambiente, except that each room has an exquisite view of the sea? How can he understand that in Spain there has suddenly appeared this alien city, most of whose inhabitants speak northern European languages, frequent Nordic bars with Nordic bands, and when the season is over, board up their apartments and go back to Berlin and Stockholm? It is a revolution of considerable magnitude, but the best place to acquaint oneself with it is at Benidorm, a charming village a few miles farther up the coast.

Here the activity has multiplied about one hundred times within five years! Where there were three dozen towering apartments to startle me at San Juan, there must have been several hundred at Benidorm. It has a spacious beach, mountains inland and an unruly sort of charm. It is preponderantly German, and while I was staying there it gained notoriety because a mad German described as the Werewolf of the Autobahn was supposed to have fled to Benidorm after having slain several girls near Berlin. He was said to be hiding out in some kind of disguise that would not attract attention, but the Spanish police nabbed him. He had been riding up and down the beach at Benidorm, dressed head to toe in a white silk suit and driving a flaming red Mercedes convertible while accompanied by four blondes. Reporters pointed out that such a disguise was scarcely calculated to avoid attention, but the police said, 'Reverse thinking on the part of a born criminal.' Later when the reporters discovered that the suspect's passport showed that he had been in Benidorm at the time of the murders and had indeed been registered with the local police, the latter said, 'That's a technicality we haven't discussed yet.' That afternoon the suspect was discharged and held a press conference at which he announced that an Italian movie company was going to star him in a picture to be called *The Werewolf of the Autobahn*. He thought that maybe the four blondes would get parts, too.

Benidorm is like that. Looking at the real estate explosion of which it is merely a part, one asks, 'What good has it done the Spaniards?' and the answer is problematic. The building gamblers who have underwrittten the initial costs of the apartment houses have used their small funds to exert a favorable leverage, and since they know how to avoid taxes they have often ended up millionaires. Laborers' wages have been kept low, and although some of the new bars and stores have fallen into Spanish hands, most are owned by foreigners. What seems to have happened is that the low cost of Spanish construction has subsidized good housing for Germans and Swedes with minimum rewards to Spaniards. Thus the precedent set by the conquistadors, who operated a good thing for themselves and for Peru but who benefited Extremadura in no way, is once more being honored. And just as the Extremaduran emigrant builds up Germany in return for a little gold exchange, so the Mediterranean builder erects homes for northerners. What profits do accrue do not benefit the country-side, except for the service jobs created by the new developments. Further-more, any threat of war over Gibraltar or any upheaval attendant upon the passing of Franco could evaporate the tourist industry overnight and leave these vast buildings vacant. If this were to happen for even a season, with the resultant defaulting on mortgages and the loss of income to stores, the Spanish economy would be seriously compromised. Morally there is also the problem of allowing impoverished Spaniards to see that their govern-ment, which cannot build them houses or schools, is able to construct luxury housing for aliens. Few Spaniards, of course, can afford these beach-side palaces.

On the other hand, in several good sites back from the beach in locations like Alicante and Benidorm, Spaniards are beginning to build high-rise apartments for themselves. An official in the Health Administra-tion explains how this works: 'I can't afford to put up the money for a beach house. Nor can the other fellows in my division. So the government has come to us and said, "We won't lend you the money to build an apartment at Alicante, because you're not a good risk. But there will always be someone like you employed by the Health Administration, so we'll lend the money to the Ministry so that they can put up housing at the beach, and it will belong to you as long as you work there." ' In this manner, even though they own no equities, a few of the benefits of the enormous building boom trickle down to Spaniards, but it should be noted that their buildings are not on the beach; those sites are reserved for foreigners because they have the money, and Spaniards, from their long association with the landed families, are habituated to seeing the best of everything remain in the hands of the few.

Wherever I looked along the coast I found evidence of its being con-verted into an endless ribbon of vacation land. New paradors of clean design were being located at the spots where tourists driving down from France in sports cars would want to spend the night on their way to Torremolinos. Good private hotels were frequent. The narrow road was being widened into one uninterrupted boulevard that would stretch for seven hundred miles. The beach areas had been given fine-sounding names which reverberated with overtones of sun and fun: Costa Brava, Costa Dorada, Costa del Azahar (Orange Blossom), Costa Blanca, Costa del Sol, and beyond Gibraltar on the Atlantic, Costa de la Luz. By this simple device Spain has enhanced the charm of its playlands manyfold. I am told that throughout northern Europe one gains cachet if he says, 'I'm spending my vacation on the Costa del Sol.'

North of Valencia on the Costa del Azahar, I began to experience a sense of excitement, for I was returning to familiar ground. To the left ran the small railroad leading through the mountains to Teruel, and I remembered my exploration years ago; next a road cut off to the right, and as I drove down it I could smell the orange blossoms which had lived in my memory with such persistence, for this was Burriana, that little shipping center where I had first landed in Spain. Could this be the waterfront where the oxen had lugged the heavy barges into the sea? It was now a spacious, jetty-girt harbor with orange boats from Denmark and Germany tied to its piers. Handsome port buildings had been erected to house officials, and almost at the spot where I had first come ashore a high-rise apartment was going up. Not a single item that I remembered still existed, except the Mediterranean, and it had been so pushed around that I scarcely recognized it. Little Burriana, a modern shipping center! Empty, bleak Burriana with its straining oxen, now a location for apartment houses. No transformation then under way in Spain represented so much personal drama as this, and once I had seen it I required no further explanation of what the Spaniards call 'The Miracle of the Mediterranean.'

Once we had passed Castellón de la Plana my wife took over, for we were now approaching that provocative region called Cataluña, which I had never seen but which she had visited some years before, to her intense pleasure. If I said, 'Madrid's an exciting city,' she said, 'But wait till you see Barcelona!' If I liked the park in Sevilla, she said, 'Wait till you see Montjuich in Barcelona.' And no matter what street in Spain I spoke favorably of, she always said, 'It's pleasant, but wait till you see Las Ramblas.'

As we approached the city she asked the driver to keep to the beach road, and there we saw that lovely chain of seaside villages which not even modern builders have been able to spoil, especially Sitges, where we spread a picnic at the farthest point of the pier so that we could look back at the low houses and the village square. 'Three parts of Cataluña are superb,' my wife explained as we finished our first meal in the region. 'Seacoast towns like Sitges, mountain towns like Vich, and Barcelona. You're going to love this part of Spain.'

Her enthusiasm began to infect me, and as we crossed the river with the beautiful name, Llobregat, she pointed to a small mountain on our right, standing with its feet in the sea. 'Montjuich,' she said. 'We'll spend a lot of time here.' When I asked why, she said, 'Half a dozen museums plus a village like none you've seen before.'

She directed the driver to make a series of tricky turns and within a few minutes we found ourselves at the foot of that tall and florid column which dominates the harbor area of the city and which carries at its top a monument to Christopher Columbus. 'When he returned from the New World,' my wife explained, 'he reported to Fernando and Isabel here. Barcelona was the first city in Europe to hear the official account.'

After we paid our respects to Columbus she began to chuckle with delight, clapping her hands and whispering, 'This is what I've been telling you about. Las Ramblas.' It was a wide boulevard consisting of two outer streets for traffic and a spacious central mall for pedestrians, the latter containing newspaper kiosks and many flower stalls. 'Look! There's the woman who sells roses. Over there's the old man who made me my bouquets. Have you ever seen so many flowers?' That day Las Ramblas was indeed a garden, for it was laden with blooms, but I had little time to study them, for now my wife tugged at my arm. 'Look! Look! The bird stalls.' At home we have many birds, wild ones of course, who feed at our window like insatiable gluttons, and we had missed them. Now we were to have, in our front yard as it were, the wonderful bird stalls of Barcelona, and although I shall not be referring to them again, the reader should know that each morning when I started out to explore the city I stopped first to visit with the birds—hundreds of them from all parts of the world—in small, clean cages, well fed and cared for. One can grow to like a city which gives its morning greeting in such a manner.

Las Ramblas proved to be as rewarding as my wife had predicted. It is a heavenly promenade, probably the best I know, and on it I spent many hours. A rambla is a ravine, and this one served as a drainage ditch in time of heavy rain. It is referred to in the plural because it is composed of different sections: La Rambla de los Capuchinos, La Rambla de los Estudios, plus at least three others. It's the center of Barcelona life: here stands the splendid opera house, so plain on the outside, so luxurious inside; here are the theaters, many of the good restaurants, some of the big hotels, and at the inland end, the central Plaza de Cataluña, where the trains and subways focus. At the seashore end, near the Columbus monument, stand the tattoo parlors and the cheap movies. The kaleidoscope is never-ending, for even at four in the morning, when the rest of Spain is asleep, sailors are prowling Las Ramblas and the late restaurants are doing good business.

What seemed to me particularly appealing was that quite close to the boulevard were the city's most varied sights. Off to this side the red light district, where contraceptives, ostensibly forbidden to be sold in Spain, are available in shops which display them in the window. Over here the vast market, one of the best I had seen, close to our hotel and selling a huge variety of fruit and seafood. One stall carried twenty-nine different kinds of olives, large gray-green ones bitter to the taste, sweet ones pitted and stuffed with blanched almonds, tiny black ones which my wife preferred. On the opposite side were the narrow streets which ran to the Gothic quarter, whose concentration of antique buildings alone would attract any visitor, and farther along were the streets leading to this museum or that.

FOLLOWING FACING PAGES: *Most travelers believe that Barcelona's Las Ramblas is the most beautiful street of the north.*

Not the least of the treasures were the bars where dozens of tapas were lined up twenty-four hours a day, including some of the best seafood one could wish. To spend a week in a room facing Las Ramblas, visiting the museums or the Gothic quarter, taking one's meals in the fine restaurants nearby and at night listening to the music of Barcelona, would be an introduction to Spain that might spoil one for what was to come later.

My introduction, following a stroll along Las Ramblas, buying newspapers from London, Paris and New York that I hadn't seen for weeks, was as appropriate as one could have devised. My wife had a letter of introduction to Dr. William Frauenfelder, the Swiss-born director of the Institute of North American Studies in Barcelona, a learned man who knew the city and had a special affection for it. He met us at our hotel and said, 'If you like music there's a concert tonight that will tell you much about Cataluña. Care to attend?' I asked what the program was, and he said, 'That's what makes it so significant. A choral group singing Haydn's *The Seasons*. You've heard the saying? One Catalan starts a business. Two Catalans organize a corporation. Three Catalans form a choral society. In this city music's important.' We said we'd join him, whereupon his manner changed and he became apprehensive. 'I must warn you about one thing. The building in which you'll hear the music is . . . it's unusual. You must prepare yourself for it.' I wondered how one prepared himself for a building, and he explained: 'When you go in, please, please, Mr. and Mrs. Michener, don't gasp or raise your voices. And above all,' here he took us by the hands, 'above all, dear friends, don't laugh. You would destroy your whole effectiveness in Barcelona if you laughed.'

Such a challenge I had not met before. Not long ago my wife and I had been present when Chagall's ceiling at the Paris Opéra was unveiled; we had sat right in front of André Malraux and had behaved rather well, craning our necks back till we were staring into Malraux's face, and shortly thereafter we had attended an opening at Lincoln Center and had not hooted, but apparently the music building in Barcelona was another matter. 'What you had better do,' Dr. Frauenfelder suggested, 'is simply go into the building and allow it to absorb you. Don't say anything. Just look.' We agreed to do this, and at a late hour that night we appeared at the Palau (Palacio) de la Música and one look at the bewildering façade satisfied me that no amount of previous warning from Frauenfelder could have prepared us. The Palau had been erected in 1900 when architects in many parts of the world were getting fed up with old formalisms and fake Greek temples, but the Barcelona architects had had the courage to do something about it. They cast aside balance and austerity and above all they avoided standard types of pillars and capitals. They invented new kinds of pillars, big and small. They devised capitals that looked like turbans and others resembling mushrooms. They tacked on balconies, offset windows, and in one area added a statue of Richard Wagner in his well-known beret. On one shelf someone who looked like Joan of Arc came striding out of a sculptural group, but she was wearing a beard. And wherever I looked I saw not stone or concrete but a mixture of colored ceramic and brick, delightful to the eye, since light played across the surface unevenly, here reflecting as if from a mirror, there deadened by the rough surface of the brick. It was an extraordinary façade, appropriate for the illustration to a Gothic fairy tale, and my wife whispered, 'What must the inside be?'

Gritting my teeth, for I had never before entered such a building except at an amusement park, I followed Dr. Frauenfelder inside, and at the door he whispered, 'Remember, let it flow over you.'

We entered a large auditorium each square inch of which seemed to be covered with florid decoration consisting of pillars covered with broken pieces of ceramic, gigantic sculptural groups featuring flying horses, and colored stones set at odd angles. The effect was that of crawling into an overwhelming grotto, but before I could embarrass Dr. Frauenfelder by laughing, I glanced at the empty stage and saw that its two side walls were covered with eighteen of the strangest statues I had ever seen. They were larger than life size and showed women in medieval costume playing a variety of unfamiliar instruments. They had been carved in a way that was new to me: everything from the waist down was painted flat on the wall in a stylized manner, using pieces of mosaic glass for effect; everything above the waist was carved in stone naturalistically and stood out from the wall like an ordinary statue. The union created an effect that was completely charming, bearing no relationship to reality but a great deal to art.

It was these curious stone women who won me over. They seemed exactly right for the stage of a music hall, and once they established the tone, all the other bizarre phenomena fell into place. Why not have the angle where the proscenium joins the roof covered by rearing horses flying through space? No other symphony hall had such horses, and when I looked closer I saw that Valkyries were riding them. Why not? If this is a place where you come to hear music, why not have a gigantic bust of Beethoven on the right of the stage and someone who looked like Josef Stalin on the left? Dr. Frauenfelder had given me good advice: 'Let it flow over you.' I sat down and did just that, and slowly the wonderful harmony of the place asserted itself; in Rome and Chicago and Tel Aviv I had been in dozens of concert halls, and they'd all been alike and quite uninspiring, but nothing else on earth was like Barcelona's Palau de la Música, and when the chorus of Catalan singers came out and stood on the stage, surrounded by the eighteen stone maidens playing their antique instruments, it was astonishing how the living and the dead united to form one majestic whole.

I fell in love with this crazy hall. I went to it night after night, and no matter what the style of music, the hall seemed to accommodate itself, and what was the more surprising, the stone girls adjusted their manner of playing, too. I heard Illinois Jacquet and Bud Freeman give a jazz concert, and the girls played jazz. I heard a tenor soloist, and they accompanied him. Best of all, I heard one of the Madrid symphonies play a Wagner program, and during the 'Ride of the Valkyries' not only did the eighteen girls join in the music, but high on the ceiling I heard stone horses neighing and warrior maidens shouting, 'Ho-yo-to-ho.'

On the left wall of the stage, as one faces it, the eighth girl plays a drum and wears a high Chinese-type hat beneath which appear long Saxon braids. She has a determined face, with distinct ridges at the corners of her mouth, and her head is twisted in an enchanting manner. She is completely adorable in a resolute, stubborn sort of way, and after the Dama de Elche she is my favorite statue in Spain, for she symbolizes for me the Catalan temperament, and often as I sat in her palace, listening to music, I stared at her and thought not of Haydn or Wagner but of Cataluña.

Next morning I had the good luck to meet José Porter, who runs a bookstore not far from the cathedral and who is a dedicated Catalan. For some time I had been searching for a book relating to one of the greatest Spaniards, Ramón Llull, and I asked Señor Porter to help, but this day he was inflamed over a fact which exacerbates all Spanish intellectuals: the United States had once more used Columbus Day as an excuse for honoring Italians.

'My God!' Porter cried in his jumbled office, his round face getting red with the indignity he was suffering. 'Only a fool believes in the face of modern research that Colón was an Italian. Don't Americans ever read books?'

I pointed out that the best extant biography of Columbus was by an American, Samuel Eliot Morison, and that he had accepted him as an Italian. To this, Porter, whose name was Catalan with French overtones, exploded, 'Nonsense. Do you know nothing of Armand Bernardini-Sjoesedt?' I shook my head, and he said with blistering contempt, 'It's time his works were known in America.'

Porter was a short man with the pugnacious appearance of a prize fighter, and now with a jabbing forefinger he proceeded to give me ten reasons why Columbus was not Italian. 'First, even the standard biographies which claim he is Italian admit that he came to Spain when he was already a middle-aged man, yet not once do we find even a shred of his writing to be in Italian. Second, those who claim he was Italian never agree as to where he was born. Third, some time ago I was invited to address a learned society in the United States, Cleveland I think it was, and the chairman, knowing my research, took me aside and said, "Señor Porter, we're proud to have you with us, but I must insist that in your speech you make no mention of the fact that Colón was not Italian. All of us who are scholars know that to be a fact, but it would be suicide to say so in this country. The Italian politicians are too strong and they'd cut off our funds." So in what you like to call the freest country in the world, the truth was muzzled. Fourth, it was a Jew of Barcelona, Luis de Santángel, who put up the money to finance Colón's trip of discovery, and we in this city believe he did so because of reasons which I will develop as we go along. Fifth, it seems to me significant that when Colón returned to Spain he reported not to Sevilla or Madrid but to Barcelona.' Here I said that this could have been because Fernando and Isabel were here at the time, but he was already into his sixth point. 'When Colón reached this city he handed Luís de Santángel a letter of appreciation for his money, and it was written in Catalan. Seventh, no existe in todo el mundo ninguna carta firmada Colombo [there does not exist in the entire world one letter signed Colombo] but only those signed Colón, which is Catalan for pigeon; in other words, he never wrote in Italian or signed his name that way, but he did write in Catalan and he used a Catalan signature. Eighth, the first missionary to accompany Colón to the New World was a Catalan, Bernard Boyl. Ninth, the foremost soldier to accompany him was also a Catalan, Pere Margarit. Tenth, none of his portraits look Italian, but they do look Catalan.'

Triumphantly Señor Porter threw his arms wide, rose from his desk and ran to stand over me. 'It seems completely clear to me that Cristóbal Colón was a Catalan. Look it up in Bernardini-Sjoesedt.'

It was that afternoon when my wife and I discovered the full flavor of Catalan patriotism. We were taken by subway beneath the boulevard which runs northwest from the Plaza de Cataluña, and at the terminus we climbed out to board a dinky little blue-and-white trolley, which deposited us at the bottom end of a funicular railway. This lifted us to the top of a very steep hill, crowned by a Catholic shrine of some importance, which was surrounded cheek-by-jowl with a rowdy amusement park. 'This is El Tibidabo,' our Catalan guide said, 'the place where the devil tempted Jesus.'

'How did it get that name?'

'Tibi, Latin meaning: To thee. Dabo, Latin for: I give. It was to this spot that the devil brought Jesus when he tempted him with the pleasures of earth.'

'Wait a minute!' I protested. 'The Bible says that . . .'

'My friend, if the devil had taken Jesus to the top of some arid hill in Palestine and Jesus had rejected a hunk of desert, would that have had spiritual significance? But if the devil brought him here, and if Jesus turned down something as glorious as Cataluña, wouldn't that signify? From the top of El Tibidabo he pointed out the glories of his land. 'Down there the seacoast, the best in Spain. Back here the sacred mountain of Cataluña, Montserrat. There the Llobregat coming out of the hills. And before us at our feet Barcelona, like a carpet of beauty. This spot . . . right here on El Tibidabo . . . ' He was overcome with emotion, but with his right hand inscribed a complete circle, encompassing one of the loveliest views in Spain. Later he said, 'If Our Lord was not tempted by what he saw on El Tibidabo, he was beyond temptation.'

Succeeding days were filled with trips illustrating many different aspects of Catalan life, and although it would be instructive to report the richness we found, it will be wiser to concentrate on our experiences with the intellectual activity of the region, because Barcelona specializes in this, and the reader may be surprised to discover how fine its quality is. That evening Dr. Frauenfelder arranged a visit to the home of a prominent hostess, where I had the good luck to sit with a spirited Catalan, José María Poal, a medical doctor eager to get me started right in his city. Approvingly he said, 'Last night I saw you at the Palau de la Música, listening to Haydn being sung in Catalan. A proper introduction.' Dr. Poal was a short man, as most Catalans are, with very dark hair, a beard but no mustache, and heavy glasses. Like many men from this region he was a brilliant talker and commanded three or four languages; ideas were a challenge to him, and when I asked a question, he would cry, 'Ah, yes! I was thinking about that the other day,' and he took pleasure in explaining his thought processes, or those of the typical Catalan, as if I were a student, which indeed I was. 'Yes! What is a Catalan? I was pondering this only yesterday and came to the conclusion that we must be understood as the diametric opposite of the Hungarian, who came out of Asia and maintained himself as an enclave in the midst of surrounding European peoples. We're the perfect mixture, a fusion of Celt-Iberian, Phoenician, Greek, Roman, French, Aragonese, Catalan, with a sprinkling of Visigoth, Mussulman and Jew. Better than any other group in Spain, we're able to see the world as a whole . . . especially Europe.'

I asked Dr. Poal to identify the salient characteristics of the Catalan, and without referring to past contemplation he cried, 'Not art. Not architecture. Not writing, although we've had some great ones. Music. Pinch a man on the streets of Barcelona and if he doesn't cry out in pitch, he's not a Catalan. Three years ago the choral group you heard last night was in financial trouble. Had to have ten million pesetas or go out of business. A group of us went quietly through the streets of this city, telling our friends, "The voice of Cataluña is about to be silenced. The chorus that inspired your father and mine in the dark days is broke . . . busted . . . the strings on the lute are torn." Within twenty-four hours we had the ten million pesetas, for a Catalan would rather miss a meal than his music.'

Dr. Poal reminded me of one fact which Americans tend to forget. 'The influence of France on Spain has been considerable, and usually positive. Much of our best thinking has been inspired by French precept, and this is particularly true of Cataluña. In this room tonight I would suppose that better than fifty percent speak French and more than that read it. At many stages of history we were part of France, and if one were to carve out a linguistic Cataluña, much of it would be found over the Pyrenees in France. A man like myself . . . I feel a tremendous pull toward the Pyrenees. They exert a kind of fascination on the Catalan mind. Always keep your eye out for the French influence in Spain. It's usually constructive.'

What Dr. Poal overlooked telling me was something I already knew, that France did not reciprocate the warm feeling of Spaniards like Poal. Agitation for a separate Catalan state, or for a separate Basque, arose in northern Spain but involved substantial areas of southern France, for there were about as many Catalans and Basques living in France as there were in Spain. Therefore, this area of Spain was something of a headache to France. Contemptuously, French thinkers repeated the aphorism 'Africa begins just south of the Pyrenees,' and most Frenchmen dismissed Spain as something so exotic that no rationalist could comprehend her. In French regions adjacent to Cataluña the feeling was exacerbated in 1939, when hundreds of thousands of Spanish patriots fled through the mountains to take up what they considered temporary residence in France; they remained for more than a quarter of a century. Finally, during many periods of history, Cataluña formed a part of France and was governed by Frenchmen, so that it can be considered a defected province but one that France was well rid of.

I thought it best not to raise such questions but I did pose two others. First, what was the future of Cataluña? 'Ah yes! I've been thinking about this a great deal and I know of no one in my acquaintance who dreams any longer of Cataluña as a separate state. At one time it could have been free . . . like Switzerland . . . or maybe a union of Basques and Navarrese of Spain and France . . . a rough confederation of some kind . . . but those days are gone. Everyone knows it. We must integrate fully with Spain, and everyone I know is eager to do so. But I would lie if I did not say that I feel more Catalan than anyone else in this room or perhaps in all Barcelona. My heart throbs to the rhythm of this land. I write poetry in Catalan. I should. It was my grandfather who compiled the Catalan grammar. Montserrat, Vich . . . these places are part of me and I would die rather than betray Cataluña. But politically our future rests in being a creative part of Spain. God, how the rest of Spain needs us!'

Second, with the continued influx of immigrants from Extremadura and Andalucía, would not the spirit of Cataluña be watered down until it vanished? 'Now, now! I've just been reading a fine book on that very subject. You've got to read it. Francisco Candel's *Los otros catalanes* [The Other Catalans]. It's a probing analysis of this very problem, and Señor Candel claims that it works the other way. The Andalusian comes up here, sees the wonder of Cataluña . . . the schools, the hospitals, yes, and the big factories where men earn a decent wage. Señor Michener, in five years he's a better Catalan than I am.' I said I doubted this because my experience in other nations had been contrary, to which Dr. Poal replied, 'Other nations, yes. But Cataluña is special. Because we are so mixed in our heritage we are not narrow-minded little provincials. We have a bigness of spirit . . . a singing of the heart. This communicates itself, especially to people like the Andalusians, who've lived in a bitter, narrow world.'

As a result of my talk with Dr. Poal, I acquired a typed copy of Dr. Salustiano del Campo's research paper, 'On the Assimilation of Immigrants in Cataluña,' completed only a few weeks earlier. To me its statistics were interesting, because I had already witnessed in other parts of Spain the passion with which poverty-stricken families had said, 'He's lucky. He moved to Barcelona.' Here was a study reporting the results of these moves.

'Why did you immigrate to Barcelona?' Nearly half replied, 'Because I wanted to find a better life,' but many made the tragic confession, 'In my village I was unable to earn a living.'

'Has the move worked out well?' More than half replied that it had exceeded the hopes they had had when they left their villages. Only ten percent said they had been disappointed.

'What kind of effect has the immigration had on Cataluña?' Among those moving in, more than half believed that Cataluña had been lucky to get them; among the Catalans who had to make places for the immigrants, only a third thought the influx had been beneficial. About half doubted that the move was for the best.

'Are the immigrants learning to speak Catalan?' The testimony of both the immigrants and the native Catalans among whom they worked was unequivocal: very few learn Catalan. This is probably for the good of Cataluña, since it will make assimilation with the rest of Spain easier, but it must create apprehensions in the minds of fervid Catalans like Dr. Poal.

Then followed a series of tables which I found fascinating. They reported on Dr. del Campo's attempt to identify the 'social distance' which separated the various groups of newcomers. People from twelve regions of Spain, such as Extremadurans and Andalusians, were listed, accompanied by people from twelve foreign countries, such as Frenchmen and North Americans. A variety of questions was then put to Catalans and immigrants alike, with the results shown in the table on page 563.

It is interesting but not surprising that in the choice of marriage partner both Catalan and immigrant preferred mates from any part of Spain, even ill-regarded Murcia, to foreigners; religion had much to do with this, because if one chose a Spaniard, no matter how lowly, he was at least sure of catching a Catholic. In all columns the social distance between the Murcian and the highest-ranking foreigner was considerable.

I concluded from my reading of Dr. del Campo's study that the dilution of Cataluña was inescapable. Immigration into the area is more massive than I have been able to convey; word has gone out to the other

As a Catalan, which region's people do you like best?	As an immigrant, which region's people do you like best?	If you were to marry, from which would you choose?
1 Cataluña	1 Aragón	1 Cataluña
2 Valencia	2 Cataluña	2 Valencia
3 Baleares	3 Navarra	3 Baleares
4 Basque region	4 Castilla	4 Basque region
5 Navarra	5 Valencia	5 Navarra
6 Aragón	6 Asturias	6 Aragón
7 Asturias	7 Basque region	7 Asturias
8 Castilla	8 Extremadura	8 Castilla
9 Extremadura	9 Andalucía	9 Extremadura
10 Galicia	10 Baleares	10 Andalucía
11 Andalucía	11 Galicia	11 Galicia
12 Murcia	12 Murcia	12 Murcia
13 France	13 Mexico	13 Mexico
14 Mexico	14 France	14 France
15 Italy	15 Brazil	15 Brazil
16 Brazil	16 North America	16 Italy
17 Germany	17 Italy	17 North America
18 England	18 Germany	18 Germany
19 Sweden	19 England	19 Sweden
20 North America	20 Sweden	20 England
21 Argentina	21 Morocco	21 Argentina
22 Venezuela	22 Argentina	22 Venezuela
23 Morocco	23 Venezuela	23 Norway
24 Norway	24 Norway	24 Morocco

parts of Spain that here is the good place to live and that for generations to come there will be jobs along the Catalan coast. I would expect the immigration to increase rather than diminish, for if I were a young Spanish laborer in some backward Extremaduran or Andalusian village I would cut out for Barcelona tomorrow. I would be homesick, to be sure, and I might long for the intimacy and love of my native pueblo, but it would see me no more. I would not subject myself to its humiliation when I could live in the freedom of Barcelona.

Since my earliest days in Spain I had wanted to see how the publishing business operated, for I bought many books and knew a few writers, but always I had been advised, 'Hold that till you reach Barcelona. It's the publishing capital of Spain.' So one morning I reported to Ediciones Destino, whose president, Señor José Vergés Matas, proved generous with his time. He was an unusually handsome man who looked to be about forty-two, with prematurely white hair and a large mobile face featuring even teeth and a modern type of eyeglass. 'The old firms die out,' he said gravely. 'You won't believe it, but I founded this company. Yes. First we published magazines and made a big success. This one here,' and he showed me his firm's leader, a magazine of opinion and news, 'sells about sixty thousand copies a week.' I looked at the cover and saw that it was in its thirtieth year.

'Did you say you founded this?'

'Yes. Thirty years ago.' He was obviously somewhat older than the forty-two I had guessed. Then he added. 'I was quite young at the time, believe me. Today I wouldn't have the courage. Well, when the magazines made money we turned to books, and in Spain that's an adventure because in this country we don't have many readers. In North America you have two hundred million people.' I was constantly being surprised at how much educated Spaniards knew about my country and how little we know about theirs. 'Some good books in your country can hope to sell a hundred thousand copies. In Spain we have one-sixth as many people, about thirty-four million, so we should expect to sell one-sixth as many books, or sixteen thousand. How many do you suppose we do sell?'

I knew that Spanish readers bought fewer books than Americans did, just as Americans bought fewer than English or Japanese, but I had no idea that the editions of important books were so minute. Señor Matas said, 'We're lucky if we sell three thousand copies. We print that number, hopefully, and we keep our costs so low that we break even if we sell twelve hundred. We put only fifteen hundred in covers. We bind the rest only if we sell our first effort. If not, and this is usually the case, we throw away the second fifteen hundred sets of sheets.

'We pay about the same royalties to authors that you do. On the first eight thousand copies, ten percent. On the next two thousand, twelve percent. Above ten thousand copies, fifteen percent. But not many writers can live off what they earn publishing books in Spain.'

I had noticed on the shelves lining his office a series of what looked like novels, all published in the same format and stretching for some distance around the room. When I asked what they were, his wide face broke into a smile of satisfaction. 'One of the best ideas I ever had. The Premio Eugenio Nadal. He was an editor of ours. We've given this prize each year since 1944, and we've found some sensationally fine books. All novels. In 1947 Miguel Delibes' *The Shadows of the Cypresses Lengthen*, in 1959 Ana María Matute's *Earliest Memories*. And of course this one in 1946, José María Gironella's *A Man*. Because we've held our standards so high, and partly because of luck, we can assure the author who wins this prize a sale of at least twenty thousand. He earns some real money if he wins the Premio Nadal. Maybe four hundred manuscripts will be submitted.'

Señor Vergés told me that of all the books published in Spain, ninety percent are handled by Barcelona firms, and of books of high quality, about ninety-eight percent. Much of the actual printing, however, is done on big presses in cities like Bilbao. 'What we're finding profitable is joint publication with houses in Italy, Berlin, Geneva and Amsterdam. We bring out expensive books in color, like the paintings of Goya or *Life in Prehistoric Times*. We print all the editions, regardless of language, in Switzerland and especially Italy, which seems to have the best color presses in the world these days, and this enables us to keep costs so low that we all make money. But here is something we do that you don't do any longer in America, and our authors appreciate it.'

He pointed to a shelf on which rested thirty volumes, bound in leather and most handsomely designed, representing the complete works of a novelist held in much esteem locally, *The Complete Works of Josep Pla*. 'They sell for six dollars and forty cents a copy and large numbers of people feel that they must have the complete set.'

'When did Pla die?' I asked.

'He's still alive. We do this for our living authors,' and he pointed to four or five other such series.

I picked up one of Señor Vergés' books and saw that it was not in Spanish but in Catalan. 'There's a problem for you!' he said. 'Of our thirty-four million population, thirty-one million read Spanish and they will buy three thousand copies of a book. Only three million read Catalan, but they will also buy three thousand copies of a book published in Catalan. Therefore, it's just as profitable for us to publish in Catalan as it is in Spanish.' I could not believe this, but Señor Vergés referred to two editions of Truman Capote's *In Cold Blood*, one in Spanish, one in Catalan. 'The publisher will sell about the same number of each,' he said. 'Catalans read. They're the Bostonians of Spain.'

Recalling the way in which English and American authors jump from one publisher to another, I pointed to the Premio Nadal novels and asked, 'When you give a man the prize, are you able to hold on to him for his subsequent books?'

Apparently this was as touchy a point in Barcelona as it was in New York, for Señor Vergés frowned and said, 'Alas, the prize is often the nudge they need to go off to some other publisher. Look at him.' He pointed at José María Gironella's novel, the winner in 1946. 'He left us, and you know what happened with his later books.'

Friends had arranged for me to meet Gironella, Spain's phenomenal success. His last three books, dealing with the Civil War, had been tremendously read, *The Cypresses Believe in God, A Million Dead* and the one currently in the windows of every bookstore, *Peace Has Broken Out.* Within a few weeks of publication the last had sold a hundred and fifty thousand copies, fifty times normal expectations, which would be comparable to the unheard-of figure of five million for the United States. In other words, Gironella was the man who broke the restraints of Spanish publishing.

I found him in a neat, book-crowded apartment, with a group of unexpected works lying handy to his desk: a life of Franklin D. Roosevelt, a critical study of Lenin, biographies of Gandhi, Stalin, De Gaulle. William Shirer's *Rise and Fall of the Third Reich* was prominent and on a table by the davenport Capote's *En sangre fría.*

Gironella was a slim, tense man in his late forties, I judged, although my experience with the publisher had somewhat unnerved me where guessing ages was concerned. He smiled easily and said, 'I'm surprised a norteamericano writer would want to speak with me. When my first book was published in America, Spanish Marxists living abroad crucified it and charged me with being a Fascist lackey. The publisher, I won't bore you with his name, wrote and told me he wouldn't be taking any more of my books because he couldn't afford to have a Fascist on his list. Later somebody told me that the real reason he cut me off was that my book didn't sell very well. I'd cut an author off too, if he was a disappointment financially as well as politically.

'Actually, I doubt that the tag "Fascist lackey" applies to me. At home I'm accused of being a dangerous liberal. I believe the fact is that I have described the war pretty much as it occurred, and to do this would enrage norteamericanos who saw it otherwise and Spaniards who had their own version.'

Gironella, who in appearance reminded me of Arthur Miller, had traveled widely throughout Europe. 'Almost all the countries. Communist too. I understand you've been to Asia. I found it wildly exciting. Japan, India, Egypt. This year I want to see Israel. I don't understand how a serious writer these days can judge his own terrain if he knows no other.'

I asked him why he continued to live in Cataluña, and he grinned. 'I grew up in a town near Gerona [Catalan, Girona]. I suppose that's where my family got its name. Gironella. The Girl from Girona. It's a grand region. The other day this fellow heard a lecture on the glories of Castilian literature, and which writers did the speaker refer to? Valle Inclán, a Galician. Pardo Bazán, another Galician. Ibáñez, a Valencian. Pío Baroja, a Basque. Unamuno, a Basque. Lorca, an Andalusian. Jiménez, another Andalusian. And at the end of the list he referred to me, a Catalan. I love the regions of Spain.'

I asked whether he thought the influx of Andalusians would modify

Flower seller on Las Ramblas.

Cataluña. 'For the better. In my little town they've opened a night club. Stiff, suspicious Catalans go there, listen to the guitars till midnight, then raise their right forefinger, whisper one reserved "Ole" and go home satisfied that they've participated in the glories of Old Spain.'

I saw a good deal of the book business in Spain and constantly had the feeling that it stood about where it had in the United States fifty years ago. There was much peddling of illustrated Bibles on street corners, where fast-talking men in overcoats spread their big volumes on collapsible tables and buttonholed people as they climbed out of the subway or left the cinema. The Bibles seemed poorly put together and were far below the quality of similar ventures in Italy or Germany.

What to me was wholly incomprehensible was the hawking of complete sets of authors like Honoré de Balzac and Victor Hugo in poor translation encased in cheap impermanent binding. Some of these sets, whose authors I cannot now remember, were truly grotesque; the average Spanish family had no conceivable need for the collected works of Bret Harte, for such books could not possibly relate to their needs. There seemed to be two reasons for this phenomenon. Spain did not encourage or at times even allow honest discussion of contemporary problems, so it was understandable that publishers would look to foreign literatures for sets of books which might sell because of clandestine reputations. Certainly the ideas of Balzac and Hugo were at odds with those of Generalísimo Franco's Spain, but they were French ideas and therefore to be discounted. For example, one could not possibly publish in Spain the kind of book attacking Franco that one publishes in the United States attacking whoever is President at the time, nor would one publish a novel on any significant contemporary issue, so for first-rate treatment of the human condition one must look abroad. The second reason we have already uncovered. Spanish families love to buy sets of books, whether they read them or not, and since Balzac wrote many books, he produces an impressive set.

This accounts, too, for the sale of encyclopedias, often wretched in scholarship. One finds sets of volumes on almost anything, not as banal perhaps as the comparable volumes now being peddled in the United States on our history, the nature of science or great moments of discovery, but still pretty bad. From time to time I consulted these miserable works in search of rudimentary data and they had nothing to offer, yet they appear proudly in many homes, gathering a dust of respectability that is rarely disturbed and never with profit.

On the other hand, Spain has produced one of the world's outstanding encyclopedias, the great *Espasa-Calpe* in some ninety volumes, publication of which began in the 1920s. It is a reputable work, unbalanced perhaps in its emphasis on Spanish history and thought, but with a mature coverage that makes one wonder how Spain, with so few readers, could have produced such a work, whereas the United States, with infinitely greater resources, has not. Of course, the *Espasa-Calpe* is not found in many private homes, but Señor Porter, the bookseller, had one in his, and I was surprised in other homes I visited to see the endless rows of this extraordinary work. It was the exhibition set nonpareil, but it was also a gold mine of material in which to prospect. For example, the article on *Don Quijote* covered pages 1117–1214 of Volume 48, and like several other such entries, was a book in itself, for the pages of *Espasa-Calpe* are quite large. Experts told me that in coverage of topics the Spanish encyclopedia surpassed Mussolini's distinguished *Enciclopedia Italiana* and in thoroughness of treating those topics, the *Britannica*. It was, however, less distinguished in scholarship than the famous Eleventh Edition of the *Britannica*, but not inferior to the later editions.

This matter of Spanish scholarship baffled me. Repeatedly I bought books whose titles led me to expect an orderly development of an idea, as for example, *History of Spanish Colonization in Africa*, only to find that the accurate title should have been *Some Casual Reflections on Random Aspects of a Gentleman's Travels in Our African Colonies and Elsewhere*, in which the first chapter dealt with a trip the author once made to Kenya, the second with a hippopotamus hunt in the Congo, the third with a hortatory essay on the need for more Catholic missions, and the fourth with God knows what. I doubt if there is another country in the world, except Japan, in which books are so poorly organized and so dependent upon the personal whims of the writer. Especially aggravating is the fact that few Spanish books contain indexes, at least none of the hundreds I have bought, and some which pretend to scholarly completeness, such as the history of the zarzuela which I have before me as I write, lack both index and table of contents, even though they are the kind of book one consults for particular items rather than reading seriatim. Can one take seriously the scholarship of a man who fails to provide even a table of contents?

On the other hand, if, as I sometimes think, the measure of a contemporary society is whether it can support poets, Spain is far ahead of the United States, for poetry is published in Spain, as it is in Russia and Israel, and it is not much published, with honorable exceptions, in the United States. A man in Spain can build an enviable reputation from a few volumes of poems and is then held in an esteem which knows no parallel in America, for poets like Lorca and Jiménez are worshiped in Spain.

I met many Spanish writers and studied the lives of more, and concluded that there is no nation in the world where it is so good to be a dead writer. Wherever I went I saw placards announcing grand assemblies of Homenaje a (Homage to) Benito Pérez Galdós (1843–1920) or Vicente Blasco Ibáñez (1867–1928) or Pío Baroja (1872–1956). I attended three such homenajes to writers, and they were moving affairs at which men rose to give orations the like of which I had not heard for fifty years. All aspects of the life and writings of the man in question were reviewed and true homage was paid him as a continuing cultural force. In the parks I found statues to these writers and in the newspapers a constant series of essays on their significance. Subjected to such a continuing barrage, I began to believe that Pedro Antonio de Alarcón, the author of the story from which Falla's *El sombrero de tres picos* was adapted, was a much greater writer than Walt Whitman, because I had never heard of anyone in Camden holding a Homage to Walt Whitman. He was dead, so forget him because in life he had been troublesome.

The case of Pío Baroja is interesting. This acidulous Basque wrote strongly anti-clerical novels, as did Blasco Ibáñez, and during their lifetimes they were anathema, but now that they are dead they are the subject of frequent homenajes and their accomplishments are praised as having brought real honor to Spain. I was present when the tenth anniversary of Baroja's death was observed, and the enmity which the state had held against him as an anti-clerical radical was forgiven and he was ushered into the pantheon with editorials and homenajes that would have been impossible even five years before. In a way, the same thing has happened to Hemingway; he was a foe of the Franco government and while he lived was more or less persona non grata, but now his greatness is being acknowledged: 'A few days before the death of Baroja, he was visited by Hemingway, who wished to tell the old man that the Nobel Prize for Literature which the norteamericano had won belonged really to Baroja. Hemingway, who was a gallant man, spoke only the truth and we are proud that he had the elegance to proclaim it when others of less pundonor would have remained silent.'

No American writer that I know is going to have in death the kind of immortality that Spain confers on her authors; I was present when Dr. Gregorio Marañón died, a kind of Charles Beard plus André Maurois, and one would have thought that the king had died. Indeed, it was a kingly role that Marañón played, that of a great medical man who wrote essays on Spain's periods of ascendancy. But when I dug deeper I found again and again that mournful refrain, 'Pío Baroja lived poorly on his meager income,' or, 'After a life of complete privation he died miserably,' and when I began to question not one person in the creative fields but many, I found that whereas it was wonderful in Spain to be a dead writer, to be a living one was something else. The Premio Nadal, which Señor Vergés' company awards each year, brings the author only $3,333, and few can logically hope to win it. Most struggle a lifetime in near-poverty, abused by society and held in contempt by its rulers. If they write honestly they run the risk of being thrown into jail; if they do not write constantly they starve; and their funeral dirge is always: 'They struggled to make a living and died filled with bitterness and remorse.' I went through a period of acute depression when reviewing the lives of the gifted men who wrote the zarzuelas; so frequent was the statement 'With his four chief works he made millions of pesetas for the managers of the theater, but himself died in poverty' that I suspended my studies. The literary condition in Spain is rather the reverse of that in the States; American writers earn a good living but play no significant role in their society; Spanish writers earn almost nothing, but when dead they are enshrined.

One of the aspects of Spanish intellectual life which struck me repeatedly was the fact, reflected in these pages, that civic leadership so often rested in the hands of medical men. They wrote the best books, made the most daring statements and were revered as the element of society that could be trusted to support good movements. The doctors of Spain formed the stable, liberal cadre and I wondered why this was. I therefore asked a government official if he could arrange for me to meet a typical Spanish doctor who might care to discuss the matter.

I was taken to a huge apartment building, Avenida Generalísimo Franco, 520, whose rickety basketlike elevator crept precariously up a good many floors, opening first on one side then on the other, for it was all doors. It ejected me onto a vast, gloomy ledge with a central well that dropped straight down to where the doorman looked like a midget; it could have been designed by Piranesi. A somber door standing back from the chasm was marked Dr. Arturo Fernández-Cruz, and when the maid opened it I was admitted to the richly decorated apartment of a man of taste. Paintings hung on the walls, which contained many bookcases. Fine rugs and antiques, including what I took to be a valuable Chinese ivory of Confucius and a Thai ceramic of a princess, occupied me until the doctor appeared, and no man could have been better prepared to explain the dynamism of Spanish doctors than he.

He was a cyclonic talker and a man of wide interests. Of medium height, with a head of dark hair that reached down toward his eyes, he wore a mustache which seemed constantly in motion. His eyes were expressive, and his cheeks puckered in when he found delight in some idea which he had begun to offer only tentatively but which had matured into a kind of truth. Because he sat with his back to a solid wall of medical books in varied languages, many of them having been printed in the United States, he gave the impression of being a good medical man, which my friends assured me he was, but it was his reaction to other subjects which captivated me, and I think it wisest if I simply repeat his flood of ideas, for they better than my comments on them will provide a picture of the Spanish medic.

'I suppose I carry a strong strain of the Visigoth in me. I was born in Sevilla, of the middle-class type that they describe as "muy fino y muy frío" [very fine and very cold], but I must have had Germanic inheritance because of the way my mind works. I was a professor at the medical school in Santiago de Compostela, in the heart of Galicia, where a man's character is all-important. "Of course Juan's a good violinist, he comes from such a good family." I prefer it here in Cataluña, where performance is what counts. "Juan claims he's a violinist. Here's a fiddle. Let's hear him play."

'The ideal Catalan, as I study the type in my office, would be Ben Franklin. If you understand his practical nature, you understand Cataluña. No, one more thing would be necessary. He'd also have to be able to sing.

'But you came here to talk about doctors. Remember this. There is no analogy between the role of the doctor in Spain and the doctor in any other country. Our tradition stems from the great Jew Maimonides and the Muslim Averroës. A sick man must be cured, factually. We are not prone to philosophizing about medicine or the good life or the nature of cure. A man is sick, cure him. We set a high pragmatic standard and this gets to be known in the community. From Maimonides and Averroës we also inherit the high position enjoyed by the doctor. This was never a Spanish trait. It was a Jewish and a Muslim trait, and fortunately for us it was adopted by our society.

'Our pragmatic attitude to medicine allows us much mental space for speculation in other fields. No group in Spain reads as much as we do. In all languages. We're the educated ones . . . in medicine and everything else. You see my books. I don't buy them because they have pretty covers, but because I need to know what's going on in the world.

'This means that we come to have the reputation of knowing more than we really do. But we try to know, therefore we are applauded by the people. Oftentimes the doctor is the only educated man a family will know. His opinion is given more weight perhaps than it deserves. But if you look at Spain's position in the world at large, you find that it is only our doctors who stand at the top when judged internationally. We produce good men who do their best to keep up with what's happening in Vienna and Massachusetts General.

'Now, because of our unusual position in Spanish life, we find ourselves constantly invited to lead liberal movements. I suppose doctors the world over incline toward the left in politics, because we see society as a whole. We are driven to become intermediaries because of the trust imposed upon us, and as learned men we must lean toward social justice and a more liberal interpretation of society.

'But let's confine ourselves to Spain. The average family knows only two persons in whom it can trust, the doctor and the priest, and since the priest is obligated to support a certain status quo of which his church is a major component, the family can look only to the doctor for the liberal interpretation toward which it may be groping.

'I've thought about this a great deal, because in Spain, doctors have been foremost champions of advance, as they are everywhere, and I've come to two conclusions. We are able to espouse liberal causes where others would be afraid to do so, because we have a prepared position to which we can retreat. If we are savagely rebuffed in attempting to get better housing, we can still live, because doctors are needed. We can absorb enormous defeats and still live. A priest might be thrown out of the Church. A newspaper editor might be fired and be unable to find work. But we have that prepared position.

'The second factor is that because medicine was for so long the prerogative of Jews and Muslims, children of the best families won't go into it. Only the middle-class families provide medical students. When I was a student in Sevilla we had a young duque in class. He asked me one day what I was going to be, and when I said, "Medico," he said, "My God, I'd rather be a bullfighter." To boys like me medicine was a form of democratic opportunity, the escape from mediocrity, and that's true of all the doctors you see. Middle-class origins, first-class brains. That's a powerful combination. But having come from such backgrounds, we have a natural interest in social betterment, as all doctors should, and I judge that accounts for our favorable position.'

The longer I talked with Dr. Fernández-Cruz the more obvious it became that he felt a personal identification with the Maimonides–Averroës tradition, and like thousands of his associates, was ready to act upon it. One of the most moving things in Spain is the frequency with which one sees in small towns the rude statue to some local doctor who had led the community's fight for social justice. In Badajoz, in Teruel, in a dozen nameless little villages I had seen these evocative monuments: 'To Dr. Teófilo Gómez, predilected son of this village, to whom we are indebted.' It seemed to me that about half the books I read on recondite subjects of Spanish life were written by medical men like Marañón, but my lasting memory is not of their scholarship but of their unfailing championship of liberal causes.

On the other hand, I also noticed that no matter where I went, it was the doctor's house that was the most luxurious, his car the biggest. If he read more books than anyone else in the community, it was partly because he alone had the funds to buy them. I felt sure that the schoolteachers I met would have enjoyed reading more, but their condition was so pitiful that they barely kept ahead of their students; if the condition of the doctors of Spain represents one of the best aspects of the country, that of the schoolteachers represents one of the worst.

There was one publishing company which I particularly wanted to see, much to the astonishment of my Spanish friends, for I thought its operations threw much light on one aspect of life in Spain. To explain, I must detour to a cinema hall on Las Ramblas that carried a banner which I had seen across Spain: 'Marisol: *Cabriola.*' Along with the banner were motion-picture stills showing a delightful blond girl of unascertainable age named Marisol; when supposed to be winsome, she was photographed as thirteen, but when sexy in a refined sort of way, she looked more like nineteen. In either case she was adorable and apparently most of Spain thought so, for her movies were the most popular then being shown. I had intended for some six years to see a Marisol show and there would never be a better opportunity.

All Marisol pictures were alike, I was told, but this one had special features in that it had been written and directed by Mel Ferrer when he was not engaged in various movies that his wife, Audrey Hepburn, was shooting in Europe. And Cabriola was the name of a famous horse ridden in the ring by the Andalusian bullfighter Angel Peralta. Shortly after completing the film, Cabriola had been killed while fighting at Alicante or somewhere in the south, so that the movie was a kind of funeral ceremony for a notable beast.

The theater and all that transpired within was a fairyland. Children were everywhere, waiting for their idol to appear, but there were also many middle-aged women, wondering why their daughters had not turned out as well as Marisol. When the curtain finally opened, after eighteen minutes of advertising slides, a lovely gasp rose from the crowd and a story of complete improbability unfolded.

Marisol, photographed with a skill that I admired, came on screen as a gamin with a beat-up old horse and a cart in which she collected garbage in the slums of Madrid. She lived with her younger brother (this was apparently de rigueur in a Marisol film, since it allowed little girls to imagine how much fun it would be if they could escape parental control) in a makeshift hovel on the edge of the public dump. In addition to the horse that pulled her dump wagon she had another, one of the most beautiful mares ever bred (played by Peralta's Cabriola, a gelding), but how she got her or why was never explained. Through a variety of plot complexities that were winsome if not logical, Marisol trained her horse to fight in the bullring, and with no explanation as to where the money came from, she suddenly appeared with the horse at the ranch of Angel Peralta on the edge of Las Marismas. She was dressed in a whipcord costume that must have cost four hundred dollars.

Now, all this time she was dressed as a boy, and part of the delight the children experienced was in whispering to their friends, 'She's really a girl but the matador doesn't know.' Since Marisol sings, an orchestra had to appear in Las Marismas. Since she dances rather well, a famous flamenco male dancer appeared with her in a dream sequence. I think one would have to be a misogynist not to enjoy such a film if seen in the presence of young girls and middle-aged women, gasping with apprehension when little Marisol found herself by accident in the middle of the bullring facing an enraged animal from whom Angel Peralta would rescue her. And of course there came that electric moment when the matador discovered that she was a girl, so that the film could end with her in another mysteriously provided costume riding behind him in the grand parade of Sevilla's feria.

The publishing company I wanted to visit was called Editorial Felicidad, and there could not have been a happier choice of names, because it published the small hard-bound books which were released in conjunction with each Marisol film. They consisted of the plot of the film, or the major incident of the plot, told in simple words and illustrated with scenes from the picture. The books did a tremendous business not only in Spain but also in Latin America, for Marisol was just as popular in Buenos Aires as in Barcelona.

'We publish an edition of thirty thousand for Spain,' one of the Felicidad people told me. 'For Latin America even larger. With *Cabriola*, because the horse is popular in its own right, we'll probably do better. And you must remember that a serious novel is lucky if it sells three thousand. The books are sold in bookstores. I saw one the other day that had sixteen separate Marisol titles, although there may have been some Rocío Dúrcal ones mixed in.' Rocío is a late rival, a marvelous young lady with a face that is perfectly square and a somewhat better figure than Marisol's.

'Some years ago we published a biography of Marisol. Huge edition. You can't buy a copy anywhere but maybe the president of our company will mail you one to North America. [He never did; no copies available.] She was born in the Calle Refino in Málaga to a middle-class family and her talent was mysterious. At the age of seven she was a professional, and the significant fact about her is that in all the following years she never made one false move. She must have had incredibly good advice. You've seen how careful they are in photographing her. Everything must be just right. A million parents in Spain pray at night, "If we must have a girl, let her be like Marisol." I feel that way myself.

'Boys starting to read will often buy our books, but mostly they sell to little girls and middle-aged women. But we find that even older boys will sometimes peep into the books and whisper to one another, "Well, if all girls were like Marisol it wouldn't be so bad." '

I observed two interesting things about the Marisol fad. The situations in which she finds herself are those which could be especially alluring to girls being brought up in the restrictive customs of the nineteenth century. *Marisol Goes to College. Marisol on TV. Marisol, Girl Reporter. Marisol, Detective. Marisol Learns Ballet. Marisol, Sportswoman.* I doubt that one can present to the young girls of Spain such a standard of freedom without its having some effect.

The other facet of the craze is that in most of her pictures the plot, as we have seen, gives her an excuse to appear in men's dress, and most effectively too, but in this respect her rival Rocío is even more appealing, for she has a figure that seems to blossom when shown in formal men's wear. This is, of course, a carry-over from the tradition we met in the

zarzuela, for when a society aggravates the difference between the sexes, postulating a completely manly man and a womanly woman, the temptation to burlesque the nonsense is great. Unfortunately, this is a low form of art, as proved by that endless flow of abominable English movies in which sailors are given an excuse to dress as women, to the boundless delight of the unsophisticated British audience. In the legitimate theater next to my hotel on Las Ramblas I had an opportunity to see a play I had missed in Pamplona, *La tía de Carlos,* which Spain's fine rubber-faced comedian, Paco Martínez Soria, takes back and forth across Spain, year after year, because audiences love to see him caper as the old lady from Brazil. He does a fine job, featuring long monologues in a crazy cracked voice; his nephew's fiancée asks him if they dance in Brazil, and this is good for a nine-minute explanation of the rhumba, but the significant fact about his popularity is that like Marisol in men's clothes, it is based on the exaggerated difference between the sexes. Also, he is very funny.

In Barcelona books are important, but music is king. My wife and I discovered this when we wanted to attend the opening of the opera at the famous Liceo, which stood just down Las Ramblas from where we were staying. 'We can get you tickets but they'll be dreadfully expensive,' the government official said, and I nodded. Then he frowned. 'But I'm afraid that even if you're willing to pay, it won't do much good, because you norteamericanos don't travel with dress suits.' I said I didn't have one, and he shrugged his shoulders. 'I could get you the tickets, but without a dress suit they wouldn't allow you in.' I explained that we would be happy to sit upstairs in one of the balconies, and he said, 'Apparently you don't understand. This is the opening of the opera. All Cataluña will be there. And the people in the balconies are more meticulous about their dress than those downstairs.' It was impossible for us to enter the building, so we went like peasants to stand in Las Ramblas and watch the limousines arrive with the great of the region, and although we had attended opera in most of the fine houses of the world, and sometimes under rather gala conditions, we had never witnessed anything like this. The dress was impeccable, the excitement intense and there must have been a couple of thousand of us in the street, watching the entry of the Catalans into the Liceo.

Later in the week, when evening dress was not essential in the upper balconies, we were allowed to buy two rather poor seats for $9.40 each to see a performance of *Turandot,* and most of those in the tiers below us and on the main floor were in formal wear. The performance was excellent, and during one of the intermissions, which lasted forty-five minutes each because the Catalans wanted to be seen parading the handsome foyers, I had a chance to study the program for that season, and better than the words of some Catalan enthusiast it demonstrated the musical taste of this city.

Fourteen different conductors from nine different nations, using sing-

577

Marisol.

ers from all parts of the world including Russia and Japan, were presenting twenty-one different operas from eight different nations, including
Russia and Belgium. What impressed me most was the fact that in the
twenty-one operas only nine war-horses like *Aïda* and *Tannhäuser* appeared, but eight that I never had a chance to hear, like the German *Zar
und Zimmermann* by G. A. Lortzing; the French *La Carrosse du Saint
Sacrement* of H. Busser; the Portuguese *Serrana* by A. Keil; and the
Mexican *La Mulata de Córdoba* of J. P. Moncayo. The charge of provincialism that can justly be made against Spanish music in general certainly
does not apply to Barcelona opera, because a season's attendance at the
Liceo would give one a wider purview of what was happening in this genre
than a season in New York or London.

I was advised that this catholic taste, like so much that was commendable in Cataluña's cultural life, stemmed from the French influence
of which Dr. Poal had spoken. A man at the opera told me, 'We have a
mania for knowing what's happening in the world. We read. We have a
constant fear of sinking into the intellectual lethargy you find in . . . well
. . . Andalucía. No norteamericano loves his English heritage the way a
Catalan loves his French. If I thought I would never again read a French
book or hear an opera in French, I think I would wither.'

A man who was listening added, 'We're not French, you understand.
We're Catalans. We don't want a separate state and a seat in the United
Nations. The world should be moving toward larger units, not smaller. And
since we have to be a part of something, it's best to be a part of Spain. But
we are not Spaniards, we are Catalans, and in the future this fact will be
stressed. We want our own language, and our newspapers, and our university. We were on our way to having these things when Civil War overtook
us in 1936. Everything was lost . . . lost. How tragic it was. That damned
war. Now we must begin over again, slowly. But we will be Cataluña. We
will be Catalans.'

I asked numerous residents of the city, 'Do you consider yourself a
Catalan?'

'What else? Did you happen to attend that great performance of
Haydn's *The Seasons* at the Palau de la Música? Notice how the soloists
imported from England and Germany sang in German. But the choir, God
bless it, sang only in Catalan.'

These attitudes naturally arouse in the rest of Spain a suspicion
against Barcelona. Time and again in other parts of Spain intelligent
Castilians or Andalusians queried me as to what I thought of Barcelona,
and when I said, 'I've never been there,' they frowned and said, 'It's a
shame you're saving it for last. It could have an injurious effect.'

Between Madrid and Barcelona there is open war. Forty years ago the
latter city was the industrial leader, with its access to the Mediterranean
and its superior contacts with Europe; the intellectual center too, the

progressive, clean, handsome, well-educated city, and as such it constituted a kind of affront to the rest of the country. Barcelona was both envied and ridiculed; often I heard the statement, 'Who would want to be a Catalan? All business and no soul. There's not a man up there who comprehends pundonor.'

In recent decades, of course, with the central government concentrating in Madrid and with Barcelona suspect because of its anti-Franco role in the war, there has been a concerted effort to draw major industry to Madrid, and it has succeeded. Madrid is now the larger city in population and much the more important industrially. An Englishman connected with the business of distributing films explains what's been happening: 'As you know, the film industry has always centered in Barcelona. Metro-Goldwyn-Mayer, J. Arthur Rank, Warner Brothers . . . all have their offices here. For good reasons. In Barcelona you have linguists, typists, people trained in business. I judge it's three to five times easier to conduct business here than in Madrid. But starting about 1950 a quiet pressure has been applied on all us Johnnies, "Move to Madrid. Move to Madrid." And I wouldn't be surprised to see us frozen out of here before much longer.

'It works this way. You require a piece of paper signed. "Bring it to Madrid and we'll handle it for you in ten minutes." So you fly to Madrid, because if you don't, you get no signature. You want to talk about quotas. "Fly to Madrid." You're interested in a peseta deal. "Fly to Madrid." After four years of this you get the message. We'll all have to fly to Madrid, but where we'll find the trained personnel no one can say.'

There used to be newspapers in Catalan, but after the war they were forbidden. Once church sermons were in Catalan, but they too were forbidden. Catalan resistance was formidable: 'After the war they installed a Madrileño as editor of our best newspaper *La Vanguardia*. To police us, and he was a true swine. One morning he happened to be in an out-of-the-way parish church when the priest, feeling himself secure, gave his sermon in Catalan. After mass the editor grabbed the priest and said things like "You dog. You've been warned not to use Catalan. I'm going to report you to the police." An old woman happened to overhear the threats, which were much worse than I've said, and she alerted the city. By nightfall almost every major business had canceled its advertising in *Vanguardia*. And kept it canceled. Well, planeloads of people flew up here from Madrid, and one general kept shouting, "We'll knock the city down." Enormous pressure was brought on us to reinstate our advertising, but our leaders were clever. They never mentioned Cataluña or the real problem. They simply said, "How can we advertise with a man who abuses a priest?" In the end the government had to give in. The editor was removed. Word swept through the city, "He's being replaced by a man who respects priests." And we were very happy.'

Today Barcelona once more has a Catalan newspaper, but it is watched closely by the police. I was in one printing plant when officers from the Guardia Civil swept in, confiscated the entire printing of a calendar and burned it. The proprietor sequestered two copies, which he let me see. At first glance it was innocuous enough, printed in Spanish as such things had to be. But at the bottom of each month appeared in fine print a list of events under the heading *Never forget these days*. I was not allowed to take the calendar or to copy the dates that had made it illegal, but I recall them as something like this: 'On this date Comte Ramón Berenguer el Gran betrayed Catalan hopes. On this date Spanish armies burned Barcelona. On this date brave Catalans defied the forces of King Felipe IV.' On and on went the litany of hopes seduced and infamy rampant; for each month the Catalans had six or seven evil events to remember, and I suppose the official who gave orders to the guardia was prudent in deciding to burn this calendar, for it was inflammatory.

At the same time that I was being inducted into the arcane mysteries of Catalan nationalism, I was walking through the museum quarters of the city and I cannot recall a more pleasant experience. Margarita Tintó, a tall and beautiful archaeologist, led me through the amazing subterranean museum that lies under the Gothic quarter, showing me the columns and viaducts of the Roman city, the remnants of Visigothic times and a few fragile relics of Muslim rule. At one point, as we climbed across a viaduct many feet below the surface, Señorita Tintó said, 'We are now under the nave of the cathedral. See where its roots begin.' I commend this unusual museum, for in no other have I ever been taken into the bowels of a living city in order to witness its birth.

More spectacular is that unparalleled collection of buildings called El Pueblo Español, where behind a stone-for-stone replica of the entrance gate to Avila hides a complete village which could house about eight hundred people. It was erected in 1929 as merely one feature of an international exhibition, but it proved so popular that it was converted to permanent status and is now one of the most enchanting museums in the world. It contains eighty-one major buildings, each faithfully copied from some famous original and so distributed that all regions of Spain are adequately covered. This attractive little house comes from Toro, where King Fernando V offered to duel King Alfonso of Portugal. Every stone in the copy is faithful to the original. These three handsome old houses have been copied from Teruel; this one reproduces a family shield we saw in Santillana del Mar. In addition to the houses, which are strung out along streets duplicating real streets in the various provinces, there is a plaza mayor where concerts are given in summer, half a dozen smaller plazas modeled after real ones, a cathedral and a full-sized monastery with a cloister. There are about eight major streets, and to see everything would require the better part of a day, but for one who has visited most of Spain, a tour through this village is an architectural treat, for at every corner he sees some famous house that he visited a month ago. For the person just beginning his tour of Spain, I could imagine no better introduction to the quality of small-town building than this; the village is a synthesis of all that is most typical in Spain.

It is difficult to describe how tastefully this has been done, or indeed how it was done at all. The village is now nearly forty years old, but it remains clean and fresh. It has deteriorated in no way and looks stable enough to weather another twoscore years. Obviously the eighty-one buildings are merely false fronts, just deep enough to permit a chain of attractive shops to function inside; here one can see the old arts of Spain performed by experts: glass blowing, printing, weaving, candy making. What perplexed me was how the buildings had been put together. Let's begin with this flight of stone stairs duplicating those before the cathedral at Santiago de Compostela. They are real stones on which hundreds of thousands of people have walked, and that wooden balcony over there on the house from Oviedo is real wood upon which people can stand. The cut stones in this arch are also real and have been quarried on the site from which the originals were cut, but imperceptibly the real merges into the unreal, because this wall is clearly stucco only a few inches thick but skillfully etched to represent stone. A builder could spend a profitable morning trying to detect the real and the unreal; I was not able to.

I visited eighteen major museums in Barcelona and the only second-rate one was the newly opened Picasso museum. In appearance, of course, even it was excellent, for it occupied one of the city's old private palaces, which had been remodeled in exquisite taste. Also excellent were the interesting materials on the life of Picasso, which could not, I suppose, be duplicated elsewhere, and these too were well arranged. For example, I here learned for the first time that one of Picasso's chief works, the enigmatic 'Les Demoiselles d'Avignon' of the Museum of Modern Art in New York, got its name not from the papal city of Avignon in France but from a well-known Barcelona house of prostitution bearing that name.

What was depressing about the museum was that it had so few paintings by Picasso! The spacious walls were covered mostly by lithographs which any private collector could duplicate for a few thousand dollars, a few etchings, a couple of drawings and a handful of paintings, rarely of top quality. I can think of fifteen American cities that could throw together an infinitely better exhibition of Picasso's work by showing only those paintings owned by collectors in the city. Picasso is a Spaniard, but Spaniards have never collected his work.

In a mournful way the museum exemplified the intellectual tragedy of contemporary Spain. Her foremost talents have either been destroyed, like García Lorca, or muffled, like Pío Baroja, or they have turned their backs on Spain, like Picasso; Jiménez, the Nobel Prize poet; and Pau (Pablo) Casals, the cellist. To me it is beyond explanation that an event of such magnitude as the Civil War should have produced no artistic syn-thesis. In Germany, Russia, England and Italy there has been such syn-thesis, but Spain has stifled hers, both in the field of plastic arts, where a new Goya should have arisen to depict the contemporary horrors of war, and in the drama and novel, where works like those of Günter Grass and Alberto Moravia could easily have been evoked. I can think of no nation of modern times, except Turkey, which has experienced such traumatic shock without its artists' having reacted to it in works of grandeur. This is the severest criticism one can make of the dictatorship and the most pertinent: it has forbidden the artistic statement and has therefore crushed it, for the authentic statement once stifled cannot later be revived.

There is, however, a commendable attempt to catch up now, and the Picasso museum is an example, for Spain is desperately eager to reclaim this man as her son. In one year I must have read fifty articles about Picasso the Spaniard: one referred to him as the jovial Málaga painter. On his eightieth birthday sincere felicitations were extended, and if the Picasso museum in Barcelona is not much good, it is certainly crowded with young people hungry to know what kind of man this fellow Spaniard was. There is also a chance that the Gironella novels may pave the way for an honest evaluation of recent Spanish history, but I doubt it. A professor said, 'It is one thing for Picasso to be brave in the safety of Paris. Hell, you complain about Spaniards having no Picassos. During most of the last twenty-five years I'd have been arrested as a suspicious character if I owned one . . . even supposing I could afford it. But for a writer, who has got to live in Spain, to write the way you're talking about . . . that would be suicide . . . now and for the next twenty-five years. We are a state that is determined to live without ideas.' In fact, twice during my stay in Barcelona I was supposed to meet with professors who were described to me as 'cautious men, middle of the road, but with profound ideas concern-ing the future of Spain.' In each instance the interview had to be called off because gangs of bullyboys established for the purpose of terrorizing intellectuals had waited outside lecture halls and had beaten the profes-sors unconscious. Their crime? They had dared to discuss serious ques-tions seriously.

This dualism, this seeking on the one hand for French enlightenment and the crushing of it on the other, explains the following letter:

> Since you left Barcelona I feel very old and defeated, but also very young and hopeful. The cause of the first is Marisol. Of the second, Gironella. Marisol has announced that she's going to get married! I had thought she was about fourteen but she's in her twenties and it all seems dreadfully wrong and I seem very ancient. But your friend Gironella has given us much courage by daring to discuss openly in the paper the deficiencies of the new constitution we've been promised. You would have been thrilled by his clear-cut, honest statement:

> In my opinion Spain has had for many years two basic problems. One, that of progressive democratization; the other, that of what's going to happen when a vacancy occurs in the Chief of State's office.
>
> I do not believe that the Ley Orgánica [Organic Law] approved with such bewildering speed by the Cortes solves either of these two problems.

Gironella continued with a lucid analysis of what the law should have done . . . The kinds of things you and I talked about so much and he had the extreme guts to end:

> In consequence, then, the new Ley Orgánica appears to me a movement of hope but not a solution.

Occasionally my inquiries into the intellectual life of Barcelona bore unexpected results, as when friends took us to see the old monastery of San Cugat del Vallés, lying some distance from Barcelona in a country region. It was there that I saw one of those plain and powerful Romanesque churches which will play so important a role in the final chapter of this book, and as I was admiring its solid simplicity, my guide said, 'While we're here, let's have lunch at El Rectoret,' which was easier suggested than accomplished, because we drove for some time about the countryside without finding it. Finally a shepherd told us which turns to take and we came upon a dilapidated farmhouse standing completely alone. Only an optimist would have believed that within those flaked and weather-beaten walls he would find food.

In a sense, we didn't. What we found was an adventure in family living in which food was incidental. That it was some of the best food in Spain was beside the point, for El Rectoret could have been called 'Cataluña at Table.' It consisted of eight or nine farm rooms, as beat up as the exterior, jammed with simple tables and chairs. I was invited to inspect the fifteenth-century kitchen, where I stayed for more than half an hour, watching a unique operation. El Rectoret serves only four dishes: sausage, chicken, lamb chops and rabbit, with the last selling about as much as the other three combined. With whatever meat you choose you also get a raw salad, a pitcher of marvelous sangría and a terrifying dessert called for some inexplicable reason 'a pijama,' that is, a large soup plate lined with mixed fruit in heavy syrup around a center of flan, the whole smothered in gobs of vanilla ice cream. Salad, rabbit, sangría, pijama! The farm tables were crowded with hundreds of stalwart Catalans, stubborn rocklike people with a passion for good food and music.

The kitchen was a madhouse of open grills, smoking charcoal and sizzling meat. About sixty cooks and waiters moved in and out, all relatives of one huge family. The grandmother checked salads to be sure they contained onions. One aunt did nothing all day long but cut the tops off huge tins of mixed fruits for the pijamas. Another unmolded flan after flan. One traffic manager stood on a little box and shouted numbers at the women tending the grills: 'I have twenty chickens waiting, fifteen sausages, ten lamb chops and forty rabbits.' At the huge fires one man kept applying charcoal as the women opened enormous flat grills and placed the meat upon them, then closed them and thrust them over the fire, where grease from the cooking sizzled all day.

Fifty years ago the grandmother and her husband had opened their farmhouse kitchen to the mule drivers of that day, and in the intervening years they had not altered the menu. Now, on Sundays, customers might wait for a couple of hours to find a place at one of the tables, but as they stood in line they could see great-grandchildren of the original couple washing vegetables in the yard for use in the salads.

Wherever we went on such excursions we met by accident Catalans who represented the best of their culture. Friends took us to the well-known Los Caracoles restaurant (The Snails) at the foot of Las Ramblas, and at the next table sat Joan Alavedra, an elderly man built square, with a rumbling voice, a wild head of hair and a thick homespun suit. He was a poet whom other Catalans respected for his integrity, and throughout the evening many came to pay their respects. When he heard we were in the room he wanted to tell us of his adventures with President Kennedy. It was a poet's story, roundabout and not to the point, but very moving in its conclusion: 'I am the man whom Pau Casals has honored, for it was my poem "The Manger" that he chose as the basis for his great choral composition. Same name. I was with him in Greece when *The Manger* was sung before the royal family. What a night of splendor. How Europe loves this noble old man. Last summer when he was at Prades over the border in France, conducting his summer festival, sixty members of the Barcelona music fraternity made themselves into a little orchestra and traveled from here all the way to Prades. With their instruments. When they got there they unloaded and stood in the street outside Casals' house and played Wagner's *Siegfried Idyl* as a present for the old man. To let him know we still love him even if he can't come home. Then they packed their instruments back into the cars and drove home to Barcelona, and as they came over the hills and saw Cataluña in the moonlight some of them broke into tears and one said, "How the heart of old Pau must break on a night like this. To be so near to Cataluña. To be so near."

'So when this great honor came to Casals in Puerto Rico he wanted me to share it with him, and I flew there to do so. We were to fly to the White House in Washington to receive in person the gold medal of freedom of the norteamericanos. Old Pau, as you probably know, speaks only Catalan in public. Only Catalan, and I would interpret for him. But the week we were to go your President was assassinated. Old Pau sat in his room, rocking back and forth, saying, "I can't believe it. He was my friend." Mrs. Kennedy invited him to participate in the funeral and I urged him to go. "Play one last piece at the grave of your friend," I said, but he was afraid of the crowds.

'The reason I'm telling you this, Señor Michener, is that when I came back to Barcelona my heart was filled with grief and I wrote a poet's account of my visit to Pau and by extension to the Kennedys. It was called "Carols and Kennedy," but in Catalan, of course, and within two hours of the time word flashed through the city that it was available, every copy was sold and I don't even have one for myself. It now sells for more than five dollars on the black market. Because Pau and your President stand for the same thing in the hearts of the Catalans. They stand for freedom.'

At another time it was Lluis Oncins Ariño, the unpremeditated Catalan painter who had spent the middle years of his life as the Spanish representative of the Reynolds Aluminum Company but who suddenly announced that he would henceforth be a painter. With a brooding palette of only four colors, 'My cuisine,' he calls it, dark purple, a blue that is almost black, a very dark red and a heavy orange, he paints heads representative of Spain's varied regions. He has a curious Goya quality, but if you mention this to him he becomes bitter. 'I am Oncins, metal merchant, with my own vision of a crazy world.' When I pointed out that his best pictures seemed always to contain groups of heads, arranged awkwardly but with force, he said, 'With four heads you can't escape dramatic involvement, which seems to be what you prefer, because it's easy to perceive. The real drama lies in the single head, if you could see it.' When I tried to look again at a canvas I had liked, he growled, 'Don't touch the paintings. The hands of the non-artist corrupt.'

I was somewhat ill at ease with Oncins, because he looked exactly like Hubert Humphrey and I expected him to talk politics; also, in his best work he reminded me much of the American painter Robert Henri, who had come to Spain from Philadelphia and had painted the grandmothers of the models Oncins was using. I started to tell Oncins of this, but he was impatient: 'I'm not interested in other painters. It's a savage job to find out what one wants to say, in one's own way.' In pursuit of this I asked him how he had settled upon his four strange colors, and he growled, 'They settled on me.' I obviously wasn't getting very far with this hard-headed Catalan Hubert Humphrey, so I paid my respects and moved on, but after I had been back home in Pennsylvania for some weeks a traveler from Spain climbed my hill with a large bundle.

'This painter in Barcelona heard I lived in Pennsylvania and he made me bring this to you. He said you were a tough man who asked sensible questions.' And with that my visitor unwrapped a good-sized board on which, in his dark colors, Lluis Oncins had painted me from memory against a background showing stylized elements of the American flag. I looked like a Spaniard, a Catalan to be exact, but the likeness was good, except that he gave me somewhat more hair than nature allowed. How-

ever, the salient characteristic of the portrait was that I was shown with a glowing heart, painted in Oncins' traditional dark orange because, as he had explained to the messenger, 'Michener's love for Cataluña was self-evident.'

With another painter I had a much different experience. Norman Narotzky was an American working in Barcelona, for he was married to a girl of that city, and while I knew him a notable storm developed over a painting of his which synthesized his reflections on Spanish history. A friend told me of the work before I had a chance to see it for myself: 'I'm afraid Norman was ill advised. You see, he's done a pair of portraits of Fernando and Isabel and titled them "The Catholic Kings." ' I said I thought this was appropriate for an American, since it was these kings who had launched the discovery of our country, but my informant said, 'I'm afraid you don't understand. The portraits, which are really very fine, serve only as the kick-off point for what Narotzky really wants to say. Accompanying them are symbols of religious repression through the ages. The swastika, the stake, the crucified Christ wearing robes used by the Inquisition. It's a real beauty! Norman has omitted nothing.'

The two paintings, which I liked so much that I tried to buy them, evoked a scandal. A government official pointed out that since Spain was officially sponsoring a movement to have Isabel declared a saint, the painting was not only offensive to the nation's historical sense but sacrilegious as well. He fulminated that his country did not intend to sit idly by and allow intellectuals to cast aspersions on the grandeur of the Spanish heritage. Others felt that for an American to speak ill of the Inquisition was unfair, unhistoric and probably subversive. Narotzky was investigated; inquiries were made at the American embassy; and the dealer who had exhibited the work was badgered by the police with all sorts of hampering restrictions.

I found it was impossible for the tourist to understand the ins and outs of Spanish censorship. Whenever a newspaper was censored and taken off the streets clandestine copies circulated, and I read them avidly to detect what had offended and almost never was I able to do so; but my Spanish friends would take a quick glance at the paper and almost always spot the article that had caused the trouble. However, even when they told me which article it was, I frequently read it without appreciating why it had been found so offensive. The only insight I uncovered for myself came in a bookstore when I saw William Faulkner's *Requiem for a Nun* published in Spanish as *Réquiem para una mujer* (Woman). When I asked the bookseller why the change, I found that he was a marked agnostic: 'On the face of it the Faulkner heroine could not be a nun because she wasn't a Catholic, so it's not illogical for our censors to deprive the author of his

This Italian painter on Las Ramblas
reminds one that European visitors have been more
welcomed in Barcelona than in other Spanish cities.

cheap little play on words. But more important is the fact that we can permit nothing that would cast even oblique reflections on the Church. All of us know that well over seventy percent of priests maintain mistresses, and the general public approves, for it keeps the priests away from our own women, but to speak of this in a book? They'd never permit it.' However, shortly after he spoke, a Barcelona publisher brought out a Catalan translation entitled *Rèquiem per a una monja.*

One Sunday morning as I was walking through the Gothic quarter, of which I never saw enough, for it is not often that one finds in the heart of a modern city an ancient one existing as a kind of soul imprisoned in stone yet mysteriously vital, I heard the lovely sound of rustic pipes and muffled drums. I could have been in a woodland except that the cathedral rose above me, and as I entered its plaza I saw that several hundred people or perhaps even a thousand, all dressed in Sunday clothes, had gathered about two orchestras that were playing a concert while worshipers heading for the cathedral or coming from it after Mass passed by and nodded approvingly, even though the music was not religious.

The orchestras were special. Each was composed of a dozen members whose instruments had been determined centuries ago: one double bass, five country oboes, one trombone, three cornets and two fiscorns, which were small and gave forth piercing sounds. I was surprised to see there were no drummers, for I thought I had heard drums, but when I approached the orchestras I saw that the oboe players had tiny drums, not more than three inches across, strapped to their left forearms, and these they struck from time to time without interrupting their playing on the oboes. One of the fiscorn players had a cymbal even smaller strapped to his wrist, and this he struck with another which he held daintily between his fingers. The music these orchestras produced, one playing while the other rested, was delicate and unlike any I had heard before, the wedding of oboe and cornet being especially pleasing. Naturally, I compared this sardana, for so the music was called, with the oboe music I had heard in Pamplona, and although I much preferred the latter as being more raw and mountainous, I respected the sardana as being more artistic. Since the orchestras played for about four hours, I had ample opportunity to judge their work.

As I was watching the fiscorn players, for I had not before seen this instrument, a strange thing happened all around me. A moment ago the Catalans in the plaza had been listening to the sardana; now, without anyone's having given a signal, large circles had formed, containing men and women of all ages down to eight years old, so that the entire plaza was covered with people silently performing the folk dance that accompanies the sardana. I was astonished at how quietly this had happened, for there were at least eleven of these large circles, some with thirty members, and the dance was vigorous and beautiful, yet how it had started I couldn't say.

The sardana was like the movement of an animated clock that ran in both directions. Slow steps left, slow steps right. Left, right. Left, right, with arms held closely to the side. Then faster steps, with hands slightly raised. Then fast, intricate steps, with hands held high above the head and the body swaying beautifully as the tempo of the music increased. Finally the entire plaza in motion, with worshipers filing in and out of the cathedral and stopping to join the dance if they felt so inspired. Then a tinkling clang of the tiny cymbals, a ruffle on the toy drums, a wail on the oboes and the dance ended. In the flash of a moment the circles disbanded and the plaza was both silent and sedate for Sunday morning. After ten or fifteen minutes' rest the second orchestra began and the dance was under way once more.

I found that if I took my eye away from the plaza for even one moment, I missed the beginning of this strange dance. The fresh orchestra would play for perhaps eight minutes and nothing would happen. Stolid Catalans in dark suits would be looking off into space as if dancing were the most remote intention of their lives, and if at this moment I looked away, I missed the whole thing, because when I looked back, there they would be, in great circles, dancing slowly left and right.

I was determined to see who gave the signal for this dance, so on several occasions I kept my eyes glued to a fixed spot where experience had told me a circle would be formed. One moment, not a sign of dancing. Then a girl, unaccompanied by any boy, sedately placed her purse on the flagstones. Nothing happened. Then a boy carefully took off his jacket, folded it and placed it atop the purse. Within seconds a dozen purses, jackets, walking sticks and coats were piled neatly in that spot, and around them the Catalans, strangers one to the other, began their slow sardana. More than anything else this strange beginning resembled the process by which ice forms across the surface of water; now it is fluid; now it is crystallized; the dance has begun.

Toward one o'clock that afternoon the orchestras combined to play a very slow and mournful sardana and for a long time no circles formed. Then an old man, with tears streaming down his face, solemnly folded his jacket and placed it on the stones. He was joined by others, and some of them were crying too, and soon the plaza was filled with solemn music as a tragic song was repeated over and over by the orchestras. I asked a man sitting on the cathedral steps what was happening, and he said, 'This piece is called "Patética." We play it when some famous person has died.' I asked whom it was memorializing, and he said, 'Yesterday Maestro'—I didn't catch the name—'he died, and he was one of our best composers of sardana music.' I went down to stand with the musicians as they played, because I wanted to see how the music was written. It was written out by hand, 'Patética,' and as the fiscorns shrilled their lament for the dead musician I saw that some of the players had tears in their eyes too, for music is something to be taken with great seriousness in Cataluña.

589

If I were to choose one man to represent the intellectual curiosity which I found so marked in Barcelona, it would have to be Luis Lassaletta (1921–1959), for although his history was unique, it was also representative. He was a slim, extremely handsome young man whose father had been Spanish manager for the Hispano-Suiza company. At the outbreak of the Civil War, Lassaletta senior was the only man in managerial status brave enough to remain in the city, which was obviously going to fall into the hands of the leftists. He paid for his bravery with his life, shot through the head without trial and for no reason except that he was an employer.

His son Luis, fifteen at the time, was thrown into jail and kept in a hole in which he could neither lie down nor stand up, with water dripping on him and a bright light shining in his eyes. He later reported that it was only through the exercise of will that he avoided going insane. When the war was over and he was released from prison, along with his younger brother José María, he was so dedicated to freedom that he was determined to go to the freest place he knew of, the African jungle. He grabbed a ship out of Barcelona, as young men like him had done through the centuries, and landed in Africa with enough money to sustain him for three months; but once ashore he exhibited skill in trapping wild animals and in training them. 'He spoke to them,' a friend says, 'and they spoke back. With his intense eyes he looked into the hearts of his animals, and although he was known as a "great white hunter" he never shot animals . . . or at least, not for sport.'

The fame of Lassaletta spread over Europe and he was consulted by zoo directors and naturalists. He was offered jobs by many different nations but his love was life in the jungle with his friends, and there he became a legend. In Gabon, in the Ubangi country, along the coastline of Lake Chad, he was the man who appeared suddenly out of the wilderness accompanied by Negroes bearing a live python or a cage containing a gorilla.

Then one day during the Christmas holidays, which he was spending in Guinea, a Gabon viper bit him in the face. 'Luis knew there was no anti-venom serum in the district, so he went to the hospital and told the doctors, "I am going to die. It will be three hours and painful but you mustn't worry, because there is nothing you can do." In the most dreadful agony he died, and the Barcelona papers mourned, "When Luis Lassaletta, who was the friend of all animals, dies from the bite of an animal, the world makes no sense." '

I of course never knew Luis Lassaletta but I did have the good luck to meet his two younger brothers, and with José María, who has inherited Luis' affection for animals, I spent some time. He kept in his back yard a tame hyena that he had captured in Africa, for it is now he who supplies European zoos with wild animals, and for some reason which I cannot explain I became close friends with this hyena; perhaps it was because I was lonely for my two dogs, whom I had not seen for nearly half a year; perhaps it was my fascination with his tremendous jaws which could bite through the thighbone of an ox. At any rate, this ugly beast and I had a great time. He seemed to know that I would play with him, no matter how rough he got, and there were times when he would take my forearm in his mighty jaws and bring his teeth against my skin and grin at me as if to say, 'Can you imagine what I could do if I had a mind for it?' I knew, and with my free hand I would bang him in the snoot, and he would roll over backward with delight.

José María went to Africa to recover his brother's possessions, among which he found a letter in which one of Luis' bearers sought help for the murder of four people:

Douala, French Cameroons
14 July 1955

Dear Sir, Professor of Help,

I have the honour most respectfully to put this humble petition towards your understanding.

My life is very poor and as such I shall be very grateful if master could give me a helping hand towards the battle of life by giving me some money for killing the understated persons as victims. Meanwhile the secret shall only remain the both of us.

Names of Victims

I	John Osungwe	a man
II	Andrew Oruh	a man
III	Sadrack Mbeng	a man
IV	Nkhnge Enota	a woman

All these are the enemies who try to kill me. I would be very grateful master could grant my plea.

Your future customer,
Joseph Ayok

I suppose that most visitors to Barcelona sooner or later make the trip to Montserrat (Serrated Mountain) but, paradoxically, few ever see it. They see the famous monastery, of course, and the shrine beloved of all Catalans, and they take one of the numerous téléphérique rides to the tops of peaks, but the mountain itself, one of the most exquisite in the world, they do not see, for this can be done properly only by going far north of Barcelona to the ancient town of Vich, which is worth a trip in itself if only to see the church decorated in gold murals by José María Sert. From Vich, whose hotel has a restaurant of notable reputation, one drops back south to where Route N-141 cuts off toward the mountains, and as one

José María Lassaletta holds a photograph of his brother Luis, killed in Africa by a Gabon viper, whose skull Don José holds in his right hand.

drives down this twisting road he comes to a spot from which Montserrat in all its wonder stands forth against the southern sky.

The mountain is prodigious, a chain of sawtooth peaks that resemble the Tetons of Wyoming except that the former are not so tall, only 4072 feet against the Grand Teton's 13,747 (of course, Montserrat starts from sea level, whereas the base of the Tetons is well above it). The peaks of Montserrat are more compact, and if one can use the word in this sense, more artistic. They blaze in the sky like tongues of flame, not one or two peaks but scores of them thrown together to make a jagged pattern. When I saw Montserrat from this ideal vantage point I'd already seen most of the world's famous mountains, but for an assembly of peaks of limited scope I had seen nothing to surpass this group.

The ascent from the north is also more exciting, I think, than the traditional approach from the south, which is how one climbs if he starts from Barcelona, but by either path the narrow road is magnificent and the final turn which throws one onto a small plateau just under the summit of the mountain is surprising, for unexpectedly one finds himself face to face with a series of massive buildings wedged into crevices below the rocky spires that rise above them like a crown. I had expected to end my climb at a shrine; instead I found enough recent buildings to house a small town and was amazed to think that all these rocks and timbers and steel girders had been lugged up this steep mountain.

Obviously, centuries had been required to build this complex. As long ago as the year 700, religious hermits had established themselves in these caves and had launched the legend of pure men hiding in inaccessible mountains. Their isolation ended after the year 880, when shepherds found in one of the caves a beautiful wooden statue of the Virgin, dark of face and majestic in manner; she had been hidden there when Muslims overran Cataluña. A Church commission affirmed that she was the last statue carved by St. Luke. She made the mountain famous; Goethe and Schiller visited the monastery that developed in her honor, as did innumerable kings and cardinals. Throughout Europe, Montserrat became identified with the legendary Monsalvat, the hiding place of the Holy Grail as depicted in Wagner's *Parsifal,* so that pilgrims had a double reason for climbing the mountain; even today the path is crammed with devout travelers who know that if they can complete this journey, some special blessing will be accorded them.

Even if one were not religious, an expedition to Montserrat would be a rewarding experience, for when the buildings are reached the day has only begun; from them téléphériques swing upward to the tips of the highest peaks, from which amazing views of Cataluña can be seen, even as far as Las Islas Baleares (the Balearic Islands). There are also picnic grounds tucked away at high altitudes and trails across the plateaus to needles which can be climbed if one has ropes and crampons.

Montserrat is the shrine of Cataluña; here couples come each day of the year to be married, a custom which became additionally popular during the years when the Catalan language was proscribed, for at Montserrat the wedding service was conducted in Catalan, no matter what the Madrid bureaucrats decreed. As one middle-aged woman told me, 'I wouldn't feel married if the priest had done it in Spanish.'

But Montserrat has always been, and still is, primarily a monastery. In many-tiered buildings, whose multiple windows, set against rocks, reminded me of the Buddhist lamaseries of Tibet, Benedictine monks maintain the old traditions of prayer and work. It is they who occupy this plateau set among spires; they operate the stores and collect the profits from the téléphériques. They live far removed from the problems of

Spain's ordinary life and seek a perfection which not even the average monk living elsewhere could attain. Says the official guide: 'The monks' chief occupation is reciting the Mass, and this they try to perform with the utmost care in every particular, so that it may be effective to the Glory of God and for the good of the Church.'

As I traveled in and out of Barcelona, and especially when I went to high points like El Tibidabo and Montjuich, I became aware of a singular

Nature forms
in La Sagrada Familia.

building in the eastern section of the city. From a distance it looked
something like a church, except that it had four main steeples and a covey
of smaller ones. When I asked what it was, a friend said, 'El Templo de la
Sagrada Familia, The Expiatory Temple of the Holy Family. But its real
name should be Gaudí's Folly.' When I asked why, he said, 'Go look. You'll
understand.'

When I told the taxi driver that I wanted to see the Expiatory Temple and so on, he interrupted: 'Gaudí, okay,' and after a short drive, put me down before one of the strangest-looking serious buildings in the world, a huge unfinished cathedral, a gaping wound in the heart of genius. For some minutes I stood in the street, just looking at the fantastic thing. All I could see was a façade terminating in the four spires I had noticed from El Tibidabo. Behind the façade . . . nothing, but off to the right I could see what looked like one spur of the transept topped by the group of lesser spires.

When I say spire I do not mean the traditional church steeple that ends in a cross. I mean something quite different. A French visitor was also in the street, looking through field glasses at the top of one of the spires, and noticing my interest, said, 'One of the true masterpieces of modern art. Regard.' He passed me the glasses, and at first I could not believe what I was seeing through them. First of all, the spires were built in such a way that they resembled pretzel sticks studded with salt crystals, except that at the upper end they narrowed down to points of rock candy, brilliantly colored. The spire was decorated with ceramic bits set in plaster and color was reflected everywhere. 'The sun lives in each part,' the admiring Frenchman said, and since many of the ceramic pieces were finished in gold, the spire seemed to be a finger of the sun.

'Have you studied the tip?' he asked, and how can I explain what I saw when I did? I said it wasn't a cross but I would be hard put to say what it was. I could think only of Angkor Wat and its repeated use of the cobra head with hood extended. Yes, it looked much like a cobra, except that it was angular, off center, totally bizarre and with the hood indicated by a score of ceramic balls that looked as if they had been racked up for a celestial billiard game. There was also something that resembled a four-leaf clover and a series of golden protuberances that looked like either sails or segments of a peeled orange.

'Glorious, eh?' the Frenchman asked.

'What is it supposed to be?'

'Who cares? It's a work of genius. So who cares?' He took back the glasses and passed into the unfinished building, but I remained in the street, studying the lower portions of the façade, for it was here and not in the fantastic towers that the genius of Gaudí had manifested itself. The entire front was a kind of garden rising vertically from the pavement. Vines climbed upward to provide niches in which statues of Biblical figures stood as if resting in some countryside grape arbor. What in a traditional façade would have been a pillar, here became a tree in whose spreading branches perched stone birds. On either side of the main entrance, at eye level, families of realistic chickens scratched, beautifully carved, and wherever human figures appeared, animal life appeared also, for it was obvious that Gaudí had loved nature; his definition of religion encompassed all that lived.

I suppose the outstanding characteristic of the façade was that when seen from where I stood, there was scarcely a square foot that was not covered with ornament in some way. One night, when I saw it illuminated by flares, it cast a million shadows and the spires looked like decorations on a wedding cake. Few lines were straight and some of the windows were wonderfully inventive; the man who designed this façade knew what fun was. It reminded me of two other structures I'd seen, one in Barcelona and the other in Watts, the Negro section of Los Angeles. The first, of course, was the Palau de la Música, and I assumed that Gaudí had also built that, but I was wrong. In Barcelona at the turn of the century there had been a flowering of the Catalan spirit, and a different group of architects had been responsible for the Palau. As for Los Angeles, in Watts in the early years of this century an immigrant Italian tile setter named Simon Rodia decided to build by himself a memorial to his love for the United States, and it took the form of a cluster of huge towers one hundred feet tall and built of iron rods handsomely interwoven. He ornamented them with anything he could salvage from junk yards: broken plates, green and blue soft-drink bottles, chipped cups and saucers, flashy tiles from old bathrooms. From the seashore he collected shells and from garbage dumps odd containers, and all this he set into concrete slabs which formed the sides of his structure. Working pragmatically and alone, he spent thirty-three years on his task, creating what has been called 'the greatest structure ever made by one man.' Today the towers have become an embarrassment to Los Angeles, for they have begun to deteriorate and vandals have worked much damage; it may be that they will have to be torn down, but if they vanish something unique and beautiful will have been lost, as subtle as the skin of a lizard, and committees have been formed to save them, for many world critics judge them to be the one authentic work of art to have been produced by California. At any rate, if one has seen the Watts towers he is prepared for the Gaudí, and vice versa.

I left the street and passed through the façade as if I were entering the church, but inside there was nothing. Not even the walls were up, except at the unfinished transept. 'How long have they been building this?' I asked a caretaker.

'A long time,' he said, pointing to a crane I had not previously seen. Some work was under way, but from the magnitude of the task that lay ahead, I judged it would take a crew of thousands forty or fifty years to finish. 'Are they proceeding with it?' I asked, but the caretaker shrugged his shoulders.

I did find a placard which explained the façade. It was intended to portray events connected with the birth of Christ, and the four spires represented the major symbols of the faith which Christ had founded: the cross, the walking stick of Joseph, the ring and the miter, though what religious significance the last three had I did not know, but I did know that

an architect of noble imagination and vast intention had drafted this memorial to the Holy Family but had somehow run out of energy. The demanding task had staggered to a halt and I saw in the gaping emptiness both wonder and tragedy and was driven to discover what had happened and why.

I asked so many questions about the building that friends arranged for me to meet the one man in Barcelona best equipped to explain. I was taken to an attractive country-style house which now stood well within the city but which must have been in a rural area when built. An old-style fence with the kind of latched gate I knew as a boy surrounded a pleasant yard, and at the door of the house a girl obviously just in from the country bowed and said in Catalan, 'Dr. Bonet will see you shortly.' She led me into a library, where I found, in addition to the ninety volumes of the *Espasa-Calpe*, whole shelves of books about Gaudí. French, Italian, American and especially German writers had compiled an impressive series of essays on Gaudí and photographic studies of his work, and from their titles it was obvious that their authors considered him one of the important men of his generation. But what was his generation? When did he live? I did not feel free to take down the books, but since they all appeared to be of recent publication, for they were largely in the new international format, I judged that he must have died fairly recently.

The door to the library swung open and a slight, old-fashioned gentle-man in dark suit and vest, in his late sixties perhaps, came into the room with that air of excitement which marks men who love to talk about work that fascinates them. 'Luis Bonet y Gari,' the man said, extending his hand. 'I am delighted to meet with someone from América del Norte who knows the work of Antoni Gaudí.' I decided not to tell him that I was there because I knew nothing about Gaudí, for it was obvious that he had much to tell. He wore a black bow tie which stood out against the whiteness of his shirt and hair. His eyes were unnaturally bright and he spoke crisply.

'I am, as they told you, the architect of the Sagrada Familia. I was a student of Gaudí's, and although no one can say what his exact plans were for finishing the structure, I am at least in harmony with his general ideas.'

'When did he die?' I asked.

Dr. Bonet was surprised that an expert like me didn't know this fundamental fact about the master, but he said courteously, 'Born 1852 Antoni Gaudí i Cornet in the small Catalan town of Reus. Struck down by an automobile here in Barcelona in 1926. Unrecognized, he was thrown into a pauper's bed in an out-of-the-way hospital, where he died some days later without having regained consciousness.'

'Then the Sagrada Familia dates from the last . . .'

From this carefully designed window
of Gaudí's Templo de la Sagrada Familia
a stork is seen on its way to Africa.

'Another architect had made preliminary plans for a traditional kind of church, but in 1882 Gaudí drew a set of sketches showing how a structure more suited to Cataluña could be evolved from the work then under way. He got the job and the result is history.'

'How did he come upon the ideas he used in the façade?' I asked.

'Ah! Where? As a young man I worked with him and discovered many secrets about building in the new style, but how he conceived that style I never knew. Obviously, he saw architecture as an outgrowth of nature. Obviously, he was inspired by the Mediterranean and all the cultural forces that grew up along its shores. But above all else he was a Catalan, and something of our essence flowered in him. He could have come only from Cataluña.'

I was afraid to ask the next question, for it would betray my ignorance, but I was caught up with the mystery of Gaudí, so I asked, 'Did he do much work in Cataluña?' It turned out to be a good question, because Dr. Bonet pulled down from his shelves a score of books written within the last decade by non-Spanish experts and in their pages showed me pictures of the work Gaudí had done.

'The amusement park here in Barcelona. Oh, don't miss that! It's a child's fairyland built in stone. Then the apartment houses with their shining roofs. And don't forget his beautiful Casa Vicens not far from here.'

What really surprised me was a sketch Dr. Bonet showed me of the church as it had been intended to look, for this showed that the façade I had been looking at was not the main one at all but merely the entrance to the south transept; the main nave had not yet been started, except for the apse, which stood under the cluster of lesser towers. The finished church would have eight more of the giant spires; and the placard I had seen earlier was wrong. The spires did not represent abstract attributes of the church but rather twelve men from the New Testament: the four already standing were those for Barnabas, Jude, Simon and Matthew.

Dr. Bonet reviewed the plan with me and I could see that he visualized the church finished as his master had intended. It would require sixty or seventy years to complete, but the determination to do so was present. 'The four existing spires of the Sagrada Familia have become for Barcelona what the Eiffel Tower is for Paris or the Statue of Liberty for New York. They are the recognized symbol of this city and of Cataluña. It is unthinkable that the remaining eight should not be completed, because the four we have are among the few works of true architecture built in the last century. Throughout the world they are recognized as such.'

But not in Spain. I was to find that among Spaniards familiar with the problem, Gaudí is looked upon as a Catalan crank and his work dismissed as irrelevant. One man in Madrid asked me, 'What can you make of those towers? At their base, Gothic. Midway up, pure Art Nouveau. At the top, Picasso cubist. It's junk architecture and it's lucky for us it was left unfinished. Perhaps a real architect can move in now and bring the mess to some conclusion.'

I heard the same arguments in Barcelona. 'The Sagrada Familia should be turned over to a committee of architects under the age of fifty. Make that forty-five. They should keep what's already up and finish the damned thing off in some kind of ultramodern simplistic style and give us a church that can be used. The four main towers can stand where they are. They're no good, but they do no harm.'

If a plebiscite on this matter were taken throughout Spain, it would be meaningless, for most Spaniards know nothing of the Sagrada Familia. If only those qualified to vote were polled, I suppose the decision would be to finish the job quickly and without regard to Gaudí's imperfectly recorded master plan. If the architects of the outside world were questioned, I believe they would vote for finishing the church with due respect for Gaudí's plan but with modifications dictated by the probable taste of 1990. (This would be my preference.) But to the devoted followers of Antoni Gaudí, the only way to finish this monument is in strict adherence to his wishes. This would require eight more towers, an additional lesser façade depicting the Passion of Christ to balance the existing Infancy, and a gigantic main entrance showing Christ in Glory with a wealth of imaginative detail that I fear only Gaudí himself could have devised. He was a unique genius who carried his plans in his head and I doubt that they could be reconstructed from the inadequate notes he left.

What will be done? No one knows. In fact, no one has even a coherent guess. Men like Dr. Bonet are convinced that sooner or later the people of Barcelona will recognize in this magic shell a Catalan treasure and will insist upon its completion. A committee has been formed to speed the work and collections are taken each year; visitors from other countries often return home and write out checks to further what one correspondent described as 'the most exciting thing I saw in Spain.' But the city fathers, faced with this gaping wound and the prospect of another century before it can be healed, are understandably impatient to get along with the work in some simplified manner. The debate is bitter.

As for Parque Güell, a garden area lying northwest of the church, it is a child's delight and faces the same problems as the church. It was never finished, really, and the dreamlike buildings have become dilapidated; I don't see how they could be properly refurbished without an expenditure of funds that could scarcely be justified. For as long as they last, however, the inventions which Gaudí poured into this park are a joy to the spirit: caves where one can rest and towers that seem made of gingerbread, flights of stairs lined with rocks of all hues and huge flat buildings whose Assyrian-like pillars lean at odd angles. It was in this park that I saw a work of Gaudí's that made my heart skip through sheer pleasure: it was a swinging gate made of wrought iron. Its basic design was a series of large squares onto which were fixed circles fashioned to look like the ribs of a palm branch with the core off center. The solidity of the squares, the beauty of the circles, the unbalanced position of the cores and the airiness of the whole concept represented invention of the highest order, and if I had seen nothing else done by Gaudí, I would have known from this gate that he was first rate.

'This is how he looked,' Dr. Bonet said, handing me a photograph taken in front of the cathedral one Corpus Christi day. Gaudí was a small man, a Catalan to be sure, with white hair and beard, ill at ease in a dark store-made suit and staring intently into space while those around him attended to the formation of the parade in which he would march, carrying a long wax taper. The thing that no one could miss was the way he leaned forward from his ankles, as if there was work to be done or a quest to be followed. He never married; he left no coherent account of his artistic philosophy; only rarely was he able to finish the great works he began; and he must have been a difficult man to deal with. But one glance at his iron gate and you know that he was a poet.

In view of what I shall later be saying about another Catalan, Ramón Llull, I should like to leave Gaudí, who moved me deeply, as described by Dr. Bonet: 'He felt the entire Mediterranean to be at his disposal. Here he used the palm trees of Egypt and the pillars of Karnak. Byzantium was very much on his mind. And the caves of Crete and the temples of Greece. He had deep affinity for the Etruscans, their hard colors and sure touch. Rome was here, the great builders, the men who were not afraid to throw aqueducts across valleys. He looked out to the Mediterranean and was in no way provincial.'

I said, when speaking of Córdoba, that I would not bore the reader with a recital of my disappointments in trying to find a good performance of flamenco, but what happened when I carried my quest to a village near Barcelona could not be termed boring. When friends heard that I was still trying to find authentic flamenco they proposed a dance hall at the water-front end of Las Ramblas, but when I looked at the program I saw that the music was to be provided by a band called something like Les Greer and his Dixie Wildcats and the dancer was The Flame of Cádiz, and I felt that I could forgo that one; but about this time I met one of Spain's best-publicized playboys, and he said, 'Michener, this country would be humiliated if a serious student like yourself came here and found no decent flamenco, so I've arranged for the best flamenco party in recent times, and you're to be guest of honor.'

I was driven to a finca in the country, an exquisite place overlooking the sea and decorated with animal skins from African safaris. Four professional bartenders served drinks and the audience was glittering: three motion-picture stars of world reputation, several writers whose books were widely known, four Spanish noblemen including a couple of condes, a famous bullfighter retired to honor and a score of similar luminaries. We had convened at midnight and the singing was to last till dawn. All but a few lights were turned off, and before the music began we could hear the whispering of the Mediterranean. This was not one of the legendary gypsy caves of Andalucía, but it was the next best thing, and my host said, without smiling, 'If you don't like this flamenco you don't recognize duende when you see it.'

I should have been warned when I saw the principal singer. Instead of a man trained over many years in the intricacies of the art, a square-built woman of forty appeared, with a voice like a bullfrog, or worse. She was apparently a great favorite of the crowd, for when she gave her deep, throaty 'Adiós, amigos,' one of the condes called something and she yelled back, 'Soy más macho que todos aquí, y tengo un par de cojones así de grande!' which a friend translated as 'I'm more manly than anyone here and I've got the biggest testicles.'

Well, flamenco types are sometimes rather tough and I assumed that this was merely her manner of speaking, and that when the music began she would sing properly, but the appearance of her guitarist gave no assurance of this; he was a kind of comedian, with a rubber face, who could play tricky little passages which went well with her kind of singing, such as it was. I groaned, and then the principal girl dancers came out, tall, willowy, beautiful gypsy girls, I thought, and the evening started. I didn't recognize the first song, but the others did. It was more like a rock-and-roll flamenco than what I had hoped for, but with the savage grunting of the singer and the simplified dancing of the two girls it was acceptable.

It was on about the fifth number that I finally realized that something was more seriously wrong about this evening than the beat of the guitar. I was sitting on a Mongolian-style hassock covered with the skin of a lion which the owner of the finca had shot, when the prettier of the girls came to stand before me and dance a sevillana, for which normally she would have had a partner. After a few steps, which I recognized as something less than top flamenco, she began a slow motion of her shoulders, which I had not seen before in this dance. She continued thus for some minutes and then began to undress, taking off one piece of clothing after another until she stood about a yardstick from me wearing only a burlesque G-string, which she proceeded to throw away while the female singer uttered her guttural nonsense and the guitarist played a music hall number. After some moments of dancing for me, as guest of honor, the young lady asked me to join her, but I did not feel equal to the task, not knowing either the steps of the flamenco or those she was improvising, but one of the condes obliged and the pair did a brief fandango of sorts, after which she picked up her bits of clothing, chucked me under the chin with her G-string and repaired to a corner, where she slowly dressed in view of everyone.

In this style the flamenco continued till dawn. There were breaks, during which casually arranged couples drifted off to nearby rooms, and occasionally one of the guests would take over the singing or even the guitar playing; once or twice there were moments of quiet beauty as the second of the strippers sang folk songs in an appealing voice, once while standing naked by a window. I remember that there was almost a fight, too. A Catalan asked a man from Madrid how he liked Barcelona, and the Madrileño said condescendingly, 'Este pueblo no es mi pueblo,' which in Spanish carries a lilting condescension because of its repetition of words: 'This town ain't my town.' 'What's the matter with this town?' the Catalan demanded. 'It just ain't my town,' the Madrileño said, but neither was drunk enough to fight.

At eight in the morning, when a cab came to drive me back to Las Ramblas, my host finally dropped his pose of seriousness and said, 'Well, you won't see another flamenco like this one in a hurry.' I laughed, and he said, 'The singer's the one who's famous. We all love her.'

On the way back to town I thought of the contradictory reputation Spain has in this matter of sex. The country is advertised abroad as the home of passionate women who click their heels with impatience, but the press, the Church and political leaders always speak of Spain in puritanical terms. The highest moral ideals are preached, yet most men who can afford it maintain mistresses with the tacit approval of the Church, which knows how far to go in these matters. The major cities boast of the absence of prostitutes, yet when a foreign male checks into a hotel alone he is barely in his room before his phone rings and a soft voice says, 'Ello, Señor Brooks of New York. This is Encarnación. Señor Keller asked me to call you.' And on all levels of society there is a circumspect, rather well-behaved circuit of sexual freedom whose operation I had witnessed this night. From what I have seen of Spain in action, it seems to me that they handle the moral problem about as well as any country I've visited . . . if one can dull his ears to the moral preachments, which at times grow downright tedious.

Under normal circumstances the high point of my stay in Barcelona would have been the Sagrada Familia, but because of the agitated political situation the thing I remember most was the aftermath of a chance meeting that had occurred some months before in a remote valley northeast of León where the road from Potes to Riaño crosses the mountain range known as Picos de Europa. There at a well beside the road I had met a Catalan university student whom I shall call Pau Lluis Freg. We had talked politics for some minutes, and after I had answered a chain of his questions, he said, 'When you get to Barcelona, look me up. I have friends who would enjoy talking with you.' I lost his address, but one night in the city, as I was about to deliver a speech to an assembly of students, he appeared suddenly out of a doorway and with conspiratorial manner said, 'I shall call on you at your hotel.'

Through him I was introduced to student life in Barcelona at a time when it was under serious stress, and I must make clear, because people who have never lived under a dictatorship are sometimes confused as to what happens in a country like Spain as compared to Russia, that I shall here report only a fragment of what students told me. We conducted a series of the most frank and open discussions I have ever held with university people; they were no more afraid to speak openly and in open places than I would have been in Pennsylvania, and if in what follows critical points are left untouched, it was only because I didn't raise them or have forgotten what I was told. The muffled hesitancy that I had known in other countries I did not encounter in Spain; yet the Spanish students were afraid in other ways and had good cause to be, for many of their associates were already in jail. If this is a contradiction, it is merely what I experienced.

'The turmoil in our university is much worse than the newspapers have dared admit,' Pau Lluis told me as we walked through the small streets off Las Ramblas. He was an earnest young man of twenty, dressed like a conservative English businessman but with the eyeglasses of a student. 'There have been six riots that I know about and my division is closed down altogether. I don't know what I shall do for an education.'

'What are you doing now?'

'We protest. We meet near the university, but you understand . . . we're locked out. There are no classes.'

'What happened?'

'Riots. We reached the end of our patience. Really, our endurance was used up. So there were riots. I think the administration was with us and could have handled the problem, but the police saw a chance to get even with us and gave us severe beatings. Real trouble in the streets. So it was the government that closed the doors. The police, you might say.'

I was vague as to what had caused the riots, for newspaper accounts had been meager, it being one of those cases in which I learned more from the *New York Times* than from the Spanish papers, which were under severe censorship. 'What are the riots about? Politics?'

Pau Lluis looked at me in astonishment. 'No! We're not radicals or anything like that. We had to strike because we were being treated with contempt. Let me tell you why I finally struck. I had four professors, and three of them were swine. True swine. They came to class about two times in five, and when they did come they stood at the podium and insulted us. Once I asked a question about a difficult passage, and the professor shouted, "I am the professor and I explain when I think it's necessary. Sit down." To show his displeasure he didn't come back to class for three weeks.'

'Who taught the class?'

'Nobody. If a professor becomes angry, there's nothing the students can do.'

'Then how do you learn?'

'You don't. Time of the examination comes and you're not prepared. So you flunk, and there's nothing you can do about it.'

I found this difficult to believe, so Pau Lluis introduced me to an English boy who was studying at the university and he confirmed the story. 'In English universities we were sometimes treated with infuriating condescension, but here we're treated as pigs. The government fears us . . . hates us, really. In Spain the educated man is held in contempt.'

This was a direct contradiction to what I had been told by Dr. Fernández-Cruz, who had emphasized the regard in which doctors were held because they were educated, and I asked about this. Pau Lluis said, 'Both points are correct. The Spanish countryside loves the medical man because he can do something and despises the scholar because he can do nothing but read. Don't forget that Don Quixote was held to be a fool principally because he read books. The idea still exists.' At another time he said in frustration, 'Of all the major countries, Spain has the greatest need for intelligence, and we distrust our universities, which are the only agencies that can provide it. Most of those people out there, even in Barcelona, honestly believe that if the students said their prayers and listened to the police, they wouldn't need the university.'

I asked whether the riots in Barcelona, which had been prolonged and violent, had anything to do with Catalan nationalism, and Pau Lluis laughed. 'Everywhere I went in the north, on that trip when I met you, people asked the same question. In the last four years I haven't once heard Catalan separatism mentioned seriously. We used to talk about it in lower school . . . the poets . . . the bad days of betrayal. But now what sensible man would believe that Cataluña could exist as a separate state? That's what you go to university for. To learn some sense.'

'Do you think of yourself as a Catalan? Or as a Spaniard?'

'As a Catalan. An American who studied with us last year said, "If I hadn't known Texas, I wouldn't have understood Cataluña. They're Texans first and Americans second. You're even worse." He was right, I suppose. But as a Catalan I'm quite satisfied to be part of Spain. It could be good for both of us. As a matter of fact, Spain without Cataluña would be a miserable place.'

'Were the priests who rioted also free of politics?'

'Quite. If you read the stories carefully you saw that the reason the priests marched in defiance of police orders was to show their support for us students. That's all it was. On the other hand, the police had begun to resent the freedom with which young priests were speaking out on social problems, so I suppose you'd call that politics. When the government gave the word "Beat up those damned priests," the police did it with real brutality. I was there, marching behind the priests, and it would have been just as easy for the police to beat us up but they were gunning for the priests and they waded in dreadfully. It was very bad to see. A priest would fall down and the police would jump on him and club him. It was the natural hatred for the priest in black showing itself in a new form.'

'How do the students feel about the Church?'

On that one Pau Lluis bit his cheeks for a long time. 'We were pleased that the priests marched in our defense. It was a ray of hope. Maybe the Church is going to abandon the big families and the army and finally help the people. Certainly the young priests know that this is what it should do.'

'The Church as a whole?'

'I know only Cataluña. Here there's a possibility, but I suppose you know that once again, when our bishopric became vacant, they refused to appoint a Catalan and brought in some fellow from Astorga. I think the Madrid government fears the Catalan church as much as it does the Catalan university.'

In the days when I knew Pau Lluis there was great agitation in the Church. Seminarians marched out on strike, something unheard of before. Junior priests signed manifestoes which they carried in person to newspaper offices, so that even though we were unable to find out what was being protested, we knew that protests of a vital nature were being made. Other priests of high rank circulated petitions demanding that the precepts of Pope John XXIII be followed in reforming the Spanish clergy. And in a small city not far from Barcelona, one priest who was outspoken in his demand for a general reform of the Church was arrested and publicly charged with having had immoral relations with a female parishioner in the back seat of an automobile. No one I met could recall ever before having heard of a public charge of this nature. It seemed to a group of Americans, some of them Catholic, who followed the turmoil, as if 'the young priests had matriculated at Berkeley.'

Pau Lluis was an unusual student in that he spoke no foreign language; we conducted our conversations in Spanish, and when we encountered a subject for which my Spanish did not suffice we sought out translators, and one Saturday afternoon while traveling out into the countryside to visit the lodgings of the student from England, I became involved in an experience which quite startled me. We were riding in one of Spain's good trains and the coach was crowded with a group of schoolgirls heading for a weekend camping trip, accompanied by four young, attractive nuns. After a preliminary half-hour of squealing as we pulled out of Barcelona, the girls subsided into informal group singing. 'My Bonnie Lies Over the Ocean' and 'Old Black Joe' they dedicated to me. I think they next sang 'Cielito Lindo,' which made their first three songs English, American and Mexican, which was properly international for a group of Catalans. Then they began a soft folk song, one of the best ever written; I have often wondered why it has not been introduced to the United States, for it seems to me to have everything a song of this type requires. I could not believe that the girls of this Catholic school were singing it, so I asked one of the nuns, 'What's the song?'

' "Stinki Rass," ' she said.

They were even singing it under its own name; in the United States some school-board member would have insisted that new words be substituted, for this was one of the great revolutionary songs. 'What do the words mean?' I asked.

'It's a song of freedom,' the nun said. 'Stinki Rass was a man who loved freedom.'

The girls were singing a Catalan version of 'Stenka Razin,' the Volga folk song that speaks of the famous revolutionary who defied the tsar and surrendered his head on the public chopping block sometime around 1700. It was an unlikely song for Spain, the apotheosis of revolt against tyranny, and I was not satisfied that the girls knew what they were singing, so I made further inquiry, and the same nun said, 'Stinki Rass fought against the tsar and was beheaded.' When I asked why he was fighting, she said, 'For freedom.'

It was not the first time I had been perplexed by the contradictions of Spanish censorship. A man was arrested for spiriting Protestant Bibles into the country, but this Catholic school was honoring Stenka Razin as freedom's hero. In a Spanish cinema house I saw an Italian motion picture about Benvenuto Cellini in which Pope Paul IV was shown defending the Catholic Church against the infamous troops of Spain, and periodically one character or another reviled Spain and Carlos V; they were the villains and were so specified, but the censor had not objected, yet not long ago an American was thrown in jail for having spoken disrespectfully of Spain.

I remember when I was visited in my hotel room in a northern city by a newspaperman. He wanted to talk with someone from the outside world and spent several hours telling me how censorship operated in his field. 'I have a friend in the French city of Hendaye, and each month he crosses the bridge into Irún and mails me the liberal journals from France.' From a briefcase he produced four or five magazines which were obviously more valuable to him than food. 'I know what's going on in the world. I'm at least as good a writer as you are. I'm a professional, and I could write brilliant articles on what's going to happen in the next ten years, where the government's making mistakes. Michener, I know.' He was close to having tears in his eyes as he translated from the clandestine magazine a series of titles which had attracted him: 'De Gaulle and the Gold Standard.' 'Harold Wilson's Four Major Problems.' 'The Failure of Johnson's Viet Nam Policy.' He tapped the magazines and said, 'That's what a man writes. What do they make me write?'

He handed me a piece of paper on which, having anticipated meeting with me, he had typed out the titles of his last three articles: '¿Existe el hombre abominable de las nieves?' (Does the Abominable Snowman

Exist?), 'El crimen en Chicago' (Crime in Chicago), and '¿Es verdad que los ingleses aman Isabel Segunda?' (Is It True That the English Love Elizabeth II?) He said that more intellectual ability was being wasted in Spain than in any other nation he knew, and he could foresee no end to it.

Pau Lluis and I debarked at a seaside resort well south of Barcelona and walked over sand to a beach house where a group of students waited to pepper me with questions. Like the newspaperman of the north, they were as intelligent as those of similar age in America. For a long time they spoke of nothing but my country, and their knowledge of it was astonishing. They wanted to know what role McNamara was playing in the government and whether Bobby Kennedy would run for President in 1968. They were, like all Europeans, especially interested in the *Report of the Warren Commission* and were unprepared to accept it, but their rejection was not based on personal prejudice; they had read of certain books contesting the *Report* and had been influenced by them.

Finally my turn to ask questions came. I wanted to explore the problem of how far politics intruded into the student riots, and as soon as the subject was broached I found a willingness to talk which quite surprised me. If students in Stalin's Russia, Hitler's Germany or Mussolini's Italy had spoken so openly of their grievances, they would probably have been shot; I suppose that in Franco's Spain if I were to betray the individuals who talked with me, they would also be in some kind of trouble, but of a much lesser degree, because these students showed no hesitancy, which they would have had to do with a stranger if their lives were endangered.

'Pau Lluis is right. This is not a political movement, essentially. It's an attempt to force choices now, before the big changes come at Franco's death.' The speaker was a girl who looked as un-revolutionary as a student could. She was quiet and obviously middle-class, with an interest in social problems. It was her opinion that the students and the young priests were trying to impress the government with the fact that they must be taken into account when the new Spain was formed. 'We can't have the old sloppy university teaching. We won't tolerate it.' To hear her and Pau Lluis one would have thought that Spain's major problem was improvement of the university.

A more radical young man, a would-be engineer, for the students I met were enrolled in practical courses, with no poets or philosophers intermixed, had a different opinion: 'Politics has had no part in launching these student riots. We've spent little time discussing specific steps to be taken when the change comes. I have no interest in politics, but of late I've seen that in the end we shall have to become involved. We will want certain things, just as the young priests do, and in the end the police will bang us over the head, and we'll be in politics.'

I asked what form this participation would take, and he said, 'The students, the young priests, the young businessmen will say, "The New

Along all the beaches of the Mediterranean it is the foreign girl who attracts and perplexes the men of Spain.

Spain must have this kind of freedom," and the Old Spain will say, "Now you be still and we'll make the decisions," and somebody will have to get banged on the head. It'll be us, and in the end we'll have to align with labor and I suppose they'll have to send the army against us, and there we are!'

We pursued this for some minutes and there were those who agreed, up to the point of army intervention. 'There will be no civil war,' students like Pau Lluis believed. The engineer asked, 'But if we are pushed too far?' The students refused to say, 'Then there will be war.' Instead they said, 'No one wants a return of 1936.'

There was agreement, however, that I would see a good deal more student agitation within the next year, and even before I had reached home it had erupted in both Madrid and Barcelona. The students also warned me that labor, having taken heart from the example of the students, would begin to strike, and this too happened as they had predicted. They also said that the government, aware of these pressures, would liberalize the constitution; they had seen reports of this in the *New York*

Times but not in their local newspapers, and again they were right, for shortly after, Generalísimo Franco announced a liberalization of the form of government, although not much relaxation in actual operation. In other words, the students understood rather well what was happening.

There was heated discussion of a point on which I was uninformed and whose intricacies I could not follow: the government in Madrid had promulgated a fake student organization with appointed representatives, 'no better than the labor syndicates,' one of the engineers said, and the students were determined to by-pass it and elect their own representatives. Whereas politics in the abstract did not arouse them, this matter of a union did, and I could anticipate the pragmatic steps whereby they would escalate from university problems to national ones, and I suppose that this was why the Madrid government had cracked down so hard.

At the conclusion of the meeting Pau Lluis surprised me by inviting me to his home, a comfortable apartment in the western end of Barcelona, where his small, attractive mother and businessman father were pleased to entertain me. They were perplexed, as all parents are, at having bred a son who had strong opinions, but they were proud that other young people sought him out as if his opinions were important. 'What should Pau Lluis do about his education?' his mother asked. She seemed no older than forty and must have married young. 'It's disreputable for a boy his age not to be attending classes.' Her husband turned out to be an aficionado of the zarzuela and had a large collection of records; he was relieved when I turned the conversation away from his son, who was in trouble no matter how well behaved he might appear, and spoke of *La revoltosa* and *Gigantes y cabezudos*. The Fregs served a formal tea, much as I might have got in London except that the cakes were sweeter and the tea weaker. Señora Freg came back to her son's education: 'From what you hear, is there any chance that the university will reopen soon?' I told her that in American circles it was believed that classes must reopen soon; it was only logical not to penalize an entire student body. 'But this is Spain,' she said reflectively, as if here it was not illogical to stamp out intelligence that seemed to be developing a mind of its own. Her husband remarked wryly that it was good to know that in California, too, people had trouble with their universities. 'It's not localized.' The Fregs were proud of their studious son and dreadfully apprehensive. They showed this by their reaction to me; Pau Lluis had shown them a clipping about my lecture and they realized that he would not have taken the trouble to make my acquaintance if he were not an exceptional boy, but they also knew that he would not have done so unless he had a kind of radical approach which must ultimately place him in conflict with the police. I wanted to tell them that Pau Lluis was as stable a young fellow as one could expect to meet under the current circumstances, but I lacked the Spanish. However, I mumbled something to that effect and I believe they got the drift.

It was now time to leave Barcelona and I did so with reluctance, for the city had been a revelation to me, and my wife was pleased that I shared the enthusiasm she had developed years earlier. When speaking of Andalucía, I said that if I were a young workman stuck away in some bleak pueblo I would emigrate to Barcelona, and the more I saw of the city the more surprised I was that the influx from the south had not been greater; but it is necessary to complete the analysis. If I were a young Catalan with intellectual promise I think I would leave Barcelona and emigrate to Madrid, and I would do so for two reasons. I am inherently suspicious of separatist movements, whether active or sentimental, political or artistic, and I fear that Catalan nationalism would in the long run weaken me. Also, I would want to be in Madrid because for the next forty or fifty years it is there that the decisions will be made, and as a Catalan intellectual I might play an important role in helping make them. The figure of speech with which I opened this chapter was more relevant than I had supposed: Barcelona has the heady and dangerous quality of champagne and should be taken in moderation.

One of the pleasant aspects of the city is that it serves as the sea terminus for the Baleares, which, with Palma as their capital, have long provided a romantic holiday land for vacationers from northern Europe. Here George Sand and Frédéric Chopin came when there were no hotels on Mallorca; today there is a heavier concentration of tourist facilities than elsewhere in Spain: sixteen hundred hotels, five thousand bars, ten thousand tourist shops and two and a half million visitors a year. Impossible as it seems, in the winter season one can leave Sweden by plane, spend three months in Palma in a top-class hotel with all meals and fly back to Sweden for a total cost of $248. At one hotel the manager told me, 'And because we happen to be outside of town, if you stay with us, we allow you the use of a car at no extra cost.'

My wife and I took a night boat to Palma, and asked the steward to call us an hour before dawn so that we could go on deck to watch the islands rising from the sea. How beautiful Mallorca was! First the mountains showed like a dark mass, sufficiently high to assure us that they would contain valleys, which are among the chief pleasures of the place. Then as dawn brightened, much of the darkness changed to green forests, so that Mallorca was going to be a verdant island. Next we saw lines of white cliffs dropping down to the water's edge and these I had not heard about, so I asked a sailor, 'Does Mallorca have so many cliffs?' He peered into the uncertain light and said, 'Hotels. They're all hotels.'

Now, as the sun approached the horizon, I saw for the first time the fortress on the hill that guards Palma, and before long its round gray towers caught the first direct rays of sunlight. I could imagine how impres-

Spain's ye-ye boys are giving signs
that they refuse to take seriously the leadership
of Church, army and landed families.

The harbor of Barcelona is a place of much coming and going.

sive those battlements must have seemed to pirates moving in to sack the place, which happened frequently, or to armies obliged to lay siege to Palma. One part of the Baleares had had a chameleon-like existence; it had been occupied by Phoenicians, Carthaginians, Greeks, Romans, Visigoths, Muslims, and in the age of stability, when it was presumed to be Spanish, by a whole parade of European powers.

As I was reviewing this turbulent history, full sunlight burst over Palma and I saw, standing beside the sea, the great cathedral which since its inception has been the conspicuous symbol of Mallorca. It was a magnificent sight, this poem of stone rising from the waves, and if one complains that in cities like Toledo, Sevilla and Barcelona one can barely see the cathedrals because of encroaching houses and shops, the deficiency is repaired here, where the cathedral stands as free as a lighthouse on a promontory. The full sun was now reflected from the white hotel faces, so that more than ever they resembled cliffs, and my wife said, 'There ought to be sea gulls flying out of them.'

I had made the trip to Mallorca not to see one of Europe's major playgrounds but rather to pay my respects to the greatest Catalan of history, a man of cloudy reputation but grandeur of spirit, a bit of a charlatan but a leader of the Church and one of the most congenial figures in Spanish history, whose fame has always been relished by a few and whose general quality must one day be recognized by the many. In the uncomplicated days of the medieval period when to be Christian was to be Catholic and when, even though heresy might crop out here or there to be speedily exterminated, there was not yet open schism, the five major nations of Europe produced five scholastic philosophers. In the order of appearance the first four were Abélard of France (1079–1142), Albertus Magnus of Germany (1193–1280), Thomas Aquinas of Italy (1225–1274) and Duns Scotus of England (1265–1308). In Spain the comparable figure was the Catalan from Mallorca known throughout Europe as the Doctor Illuminatus, Ramón Llull (1235–1315). In English he is known as Raymond Lull (or sometimes Lully) and in Latin as Raymundo Lulio, but each of these names is deceptive as far as pronunciation is concerned, for it is Yool.

The date of his birth to a noble family of Mallorca is significant, in that Christians recaptured the island in 1232, only three years before Llull was born, so that in effect he was a child of Muslim–Christian inheritance. For the first thirty years of his life he proved to be an ordinary fellow with certain extraordinary habits. He was a roisterer, married early to Blanca Picany, who seems to have been a stable woman of deep sensibility by whom he had children, including a son to whom he wrote a delightful book about growing up. The first unusual thing about Llull was that he wrote poetry, and very good poetry too, of a high lyrical pitch but not much spiritual content. Mallorca legend says that his life would have gone forward in customary routine, focusing on his good wife and his beloved children, except that one day he conceived a passion for a young unmarried woman of the city. He was driven to confusion by her pale beauty and one day rode his horse into the center of the church during worship so as to impress her with his love. She rebuffed him in various ways and there was talk of calling in her male kinsmen to chastise him, but at this point she chose a more dramatic gesture. She had her duenna arrange an assignation, and when she was alone with Llull she confessed that she was smitten with him but that one thing had deterred her from confessing her love, and having said this, she undressed to the waist and allowed him to see her breast eaten away by cancer and she only weeks from death.

The impact upon Llull was so staggering that he became more or less unhinged. The girl died on schedule, and he began that withdrawal from life which became so pronounced that his wife had to sue the court for the appointment of a custodian for his possessions, and this was done. Henceforth Llull was in effect a penniless friar. After a pilgrimage on foot to Santiago de Compostela, he joined the Franciscan Order; and after a sustained mystical experience in which he beheld Christ five times, he conceived the idea that he had been chosen to convert Islam to Christianity. Later he realized that to accomplish this he must know Arabic; finding that faithful Muslims would not teach him the language when his avowed purpose was to subvert Muhammad, he escaped their boycott by borrowing enough money from his wife to purchase an Arab slave whose only job was to teach him Arabic. When the task was done and Llull could speak the language—he never learned Latin—he tested his powers by conducting a theological disputation with his slave, but the latter must have been a courageous man, for either he bested Llull in the argument, proving that Muhammad was superior to Christ, or he blasphemed Christianity; whatever the case, Llull flew into a rage and killed his slave. His remorse was so great that from this time he lived by only one rule, 'He who loves not, lives not.'

It would be a pleasure to recite the accomplishments of this brilliant man, but recently I came upon a passage from Havelock Ellis' tribute to Llull, written in 1902 when Ellis was among the first writers in English to bring the Catalan philosopher to the attention of Europe, and this sums up the matter:

> The multiplicity of Lull's acquirements remains astonishing. He wrote, as a matter of course, of metaphysics, logic, rhetoric, grammar, dogmatics, ethics; these were within the province of every schoolman. But beyond these, he dealt with geometry, astronomy, physics, chemistry, anthropology, as well as law and statecraft, navigation and warfare and horsemanship. He foresaw the problem of thermo-dynamics, the question of the expenditure of heat in the initiation of movement; he discussed the essential properties of the elements; he was acquainted with the property of iron when touched by the magnet to turn to the north; he endeavored to explain the causes of wind, and rain, and ice; he concerned himself with the problems of generation. He foresaw the Tartar invasion before the coming of the Ottomans, and he firmly believed in the existence of a great continent on the other side of the world centuries before Columbus sailed out into the west. He was not a great scientific discoverer or investigator, he had not the exclusively scientific temperament of another great Franciscan of that day, Roger Bacon; but his keen and penetrating intelligence placed him at the head and even in front of the best available knowledge of his time, and we can but wonder that a man who began life as the gay singer of a remote centre of chivalry, and ended it as a martyr to faith, should have possessed so much cold, intellectual acumen, so much quiet energy, to devote to the interpretation of the visible world.

Ellis' imposing catalogue fails to touch the two facets of Llull's career that attracted me to him. I do not mean his perfection of the astrolabe, whereby travelers were able to ascertain where they were on the ocean, nor his writing of two hundred and twenty-eight treatises on almost every important topic of his age, but rather the fact that it was Ramón Llull who intellectually initiated the cult of the Virgin; his philosophical expositions paved the way for the doctrines of Immaculate Conception, Intercession and Assumption. (The theological underpinning was provided by Duns Scotus.) Therefore, since the cult of the Virgin has become the central fact of Spanish theology and perhaps of Spanish thought in general, Llull must be recognized as one of Spain's prime movers.

The second reason why I regarded him so highly had to do with other matters. Years before, when I was studying Muslim and Jewish thought in the eastern Mediterranean, I came upon an essay whose title and author I have forgotten, because at the time I was not concerned with the problem it discussed; it was called something like 'Raymundo Lulio and the Last Crusade' and was by a Jewish author who took a rather dim view of Llull, because the Franciscan had conceived a scatterbrained idea of converting all Jews and Muslims to Catholicism by means of his rational persuasion alone. It was a brilliant essay, and long after I had read it and apparently forgotten it, the picture of Ramón Llull returned to stand with me at unexpected places. In Cyprus I recalled that Llull had journeyed there in hopes of converting the Tartars, whom he mistakenly believed to have overrun the Holy Land. When I wandered among the barren rocks of Carthage, Llull appeared, and at Tunis he was very much present, for he had gone there to argue with the sultan and to prove deductively the superiority of Christ. In Paris there was Llull; in Rome, where he went so often to plead with the popes for a crusade of the intellect and not of the sword; and in a half dozen other cities of the Mediterranean where he had engaged in disputation with Jews and Muslims, trying to convert them by his logic.

'I see many knights going to the Holy Land beyond the seas,' he reasoned with the Pope, 'and thinking that they can acquire it by force of arms; but in the end all are destroyed before they attain that which they think to have. Whence it seems to me that the conquest of the Holy Land ought not to be attempted except in the way in which Jesus Christ and his apostles acquired it in the first place, namely, by love and prayers and the pouring out of treasure and blood.' He ended all his exhortations with the reminder 'He who loves not, lives not.'

It was with these recollections of a man who had become a brother to me that I watched our ship dock at Palma, where Llull had galloped his legendary horse into church to seek an assignation with his reluctant lady. As soon as the gangplank was lowered I set off for the Basílica de San Francisco, whose three-tiered cloister marked by palm trees is one of the choice sights of Mallorca. There I had the good luck to meet the young Franciscan who directed the monastery attached to the basilica, Father Antonio Riutford, who seemed scarcely old enough for such a job. He was a scholar and well versed in the life of Ramón Llull, of whom he said, 'Fine philosopher. Poor theologian.' To confirm this judgment he led me to the stained-glass window which showed St. Francis and St. Dominic watching with approval as Ramón Llull in purple robes and Duns Scotus in blue announce their doctrine of the Virgin. 'Llull for ideas. Scotus for sanctity,' Father Riutford said. He then took me to a second window overlooking the nave of the church, and here Llull appeared in the brown robes of a Franciscan, preaching to Muslims with more success than he enjoyed in real life; the window is striking in that the unbelievers are not struck dumb by Llull's eloquence. They listen with dignity to the Doctor Illuminatus and some of them have voluntarily moved into the ranks of his converts.

Next Father Riutford showed me a painting which has caused much discussion. It shows Llull twice: first as a bearded old man of eighty preaching on the shores of Africa as an angel brings him a martyr's crown; second as he dies a miserable death supported by his defenders, who are unable to save him from his Muslim executioners. 'A very dubious work,' Father Riutford admitted. 'Had he died so, he would surely have become a saint. The fact seems to be that he went to Africa, preached to the Muslims, accomplished nothing and sailed back to Mallorca. When his ship was in sight of Palma, he died.' Through delicacy, perhaps, Father Riutford did not bore me with the unbecoming struggle that enveloped Llull in death. Franciscans insisted that he had died a martyr and must be made a saint; Dominicans laughed at the claim and charged instead that he was a heretic and should be posthumously excommunicated. Through the centuries one pope inclined toward one interpretation, his successor to the other; as a result Ramón Llull has not even yet been proclaimed a saint.

This Papal ambivalence was duplicated among the citizens of Palma, who could not decide whether Llull was saint or heretic. 'This nave summarizes the story,' Father Riutford says. 'Originally Llull was buried in this chapel over here, but antagonisms between his supporters and his detractors became so vicious, with brawling and the defacing of his grave, that the Franciscans judged it might be wiser to hide his ashes down there, in the ground under the altar. Long after this was done, it was decided that it was a humiliation to a great man, and if he couldn't stand forth in his own church, where could he? So the hidden urn was dug up and Llull was buried anew in this other chapel back in the apse. It's a beautiful tomb, but as you might have expected, it's been left unfinished for these last five hundred years. Those responsible for the church have not yet been able to agree as to what kind of man Llull was.'

It was a strange tomb that Llull's followers erected in the 1450s. Well above the level of the eye rests a stone sarcophagus decorated with the jacent statue of a bearded old man holding a rosary in hands clasped for prayer, but the statue does not occupy a normal position on the lid of the sarcophagus; it is carved on the side facing the viewer. Llull, therefore, does not lie parallel to the floor but sleeps on his elbow and looks as if he might fall off the side at any moment. There were supposed to be two statues flanking his tomb, Philosophy and Theology. Below, so that their heads would have stood at eye level, should have been seven additional statues representing: Grammar, Logic, Rhetoric (the trivium) and Arithmetic, Music, Geometry and Astronomy (the quadrivium). The niches are waiting, set off by Gothic pilasters, and angels stand by with crowns to grace the missing figures, but the statues have not been completed even though sculptors have had five hundred years to do the job.

'Mallorca has never been able to make up its mind,' Father Riutford said, showing me a crypt which had been dug under the altar in 1915, the sixth centenary of Llull's death, with the idea that his body should be identified with the Host and thus to serve as the focus for a cult. The crypt was prepared, even though many graves occupied by friars buried there over past centuries had to be dug up, but when it was finished the old animosities against Llull prevailed and the move was not permitted.

Spain as a whole has not been easy in its attitude toward Llull, who seems to have been more a Frenchman than a Spaniard; his orientation was to Paris and not to Toledo, certainly to Rome rather than to Barcelona. One of the scholars at the Madrid tertulia had told me, 'Llull is a man you can't trust. You think you have him, and he slips out of your fingers.' As the man spoke I recalled the poem Llull had written at the age of sixty-five:

> I am old, poor, unappreciated and without assistance from anyone. I have undertaken superior tasks, insofar as my ability would permit. I have journeyed through a great part of the world. Very fine examples have I given of learning, but nevertheless I am little loved and less known.

(Later, when I returned to the tertulia in Madrid, I asked Martínez López of Texas and Cossío of the Academy their opinion of Llull, and they agreed that he was one of the supreme Spaniards, whose theories have yet to be exhausted.)

I revere Llull because in his day he saw the interlocking nature of the world and was willing to sacrifice his life to help achieve unity. To him the Mediterranean was infinitely larger than the Atlantic and the Pacific are to me, yet he went forth to all the shores, preaching one message, 'He who loves not, lives not.' If the Tartars overran older civilizations, he was ready to talk with the Tartars. If the Muslims held Africa in slavery, he was prepared to walk on foot through Africa and debate with its rulers. If he came upon an island, he said, 'Let's build a university.' If a subject was obscure, he wrote a book about it, explaining its intricacies and relating them to all other known fields. Beaten and expelled from Bugia (today Bougie in Algeria), the Muslim capital on the northern coast of Africa, he blamed no one but himself, reasoning that if his logic had been more persuasive the Muslims would have listened; so after surviving shipwreck on his way to Pisa he retired to perfect his argument, after which he returned to Bugia alone to see the sultan face to face. And in spite of the defeats he met, he remained a poet to the end.

His reputation in the Church has been much damaged by one of those perplexing historical accidents that one can neither explain nor correct. In the eighteenth century a fable circulated to the effect that Ramón Llull, the world's master alchemist, had succeeded in compounding an alkahest that would speed the transmutation of lead to gold. For prudent reasons he had refrained from committing his formula to writing, but if one studied his numerous books on alchemy one could deduce the formula and with it make gold. Understandably, there was a run on Llull's alchemical works and he became famous throughout Europe. What were the names of his books on the subject? He wrote none. Close study of his major work proves that he held alchemy in contempt; certainly he ridiculed the idea of transmuting metals and frequently spoke poorly of those who tried. He was, in effect, his age's principal foe of alchemy; but because he was known to have written on chemistry, and partly, I suppose, because pictures of him showed the long beard of the typical Faustian alchemist, he became the symbol of the movement and it would have been fruitless to deny that he was its leader.

As for the alchemy books attributed to Llull, which do exist and in extraordinary number, they were all forgeries, done mostly in Germany and very late. For a book on alchemy to sell, it almost had to be signed by Raymundo Lulio, and so they proliferated. Even today the few persons who have heard of Ramón Llull are apt to remember him only as Europe's chief alchemist. For a man who founded his intellectual life on rationalism, it is a bitter trick.

I was surprised in Mallorca to find no monument to Llull, as I had been surprised in Córdoba to find none to Averroës, but at lunch I discovered why. A friend in Barcelona had asked a young scholar in Palma to supervise my lunch, and when we were seated I asked him why Llull had been ignored, and he said, 'But he wasn't. In 1915 plans were laid to erect a statue on the waterfront. The site was selected and the base was built. But . . .'

'There were objections?'

'Yes. I'm a great admirer of Llull's. He was probably the best man these islands ever produced, but there are many who consider him a heretic. So the monument was not permitted.'

It so happened that at a nearby table a medical doctor was having his lunch, and when he heard that I was from the United States he introduced himself, Dr. Antonio Bauza Roca from the Mallorcan city of Petra. 'We make many shoes there for shipment to your country, but we are famous for something quite different.' He was a peppery little man with a rim of dark hair about his bald head and a set of very dark eyebrows; he had many interests and spoke with fluency on economics, politics, shipping and literature, but when he handed me his card it was as El Presidente de la Asociación de los Amigos de Fray Junípero Serra. 'He was born in Petra,' Dr. Bauza said proudly, 'but it was in California that he found his immortality. He's buried in Carmel and we've been told he's practically the patron saint of California.'

Then, with his eyes dancing beneath their large brows, he explained why he had wanted to speak with me. 'In 1969 we celebrate the two-hundredth anniversary of Fray Junípero's arrival at San Diego. Festivities here and bigger ones in California. At that time our great project will come to fulfilment . . . the one we've been working on so hard.'

I asked what it was, and he said, 'The rich people of California consider it shameful that in Mallorca there is no fine statue to Fray Junípero, who is the greatest man ever to come from these islands. So they're collecting money and we're going to build a tall statue . . . right over there. Fray Junípero Serra, the patron of Mallorca, rising like a giant and looking across the sea toward California, the land he went to convert.'

I noticed that my luncheon partner did not respond to this news but sat with his hands clenched. When Dr. Bauza, having invited my wife and me to attend the celebrations enshrining Fray Junípero, departed, he cursed and said, 'Can you guess the spot they've chosen for their monument? The very one where the statue to Ramón Llull was to have been built. I wouldn't be surprised if they used the same base. And what did Junípero Serra ever do? He stumbled his way into California. Oh my God!'

Sadness possessed my friend as he reflected on the world's unjustness: 'A man like Ramón Llull can have the foremost mind of his age. Write more than two hundred books that kept intelligence alive. Identify the true nature of the Virgin. He can work to unite the known world, and it all comes to nothing. Even his own Church rejects him . . . his tomb is left unfinished. And all because he worked in the field of the intellect. But let an ignorant friar happen to wander across land where oil is to be discovered . . . and where American millionaires are to flourish. And all the money you would need is made available for erecting a statue to that friar.'

He turned to me in mock bitterness and said, 'You norteamericanos are ruining Spain.' Then like a conspirator he drew close and whispered, 'But if you do put up that statue to Junípero Serra . . . on the site reserved for Ramón Llull. Well, don't be surprised if some dark night the damned thing's dynamited.'

I thought it wisest not to tip my hand at this early stage, but if his plot goes forward, I plan to be in on it.

FOLLOWING PAGE:
This noble animal lost its ears in the arena
in proof of the great fight he gave.

XI

THE BULLS

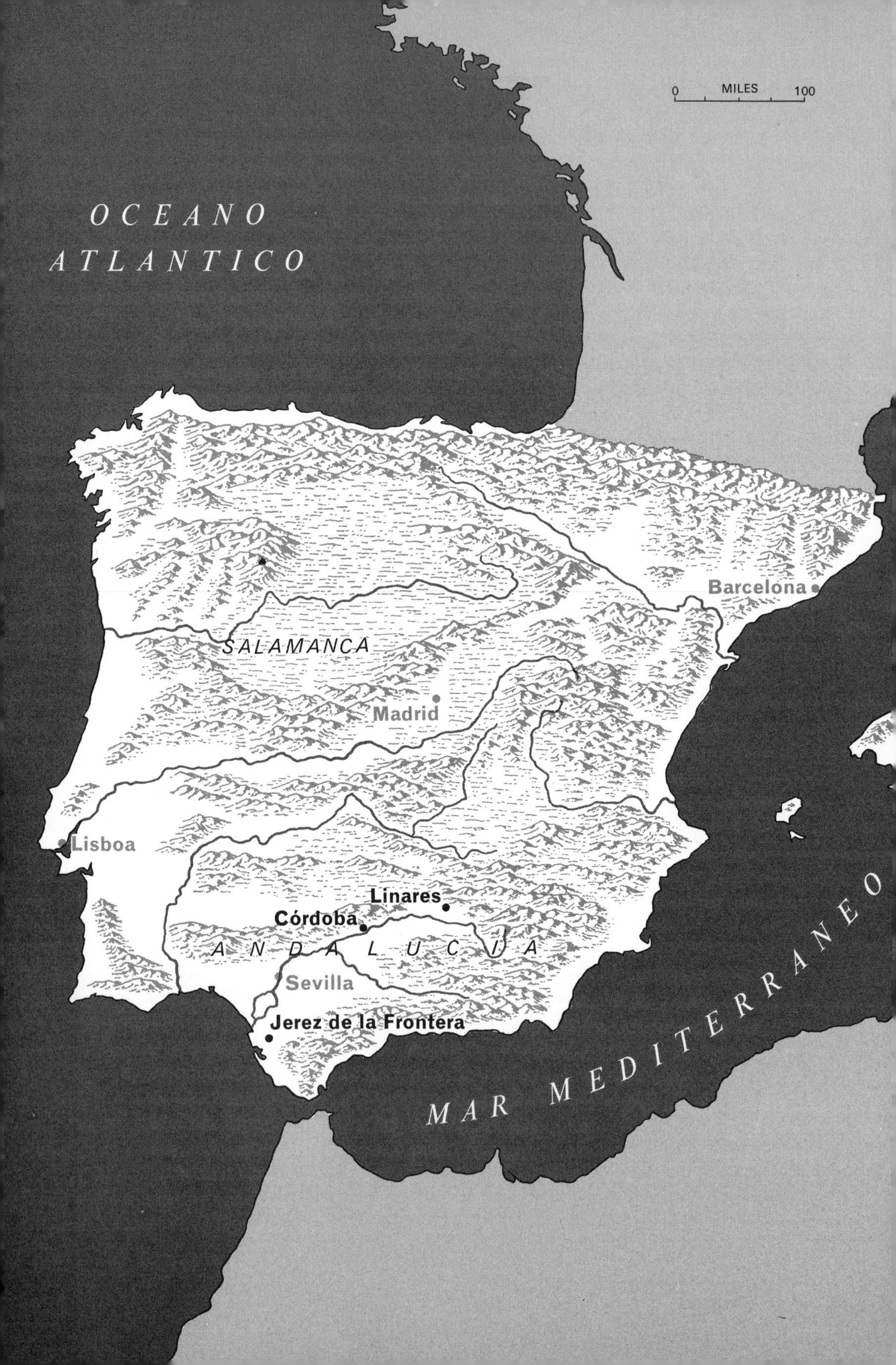

OCEANO
ATLANTICO

MILES
0   100

Barcelona

SALAMANCA

Madrid

Lisboa

Linares
Córdoba
ANDALUCIA
Sevilla
Jerez de la Frontera

MAR MEDITERRANEO

F rom that first Sunday in Valencia when I watched La-
landa, Ortega and El Estudiante fight six bulls I have been a devotee of the
bullring. Over a period of thirty-five seasons I have seen all the great
matadors in Spain and Mexico save Pepe Luis Vázquez the Spaniard,
although strangely enough I was a good friend of the Mexican matador of
that name. I have traveled with bullfighters in both countries, have read
almost everything in print in both Spanish and English, plus many fine
books in French, and instead of losing interest as the years passed, I have
found my appetite for this art increasing.

I suppose I have seen over 250 fights with full matadors, which is a
far cry from the 750 which a professional bull-follower like Kenneth
Vanderford has seen, or the amazing 114 which the American girl Virginia
Smith saw in one year by dint of driving her Renault like mad back and
forth across Spain during the bullfight season. I have long since stopped
making apologies for my interest in the bulls, but I do believe that the
following observations by a Spaniard who had lived in America will prove
relevant.

American: How can a civilized man like you tolerate bullfighting?

Spaniard: A fair question and one deserving a serious answer. I suggest
that you think of bullfighting in Spain as you would boxing in America.

American: Exactly the point I wanted to make. All decent Americans are
opposed to boxing. Each time after a boxer is killed in the ring, there is
an outcry from our responsible press, questions are asked in Congress
and movements are launched to end this bloody business.

Spaniard: Rightly so, because boxing is much more brutal than bullfighting.
And of course far more men are killed in the boxing ring than in the
bullring. Statistically boxing is more dangerous. Morally it's more
debilitating.

American: I agree. And that's why we're all against it. Why aren't you Spaniards against bullfighting?

Spaniard: To a certain extent we are. Many decent Spaniards oppose bull-fighting on precisely the grounds that decent Americans oppose box-ing. But on the other hand, there are decent Spaniards who rather like bullfighting and feel that the brutality is a small price to pay for so much beauty.

American: That's what we Americans can't understand. How can anyone argue that fleeting beauty, fine as it is, justifies a thing like bullfight-ing?

Spaniard: To understand this I invite you to compare bullfighting not with a rejected American sport like boxing, but with an accepted one like football.

American: (*aggressively*) What do you mean, football?

Spaniard: I've been following your statistics for some years, and each year your American-style football kills more than forty of your finest young men.

American: There's an accident now and then.

Spaniard: Forty men, year after year. And not dead-end kids like boxers. But the best young men of your country, many of them fine scholars. Yet I hear no outcry against football.

American: Well, football's different. Our best colleges play football.

Spaniard: Why is there no public outcry against a sport which kills forty of your best young men each year?

American: Well, football's part of the American way of life. Everybody's for football.

Spaniard: Exactly. Football's part of your way of life. Universities pay for their stadiums with football. Television earns enormous sums from bringing it into your homes. Automobiles and razor blades are sold by means of it. Newspapers, who might be expected to lead the fight against such brutality, earn much of their profits from emphasizing football. It would be ridiculous to attack something that earns every-one so much money.

American: But we don't look at football as a way to earn money. It's a manly sport.

Spaniard: To a European like me, the amazing thing is that while you're killing your forty a year, you have at your disposal a much finer version of football which kills nobody.

American: You mean soccer? The sissy game?

Spaniard: All the rest of the world plays what you call derisively the sissy game and finds it the best team game ever invented for professionals. Millions of people watch it with interest. It sells just as many automo-biles and fills just as many pages of newsprint. And it kills no one.

American: But fundamentally it's a sissy game. And it's not part of the American pattern.

Spaniard: Precisely. Because Americans demand a more brutal game. And if fine young men are killed each year, that's a small price to pay for your entertainment.

American: I've never seen anyone killed.

Spaniard: And the maimed?

American: Well, a broken neck now and then. Or your front teeth knocked out. But boys get over things like that.

Spaniard: And walk with a limp the rest of their lives. The solemn fact, according to fatality statistics, is that your football is some six hundred times more dangerous than our bullfighting. Yet you want me to go out and protest against bullfighting while I am not allowed to demand that you protest football.

American: There's this difference. In football the young man can either play or not play . . . as he wishes. In bullfighting the animal has no choice. And he's killed.

Spaniard: If you want to lament the death of a bull and forget the death of young men, it's your decision. What we might conclude is that bullfighting is a relatively safe brutal sport, and Spaniards like it. Football is a relatively dangerous brutal sport, and Americans like it.

American: Yes, but bullfighting is somehow degrading.

Spaniard: If you say so.

Although I have known most of the great matadors, some fairly well, my major interest has always been with the bull, for I find this noble animal one of the most praiseworthy beasts existing. When left with his fellows he is gentle and can be easily handled; when separated and alone he will fight anything that moves. His stubborn heroism is unmatched, for he has attacked and sometimes conquered automobiles, trains, airplanes, trucks; in organized fights with lions, tigers, elephants, bears and dogs it is seldom he who slinks away. He has a tenacity of purpose not equaled in the animal kingdom; on July 10, 1966, in the plaza at Pamplona a bull raised by César Moreno was pitted against the matador Tinín in third position. He gave a notable fight, was brave as a bull could be and was killed by a good thrust of the sword. I say killed, for the bull was technically dead, but in the waning moments of his life he walked stolidly nearly twice around the entire circumference of the ring, seeking some spot in which he could defend himself in this battleground where he had behaved with such honor. Up and down pumped the mighty hooves, here and there probed the doughty head. If men molested him, he fought them off, conserving his strength and dealing with them as he would with pestering flies. On and on he went, refusing to die, marching like a Roman legion that had been assaulted in the north of Spain, resolute and beaten and magnificent. Men standing beside me had tears in their eyes, and an awe-struck Englishman whispered, 'My God, he's a Winston Churchill of a bull.' Finding no protecting corner in which to make his final stand, he backed against the wall, his feet wide-spread, his horns still dangerous.

Lower and lower dropped the magnificent head, and at last he died. The mules dragged him in a circuit of the ring so that men could shower flowers upon him and hosannahs, but his triumphal tour dead was as nothing to the two he had made alive. It is this kind of animal one sees occasionally in the ring, and he reminds us of the quality that inheres in all animals.

The fighting bull is a special breed, and some of my happiest days in Spain and Mexico have been those long and lazy afternoons spent watching bulls in their native habitat. Dark against the brown fields, they stand in monumental groups, serenely indifferent to the stray men who happen to move upon them. My lasting memory of such days is of a group of Concha y Sierra bulls in Las Marismas, raising their heads at my approach, watching me for a few moments, then returning to their browsing. I have always loved animals and have spent many hours comparing them: the elephant is more majestic than the bull; the lion is more animated; the tiger is certainly more terrifying; but for the inherent nobility of the animal kingdom, a nobility which I have observed in dogs, in horses, in kestrels, in ants, in groundhogs, in antelope and in the three kingly beasts just named, I prefer the bull, as men of a philosophical mind have done since the beginning of time. It is not by accident that the bull marches across the rocks at Altamira and Lascaux; the young nobles of Crete could have tested their skill against lions or bears, but the adversary they chose was the bull; and the mystic rites of Mithras could have been composed around any well-proportioned animal, but it was only the bull that gave power and significance. I respond to the fighting bull of Andalucía exactly as my ancestors responded to his ancestors at Altamira and Crete.

In writing of Pamplona, I pointed out that in 1966 the last day of running with the bulls through the streets was not the last day of the fair, and this requires some explanation. That year San Fermín covered eight days, and on the first seven the running with the bulls occurred each morning as planned, but on the eighth day there was a fight but no running, and for good reason. On the first seven days the bulls to be fought each day all came from a single ranch, and what was more, all from the crop of bulls born four years earlier and raised together since birth; on the final day one bull from each of six different ranches was fought in what was called a concurso. This is a formal competition with two characteristics: a panel of judges awards a prize to the bravest bull, so that the reputation of the competing ranches is at stake; and the public is attracted by the possibility that it can, if some bull proves to be extraordinarily brave, spare that bull's life. I have seen only two concursos, the classic one held each year in Jerez de la Frontera and this one in Pamplona. I have, of course, seen several fights in which six bulls from six different ranches

The calf, bloodstained and wet, struggles to rise from the earth.
At the end of his life he will struggle just as valiantly
to avoid returning to the sandy earth of the arena.

were brought together haphazardly, but these could not be termed concursos because there was no competition for the bravest bull, nor did the public have the right to excuse a bull from death in case he proved unusually brave. In general I have found fights built around bulls from different ranches disappointing; one gets a better sense of the bull if all six come from the same ranch.

To attempt to run the six bulls of the Pamplona concurso through the streets would have proved impossible, for since they came from different ranches and were strangers each to the other, if they were lumped together in the holding corrals at midnight, by dawn five would be dead. Bulls will not tolerate other bulls whose smell they do not know and will duel such intruders to the death. In fact, if from the same ranch a five-year-old bull were to be thrown in with a group of adjusted four-year-olds, the latter would probably kill the former because they would not be accustomed to his smell.

I remember at the Sevilla feria of 1961, when Robert Vavra and I spent about ten hours during visits to the Venta de Antequera corrals, studying two strings of bulls to be fought later. We were fortunate in the bulls we chose to concentrate upon, because one string came from the ranch of Benítez Cubero and were to give the finest six fights I have ever seen a set of six bulls give; in the corrals they were magnificent, relaxed yet quick to respond to anything unaccustomed, and we were able, by dint of careful comparison, to determine fairly well the kind of fight each bull would give and how he would be differentiated from his fellows. Our error was that we consistently underestimated the bulls; I had never seen a finer group, but I did not discover this until the fight unfolded.

The second string was not so fine but in some ways it was more interesting, and to it we gave the bulk of our attention. It was a group of six Miura bulls from the famous ranch whose animals have killed more toreros than any other and against which, at the beginning of this century, a group of matadors went on strike. Even today, when Miuras are fought, the matadors are apt to be the hungry ones of fading reputation who cannot get other fights; well-established matadors consent to fight them only rarely. Part of their evil reputation stems from the fact that the Miura ranch has been in unbroken existence longer than most others and has thus had time to build up its list of fatalities; at any rate, it is the most feared of the existing ranches and along with that of Tulio Vázquez one of the most prestigious. The Miura is noted for a sway-back body, a long neck and a relatively small head. They turn with incredible swiftness and are said to be 'all over the matador in an instant,' so that many matadors refuse to fight them. As we studied these six we began to isolate obvious characteristics: one of the bulls appeared to have homosexual tendencies, which so perplexed him that he was not going to give a good fight, nor did he; another was shy and nervous, apt to jump at unusual phenomena and always away from the source of the surprise, not toward it, but he was a splendid animal and we felt that although he would be dangerous in the first portion of the fight, when he struck the horses and was made to know the seriousness of the battle by the picadors jabbing at the hump of muscle over his neck, he would quieten down and give good combat, which proved to be the case; there were two bulls from which nothing much could be expected, for they simply lacked class, and in the arena some days later they proved to be as poor as we suspected; and there was a powerful red bull who might go either way.

He was a contentious beast and accepted no nonsense from any of the others, but he was far from suave, which a great bull should be. The more we watched him the more complex he became, for although he wanted to fight he was fundamentally unsure of himself. He fascinated us, for he was obviously a beast of much potential, and then on the morning of the fight, before the hour when the bulls are put into the little cells from which they emerge into the sunlight of the arena to give battle, that solemn hour at high noon when the peons of the matadors who are to fight that day assemble at the ring to determine how the bulls can be most fairly matched in pairs and to draw lots to see which man will fight which pair, a sly and tricky negotiation, we saw the big red bull for the last time, and he had become so self-contained, so suave that we knew he was going to be one of the memorable Miuras. He was fought by the matador Limeño from Sanlúcar de Barrameda, and he responded so well to all elements in the fight, charging the first capes, assaulting the horses and ignoring the picadors, following the red muleta at the finish, that all agreed he was the notable bull of the year.

It is by such study that men come to know bulls and to love them for the simple, brave things they are. I remember once in Madrid when Vavra and I went out to the Venta de Batán corrals to see a set of Cobaleda bulls from Salamanca. (For some inexplicable reason bulls from Andalucía are apt to be brave and strong, bulls of Salamanca quite the contrary. Of course, a fine Salamanca bull, and each year there are some, is superior to a poor Andalusian, but in general it is the bulls from the south who give good fight. Several wild guesses have been made on this subject, none of which satisfy me. It is claimed that grass in the south is richer in vitamins and the water in minerals, but analysis does not bear this out; the more even length of day in the south has been suggested, but this makes no sense at all; one argument has been persuasive, that the rocky land of Andalucía develops stronger hooves and leg muscles than the softer soil of Salamanca. Persuasive, that is until one recalls that in the swamps of Las Marismas are grown some of the finest fighting bulls so far produced, and during half of each year these animals walk only on a soft and marshy

FOLLOWING FACING PAGES:
*Like members of the Guardia Civil, their
weapons poised, the bulls maintain a vigil.*

soil. Experts, of course, argue that it is the effort required when the bull drags his feet out of the sucking mud that builds up his muscles.)

Well, these Salamanca bulls at Madrid looked fine. They were big and in the corrals they comported themselves with dignity. But they were very heavy and their fore knees were weak. Even from the barrier Vavra could detect signs of weakness. 'Those knees won't stand up in the fight,' he predicted, and later when these pathetic creatures came into the ring they made one or two charges, as their taurine hearts commanded, but then their knees gave out and they fell into heaps around the ring, too heavy to get back up on their feet. The fight degenerated into a dismal spectacle of one pass, bull down, haul the bull back up, another pass, bull down again. Two of the poor creatures, their hearts still willing but their legs played out, simply lay on the sand and protected themselves by cutting swaths with their horns; to get them to their weakened legs proved most difficult. The afternoon was a travesty, the worst I've ever seen. My only consolation was that long before the fight we had guessed that it would probably be so.

As I explained in the chapter on Badajoz, I am loath to introduce unfamiliar Spanish words which are not essential, and foreigners who write about bulls offend in this respect, peppering their pages with italic instead of information, but for what I wish to say from here on, a limited taurine vocabulary is necessary, with as many of the words as possible kept in English:

Torero includes all men engaged in the fight, whether matador, picador, peon or banderillero.

Cuadrilla (crew) is the team working in support of one matador. It consists of two mounted picadors who ride on horses supplied by the ring, and three peons, who are called banderilleros when engaged in placing the banderillas.

Corrida (a running) is the complete bullfight, customarily consisting of six bulls from the same ranch fought by three matadors. The senior man in point of service fights bulls number one and four; the second, bulls two and five; and the junior, bulls three and six. Since it requires about twenty minutes to fight one bull, the corrida lasts about two hours. In June fights may start as late as seven; in the autumn as early as four. I have often seen acceptable fights on rainy days but never on windy.

Single fight is the action of one matador against one bull. It has been described by earlier writers as a ritualistic drama in three unequal acts, plus prologue and epilogue. One advocate of this interpretation has said, 'The prologue, which consists of the matador's testing the bull with the cape, might be thought of as *A Midsummer Night's Dream*, with its airy joy. The first act with the picadors is heavy like *King Lear*. The relatively unimportant but poetic second act of the banderilleros is *Twelfth Night*. The stupendous third act, heavy with emotion and impending tragedy, when the matador alone faces his destiny, is of course *Hamlet*, while the overpowering epilogue of death can be likened only to Aeschylus.'

Don Quixote . . . a wash drawing by Picasso . . . an echo from the Caves of Altamira . . . a bull and picador separated from their forms . . . all these can be seen at certain moments of the corrida.

Cape is the large stiff-fabric cloth, magenta on one side, yellow on the other, used by the matador in the prologue and first two acts and by the peons throughout. The bull will charge either color equally.

Pic is the long steel-tipped pick or lance used by the picador in the first act.

Banderillas are the colorfully decorated short sticks with barbed steel points which are placed in pairs by the banderilleros in the bull's shoulders.

Muleta is the red-flannel cloth, smaller than a cape, used by the matador during the third act and epilogue.

Faena is the vital third act in which the matador exhibits his skill with the muleta. Tradition requires that during the faena he keep his sword in his right hand, which usually also holds the muleta. Experts judge that the excellence of any single fight depends about sixty to seventy percent on the faena, which can excuse poor work elsewhere.

Kill is the tragic epilogue that ends the fight.

Let me make one thing clear. Most corridas are a disappointment. Six bulls are fought, and of them, five are apt to be so difficult that the matador cannot parade his skill. In all the years I've been seeing corridas, only the six Benítez Cubero bulls of which I have spoken gave a uniformly excellent show. No other set has ever provided even as many as four good fights, and the vast majority have provided none. Of a hundred corridas taken at random at least eighty will be bores; ten will be reasonably good; five will be unquestionably good; four will be worth remembering; and one might be superb. Therefore, the mathematical chances of buying a ticket on impulse and seeing a good fight are at least four to one against. At one catastrophic San Isidro feria in Madrid of sixteen fights, fourteen were very poor and the other two barely acceptable.

At the Pamplona feria in 1966, government inspectors found that sixteen of the forty-eight bulls failed to meet legal standards, being either underage, underweight or with the tips of their horns shaved off. Fines of 265,000 pesetas were assessed, and this in a feria which was supposed to emphasize the excellence of the bull. In the two hundred and fifty corridas I've attended my luck has been poor, for I have seen even fewer good fights than the averages would have indicated.

In watching a single fight I have said that it should be considered as a ritual drama, and philosophically this is correct. Occasionally one can receive from this tragic play a catharsis precisely like that described by Aristotle, and that is why so many foreign writers have been attracted to the bullfight. I have found it more practical to see the single fight as a spectacle built up of several identifiable skills, for in this way I can better judge what I am seeing. A really complete single fight would consist of six components, each performed with art, as follows: one, after the bull enters the ring and has been tested by the peons, the matador must initiate his part of the fight with a series of delicate and artistic passes with his large cape; two, the bull must then three times attack with resolute bravery the picador and horse, and the picador must handle his lance properly; three, after each pic the three matadors in proper turn must lead the bull away from the horse and execute artistic and sometimes intricate passes with their large capes; four, three separate pairs of banderillas must be placed correctly and with art; five, the matador with his muleta must build an artistic faena consisting of a series of linked passes that make sense; six, the matador must kill proudly and honorably, going in over the horn and finishing the bull with one thrust.

Well, that makes six components for each bull or a total of thirty-six for an afternoon, and if on a given day you see out of thirty-six as many as four items properly performed, you've not been cheated. On some afternoons you see none. To see all six performed well on a single bull is so rare as to be historic, and to see the six performed well on each bull of the

Matador Fulton with cape.

afternoon would be positively impossible. It has never happened and never will. At the beginning of the Pamplona feria in 1966, I had seen some fifteen hundred bulls fought and had never seen one on which the six components were properly performed, and I did not expect ever to do so.

These doleful facts are summarized in a saying which reports as a permanent truth: 'Si hay toros, no hay toreros; si hay toreros, no hay toros.' (If there are bulls, there are no bullfighters; if there are bullfighters, there are no bulls.) This applies equally to golf, to love-making, to buying stock in the Xerox Corporation and to most other human endeavors: 'When everything looks right, some one thing is bound to go wrong.'

For the uninitiated foreigner, especially one who loves animals, a corrida is usually an unrewarding experience; he sees a confusing spectacle in which the bull appears only as a necessary and fractious evil who, after disrupting everyone's plans, ends ignominiously as a kind of ani-

637

mated pincushion. The animal is without individualized personality; and it is not illogical for the foreigner seeing his first fight to hope that the bull will catch or even kill the matador, for that would introduce into the mysterious rites at least a focal point of comprehension. But when one has attended many corridas and has begun to catch a glimmer of the intricate and subtle construction of a bullfight, he begins to center his attention on the animal, and occasionally he will sense the overtones of the tremendous drama being enacted before him: the confrontation of man and primordial animal. The devotee therefore finds something of interest in every corrida, for this confrontation can take any of various forms and all are challenging.

What have I found in the Spanish bullfight? A flash of beauty, a swift development of the unexpected, a somber recollection of primitive days when men faced bulls as an act of religious faith. In the bulls I have found a symbol of power and grandeur; in the men I have seen a professionalism which is usually honorable if not always triumphant. I have never seen a corrida which did not teach me something or which did not at some point develop unexpectedly, and I am willing to settle for this limited experience. No matter how disastrous the fight, and some of them can be dreadful, there is the ancient drama of hopeful man and savage beast and the mysterious bond that exists between them.

I have stressed the professionalism of the matador because when one enters a plaza, having paid up to twenty-five dollars for the privilege, he can be reasonably assured that if a good bull thunders into the arena, the man facing it has served an apprenticeship which taught him to give a decent fight. Since top matadors earn enormous sums of money, say seven thousand dollars a fight for eighty or ninety fights a year, the competition is grueling, for the bullring is the traditional route by which boys from impoverished families attain bull ranches of their own, and fame, and wealthy wives. It is a matter of endless training, the fighting of imaginary bulls day after day in the public parks of Madrid or Sevilla. One boy grasps a pair of horns, bends over, snorts like a bull and charges into the cape or the muleta held by another boy. Hour after hour they practice, first one boy playing the bull, then another. At home they practice passes before mirrors to attain grace, and always they bum about the countryside seeking invitations to those testing exhibitions in which the young heifers of the bull ranch are thrown against picadors and matadors to see whether they are brave or not. If the heifer charges the horse bravely, and we have seen at Trujillo and Pamplona how these scrawny, awkward beasts attack, driving at any moving object time and again, she is set aside for breeding purposes. If the heifer proves faulty or unwilling to attack when hurt, she is ticketed for beef. (If you think for a moment, you will understand why it

In each bullfight come moments of nightmare intensity
when forms melt together and strange combinations appear.

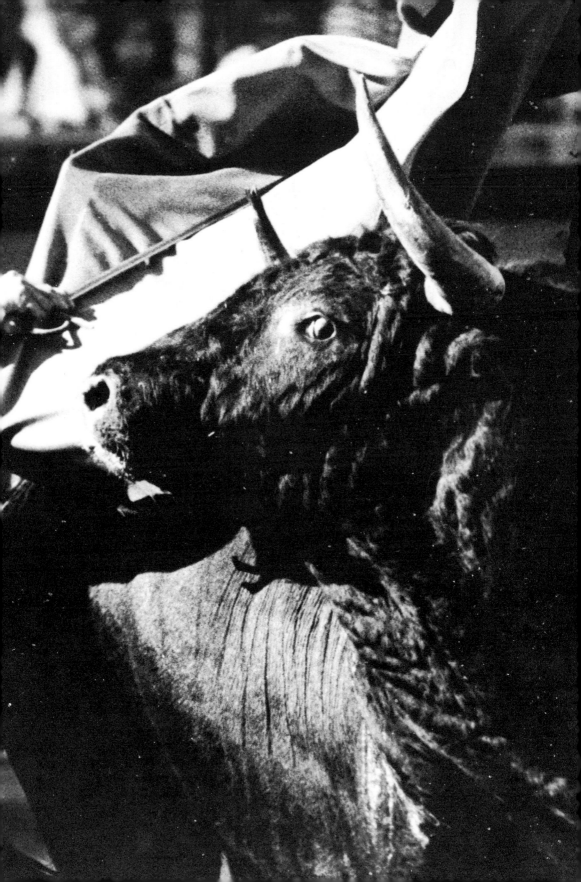

is the heifers who are tested and not the young bulls; these animals learn so quickly that if the males were tested with capes when young they would remember, and when they entered the arena against the matador they would kill him. Since the bravery of a bull is determined primarily by his mother, she must therefore be tested to see if she is brave; the father contributes only the young bull's physical conformation, and a visual inspection tells whether it is satisfactory or not.) At any rate, the would-be matador must seek out these testings to familiarize himself with the bull family and to exhibit the skill he has learned in the parks and before the mirror. Especially he must keep his ear tuned for word of any village festivals in which improvised arenas are set up in the main plaza, with upended carts forming the barriers and boards protecting store windows, for at these rowdy festivals wise old bulls are turned loose on which aspirant matadors can try their skills without killing the animal. The bulls have attended so many festivals they know better than the young fighters how to position themselves and when to react to the passes. 'That bull speaks Latin,' is a customary description. I once heard a young fighter say, 'After I gave him two good passes he tried to borrow money from me.' The Mexicans have a wonderful word for such goings-on. Pachangas, they call them, and the syllables evoke the madness; capeas they're called in Spain, and they do not always end humorously. Each year some aspirant is badly gored by the canny old beasts and sometimes death results. But the competition to become a full matador is so keen that young men must take these chances.

Of a thousand boys who begin at age twelve to learn the bullfighting passes, perhaps a hundred will succeed in fighting one of the old bulls at a capea; far fewer will ever face a heifer at a ranch. Of a hundred who progress to the point where they have actually fought bulls as beginners, only four or five will become full matadors. And of a hundred full matadors, only four or five will become big stars. The adverse odds in this profession are overwhelming.

But since the rewards can be overwhelming, each year the horde of boys at practice remains about the same, and some very moving literature has grown out of this drudgery. Anyone interested in the purely seamy side should read Luis Spota's *The Wounds of Hunger*, which has been translated into English by Barnaby Conrad. It is based on the saying that for a bullfighter the wounds of hunger are more terrifying than the wounds of the horn.

There are several fine recent books on bullfighting, and as in the case of Spain generally, the best are by Englishmen; Kenneth Tynan's perceptive *Bull Fever*, which analyzes the mystique of the art; Angus Macnab's *The Bulls of Iberia*, which has some excellent summaries of individual

The horns, which might be seen in any pueblo in Spain, are those of an old bull. The face is that of an old man.

fights; and John Marks' *To the Bullfight*, of which Hemingway said, 'the best book on the subject—after minê.' Of recent American books the three best are, perhaps symbolically, compendiums featuring photographs, but they are very good: Peter Buckley's *Bullfight*, which gives a fine account of how matadors cruise back and forth across Spain; Barnaby Conrad's *La Fiesta Brava*, which is well informed; and Robert Daley's *The Swords of Spain*, the classic photograph of which has a heroic tourist running into the arena at Pamplona in sheer terror, full speed and at least three hundred yards ahead of the nearest bull. El Valiente, Daley calls him, and every time I see him bursting into the arena I think of myself.

Of course, the best thing so far written on bullfighting is Ernest Hemingway's *Death in the Afternoon*. As his friend Quintana says, 'It's amazing that a man who spoke no Spanish to begin with could have so quickly caught the spirit of a foreign art.' It remains a masterpiece of insight and persuasion and is as popular today as when it was first published in 1932. Recently an American, John McCormick, aided by a Mexican, Mario Sevilla Mascareñas, has produced an opinionated but highly literate and well-informed philosophical analysis, *The Complete Aficionado*.

The period during which I have seen bullfights may be divided into three epochs, each named after a matador: the Epoch of Belmonte, 1914–1936, the Epoch of Manolete, 1939–1955, even though Manolete himself died in 1947, and the Epoch of El Cordobés, 1955 till today. Of the three, the most varied and rewarding was the first, for then one had normative figures like Belmonte, the peerless Joselito, Chicuelo, the preposterous El Gallo and Marcial Lalanda. The middle period was the most dramatic, with the confrontation of the tragic Manolete and the Mexican Carlos Arruza, ornamented by half a dozen additional figures of first category. The third period, running into the present, has been for me more difficult to categorize. I have found it dull, marked by certain honorable matadors but none of supreme excellence, and while it has given us El Cordobés, the most popular matador of all times and the one who has earned the most money, it has provided neither a classic figure nor a tragic poet. To such judgment authorities like José María Cossío and Vanderford say, 'Nonsense. Antonio Ordóñez has been at least as great as Joselito.'

My favorite in this long procession has been none of the men named but the austere classicist Domingo Ortega. He was so pure a bullfighter that men wrote long books about his art, claiming that he had saved the bullfight from becoming a mere ornamentation. Philosophers invoked him as a reincarnation of Seneca; motion-picture theaters throbbed to the classical emotion which he was able to cram into a few controlled passes; and at the plaza men were alternately perplexed by the rigidity of his style and enchanted by its purity. If I had been a bullfighter I should have wanted to fight like Domingo Ortega, and my memory of him in the ring has had a

Rehearsal for what? Applause, money, the wounds of honor, death? The pain of disillusionment?

profound influence on the way I think and especially in the way I evaluate work in the arts. I would say that he has had an impact on me as great as that of Johannes Brahms.

The quiescent third epoch, in which I have seen most of my fights, did produce the much publicized Dominguín-Ordóñez confrontation, in which the latter excelled, and some, including Hemingway and the experts just cited, have believed that Ordóñez has been the greatest fighter of this century; but as I described in the chapter on Pamplona, I have never seen

643

him good but have seen him when his arrogant contempt for the audience was unbearable. In this period most of my knowledgeable friends have tried to convince me that the great figure is Curro Romero, and I well remember the afternoon I sat in the stands at Pamplona and happened to mention another matador as my favorite. A voluble Spanish gentleman next to me, who had remained unmoved by all my other judgments over a period of six days, exploded with rage, and Vavra caught a series of eight snapshots showing his disgust. 'There is only one matador in Spain worthy of a man's respect,' he shouted. 'All the others are what? Nothing! Poof! To see Romero on one of his fine afternoons is like seeing God Himself descending to supervise a performance. Then the cape stands out like sculptured gold, the muleta is like a thread of silk binding the man and the bull together. It is exquisite, the stuff of dreams, and one feels tears in his eyes, a profound exaltation in his heart. I have seen Curro when he molded fifteen thousand people in the plaza as if he were an angelic child playing with sand. You hear the phrase "he and the bull were one." With Curro it's different. There is no man. There is no bull. There is merely a golden moment, and when it's past you turn to your neighbor as I'm turning to you now and ask, "What was that I saw?" And he explains very humbly, "My friend, you saw a miracle." Therefore, please don't speak to me about so-and-so. At least not in the same plaza where I have mentioned the name Curro Romero.' John Fulton, Orson Welles, Kenneth Vanderford, Robert Vavra and scores of others all felt the same way, although they tended to express themselves more forcefully than did my Spanish friend at Pamplona. To have seen Curro Romero was to have seen the ultimate.

Well, finally I saw him. At Sevilla he came into the arena, a rather pudgy young man of undistinguished height, carriage, feature and bearing. He was a disaster. I saw him four more times in Sevilla, always miserably bad. He seemed to take one look at whatever bull fate had allotted him and to decide, 'This animal is not for me.'

'You mustn't judge him until you've seen him good,' Fulton insisted, paying him the cherished accolade that comes when one matador praises another. 'It's not a question of the bull's being good or bad—he must be right for Curro.' Now, one of the attributes of Domingo Ortega that I remember best was that he could take whatever came out of the chute and give it a majestic fight. If luck gave him a bad bull, he made it good; if his lot was a good bull, he made it great; and on those rare occasions when he received a naturally great bull, he handled it with such noble precision that its head was subsequently mounted. Ortega gave new meaning to the word pundonor.

Curro Romero must have had his own analysis of this word. At Jerez he was abominable because he would not try to accomplish anything with

Last known portrait of Juan Belmonte (not Somerset Maugham), the man who revolutionized bullfighting, taken shortly before he shot himself.

average bulls, although his competitors did passably well with theirs. 'You've got to catch him on the right day,' Vavra explained, while Vanderford growled in his beard, 'With Curro you must not use the words pundonor or sinvergüenza. They do not apply. He is honestly terrified of a dangerous bull . . . or of a good one. Lack of courage? Yes. Lack of honor? Never.'

I remember the agonies Orson Welles went through at one San Isidro, for since Curro's first appearance in the ring, Welles has always held that he is the one bright light in the taurine world and he had been warning us not to miss his boy's performance. First day, horrible. Second day, nothing. Third day, deplorable. 'Wait till he gets a good day,' Welles advised.

In Barcelona the bull came out the chute wrong, and Curro quit. At Valencia there was wind, and he attempted nothing. Back in Madrid he screwed up his courage and like Ortega tried to make a good bull great, but in the end he ran in palpitating fright past the bull, jabbed his sword out sideways and punctured a lung. The audience wanted to annihilate him on the spot, and would have done so had pillows been concrete blocks, for they showered him with the former while officers of the Guardia Civil kept them away from the latter. 'This wasn't his day,' Welles said sadly 'But just wait.'

I had now waited through more than twenty fights. I'd seen Curro face forty-odd bulls and never had the magic moment come. Never had the magic moment even been in the same province. I had seen him bad, and I had seen him worse, and I had seen him disastrous. And I no longer hoped. Each of my bullfighting friends had seen him in apotheosis, and apparently he could be something wonderful, running the bull slowly and majestically in passes of impossible beauty. My testifiers were not liars, nor were they combined in a conspiracy to create a White Legend. The agitated poet to my left at Pamplona had not compared notes with Orson Welles or Kenneth Tynan. That was his judgment, founded on fact, but it was a fact I was apparently destined not to see. To me Curro Romero would remain a legend, a reward which good fairies brought to good little boys. Alas, I was bad.

There was, however, in these same years a tall, ungainly, angular and thin young man from the village of Vitigudino near Salamanca who entered the arenas with little fanfare. I was in Madrid on May 13, 1961, when he underwent the ceremonies which confirmed him as a full matador; he took his sword from the hands of Gregorio Sánchez while standing a few feet from me, then strode with austere dignity toward the bull to give battle in the time-honored way. He was El Viti, and in Madrid he was a sensation. In Sevilla he was extraordinary. In Málaga and Jerez and Barcelona he was cold and precise and clothed in honor. Wherever I went I saw this reserved young man with the grave sculptured face and the long thin body fight in a manner I had thought forgotten. He engaged in no heroics and there was nothing of lyric poetry in what he did, but there was a distant echo of the epic. He never allowed himself to be hurried and I doubt if he could perform an arabesque with a cape if he wanted to, and I'm sure he never wanted to. Because he never once smiled in the ring, his detractors called him cold and frigid and rooted. Vavra and Fulton spent hours explaining to me why he failed to excite the crowd. In Pamplona it was my mention of his name that had started the argument with my poetical neighbor. 'Viti's nothing!' he exploded. 'An iceberg!'

Yet day after day this quiet young man with ice-cold manner, this youth who never smiled, who never displayed even the slightest emotion, not even when gored a few feet from where I sat, turned in a beautiful performance and won awards that others missed. He became for me the epitome of what I looked for in the ring, and almost never did he disappoint. I'll correct that judgment: never did he disappoint, for even when the bulls were bad he tried. Like Domingo Ortega before him, he brought new distinction to the word pundonor, for he was composed of this manly virtue.

The finest single component of any fight that I have so far seen was the work with the muleta that El Viti performed one day in Madrid. Luck had given him an evil bull, a little worse than those the other matadors had walked away from in disgust, slaughtering them shamelessly. El Viti took his fractious bull and with masterful low chops began to give it both direction and confidence. Never did the animal have to charge more than a few feet and always its horn was so placed that with a bad toss left or right it could impale El Viti. Slowly, with infinite precision, the fight continued, and bit by bit the matador made of this bull a noble animal that charged with fury and followed the cloth as it should. The process continued long, until El Viti was making all the passes that a matador should make with the cloth, and the ungovernable bull was kept as close to him as I was to the man sitting next to me. It was a culminating performance, so wonderful that people were screaming with admiration of the sheer mastery.

Finally El Viti took his stance before this once most dangerous of bulls and raised his sword for the kill. He waited. The bull would not charge. He waited. He waited some more, what seemed to be an infinity of time. At last the bull charged, the most dangerous moment of the fight, for the man must move forward, go in over the horn and somehow make his escape as the sword plunges home. But this time El Viti did not move. He kept his rigid posture and allowed the bull to bear down upon him; as the animal threw his great weight forward, the man stood fast, lured the bull off to the right with the muleta and directed the tip of the sword toward the lethal spot, where it was driven home by the weight of the charging animal. El Viti had killed recibiendo, that is, receiving the bull while keeping his feet motionless, and you can attend a hundred fights without seeing this done properly, or done at all, or even attempted. But to have done it successfully on such a bull was miraculous.

During this epoch there was a very brave young man who was to give his name to the period, El Cordobés, an illiterate street gamin from a town near Córdoba who electrified the bullfighting world by the animal vitality he exhibited in the plazas. Part vaudevillian, part satyr, part inspired improvisator, he sold enormous numbers of tickets and charmed huge numbers of people but not me. In the remotest towns of Mexico, where impresarios had experienced trouble half filling their bullrings once a season, they could now hold three corridas in three days and cram the ring each day by merely announcing the name of El Cordobés. With a shock of unruly hair, a rock-and-roll manner and a mouthful of unusually handsome teeth, he revitalized bullfighting, but I am not sure that it was any longer an art. It was something else.

I would have to confess, however, that three times I saw him perform a feat that even now seems impossible. Eager to make a good impression in classical Sevilla, he came out to cite his bull from a distance four times as great as the ordinary matador would normally choose, and as the bull charged at him, eleven hundred pounds of furious power, El Cordobés whirled in a tight circle, his small protecting muleta furled tightly about him and he in direct line with the bull's charge. At the last moment he stopped his whirling, dug his feet in and unfurled his muleta, allowing the bull to thunder past a few inches from his chest. It was exciting, but it wasn't bullfighting; it was vaudeville, and after a few performances I lost my taste for it. But not even the young man's severest critic could deny him extraordinary courage and the ability to spread his charisma over an entire nation.

In any discussion of matadors the question arises: 'How good are the Mexicans?' This needs careful analysis. First, Mexican bulls are decidedly inferior to Spanish. They are smaller, more difficult and less likely to give good fight. Therefore, the Mexican faces obvious limitations. Second, whereas in Spain there are scores of bull ranches where a would-be matador can work with heifers, in Mexico there are few, so that the training of Mexicans is apt to be less thorough. Third, in raw bravery nothing can surpass a Mexican matador, and in this department they have no cause to defer to anyone. You will see exhibitions of pundonor in Mexico that you will see nowhere else. Fourth, the Mexican crowd is rowdy, largely uncritical and a joy to be with. Therefore, the Mexican matador can get away with nonsense that would not be permitted in either Madrid or Sevilla. Finally, a good Spanish matador may fight sixty or seventy fights a year; the finest Mexican is lucky if he performs forty times, so that the Spaniard obviously has more chance to perfect his art.

One curious distinction needs to be made. The art of placing banderillas, which can be a graceful and lyric performance if the man doing the job has skill, has declined so badly in Spain that not often does one see a pair placed properly; since 1960 I have seen only four or five pairs done with any style by a Spaniard, whereas in Mexico almost every matador is master of this art and one can see almost any afternoon pairs of banderillas sent home with a delicacy that elicits shouts of admiration from everyone. Spanish bullfighters could do as well, I'm sure, but the public no longer demands that they do so.

In this century there have been three Mexican matadors the equal of anything that Spain has produced. In the Age of Belmonte there was Rodolfo Gaona, a large man with a complete repertory and the personality to support it. At the transition period between Belmonte and Manolete there appeared a string-bean-thin Indian with a style so exquisite that he seemed to float across the sands. Fermín Espinosa is known in history as Armillita, but in accuracy he should be called Armillita Chico, since his older brother Juan, using the name Armillita, became a full matador in 1924 but surrendered the rank in 1933 in order to serve as peon for his more gifted brother. Armillita Chico was, if I understand correctly, the only major matador who fought a lifetime of complete seasons without once having been seriously gored, and he is reputed to have understood the psychology of bulls better than anyone else who ever got into the ring with them. And in the Age of Manolete there was Carlos Arruza, the golden boy of bullfighting who could do everything with diffident grace. He was the equal of Manolete, and the great confrontations between these two consti-tuted one of the highlights of the century; even in their deaths there was a kind of competition: in 1947 Manolete was killed by the Miura bull Islero; in 1966 Arruza was killed in a violent automobile accident.

Many Spaniards refuse to acknowledge these three Mexicans as top caliber. Gaona they denigrate, and the lovely floating pass which he perfected whereby the cape, held behind the body of the fighter, sways first to this side, then that, and which throughout the rest of the world is called a gaonera, is in Spain called de frente por detrás (facing the bull but with the cape behind the body). Armillita they dismiss in silence, for his cold Indian style repelled them and they could not believe he was as good as he was. And Arrruza, whom they cannot deny as one of the great, they embrace by insisting that he was a Spaniard, which his parents indubita-bly were before they emigrated to Mexico. Arruza considered himself a Mexican.

However, when one drops below the category of Gaona–Armillita–Arruza one finds few Mexicans who equal the middle echelon of Spaniards, and the record books are replete with names of Mexicans who stood at the top of their profession at home but were disasters when they faced the bigger bulls of Spain. Of course, there have also been a few matadors of good reputation in Spain who were found inadequate in Mexico, but not many. Furthermore, in the past twenty years there have been no Mexicans of major reputation, and in this period it would be impossible to claim that Mexican matadors were as good as those in Spain.

Four Americans have become full-fledged matadors. The first, Harper Lee, was born in Isletta, Texas, in 1884, and after drifting about the plazas along the Mexican border, finally took his alternativa in Monterrey in 1910. Lee never fought in Spain but he gave commendable performances throughout Mexico and seems to have been a thoroughly engaging human being. His life has been favorably summarized in *Knight in the Sun,* by Marshall Hail, published in 1962.

Sidney Franklin, a Jewish boy from Brooklyn named Sidney Frumpkin, took his alternativa in Nuevo Laredo, Mexico, in 1932, from the hands of Marcial Lalanda, and confirmed it much later in Madrid in 1945 at the hands of El Estudiante. He fought well both in Mexico and Spain and won commendation from Hemingway. His autobiography, *Bullfighter from Brooklyn,* is a hilarious affair, no single statement of which should be taken too seriously. I once had the pleasure of knowing Franklin and dining with him over an extended period, and never have I met a man whose conversation was more engaging. A group of us used to frequent his company simply to hear what he was going to come up with next, and one of the pleasures of my home in eastern Pennsylvania is that every Saturday night at eleven Sidney Franklin is available on television, broadcasting the fights from Mexico City. His chatter on the air is almost as diverting as it was in person.

In 1966 Robert Ryan, of Los Angeles, took his alternativa in Mexico and performed well in the Tijuana plazas.

John Fulton, the boy from Philadelphia, is the only American ever to have earned his alternativa in Spain. He took it in Sevilla in 1964. His doing so is an epic of determination and I hope that one day he will write his account of how it was done. Since he is also a gifted artist, his black-and-white drawings of what he was talking about would enhance the narrative.

His is a tale of a young man with an idée fixe plus the grim resolve needed to carry it out in one of the cruelest ambientes on earth. For three years Fulton in Sevilla rarely sat down to a meal, eating at most twice a day from a stand-up bar where the bill was a few pesetas less if one did not take up space at a table. Once when money from home enabled him to sit and eat a regular meal, the waiter rushed up and asked, 'Fulton, are you sick?'

Like his idol, Rafael Gómez, called El Gallo, Fulton has a running sequence of sardonic observations on the difficulty of becoming a matador. 'It's as easy for an American to be a bullfighter in Spain as it would be for Cassius Clay to be mayor of Birmingham!' When asked by a lady if he feared the bulls: 'Not half as much as I do the men who manage the bullrings.' On being complimented for speaking idiomatic Spanish: 'I had to learn Spanish. The bulls won't speak English.' Of a famous Sevillian who sponges off matadors: 'That man is well known . . . at lunch.' Of the determination of a young aspirant: 'If he gets one foot in the door, he'll keep it there till gangrene sets in.'

I know of no ambiente more totally corrupt than that of bullfighting.

It is said, and properly so, that in this miserable racket the only honorable figure is the bull, and him they mutilate by shaving down the tips of his horns so that he has difficulty in locating his target. They try to drop sedatives in his drinking water to make him drowsy and sacks of cement on his back to make him weary. On one occasion when the draw for the bulls required a matador to face a particularly tough beast, his brother tried to shoot it in the corral with a rifle.

I suppose one could argue that the management of American boxing is as corrupt as bullfighting, but I doubt it. There must be one or two people in the boxing hierarchy who are comparatively honest; but in the management of bullfighting I have not met any. Symptomatic of the general corruption is the case of the typical newspaperman who reports on bullfighting in the daily press or in the many colorful magazines devoted to the art. With several honorable exceptions he receives no salary from his employer; indeed, he is often required to pay the employer for the privilege of writing in the journal. He must therefore steal his income from the matador, whose future bookings depend on what is said about him in the big-city papers. Suppose a matador has a disastrous afternoon in Sevilla. Everyone in that city who was at the ring will know about it, but there's nothing to be gained by having people in Barcelona and Madrid know about it too, so for six thousand pesetas to each of five strategically placed newspapermen (or one hundred dollars in all), the matador can see to it that in all other cities in Spain the bullfight fan will read on Monday morning that 'Juan Diego had a sensational triumph in Sevilla, with the fans clamoring wildly and carrying him from the ring on their shoulders.' The really bizarre thing about it is that even in Sevilla, the same stories will appear if the matador pays enough, so that a bewildered American or French fan who went to the fight and who can read Spanish begins to wonder if he can trust his own eyes. His eyes are all right. It's the newspaperman that he can't trust.

I once had dramatic proof of this venality. I happened to be in Jerez de la Frontera on Monday, May 10, 1965, for a novice fight in which the youthful sensation of that year was appearing, Sebastián Palomo, called Linares. He came into the ring—an extraordinarily handsome boy of fifteen, very small, very slim and very brave. The afternoon was a complete disaster; the ring was showered with the cushions of disgust, and if the fans could have got hold of Linares they might have lynched him, but the police saw that this did not happen.

I drove the next day to Badajoz, where the newspaper in its edition of May 12 carried a report that I clipped: 'In the brilliant fight held yesterday at Jerez, Sebastián Palomo Linares, fighting large bulls, heard loud applause on the first and an ovation on his second.' This was so blatant that I asked one of the men connected with bullfighting in Badajoz about it, and he said, 'Look, we have a contract with Linares to fight in Mérida. The boy is sensational news. We have to pay him a lot and therefore we have to sell a lot of seats. What does it matter what actually happened in Jerez? Everybody in Badajoz wants to believe that when Linares appears in Mérida they're going to see the new Belmonte.' And he showed me a poster which proclaimed the forthcoming appearance of Linares: 'Destiny Sent Him as Special Envoy to Save the Fiesta Brava. Fresh from his sensational triumph in Jerez.' Looking at the poster, with its gallant young man facing a bull of tremendous size, I began to wonder what I had seen in Jerez, and I realized that the man was right. It didn't really matter.

I was to see Linares twice as a beginner and twice as a full matador, to which he was promoted long before he was ready, and each time he was miserable. In fact, cushions were thrown at him, but I could see that the boy had the figure to be a matador, the courage to face bulls and a charisma that simply radiated. The last was enhanced by the release of a well-calculated motion picture called *First Time in This Plaza,* in which he was both a winsome little boy whom women could love and a brave man whom men could envy. Wherever he was due to fight, his manager scheduled this film in the movie houses, and when I last saw Linares he was besieged by screaming girls wherever he went. Vavra thought he might become the new El Cordobés.

This business of making a motion picture to enhance one's reputation, or even to create it, is amusing, because the plots are so invariable. A poor boy who wants to become a bullfighter has a serenely faithful manager who believes in him and two girls who are competing for him, one blond and good, the other brunette and bad. There is always the testing of heifers at the country ranch, where we see the good girl, and the flamenco party at which the bad girl makes advances. There has got to be one bullfight in which he is, as they phrase it, 'a clamorous success,' and one in which he is not, the latter being used to show his courage under adversity. In recent films a new ingredient has been added after its successful introduction in one of the El Cordobés films: the hero, frightened by his bad afternoon, sleeps fitfully, during which it is obligatory for him to dream in color of his own wounding in the plaza of destiny. Next we see the fatal ring, with him in civilian clothes kicking at the sand and stopping in long-drawn horror when he sees, always unexpectedly although he's been in this ring ten times before, the door marked Enfermería. We now switch to the good girl, who is kneeling before an altar graced by one long, tapering candle. As she prays the candle gutters and goes out, and from the wall behind her a picture of the matador falls mysteriously to the floor. When she picks it up the glass is cracked, at which moment we cut back to the ring, where one hell of a big bull is bearing down on our boy and giving him the works. An operation is required, with dozens of doctors in white and the anguished manager biting his lip, after which the wheels of a Mercedes-Benz squeal and the good girl rushes to the bedside of the dying matador. While she is weeping there an ordinary taxi pulls up and the bad girl dismounts, but she is prevented from entering the infirmary by a kindly priest who explains that now the matador is with the girl who truly loves him. But as the priest leaves, we see the face of the bad girl, and it is bathed in tears and she bites the corner of a handkerchief and slowly climbs back into the taxi, which takes her off into the shadows, leaving the impression that she too, at heart, is a good girl.

Many of the matadors have made films, always to critical acclaim and to the satisfaction of their fans. One of the best was Luis Procuna's Mexican film *Bullfighter*. The most successful was El Cordobés' *Learning to Die;* the most artistic was an Italian film starring the matador Miguelín, *The Moment of Truth;* but the one with the right blend of ambiente and pathos was the one I mentioned earlier, *Afternoon of Bulls,* featuring Domingo Ortega and Antonio Bienvenida. This one I would like to see again. The worst I ever saw was an epic turkey made by handsome Jaime Ostos, and it, too, is worth seeing if only because it is so bad that it evokes memories of the grubby world which it portrayed.

I suppose many readers have been either irritated or perplexed by my insistence that bullfighting is an art and not a sport, but in this I am correct. It is so reported in the Spanish press and is so considered by anyone really concerned in the matter. I was reminded of this one day on an airplane, when I had been absent from the bullring for some years and had forgot the wonderful sleazy world that envelops it. I picked up one of Spain's best newspapers and found it engaged in a public brawl which had been started by an article that spoke disrespectfully of El Cordobés. Within a few weeks the paper received 17,000 letters, of which 15,107 supported the matador, 1624 the journal, while the remainder 'were so confused that we couldn't decide where to place them.'

There was no confusion on the part of the people who defended El Cordobés. In various letters he was compared favorably with Velázquez, Goya, Zuloaga, Picasso and Dali, which should give some indication of whether Spaniards think of their matadors as artists or sportsmen. Many writers referred to 'the crazy month, in which El Cordobés fought thirty-one times, a feat never equaled before.' To accomplish this he had to fight one day in the morning in one town and in the afternoon in another a hundred miles away. One enthusiast let himself go: 'To compare the average bureaucratic bullfighter with the great El Cordobés is to compare one of those elegant white-glove comedies we see on the stage with a great drama like *Oedipus Rex, Medea, Othello,* or *Death of a Salesman.*'

My favorite letter, however, summed it up concisely: 'I have for a long time considered El Cordobés the Johann Sebastian Bach of bullfighters, but after his recent performances I suspect we shall soon have to refer to Johann Sebastian Bach as the El Cordobés of musicians.' I have not quoted the letters which indulged in hyperbole or in which the writer allowed his emotions to get the better of him.

I once had a full day in which to contemplate the sordidness of the bullring, for at eight one morning I reported at the box office in Sevilla to purchase a set of tickets for the feria. I was fourth in line. When the window opened I was fourteenth, men connected with the racket having edged in ahead of me with the connivance of the police. At one o'clock, when the window had been open for five hours, I was twelfth in line, because all morning drifters had sidled up to the window with bribes to the ticket sellers. At one the police announced that the windows would now be closed, but at four we could resume our positions, which would be noted and honored. At four the best I could do was sixteenth.

I was determined to stick it out; in fact, I was enjoying this first-hand experience of what the devotee of the art goes through, and my long vigil was lightened by the fact that a most engaging American wound up behind me in the line, Charles Moore, an ice-cream salesman from El Paso, Texas. 'We'll see if they have the nerve to keep us standing here all day without selling us a ticket,' I suggested.

'Okay by me,' Moore said, and we watched the comedy.

The closest we ever got to the window was eighth. Where the connivers and drifters and the slinky individuals in long coats came from I'll never know, but sometimes an hour would pass without our moving up one slot. A policeman finally came up and said, 'They prefer it if foreigners buy their tickets on the black market. You're expected to.'

'We'll wait.' He shrugged his shoulders and escorted two more characters to the head of the line.

At eight o'clock that night, when they closed the windows, I was fourth in line and Moore was fifth. The men inside, who had seen us all day long, were quite prepared to have the day end this way, but the policeman told them, 'You'd better do something about the norteamericanos. I saw the one with glasses taking notes and he may be a writer.' So at five after eight Moore and I were allowed to buy our tickets. The man at the window couldn't have been more gracious.

John Fulton has a more harrowing story to tell. For an American without friends to arrive in Sevilla determined to become a matador, and for him to buck the prejudices of Spain, where honest men are convinced that no one but a born Spaniard, or at the very least one of Spanish ancestry, can ever truly understand the ambiente, required a courage that few young men could muster. It is interesting to observe that the Spaniards are nearly as reluctant to accept Portuguese as they are Americans, even though I have seen Portuguese like José Julio give fine performances against the big Miuras in Sevilla. Spaniards are convinced that Portuguese and Mexicans and Venezuelans and North Americans never quite catch the hang of this peculiar art.

They were much relieved, therefore, when John Fulton ran into trouble in his presentation in Madrid. In all ways possible they stacked the cards against him, then sat back amused when he failed. 'A fine boy, an intelligent one, too, but not a bullfighter,' they said. 'How could he be? He's a norteamericano.' But when he had a splendid afternoon in Sevilla and was carried from the ring on the shoulders of Spaniards, they said, 'Interesting, but not true bullfighting. How could it be? He's a norteamericano.'

I've seen motion pictures of some of Fulton's good afternoons in Mexico, and they were indeed good. His tall and very graceful body moves well against the dark mass of the bull and he has a repertoire of passes that is wholly professional. If he is no Belmonte or Manolete, few are; he is certainly as competent as the average Spanish matador and better than many, but he is a foreigner, and no Spaniard is eager to sponsor him.

Critics of this insular Spanish attitude point out: 'In American baseball we accept players from any part of the world, especially Spanish parts. Luis Aparicio gets off the plane from Venezuela at the Baltimore airport and ten minutes later he's a full-fledged member of the Orioles. Or Tony Oliva flies in from Cuba to Minneapolis, and next thing you know he's leading the American League in batting. When the Alou brothers arrive from the Dominican Republic it is an invasion. Felipe plays for Atlanta, Matty for Pittsburgh and Jesús for San Francisco. But let someone try to break into Spanish bullfighting and even if he arrived in Madrid on the wings of the Archangel Gabriel accompanied by the ghost of Juan Belmonte, he couldn't make it.' The analogy is not fair to Spaniards. What has been said of their insularity is true insofar as bullfighting is concerned, but it is not true in professional soccer, which is the true parallel to our baseball. When Real Madrid reigned as the best team in the world it employed international stars like Ferenc Puskas of Hungary, Alfredo Di Stefano of Argentina and Raymond Kopa of France. In fact, when I first looked at the roster of Real Madrid in 1961, I found it difficult to believe that it was a Spanish team.

Say the Spanish: 'In the international sport of football we want the best, and to get the best we have to buy in the world market. In the Spanish art of bullfighting we also want the best, and that can be found only in Spain. No one else can master the nuances of this art.'

One of the side attractions of bullfighting is the bizarre gang of fans addicted to the art. Everyone who has followed the bulls has known the epicene from Peru or Chile who drives his Hispano-Suiza back and forth across Spain, enamored of some young man whom he attends slavishly and without regard to the pathetic figure he is cutting before his friends. He doesn't care. He has bull fever interlaced with sex, and few diseases are more virulent.

One also gets to know the American widow of forty-six whose husband left her several hundred thousand dollars and a passport, and with these she travels from feria to feria, passionately in love with some matador who has not yet spoken to her, for he does not know that she exists. If I were to describe faithfully even one of these women, and I have known several dozen, American readers would be incensed and would claim that I was burlesquing the species. 'Such women couldn't exist!' my friends have protested on the few occasions when I have tried to describe them orally, but they do exist and some of them are dear friends whom I regard with affection. They happen to be nutty about bullfighting, and some of my other good friends are nutty about other things.

One hears much of integrity these days, and I have indicated that I prefer El Viti among the current crop of matadors because of his integrity. Once when the crowd had petitioned for, and the judge had awarded, an ear, El Viti turned it back, saying, 'Today I did not deserve an ear.' But no one connected with the art ever exhibited such integrity as an American woman I know who pined for one of the leading matadors. She followed him about Spain as if she were a puppy and he a wise old bulldog. At the arena she showered him with roses; at his hotel she would stand for hours waiting for him to make an appearance; she suffered humiliations by the score; and then one day when she had already paid for a ticket to a good fight in Madrid she heard belatedly that her idol was to fight that afternoon in Aranjuez, some thirty miles to the south.

She thereupon gave away her ticket to the fight in Madrid, paid a scalper's price for a ticket to the new fight, bought an armful of roses for her matador and hired a taxicab to take her to Aranjuez, where she found as she was about to enter the plaza that her beloved, to whom she had so far not spoken a word, had been injured the day before in another town and would not fight this day. His place was being taken by a matador of higher category, so that the fight was probably going to be better than the one scheduled, but to her this was inconsequential; if the object of her passion was not going to perform, the fight was not worth her attendance. She handed her ticket to a young man hanging about the entrance in hopes of just such a miracle, gave her roses to an old woman selling flowers and climbed into her taxi, announcing with a certain grandeur, 'Take me back to Madrid.'

The aficionado from whom I have learned most is Angus Macnab, who has been described as 'the Scotsman's Scotsman.' To hear him explain, in Scottish accents, the merits of a particular fight is to enjoy language and emotion at its best: 'Mind you, I'm not one to question the judgment of Ernest Hemingway, nor of matador John Fulton, but when I hear people assure me that in the great hand-to-hand at the Málaga feria in 1959 Antonio Ordóñez and Dominguín presented between them the fight of the century . . . some even claim the fight of the ages with six bulls killed by six single sword strokes, et cetera. Well, when sensible men tell me this with their smiles on straight and I'm expected to believe them, I keep my mouth shut and ask myself one question: "Has no one bothered to read what Alberto Vera, who wrote under the name of 'Areva,' said about this so-called magisterial fight?" Have you bothered to read it, Michener? No? Then I'll quote: "This afternoon we saw two famous matadors fight six bulls, and each animal had two distinctions. It was barely three years old and was therefore more truly a calf. And what horns it did have were mercilessly shaved." Michener, if you want to select one afternoon as an example of what bullfighting can be, at least choose one in which bulls were fought and not calves with their horns removed.' Even the most trivial of Macnab's opinions on matadors and bulls are expressed with similar force. 'Biggest bull I ever saw was at Pamplona one year. A Miura of nearly fifteen hundred pounds. Can you imagine how big that was? Killed two horses just by running into them. But the best man-and-bull together I've ever seen was Domingo Ortega and a runty bull of admirable courage to whom he had given a great fight. At the end he dropped on his knees before the fine animal, then turned his back to the horns and remained so with the bull's right horn in the middle of his spine. Still on his knees he crawled away to pick up a hat that an admirer had thrown in the ring and this he placed on the bull's shoulder. Then, standing back, he sighted with his sword, moved forward and pushed the sword right through the hat and into the proper spot. The bull took one step and dropped dead.'

The addict with whom it is most fun to attend a fight is Kenneth Vanderford, who has a sardonic wit and a dry skepticism concerning everything. At his apartment in Madrid, where all writers interested in the fiesta brava sooner or later converge to check facts, he has a modest library of taurine material, including complete files of most of the bullfight journals for the past eight years. Apart from the nonsense of looking like Hemingway, from which he derives much amusement, Vanderford is unusually erudite, with a Ph.D. in Spanish from the University of Chicago. When I last saw him he was engaged in a newspaper duel with a learned Spaniard who had written an essay lamenting the fact that the Spanish language does not permit words to begin with the letter s followed by a consonant, so that English words like scarp, spume and stupid became in Spanish escarpa, espuma and estúpido. This meant, the essayist had pointed out, that the two radically different English words, eschatology which means the philosophical analysis of ultimate goals, especially those religious, and scatology, which means preoccupation with or study of excrement, had each to be translated by the Spanish escatalogía. Vanderford, a remarkably irreligious man (he calls himself a humanist), humorously proposed that since no intelligent man really believed in the future life any more and since there was not much to be gained by continuing to talk about it, maybe it would be better to drop the first meaning and cling to the second, which is concerned with an inescapable fact of life that is always with us. He continued with the suggestion that on second thought neither meaning need be dropped, since further study of the conflict had revealed an intimate relationship between the two meanings of the word, psychologically if not etymologically. He pointed out that the famous ascetics of history, who have always been interested in eschatology, have also notoriously been interested in scatology, since the French Catholic writer Viscomte Maxime de Montmorand, in his *Psychologie des Mystiques Catholiques Orthodoxes,* holds that nearly all Christian ascetics have been scatophagous. Vanderford holds equally recondite and stubborn views on bullfight matters.

'You say it. Hemingway says it. Tynan says it and Macnab says it, so I suppose I can't fight you all. But to say that at the kill a matador "goes over the horn" is pure nonsense. Let him go in that way and he'll get a horn in the gut every time. What he does is to trick the bull into charging one way while he slides in on a curving trajectory the other way, thus avoiding the horn. Over the horn? Never.'

It is Vanderford's opinion that 'the best-informed and most dedicated foreign bullfight expert of either sex is Alice Hall.' This tall, slim gray-haired spinster was, until her recent retirement, a teacher of Spanish in a fancy private school in Atlanta, Georgia. She came originally to Spain for the laudable purpose of improving her pronunciation, little aware of what was in store. Like any dutiful tourist she went routinely to a bullfight, had the good fortune of seeing César Girón on one of his great days, and promptly surrendered. Year after year she returned during her vacations and applied to bullfighting the tenacious scholarship which had made her a fine teacher. A friend says, 'Alice feels intuitively what the bull and the man are going to do next . . . what they must do . . . and she is in the ring with them when they do it.' 'Each autumn when I go back to Atlanta and face my first class of girls,' she says quietly, 'I feel as if I have been sentenced to exile, that I am in a strange land surrounded by strangers. My heart was left behind in Andalucía.'

My favorite aficionado was a Frenchman. On the afternoon of the first fight at Pamplona, which is quite near to France and therefore attracts many Frenchmen, this doughty little bourgeois, with mustache, close-buttoned black suit and lunch in a briefcase, became so enraptured with the performance of Paco Camino that as the matador took a turn of the plaza he threw his bota of wine into the ring, and Camino drank from it. The crowd applauded. Later my Frenchman did the same for Diego Puerta, and again the crowd cheered.

It was not until the fourth day that I was close enough to see why the crowd kept cheering this modest Frenchman, but on this day, when he tossed his bota at the feet of Miguelín, his section of the plaza rose en masse and accorded him a round of applause usually reserved for generals or generalísimos. Why? Because when this prudent fellow tossed his bota into the ring he kept it attached to a long length of French fishing cord, so that when the matador finished taking his drink, the valuable leather bottle, worth about forty cents, could be reeled back to its owner.

The aficionado who best exemplifies the emotional hold that bullfighting can exert is a man I have not met. George Smith, a retired high school Spanish teacher from Los Angeles, saw his first fight in Mexico and subsequently came to Spain on vacation, developing an intense interest in the bulls. He began to acquire a bullfight library, and with the help of a former matador who in retirement became an expert on old books, has built up what many call the finest library of its kind in the United States. He intends leaving it to the Los Angeles public library. Sudden and protracted illness has prevented him from returning to Spain but he is so infatuated with the ambiente that each spring, during San Isidro, he sends his matador-bibliophile a substantial check in order to assemble in Salvador's taurine restaurant a group of aficionados to partake of the feast that he would like to give in person. In 1967 Nicanor Villalta, one of the finest and bravest of the old-time matadors, attended. Also present was the critic who wears the gold watch that once belonged to Manolete: 'The mother of Manolete to Antonio Bellón, loyal and unselfish friend of her son.' Vanderford was there and several others who appreciate the bulls, and as the meal drew to an end, Vicente Molina, the book dealer, proposed the toast, 'To a man who truly loves our crazy world.'

Some travelers in Spain, seeing the crowds of such tourists at bullfights, conclude that it is only the thrill-seeking foreigner who keeps the art alive, and it is true that along the Mediterranean coast the rings are populated mainly by travelers from northern countries who understand little of what they are seeing. I remember the last fight of the season in Barcelona, when more than two-thirds of the meager audience consisted of white-hatted sailors from the visiting American fleet. In Mallorca foreigners constitute a majority of the audience, and standards have degenerated so badly that a local impresario has rigged up his private plaza and keeps a tame bull therein for tourists to 'fight' at five dollars a throw. For two dollars they rent gaudy matador suits, and for an additional two dollars they can have their photographs taken facing the bull. When they get back into street clothes for another dollar they can purchase from the Plaza Mallorca a colorful poster showing their name printed between that of Manolete and El Cordobés.

'We call that animal El Toro de Oro, the Golden Bull,' Bartolomé Bestard, honorary American consul in Mallorca, told me. 'He's so smart that when he sees a camera he shows the one-day matadors where to stand. But don't laugh! That bull personally has paid for those three apartment houses over there. A fabulous animal.'

As my Spanish friend implied in the dialogue which opens this chapter, many intelligent and progressive Spaniards decry bullfighting as a blemish upon their country's reputation. In 1965 I saw a series of excellent fights on government television, but in 1966, following a disastrous corrida which revolted many people, the broadcasts were quietly eliminated. Word went out that the government had decided that public reveling in bull-fights must stop, at least over television. (In 1967 the programs were resumed.) More significant was what happened on Sunday afternoon, September 18, 1966, when Vanderford and I attended a corrida in Madrid, only to find that without previous warning members of the Guardia Civil had stationed themselves at all entrances and were turning away children under the age of fourteen. Later the government encouraged the rumor that this was henceforth to be the law in all cities. 'They've determined to stamp out bullfighting by driving young people out of the arena and onto the football field,' a matador told me. 'In the end they'll succeed.' (In 1967 this ban was still in force.)

The best-reasoned and most forceful condemnation of bullfighting to have been voiced in recent years is that published in 1962 by Eléna de La Souchère, a Barcelona woman of French descent who fled Spain after the Civil War:

> Beginning in the eighteenth century, the uprooted and somewhat indolent masses who pushed into Madrid and Sevilla conceived a passion for the arena. Bullfights, which until this time had been occasional single combats for the pleasure of the knights-combatant, now were transformed into periodic spectacles; the professionals of the arena reappeared. . . . These games were the response to a deep-rooted psychological need. The people had ceased to participate in public life and the psychologically passive plebeians refused henceforth to take any risk or assume any effort; nonetheless, they craved a chance to demonstrate their aggressive instinct. . . . In Madrid, as formerly in Rome and Byzantium, the people continued to fight and to triumph but through an interpreter—an appointed slayer-of-beasts—with whom they could identify. . . .
>
> The *corrida* in fact completes the destruction of the conditions which gave it birth. The games of the circus are costly, voracious. There is not enough bread—and the wheat fields lie fallow as far as the eye can see, giving graze to the *corrida* bulls. The farmer trudges behind his antique wooden plough: The bullock is a luxury, reserved for the minority of wealthy cultivators. Thousands of bulls are sacrificed each year to the arenas. The circus devours the unsown harvest, the bull unharnessed to plough the scanty soil, the glebe land, which is the raw material of bread and of man's labor.
>
> Each village should awaken from the torpor into which all have fallen. But the *corrida* is an obstacle in the path of necessity which orders man to work. This torpor is born of and nourished by the perpetuation of man's resignation. Every Sunday, the circus games sap his vital energy: the intensity of a prolonged and repeated emotion summons all his energies,

gathers them, strains them to paroxysm, breaks them by an abrupt relaxation, knots them together once again, breaks them once again, to the
rhythm of the bull's charge and retreat, charge and retreat. In this impassioned catharsis, the active energy of a people becomes so many nervous
sparks strewn on the sterile sand of the arena. Becoming accustomed from
an early age to the death-spectacle, the dolorous diversion, destroys the
sensitivity of the human being. Henceforth, he is predisposed to any abuse,
any cruelty. Familiarity with bloody spectacles goes a long way toward
explaining the sadistic abuses which have marked the revolutions and the
civil wars in nineteenth- and twentieth-century Spain. By tolerating the
arena games, by promoting them and allowing children to witness them,
the Church and the public authorities have shown to what extent they
submit to the *terratenientes,* landowners, who raise the bulls; and they
show once again how indifferent they are to their esential task: education
of the masses.

On the other side of the ledger, the idolatry of these circus games has
been condemned by all the great figures of late-nineteenth- and early-twen-
tieth-century liberal Spain, from Blasco Ibáñez to Pío Baroja and Ortega y
Gasset. In that era all of the progressive forces, particularly the liberals and
the anarcho-syndicalists, were alarmed by the psychological effects of the
corrida. Their alarm was all the more pronounced because the ravages of
the arena, physical ravages first of all, are felt most in the lowest classes:
each Sunday during the bullfight season is marred by several accidents. In
a special issue, September-October, 1962, devoted to bullfighting, the
Madrid magazine, *Indice,* published the complete list of Spanish *toreros*
killed in the arena since the end of the eighteenth century. Listed were the
names of some 278 victims between 1900 and 1962; in other words, considering the brevity of the bullfight season (from Easter to the autumn) one
death every six weeks.

But the *corrida* perverts even more than it kills. Its false prestige has
demoralized generations of young workers; in presenting a gilded mirage
and factitious universe it tempts their appetites for luxury, for vainglory,
and instills in them a disdain for useful work. Yet the majority of appren-
tice *toreros* have not even a chance to prove themselves in regular *corridas.*
While casting about for engagements they subsist on shady deals.

A varied fauna buzzes about the walls of the arena . . . these down-
and-outs perhaps were once the hopes of a season; ever suppliant, they
cling to the neighborhood of the plaza in low taverns filled with the stench
of refried oil. The adolescents who hang about the arena in search of work
will join them one day. And others, and still others . . . The arena wins.
It spreads out. It eats into the city, as an ulcer eats into healthy flesh; the
ulcer is devouring the city.

Señorita de La Souchère speaks for many, but her figures on deaths
from bullfighting apply primarily, of course, to a previous condition. One
man altered the trend of those figures, and outside the bullring in Madrid,

*The old, who used to dream of becoming bullfighters,
now hang about the young, who still have hopes.*

matadors have erected a statue to him: 'Dr. Alexander Fleming, discoverer of penicillin.' Four-fifths of bullfight deaths in times past came because horns infected with animal manure produced instant gangrene; most of these men would have lived had penicillin existed in their day. Today Fleming's miracle drug saves literally dozens of bullfighters, and he is properly their patron saint.

In her criticism, Señorita de La Souchère implies that the meat of the fighting bull is wasted; this has never been true. In the old days the carcasses were butchered at the bullring and passed along without charge to hospitals and poorhouses, but today the meat is carted to selected butchershops throughout each city and sold at a slight reduction. At the ring in Pamplona, I came to know Señora Aniceto Oloriz, a small, doughty woman with a marvelous smile and reddish hair who supervised the butchering of the dead bulls as promptly as they were hauled from the arena. About ten minutes after Paco Camino killed a bull, Señora Oloriz had it cut into quarters and early next morning was hawking it at her stall in the Pamplona market.

In recent years bullfighting has been increasing in popularity and probably more people are seeing it now than ever before. New arenas are replacing old in cities like Burgos, Avila, Badajoz and Córdoba, while completely new ones are being erected where none existed before. The number of corridas fought and attendance at them have grown. For every great Spaniard who has opposed the art, one could name two others who have supported it.

Much nonsense is perpetrated when foreigners compare bullfighting with football, especially when they see the huge stadia used by the latter or read that a hundred and ten thousand fans have attended a football game, as compared to a maximum of twenty-four thousand at a bullfight. Also, they see boys all over Spain kicking footballs in the street, and it is not illogical to conclude, 'In Spain football is the rage. It's all that kids play, so bullfighting must be dying.' The first two statements are true. Football has become Spain's lovely madness, as I have shown.

But this does not mean that bullfighting is dying, for the two seem not to be in competition. The truth is that football is a popular sport which commands an enormous following, and bullfighting is an artistic spectacle which retains its traditional adherents. An analogy might be the popular movies in Japan as compared to the classical art of kabuki. One does not eliminate the other, and no football player has attained in Spain the popularity enjoyed by El Cordobés. The status of bullfighting, as of 1966, is summarized in the accompanying table.

These figures require comment. They summarize the season of 1966 in Spain only and do not take into account corridas in Portugal, France, Mexico and South America. Contrary to what some say, the total number of corridas fought each year has been increasing rather than diminishing.

A Typical Year–1966

	Full matadors	Novice matadors
Total corridas	599	480
Number of bulls killed	3647	2836 [1]
Number of matadors eligible to fight	172	8162 [2]
Number of matadors fighting	116	247
Average corridas per matador	5.2	1.9
Median corridas per matador	7	3
Number of matadors fighting only:		
Three times all season	9	29
Two times all season	10	42
One time all season	17	77
Number of promotions to full matador		24
Top pay one matador one corrida	$25,000.	$1,600.
Bottom pay one matador one corrida	—$100.	—$50.
Corridas fought in:		
Madrid	51	43
Barcelona	51	16
Palma de Mallorca	31	1
Sevilla	18	14

TOP MATADORS

Full Matadors	Fights	Novice Matadors	Fights
Paco Camino	95	[4] Flores Blázquez	58
M. Cano 'El Pireo'	78	[4] Pedrín Benjumea	53
M. Benítez 'El Cordobés'	74	[4] J. L. Bernal 'Capillé'	50
Diego Puerta	71	Ricardo de Fabra	48
José Fuentes	70	[4] Paco Ceballos	45
S. Martín 'El Viti'	68	[3] F. Rivera 'Paquirri'	38
[3] J. M. Inchausti 'Tinín'	68	A. García 'Utrerita'	38
[3] S. Palomo 'Linares'	64	Fernando Tortosa	35
Jaime Ostos	53	[4] A. Sánchez Bejarano	35
[5] Fermín Murillo	51	[6] F. Rodríguez 'Almendro'	31

[1] Not counting 193 bulls and 85 novillo bulls killed in France and 4 Spanish bulls fought in Portugal but not killed, since that country forbids the fight to end with the death of the bull.

[2] Men carrying cards issued by the matadors' union.

[3] Novice matadors who were promoted to full matadors during the season; their figures are for the two categories combined.

[4] Novice matadors who were promoted to full matadors during the 1967 season.

[5] Retired from bullfighting at end of the 1966 season.

[6] For purposes of comparison, in 1966 Curro Romero fought 24 times.

*One of the four Córdoba memorials
to Manolete.*

To me, the startling figures are those for the total number of aspirant matadors and the minuscule few who make the grade. Most depressing is the number of established matadors who are able to fight only two or three times a year. These are the proud and gallant men with whom the citizen who follows bullfighting becomes so familiar. In his three fights a year such a full matador down on his luck may earn for himself a total of a thousand dollars, and on this he must support himself, keep his hair cut so that he looks prosperous, his shoes shined and his clothes sharp. And he must frequent the popular bars so as to be seen. Since his professional pay will not permit these things, he must scrounge from his family, his wife or his girl friend; if unusually lucky he will be able to attach himself to some well-heeled businessman who in his youth vaguely wanted to be a matador and who now finds pleasure in supporting a matador so as to feel himself

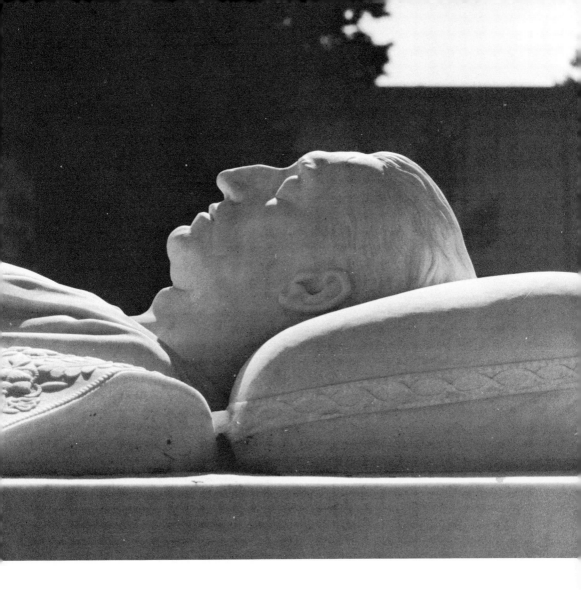

part of the ambiente. It is this situation that accounts for the minus figures at the line 'Bottom pay one matador one corrida,' for many times unscrupulous impresarios will allow a beginner (and not infrequently a full-fledged matador) to fight in a given city if the matador pays for the privilege. If a man has prospects of only one or two fights a year, and if he has a friend who will foot the bill, he will accept and will pay for the privilege of once more appearing in the suit of lights, once more leading the parade as the band plays. As for the number of times full matadors are bullied into fighting for seventeen dollars an afternoon or nothing, these are so common as not to warrant a special line in the statistics.

To understand the lure of bullfighting, one must go, I think, to Córdoba, where the city operates a taurine museum dedicated to the five so-called Caliphs of Córdoba: Lagartijo (1841–1900), Guerrita (1862–

1941), Machaquito (1880–1955), Manolete (1917–1947) and El Cordobés (1936–   ). The numerous rooms are evocative of these peasant boys who attained folk immortality, and as one moves among the ancient costumes and posters and sees the mementos of their dramatic lives he can catch a glimpse of what bullfighting meant to the underprivileged; but more can be gleaned, I believe, from walking the streets of Córdoba and seeing those grandiloquent monuments to Manolete, whose death at the horns of a Miura bull in Linares stunned the city. Fronting the church of Santa María in the peasant barrio there is a huge monument; a little farther along, at the square where his once-impoverished mother lived, there is a second huge monument which must have cost more money than she has spent in her life; beyond, there is a plaque in the wall indicating where the great man was actually born; and in the cemetery there is a monument surpassing them all, showing the matador recumbent. But more impressive to me than the museum and the monuments, which are, after all, dead recollections, is the Bar San Miguel, not far from where I lived in Córdoba and into which I stumbled by accident. It is run by a fine-looking man in his thirties, Manuel Barrera, and it consists of five rooms literally covered from floor to ceiling with mementos of El Cordobés: three different niches built into the walls display full-sized plaster statues of the matador; half a dozen carved heads stand about; and at least five hundred framed photographs hang in rigid order.

Before he became famous El Cordobés used to hang out in this bar, Barrera says proudly, 'and I was one of the first to recognize his ability. The world's first Club El Cordobés was launched right here . . . in my bar. My sister carved the first full-sized statue of him. That one. We make plaster casts of it and sell them to El Cordobés clubs throughout the world. He's the greatest man Córdoba ever produced. He's immortal.' In the bar hangs a framed slate with categories painted on in white enamel with space for the relevant figures to be added in chalk.

EL CORDOBES

THIS YEAR

CORRIDAS	82
EARS	138
TAILS	28

THIS WEEK

MALLORCA	1 ear

There are many such bars throughout Spain, each dedicated to a predilected bullfighter, and if the art is on the wane, the habitués of these

One of the statues carved by Barrera's sister.

Among the bronze figures who carry the casket of Joselito, beau ideal of matadors, walks a boy who bears an even graver burden: the gnawing worm of bullfighting.

bars, the members of the numerous clubs and the other fanatics do not know about it.

On the other hand, the perceptive traveler soon discovers that bull-fighting is an anachronistic spectacle; if the Republicans had won the Civil War in 1939 I suppose they would have outlawed it in deference to progress, and most progressive Spaniards would have approved. The victory of Generalísimo Franco provided the art with a reprieve, for bullfighting is essentially a reactionary operation dependent upon large areas of uncultivated land and a feudal system; now that a new generation of managers is about to take over responsibility from Franco, men alert to opinion in Berlin and London, it is quite possible that bullfighting will come under serious pressure. It will be interesting to see if its 1967 return to television will become permanent.

Why does one bother with a spectacle so archaic and so often disappointing? On July 13, 1966, when I got up extra early in Pamplona to be with the bulls on the last day of the running, I went to Marcelino's restaurant after the bulls had passed and had a breakfast of bacalao (steamed salted codfish) and then went on the unforgettable picnic at the Pass of Roncesvalles. In the patio de caballos I renewed acquaintance with Domingo Ortega and El Estudiante, and had my picture taken with Antonio Ordóñez, who had been miserable on his first appearance and who wanted to recoup this day. In the plaza I exchanged amiable greetings with the Curro Romero devotee on my left, who took the opportunity to remind me that, by all accounts, Curro had been sensational a few days before in Madrid. 'The kind of matador we dream about,' he said, repeating himself.

The fights this day were ordinary, with here and there a few details, and then the fifth bull, a big red one, came out. Looking back on it, I can scarcely believe that in the early morning this extraordinary bull had passed my doorway with only a few inches separating us, but I had been so excited that I failed to notice. 'A big red bull like that? You didn't even see him?' friends asked afterward. I said, 'He wasn't there,' nor had he been, so far as I was concerned.

But he was certainly there that afternoon. He pertained to Andrés Vázquez, a matador of only ordinary qualifications but who was to prove the truth of what I claimed earlier, that any professional, when he gets the dream bull, will at least have the basic techniques for giving it a great fight. Whether he does so or not is another matter, and much can go wrong in the process of leading a noble bull from the first cape work, to the horses, through the muleta work and on to the moment of death, so that many fine bulls are wasted.

On this day nothing went wrong. The bull entered the arena at a gallop and roared to the center of the ring, where he stopped, motionless, as if posing for a poster. He then charged toward the first cape that showed itself, and as soon as the crowd saw how true he moved, a loud shout rose from the stands, applauding the bull and expressing the hope that at last we were to see a good fight. Vázquez, recognizing the quality of the beast the luck of the draw had thrown him, ran into the ring and took charge, unfolding a series of slow and majestic passes in which the bull followed the cloth as if his nose were pasted to it. I had not seen such passes for some years, nor had the crowd, and the applause grew, with six or seven bands playing at the same time in a kind of super-bedlam. The horses now entered, and for once we saw a powerful bull charge the horses three times, take all that the picadors had to offer, then slide each time off the horse and into the cape of the waiting matador. Vázquez, El Pireo and Ordóñez in turn launched beautiful series of passes in which the bull followed the arabesques of the cape with arabesques of his own, more astonishing in that he used his long and powerful body to execute his passes. It was magnificent and the bands roared with delight.

Now came the highlight of this fight. Vázquez and his banderillero Mario Coelho came into the ring, dismissed the two peons who would normally protect them with capes and the other two matadors who stood by in case of danger, and ran in a series of exquisite ellipses before the bull's nose in such a way that whenever the bull was about to catch Vázquez on his horns, Coelho would mysteriously appear at the apex of his ellipse and lead the animal away to the point at which the red beast was about to catch him, whereupon Vázquez would suddenly appear and the bull's charge would be diverted. In the midst of this chinoiserie, Coelho stopped long enough to place the first pair of banderillas, and it was done so flawlessly that the crowd exploded with joy. Now the brass bands grew silent and allowed the primitive oboes of Pamplona to take over, and a rustic melody from centuries ago filled the arena, as fine music as I have ever heard at a bullfight. Suddenly the running figures converged with the arc being described by the bull's horns, and in some fantastic manner Vázquez placed the second pair, almost as perfectly as the first. The matador now left the ring, and no protecting capes appeared to guard Coelho. Very slim, very quiet, the banderillero took his position close to the red wall of the arena in a spot from which escape would be difficult if he misjudged the bull's charge. Keeping his feet rigidly planted, he cited the bull from a considerable distance, and as the animal started his charge, Coelho moved his body but not his feet to the left and when the bull lowered his head and charged at him there, he swiftly brought his shoulders over to the right and as the bull thundered past, planted two perfect banderillas in his shoulders.

Bands and oboes alike sounded their approval. The fight stopped while Vázquez and Coelho came repeatedly to the center of the ring to acknowledge the tumultuous noise. They were forced to take a turn of the ring, with the music rising to a higher pitch, and gifts were tossed to them in honor of banderillas such as had not been seen in Pamplona for years. On July 8, 1915, the great Mexican Gaona had placed a pair here in a manner which seemed impossible; a camera fortunately caught the moment of impact and even today men looking at that photograph will swear the bull must have caught the man. The event has become historic and is called 'The Pair of Pamplona.' Statues have been made of it and the photograph is remembered as one of the most famous in bullfight history; if there were a fine snapshot of Coelho's performance it might properly be called 'The Second Pair of Pamplona.' The set of three was one of the best

Alone in the blazing center of the ring, in terrain as alien as the craters of the moon, the fighting bull waits for the challenge.

offered in Spain in recent years. This seems to contradict what I said earlier about the mediocre quality of Spanish banderilleros, but it doesn't necessarily, because Mario Coelho is a Portuguese and his performance had the stamp of Portuguese excellence about it.

So far the fight had provided four above-average components, but the major tests were ahead, for a bullfight is judged not so much by early cape work or banderillas as by the faena and the kill. Bullfighters say, 'With the cape a matador wins applause; with the muleta, contracts; and with the sword, money.' Vázquez came forth for his faena, and the audience grew hushed as he started slowly to test the bull with the muleta. Finding the animal as good as ever, he began the first of what would ultimately be seven series of intricately linked passes, each series building in intensity on the one before. Before he was through, Vázquez displayed a good selection of the known muleta passes, executing them with a cool firmness that kept the crowd roaring its approval. He ended with a series of spinning passes, in which as the bull rushed past he whirled about in the direction contrary to its charge, drawing the red cloth away from the bull and wrapping it around his own body, unwinding quickly so as to be ready for the next charge of the animal. They were beautifully done, and the braying of the bands left no doubt that Vázquez had passed with honor the fifth test, but now came the kill, and many a matador had come to a culminating moment like this only to dissipate it with inept sword work. (In the twelfth fight of Madrid's 1967 San Isidro feria El Cordobés accomplished a feat rarely seen. With a splendid Antonio Pérez bull he performed such a dazzling faena that in spite of botching the kill and messing around until two warning signals had to be sounded, the public launched a blizzard of white handkerchiefs and screams, demanding that he be given two ears, and this was done. Previously I had not seen even one ear awarded under such circumstances.)

Silence fell over the plaza again, but the suspense was to be short-lived. Addressing the bull with meticulous care, Vázquez prepared everything as properly as he could, squared the animal so that his two front feet were together, and sighted the fatal spot along the extended sword. Rising on his toes, he started forward with full power, and if at that first moment the bull had raised his head unexpectedly the horn would have caught him full in the chest. On and on he came, his abdomen and groin wholly exposed to the horn, and at the last moment he pressed the point of the sword precisely into the target, and with his stomach almost on the bull's shoulder, drove the steel in up to the hilt, so that his fingers could have touched the bull's back.

Vázquez fell away, miraculously untouched. The bull staggered forward with this new burden of steel in his vitals and after a half-dozen bewildered steps fell in a heap. A great sigh rose from the crowd and for a moment there was unbelieving silence.

Then the arena practically fell apart. Brass bands and oboes, men and women screamed their approval. For once in my life I saw a plaza truly covered with white as practically everyone inside waved a handkerchief to the judge, beseeching him to award honors to Vázquez; normally some time passes after such a petition to allow the judge to study the propriety of the request, but on this day there was none. One ear, two ears, the tail,

almost as quickly as that. The grave alguacil in seventeenth-century costume stepped forward to detach the trophies, but before they were handed
to the matador the dead bull in grandeur was dragged about the arena and
the bands played for him.

When the bull departed through the gates, trailing glory in the dry
sands, Vázquez stepped forth to accept the trophies, but when they were
handed him he did an unusual thing: he forced Mario Coelho to share the
applause with him. He gave one of the ears to the Portuguese whose
phenomenal pair had been the emotional highlight of the fight, and the
two men made their parade together, two times around the ring, or was it
three, gathering roses and women's handbags and cigars and wallets and
God knows what.

After some fifteen hundred bulls, the vast majority of which were
disappointments, I had at last seen my one complete fight. Of the six
components, each had been performed properly, and I never expect to see
this again.

I must point out that in this fight no one of the six components was
the best of its type that I have seen; it was the conjunction of the six that
was so unprecedented. As to opening cape work, I had seen Marcial
Lalanda do better. Regarding the picador who fought the bull so cleanly
and so well, he did not compare with fat Felipe Mota, whom I had watched
in Mexico. The cape work by the three matadors after the pics did not
equal what Ordóñez and Dominguín are said to have done one afternoon
in their famous series of hand-to-hand confrontations. The banderillas, as
I have explained, were wonderful but not to be compared with the things
performed by Carlos Arruza at his greatest. The work with the muleta was
better than one sees in twenty typical fights but not so good as Domingo
Ortega used to offer. And the final kill did not equal the recibiendo of El
Viti. But if one records honestly what he has seen happen to one bull
alone, I doubt if he could find an instance in which a more complete fight
had been given.

I can compare it only to an opera I once saw in which Gigli, Rethberg
and Pinza sang, each at the very top of his career, each in flawless voice. A
great deal can happen to spoil an opera and does, but once or twice in a
lifetime one sees a *Carmen*, a *Lohengrin* or an *Aïda* in which all things
blend in due proportion: the horse performs without going to the toilet on
stage, the swan floats get past without getting stuck at the outskirts of
Antwerp, the tenor is as good as the soprano and the ballet dancers do not
bump into one another, and this kind of performance one never forgets.

FOLLOWING PAGE:
Gravedigger.

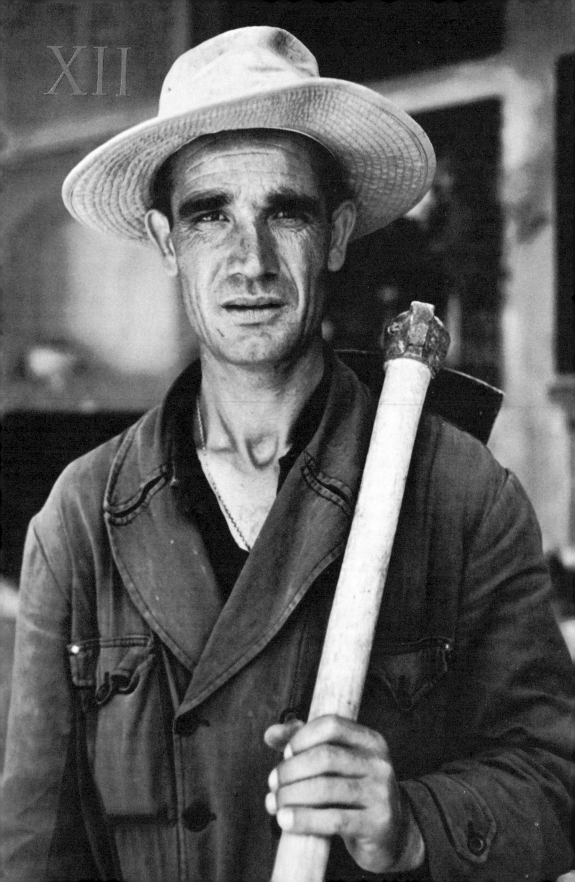

XII

TERUEL

OCEANO
ATLANTICO

MILES
0   100

Zaragoza
Barcelona

Albarracín • Teruel
Castielfabib

Madrid

Valencia

Lisboa

Sevilla

MAR MEDITERRANEO

I was lost, and I was unhappy about it. I had been heading for Teruel, of all the Spanish cities the one with the most personal meaning for me, and it was late afternoon when I saw ahead of me the dirt road ending in a high solitary peak on whose top perched a little town. It was a heroic sight, one which evoked memories of sieges and a handful of men defending themselves against infidels or Christians, as the fortunes of war had directed. Then, as I progressed down the road, I spotted on the far edge of the peak a remarkable church whose slab-sided, unbroken walls dropped from a great height precipitously into deep gullies, so that it gave the impression of occupying an entire peak. From where I first saw it, the building was totally unapproachable, and the closer I drew the more convinced I became that there was no way by which human beings could get into that church. On all sides it was impregnable, alike to the infidel who might seek to capture it and to the Christian who might want to pray in it.

I studied my map again and concluded that the village ahead could only be Castielfabib, a settlement I had not heard of. I had no intention of ascending that formidable hill, but since the road ended there I had no choice but to plow ahead, and finally I came to a point at which the road turned abruptly left, passed into a tunnel which carried it beneath the lofty town and broke out onto as fair a valley as I had seen in Spain. Hills rolled away in soft battalions and a bubbling river was coaxed into irrigation ditches. Fruit seemed to be growing everywhere and it was obvious that Castielfabib, in spite of its strange location and stranger name, commanded an area of some prosperity.

The road now swung back on itself and began a very steep climb, up and up until the church hung directly overhead, at which point I satisfied myself that my earlier conclusions were right; the preposterous building did occupy every inch of a peak and contained no visible entrance; yet it was so massive that it could obviously house the worshipers of a community many times the size of Castielfabib. Forgetting the church, I entered the village and found myself in a kind of fairyland that history had forgot. After a cursory exploration which showed far vistas in all directions, including a deep canyon that led the river through bright cliffs, I came upon an inn, if such it could be called, where on the very edge of the steepest cliff a small house perched, with one public room containing some thirty low rush-bottomed chairs placed in rows before the town's only television set. The room was miserably lit by one narrow window which cast a pale light on the gloomy interior. The man who grudgingly tended bar seemed embarrassed by my presence and said he did not have any of the first three drinks I suggested. I concluded that Castielfabib had a negative influence on its inhabitants, making them as aloof and lonely as it was.

Then the door banged open to admit a woman of enormous vitality. She was about five feet two inches tall, was not thick through the body but was strong in the shoulders, and owned a face of lively, amused dignity. Like many Spanish women in their late thirties, she was dressed in black, but her face was so animated that she made the dark clothes seem a party dress.

'Ah!' she cried warmly, 'you've come to the loveliest town in Spain. It's older than Valencia, twice as old as Madrid. Have you ever seen anything finer than our little plaza?' She led me to the door to study the Plaza del Caudillo, which my own eyes had dismissed only a few moments before. Now, looking at it with her, I saw a severe lopsided square delineated by a series of ancient buildings with classic façades. Several trees threw congenial shade and in the middle a fine, simply carved granite fountain produced four jets of constant-running water from which village wives, all dressed in black, were filling large clay jars which they carried sideways on their heads, the nozzles so tilted that the water did not run out.

'Beautiful town, eh?' she cried with real love. 'And look at our fortress of a church.'

'How does one get inside?' I asked.

'And up there the ruined walls of the old Moorish fort. Have you ever seen a town more exciting than this?'

She led me back to the bar and ordered me a bottled drink. 'You'll like it more than what you wanted,' she said. Kicking at the low chairs, she said, 'You ought to see this room when there's a good show on television. Forty people. We don't charge admission but we do sell drinks. Forty people can sit here laughing for two hours and not one ever gets thirsty.

'Husband!' she called. 'Run to Rodríguez and get his book of photographs.'

Village cart.

Her silent husband disappeared, and while he was gone a delightful girl of ten ran in, duplicating her mother's vitality and joy in living in this mountaintop village. The child insisted that I climb to the roof with her, for from there I would see the whole area, and the steep approach was worth the effort, for from the top of the building I could see a miniature presentation of Spain at its best. Hills closed in the valley on all sides, except to the north, where a distant village showed its red roofs. Lush fields of wheat and corn glistened in the sunlight, forming a golden checkerboard in which the darker squares were fields of apple trees and pear and apricot and cherry, with here and there large areas of low-growing grapevines. 'Show him the ruined convent!' her mother called from below, and the child pointed out the gray, weather-beaten relics of a building that must have been impressive in the late seventeenth century, standing as it did at the edge of the red-walled canyon. The little girl also traced out for me the footpaths used by the farmers, and I understood why those who lived in this remote village loved it.

'What do you suppose is under us, as we sit here?' the woman asked

when we had descended to the bar. 'A tunnel, right through the heart of
this mountain. And what do you suppose the tunnel was for?' I said I had
just driven through the tunnel, whereupon she shouted, 'Not that one. I
mean the old one. The big one!'

She launched into a history of Castielfabib. The name, she supposed,
was a corruption of Castillo de Habib and referred to an age when the
Moors had occupied the fortress at the peak of the mountain, more than a
thousand years ago. The area had been rich in silver and copper, and the
tunnel had been scooped out for a foundry in which coins and metal
objects had been minted for more than a millennium. In this tunnel the
bells of the church had been cast . . .

682

View from Castielfabib.

Her narrative was broken by the return of her husband, bringing Señor Rodríguez's photographs of the town, and with much civic pride she pointed out the features, and as she spoke I reflected on the peculiar fact that around the world generally, Spain is known as a man's country, but the women of Spain seem not to have been informed of this fact. In England the proudest sign that can appear on a shop is 'Henry Thompson and Son,' signifying that the male line of the Thompsons is strong and that Henry's son is prepared to carry on the traditions. The same is true of France, where 'et Fils' is a blazon of commercial nobility. In Spain, however, the proud sign is quite different: 'Viuda de Juan Gómez,' or more often the abbreviation 'Vda. de Juan Gómez.' This means that the widow of

Gómez is carrying on the business and assures her patrons that she will give the same distinguished service she gave while her husband was still alive, except that now she will be relieved of his bumbling interference.

'But how do you get into your church?' I asked again.

'You'll be surprised when you see.' We left the plaza and followed an extremely narrow footpath which appeared to end at the edge of the cliff; however, at the last moment it swung to the right, then ducked swiftly into a tunnel that ran completely beneath the church. At a midway point, as one stood under the huge structure, a door led upward from the tunnel, and it was by means of a very steep flight of stairs that one entered the church. It was indeed a church founded on a rock.

This unplanned excursion to Castielfabib, one of the more rewarding interruptions of my tour, meant that it would be nearly night when I reached Teruel, but this was not a loss, for as I wandered down from the hilltop and picked up the Río Turia, which would lead me in to Teruel, I came upon one of those memorable evenings in Spain when low-hanging clouds provide a darkened sky against which the sunset can reflect from below, so that one seems to move in a sea of color. How beautiful the little villages were as I drove through them. Take Villel, for example, with its enormous tower rising against red hills, streets lined with flower boxes, doorways glistening in blue-and-white tiles, cypresses lining a cemetery. Not many villages in Spain are prettier than those along the Turia. I also saw the imposing sign welcoming travelers to the province of Teruel:

BIENVENIDO	WELCOME
BIENVENU	BENVENUTO
WILLKOMMEN	

with the coat of arms that I remembered from my first visit, a ferocious-looking bull over whose head hovered a star.

It was now past eight-thirty but the sun still lingered on the horizon, throwing a blaze of light across the eastern sky; over the earth itself a dull red glow lay like a fog, while at my feet ran the dark Turia, the combination of colors forming a most dramatic entrance to a city. My breath came more quickly when I realized that at some unpredictable moment I would turn a bend in the road and see once more that city which had been so often in my mind and so deeply in my heart. I was actually nervous at the prospect, but then the river turned abruptly and I saw before me, on a hill in the distance, the outlines of Teruel, and I remember thinking, Those buildings to the left and those big apartments to the right. They weren't here when I knew the place. And the more I saw the more I realized that Teruel was not going to be the way it had been thirty-four years ago; the changes were to be of a magnitude that I would sometimes be unable to comprehend.

Teruel today from a bunker of yesterday.

But then, as if to make my return to this mystical city simpler, on my left I came upon a cluster of five once-handsome buildings, now torn and roofless, their yellow bricks crumbling in the night air. They looked as if they must have been there when I was first in Teruel, but some tremendous force had ripped them apart, say an artillery bombardment during the Civil War. What had they been, these handsome structures? And why so many in one group? A convent? A monastery caught in the cross fire of armies? I stopped three passers-by, old men walking home from their work, but they did not know.

685

In considerable excitement I entered the city, and my first superficial impressions allayed my fears on the road, for Teruel looked pretty much as I had remembered it. The railroad climbing the mountains from Valencia still deposited passengers at the foot of that splendid flight of stairs. The Moorish towers, the finest still standing in Europe, were as handsome as ever in their coats of tile. The public square was still small and poorly designed and congested. And from his Roman tower the bull of Teruel still looked down upon the community of which he was the symbol. As I paid my acknowledgments to the bull, I thought of the strange manner in which this city had been born, because Teruel is one of the few settlements on earth whose moment of birth can be specified.

Teruel is a young city, not much older than Madrid, and it is small. Its birth had been auspicious but there things ended, for it was now the least of Spain's fifty provincial capitals, with less than nineteen thousand population. In October, 1171, when El Cid had been dead for three-quarters of a century, King Alfonso II was endeavoring to establish a defensible frontier between Christian Zaragoza and Moorish Valencia; one evening his troops decided to give battle next morning at a favorable spot marked by a hill; but the Moors offset his advantage by collecting that night a herd of wild bulls and fastening to their horns bundles of firewood which were set ablaze. The maddened bulls stampeded toward the Christian lines, with the Moors following behind. In previous battles this tactic had worked, for in the confusion caused by the fiery animals the mounted Moors had overwhelmed the Christians.

But this time Alfonso's men stood fast, and with catapults which lobbed boulders at the onrushing bulls, with long half-moon lances that severed their hamstrings, with pikemen who formed solid walls of spear points, the onslaught was repulsed. Infidel power was broken in the area and it would now be possible to establish a permanent border between the two forces. It was a crucial victory.

While celebrating, the victorious Christians saw a sight which became the symbol of their triumph: one bull, the only survivor of the stampede, remained on the crest of the hill, shaking his head at the heavens in such a way that the brand still burning miraculously between his horns shone as if it was a star. 'He has been converted to our side!' the Christians shouted, and the hill which the bull had chosen for his last stand became the site of Teruel.

The next thing I did proved symbolic. I got a haircut at the barbershop of Maximiano Gómez, Calle del Mariano, 12, which was an event of no importance except that as soon as Maximiano heard that I was interested in Teruel, he stopped cutting my hair, ran to a friend's house and brought back a pamphlet on the city, which he insisted that I take and for which he would accept no money. 'I want you to have the best visit possible in my city,' he said. 'It's small and during the war it was much abused. But

The bull of Teruel.

now it's fine again.' This meeting with Maximiano set the standard for all that was to happen to me in my chosen city.

On my earlier visit I had stayed at a small hotel; this time a new parador was available, and in its dining room I was introduced to a specialty which I commend. The menu said simply 'Entremeses variados,' which from my attendance at theater I could translate only as 'Theatrical entr'actes varied.'

'What might they be?' I asked the waitress, and she smiled condescendingly as if I were a relative come in from the country.

'You don't know what entremeses are?' she said loudly enough for all in the room to hear, and without waiting to determine whether or not I wanted them she hurried into the kitchen and appeared sometime later with an enormous tray, from which she placed on my table, for me alone, twenty-one small saucers, each with a respectable portion of hot or cold food. It was a feast both to the palate and the eye. There were four kinds of fish, three meats including little balls of mutton highly spiced, eggs in aspic, four or five vegetables including the finest fried eggplant, olives, pickles, pimientos, potato salad, potato chips and hot toasted almonds. And it must be remembered that entremeses were merely the first dish of a four-course meal.

Next day my bland good luck continued, for I met Señor Don Francisco Cortel Zuriaga, a native of Teruel and for the past fourteen years its director of publicity. He was a lively man of middle years and height, with a dark mustache and grayish brown hair; his stocky, rugged appearance made me think his ancestors must have come from the mountains of Spain. He could not be considered a literary man, but he possessed an unusual sense of what a writer might like to see, and he would not rest until it had been seen.

'You know the Lovers of Teruel, of course?'

'No, I haven't heard about them.'

His jaw dropped. 'You were in Teruel thirty years ago and you didn't meet the Lovers?'

'That's right.'

This information was so disgusting to Don Francisco, so incredible, to judge from his reaction, that he sent out for a guidebook and sat twirling his thumbs while I read the section on the Lovers. As soon as I had done so, he whisked me out of his office and across the square to a narrow alleyway that led up a small hill. 'No man can know anything about Teruel unless he understands the Lovers.' He took me to a tiny chapel attached to a church and there, as we stood surrounded by the tapestries that enclosed the place, he showed me a pair of marble tombs, one topped by the jacent statue of a handsome young man, the other by a girl of most exquisite beauty.

As I contemplated the tombs, Don Francisco was on his knees with his eyes at floor level. 'See for yourself. Not legends, these two. Real people.'

He invited me to kneel with him, and when I had done so I found that the lower portions of the tombs consisted of slabs of marble carved in an ornate geometrical design; it had many holes through which I could see into the caskets, lit by electricity and containing the mummies of the Lovers, dead for more than seven centuries.

As I knelt there, a bus drew up and thirty or forty tourists from a distant part of Spain filed into the little chapel to pay homage to the only two people who have ever brought fame to Teruel, and I should like to

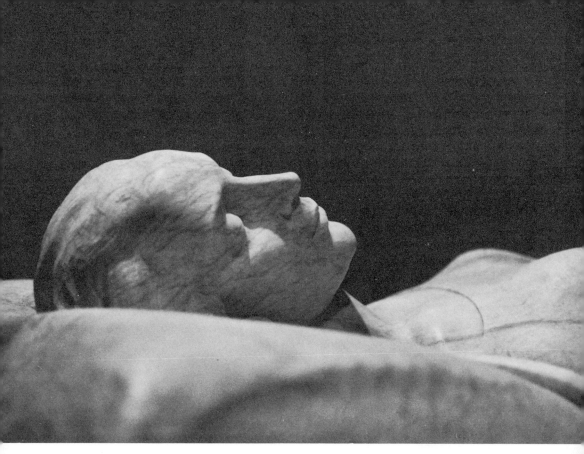

Isabel Seguras.

report the history pretty much as the singsong guide recited it to the visiting group.

'The year was 1217, Don Domingo Celada being judge of Teruel. In his city were two noble and influential families, Segura and Marcilla. Daughter of the first was the beautiful Isabel, whom you see here. Son of the second was the brave Diego over there. From the days when they played together as children they loved each other, but Diego's family had fallen on hard times and was poor, wherefore Isabel's father, the richest man in town, forbade their union.

'However, Diego sought and obtained an agreement whereby he would leave Teruel and for five years try to build his fortune in the world, at the end of which time, if he had succeeded, he would return and wed Isabel. With the fire of youth he left the city, and since no one heard from him for the next five years, at the expiration of the term the head of the Segura family forced his daughter to marry the very rich Don Pedro de Azagra of nearby Albarracín, the hill town which we visited this morning.

'The wedding was convened. The couple were married, but as the bells ceased ringing, there was a clatter at the Zaragoza gate and watchmen ran to advise the townspeople that Diego Marcilla had returned from his five years' exile with great riches, ready to marry his beloved. Diego had not counted in his five years' grace that first day on which he had fled Teruel. Isabel's family had.

'The young man ran to Isabel and pleaded with her to marry him, but she pointed out that this was impossible as she already had a husband. Diego then begged her to give him one kiss which he could bear with him as he wandered through the world. This, too, Isabel refused, whereupon, as a book in our archives reports, "Diego was not able to bear the anguish and tension of his enforced departure, and with a sigh died from pain at the feet of her."

'Next day, at this church of San Pedro his funeral services were held, to which Isabel came, dressed in her wedding gown. Silently she walked down the nave and advanced to the bier, where she knelt in order to give Diego the kiss which in life she had denied him, but as she did so, she died, falling prostrate upon the corpse of her beloved.'

The two deaths from love, something never before heard of, so impressed Teruel that the citizens demanded that Isabel and Diego be buried side by side in the church, and it is surprising to find that the religious authorities acceded to this improper demand. Throughout Spain and the medieval world sped the fame of the Lovers of Teruel, and during repairs made to the church in 1560, the graves of the couple were uncovered and their mummies translated to the spot where they now rest.

Naturally, the authenticity of a tale like this was bound to be challenged in later years, especially since the Italian Boccaccio in 1353 told practically the same tale under the title 'Girolamo e Salvestra,' except that he introduced considerable salacious and amusing material. The question thus became: did Boccaccio in 1353 hear reports of an event which actually happened in Teruel in 1217 and adapt it to his pen, or did someone from Teruel in 1400 happen upon the tale of Boccaccio's and adopt it as a local legend? Powerful minds have addressed themselves to this problem, and for some decades at the beginning of this century it was pretty well agreed that the yarn had originated with Boccaccio.

But recently this conclusion has been subjected to serious review, and in 1963 Señor Don Jaime Caruana Gómez de Barreda, cronista of Teruel, summarized all available studies and offered substantial reasons for believing that the tale had originated in real events which occurred in Teruel as stated, in the year 1217, when Don Domingo Celada was judge. (One wonders what might have happened to the cronista's job had he concluded otherwise.) An aspect of the argument that has carried much weight with me is one which I have not seen in print in any books relating to the lovers. I offer it to Professor Caruana for consideration in his next edition: When a story is told in two different versions, only one of which stresses erotic elements, it is likely that the more erotic version came second; specifically, it is difficult to find instances in which popular taste borrowed an erotic tale from a professional writer and retold it with the erotic elements missing. Applying this tentative theory, it is unlikely that the simple folk of Teruel borrowed a naughty tale from Boccaccio and cleaned it up in their retelling; whereas it would be within reason for a sophisticated writer like Boccaccio to borrow a sentimental folk tale emanating from Teruel and to introduce erotic elements in his version. It therefore seems probable that it was Boccaccio who did the borrowing and the 'sexing-up,' as Hollywood terms it. Other curious reasonings supporting the authenticity of the Teruel version can be found in Professor Caruana's book.

In recent years Teruel, aware that it had on its hands one of the top attractions of Spain, enclosed the mummies unearthed in 1560 in a reverent new chapel and engaged the sculptor Juan de Avalos to fashion the two new tombs which we have seen. In doing so, he created a masterpiece of popular art. The caskets are made of grained marble and emblazoned with shields of the Segura and Marcilla families, but it is the lids that draw the crowds. On the Marcilla casket Diego lies, very tall, barefooted, sallow-cheeked and handsome. His hand reaches out across the open space separating the two and almost touches Isabel's, but not quite; religious propriety would not permit him to do so since Isabel was already married. Isabel's figure, draped in a loose-flowing gown, her fair head resting on two pillows, is one of the most charming portraits carved in recent years, and what is surprising, one of the sexiest. Indubitably she is a woman; indubitably she is lovely. As Don Francisco says, 'Whether the Lovers lived or not, I want to believe they did.' And so, apparently, does most of Spain.

There are, of course, dissenters. Schoolchildren herded in to see the mummies sing a blasphemous little jingle:

> Los Amantes de Teruel
> Tonta ella y tonto el.

Reversing the order of the last line so that it conforms to the chronology, this might be translated:

> Ah, the Lovers of Teruel,
> He was a dope and she as well.

Without being aware of what I was letting myself in for, when I returned to the parador I studied the various books Don Francisco had brought me, and in cronista Caruana's essay I came upon the passage in which he tries to explain why the Italian Boccaccio, hundreds of miles away from the scene, had dealt with the strange deaths, whereas no one in Teruel had even so much as mentioned them in writing until a good three hundred years later: 'In Teruel nothing was written during the thirteenth, fourteenth, and fifteenth centuries, nothing that had any literary character, neither a novel, nor a poem, nor any other form or genre of literature . . . Naturally, since Teruel had neither a great poet nor a literary man of any quality, no one sang or conserved the true happenings in the epic or lyric form which such a tradition merited.'

That night I lay awake, pondering the case of a city in which for three hundred years no one wrote anything of merit, and I wondered what the citizens of that city had visualized their major responsibility to be. It would be difficult to find another city of nineteen thousand in which, during three centuries of vast change and heroic impulse, no one had written anything or painted anything or composed anything, especially when one of the most compelling natural incidents in world literature had occurred within the city boundary. It is not difficult to imagine Boccaccio's hearing from some traveler the account of the Lovers of Teruel and starting that night to write his version; it is difficult to imagine the citizens of Teruel living with the story for three hundred years without any inclination to do anything constructive about it, but that seems to have been the case.

I then began to imagine how different the results would have been had Teruel in those days produced one young man like Thomas Hardy or Truman Capote, and my imagination began running wild through the long dark hours as I tried to construct what these talents would have done with this story in medieval terms. It was a game of vast dimension and unexpected twists: it was not difficult to imagine Capote tracking down each nuance of the story and taking delight in depicting the journey of rich Don Pedro de Azagra from Albarracín to Teruel to claim the bride he was to know for only eighteen hours, and I could visualize Hardy working slowly to construct a study of rural passions.

But then the strange affliction of being a writer overtook me, and I was no longer concerned with Thomas Hardy; I was in bed in Teruel, imagining what my responsibility would have been had I been a citizen of this beloved town during the days of its intellectual aridity, and I started to draft my medieval epic on the legend. At first I was perplexed by what had happened to Diego Marcilla during his five years' absence and for a couple of hours I wasted my time devising an explanation for this lacuna; finally I recalled that every writer who had dealt with the legend after Boccaccio had ruined his story through bothering about what the boy had done during these years. Whoever had told the story originally had hit upon an idea that could not be improved: 'After five years' adventuring in the great world, Diego returned to Teruel, entering by the Zaragoza gate.' Take it or leave it; he was absent for five years and he came back.

What was important, I realized, was not the detail but the universal fact that young men leave their villages in search of adventure that will make them famous or success that will make them rich, and the problem for the storyteller was to reflect the permanence of this theme. At about five in the morning, as dawn was breaking, I began to visualize the Zaragoza gate as it must have been in the Middle Ages. Now, when Diego left Teruel on his five years' pilgrimage I could hear the stones of the gate admonishing him, saying that they had watched many young men leave on missions such as his and that the fame they had sought proved meaningless; the riches they had won were unrewarding, for the love they had abandoned would not be recaptured.

Like most men, on the rare occasions when I am kept awake through a night I fall asleep at dawn, but on this long night I didn't, for the dialogue of the stones preoccupied me during several more hours, after which I began pondering how a medieval writer might have depicted the triumphant homecoming, and I was thrown into a Greek-chorus type of passage in which the stones of the Zaragoza gate both welcome him as their long-absent son and comment on his journey, and I was winging away for another two hours. When I finally went down to breakfast the people I was with said, 'Michener, you look all beat up. Where have you been?' I replied, 'If I told you, you wouldn't believe it,' for I had spent my night at the Zaragoza gate.

(Late in the editing of this manuscript friends brought to my attention the fact that an art cinema in Philadelphia was offering a French motion picture titled *The Lovers of Teruel,* which had won a top prize at the Cannes Film Festival of 1962. A Russian–French cast headed by Ludmila Tcherina had been photographed in marvelous color patterns by Claude Renoir, son of the painter, and the result had been highly regarded by critics. I took the long trip and was more than gratified. Poetic and surrealistic, the picture told of a grubby little traveling show which had set up its stage opposite the railroad yards of a small French town in order to present a mime-dance version of the Spanish legend, but the real-life actors were finding their personal lives paralleling those of Diego and Isabel. Scenery, acting, fantasy and movement were exceptional, and a splendid sense of the old legend was achieved, but unfortunately neither in the real-life nor in the inserted play was the overpowering simplicity of the original achieved. Diego died not of love but from the dagger of his rival. Isabel died from the same dagger. Great folk-sentences like 'The year 1217, Don Domingo Celada being judge of Teruel' and 'There was a clatter at the Zaragoza gate' were not caught, and I went away supposing that the legend was so primary that it could not be reproduced in art; but upon reflection I cannot believe this. I therefore draw attention to the legend, trusting that sometime within the next hundred years someone with talent will direct himself to it.)

For a chain of happy days I wandered about the city, nodding to the bull on his pillar, revisiting the places I had known before and talking with groups of men wherever I found them. And then on the third evening as I was standing in the garden of the parador I felt a voice within me saying in an accusatory manner, 'You didn't come to Teruel to feast on entremeses or to wander about looking at bulls and mummies. Get to the main problem.'

What was the main problem? In 1932 I had seen, by merest accident, a Teruel which existed for all practical purposes in the sixteenth century.

Men of Teruel.

It was the most backward of the provincial capitals, and when judged by ordinary cultural indices, had least to commend it. But it had caught my fancy as typical of the problems of Spain, and during the years that followed, I kept it much in memory. This, however, would not alone have accounted for the striking significance of Teruel in my life nor for the fact that when I approached it from the Río Turia my hands were wet with perspiration.

For a brief moment, in the winter of 1937–38, the chances of history

made Teruel the most important city in Europe, where decisions of great moment were in the balance. It became also, for men in all parts of the world, a source of moral anguish and has continued to this day to be a source of moral guilt. I doubt that many men live entire lives without incurring some sense of regret; for many of my generation their regret centered on Teruel, and the guilt which it evoked has never been discharged, not at Anzio nor at Guadalcanal nor at Bastogne.

In 1936, when the Spanish Civil War broke out, I was at an age when it would have been relatively simple for me to have broken loose from my prosaic job of teaching in Colorado and come to Spain to fight in the Abraham Lincoln Brigade, composed of Americans who wanted to help defend the Republic. Some of the men I respected most in American life were so serving, and when I thought of them doing the job that I should have been engaged in, I felt ashamed, for most of them knew nothing of Spain and had no spiritual connection to it, whereas I did know and the ties which bound me were strong indeed. I had watched at close hand the birth of the Republic and had seen its first faltering steps; I had spoken with the president and while he had not impressed me I had applauded many of the changes his party had introduced into Spanish life. I had read the brave words of his lieutenants and had picked out of the Spanish newspapers to which I subscribed the doings of this group of dedicated men. That change was overdue in Spain, I knew better than most, and when an army revolt arose to end that change I was desolate. Of all the young men available in America in those crucial years, I should have volunteered to defend the Republic, for I saw clearly what must ensue in Europe; I was convinced that a world war was upon us and that in the end my country would be involved.

Then why didn't I fight in Spain? For three reasons. First, I was not invited. Recruiting campaigns for the Abraham Lincoln Brigade were conducted mainly in the big cities, and although some of my friends were active, they were in New York and made no approaches to me, for they were seeking a different kind of person. In the absence of a specific opportunity to join, I was never confronted by a hard choice. Why didn't I volunteer? In my life I have rarely volunteered for anything, nor sought anything, even though I have been willing to take unusual risks when they evolved, and I still find this a logical attitude. Second, since I was convinced that America would soon be at war and since I had taught my students that our survival depended upon its successful prosecution, even pinpointing Singapore and the Philippines as the spots where the war would probably begin (one student had asked, 'How about Hawaii?' and I had explained, 'Impossible. The Japanese would never dare'), I was willing to wait until we made our entrance, satisfied that the Spanish Republic could hold out till then. Third, and I believe this was the most important, those men and women engaged in enlisting Americans for the Brigade, even those who were my personal acquaintances, were people whose general judgment in other matters I did not respect. For some years certain of them had been goading me to join the Communist Party, a step which I refused for the good reason that in Europe I had known many Communists and had found them ill-informed on politics, corrupt in personal judgment and ruthless in their attempts to force others into their orbit. In Europe they had posed a difficult problem for me, and now in America they did the same, for although I sympathized with many of their objectives, as did many of my generation who had watched the depression puncture pompous old verities, I was suspicious of their immediate judgment and their long-term intention. I was especially schizophrenic regarding the Communist relationship to Spain; as a sensible man I had to applaud the efforts of this long-misruled nation to achieve a modern government, but the manner in which my Communist friends proposed to dictate to that government disgusted me and I could not find it within myself to support them. Did I, in 1936 and 1937, suspect that they might have a goal beyond the apparent one of defending the Republic? Did I anticipate that their ambitions would quickly escalate to the point where their goal was no longer a Republic but a Communist dictatorship? I did not. Such conclusions would have required greater insight than I possessed. I believed that the Communist commitment was deeper than mine and that it was only this enthusiasm which caused them to say and do things which I considered nonsense. But in the latter months of 1938 I began to read in impartial journals reports which made me wonder if a serious change had not occurred in Republican ranks. The defense of a free democracy had been subordinated to the expanded goal of establishing a Communist government, and the intuitive suspicions that I had entertained in 1936 matured.

One obvious question must be asked. Are the three reasons cited above mere ex post facto rationalizations masking the fact that I was afraid to volunteer? In any sensible man fear of battle will always be a partial motive, and in my case it could have played a decisive role. On the other hand, in World War II, I was exempt from military service because I was a Quaker, but I joined the navy anyway. In Asia, I have seen a good deal of war, more than most, and I cannot recall ever having shied away from battle. I therefore conclude that the reasons cited above are not spurious and did actually govern my behavior.

It was with a sense of doom that I followed the news which began to come out of Teruel in late 1937. We have seen that in 1171 the city was founded because a fortress was needed to stabilize the battle line that existed between the Christians in Zaragoza and the Moors in Valencia. Now, almost eight hundred years later, Teruel found itself serving the same function, except that this time it was General Franco's troops that were in Zaragoza and the Republicans that were in Valencia. It had become the keystone of the Republican line running between Valencia and Barcelona and its retention would determine who would win the war.

In October, Franco's army occupied Teruel and in forays from it began to cut the Republican lines. If the Republic were to survive, it must recapture this city, even though winter was approaching.

Teruel was defended by some ten thousand Franco troops under the command of a colonel bearing a French last name, Rey d'Harcourt, who had ordered the building of defense positions on all slopes leading up to the city. Teruel would be difficult to assault, but for the job the Republicans had assembled a force of a hundred and ten thousand well-trained men, and on December 15 they began the attack.

It coincided with the beginning of one of Teruel's famed winters; for several weeks the thermometer dropped each night to zero degrees Fahrenheit, bringing some ice and much snow, which helped the Franco men inside the city. Nevertheless, the Republicans attacked, only to be repulsed by slanting fire. Again and again the Republicans tried to climb the sloping flanks, but had to retreat, leaving their wounded to die between the lines. Here in this significant city, which I had stumbled upon years ago, developed the most terrible battle of the war; and here the fate of the world, at least for this period, was being decided.

The Republican attack continued for twenty-four gruesome days, during which frightful crimes were perpetrated by both sides. Prisoners were shot. Bystanders were executed. Dead bodies were mutilated. Buildings were wantonly destroyed and vengeance was exacted on any enemy at hand. If the brutality of the two armies was about equal, so was the heroism. To storm the hills of Teruel over ice and snow and then to penetrate the rubbled defenses required courage of an absolute order, and this the Republicans had; to remain inside the city walls, with no water, no food and diminishing supplies of ammunition, while determined assaults came hourly, required of Franco's men a determination which never faltered.

In America, I followed the siege with a sense of tragic despair. The hills I had tramped were the ones under contention and the city streets I had found so meaningful were those where the shellfire struck with such fury. Reports said that several columns of Franco's troops were rushing south to relieve the handful of men inside Teruel, and I prayed that they would not arrive before the Republicans had won the city.

Shortly after January 8, 1938, I read with enormous relief that Colonel Rey d'Harcourt had surrendered Teruel to the Republicans. His men crawled down out of the rubble, looking like emaciated ghosts, and women who had undergone the siege and the bombardment appeared half dead as they begged for water. It was a tremendous Republican victory and aroused hopes throughout the eastern half of Spain. In Fascist capitals like Berlin and Rome, especially the latter, it caused despair, for it seemed the first of what might be many Republican triumphs. In America, I breathed deeply and looked at the new map. The great cities, Madrid, Barcelona and Valencia, remained in Republican hands, and the war had obviously become a contest between the reactionary rural sections and the liberal metropolitan ones, and I could not believe that in an age of technical development rural areas could win a war.

But almost immediately the relief columns which Franco had set in motion toward Teruel began arriving to start a new siege. This time it was the Franco forces who had to attack up the dreadful slopes; it was the Republicans who were trapped inside the city, with inadequate food, water or ammunition. Only the cold remained the same. At first the ice and snow

Wall in Teruel.

exacted more casualties than the bullets, but finally the Franco forces moved heavy Italian batteries into position and these began the systematic destruction of the city. Row after row of houses were pulverized. In early February the Republicans had to evacuate the commanding hill on which the Bull of Teruel had appeared, and it was soon occupied by an Italian battery which fired point-blank into the city.

Throughout the middle weeks of February, in intense cold, the Franco forces inched their way forward, and it was during this fatal time, when the result of the battle was obvious, that the worst atrocities were committed. On February 20, Franco assault troops broke through to the first line of houses and bayoneted all in sight. On February 21 the Franco men swept into the heart of the city, took all the major buildings and began those reprisals which would permanently remove from Teruel any persons with Republican connections.

The battle had lasted sixty-nine days. Twenty thousand Republican troops were dead, ten thousand Franco men. Twenty-eight thousand prisoners had been taken and the number of wounded could not be calculated. Thousands of civilians were dead; on each side thousands had been assassinated under one pretext or another. But at last the battle was over and Teruel, almost totally destroyed, was permanently in Franco's hands. The Republican lifeline from Valencia to Barcelona and to Madrid was threatened if not wholly cut, and the uprising of the rural areas against the cities had succeeded. Germany and Italy had won the first round in the test of arms, and a world war was inevitable. Of course, the war in Spain would struggle along for another year, with the terrible Battle of the Ebro still to unfold and the final siege of Madrid, but after Teruel sensible observers knew that the outcome was determined.

With the death of this mountain city I experienced a spiritual agony that has not diminished through the years. A noble effort of men to govern themselves perished with the collapse of Teruel, and not all the rationalizations of the postwar period can deny that fact. Now it is popular to describe the whole war in terms of white (the victorious forces) and red (the Communist), but when the war began this was not the distinction nor was it the commanding consideration at the Battle of Teruel. When I read, as I do in the book before me, that 'finally the white forces of freedom triumphed over the Russian-led reds,' I feel sick at my stomach. When I see official publications which seek to prove that all Republicans were Communists, that only Republicans slaughtered civilians, that only Republicans were guilty of heinous crimes, my reason balks. The war had begun on different principles, even though I do now admit that it ended in a debacle in which those original concepts were engulfed.

On March 11, 1939, Almería, Murcia and Cartagena surrendered and the long struggle ground to a halt. About 900,000 Spaniards were dead, of whom some 175,000 had been assassinated. More than 170 monasteries and convents were burned and nearly 1900 ravaged to the point where they could not be used. Some 3000 others were wrecked in part. More than 250,000 homes were destroyed, and nearly 400,000 Spaniards preferred exile in countries like Mexico and France to the reprisals that awaited them in Spain. Any rehabilitation of the country was made more difficult by the fact that 8,000,000,000,000 pesetas had been sent out of the country by the Republican government to purchase arms; 1,500,000,000,000 were subsequently recovered by the Franco government, but the remainder stayed abroad, mainly in Russia and Mexico. (The data in this paragraph come principally from Georges-Roux, *La Guerra Civil de España*, translated from the French, 1964.)

As to the number of priests and nuns assassinated in the early days of the war, the figures are uncertain, but at least fifteen thousand perished, including fourteen bishops, not one of whom would commit apostasy in order to escape martyrdom. In one town after another, where for the last two hundred years observers had reported that the citizens were above all else Catholics who loved their priests, one of the first things that happened when war started was the indiscriminate slaughter of clericals, and this occurred even in areas where Communists were not in control. On the other side, events such as those at Málaga, where eighty suspected Masons were garroted, were common.

Today, looking back at such evidence as has so far been made public, I must conclude that the apprehensions which kept me from volunteering in 1936 were sound. I was a better judge than I knew, for the seeds of the final Communist debacle in Spain began to mature fairly early in the fight, even though at the time I was not intelligent enough to identify them. I think that no one can see the photographs of Barcelona, Valencia and Madrid taken in the final winter of 1938–39 without realizing that Communism had pretty well taken charge of the Republic; if the leadership of that time had somehow triumphed, there can be little doubt but that it would have organized a Communist dictatorship. But during the Battle of Teruel, Communism was not inevitable.

But I had not returned to Teruel to exacerbate the feelings of guilt occasioned by its fall. I had quite a different purpose. During the war no city had given Franco's army more trouble than this, and at various points in Spain I was warned not to bother with Teruel: 'The victors are disgusted with it. They hated its stubborn people, and the Franco government would give the city nothing.' Others said, 'If you want to see Spain at its worst, go to Teruel. It's a ghost town.' In a well-produced volume called *The Spain of Each Province,* sponsored in part by the government, native sons write about and illustrate each of the fifty provinces, but apparently Teruel still produces no writers, for its essay is written by a man from Madrid. It is a beautiful thing, an elegy for a dead city, and the painting which illustrates it is a handsome, mournful black gash, recalling barbed wire and broken bottles. Because I had an affinity for Teruel, I wanted to see what had happened to it in defeat, for this would constitute a real test of contemporary Spain: How did the victors treat the vanquished?

First I went out into the country to see if it had changed much. I chose the remote village of San Agustín, on the border of Castellón Province, and there under a perfect July sky I walked for several miles through ripened fields where the reapers were at work according to a division of labor laid down prior to Bible times: a young man swung the large scythe; his strong wife gathered the fallen grain; an old man twisted stalks into a rope and tied the bundles. As I watched them I said, 'The recurring sound of rural life has been the swish of the scythe over stubble and rocks, but no musician has been able to put it into music.' In the fields at least nothing had changed, and the trio at work looked just as poor and just as tired as their predecessors had looked thirty-four years before.

Nor had the village changed. The central square was still unpaved; most of the houses were still unpainted; the dust was omnipresent and the heat still kept people indoors. The meanness of the life continued too: the earthen floors, the sparse furniture, the inadequate clothing, the harsh

The spirit of Teruel.

poverty of Spanish rural life. I recalled that day in Badajoz when our car had taken the injured man to the hospital, and in San Agustín the standard of living was the same. Of all the countries in which I have traveled, only India and Turkey have had a rural poverty as grinding as that in Spain, and the much publicized 'Twenty-five Years of Peace' have brought little to the farmers.

Yet even as I thought this, I became aware of the improvement. Out beyond the village I could see electricity wires which had not been there a generation ago; in what once had been barren fields I could see where millions of young trees had been planted, as they have been throughout Spain. The roads were better and the village even had an automobile and two television aerials. The farmers looked poor, but nowhere did I see any in rags, nor did any look underfed. On balance I would say that in the country things were a little better than they had been before; but when one considered what had been accomplished in rural areas in Germany, Denmark and Britain, the comparison was disadvantageous. On the other hand, Spain had accomplished more than Turkey and much more than India.

On my return to Teruel, I picked up, along the road, a fine-looking young man in clerical garb who said he was hitchhiking home from his studies at the seminary in Valencia, and his pleasant chatter was so charming that I shall repeat it without interruption: 'I'm twenty-two years old and entered seminary training at eleven. I was an orphan, you see, and was stuck away in an orphanage and this was the only way that I could see of getting out. I wasn't a real orphan, I suppose, because my mother and three sisters were living, but my father died and we could scarcely live on what my mother earned, so it was decided that I should go to the orphanage, and I made up my own mind to go to the seminary. We have no students there from the upper class and none from the lower class, so today all priests come from the middle class. I suppose when I become a priest I'll be sent to some small village like the one you've been visiting, and I'll bring my mother to live with me and I'll find jobs in the village for my three sisters, who will live with me until they're married. I've noticed a priest can usually find jobs of some kind for his relatives. You mention the novels of Pío Baroja, but we're not allowed to read them. He's much too anti-clerical, but the disappointing thing is that the Spanish novels we are allowed to read are so pro-clerical they aren't much fun. But I understand the Church's problem and obey its suggestions. I saw your motion picture *Sayonara*. All of us at the seminary did. It's about two soldiers and two Japanese girls. Japan must be a wonderful country and I wouldn't be unhappy to be sent there when I'm graduated, but I suppose I'm destined for Spain. This is a great country and there's much work to be done.'

When the seminarian left me in Teruel, I was assaulted, there can be no other word for it, by noise such as I had not heard for some years. At first I couldn't identify it or its direction, but as I drove toward the center of the city I heard the rhythmic roar of motors off to the west and decided that Teruel must be holding some kind of auto race, and I set out to find it. I was wrong. It was a motorcycle race around a circular course that ran through a handsome new section of Teruel which had grown up in recent years on the other side of the ravine down which the Saracen bulls had charged the Christians in 1171. Before the war this area had contained no houses or even any barns. I took my place behind some bales of straw that marked a turn in the course and decided simply to look at what was on display in this new Teruel. The thirty or forty motorcycles which kept roaring past were the best that Europe built, and each driver wore an expensive leather suit with goggles to match. The competition was keen. Number 1, in green, drove at a sensational speed and could not be overtaken, but a real battle developed between 11 in red and 15 in the same color. The latter tried to drive 11 into the wall at the turns, and when 11 protested, rowdy 15 yelled the Spanish equivalent of 'Up your bucket.' The

noise was unbelievable, for not only did the motorcycles thunder with their mufflers open, but as usual three huge loudspeakers suspended from public buildings kept up a constant chatter, while a Coca-Cola truck below played records over its public address system. The streets along which the race careened were wide, well paved and finely planted with trees. The houses, all of recent construction, were about what one would find in southern California, except that since Teruel has bitterly cold winters, said to be the worst in Spain, its houses had more provision for heating than California's would have had.

It was the people, however, who were most impressive. To watch the race cost about twenty-five cents, but the course was jammed, and I saw no one poorly dressed; their clothes would have fitted in without comment in Chicago or Edinburgh. It was a well-fed, well-groomed audience, and as the motorcycles roared around the walls of the bullring for their dash right at the bales of straw where I stood, I saw at least as many pretty girls wearing make-up as I would have seen in a similar American city. Their dresses were about as short, and if they were accompanied by young men, they walked hand in hand as they would have in a small English city. In fact, except for a rather heavy concentration of men in clerical garb, I could see nothing that would indicate I was in Spain.

In this cautious manner I checked each experience I was having in Teruel and could find no evidence that this was the city on which Franco's forces had broken their teeth in the Civil War. The visible scars were healed. If in the sieges of 1937–38 the city had been mainly destroyed, it has now been well rebuilt. Not even in the ancient Jewish quarter, with its crowded streets, were there evidences of the war, but I did see set into the wall of a house built in 1400 one sign which startled me: 'This building is insured against fire by the Great American Insurance Company of New York.' If the Franco government has rebuilt Teruel in a spirit of forgiveness, no matter how grudging, then the outward bitterness of the Civil War has subsided. In the new suburb where the motorcycle race took place I saw much evidence of new construction sponsored by the government: new schools, new homes, even a new bullring, and a handsome new sports center where for fifteen pesetas (about twenty-five cents) a month young men can enjoy a swimming pool, a large gymnasium and a basketball court as good as that in any American city of comparable size. A sign said that the sports hall had been erected with funds from the Youth Front, so I suppose that only those boys whose families support the government can participate. I saw the tennis courts on an emotional morning: the day before, Manuel Santana had won the world's tennis title at Wimbledon, Spain's first title of the kind in history, and Teruel was celebrating.

Today, even though the sore of Teruel has not healed in my heart nor will it ever, I can accept most of the statement which the Franco govern-

705

Guardia Civil headquarters.

ment has recently drafted in English for inclusion in any tourist publication where reference to the war cannot be avoided.

> For a century and a half Spaniards had tried to live in peace according to the formulas laid down by the French Revolution—generally speaking under a Monarchy, though twice under a Republic. It was impossible to implant a purely liberal policy in a country without a middle class, and with an almost feudal structure. And so we spent a century and a half hitting each other over the head, familiarizing the world with the spectacle of civil war, and introducing the word *'pronunciamiento'* into most languages. The nation was filled with hatreds, and those hatreds provided a fruitful field of action for ideas and political groups which ended up by dominating the rest— Anarchism and Communism. And this was the outcome of a policy full of liberal phrases!
>
> One day, in 1936, those hatreds exploded. The world still remembers that three-year war to which the Catholic Church gave the name of Crusade. We don't pretend that all the goodies were on one side, and all the baddies on the other; for one thing, goodness and badness are always mixed. But what we can and do claim is that the war was won by that section of the people who preferred a Spanish Spain to a Spain turned into a satellite of Russia.

And then, when my opinion about modern Teruel had about crystallized, I stumbled upon an extraordinary building, a modern hospital built on the skyscraper design, with an elegant reception floor topped by tiers of rooms bursting with every modern medical device. I was shown around the building by the administrator, Don José Callado Ruiz, who had been born in nearby Cuenca and educated in Madrid. He was indistinguishable from hospital administrators in England or Holland, efficient, knowledgeable and proud of his institution. Where the ordinary hospital might have one iron lung, his had two, and incubators for premature babies, and gleaming trays of all the latest medical tools from Solingen in Germany, and x-rays galore and a splendid medical library. It was the kind of hospital that put the ones I knew in America to shame.

It had one fault, however. It had almost no patients. There were, I believe, four women on one floor awaiting childbirth; the rest of the gleaming installation was unused and had never been used. I tried to pierce the secret of this amazing building, for I had recently been in a hospital in America, and judging by the overcrowding there, this Teruel installation had space for about four hundred patients, and certainly in the villages I had been visiting there were candidates who could have profited from admission. Then, as I waited in the foyer, I understood a little better, for on the far wall, gazing balefully at whoever entered the hospital, was the frightening portrait of a fleshy young man in an open shirt. I had seen this hypnotic portrait before in many public buildings, this all-seeing, all-knowing young god of modern Spain, and his counte-

José Antonio.

nance was the only thing that had ever frightened me in the country. He was José Antonio, son of the tough dictator Miguel Primo de Rivera, Marqués de Estella. Born in 1903, José Antonio had organized the Falange at the age of thirty and had been the bullyboy of the street-rioting that had helped discredit the Republic. His adherents roamed the streets in trucks, machine-gunning their opponents, and most Spaniards believe that if José Antonio had lived he would have challenged Franco for the leadership of Spain and might have become the country's Fascist dictator, but shortly before the outbreak of war he was arrested by the Republicans and some months after the beginning of hostilities was tried, condemned and shot. Alive, he was a danger to Franco's claim to leadership; dead, he became a patron saint, and at the end of the war his body was carried on shoulders from Alicante in the south to El Escorial, where he was temporarily buried among the ancient rulers of Spain. Later his corpse was translated to the newly built basilica of the Valley of the Fallen, where it lies in enormous solemnity before the high altar. I say that the visage of José Antonio is frightening because he looks exactly like a younger Hermann Goering, and had he lived and triumphed he would each year have resembled Goering more. He would now be only sixty-three and good for another fifteen years' rule, which is a frightening thought.

At any rate, the hospital he now supervised in absentia, the finest I had visited in a dozen years, was reserved for those who, like himself, were dedicated to a certain way of life. For members, the rates of the hospital were low and the service provided by the medical head, Dr. Antonio Moreno Monforte from the college in Zaragoza, was, I am sure, excellent. In England such a hospital would be crawling with patients and overworked nurses and grumbling doctors, for members of the Labor and Conservative parties alike would be eligible, and one had to sense the difference.

On the last day of my sentimental return to Teruel, Señor Cortel Zuriaga, the man who had shown me the tomb of the Lovers, took me to a high point overlooking the city, and with the cemetery at our backs, explained how the fortunes of the great battle for Teruel had fluctuated, and he spoke with decent respect for each side: 'If the Republicans were to win the war, they had to capture this city. They did so, and then General Franco knew that he must retake it. It was as simple as that.' And he pointed out the routes used by Franco's rescue columns as they brought pressure to bear on the city then held by the Republicans. 'For anyone in Teruel it was a terrible war,' he said. 'It was a blessing when it ended.' Then he said something about the bull that stood in the plaza, representing the city, and in these words summarized the spiritual significance of Teruel: 'We saw the other day that the symbol of Teruel is a bull. But which particular bull? A Saracen bull sent against the Christians as an

Here lies Esteban Pérez Moral. Brigade of Engineers.
Died on the front Teruel the 18th day of December 1937
at the age of 24 years. His father and
brothers dedicated this remembrance. R.I.P.

The survivor.

enemy. It came to destroy us, but we converted it. If the Spaniards in 1171 were able to accept such a bull as the symbol of their city, then other Spaniards in 1939 should have been able to accept their recent enemies.' Apparently, after the first long year of revenge, that is what has happened.

As I stood looking down upon the city that has meant so much to me, I asked myself the question which perplexes many people who wish to visit Spain: 'If I was once so committed to a Republican victory, how can I bear to visit Spain now?' I have often wondered, for after the destruction of the Republicans, I went through a period of bitterness in which I did not care ever again to see Spain, and I.would schedule my trips through Europe so as to avoid it. Then two things happened. One day, while talking to a group of Spanish exiles in Mexico, I asked myself, 'Why should I allow Franco to deprive me of a land which is almost as much mine as his?' More important, as I studied the world I came to the conclusion that each nation, at the end of a cycle of about twenty-five years, starts anew. What went before is historically important and probably sets a limit to what the newborn nation can become, but the fact is that the past is past and a new nation is in being, with fresh possibilities for success or failure. That is why General de Gaulle has been so right in France; he is governing an entirely new country not bound by the debacle of 1941. That is why the young Germans are so right in disclaiming responsibility for 1935–1945; they're a new nation, almost as if they had been discovered on the moon, and they are correct in insisting that they be so treated. It is obviously true of China, though most of us have been reluctant to admit it. And one of these days it will be true even of Russia, and we had better be prepared to admit that, too.

It also applies to the United States, though we fight against it and blind our eye and conscience to the fact. The median age of our population is lower now. We are more overcrowded, more urban, and whether we like it or not, a permanently mixed nation racially. We are in the midst of swift change in education, technology, labor relations and religion. We are evolving a new morality, a new posture in world politics. Yet we refuse to understand that the advent of such change signifies also the advent of a new nation. The people of Spain seem more prepared to accept their new nation than we are to accept ours, and it may be this reluctance to accept the new that will destroy us.

As a matter of fact, I suspect that the rebirth of each nation occurs about every seventeen or eighteen years, but only the rare social scientist can recognize the change as it occurs. I usually seem to be about seven years tardy. America's present cycle will end sometime around 1970, and if we try to govern our new nation by 1920 policies we shall be truly doomed. Spain's last cycle ended about 1964, and it is the opportunity to watch a new nation coming into being that makes a visit to Spain so instructive and rewarding.

FOLLOWING PAGE:
Stoned roadway.

XIII

SANTIAGO DE COMPOSTELA

OCEANO
ATLANTICO

MAR MEDITERRANEO

Paris

Orléans

Vézelay

Tours

Nevers

Poitiers

Limoges

Toulouse

Montpellier

Arles

CABO FINISTERRE

Pamplona

Roncesvalles

Estella

Eunate

Puente la Reina

León

Logroño

Santiago de Compostela

Astorga

Santo Domingo de la Calzada

Vigo

Ponferrada

Burgos

Cebrero

Castrogeriz

Bayona

Villafranca del Bierzo

Frómista

Barcelona

Madrid

Lisboa

Sevilla

0   MILES   100

$\mathbf{A}$ny reader who has come with me so far through the Iberian peninsula should be prepared for a pilgrimage across northern Spain to the sanctuary at Santiago de Compostela, the finest journey in Spain and one of the two or three best in the world. It is a twofold pilgrimage to a long-dead form of art and to a living religious shrine. To understand the latter, certain things must be known.

Fact. Two of the earliest disciples chosen by Jesus were the brothers James and John, sons of the Galilee fisherman Zebedee and his wife Salome. So energetic in their support of the new religion were the brothers that Jesus gave them the honorary second name of Boanerges, the Sons of Thunder. Salome, sister of the Virgin Mary, which meant that her sons were cousins of Jesus, appears to have been a woman of some wealth, for she underwrote many of the expenses of the group and may have paid the tavern bill for the Last Supper. At any rate, both Mark and Matthew, in their gospels, relate the story of how Salome, hoping to gain some return for the money she had spent, requested that Jesus give her sons the positions on his right and left hand in heaven, but he rebuked her, saying, 'Ye know not what ye ask. Are ye able to drink of the cup that I shall drink of, and to be baptized with the baptism that I am baptized with? . . . to sit on my right hand, and on my left, is not mine to give, but it shall be given to them for whom it is prepared of my Father.' In A.D. 29 the brothers were present at the Crucifixion, and in 44, James, having persisted in his energetic propagation of the faith, was beheaded, perhaps at Caesarea, by order of King Herod Agrippa, thus becoming the first of the followers of Jesus to attain martyrdom.

Tradition. In the Book of Acts it is suggested that after the death of Jesus and before the martyrdom of James, the disciples scattered to different portions of the world and proselytized for the new religion, without specifying as to who went where and with what results. Tradition, unsupported by documentation but strong in folk persistence, claims that while Matthew went to Ethiopia, Thomas to India, Jude to Persia, Simon to India and Bartholomew to Armenia, James Boanerges came to Spain, where after extensive labors he succeeded in converting nine Iberians to Christianity and was rewarded by the supreme gift of being visited at Zaragoza by the Virgin Mary, who was still living at the time. This tradition is popular in Spain but textual and historical critics in other countries find it difficult to accept. It should be noted, however, that the tradition specifically states that after this missionary effort in Spain, James returned to the Holy Land, where he suffered martyrdom.

Legend. Late in history a beautiful legend developed in Europe to the effect that following the decapitation in Jerusalem and burial in Caesarea of St. James, his body was mysteriously disinterred and found to have its head once more intact. Into the port of Jaffa, where shipping for Jerusalem customarily landed, came a ship made of stone and manned by knights; the body of James was rescued and brought in seven days to the harbor of Iria Flavia (now Padrón) on the west coast of Spain in the region now called Galicia. Here a willful pagan queen denied burial to the cargo of the stone ship, but miracles awakened her to a Christian understanding, and she allowed the saintly body to be taken inland to an unlikely spot where a Roman burial ground had long existed; here St. James was buried, sometime around the year A.D. 44. It was nearly eight hundred years later, in 812 (some say 814), that a hermit happened to see in the heavens a bright star hovering over a vacant field, a phenomenon with which we are familiar, and when he reported this fact to his religious superiors, excavations were begun and the body of St. James was brought to light, uncorrupted by the passage of time. As a saint descended from heaven, he assumed personal leadership of the Christian remnant who were battling the superior Muslims who had overrun Spain, and at the crucial but legendary Battle of Clavijo in 844, was clearly seen by the Spanish Christians, riding before them on a white horse, swinging a great sword and killing Moors by the thousands, from which he gained the name by which he would henceforth be known in Spain, Santiago Matamoros. It was under his banner that Christianity reconquered Spain; it was following his white horse that Spaniards expelled the Moors, drove out the Jews and conquered the Americas. St. James became the patron saint of Spain, as well he deserved, and his burial place became the most sacred spot in Spain, Santiago de Compostela, the last word of which could have been derived from either the Spanish Campo de la estrella (in Latin, Campus Stellae, meaning Countryside where the Star Shone) or the latin Compost Terra (from compostum, burying ground). In Spain the name James appears in a variety of forms. In Latin it was, of course, Jacobus, so that the pilgrims' road we are about to follow has always been known as the Jacobean route; in Old Spanish it was Iago and evolved into Jacóme and Jaime, the latter of which is still preferred along the eastern Mediterranean coast; as the name of our saint it became the composite form Santiago, which is the prevailing Spanish form today; through a false division this produced Diego; and in nearby France it became, of course, Jacques. In some years all these names could have been heard along the way.

History. We have seen, during our visit to Córdoba, that the Moors of southern Spain kept in a vault in that city a relic of considerable emotional significance in their wars against the Christians: the visible arm of the Prophet Muhammad, and there are historians who believe that much of the advantage which the Moors enjoyed in their triumphant sweep across Spain derived from their belief that they were invincible as long as the arm of the Prophet led them into battle. The Christians, on the other hand, were supported by no comparable relic from their New Testament, and we know from documents that a kind of fatality overcame them when without heavenly assistance they had to face Muslims who had such assistance. I think it neither ungenerous nor unlikely to suggest that the body of Santiago was found not by a hermit following a star but by hard-pressed soldiers who needed a rallying point; certainly it arrived on the scene when some kind of counterbalance to the Prophetic arm was needed, and over the centuries this heavenly figure riding his white horse, sword in hand, proved more potent and of farther-reaching significance, if we consider his role in helping conquer the New World, than the arm of the Prophet.

At any rate, we can be certain that after the year 812 Christian fortunes took an upward swing, but not all the miracles connected with Santiago were military. A bridegroom riding his horse along the sands to his wedding was swept into the waves and drowned, but his bride appealed to Santiago and from the sea rose the groom, his garments covered with white cockleshells, after which this beautiful symbol of the shell shaped like human hands extending alms became the mark of all who fought the infidel and the badge of those who made the pilgrimage to Compostela.

It is not surprising that at the scene of such miracles a series of churches should have risen to mark the grave, culminating in the early 1100s in a cathedral of majestic proportions, much of which can be seen today. It was to this ancient site that pilgrims from all over Europe made their way for more than eleven hundred years.

It is difficult to describe, in a scientific age, the spiritual hold that pilgrimage had on citizens of the Middle Ages. There was, of course, in those days but one Church, and so far as the Christian world was concerned, it was truly universal. Existence outside the membership of this religion was unthinkable, and the three physical locations upon which the

717

imagery of the Church depended were Jerusalem, where Christ was crucified; Rome, where Peter founded the organization of the Church; and
Compostela, from which point Europe had been evangelized. Any Christian who made a pilgrimage to one of these places was assured of extraordinary blessing, but a man who had journeyed to all three had a right to
consider himself in an almost heavenly state. Those who went to Jerusalem were called palmers, since they returned with palm branches; those
who went to Rome were romeros; it was only those who made the terribly
hazardous trip to Compostela who were entitled to be called pilgrims, and
no devout man in that age bothered to estimate which of the three
journeys was most important, for in sanctity they were equal.

The Way of St. James, as it is customarily referred to in English, was
primarily a French road, and I suppose that in its years of maximum
greatness some eighty out of every hundred pilgrims who traveled it were
from outside of Spain, and of these the bulk came from France, although
the road was also popular with Englishmen and Germans. In the famous
monasteries we shall see, French was spoken, and in the cathedrals French
priests officiated. Indeed, the road started at that curious tower in the
middle of Paris which still stands to excite the imagination of the visitor,
the Tour St. Jacques on the right bank of the Seine not far from Notre
Dame. Here, in all ages, pilgrims from various parts of Europe used to
convene to form bands for the long march to Compostela, some nine
hundred miles away. Kings and beggars, queens and cutthroats, butchers
and knights, poets and philosophers all met here, and for a wild variety of
reasons.

To appreciate those reasons, let us gather with the crowd that clusters
around the Tour St. Jacques one spring morning in the Middle Ages.
Some two hundred pilgrims have assembled from Germany, England,
France and the Low Countries. A few have even drifted down from
Norway and Sweden, and all are divided into seven fairly well understood
groups. First are the devout Christian laymen who seek salvation at the
tomb of the saint; since many are advanced in years, there will be frequent
deaths en route. Second are knights who in battle vowed to make the
journey if they survived; they ride horses and take their ladies with them.
Third are the monks and priests, and sometimes even cardinals, who have
dreamed for years of visiting Santiago as a crown to their life within the
Church.

Fourth are those criminals who were told by their judges, 'Five years
in jail or pilgrimage to the tomb of St. James, whichever.' These criminals,
if it is proper to term them such, for many of their offenses were petty, are
required to get a certificate at Compostela proving that they have completed the pilgrimage, and in Spanish border cities like Pamplona a lively

Give me my scallop-shell of quiet,
My staff of faith to walk upon,
My scrip of joy, immortal diet,
My bottle of salvation,

My gown of glory, hope's true gage,
And thus I'll take my pilgrimage.
—Sir Walter Raleigh

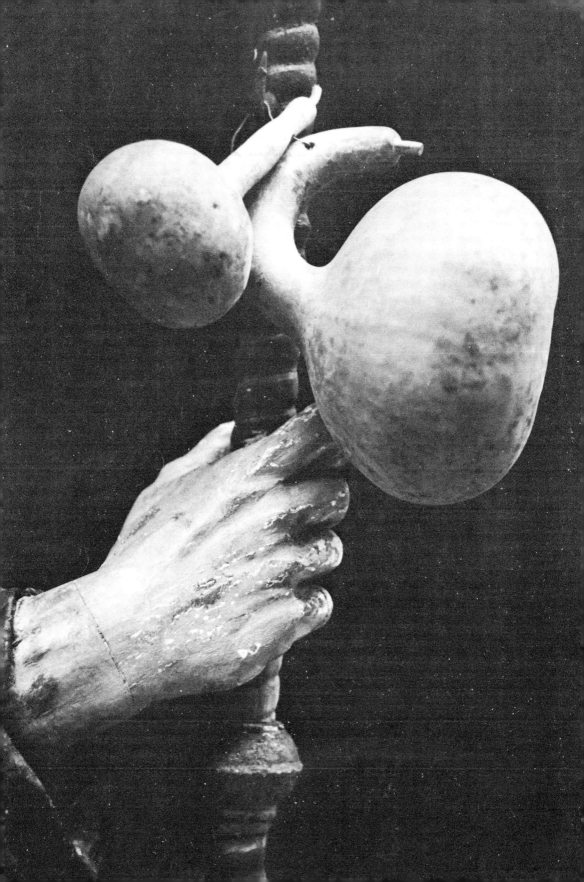

trade operates in these 'Compostelas,' for venturesome businessmen make the journey frequently, collect their certificates and sell them to those who do not wish to undergo the hazards of western Spain. The criminal, having laid out good money for the 'Compostela,' stuffs it in his pocket, has a high time in Spanish inns and returns seven months later to submit his proof to the sentencing judge. Fifth are the beggars, forgers, thieves, robbers and others who hope to make financial gain from the journey, and of this unsavory group some move backward and forward along the endless pilgrims' road, living off the devout for years at a time. Sixth are the merchants, the architects, the itinerant painters, the weavers and that horde of people who use the road as a marketplace. Finally, there is a fairly constant movement back and forth of government agents who keep watch on what is happening in northern Spain, for this is an unquiet land coveted by France and England, by Austrian adventurers and Italian, and among these watchful persons are those French clerics who are inspired more by colonialism than by religion. The buildings they erect are outwardly monasteries and churches, but inwardly they are intended as stepping stones for the French king.

But all groups this morning have one thing in common. All wear the same uniform, famous throughout Europe: a heavy cape which will serve as raincoat, comforter and nightly blanket; an eight-foot stave with gourd attached at one end for carrying water; the heaviest kind of sandal for hiking the nine hundred miles to Santiago; and a curious kind of broad-rimmed felt hat, turned up in front and marked with three or four bright cockleshells.

'I shall take the cockleshell,' becomes the pilgrims' cry throughout Europe, and already a famous dish has been invented, scallops in wine sauce served in a cockleshell and known as coquille St. Jacques.

On this medieval day, as we wait under the chestnut trees of Paris, officials move out from the great buildings that cluster about the Tour St. Jacques. Priests bless the throng, musicians lead the pilgrims to the outskirts of Paris, and a detachment of cavalry rides along to provide protection during the first days of the journey.

Through the most beautiful river valleys of France moves the sprawling army at the rate of nine or ten miles a day. Sandals wear out and new ones are bought. At crossroad shrines the faithful pray, and in each cathedral town the marchers crowd into sanctuaries to offer thanks to local saints. Food is never plentiful, and villagers guard their stores with pikes and dogs. However, each community has designated a small body of Christians whose duty it is to bury those pilgrims who die within its gates.

And so our great, inchoate mass drifts southward through France: Orléans, Tours, Poitiers mark one well-traveled road; Vézelay, Nevers, Limoges define another; Arles, Montpellier, Toulouse are on the famous southern route. And finally there are the Pyrenees leading to Roncesvalles and Pamplona, where Spain begins.

We can speak with accuracy of this vast movement of people—the incredible number of more than half a million moved along the road each year—because in 1130 what is generally held to be the world's first travel guide was written, describing the glories and hardships of this route. It was written at the request of the Church, which hoped thereby to encourage pilgrimages, by a French priest, Aymery de Picaud, who lived along one of the pilgrim routes and set the pattern for future travel writers: things near at home he praised, those farther away he questioned, while those distant he condemned. Of the Poitevins, who lived near at hand, he says: 'They are vigorous and fine warriors, courageous at the battlefront, elegant in their fashions of dress, handsome in appearance, spiritual, very generous and easy in their hospitality.'

Of the Gascons, who lived suspiciously close to Spain, he writes: 'They are nimble with words, great babblers, mockers. They are debauched, drunkards, gluttons, dressed in tatters, and destitute of money. They are not ashamed to sleep all together on one narrow bed of rotten straw, the servants beside the masters.'

But when he reaches the peasants of Navarra, whom he does not consider Frenchmen at all, he says with scorn: 'These people are badly dressed. They eat poorly and drink worse. Using no spoons, they plunge their hands into the common pot and drink from the same goblet. When one sees them feed, one thinks he is seeing pigs in their gluttony; and when one hears them speak, he thinks of dogs baying. They are perverse, perfidious, disloyal, corrupted, voluptuous, expert in every violence, cruel and quarrelsome, and anyone of them would murder a Frenchman for one sou. Shamefully they have sex with animals.'

This ancient book can still be read with interest, for it evokes the dangers faced by the pilgrims: the water in most of the rivers is contaminated and brings certain death; in many regions food is almost impossible to come by; hospitals are infrequent; and rogues lie in wait to ambush and murder.

In one group of twenty-five, all but two will perish because they drink from the rivers. Of another, half will be slain by brigands. One morning in Spain we wake to find all our animals stolen. But still we push on, the pilgrims of the cockleshell, en route to salvation.

To understand the magnificence of this road, consider a few of the pilgrims we might have met upon it:

    778   Charlemagne, legend says, but tomb not discovered till 812
    813   King Alfonso II, to see what has happened at Compostela
  1064   El Cid Campeador, about to make his dramatic moves
  1130   Aymery de Picaud, author of the French travel guide

In the blazing summer of 1966 my pilgrimage along the Way of St. James began at a spot south of Pamplona, on a bare and lonely plain marked only by dusty weeds, where the various routes converge for the long westward thrust to Compostela. On this plain I came to the forsaken church of Eunate, surrounded only by haunting emptiness, and I could not have found a more appropriate introduction to the dead art form that was to dominate my pilgrimage. The architecture of this church is Romanesque—that is, it dates from sometime after the beginning of the eleventh century, that transition period when the ancient Roman style of architecture had not yet been replaced by the Gothic. Rome had almost nothing to do with Romanesque; it developed principally from northern sources, but before we try to define what the new style was, or where it came from, let us see how it looks in the church at Eunate.

The principal characteristic of the church is its low, sturdy weight. It is a church that relates to the soil: its arches are low and rounded, as if they preferred to cling to the earth; its pillars are heavy and rooted in the earth; it does not provide enormous Gothic perspectives. It is solid, well proportioned, weighty with the judgment of intellect. The capitals of its pillars are simple and straightforward: walls are neither adorned nor soaring; windows are small and interior vistas are intimate; there is an impression of almost Scandinavian modernity. It has a tower, but not a tall one; it is built with eight sides, for some reason that no one now remembers, and is surrounded by a curious unroofed cloister of austerely beautiful construction.

The church remains a mystery. To what organization was it attached? What priests served here, what peasants formed its congregation? Who built it and when? Is there truth in the local tradition that it once pertained to the Knights Templars, that tragic order whose memorials we shall see again on this pilgrimage? Was it, as some think, a kind of Valhalla for knights who died fighting the Muslims? There it stands, a simple, lovely Romanesque construction in weathered brown stone, a forgotten memorial to the millions of pilgrims who passed it during its eight or nine hundred years of existence.

The Romanesque style, which is the master design of northern Spain, was introduced from France, but once it crossed the Pyrenees it was subjected to Visigothic and Moorish influences, so that it became something new and peculiarly Spanish, especially in the sculpture that came to festoon the semicircular arches that topped the massive doorways. Of all the beautiful things I have seen in Spain, I suppose I liked best the Romanesque churches of the north. To me they were a form of poetry both epic and elegaic; the rows of human beings carved in the doorways were people I have known; the use of space and simple forms produced an impression as modern as tomorrow; and if on my various trips to Spain I had found only these quiet and monumental buildings, I would have been amply rewarded.

Technically, I suppose one should think of the Spanish portion of the Way of St. James as beginning a little farther to the west, where that remarkable six-arched bridge at Puente la Reina unites the main roads leading down from France. It is one of the most beautiful bridges I know, exactly right for the little town that supported it in pilgrim days. It has two sets of arches, large ones over the river and smaller ones set into the pillars, so that rising waters can pass through in time of flood. The resultant design is so pleasing that I, like many others, have often been content to sit and study its perfection. Thus, at the start of the route we have two handsome structures to serve as a kind of foretaste of what we are to enjoy on this pilgrimage.

I had been gone from the famous bridge only a short time when I saw ahead of me a small town which has always excited both my imagination and my pleasure. It is the only town in Spain where women are permitted to fight bulls, and because its ancient buildings have been so well preserved it is better able than most to evoke a sense of what life was like in the apex years of pilgrimage. It is the little Navarrese town of Estella, and if I were to live anywhere in Spain, I suppose it would have to be here.

Prior to 1966 I had made two other pilgrimages to Santiago de Compostela and on one of them had met the distinguished scholar who now greeted me at the edge of town, Don Francisco Beruete Calleja, president of the Center of Jacobean Studies and leading authority on the Way of St. James. Each year he convenes a seminar of scholars from European and American universities and for two weeks conducts discussions on life along the pilgrims' route.

This year the following lectures were to be offered:

The Cult of the Bull in Navarra, in Spanish
St. James and Charlemagne in Legend, in French
The Way of St. James in Italian Culture, in Italian
Islamic Eschatology in the Sculpture at Compostela, in Spanish
The Way of St. James in Portugal, by Dr. José Filgueira-Valverde, alcalde
    of Pontevedra, whom we shall meet later

On this bright morning Don Francisco took me to the high plateau of El Puy, where on the night of May 25, 1085, occurred once more the familiar miracle: two shepherds saw a group of lights which formed themselves into a star. They said nothing, but on successive nights the star reappeared; so they warned the authorities, who as usual dug at the indicated spot, this time coming up with a delectable wide-eyed statue of the Virgin. The archaic and highly pleasing statue is now enshrined in one of the most beautiful churches in Spain, a silken web of a building constructed of slim stone pillars and wood in 1930 to replace an older one and to show how the Gothic style can be adapted to modern tastes. As one might guess, stars of various size dominate the interior: on the backs of benches, in the chandeliers, on the candlesticks, in the cupola over the ancient statue of the Virgin and in the wooden ceiling. The Virgin of El Puy, as she is called, has always been an object of extreme veneration and in her bright new home, is more so.

But this morning we did not talk about this old pilgrim shrine, because Señor Beruete had other things on his mind. 'Is there a more exciting spot in Spain than this?' he asked. 'Below us the little city with its great wealth of monuments which the pilgrims knew. Around us the rim of hills and small mountains which have always been the protection of Estella. And everywhere the echoing march of pilgrims' feet, by the thousands and thousands, as they came into this important stopping point.'

'If I had to choose one year which represented Estella at its height,' I asked, 'which would you suggest?'

Señor Beruete is a congenial man whose love for the old days shimmers in his eyes, and now he grew excited as he talked. 'Imagine you are approaching the city in the year 1262, when pilgrimage was at its height. Last night you slept at Puente la Reina and early this morning you crossed the bridge. Now as you enter Estella you pass a circle of stout walls and find fourteen separate hospitals and dormitories awaiting you. If you should be Jewish, as many of the business travelers were, you'd find over in that quarter a fine synagogue. It's a church now, Santa María Jus del Castillo, but in 1262 it was the center of a Jewish quarter which occupied much of the city. But I suppose you'd be a Christian, so you'd walk down the Street of the Pilgrims, which still stands, and ask at the plaza, which today looks exactly as it did then, for the best place to stay. If you were a Frenchman, you'd be sure to halt before the carving on the Palace of the Kings of Navarra showing Roland jousting with Moor Ferragut. Oldest representation of Roland in the world. And as you stood staring at it, some fellow Frenchman would take you in charge.

'What did you look like in 1262? You wore very heavy shoes and would probably wear out two pairs walking to Santiago. You wore a linen undershirt with a heavy woolen robe over it. And you displayed the four essentials. Long staff. Gourd. Big hat and cockleshells.'

'How many pilgrims a year might have reached Estella in those days?'

'We had, as I say, fourteen separate establishments for them within the city, and outside the walls a series of large monasteries. On some days a thousand arrived, on others less than a hundred. Who can estimate the total? Perhaps a hundred and fifty thousand, year in and year out. We do know that in 1965, which was a special holy year for Compostela, two and a half million pilgrims appeared at Compostela, but of course they didn't all pass through Estella. Eight hundred thousand, perhaps.'

He led me down into the town and to the church of San Miguel, built around 1200, and there I was to see a carving which captivated me. The door of San Miguel presents the typical Romanesque arch composed of five receding semicircles, each containing a wealth of carving and a chain of human figures. Some critics have called it Spain's major Romanesque work, but I prefer the portico we shall be visiting at Compostela. Here the door is guarded by a large stone panel depicting the Three Marys at the tomb of Jesus. The stone drapery of these figures is extraordinary and the gestures of the women so real that many critics consider this plaque the masterpiece of the doorway, but it was a less conspicuous part that attracted me.

The pillars which support the semicircles are topped by capitals adorned with scenes from the life of Christ. The one which appealed to me was the scene showing King Herod at the moment when his scribes are endeavoring to unravel the significance of the birth of Jesus. It is a tableau so brilliant, so handsomely preserved and so psychologically sound that it seems a marvel. The capital has two faces at right angles to each other, and on the left-hand face a worried soldier reports what has happened at Bethlehem. On the right-hand face two excellently differentiated scribes consult the omens, while on the corner where the two faces meet, a worried King Herod ponders the news. The face of Herod is as fine as anything I have seen in stone, a masterful presentation of a bewildered and anxious king.

Some years earlier, in preparation for a work in hand, I had read almost everything in print about this ugly and fascinating king, and I suppose I then knew him as well as a layman could; but nothing I encountered gave me a better understanding of Herod than I acquired from this statue in Estella. The variation between the two faces of the stone, the penetrating quality of the human countenances and the subtle arrangement of the tense bodies make this one of the finest statuary groups I have seen, and for me it surpasses even the Three Marys.

Estella is so rich in such monuments that one could spend days here, tracing the secrets which have come down to us from the Middle Ages, but at lunch a stray question of mine catapulted us out of the pilgrim days and into the present. The lunch itself was commendable: savory snails in garlic sauce, followed by lima beans cooked with quail. The latter was so good that I would have been content to accept it as hors d'oeuvres, main dish and dessert in one; the squab was flavored with strong country herbs and the beans were so tasty and mellow that they seemed a different breed from the unsavory ones I had known elsewhere, but the meal ended with trout Navarrese, a large firm fish sautéed with bits of very salty ham. When I had finished I asked, 'Am I confused about this? I seem to remember that Primo de Rivera, the dictator of the 1920s, bore the title Marqués de Estella. Did he come from this town?'

I had asked the right question. 'How astonishing!' Señor Beruete cried, his eyes alight with excitement. 'It was my grandfather, defending the city of Estella in 1876, who had the ugly task of confronting General Primo de Rivera. Same name but uncle of the dictator. The government forces were bent upon destroying Estella, which had given Madrid much trouble, but my grandfather worked out a plan whereby the city was surrendered without too much destruction. Because of his victory Primo de Rivera was made Marqués de Estella, a title which passed on to his nephew. José Antonio inherited the title and was Marqués de Estella when he was executed by the Republicans.'

'What was the war about?'

'Carlists,' Señor Beruete said, and that was all.

It was a touchy subject, for Estella had been the capital of Carlist agitations in Spain and on several occasions had led in civil wars against Madrid. The trouble was deep-rooted and began in this way. In 1700, when the Habsburg line died out in the person of Carlos the Bewitched, Europe agreed to the installation of the Borbón, in the person of Felipe V, but only if it was understood that the Spanish and French thrones must never be united under one ruler. To give effect to this undertaking, Felipe V in 1813, as part of the Treaty of Utrecht, which we met earlier when discussing Gibraltar, took public steps to abrogate ancient Spanish custom whereby women like the great Isabel had ruled, and to substitute therefor the French Salic law, which excluded females from the inheritance. So that his intentions could not later be misconstrued, Felipe announced, 'I ask the formation of a new law to govern the inheritance of this monarchy by the male line rather than the female, preferring that the most remote male, descendant of a male, be always put before the closest female and her descendants.' As an additional safeguard against the French it was decreed that to be eligible, any heir must have been born in Spain.

In 1788, when the danger of French meddling had receded, Carlos IV was allowed to take the throne, even though he had been born in Naples, but to be on the safe side he asked the Cortes to annul the Salic law without announcing this fact to the general public, and this was done by the step known as the Pragmatic Sanction of 1789. Spain, although not aware of it at the time, was once more governed by its own ancient customs and a female could inherit the throne.

So things continued until 1808, when Carlos IV abdicated, leaving behind two sons, Fernando, who became king, and Carlos, who had to be content with the insignificant role usually accorded royal younger sons.

Fernando married three times without producing an heir, so it was understood that when he died his brother Carlos would become king; but Fernando, although decrepit and debauched, took a fourth wife who astonished Spain by quickly producing a daughter. Now who was entitled to the throne when Fernando died, his brother Carlos in conformity to Salic law, or his daughter Isabel in accordance with old Spanish custom?

Fernando had compounded the confusion by first announcing, when it seemed likely that he would have no heir, that the inheritance should be governed by Salic law; but when his young wife became pregnant with her unborn child, who might well turn out to be a daughter, he changed his mind and informed the public of the existence of the secret Pragmatic Sanction of 1789, which restored the old Spanish tradition and thus legalized the succession of his daughter. Before his death he changed his mind several more times, back and forth until no one could say where the law rested, and a real uncertainty gripped Spain; but at his death the partisans of his three-year-old daughter were in positions of command and were able to install the child as Queen Isabel II, with effective control resting in a regency. Such a theft of the throne the followers of Carlos could not tolerate, so the fuse of the Carlist rebellion was lighted.

I have dealt in some detail with this matter of the technical succession to the throne as a cause of Carlism, and of course the rebellion was legally rooted there, but many historians feel that this was merely a cover for what was in fact a revolution to the right in Spanish politics. Fernando VII was about as absolutist as a king could be—one British historian calls him 'the most contemptible monarch ever to occupy the throne of Spain'—but even he was not reactionary enough to satisfy the social and religious fanatics of the north, who had developed a four-pronged mystique: dedication to the principle of legitimacy as interpreted by the Salic law; a profound commitment to Catholicism as the one basic principle on which Spain existed; a preference for an absolutist and theocratic form of government (when Fernando assumed the throne they had shouted, 'Death to liberty and long live the absolutist Fernando'); and a determination to force the reinstitution of the Inquisition, which they described as 'that most august tribune, brought down by angels from heaven to earth.'

By a curious accident of history, this religious movement coincided with the separatist movements of regions like Cataluña, Navarra and the Basque lands, so that many strands were tangled in the Carlist flag and no one could be sure of what a given group stood for. The bulk of Spain was moving along lines directly opposed to the Carlists, except for the plank of fidelity to the Catholic Church, so it is not surprising that the Carlists lost their wars. But during the progress of the fight they did create a northern militia, the Requetés, who wore red berets and who were probably the best troops Spain had produced since the 1500s.

The outnumbered Requetés lost their uprisings in 1833–1840 and

1870–1876, but in 1936, when they found that General Franco and his rebellious generals had views close to theirs, it was the Requetés who stormed to Franco's aid, defeating the Republicans in one crucial battle after another. Indeed, without these shock troops trained originally as Carlists, Franco might not have won, so in a real sense Carlist ideals did eventually triumph. Ironically, they seem to have helped their bitter enemies, the non-Carlist side of the royal family, back to the throne, for it is the legitimate descendants of Fernando VII and Isabel II, the daughter whom the Carlists opposed, who appear to be in line for the crown, although which of the descendants will get it no one knows. Prince Juan de Borbón, born in 1913 as the son of Alfonso XIII, now lives, as we have seen, in exile in Estoril, near Lisboa. During World War II, while Franco inclined toward the Germany–Italy–Japan Axis, Juan openly backed the Allies, thus surrendering much of the support he could have had in the present regime. His handsome but weak-willed son, Prince Juan Carlos, was born in 1938 and has since been a virtual prisoner of Franco in Madrid. He is generally understood to be Franco's choice for the throne, although a secret vote among top army officers showed that they preferred the young man's father, Prince Juan. The Carlists seem further removed from the throne than they were in 1833. The direct descendants of the original Carlos lived in exile in France and Austria until 1936, when the last of the line was struck by a police van while crossing a street in Vienna. He died childless, but a few months before, he had issued a document which designated a nephew, Xavier de Bourbon Parma, as his legitimate heir, and this man's son, Hugo Carlos, who recently made news by marrying Princess Irene of Holland, is now the Carlist claimant. Thus Juan Carlos and his Greek wife Sophia have the inside track for the throne, but the hopes of Hugo Carlos and his Dutch bride are kept tenuously alive.

Each year on the mountains back of Estella, the Carlists of northern Spain convene in almost Druidic rites of dedication to the cause of placing their contender on the throne, and it has perplexed many as to why Franco has allowed these demonstrations. Some claim that like a canny emperor he allows first one potential successor and then another to grow strong. As we saw in Madrid, he appears to prefer Juan Carlos and Sophia of Greece but is said to be impressed by the Carlist plank: 'Old-fashioned respect for established principles rather than adherence to so-called new legislation.' But he must be alienated by the Carlists' final plank: 'The various distinct regions with their traditional laws and liberties to exist in a federation.' This is northern separatism under a new name, and Franco will have none of it.

This is the kind of anachronism that flourishes in Estella, and normally I would be opposed, but I found that I liked Estella precisely because it had always been such an ornery little town. If you read the history of this part of Spain, it becomes a repetitive account of how people who were against the government holed up in Estella and fought it out when all others had surrendered. When Fernando and Isabel decreed the expulsion of Jews from Spain, Estella refused to abide by the edict and gave them refuge. When Navarra was subordinated to central authority, it was Estella that led the banner of revolt. King after king broke his front teeth on this stubborn principality, and not even the Moors were able to destroy it. 'For two hundred years the Muslims occupied that mountain over there,' Señor Beruete says proudly, 'and we remained Christian in this valley, and never were they able to cross the river and subdue us.' How many sieges did the walls of Estella repulse? It must have been in the dozens. How many times did it resist overwhelming moral pressures? Ten at least. How many times did it go down to defeat still fighting? A good many. One king hauled his cannon right to the top of a nearby hill and fired point-blank into the city for a week, knocking down churches and cloisters, but still the people of Estella defied him. I can admire such a city, even if I do not share its chauvinism.

Of Logroño, I have only the vaguest recollections, but they are most amiable. My ignorance can be blamed only on my friend, Don Luis Morenés, Marqués de Bassecourt, whom we have already seen hunting in Las Marismas and working in the government at Madrid. On my first pilgrimage to Compostela I had been accompanied by Don Luis, and to travel through Spain with him is an experience for anyone who might have believed that Spaniards were indolent.

Don Luis had us up at seven, offered us a standard Spanish breakfast of one roll and tea, then started us off to the next halting place on the pilgrims' route. All morning we explored the secrets of this dusty and historic path; rarely did we hold to paved roads and rarely have I worked so hard. Since I took no breakfast, I preferred to lunch, but then we were usually in the midst of work, which would continue till about three in the afternoon.

At this time we would head for the nearest large town, where a deputation of scholars would be awaiting us, and for an hour or so we would discuss what we had seen that morning. At four we would sit down to lunch, but the first hour would be occupied with drinks and further talk about the Way of St. James. At five we would eat, remaining at the table till seven, when Don Luis would shepherd us to a further series of towns whose scholars waited in the dark. At eleven we would reach our halting place for the night, and our dinner would be served about midnight, with more drinks and more fine conversation. At two we would retire, and at seven Don Luis would be waiting in the breakfast room with that cold roll and lukewarm tea. I doubt if any of the twelfth-century pilgrims worked as hard as I did under the lash of the marqués, and I am sure none could have seen so much of the road.

Well, at Logroño, which I am told is a fine-looking city, the lunch was

The pilgrims walked, they rode horseback, they used mule carts, but always they passed through landscapes of exquisite beauty.

long delayed but the wait was worth it, for in the interim I was introduced to one of the glories of Spain, the red wine of Rioja. It takes its name from a geographical district bordering a river, but of only one thing am I sure: the grapes that grow in this district have received a special dispensation which enables them to produce as fine an ordinary wine as any I have ever tasted. I liked it as much as the great Châteauneuf du Pape, which I came upon years ago in Avignon and which I have cherished ever since, discovering bottles in strange and out-of-the-way places, for Châteauneuf is widely valued by those who have encountered it.

It was now past five in the afternoon and I had eaten nothing for seventeen hours, when the alcalde of Logroño said, 'You must try our Rioja. We're very proud of it.' It was good.

One of the alcalde's assistants said, 'That bottle came from central

Rioja. Have you ever tasted one from lower Rioja?' I hadn't, but it too was good.

A patriot from upper Rioja now proposed, 'Our wine is the one that travels well, and when you're in a foreign country and want a breath of Spain, order a bottle from our region.' I found it to be extremely good.

There were, I seem to remember, four or five other districts with outstanding qualifications, none of which disappointed me, and after I had done impartial justice to all I was introduced to a delightful newspaperman, Don José Vidal Iborra, who handed me a small book of eclogues that his friend José María Lope Toledo had composed in honor of Rioja wine, the titles of the chapters indicating the somewhat reserved praise that was here sung of this rare wine:

II	Hallelujah
IV	One More Time
V	Rioja and Nymphs
XV	A Poet Meets Rioja Head-on

I was a novelist who had met Rioja head-on, but when I had studied through somewhat wavering eyes this book of prose lyrics I felt that the honor of American letters was at stake, and with my cup overflowing with Rioja, and I use the word overflowing not symbolically (I was holding my cup at a decided angle), I proposed a toast to Rioja and explained in what satisfied me as fluent Spanish that the first thing I had ever written in my life, so far as I could remember, was a translation into English verse of that memorable passage in Calderón de la Barca's *Life Is a Dream* in which a shoeless man complains of his bitter lot until he meets another with no feet, and I proceeded to recite both the Spanish original and my sturdy rendition into English. At the end I contrived a nebulous connection between Calderón and Rioja wine, and although I fear I did not make myself wholly clear, I was roundly applauded, except that Señor Vidal muttered, 'He's got the wrong play.'

I have only the kindest memories of Logroño, and if I cannot remember a single monument in the city or any public works, in Rioja wine I found a friend whose dark red countenance and crisp syllables evoke for me the spirit of pilgrimage wherever I encounter him.

We entered the next town, Santo Domingo de la Calzada, at about nine at night, and I had the good luck to visit the church before I became entangled with the bibulous members of its confraternity, for thus I was relatively sober and was able to see the famous hen and rooster who account for this town's fame. Santo Domingo was a real man who had lived nearby and had attained sainthood in one of the most attractive ways listed in the hagiographies. He was born sometime between 1010 and 1030 and died between 1090 and 1109, but where he came from is most uncertain. Spaniards claim him as a local lad; tradition says he probably came from either Italy or the French part of the Basque lands. At any rate, he felt himself drawn to a religious life and tried to enter various monasteries, but the examining monks found him too stupid. Accordingly, he built himself a small house by the pilgrims' route and from this served the travelers, never seeing them in person, for he considered himself too dull for the great ones to bother with. Where roads were bad, he paved them, and is today honored as the patron saint of all who work on roads. Where rivers were high, he built bridges, and some that he built still stand. Where food was bad, he provided kitchens. And where the sick accumulated, he built refuges. He was as saintly a man as Spain has produced, and toward the end of his life, I believe, one of the monasteries which had rejected him was proud to accept him as a brother.

Often as he worked he must have contemplated that delightful incident which had taken place to the east in the French city of Toulouse around the year 1080, when a German pilgrim and his son were much abused, only to be saved in the end by the miraculous intercession of Santiago. Word of the miracle flashed across Europe and was referred to in many documents from the last decade of the eleventh century, and it so typified the spirit of the Way of St. James that it became in time the Golden Legend.

Three centuries after Santo Domingo's death the good people of his village borrowed the miracle of Santiago at Toulouse and transformed it into the miracle of Domingo at Calzada. Today the story is told in this way:

> A German couple and their handsome young son, from near Cologne, stopped on their way to Santiago de Compostela at one of the shelters built by Santo Domingo de la Calzada. The innkeeper's daughter became enamored of the young man and (in one of my favorite versions of the legend) 'wolde have had hym to medyll with her carnally,' but he resisted her advances. Next morning the family resumed its pilgrimage, but the girl, her love now turned to hate, denounced the son for having stolen a silver cup, which she had secreted in his knapsack. Constables were dispatched to overtake him and he was dragged back to the town and hanged for the crime, but Santo Domingo, aware of the lad's innocence and chastity, kept his hands under the young man's feet and prevented him from strangling. When the parents saw that their son remained alive on the gibbet they went to the justice to ask that he be cut down and set free. The justice, who had at that moment seated himself before a banquet of two roasted chickens, one a cock and the other a hen, replied, 'Your son is no more alive than these chickens,' whereupon the chickens sprang to life refledged and flew off the table. Astounded, the justice restored the young man to his family, none the worse for his experience, and they resumed their march to Compostela.

To this day, on one of the pillars of the church of Santo Domingo de la Calzada chicken coops are maintained; they are decorated with life-size ceramic figures of a cock and hen, but inside, real chickens are kept to crow or cackle during services, and one of the prized mementos that a pilgrim can carry with him from his journey to Compostela is a white feather from one of these living chickens as a reminder of the fowl whose return from the dead proved that Santo Domingo had really saved the hanging boy.

The confraternity of Santo Domingo, whose members look after the church and the chickens, meets in a marvelous old monastery which, since the time of my visit, has been converted into a government parador. I was led to the six-hundred-year-old cavern, which served as the meeting room, by certain members who had heard I was in town, and they launched the evening with some bottles of Rioja wine from a district near their town. I found nothing to complain of, so we tried a different kind and it too was satisfactory. In fact, we tried quite a few samples and they were all good, and I recited again and the evening grew so congenial that the confraternity elected me a full-fledged member; I have the certificate still, proving me to be the only Quaker in history obligated to watch over chickens used in the ceremonies of a Catholic church. For the patrons who will occupy the new hostel I can only wish that they have as much fun in the new rooms as I did in the old.

Of Burgos I remember little. When we arrived at the reception which Don Luis had arranged, we were ridiculously late; it was around midnight, I think, but the hosts had thoughtfully arranged some bottles of Rioja, which was as good as ever. I believe that somewhere in the city there is a statue of El Cid Campeador, who came from these parts. From below, at three in the morning, it looks enormous.

And then the next day, in the mysterious manner in which such things happen to pilgrims, I came upon four solemn events which stunned me with their power to evoke the past. The day started routinely with a cold roll and a cup of tea, neither of which I could touch. Then came an inconsequential thing but one which I remarked at the time as a good omen: we visited the famous Royal Abbey of Las Huelgas (The Leisure Times) whose mothers superior were so powerful that it was said, 'If the Pope had to take a wife, only the abbess of Las Huelgas would be eligible.' I roamed the place with double fascination, for it held an articulated statue of Jesus, which reminded me of Alvaro de Luna's statue in Toledo, and it was to this abbey that Doña Ana de Austria finally came as abbess after her long imprisonment because of her love affair with the demon pastry cook of Madrigal. She seemed very real to me as I studied the stones which had once known the passage of her feet, and I thought how rewarding it was to travel when one had such chances to meet old friends and to review old conditions.

When we left Las Huelgas, Don Luis said, 'I think you'd enjoy it if we got off the paved roads and used the ancient routes followed by the

733

pilgrims,' so we departed from the highway and went through much dust, which I did not enjoy, until we saw looming ahead a small mountain which carried on its crest the walled town of Castrogeriz, which was to be the scene of the day's first adventure. It was an echo of a town, really, a set of near-ruins that had once been great in majesty but which were now occupied by shadows and old people; where thousands had once lived in a busy luxury, a few score now eked out a gray existence. We left our car because we wished to walk into Castrogeriz as pilgrims had done a thousand years ago, and as we marched across the flat and dusty land the city became a shining target. How pleased the hungry pilgrims must have been to see such a magnificent settlement rising in the sky before them! The ancient road climbed the hill, entered the walls and led down a very narrow street. Only a few shops were still in existence; the huge hostel that had once provided accommodations for hundreds each night was shuttered; the mammoth church, once glorious and filled with incense, now seemed close to falling down, and its sacristan was irritable, complaining of the trouble I was causing in wanting to see the gloomy interior.

It was this voice that did it! As I heard the whining I was overcome by the most compelling sense of what it must have been like to be a pilgrim in those days. 'They said its name is Castrogeriz. On a hill. I wonder if they'll let us through the walls? See the townspeople protecting themselves behind their shutters. No food from them. That shopkeeper would cut your throat for an empty gourd. Even the church is closed. But look. That's where they said it would be. The hostel's open.' And into the cavernous building the pilgrims poured, assured of hot soup and a place to sleep for one night . . . if they behaved themselves. As the guidebooks of the time said: 'At Castrogeriz good bread.'

Why should a complaining voice in this inconsequential town have had such power to evoke a sense of pilgrimage? I don't know. Once I had walked sixty miles through this peninsula, carrying a pilgrim's staff eight feet long, and as it swung methodically through the air (the point coming down every eight steps when I was walking fast, every twelve steps when I was tired) I had discovered what it must have been like physically to lug such a heavy staff across Spain; the kinesthetic sense of the staff swinging ever onward had drawn me forward with it. But not even the staff and the long walk had told me much about how the pilgrim had felt inwardly, but here in Castrogeriz, as I swung along the road and into the town, I became a pilgrim in reality as well as in imagination, and from that moment on I was to have a sense of what these distant hordes of people experienced as they picked their way from town to town across an inhospitable land, finding occasionally at some monastery or hospital a friendship so warm as to reward them for all the hours of isolation.

My second adventure that day came in the equally small town of

Frómista, where the serene little church of San Martín, built in 1066, is considered by many to be the finest complete piece of Romanesque architecture on the route. It is so pure and unblemished as to be something of a miracle, and its apse is so cleverly constructed of three interlocking semicircles of white stone as to constitute a triumph of the ordinary. Anyone who believes that stone, to be impressive, has to be ornate Gothic or delicate Corinthian should visit Frómista, whose simple church could profitably occupy a dozen pages of this report, except that in just a few hours I was to savor the essence of Romanesque elsewhere; my more lasting memory of Frómista is of something quite different.

It was, as I recall, a very hot day when I studied this sturdy old church and I did not know where we were going to eat, for I had put my foot down and warned the marqués that I couldn't undertake many more lunches at five o'clock, especially when they were preceded by an hour's investigation of Rioja. Don Luis accepted my caveat with grace, canceled a luncheon in some nearby town and set out to arrange a picnic which we would hold at some convenient spot along the pilgrims' road. I considered this appropriate, since in the old days most pilgrims must have eaten along the way, but as we were standing in the doorway of the church, wondering where to spread our picnic, we were hailed by a singular man. 'If you're going to eat anyway, why not do so in my garden?' he shouted.

It was Father Miguel Bustillo Pérez, parish priest of Frómista, a tall, sixty-year-old man of rugged proportions. He had an impressive manner and a booming voice and looked more like a successful bricklayer than a priest. He led us to his small parish house, in back of which he had a lovely garden with trees and benches, and there we spread our picnic. He supplied the wine and much of the conversation; speaking of the old days in Frómista he reminded me of a friar who might have wandered out of the pages of Chaucer, and as he spoke, so fast that I often lost the thread of what he was saying, I saw in him a revenant of all the hard-working and hospitable friars who had helped pilgrims along this way. When he called to us he had known none of us and was certainly not obligated to extend any courtesies, but his inherent conviviality had made him do so. What was more important, it had made his powerful old church come alive and underlined the significance of my experience a few hours earlier at Castrogeriz. It was a fine, lingering afternoon we spent with Father Bustillo, in his garden, one of our better Spanish picnics.

The day's third meaningful experience started with one of the best things that can happen on a journey: I met an old friend. On an earlier visit to León I had been instructed in its history by a witty scholar-priest, Don Antonio Viñayo González, who looked like a figure from Giotto. He now had the pleasure of informing me that his guidebook to León had just been published; he did not think much of it, but I was to find it one of the best because of its erudition. He said that he wanted me to spend my time in the handsome old church and museum of San Isidoro because of its choice twelfth-century frescoes, well regarded by all historians of the Romanesque style. In one dome I found the best representation I had so far seen of that mysterious religious symbol, the tetramorph, in which the four evangelists are represented, for reasons which I did not then know, by human figures with heads of animals: Mark the Lion, Luke the Bull, Matthew the Man and John the Eagle. Among them Christ sits in starry glory, in robe of faded blue and gold and shawl of brick-red. The frescoes are very medieval, and their state of preservation is extraordinary, this crypt having always been cool and dry.

Father Viñayo pointed out one aspect of the vaulting I had not read about: along one set of ribs the twelve months of the year are represented by peasants performing the chores appropriate for each season: March prunes the vineyards; July is a handsome young man reaping wheat; September makes wine; and October fattens his pigs on acorns. February, alas, which is my month, was a hunchbacked peasant of ugly mien, accomplishing nothing as he warmed his hands at a meager fire.

I was about to leave, well content with what I had seen, when Father Viñayo, with that sixth sense which men who love inanimate things sometimes have, said, 'I think you might appreciate the cloisters,' and he led me away from the vaulting and into as drab a cloister as I have ever seen. It had been built, I judged, in the eighteenth century of a gray stucco and was totally undistinguished. Indeed, I doubt if I could find in all Spain another so unpleasing as this, and I wondered what had gotten into the slim priest that he would think me interested in this mediocre thing.

'It is this side,' he said quietly, directing my attention to the fourth side of the cloister, the one nearest the mausoleum. And there I saw what had happened. San Isidoro had originally been joined to what must have been one of Spain's most grand and somber cloisters, built in the earliest days of Romanesque art, but wars and other catastrophes had destroyed three of the sides, and at some point in the eighteenth century, as I had guessed, a local nobleman had paid to have a new cloister built. Three new walls were put up and plastered in a drab and conformist pattern, where-upon the original remaining side had also been hidden in plaster to bring it into harmony with the others. Thus, without appreciating what he was doing, the eighteenth-century renovator had preserved in a plaster cocoon one of the treasures of Romanesque art. It had been less than ten years ago, Father Viñayo said, that a workman had uncovered the original.

It is difficult to explain what now stood exposed in crystal purity, its stones as clean and white as when they were laid down. It is simply a cloister wall, with four or five arches, I don't remember which, each low, unadorned, tremendously powerful and right, and each different in size and structure from its neighbors. It is a plain wall dating back to the early 1100s, but to me it was the soul of the Romanesque spirit, the secret of what I found beautiful along this pilgrim route. I would rather see these arches than the chapel at Eunate, handsome though it is on its barren plain, or the gemlike church at Frómista, or even the portico of San Miguel in Estella with its marvelous carvings, for those are all the externalization of the Romanesque spirit; at San Isidoro in León one sees the spirit itself, laid bare after years of encrustation.

Why do I like Romanesque buildings so much? Why do I prefer them to Gothic? Or baroque? Or Corinthian? I can't say, but I suppose it's for the same reason that I prefer Brahms to Schubert or Keats to Shelley. When I see a fine example of Romanesque, I feel that I am in the presence of the very best that an age could accomplish, and it was an age that accomplished much. I am at the wellsprings of art, those solid beginnings without which no later art could have achieved much. I am standing with stonemasons who saw things simply and who resisted the temptation of flying off at strange tangents. There is something perpetually clean and honorable about the best Romanesque, and when I see it my whole being responds, as if the artisans who perfected this style were working for me alone. I hear voices singing in plainsong, or the oboes of Pamplona playing without harmony. I am in a different age, with a different set of values, and I find its simplicity exactly to my taste. The separatism of Martin Luther, which is to come, does not yet assault me or confuse. From those first days in northern Spain when I saw Romanesque at its best, I have known that this was an architecture put aside and saved until I should come along; in a strange city I can almost smell on the evening breeze those quarters of the town that house great monuments in this style; but never have I seen any that have seemed more beautiful to me than the recently uncovered cloisters of San Isidoro.

Yet how strange travel can be. Even as I formulated these judgments, which in a sense constitute a condemnation of the Gothic, which I have never appreciated or understood, I was about to be shown this style at its most exquisite, and to have had these two experiences side by side, in a city where I had least expected either, still overwhelms me.

It was a surprise that Father Viñayo had arranged. We dined extremely late, I remember, and it must have been toward two in the morning, when I was about to go to bed, that the marqués said, 'Father Viñayo has a little surprise for us. Are you game?' I would have been ashamed to back down at such a moment, so I accompanied the learned priest into the summer night and walked some distance to León's cathedral. There was a partial moon, and in the looming darkness we began gradually to make out the spires of what Father Viñayo said was Spain's purest and simplest Gothic building. In the night it looked like an ordinary Gothic church, plain yet soaring, controlled but with a certain flamboyance. Its two towers were well proportioned and its transept was prominent enough to be a little cathedral in itself. If one appreciated an unornate Gothic, León's cathedral would be above average but no more.

But as I studied the building in the starry night, with León sleeping around me, one of Father Viñayo's assistants inside the cathedral threw a switch, and from different vantage points around the square, large flood-lights came on, and the sudden transition from shadowy gray to brilliant whiteness was startling, and I saw for the first time the feature that makes León unique among the world's cathedrals: more than half its exterior surface is composed of glass. It is a symphony of windows, and where the ordinary cathedral might have six, León has one hundred and twenty-five, plus fifty-seven circular ones and three gigantic roses. At first sight it seems impossible that a massive stone building could contain so much glass and still stand.

Father Viñayo led us inside, and as we looked up we saw, illuminated from outside, the famous stained-glass windows, one atop the other, then others on top of them. I am not speaking of small windows, but of full-sized ones twenty and thirty feet high, each composed of myriads of pieces of colored glass. The apse was a true miracle. It was when he saw this cascade of windows that the future Pope John XXIII exclaimed, 'León has more glass than stone and more faith than glass.'

As I stood in the silence of the night and the vastness of this huge building, I recalled my conclusions at San Isidoro, and while I did not retract any of my love for the Romanesque, I had to soften my criticism of its descendant. We left the cathedral, and when we were in the street Father Viñayo's helper turned off the spotlights and the great pile of glass and flying stone resumed its posture in the night. If one had to have Gothic, I thought, this isn't too bad, and I turned to thank Father Viñayo for having shown me the windows.

'Ah, but you haven't seen them yet!' he said.

'The surprise is about to begin,' Don Luis assured me, and I wondered what he meant.

Then, as we stood there toward three in the morning, with the soaring cathedral above us in the darkness, the helper inside threw another set of switches, and this time it was from within the cathedral that a battery of powerful lights flashed on, so that from the street we saw what men had never seen before, until a few years ago: a vast cathedral composed mostly of glass illuminated from within, so that all the stones that supported the cathedral were invisible and only the windows could be seen, each one an incandescent jewel of the most intense color and variation.

The Spanish have a saying that sums up their attitude toward religion: 'To appreciate the cathedral you must at least go inside.' Now this was reversed, for to appreciate León one must stand off in the darkness and see with fresh eye the miracle as an ordinary building springs suddenly to life, and with such brilliance that no previous experience with light and glass and stone could possibly compare. We stood in the street,

The eight windows above
are reflections only.

awe-struck by the beauty of the walls above us. We walked three times around the huge edifice, or as far as the streets would permit, and finally we agreed that it was at the apse, with its incredible windows, tier upon tier shining like suns, and its forest of flying buttresses—which explain how the curved space with so little stone remains upright—that León's cathedral looked its best. It is a rare sight, and if I were in Madrid and someone proposed, 'Let's drive up to León to see the cathedral lit from within,' I would not hesitate to make the journey, for to see this thing is to see something so different as to illuminate a lifetime of travel.

I have seen most of the fine sights of the world and know how exciting Angkor Wat can be at midnight with tiers of Cambodian dancers, or the Acropolis at dusk, or Borobudur in a jungle storm, but so far as sheer visual pleasure is concerned, I have seen nothing to excel León's cathedral at three in the morning, lighted from within, and I say this as a man who likes neither stained-glass windows nor Gothic.

On my earliest trip to León, I had had the pleasure of meeting an inventive architect, Alfredo de Ramón-Laca, who had been given the job of renovating a crumbling Renaissance hostel at the edge of town and converting it into a modern hotel to be called the Hostal de San Marcos. 'It'll be the finest in Europe,' he promised me, and we spent a day climbing over the ruins as he explained each step. 'We're putting steel ribs right through the heart of the old building, and when we're through, all the original beauty will remain, but in addition we'll have three hundred bright new rooms.' He was especially pleased that a functioning church, which formed the left wing of the building, would be retained. 'It will be this church which gives the place character.' 'I don't think anybody can make much of this,' I said. 'Come back in eight months and see,' he said.

This year I was able to stay in the hotel that Señor Ramón-Laca had built, and his earlier enthusiasm proved justified, for he had done what he promised: taken a classic building dating back to the early 1500s and preserved its magnificent façade, converting the whole into what is probably the finest hotel in Europe. At least it's one of the most reasonably priced.

I asked the manager to show me his prize suite, and he said, 'We have one reserved for heads of states.' I told him I wanted to see one reserved for the heads of a Buick agency in Tulsa, Oklahoma, so he showed me the Condestable Suite on the third floor, overlooking both a plaza outside and a patio inside. It consisted of two bedrooms, sleeping four people, with seventeenth-century brocaded baldacchinos over the beds, a large living room, all kinds of foyers and two baths. Each piece of furniture, especially the heavy antique tables and the cowhide chairs, was a work of art. The east wall of the suite consisted of the original stone wall of the fifteenth century, gray-beige in color and magnificent in appearance, and all colors used in the rooms harmonized with this wall. The spacious corridors connecting the rooms were once cloisters, and a special feature which attracted me was that the suite connected directly with the choir of Señor Ramón-Laca's church, so that one had what amounted to a magnificent fifteenth-century carved hall as a private chapel, with services taking place some sixty feet below at the main altar. Private to this suite was a spiral stone tower leading to a dungeon, plus a high-fidelity system for playing either popular or classical music twenty-four hours a day, should one desire. The cost of what must be one of the choice suites in Europe was ten dollars a day per person, or somewhat less than the cost of a Spanish-type motel in Tulsa. And to remind one that pilgrims actually used these quarters, along one wall was scratched:

STANISLA° OZEN

KOWSKI. 1,585

The financing of such a hotel is interesting. A National Institute of Industry was established some years ago, using partly governmental funds, partly private. It has three main responsibilities: to provide tourist facilities, and this function is financed one hundred percent by the government; to produce the Seat motorcar on franchise from the Fiat people of Italy, and this is only fifty-one percent government financed; and to build autobuses, which are so important to Spain, and this is financed twenty-five percent by Leylands of England, ten percent privately and sixty-five percent by the government. So far the ventures of the institute have prospered.

One of the pleasures of traveling as I do is that when it is known that I am interested in any esoteric aspect of society, people introduce me to the cronistas and other experts, and now, at lunch in León, I found myself sitting opposite a man who could well serve as an epitome of the scholar in Latin lands, where men of learning find it difficult to make a living when young but find themselves honored sages when old. In America it is the other way around.

The cronista, Don Angel Suárez Ema, was in his late sixties, a big man with a fine expressive face that lit up when he talked, which was most of the time. His sole topic, at least on this day, was the glory of León, for he was also the poet laureate of the city and its cronista. When he spoke he had the capacity to project himself into whatever past age he was dealing with, so that in turn he was a Roman commanding a legion, an impoverished king trying to bind up the remnants of the kingdom, or a princess unjustly treated. To listen to Don Angel for some hours was an exhilarating experience, something like a whiz-bang ride on a historical loop-the-loop. Spain is filled with such cronistas, learned old men who have studied all their lives and who love to share what they have learned.

I already knew a good deal of what Don Angel told me, but one of his stories was new and reflected the spirit that animated the pilgrims' road.

The narrative began with an innocuous question, thrown off by Don Angel in confidence that I would answer it affirmatively. 'Of course you've stopped at Río Orbigo to pay homage to Suero de Quiñones?'

For some unfortunate reason I thought that Quiñones were something to eat and replied that I hadn't tasted them yet, whereupon Don Angel slapped the table with his big right hand, stared at me in disbelief and cried, 'My God, man! You don't know Quiñones?'

'No.'

'The knight-errant sans reproche, except that he was crazy?'

'I haven't heard of him.'

'And yet you make a pilgrimage along his road!'

I asked the cronista to tell me of Suero, the knight-ideal who was a little cracked, and he looked at me with a sort of scholarly love, thanking me for an opportunity to speak about a character who obviously attracted him. 'You understand that in the old days many evil men, especially from Germany and France, infested this road, so that bands of knights were required to patrol it, protecting the innocent. It was for this reason that the Order of Santiago was established, composed of Spaniards. But fine knights from foreign countries formed their own order to protect pilgrims, too, so that along the way there grew up a congenial fraternity. It had, however, one weakness. A garrulous knight, say at Estella, could sit in the tavern, knowing that any competition might be miles away in León, and shout, "I am the strongest and bravest knight on the Way of St. James," and get away with it, while another knight here in León could bellow, "I am well known as the strongest and bravest knight on the Way." In the early 1400s this kind of thing had become common, so one day Suero de Quiñones from a village not far from here decided single-handedly to put an end to the nonsense. He announced, with the king's approval, that he was going to stand for thirty days at a bridge over the Río Orbigo and fight every knight who approached from either direction, which could mean thirty or forty fights a day, until it was made clear who was the champion of the Way of St. James. This was in the year 1434.

'Now, I'm not claiming that Suero de Quiñones was a normal man of the period. For some years he had spent each Thursday wearing about his neck an iron collar which must have caused him much discomfort but which he offered as proof that he would undergo any hardship to prove his love for a lady who did not return it. In fact, the nature of the challenge which he threw down at the bridge was that no knight could pass until he acknowledged that Suero's lady was more beautiful than the knight's lady. He expounded other ideas that were equally heroic.

'As I said, he made the challenge alone, but after he had done so he was joined by nine fellow Spaniards who wished to test the foreigners, and for thirty days these men stood at the bridge and fought all comers. Some chroniclers say that seven hundred jousts were held, which seems a large number, but we do know that Claramont of Aragón died in his fight with

Quiñones, but not because our knight was vengeful. Claramont's horse shied and his own lance snapped and passed through his eye. Where to bury the dead knight? The Dominicans of León wouldn't accept the body, because it had been slain in a jousting unapproved by the Church. And the Bishop of Astorga refused burial for the same reason. So Quiñones himself bought a piece of land next to a chapel burial ground, and we believe that when no one was looking he may have slipped the body underground into the holy burial place.

'At any rate, it was a splendid thirty days, with music and dancing and banquets every night after the fighting was over. Quiñones seems to have won every joust he entered, and it was some years along this road before any loud-mouthed knight dared to announce that he was the most powerful, for all knew Quiñones was.'

Next day, after we had paid our respects to the ancient Roman bridge at which Quiñones had defied Europe, we came to a hill from which we could see the modest but very old city of Astorga, and if Don Luis had at that moment told me that down there I would have the best meal I was to encounter in Spain, I would have derided the suggestion, because Astorga did not look like a place that would have good restaurants. Nor did it. Don Luis said, 'There is, however, this little place owned by a woman whose husband helps her, and it will have something acceptable.' He led us to the Restaurante La Peseta in one of Astorga's little streets, and as I entered and saw one small room and a crowded old-fashioned kitchen, I had only modest expectations. But before we sat down to eat we happened to look into the kitchen and there we found some six or seven elderly women tending a collection of pots which bubbled in a very businesslike way.

'You looking for some real Spanish food?' one of the old women asked me.

'Yes,' I said tentatively, and she took me to her part of the kitchen where she worked at a table positively cluttered with slabs of raw meat, herbs, vegetables and shellfish.

'What would you like?' she asked. It was a hot day and I doubted that I wanted heavy food, but she whispered in confidence, 'Take the lomo de cerdo adobado.' I signified my ignorance and she pointed to a long square chunk of dark meat and to myself I translated the name she repeated: 'Loin of pork adobado.' But what was adobado?

'Is it good?' I asked, for it certainly did not look so, and loin of pork was scarcely something that I would normally order from a menu, especially in midsummer.

'When I finish cooking it,' she began, abruptly stopping and sort of shouting at me, 'Garbanzos, too.'

'Garbanzos?' These are the heavy, tasteless chickpeas which spoil so much Spanish cooking. Garbanzos I did not want, but she took me firmly by the arm and led me to the pot for which she seemed to be specially responsible.

'You have never tasted garbanzos,' she said sternly. 'Now sit down and order some Rioja wine.'

Don Luis asked what I had ordered, and when I said, 'Lomo de cerdo adobado' his face brightened, and while we waited, tasting the Rioja, he said, 'In the old days when I was a boy many families butchered one or two hogs, and when the loins were cut out, long slabs of meat squared on the sides, they were marinated five or six months in a mixture of parsley, garlic, onion, oregano, salt, pepper, oil and vinegar. Then they were smoked until they became one of the best-tasting meats on earth. Michener, you've stumbled into a gastronomical gold mine.'

'But it's being served with garbanzos,' I said, and his face fell. 'With garbanzos you can't do much,' he said.

Finally the dishes arrived. The regular waiter brought the ordinary ones for Don Luis and the rest of the party, but the old woman brought mine, a huge country plate with five slices of pork neatly arranged on one side, plus a heap of garbanzos on the other. As I took my fork, the woman grabbed my wrist and whispered benevolently, 'What you're about to do you won't forget.'

It was not hyperbole. The meat was something unique into which all of rural life had somehow been compressed, for it was both savory and smoky; it was firm to the knife but succulent to the tooth; it had no trace of fat, but the forests of northern Spain seemed to have crept into it, and I have never tasted a better smoked meat. It was, however, the garbanzos that astonished me, and the others too, for when I said how good they were, everyone nibbled from my plate and we called the old cook to bring us additional dishes. She put them on the table and smiled approvingly as we dug in. Softly she said, 'My garbanzos are soaked for two days in cold salt water. They are cooked slowly, and when they are sure of themselves I throw in some salty ham, three different kinds of hot sausages, some potatoes and cabbage, and they stew for eight hours. If you're a workman with little money, you eat garbanzos as your only dish, with meat and vegetables thrown in. If you're wealthy like a norteamericano, you can afford the garbanzos plain. Because I charge you as much as if you'd taken the meat too.'

As the excellent meal was about to end we were visited by the alcalde of Astorga, who said, thinking that I was British, 'We are pleased to have you among us . . . in spite of what happened.' When he had gone I asked Don Luis what had happened, and he replied, 'He was referring to those unhappy days at the beginning of the last century when Napoleon besieged the city and knocked down many of the walls, the time when Sir John Moore allowed his troops to sack the place.'

'Sir John Moore?' I asked, surprised by such an accusation against my old friend.

'Yes. He may be a hero to the British . . .'

'He is to me. To everyone,' and I recited the opening lines:

'Not a drum was heard, not a funeral note,
As his corse to the rampart we hurried . . .'

'Actually, he was a miserably poor general who made a botch of the whole matter. He came to protect Spain from the French but ended by destroying more than the French ever did.'

'Are you talking about the great hero who died at La Coruña?'

'I would advise you not to speak of him that way in a public restaurant in Astorga. Here we remember him as the general who abandoned his Spanish allies, the people of Astorga and the wives and children of his own British troops. Unlike other armies of the time, the English army still encouraged its men to bring their families along, and Moore sacrificed the lot.' He then referred to a book he had recently read, the memoirs of General Baron de Marbot, aide-de-camp of Marshals Murat and Masséna and personal courier of Napoleon. 'Marbot claims that Napoleon lost his world campaign in Spain, and his Spanish campaign in Astorga.'

'But I thought you said Moore was defeated here.'

'The point Marbot was making was sardonic. In the days following the victory at Astorga, Napoleon made three fatal mistakes that ensured his ultimate defeat. He took prisoner the Spanish royal family, which gave us something to rally around. He sorely underestimated the patriotism of the Spanish people, who were not going to be supine like the Italian and German collaborators he had met elsewhere. And worst mistake of all, at La Coruña he killed Sir John Moore, who was the most ineffectual general he faced, thus making way for Wellington, who was the best.'

The purpose of the alcalde's visit had been to extend an invitation to see Astorga's cathedral, but this I did not see, for as we were approaching it my eye was taken by a black-and-white structure so far removed from normal experience that I cried, 'The Brothers Grimm must have built it,' for what I saw was a delightful fairy-tale castle, the epitome of all the towers and moats one has imagined as a child. Yet it was very real and four stories tall. I was about to ask what it was when some detail of its construction caught my eye, an inspired portal that reminded me of Barcelona, and I cried, 'Don't tell me. It's Gaudí!' Don Luis nodded. Only the elfin architect of the unfinished church in Barcelona could have built such a fantasy. 'How did he get to Astorga?' I asked.

And Don Luis explained, 'In 1887 Astorga's bishop was a Catalan, the inspired Juan Bautista Grau Vallespinos, and as you already know, Catalans are cliquish, so when the tempter Gaudí came whispering to the bishop, the latter was inclined to listen. It was from this conspiracy that the grandiose plan developed for building near the cathedral of Astorga a supermagnificent bishop's palace.' The two Catalans dreamed up a building which was not an ordinary religious edifice but the grandest episcopal palace built since the days of the Piccolomini in Siena.

It would be Gothic in basic design, but a grander Gothic than men had seen before. It would have spires and turrets to tease the eye, donjons and mighty winged angels and drawbridges and battlements galore. There would be no flat walls, for each would be broken by arbitrary round towers; only pure white stones would be used, so that the building could be seen from afar, but between them a black cement would be laid so as to emphasize horizontal lines.

Inside, the palace would be as luxurious as the nineteenth century could produce, with ornate halls, complete chapels, audience rooms that would have delighted a Medici, dining salons that would seat scores of prelates, and lesser rooms by the dozen, each its own work of art. The finest contemporary painters, sculptors and tapestry weavers would provide ornament for the palace, and every window would be a masterpiece in stained glass.

Grandiose as the dream was, it came true. When I first saw the result, as lovely as the two inspired Catalans had intended it to be, I liked it, and the more I saw the more I liked it. From top to bottom there is not a false note, on either the outside or the in. The two men who contrived this building were men of vision and joy, but I shall not try to describe in detail the perfection of their construction: the beauty of arch ribs made of red brick with lines of white cement, the manner in which the afternoon sun comes through the tesselated windows, the Moorish arches on one floor, as lovely as anything in Córdoba, the Gothic arches on the floor above, the grandeur of the paintings, and the sweeping splendor of the circular staircases. What I should like to point out, however, is that even in the basement the excellence of Gaudí's inspiration is visible; in fact, it is more apparent there than elsewhere because one least expects it. The pillars are so varied that they have a kind of orchestral beauty, yet each with a function that proves Gaudí to have been well trained in classic architecture. One of the most impressive modern sights I was to see in Spain was this simple yet magnificent basement.

I spent profitable hours studying the place and concluded that it was a monument to the expensive relationship between any architect and his client, for I could hear Antoni Gaudí assuring his bishop, perhaps in the Restaurante La Peseta over a dish of marinated pork and garbanzos, 'Look, Bautista, you're already in up to your neck. Why not find a little more money somewhere and we'll dig a moat around the whole thing.' The moat is there, deep and wide and paved.

Unfortunately, Bishop Grau died in 1893, when construction had been under way for only six years, and work was halted. Gaudí was fired as architect and the unfinished palace stood as a Church scandal. A poor district like Astorga had no excuse for having such an edifice and for years it stood empty. When in 1905–1909 it was brought to grudging completion, subsequent bishops were ashamed to occupy it, but in the 1960s Bishop Marcelo Gonzáles Martín, who many believe may one day be the primate of Spain, cut the Gordian knot and decreed, 'The palace will be a museum dedicated to showing life along the Way of St. James in the Middle Ages.' At last the dreamlike building has a function, which it performs well.

I cannot join in the chorus of abuse which has been heaped upon both the palace and the bishop who authorized it. It is not something that I as bishop would have constructed for a city like Astorga, nor is it a building I would have planned had I been the architect. It is about as unfunctional a structure as one could imagine, and yet, of all the buildings erected along the Way of St. James in the last three hundred years, it and the new church at Estella are the only ones that capture the spiritual grandeur of the pilgrims' way. I believe that the millions who trod these stones in ages past would approve, in a contrary sort of way, of what the two crazy Catalans did, for in its flamboyant yet dedicated style, this bizarre palace represents the continuity of the spirit which animated the pilgrims. A church ought to be big enough to absorb unique personalities like that of Gaudí and Bishop Grau. I for one was totally delighted with their majestic nonsense.

At Ponferrada, on the other hand, I came upon a structure which elicited no delight. There, on a high hill overlooking a network of valleys, which because of the gold and silver they contained have throughout history been of strategic importance, a massive castle was erected in the early eleventh century. Manned by the Knights Templars, it played a major role in policing one of the wilder parts of Spain, but today the empty old building sleeps quietly on its hill, one of the best-preserved ruins of its age in Europe.

Why does the old fortress provoke mournful connotations? Not because of what I know took place here but because of what I can imagine. In the Crusades the Knights Templars played an honorable role, even though they sometimes found it necessary to reject kingly and Papal leadership and go their own way. During a report I once made on the siege of Acre in 1291, the final Christian defeat in the Crusades, I found occasion to study the Knights Templars in some detail as they evacuated the Holy Land in retreat to Cyprus, where they set about establishing that kind of semi-autonomous kingdom which had marked their occupancy of Jerusalem. In the Holy Land they had been too powerful for kings to discipline; they disciplined kings. But now they had come on evil days, so in 1306 the King of France, Philip IV, and his Francophile Pope, Clement V, decided that the time was at hand to exterminate these fractious knights.

Accordingly, in 1307, in what has always seemed to historians one of the worst connivances in history, brutal charges were brought against the

Templars, and dissident members were produced to testify that when they had joined the Templars they had been forced to submit to sodomy, that the rulers of the order expropriated funds rightfully belonging to either Pope or king, and worst of all, that at initiation ceremonies the Mass was said backward and made a mockery.

In hideous manner with fire and torture the leaders were executed. Lesser members were hanged. The rank and file were scourged from their castles and turned loose to wander across the countryside, and by 1312 this once-great order was eradicated, its holdings absorbed by Church and king. Looking at the Templars' castle in Ponferrada, I could not help speculating upon the terror which must have overtaken this mighty fortress when word reached Spain that the King of France and the Pope had found the order heretical and had ordered it dissolved at whatever cost. Which disgruntled underlings, thirsting for revenge, lied about their superiors in this fortress? Which addlepated young men swore that their seniors had forced sodomy upon them or had profaned the host in ceremonial mock Mass? Sitting within the stormy old fortress, I wondered what the death agonies of the last master must have been. Was he one who abjured the order in forced confession or was he one of those Templars who endured all manner of torture to die at the stake in flame and silence?

In my report on Acre, I wrote some fairly harsh words about the Templars, their selfishness and lust for power; but never did I find them cowardly or deficient in honor, and the manner in which they vanished, leaving their embattled castles behind, seems one of the most poignant historical tragedies, and I know of no spot more appropriate for brooding upon this matter than Ponferrada, because in this same region, in 1476, Fernando and Isabel, and more particularly the latter, faced a similar problem and solved it in a more humane way. The Catholic Kings decided that the powerful Order of Santiago, the Templars of their age, had served its purpose; it had defended the weak pilgrims and brought security to the Way of St. James. Now it had become a mighty force generating its own power and direction, and like the Templars, it had to be suppressed; but the Catholic monarchs, unlike the French, brought no shattering charges against the knights of Santiago. Isabel simply maneuvered so that her husband was elected head of the order, from which position he quietly disbanded the knights, and anyone who has seen Henry de Montherlant's moving drama *The Master of Santiago*, dealing with the last legitimate master, knows with what dignity Spain eliminated its equivalent to the Templars.

At unexpected spots along the Way of St. James the traveler finds a crucifix or a shrine reminding him that he is passing through a religious country, or he hears an old legend which recalls the age of faith. Few

To the Spaniard a crucifix is a reminder of the central emotional event of his life.

surpass that of Noriberto, the citizen of Luxembourg, who in the year 1080 joined five other knights for a pilgrimage to Compostela. They composed an oath of fealty, whereby each man volunteered to protect to the death each other, and five swore, but Noriberto, aware that he was not a courageous man, said that he could not. Nevertheless, as a secondary member of the six he was allowed to tag along, and when Felix, the originator of the oath, fell ill in Spain, the others, each eager to be first at the cathedral, forged on ahead, but Noriberto stayed behind to nurse the sick man. Through his agonies Felix called for help, and always Noriberto was there, but in spite of all that he did, Felix died and Noriberto abused himself for his failure. 'I knew I was not worthy,' he mumbled. But when the faithless four reached Compostela they found that Noriberto had preceded them, borne on a white charger by Santiago himself.

At the little town of Villafranca del Bierzo, I was to have two experiences, and since neither was due to planning on my part, they were doubly rewarding. At a roadside café I was accosted by a man I did not know, an English traveler heading in the opposite direction, and he handed me a book which he had finished, saying, 'You might like it, seeing that you're headed west.' It was *Corunna,* written by Christopher Hibbert and published in London in 1961. I was happy to get a copy, for Corunna is the English name for La Coruña; this was an account of Sir John Moore's disastrous retreat through Villafranca and his death in La Coruña on January 6, 1809. For the next hours I was immersed in this mournful history, marking on the map the battlegrounds through which I had just passed; over this terrain Moore had led his disintegrating army, deserted by his disillusioned Spanish allies and harried by Marshal Soult, and the behavior of the English had become so barbarous that I began to understand why Don Luis had spoken so harshly of Moore, for in the retreat, and particularly in the events centering on Villafranca, one saw a rare thing: the degeneration of a British army and the ineffectual efforts of General Moore to hold his remnant together and to maintain them in some kind of decent discipline. The true tragedy of Moore was not the incompetence about which Don Luis had joked nor the burial about which the poet sang, but that he allowed the spiritual control of his army to slip out of his hands.

By the time the English reached Villafranca, discipline had vanished. English soldiers abandoned the English women who had accompanied them; when one woman stumbled into a swamp the men following did not try to help out but used her head as a stepping stone to their own safety. Food depots belonging to the English were looted and those established by the Spanish army were expropriated with no regard for the native troops. Monasteries were sacked; homes were ripped apart; castles were assaulted as if the Spanish were the enemy and not the French. There was murder and pillage and insubordination, and never in the long account of British arms did an army behave worse. Whatever discipline did appear in the ranks seemed to come from German mercenaries serving with the British; what personal courage and good spirits, from the Irish.

A handful of stern-willed English officers did try to maintain some kind of order: floggings were administered, a looter was shot, rapists were ordered to be hanged. But nothing substantial was accomplished, and when even greater tribulations overtook them on leaving Villafranca, the army came close to actual rebellion.

I was interested in what memories Villafranca retained of this debacle, and in making inquiries I encountered a second bit of good luck. I met a distinguished gentleman whose ancestors had owned the castle of Villafranca during that terrible winter of 1808–1809. The Condes de Peña Ramiro occupy one of the surprising castles of Spain, a low-roofed, round-towered structure that looks rather more like an enclosed Norman farm than a castle; but it is so definitely a part of the peculiar terrain of this region that it has an ingratiating charm. It looks, for once, like a castle in which somebody really lives.

The Condesa de Peña Ramiro is a handsome, hard-fibered woman in her middle years, with a face that reminded me of two things: some of the paintings by Velázquez, and those strong-featured Quaker women of Philadelphia who use no make-up except a flawless complexion and a radiant inner beauty. When I presented myself at the garden gate that gives access to the castle grounds, she led me to a cool, tree-shaded part of the lawn, where we sat on old stone benches and discussed many things before we got around to Sir John Moore and the catastrophe of Villafranca. She said, 'I trust you've stopped by our beautiful Romanesque church of Santiago and seen the Puerta de Pardón. It was very necessary in the old days, that gate, because the road from here on to Compostela is terribly difficult. The old and sick who reached this far often knew they couldn't survive the last hundred miles. So we established this door in our church which anyone of faint spirit could enter and receive thereby all the indulgences he would have gained had he persevered to Compostela itself.'

Later she showed me the door, a stolid, heavy thing consisting of five recessed semicircular arches displaying figures in pairs. It was a simple yet very effective portal, with a prudent, peasant-like roof projecting out from the church wall to protect the sculptures from rain. Standing before it, I could imagine the spiritual relief attained by those pilgrims whose strength had permitted them to come this far but no farther; for them the long pilgrimage was over; they had been excused from the final drudgery by a very real pardon.

'What happened to places like this when Napoleon was chasing the English out of Spain?' I asked, and the condesa summoned a young man of the town who understood these matters, and he sat with us through a long afternoon and said, 'For a hundred years the peasants remembered that winter. They looked on the English and the French alike as the enemy, and there was no jubilation when either entered the town. Burning, looting and hunger. When I was a boy old men said that of the two the English were worse, but technically it was the French who were the enemy. It was all very confusing.'

I look back upon the time spent with the Condesa de Peña Ramiro as one of the most gracious experiences I was to know in Spain. The woman was so simple in her manner, yet so profound in her concern about the things that interested me, that to share her information was a privilege. On her dining-room wall hung a portrait of King Alfonso XIII inscribed to the conde; in a corner stood the framed commission of an uncle who had governed the Philippines; old photographs told of old glories that had come to the distinguished family in the nineteenth century, but it was not a family which lived in the past, for the conversation was alive with present references, and I wondered how the conde and his condesa managed this. At the end of our long discussion I asked the condesa, 'From what part of Spain do you come?'

'From Galicia, of course.'

Then her unusual quality became explicable; she was one of those granite-hard Galicians whom I like so much. She came from the part of Spain I was about to enter, a part I had remembered, in absence, as one of the best segments of the Spanish scene; and she was an ideal representative of that region.

But before I reached Galicia I was required to follow the final agony of Sir John Moore's collapsing army as it left Villafranca to try to reach the evacuation ships waiting at La Coruña, forerunners of those later ships that would wait for another defeated British army a hundred and thirty-one years later at Dunkirk.

It was in their approach to Cebrero, the highest point on the old pilgrims' route and surely the most desolate, that the British army suffered its Gehenna. All through the preceding year the army had been pleading with both the English and Spanish governments for money to speed the war, and at last they had got some, but now on the dreadful cliff-lined pass to Cebrero the paymasters had to back their wagons to the edge of the precipice and throw away their funds, a hundred and twenty-five thousand dollars in gold coins, too heavy to carry any longer, and starving foot soldiers had to listen impotently as the worthless gold clinked down the mountainside. It was January, 1809, the coldest part of the winter, and men froze to death in the heavy snow. Women died of starvation and their bodies lay covered with ice beside the road. Horses had to be killed by the hundreds; to save ammunition they were herded to some precipice and forced to jump to their own screaming deaths. At every Spanish village, houses were looted and soldiers would lie down in the ditch, a bottle of wine to their lips, knowing that if they got drunk they would not rise again, but they drank on and hundreds made the noiseless transition from drunkenness to death.

Now, as I stood in this miserable pass, a summer sun radiated from the rocks where low shrubs flowered and it was difficult to visualize the vast debacle that had overwhelmed the British army, one of the worst in its history, but I did take a perverse pleasure from the fact that it was under these circumstances that my hero, Sir John Moore, did finally bring his rebellious troops under control, did lead them on to La Coruña, did stand off a constant series of attacks by Soult, did preserve his men for embarkation upon the ships as planned, and did save for General Wellington's later use in Spain a hardened cadre of men and officers who would ultimately whip both Soult and Napoleon. He, of course, was dead before even the embarkation took place, killed on the field of battle by a French cannonball which carried away most of his left shoulder, exposing the heart and lung. He had lost eight thousand men and himself, but he had saved what he had set out to save: the mobility of the British Army.

During one of my earlier pilgrimages to Santiago I had traversed Cebrero pass in the snow of winter and had experienced some of the misery that had afflicted pilgrims who passed this way. It was night and I was accompanied by Don Luis, who had said, 'It's dark and it's snowing but I'm sure you'll want to see the amazing village perched up there. I doubt if it could be equaled in all Europe.' We left our car at the highest point of the pass and climbed on foot a rather steep hill, at the top of which I saw two flickering lights glimmering through the snow, and it required no imagination on my part to see myself a pilgrim struggling to find a night's lodging. We came upon an extraordinary village, a hilltop cluster of very low thatch-roofed houses unmodified since the days of the earliest Celts. Open fires burned in the middle of the floor and no chimneys allowed the smoke to escape. Wind howled over the place all winter and clouds obscured it much of the time, as they did now. It is maintained in the midst of modern Spain as a memorial to the manner in which hill Spaniards used to live, a huddle of eight or ten houses centering about a low, rugged stone sanctuary which looked in the darkness of night as if it had been built of pinkish stone without the use of mortar. It was unoccupied and unutterably lonely, a rough thing that must have dated far back before the beginning of Romanesque or Gothic. Possibly it was of Celtic origin.

At any rate, in this rude spot I somehow lost Don Luis, and in the snow I spent the better part of a half-hour shouting, 'Halooo, Don Luis!' but I could find neither him nor the footpath leading down to our car. So there I was, as many a pilgrim must have been in the old days, lost on the mountain that had destroyed an army and had caused the despair of millions of pilgrims. It was really a rather bad experience, for the low houses, with no lights or chimneys showing sparks, hid from me and I wandered back and forth in the stormy darkness.

An old shepherd finally heard me and showed me how to open the door of the desolate sanctuary, and there I waited in the dank night till Don Luis should find me. I was standing in shadowy darkness, for there was only one candle guttering behind a pillar, when I heard the shepherd speak from his share of the darkness. He had white hair which showed beneath his cap, and no teeth, but he told a strange story of Cebrero.

'It was during a winter like this,' he said, 'with wind and storm and snow and frozen sheep. A monk was left here to say Holy Mass for any pilgrims who appeared at the sanctuary, but no one ever came except an old shepherd like me. Juan Santín his name, and each day in the storm he would present himself before this altar to hear Mass, so the grudging monk would have to leave his fire and come to this cold place to celebrate the mystery.

'One special night, when the storm was worse than ever before, the monk aspired to stay by his fire, but Juan Santín appeared for evening Mass. It was his only pleasure in life besides caring for his sheep, so the grumbling monk had to leave his fire once more. "Poor me, persecuted me! That I should be driven through the storm just because this idiot of a shepherd comes to hear how I pronounce a few words of Latin before this bit of bread and drop of wine."

'And as he spoke, a clap of thunder roared through the storm, and a great flash of light filled this sanctuary, and on that altar the bread turned into the Body of Christ itself, and the wine in that very chalice which you see tonight, became His blood. And the voice of Jesus Christ said to the monk, "I too have come to hear Mass said this night, for I too am a shepherd." '

The miracle of Cebrero echoed through Spain and France and the shrine became one of the most sacred on the Way of St. James. Queen Isabel was especially moved by it and donated some of the treasures to be seen here now; to me as a writer the old man's story had special meaning, because of all the pilgrim legends told along this road, this seemed the one that applied most closely to the life of the artist. Just as the grumbling monk read his Mass day after day, practically alone, never knowing when he would entertain an audience, so the beginning writer sits alone through many months putting down words which he himself doubts the meaning of, and he wonders if anyone will ever bother to read them. Then, long after they are finished and even forgotten, he may receive a letter from a strange part of the world saying, 'Tonight I was in the sanctuary of Cebrero as I read your words.'

Don Luis finally found me and led me back to the car. In storm we crossed the lonely hills of Galicia and at midnight came to that last small rivulet separating us from Compostela. Here in past centuries guards had been posted to ensure that all pilgrims disrobed for an obligatory bath. Priests claimed, 'It's to clean ourselves before we kneel before St. James.' But wise men knew it was to wash away the lice.

As we climbed the hill beyond the rivulet I knew that from the next high spot the lights of Compostela would be seen, but I was not prepared

Father Jesús Precedo Lafuente.

for what Don Luis did as we rode through the night. 'Mountjoy!' he suddenly cried. 'I am king.' He had revived the most ancient rule of the pilgrims' road, that whoever should first spy the towers of the cathedral would call out in French, 'Mon Joie,' and he would be recognized as king of that group. It is amusing to think that most people in the world with family names like King, König, Leroy or Rex obtained their names because some keen-eyed forebear had been first in his pack to see Compostela.

In the summer of 1966 I was in the city only a few minutes before I received a phone call from a valued friend, Father Jesús Precedo Lafuente, a youngish priest then serving as canon of the cathedral and a man of whom much was expected in the future. He had started his studies at Rome with the Gregorians and had finished them in Jerusalem with the Franciscans. He was a Galician from La Coruña and the best kind of clerical intellectual in that he wrote with professional skill and argued with facility on all matters regarding the Church. As he spoke on the phone I could visualize him as I had last seen him: late thirties, a dark handsome man with Galician features and a disarming smile, the kind of priest on whom the Church in Spain has been depending more and more in recent years.

His message characterized the man. 'Tomorrow's Sunday, and I know you aren't Catholic. This being the shrine of Spain, it's understandable that we have no Protestant church here for you to attend, but there's a good one not far away, and if you'd like, I'll send a car around for you in the morning.'

I replied, 'From the canon of the cathedral, that's more than generous and I appreciate it, but I'd rather spend the time revisiting the cathedral with you.' So early the next morning we set out together to explore again one of Spain's most sacred monuments, and much of what I have to report about Compostela comes from what Father Precedo has said or written about his cathedral.

It is unique in Spain in that it can be seen from four different sides, each set off by its own plaza, all of which are architectural treasures. At first glance, of course, it is the western facade that dominates, not only because it is extremely ornate, topped by two soaring and poetic towers, but also because the plaza in front is the second finest in Spain, ranking only slightly behind that gem in Salamanca. It is a huge plaza, and one night I saw many thousands of people occupy it without crowding. Four handsome buildings delineate it, each with its distinctive style of architecture, so that poets have said that at night one can hear a whispered colloquy among the architectural styles that have made Spain beautiful: Romanesque at the religious college, plateresque at the Hostal de los Reyes Católicos, eighteenth-century neoclassical in the city hall, and the wildly ornate baroque of the cathedral.

If one were to see only the western façade of the cathedral he would have to conclude that it was an eighteenth-century work, built upon the site where a series of older churches had stood; but move around to the southern façade and you will see what might be called the true cathedral. The Plaza de las Platerías (Silversmiths) is a delightful, closed-in, antique little square dominated by the huge bell tower of the cathedral and by this southern façade, which is a pure and stately Romanesque. I could very happily devote much of my time to this beautiful wall, but I have something even more compelling drawing me on, so I shall merely say that to see the cathedral pretty much as it originally was, one must come to this Plaza de las Platerías, where the statue of an insouciant King David playing his fiddle on the left doorjamb is a joyous work, probably the cathedral's best-known piece of sculpture.

The next plaza, the eastern, is my favorite, for from this vantage point, especially from the top of the steps at the extreme right, one can see the great cathedral to advantage. The plaza itself is nothing more than a huge empty square hemmed in by the bleak wall of a convent, some low arcades and the beautiful Romanesque wall of the cathedral, into whose face has been let one of the finest things in Compostela, the Puerta Santa (Holy Door), which is opened only during the years of special pilgrimage and is a sculptural masterpiece. The door is protected on each side by twelve finely carved figures of apostles and prophets and along the top by larger figures of St. Athanasius on the left, St. Theodore on the right, and in the middle the best-known representation of Santiago in pilgrim's attire, with wide-brimmed hat, gourd and cockleshell. When I think of Santiago, I think of this notable figure carved in 1694 by the Portuguese artist Pedro do Campo. The twenty-four figures which guard the Holy Door are active in the life of Compostela. Who stole the widow's cow? 'One of the twenty-four.' Who ran off with the municipal funds? 'One of the twenty-four.' Not long ago, when the university administered an especially difficult examination, one of the students responded, 'For the answer to this question you'll have to consult the twenty-four.' And there they stand, twenty-four wonderful figures from the Romanesque age, clothed in massive simplicity, topped by the three plateresque figures of Pedro do Campo. For a dusty pilgrim to have entered through this beautiful door to the cathedral which had lured him on for nine hundred miles must have been a culminating spiritual experience.

The remaining north plaza, known as the Plaza de la Azabachería (The Place Where Trinkets of Jet Are Sold), would be world-famous if it were located, say, in Toledo, whose cathedral cannot be seen from any vantage point, but in Compostela, where it must compete with three finer plazas, it seems ordinary, for the façade which faces it is a dull baroque affair of jumble and confusion. However, from the steps of the monastery

FOLLOWING FACING PAGES:
The twenty-four figures guard the Holy Door,
which is opened only during the Holy Years.

across the way one obtains a good view of the cathedral as a whole, with its varied towers and turrets, and one can begin to unravel the complexity of this strange monument. The earliest church must have been a wooden affair built shortly after the discovery of the body of St. James in 812, and we know from excavations that it was built upon the ruins of an extremely ancient Roman cemetery which dated back to before the time of Christ. This wooden church was quickly replaced by the stone church of Alfonso II, which was in turn rebuilt by Alfonso III at the end of the ninth century. The Muslim al-Mansur al Allah (Victor by the Grace of Allah) destroyed everything in his invasion of 997. A temporary replacement was erected in the early 1000s, but in 1075 Alfonso VI authorized the building of the Romanesque church which has ever since formed the core of this magnificent edifice. In the early 1100s Alfonso VII and his cantankerous Archbishop Gelmírez completed a cathedral which in outline must have looked pretty much as it does today. To this permanent nucleus was then added one feature after another, the last major change being the erection in 1738–1750 of the tempestuous baroque main façade by Fernando de Casas y Novoa.

All this, one can decipher from the supposedly uninteresting northern plaza, but one can see a great deal more. When I looked up at the pile of figures topping the neoclassical monastery facing the cathedral, I asked a guide, 'Who's the man on horseback?' 'Santiago,' he said without hesitating. But as I studied the figure I saw that the rider was cutting his cloak in two with a long sword and I realized that I was looking not at Santiago but at one of the most popular saints of the medieval period, the jovial Hungarian known as St. Martin of Tours, patron of roustabouts, tavern brawlers and reformed drunkards. And this reminded me that I was standing in what for centuries had been the powerful French section of Compostela and the financial capital of this part of Spain. Just as Medina del Campo had determined the value of international coinages in the Renaissance, so the Azabachería had determined it in the Middle Ages, and through this plaza every pilgrim from northern lands was required to pass when he entered the cathedral. This was where the journey from Paris and Brussels and Stockholm ended. This was the French town within the Spanish town, and to reach the Plaza de la Azabachería and to know that you were again within the protection of French power must have been reassuring.

To see the work of art for which this cathedral is famous you must go back to the main plaza, climb the long flight of stairs to the entrance and pass through one of the doors of the façade. Immediately inside, and before you enter the cathedral itself, you find yourself in the enclosed Pórtico de la Gloria, fifty-one feet long, thirteen feet wide and some sixty feet high, one of the major glories of world art which a week of visits will not exhaust. On the floor there is nothing and on the ceiling only routine carving on the ribs of the vaulting. On the two small end walls, nothing, and on the western wall, which is, of course, the back of the baroque façade, merely a set of sculptured Biblical figures and angels: Mark stands by himself in the left corner; then Luke and John the Baptist together; Esther and Judith; and off by himself, Job. The angels aloft are not noteworthy; those who play trumpets direct the bells of their instruments down toward the observer.

So for five-sixths of this portico there is not much to comment about, but the remaining wall, through which one enters the cathedral, contains such a wealth of sculpture and of such stunning quality that I am perplexed as to why it is not better known. It is a masterwork of Romanesque art, an enticing summary of medieval thought, yet as modern in execution as a painting by Picasso. Psychologically it is profound; humanistically it is one of the most delightful works ever composed; artistically it is of the first order; and religiously it recapitulates the faith of an epoch. But having said this I have still missed the essential quality of this masterpiece. It is fun. It has a throbbing sense of real human beings. It depicts laughter, not tears. It contains hundreds of separate figures and a huge proportion of them are having a good time. The oppressive heaviness of much medieval art is here missing and a kind of jollity suffuses the figures. Even Jesus himself is staring wide-eyed at the world about him and finding it good. The Pórtico de la Gloria is not only one of the world's supreme artistic creations; it is also one of the most human, alive and joyous.

The massive wall is broken by three large arches which give entrance to the nave and aisles of the cathedral. This means that from left to right as one faces the wall he sees, in this order, a corner column, the left doorway over which is a large curved area, then a large composite pillar, then the central doorway and it, too, has a very large curved area above it, then a second composite pillar, then the right doorway with curved area above, and at the far right-hand end, a final column. It is in the harmonious utilization of these seven separated areas—four columns, three arched spaces—that this wall is so superior artistically. Actually, there is a fifth column, because the span of the central doorway is so great that it requires this column for support, and there is no better point at which to start enjoying the portico than here. Observe that I say enjoying and not studying, for this is a wall to be chuckled over, and pedantry would kill it.

The slender central column is, like all the others, built up from separate pillars, in this case five plain ones plus one highly carved. Its base is noteworthy in that it depicts the defeat of Hercules, representing old religions, by Christianity. Two lions who accompany the fallen hero have their mouths wide open for the purpose of admitting light into the vaults below. The carved pillar is extremely lovely. It shows the Tree of Jesse,

from which Jesus sprang, and by itself would be a memorable work. Some time after it appeared at the gateway to the cathedral a pilgrim whose name is unknown discovered that among the vines and leaves of Jesse's tree were five indentations, perhaps put there intentionally by the artist, into which a thumb and four fingers would fit, and it became the custom for newcomers to the church to stand before this column and insert their fingers into the spaces and pray. Now, eight hundred years later, the weightless force of these hundreds of millions of fingers has worn deep indentions into the marble, so that the dead Tree of Jesse seems to have acquired a kind of life.

Sitting on a platform atop the tree is a benevolent statue of Santiago, and with him we begin to discover the characteristics of this massive work, for he is calm, his robes are at rest and are not exaggerated, his hands are big and capable and his feet are the ordinary feet of a workman. His face is almost beautiful in its repose and his cheeks are ruddy, for from the beginning the statues were polychromed, and in 1651 their faces were repainted; now they exude only a faded glow.

With this tender and human carving of Santiago the pillar itself ends. Its capital, extremely well carved, depicts the divine origins of Jesus. Atop the capital, and therefore in the main body of the work, sits Jesus enthroned, showing his wounds and surrounded by angels. This, too, is a remarkably human statue of a patient and loving man, as unpretentious as the Galician farmer or fisherman who probably posed for it.

We were now in the central tympanum, a work bewilderingly rich in images and joy. About the figure of Christ rest the four evangelists in the animal evocations we saw earlier in the tetramorph at San Isidoro's in León and which I could not then decipher. Father Precedo now explains that this tradition stemmed from an apocalyptic passage in the first chapter of the Book of Ezekiel, in which the prophet sees a fire: 'Out of the midst thereof came the likeness of four living creatures. . . . As for the likeness of their faces, they four had the face of a man, and the face of a lion, on the right side: and they four had the face of an ox on the left side; they four also had the face of an eagle.'

Another Church historian told me later that the identification of the four figures came from the recension of the above passage in Revelation, in which John beholds the throne of God: '. . . and round about the throne, were four beasts full of eyes before and behind. And the first beast was like a lion, and the second beast like a calf, and the third beast had a face as a man, and the fourth beast was like a flying eagle.' It was the early Church fathers who conceived these animals to be allegorical representations of the evangelists, but they found no key as to which symbol applied to which evangelist. St. Jerome made the definitive application on the basis of the way in which each Gospel opened. Matthew was assigned the man since his account begins with the human genealogy of Jesus; Mark, the lion, because he opens with the loud voice of John the Baptist crying in the wilderness; Luke, the bull, for the sacrifice of Zacharias; and John, the eagle, for the high-soaring flight of his thought in the prologue.

Outward from Jesus and the evangelists stand eight wonderful figures, four on each side. These are the angels who bear the instruments of the Crucifixion, on the left the column to which Jesus was tied, the cross, and the crown of thorns; on the right the nails and lance, the parchment of the verdict, the jug of water with which Pilate washed his hands, the lash, and the lance with the sponge which carried vinegar to the dying Christ. In spite of the lugubrious mission of the eight angels, they are themselves gentle and in repose. The anguish is past and they hold the cruel instruments in loving remembrance rather than in passion or resentment. In this respect they typify the recurrent theme of this wall, that Jesus has ascended to glory and the world rejoices.

Skipping over the multitude of angels who hover above the Lord, singing and rejoicing, each face a separate identity and all of them delightful, one comes to a unique feature of the work and one of the best loved. It is an outer semicircle depicting the twenty-four elders of the Apocalypse: 'And round about the throne were four and twenty seats: and upon the seats I saw four and twenty elders sitting, clothed in white raiment; and they had on their heads crowns of gold . . . four and twenty elders fell down before the Lamb, having every one of them harps, and golden vials full of odours, which are the prayers of saints. And they sung a new song.' In accordance with this passage, the twenty-four are shown with musical instruments, providing us with a portrait of medieval music: fourteen zithers, four psalteries, two harps, two lutes, plus a surprising device I shall speak of in a moment. They are grouped two by two, not ostentatiously but with rare subtlety, and according to the text they should be singing, but it seemed to me as if they were talking amiably among themselves. My two favorites are the fifth and sixth in from the right. The fifth plucks a lute or some such stringed instrument and the sixth has a harp. They talk together as if they had played in many different bands, and I wish I could overhear the conversation, for the harpist seems much pleased with himself as his fingers strum the strings. If I had to choose two figures who best established the serene atmosphere of this great work, I would take these, for whenever I look at them I chuckle.

If the sculptor had disposed his twenty-four musicians into twelve facing pairs, the top of the semicircle, that is, the point immediately above the head of Christ, would be empty, for the two musicians who bordered that spot would be looking away from each other, and this would be artistically displeasing. The artist obviated this by taking the four top figures in the semicircle and arranging them in this way: the two outer figures have no partners but look toward the center, while the two central figures share across their knees a strange contraption called a zanfoña, the left half of which looks like a large guitar while the right half consists of a series of cranks. It is the world's first instrument for cranking out automatic tunes, or more precisely, semi-automatic tunes, because I suppose the man on the left had to finger the strings in order to insure that the man on the right cranked out the correct notes. At any rate, these four central figures, so disposed and with the zanfoña across the knees, bind the massive composition together in a manner that is positively pleasing.

Of the two lesser arches, the left is a construction of quiet poetry suffused with mystical implications. It is built up from three concentric and receding semicircles, each of which is tied together by luxuriant foliage. The inner circle consists of eight crowned figures accompanying a nude Adam and Eve and a benign Jesus. The middle circle contains eleven patriarchal figures seated behind what could be a stylized table but which is more probably a representation of a massive rope symbolizing the continuity of life. The impression one gets from this beautiful arch is order, dignity and a mass of men living together within the boundaries of nature. An undocumented tradition claims that this arch represents the Jewish concept of life as it flourished before the coming of Christ and is a fantasy lifted from the apocryphal Book of Enoch. If so, it contains one of the gentlest commentaries on Judaism ever constructed by a Christian artist, in that the whole archway of Judaism is linked to the central archway of Christianity by a simple, symbolic device. What do you suppose it is? Two little children holding a long parchment indicating the New Testament, which the Jews merely have to accept to be saved.

The right archway is a much different matter. Here the artist is dealing not with alien Jews whom he hopes to conciliate but with Christians who ought to know how to behave within the body of the Church. The right half of this arch is a terrifying depiction of those condemned at the Last Judgment. In the quaint English which is apparently obligatory for all guidebooks in Spain: 'To the right, small reptiles and horrible big monsters harass and tear off the flesh of men, slaves of vice, with their claws and fauces. It is surprising the Dantesque expressiveness of this composition.' The left portion, that is, on the right hand of God as He and His son sit in judgment, are the saved, and they are a happy lot. I have studied this great arch for many hours, finding in it always something new and compelling, but in the end I think the excellence of the work can be reported in two facts: here paradise seems really more to be preferred than hell, which is not always the case in medieval and Renaissance art; and the conspicuous aspect of this work, an aspect not before commented on by writers but one surely planned with much care by the artist, is that we see both hell and heaven through the eyes of little children who share the torment and the glory with their guilty or saved parents. The children shown in this panel are among the finest ever portrayed in art, and I cannot praise them highly enough. In hell they perish in dreadful agony, and in heaven they rejoice with parents who love them, making each aspect more psychologically believable. Spanish religion features this involvement of children in the faith, and one of the most fearful aspects of the Inquisition was that it insisted upon the display in the parish church of a condemned man's sanbenito for at least ten generations with his name clearly upon it, the purpose being to condemn that man's children throughout those same ten generations. It could well be that this harshest of the Inquisitional laws stemmed from this right-hand arch at Compostela; at least, it was an extension of the majestic idea here represented, that heaven and hell are more meaningful when seen through the eyes of children.

Again, just as the Jews were offered salvation through the intervention of two small children, so in this panel the saved are led into paradise by two other children who show the way into the central archway.

We have now seen the six walls of this remarkable portico and more than a hundred and eighty-five different figures, but we have not yet come to the feature which has always been its chief claim to artistic fame. About the four principal columns are ranged, their feet resting at about the eye-level of the viewer as he studies them, sixteen life-sized statues of men in robes, and no matter how much one enjoys the twenty-four bearded musicians or the children of the Last Judgment, he must finally admit that this parade of splendid men is the highlight of the wall.

They are unbelievably well carved, tall, bending slightly forward, extremely human in aspect and mobile of face. Tradition says that each was modeled after a specific man who lived in Compostela at the time, and I find this easy to accept, for this gallery of men could not have happened by either accident or imagination. They are so real they could speak, yet so artistically contrived that in their silence they sing, and to have seen them intimately, day after day and in all lights is to have shaken hands with the Middle Ages.

Meet them. On the left-most pillar, below the world of the Jews, stand long-bearded Joel and quizzical Abdias. ('What name do we know Abdias by?' I ask Father Precedo. 'Abdias,' he replies. 'Everybody knows him by that name.' Back in America I would learn that he was Obadiah of the King James Bible, Abdias of the Douay.)

On the left-hand edge of the first main column stand Hosea, who had such a miserable time with his wife, and Amos. The remaining portion of this column contains the most famous of the sixteen. Jeremiah is properly grave and heavy, but Daniel is a young, beardless man with one of the most ingratiating smiles in the history of art. Standing on one leg with the other playfully crooked at the knee, he seems like a schoolboy about to play some mischievous trick, and he is by far the most popular of the figures in the procession. Since his roguish grin is directed across the portico to the enchanting figure of Queen Esther, who faces him on the opposite wall, tradition says that one of the self-righteous kings of northern Spain directed that Esther be made to appear less attractive, for she was disturbing the propriety of the cathedral, whereupon the artist shortened her nose and made other alterations, without much success, for Daniel still gives her the merry eye.

Next to Daniel comes my favorite figure, an old, smiling Isaiah, heavy with beard and marked by a golden cap, which none of the others wear. To me it seems no great accomplishment for a young man like Daniel to smile; but it is reassuring when old Isaiah with his burden of prophecy should still be able to raise a muffled laugh. Beside him stands Moses with the tablets, and his burden of law is so heavy that he cannot smile.

On the comparable portion of the main right-hand pillar stand Peter with his massive keys, Paul with a book, James the brother of Jesus, and John the Divine, also beardless and with a face of heavenly purity. He seems wide-eyed with surprise that revelation should have been accorded him, but he is not ponderous about it. On the smaller portion of this column, and facing the arch of the Last Judgment, stand solemn Matthew and conversational Andrew, while in the corner, on the last of the pillars, stand heavily bearded Thomas and preaching Bartholomew.

It is a magnificent parade from which Judas Iscariot is missing. The Middle Ages found it objectionable to picture him in such scenes, so he is often omitted. But the others march in a grandeur which seems the more impressive because of its compelling simplicity. With their appearance we leave the Pórtico de la Gloria, but not before we notice one small detail.

I spoke earlier of the angels who appear on the west wall of the portico and of how the two bearing trumpets direct them down as if playing for the delight of the observer. At each end of the opposite wall, which contains the Gloria, appears an additional angel so placed as to form part of both the Gloria and the end wall, constituting a harmonic link between the two unequal halves of the composition. They, too, point their trumpets below, and if you look at these four figures, who form a kind of thematic material for the whole composition, you realize that they are trumpeters announcing the day of resurrection, and they are summoning you to that paradise where music and joy and laughter and winking saints and beautiful queens and the benevolence of children abound, and you may well recall the John Donne sonnet on this theme:

> At the round earth's imagined corners blow
> Your trumpets, angels, and arise, arise
> From death, you numberless infinities
> Of souls, and to your scattered bodies go,
> All whom the flood did, and fire shall o'erthrow . . .

What of the cathedral itself? Could any church be worthy of such an entrance? At Compostela the interior is about what it should be, if one thinks of this building as the spiritual center of a religious nation. It is beautifully Romanesque and cluttered with just enough paraphernalia to remind one that this is Spain. In spirit it is very warm, in aspect majestic, and in its operating manifestations devout. The first thing one encounters inside the church itself is a statue to the man who carved the portico, for the intricate work which I have just described appears to have been accomplished by one man whose name is known: Maestro Mateo (in Galician, Mestre Mateu), a Spaniard who worked in northern Spain during the last third of the twelfth century. Documentary records state that he finished the portico in 1188 and it is supposed that it occupied him for about twenty-five years. His statue, which he may have carved himself, is a properly jaunty thing whose head is covered with lively stone curls, and through the centuries it has been the custom for all who visit Maestro Mateo's supreme work to bow before the kneeling statue and to touch one's head against his in hopes that some of his genius may rub off. O Santo d'os Croques, he is known in Galician, the Saint of the Bumps, and I, like many others, have touched my head against his, hopefully. When I reflect that this great artist is generally unknown, while much lesser figures of the Italian Renaissance are treasured as geniuses, I wonder at the unfairness of history, for to compare Maestro Mateo with those lesser but more famous artists is like comparing the Himalayas with the Poconos of my home district. The Poconos are lovely, for sure, but to mistake them for the Himalayas is an error.

I was fortunate in reaching Compostela at the precise point in the year when I could best witness the significance of the town and its cathedral in Spanish life, for El día de Santiago (The Day of St. James) occurs each year on July 25 and is the occasion for a religious celebration of great dimension. Toward midnight on the evening of the twenty-fourth it seemed as if everyone in the city had crowded into the plaza before the cathedral, where for two days workmen had been hiding the façade behind a huge wooden imitation featuring a panel with the words 'Al Patrón de España.' Now, at eleven, two large rockets were sent aloft to explode with a force so strong that my coat was lashed by the following blast of air. Then to constant applause one rocket after another lifted into the air for about half an hour. I had noticed earlier that this display, which had been publicized during the preceding week, was to be in the hands of a firm from La Coruña, and since the best fireworks are generally considered to come from Valencia, I expected little, and during the first half-hour saw nothing to make Valencia worry.

But after the regulation rockets had been fired, those that exploded in shimmering white or red, the good men of La Coruña let go. On a series of wagon wheels stuck on poles about the plaza they set loose some contraptions that were dazzling, each consisting of at least eight radically different sequences timed to explode one after the other over a period of at least two minutes, so that one wondered how the first charges could ignite without detonating the others. While the crowd was marveling at this, the La Coruña men produced their specialty: a large rocket which climbed in a zigzag pattern to about a hundred yards in the air, then stopped, dashed off parallel to the earth for a hundred yards, where it died in a soft hissing sound, but when it had almost reached the earth it gave forth a huge burst of flame, another rocket fired, and the whole thing went back into a giant orbit that took it higher than before, ending in a loud explosion and a blaze of multicolored lights. It was quite a rocket, much more complex than anything Valencia had shown, and the crowd cheered.

But there was still more! On a distant building far across the plaza a brilliant ball of light began to blaze, and on a thin wire that none of us had noticed before, it sped in wild flight some two hundred yards and crashed directly into the false façade of the cathedral, after which it sped back up the wire to the point at which it had begun; but few saw its journey end, because when it struck the cathedral the entire false front burst into flame and for at least four minutes we saw such a popping of lights, such a rain of rockets and such a confusion of colors that no eye could possibly have followed all that was happening. The whole cathedral seemed to be ablaze, and at the end some sixty standing rockets were automatically ignited and these went off in all directions, filling the sky with flaming color.

Apparently the residents of Compostela are more accustomed to fireworks than I, because next day the local newspapers reported that 'the traditional illumination of the façade went off as usual with nothing special to report.'

At dawn on the twenty-fifth, large black limousines begin to arrive at the Hostal de los Reyes Católicos. In the early 1500s this had been the foremost hospital in the world, a center of medical learning reputed to be without equal, for it had been established by Queen Isabel and King Fernando as a refuge for those many pilgrims who reached Compostela in a state of exhaustion after negotiating the pass at Cebrero and the bitter mountains of Galicia. Now the majestic building, constructed around four different courts, each an architectural masterpiece, serves as a luxury hotel, and in its spacious lounges the early-morning visitors munch cakes and fruit with their coffee.

They are politicians from Madrid and officers from the naval base at El Ferrol del Caudillo, the Galician birthplace of Generalísimo Franco at the northwest tip of Spain. Spaniards say that if Franco had been born one step farther west, he'd have been a norteamericano.

By midmorning the plaza is filled with army units in brown uniforms, accompanied by a competent brass band which plays marches. A small cannon booms out a nineteen-gun salute to Santiago, a military greeting to a military saint, which is not surprising in a land where in 1962 the mummified left arm of Santa Teresa, during a grand tour of the nation, was officially received in Madrid with the military honors due to a 'captain-general in active command of troops.' Additional dignitaries appear in full morning dress, and soon one portion of the plaza is filled with handsome-looking men in various costumes, all prepared to pay homage to the great saint who had led the nation to victory over the Moors, over the Incas and Aztecs and over most of the armies of Europe.

At ten a large parade forms, composed of military units, the civil officials, red-caped priests and green-clad members of the Guardia Civil. These march about the plaza in a show of national solidarity before heading for the cathedral, where at the Pórtico de la Gloria a mitered bishop in red waits to grant permission to enter, and all bow to kiss his hand.

I have not previously mentioned the extraordinary size of the cathedral, but this parade of several hundred led by a brass band will be absorbed in the vast expanse of pillar and chapel without causing much stir. On this day the interior is redolent of past glories: enormous throngs of worshipers crowd the aisles while the massive organ thunders out Bach's Toccata and Fugue in D Minor. Prior to the entrance of the parade a tall priest leads four men clothed in red in a procession that moves along all aisles and transepts of the church. They bear on their shoulders an ornate reliquary containing a statue and memorials of St. James the Less, and on his statue one sees a highly decorated silver collar which has a most curious history: it was given to the cathedral in 1435 by that same Suero de Quiñones who held the bridge over the Orbigo for thirty days. And as this strange gift makes its slow way through the cathedral, it passes the chapel in which hangs the bejeweled pendant delivered later by an equally famous Spaniard of the heroic age, Don Juan de Austria, who came here on pilgrimage after his crucial victory at Lepanto. In the left transept the relics pass the little chapel of St. Andrew, where a niche was recently let into the wall to house a sickly-sweet modern statue of the Virgin dressed in robes of pale blue and white and framed by a bouquet of asters and white lilies. A halo of small electric lights illuminates the head of this very popular statue, for even now with the procession in full swing a group of women prays before the shrine. Before each woman kneels she takes from beside the Virgin a printed slip of paper, and with a pencil hanging from a cord ticks off the subjects in which she is most interested, depositing the marked slip in the prayer box:

9. Peace in the family.
10. A termination to a bad love affair.
16. Success in studies.
23. Peace in the world.
25. For the unity of all Christians.
29. Reconciliation of a married couple.

The niche in the wall has a special appeal to women because the statue of the extremely beautiful Virgin was given by Evita Perón.

Now the procession from outside the cathedral has completed its entrance, and as it moves down the right aisle the organ produces a new song, and eight men in red robes move into action, ready for an exhibition seen in no other cathedral in the world.

Two bear on their shoulders a massive pole from which hangs an iron censer about three feet high. Silver-plated and of a handsome design, it was made in 1850 by the silversmith Losada and is the most recent of a long line of Botafumeiros (Smoke-Throwers) to have been used in this cathedral.

The other red-clad men are busy with another detail. From one of the nearby pillars they have released a very stout hempen rope possibly three inches in diameter and a couple of hundred feet long. This rope reaches up to the highest part of the cathedral, where it passes over a complicated system of pulleys, dropping down so that the Botafumeiro can be attached to its loose end, which is passed through a huge iron ring at the top of the censer and securely lashed. The eight men then grab the other end of the rope and slowly pull the huge object a few feet in the air.

A priest now opens the top of the contraption and pours inside a large bucketful of charcoal and incense and gives the censer an initial swing to start it moving. What happens next I do not understand, but by a series of skillfully timed pulls on their end of the rope, the eight men succeed in getting the great silver chalice to swing in ever-growing arcs until at last, in an unbelievable surge of power, the enormous thing is flying right up to the ceiling of the cathedral some ninety feet away, hesitating there a moment, then roaring down with sickening speed, skimming over the heads of watchers, only to be held in restraint by the rope and swung up to the ceiling on the other side. And as the huge thing flies through the air, perforations admit a flow of air and set the charcoal ablaze, so that sparks fly out in the swift descent and incense fills the cathedral. It is a most extraordinary sight, a thrilling display of motion, power, fire and mystery.

I ask Father Precedo what all this signifies, and he says, 'The people like to believe that the custom started in the Middle Ages when thousands of pilgrims slept in the cathedral and smelled up the place. The incense was supposed to be a germ killer. Actually, the custom may have started in the time of our great Archbishop Gelmírez, who did everything possible to maintain the credentials of Santiago de Compostela on a par with those of Rome. He probably invented the huge censer as a gesture of Compostela's uniqueness within the Church.'

The men who pull the ropes are employed as caretakers by the cathedral, and their origin, according to legend, antecedes that of the present building. When Alfonso III was king of the north, Bishop Adaulfo of Compostela was accused by three men of the village, Isadón, Cadón and Ensión, of 'nefarious vices too ugly to be announced.' The king's judgment ordered Adaulfo to be thrown before a wild bull, but when this was done the animal, knowing that the bishop was blameless, came and placed his

Elaborate rituals are maintained in the smaller chapels of the cathedral for the sanctification of pilgrims who come from parts as far away as Denmark and Turkey.

head in the good man's hands, whereupon the king thundered, 'Isadón, Cadón and Ensión and all their offspring are sentenced to perpetual servitude at the cathedral which they have shamed.' It is their descendants who pull the ropes.

Now they stop, for if they continued they'd send the censer banging into the ceiling and then down into the crowd, as happened in 1499 when ill-fated Catalina, youngest daughter of Fernando and Isabel, stopped here on her way to London to marry Arthur, Prince of Wales. Again in 1622 the Botafumeiro fell, landing in the middle of a large crowd without injuring anyone.

It is now time for the solemn high Mass celebrating Santiago as patron protector of Spain, and what happens next is so strange to Americans reared on a theory of separation between Church and state that I had better translate a portion of the speech which Admiral Francisco Núñez Rodríguez makes to the massive stone statue of Santiago, addressing him personally as if he were present in his role of Matamoros:

> Glorious Apostle of Spain, Señor Santiago, in obedience to the most honorable responsibility given me by the Chief of State, I come here to present you with the traditional offering whereby our people wish to testify to their gratefulness for the protection and aid which they continue to receive from you.
>
> Spain will never forget that she received the Light of Faith and the Doctrine of Christ from your lips nor that you selected these marvelous lands of Galicia for the repose of your glorious remains. Every year on this day we come to hear your message of apostolic impatience, which is like a sunrise testimony which reaches into our blood and fills it with fidelity and missionary zeal.
>
> It was in continuance of your example, O Glorious Apostle, that in the past we sanctified our power and sublimated our ambition, orienting them toward difficult enterprises like the recovery inch by inch of our national heritage and the evangelization of half the globe. A new world we brought you, and later an eighth part of the earth.
>
> We will never permit either error or false doctrine to snatch away our great treasure of Religious Unity, the foundation of our political and social unity, which thanks to you, O Glorious Apostle, we have enjoyed during these past thirty years.

Mighty and tall in his red robes and biretta, Cardinal Fernando Quiroga Palacios, primate of Santiago, and because of the advanced age of the Cardinal of Toledo, president of the council of cardinals governing the Church in Spain, replies on behalf of Santiago, accepting the homage of Spain and promising that as long as the nation is faithful it shall prosper. At this moment the pealing of the organ, signifying the majesty of government, is joined by the sound of bagpipes marching into the cathedral on the shoulders of the common people. All Spain appears united under a single banner, that of Santiago, and dedicated to a single ideal, that of the Catholic Church.

At this point it is appropriate to consider the role of the Church in modern Spain, and I shall be drawing only upon conversations conducted outside of Compostela. The central fact of Spanish history in the past five hundred years has been the country's willingness to sacrifice for the welfare of Catholicism, and if one doubts the sincerity under which Isabel, Cisneros, Carlos V and Felipe II did so, there is no chance for him to understand Spain. The cost in gold, in armies, in commerce and in freedom has been stupendous; the rewards have been a sense of mission and the building of a nation committed to one Church. Most Spaniards deem the bargain to have been a good one and the cost not excessive. In various parts of Spain I was told what I believe to be true: 'Eighty percent of the men of Spain, as contrasted to the women, inwardly ridicule the involved ritual of the Church, but of those who scoff, eighty percent would take arms to fight anyone who tried to change our religion to something else.' One fatal miscalculation of the Republic in 1936 was its underestimation of the number of Spaniards who would defend Catholicism if it were threatened.

The next point is difficult to explain, for although Spain has been the chief defender of the faith, it has often given popes a bad time. Fernando and Isabel were not loath to rebuke the Pope when he issued edicts they didn't like. Stout Gelmírez, Archbishop of Compostela, openly opposed the popes of his day. Many a law promulgated by Rome was denied proclamation in Spain, for Spaniards have usually done pretty much as they like in governing their Church. Even today the Pope has a more difficult time appointing a bishop in Spain than in any other country where the Church is recognized, for the government, in consultation with the Papal Nuncio, draws up a panel of six acceptable names. These are submitted to the Pope, who designates the three who are most acceptable to him, and from this list the Spanish government selects its new bishop. In many parts of Spain, as we have seen, the memory of Pope John XXIII is poorly regarded and his more revolutionary ideas of ecumenism are opposed by at least half the clergy. It is common to hear a Spanish priest say, 'It is now the role of the Spanish Church to save Rome from itself.' What percentage of the ecumenical reform of the past decade will operate in Spain remains to be seen.

The extent to which the Church dominates civil life is often surprising to visitors. Marriage, family life, education, publishing, health and motion pictures are only a few of the areas in which religious control is supreme. The Church is vigorously supported by the other members of the ruling triumvirate, the army and the landed families, and by the Guardia Civil and the police as well. A citizen is ill advised to tangle with any agency of this group, for the others will jump on him. A man I know was visiting Valencia when a religious procession passed and he alone of the bystanders refused to rise and doff his cap as the Virgin went by. He was arrested and asked by the police, 'What are you, some kind of a radical or something, not paying homage to the Virgin?' He escaped serious trouble only by claiming that his knee had been damaged in an automobile accident. He was warned that in the future he must be more worshipful.

This kind of interlocking directorate between the right-wing politicians and the Church has existed for two centuries and explains why, at recurring intervals, the people of Spain, judging the Church to be indifferent to their needs, have risen blindly to slay their priests and burn their churches. This has happened so often and in such identical patterns that one must consider the killings and burnings following the outbreak of the Civil War in 1936 as merely the latest in a doleful sequence. It is misleading for the Franco government to place marble tablets in churches proclaiming that it was Marxists who killed the priests. Most of these atrocities occurred months before Marxists were in control and should more accurately be considered a typical explosion of Spanish resentment. One incident not related to the war typifies those that were. In July, 1834, a cholera epidemic threatened Madrid, and when a rumor spread that Jesuits and friars had been poisoning wells, a mob swarmed into the Puerta del Sol and fanned out to burn churches and slaughter more than eighty friars and monks. In 1835 similar burnings and killings broke out, almost as if by prearrangement, in all the major Spanish towns.

During the Civil War it was natural and necessary for the Church to ally itself with the army and the landholders, but the continued alliance for more than thirty years has encouraged the lower classes to believe that the nineteenth century is being repeated and that the Church continues to be their enemy. This is why many younger priests and possibly half the seminarians want to create a Church which is divorced from the army and landholders. In Barcelona, as we have seen, priests agitating for social liberalism were clubbed publicly by the police and won much sympathy from the public. In Sevilla sixty seminarians struck for a more liberal interpretation of Church law. In Madrid priests wanted to know what was being done to implement the decisions of the Ecumenical Council, and petitions were circulated within the Church. I never knew, when I began talking with Spanish priests, what unpredictable thing they might say, and among them I found a wider spectrum of opinion than I do among my neighbors at home. Older men seemed determined to keep Spain as it has always been and to defend the country against what they regard as the recent errors of Rome; some of the younger men were surprisingly outspoken liberals.

The recent ruling which permits a degree of freedom for non-Catholics is more significant than would at first appear, and frankly I did not expect such liberalization so soon. Only a few years ago a Protestant chaplain at an American military base was arrested when he held a Sunday School picnic in an open park, for this was held to be in violation of the law forbidding any religion other than Catholicism to conduct ceremonies or meetings for worship in public, yet I have explained that when I arrived at Santiago de Compostela, the very heart of the Church in Spain, the Church itself offered to facilitate my attendance at a Protestant chapel. And when I was last in Madrid the newspapers carried long illustrated accounts of the ordination of a native-born Protestant bishop, but with the caption 'Married and with two children.'

Spain will remain Catholic, more completely so than either France or Italy; newspapers will continue to report ecclesiastical developments as headline news; and the Church will continue to be a major force in the land. But a lively argument within the Church will determine the social and political course it will take. For example, during my last trip Spanish newspapers were giving an inordinate amount of coverage to discussions in the Italian parliament of a limited divorce law. I asked, 'Why this sudden interest in Italian politics?' and a newspaperman told me, 'We don't give a damn about Italy. But we're much interested in the attempt of a Catholic country to get a workable divorce law. We're forbidden to discuss a Spanish law. So we write about Italy as if it were Spain. Everyone understands.'

As for the grandiloquent exhibition at Santiago de Compostela on El día de Santiago, the outside observer has the suspicion that whereas the oligarchy want desperately to believe that the present system will prevail permanently, they have not convinced the general population. When Admiral Núñez thunders, 'We will never permit either error or false doctrine to snatch away our great treasure of Religious Unity,' he is voicing more a hope than a fact. If religious unity continues only as it is, the handmaiden of those who rule, it must eventually be challenged; but if under the pressure of younger priests it can change and adjust itself to the spirit of Pope John XXIII, there could be real hope that in the next time of change the churches and the monasteries will not be burned.

It is rewarding to visit Compostela at any time, but in Holy Years— that is, any year in which July 25 falls on a Sunday—there are additional inducements, for then northern Spain holds continual festival in honor of Santiago. The Holy Years fall in an endless sequence of 6-5-6-11, and since the last occurred in 1965, the next will fall in 1971 and 1976. I asked Father Precedo specifically, 'Are non-Catholics welcomed here during a Holy Year?' and he gave me a document which showed that during the preceding celebration the senior government official in Galicia had been Mohammed ben Mezian bel Kasem, a Muslim from Spanish Morocco. 'If we can tolerate a Muslim at the spot where Santiago went forth to battle the Moors, we can surely welcome Protestants.'

There were long periods when Holy Years meant little at Compostela. In the early 1600s, after more than seven hundred years as the spiritual center of northern Europe, it fell on bad times because of an English pirate and a French king. In 1589 Sir Francis Drake put together a large fleet with fourteen thousand soldiers, with the announced intention of destroying Santiago, 'that center of pernicious superstition.' As his armada approached the Galician coast, priests hid the bones of Santiago, and when Drake retired, the location of the once-famous grave was forgotten.

In 1681 King Louis XIV declared that thieves and pickpockets and false priests were so brazen in their robbery of pilgrims that no Frenchmen would henceforth be allowed to make the journey. Cynics suggested that what Louis was really trying to do was to cut off the flow of money and trade goods into Spain, and he succeeded.

For the next two hundred years the Way of St. James was largely deserted, and then in 1879 devout priests rediscovered his grave. From Rome special investigators arrived to check the authenticity of the find, and after scientific studies by medical men and archaeologists, declared this to be the ancient grave of Santiago. The flood of pilgrims resumed, and a wise priest who worked at Santiago wrote, 'These remains, be what they may, have revived the spirit of pilgrimage.' Today that spirit continues as powerful as ever.

There are within the region of Compostela four additional pilgrimages worth taking which I had always felt constrained to make. Two lie within the city itself and two outside, so it was to the former that I now moved. On a bright sunny afternoon, when giant figures on stilts paraded to the delight of children, an enormous Moor proving especially popular, to judge from the squeals he provoked, I walked through a chain of medieval alleys to find myself at last on the edge of the city at a spot where the small Río Sar became visible, and there, along its banks, I came upon one of the most remarkable churches in existence, a structure so bizarre that I find difficulty in believing that it still stands in this century.

As I approached the small stone building a band of children gathered about me, singing sentences from a popular song, with one enterprising boy of eleven shouting as the others sang, 'Ten pesetas, Englishman. Your only chance in this world to hear songs in true Galician.' I told him I doubted if he knew a word of Galician, whereupon he joined the others in hideous wailing, none of whose words I could understand. 'That's not Galician,' I replied, and instead of arguing with me he halted his choir and said solemnly, 'All right, you want me to take you to the church that's falling down?'

I told him that I wouldn't require his services; the church lay directly ahead of me and I couldn't miss it if I wanted to, whereupon a devilish smile came over his childish features, and he watched with growing pleasure as I approached the church and found the door tightly barred. 'You found it,' he said with evil glee, 'but you can't get in.'

'Can you get me in?'

'Yes.'

'For how much?'

'The same ten pesetas.'

I handed him the money and with a benign smile he led me to the woman sacristan, who had been on her way to open the church from the moment I had first seen it. 'You will like it,' the boy said. 'It's the only church in Spain that's always falling down.'

A short distance from the cathedral an ingratiating barker shouts to the pilgrims, 'Step this way, ladies and gentlemen. Try your skill. You too can win a bottle of wine or a kewpie doll.'

He was correct. It was the only church in Spain or elsewhere, so far as I know, that is always falling down, and I did like it. The Colegiata de Santa María la Real de Sar was built in Romanesque style in the early years of the twelfth century and had a rugged cloister attributed to Maestro Mateo of the Pórtico de la Gloria. What makes the church unique, however, and a center for pilgrimages by those who love architecture, is the fact that its two lines of heavy interior columns are not perpendicular, like those of a self-respecting church, but are cocked outward from the central nave to such an extreme degree that they seem about to topple over into the aisles.

The effect of this unnatural pitch is such as to induce vertigo. You are reluctant to believe that anyone would build a church like this on purpose, and your first impression is, 'I must be dizzy.' Then, when your senses have adjusted to this weird visual sensation, you begin to argue with what you are seeing. 'They couldn't lean so far over and not fall down.' But they do, and when the sacristan shows you the spot from which the pillars exert their maximum effect, some leaning this way and others that, your eye jumps back and forth between the extremes, unwilling to accept what stands before it.

'What happened?' I asked the sacristan.

'The builder intended to show the majesty of God,' she replied. 'Even though the pillars are falling down, He can sustain them.' She then took me outside to show me the massive flying buttresses that had obviously been added at some later time. 'When the great earthquake struck Lisboa in 1755 the effects rumbled right across Galicia and we lost many buildings. When the quake stopped, people ran out to see if the church was still standing. It was, but the walls were weakened. So these buttresses were needed to reinforce the pillars at the top.'

Later I asked Father Precedo about the bewildering little church, and he said, 'We believe that the architect originally planned it to look somewhat as it does today. For some reason we can't comprehend, he wanted to show what could be done with pillars off the perpendicular. But when the church was up, an underground river was found to be eating away the foundations and for that reason the flying buttresses had to be added, probably long before the earthquake.'

Whatever the genesis of this strange church, it is worth a visit. It defies reason and abuses the senses, but it is a rugged building that has been in the process of falling down for the last eight hundred years, and barring further earthquakes and wandering subterranean rivers, it looks good for the next eight hundred.

The second personal pilgrimage which I took in Compostela required only a few steps from the cathedral, for the far side of the Plaza de la Quintana, the austere one which contains the Puerta Santa with the twenty-four, is delineated by the wall of the Monasterio de San Payo, now a Benedictine convent, deeply engraved with that ever-present rubric: JOSE ANTONIO. I have seen so many of these fearful signs on churches across Spain, and without anyone's ever commenting upon them, I suspect that Spaniards may be just a little embarrassed by the whole-hearted manner in which their bully-boy has been identified with their religion. Had Germany and Italy won World War II and had beefy men like Hermann Goering and Count Ciano been forced down the world's throat as authentic gods, then surely José Antonio would have been their Spanish counterpart; but the ideals represented by these three deities did not prevail, and today when one sees the name of the Spanish Fascist cut into the walls of so many churches, one feels a sense of anachronism.

At the end of the blank wall so emblazoned, one comes to the inconspicuous church of the convent which contains an altar so baroque, so outrageously gingerbread, that it serves as a corrective to Romanesque austerity. Even the purist needs a touch of the bizarre; any man who loves the cold asperity of El Viti ought to relax now and then in the sunny warmth of Curro Romero's arabesques, and for me such relaxation is found in this convent church.

Two very large pillars, flattened out to provide space for decoration, flank the approach to the main altar, and from the moment one sees these warning sentinels he prepares himself for an orgy of gilt and exaggeration, for the pillars are twisting Solomonic columns in which foliage intertwines with plaster angels, with horsemen whose mounts are rearing furiously, with wreaths, whole landscapes, bas-relief scenes from the lives of saints, and with a host of odds and ends thrown helter-skelter in hopes that some might stick. Most did.

The two pillars are a mere warming-up for the main altar, forty feet across and seventy high, which stands well to the rear. Every inch of this huge construction is plastered not only with gold leaf but also with figures of saints unnumbered, niches carved deep with flowers, propitiatory tablets set off in high relief, life-sized horsemen galloping forth at strange angles, good men ascending to heaven and other good men being beheaded by pirates. Here the smaller pillars which outline the altar are covered with so many golden vines, shields and flying angels that they seem to be crawling, while over everything there is such a wealth of glitter and gold, of precious stones and violent movement, that the eye is not permitted a moment of repose. Yet the altar and its two forward pillars are so harmonious in their relationship that the overall effect is pleasing.

The two excursions outside Compostela take me through the countryside of Galicia, which hardy English travelers have considered the best region in Spain. I like it very much, a hard, cold, dour land resembling Scotland, where I took my graduate education. The food is heavy, like Scottish food; the dress is colorful, like Scottish dress; like Scots, the Galicians have to be cautious if they are to subsist on their harsh land; the bawdy sense of humor of the two peoples is alike; and the music of Galicia comes from the bagpipe, an instrument almost identical in construction and sound to that made famous by the Highlanders of Scotland. Of course, when I compare the sturdy Galicians with the Scots I knew in my youth I am not, God forbid, referring to the pasty Lowlanders of Robert Burns and Walter Scott but to the honest Highlanders of Ross and Skye and the Outer Isles.

Even a few miles' travel into the countryside of Galicia shows the observant traveler the secret of this land: the granite rock which is both the glory and the curse of the region. From deep quarries, which seem to abound, the Galician digs out a gray-and-white-flecked granite which he uses for everything. A farmer wants a barn? He builds it of granite. He wants a corncrib to protect his grain from rats? He builds one of solid granite. Garages, lean-tos, small homes and large are all built of this fine stone, and nowhere else in Europe could one find so many skilled stonemasons. This sounds ridiculous, but in the fields even fences, which in other parts of the world would be built of wood, are here built of granite: long thin slabs, beautifully cut and stood on end to form stony palisades. Galicia is the granite land.

But this prevalence of stone is also the curse of the region, for land is inherited not by the eldest son alone but by all, so that fields are divided and subdivided so often in the course of a hundred years that the resulting areas are scarcely big enough to support a family. What makes it worse is that each canny Galician insists upon outlining his new field, however small, with granite walls, until the area absorbed by stone equals about thirty percent of the tillable land. And with each death, the fields grow smaller and the fences bigger.

The results: During the last sixty-six years Galicians have been going into voluntary exile across the world, so that the voluntary depopulation of Galicia in this century equals the involuntary depopulation suffered by the Scottish Highlanders in the last century, and that was one of the most notorious land scandals of history. The difference is this. In Scotland peasants were expelled by greedy landlords. In northern Spain the crime against land was perpetrated by the farmers themselves.

Galicians are said to have many superstitions, but these often resemble the monitory yet enticing belief which one of them described: 'Like all country people, we have a mania about protecting our girls until they are safely married. Now, where does a country girl run the greatest risk of being seduced? At the village well, of course, to which she must go daily and without chaperones. In any village one can see girls swinging their way provocatively to the well, hoping, one might say, to be propositioned. So ages ago we created the water rat. Each well has one and sometimes more of these fearful creatures. A water rat can look at a man and nothing happens. But if he looks at any girl, she dies. Then and there. So you can be sure our girls watch carefully and behave themselves when they're near the well. But we're also Galicians, as well as parents, so the myth doesn't stop there. For although the water rat does kill instantly, the death is very sweet. So our girls aren't too careful.'

The glory of Galicia is its chain of rías, those fjord-like indentions of the sea that reach far inland with a burden of fish and salt air and noble landscape. In some places the rías run between meadowlands to create pastoral scenes of deep loveliness; at other times they cut through low hills to produce islands, and I have often picnicked beside them; here a sandy beach for swimming, a forest reaching down to the water; there a ruined castle on the hill; on that headland a long-forgotten church; and each day a golden sun, the smell of salt, the unannounced appearance of a low-sweeping fog and then the sun once more, with everywhere the soft, sweet motion of the sea wandering inland. Galicia has about a dozen of these rías, nicely differentiated, and tourists in general seem not to have discovered them.

But when I headed for the southern rías it was not to go picnicking; I sought the small city of Pontevedra, near the border of Portugal, through which a branch of the pilgrims' route had led up the coast from the seaports of Lisboa, Porto and Vigo. English pilgrims in particular liked to come by boat to Vigo so as to have a relatively short trip overland to Compostela. But Portuguese also followed the route in large numbers and their movement made Pontevedra a center of some importance.

The reader has probably noticed that the Way of St. James lacked one thing to make it an almost perfect pilgrims' route: nowhere was the cult of the Virgin Mary exploited, so that a good half of the mystical wonder of the Catholic Church was unprovided for. At Oviedo, north of the main route, one could detour to see relics of Christ himself, while international saints like Martin of Tours, Nicholas of Bari and James of Compostela could be known familiarly; but the Virgin Mary was not much in evidence, and with her increasing importance in the Church, this lack was felt.

It fell to the little town of Pontevedra to correct this. There, in the years when pilgrimage to Compostela had diminished to a trickle, a new cult grew up around a legend claiming that the Virgin Mary had been the first pilgrim to the tomb of Santiago, who had given his life for her son.

I went to a delightful little gingerbread sanctuary built in 1778 in the form of a combined cross and scallop shell, inside which in a place of high honor I found a most saucy religious statue. It was the Pilgrim Virgin, representing her as a primly dressed eighteenth-century traveling lady in stiff German brocade, a comfortable shawl with tassels, long black Restoration curls, bejeweled staff and gourd, and a positively enchanting Jesus dressed like a child's doll. Atop the Virgin's head stood a jaunty cockaded hat festooned with cockleshells. To be accompanied on one's way by such a delightful lady must have been enjoyable, but the true pilgrim, remembering the dangerous adventures of preceding generations, must have longed for the harsher reality of Santiago with his heavy road-worn shoes and staff. At a kiosk near the sanctuary I bought a portrait of Santiago, and he too had become a sickly-sweet cardboard figure; the granite-hard Matamoros who had led Spain to victory, who had incited whole armies and who had sustained pilgrims on their foot-weary march of nine hundred miles had degenerated into a sentimental nineteen-year-old high school senior with a premature beard. Thus did the impetus of pilgrimage diminish.

It was in this gloomy frame of mind that I met José Filgueira-Valverde, alcalde of Pontevedra and my favorite Galician. A very tall and robust man, he thundered onto the scene, crying, 'Michener! How fine to see you back in Pontevedra.' Before I had a chance to speak he had laid out the day for me. 'A few minutes to see what we've been doing with the museum, a short tour of the city to see how we're saving the old buildings, then a drive to Bayona, where I have a little surprise for you.' The mayor is so dynamic as to be exhausting, yet his delight in what he is doing is so obvious that one keeps up. The museum, for example!

'I told the government, "It's foolish to have all the museums in Madrid," so we determined to have one here,' he explained. I had seen it some years before as a small building exemplifying what one energetic man could accomplish, for even then the museum was well known. Through the generosity of a local benefactor it had acquired an excellent collection of prehistoric goldware. It displayed whole cases of stone axes, Roman pottery and Greek coins. Filgueira-Valverde had also encouraged the Pontevedrans to do certain unusual things: 'This is a Galician city, so I said, "Let's have a room which shows what a Galician kitchen is like. Women would love it." We're also a seaport, very important in Spanish history. So we found the shipboard cabin of one of our sons who became admiral of the Spanish navy. We rebuilt it board by board so our children can see what their heritage is.'

In those days the museum was a positive delight, rambling as it did over two old buildings joined together by a kind of drawbridge. I liked especially two very old life-sized statues of Biblical figures. When I first saw them I thought they were familiar; I had seen them or their brothers somewhere before. Now Mayor Filgueira-Valverde told me what these rare pieces were. When Maestro Mateo's Pórtico de la Gloria was originally installed in 1188 it was an open-faced porch giving onto the public square, but in 1738 when the new façade was added, making what had been an open portico into an inside room, some eight statues no longer fitted; they were removed and kept in a stable for nearly two centuries. In 1906 their Compostela owner concluded a deal whereby they were to be sold en bloc to a museum in America, where they would have formed one of the Romanesque glories of our museum world, but the Spanish government interceded and offered them at the same price to Spanish museums, and these two masterworks wound up in Pontevedra.

For what Mayor Filgueira-Valverde showed me next I was unprepared: a new statuary wing as big as most ordinary museums. He had just presided at the opening ceremonies of what I judged to be a memorial to his own energy, for how such a granite edifice had been paid for out of a small community budget I could not guess. I would recommend this museum to everyone, for it has been done with taste. 'And pull,' a Spanish friend whispered. What this signified I was not to learn till lunch.

At breakneck speed the mayor bundled me out of Pontevedra and down to Vigo, which he passed with a merry tattoo of praise for that famous seaport. His objective, however, lay beyond at the ocean port of Bayona, a town I had not heard of before that day, situated near the Portuguese border, and there he showed me something I could scarcely believe. On a high peninsula which juts out into the Atlantic Ocean the Spanish government acquired an abandoned castle completely surrounded by handsome walls which overlook the sea from a considerable height. The castle has been rebuilt to serve as a parador where rooms have one of two exposures: the choice ones look out upon a series of colorful bays, spotted with islands and marked by half a score of distant headlands against which the Atlantic breaks in silvery splendor, forming one of the most exciting vistas I have ever seen from a hotel; the poor rooms merely look down upon eighty miles of the surging Atlantic, one island and not more than four fine headlands, reaching into Portugal. I doubt if there is any hotel with a setting to equal this, yet the best accommodations cost only eight dollars a day for a double room, while a four-course dinner can be chosen from some fifty dishes for only two dollars and sixty-five cents. Not many Americans will revel in this luxury, because as soon as the parador was announced, Monte Real it is called, the English reserved it for almost a year ahead, having learned from experience that one of the finest places in Europe in which to vacation is this Portuguese–Spanish coast.

At lunch the mayor introduced me to an adventure which I could have done without: he plopped before me a plate of the ugliest food that the human being is capable of eating. They were percebes, a kind of barnacle, which attach themselves to rocks standing at the point where breakers crash in from the Atlantic, and much of the excitement to be found in eating percebes stems from the fact that each year men lose their lives gathering the repulsive things. When served, they look like a plateful of miniature rotting turkey legs with the skin on the leg turned black and flabby and the nails on the toes become coarse. But when the skin has somehow been torn away, beneath lies a stem of delicious, chewy meat somewhat like octopus, while the hideous toes, if properly gouged, can be tricked into giving up morsels of solid meat that is much like the best crab. I enjoyed the repulsive things, the more so later when I heard one morning a lusty old fisherwoman shouting in a quiet street in Pontevedra, 'Buy my percebes! Buy my percebes! They are firm and thick like a fisherman's penis.'

The surprise that the mayor had prepared for me, however, had nothing to do with seafood. Across from me sat one of the most reserved and courtly Spaniards I was to meet, a man in his early sixties, tall, aloof, gray in both dress and manner. He was Francisco Javier Sánchez Cantón, the director of the Prado Museum, whom I had tried in vain to see in Madrid. Introductions were made, and then ensued another of those rare and memorable luncheons which can take place only in Spain. It was about three-thirty in the afternoon when we sat down to eat. It was after six when we finished, and in the interval we talked of only two things: first of the Prado, and I surprised the director by saying that one of my favorite pictures in his care was Correggio's 'Noli Me Tangere.' Filgueira-Valverde, with explosive enthusiasm, interrupted to say that he had eyes only for Spanish painting, and he expatiated on how vibrant the Spanish school had always been, from the earliest primitives through Zurbarán and Velázquez and down to Goya. For him there could be only one school, the Spanish, but when forced to state which of the Prado paintings pleased

784

Madonna of the Pontevedra Museum.

him most he said quietly, 'Roger van der Weyden's "Deposition from the Cross." There can be nothing better than that.' Dr. Sánchez Cantón, as custodian of all the paintings, refused at first to nominate a preference but did grudgingly admit that Velázquez was good, and he told two stories about his favorite painter. 'An American woman who loved painting walked into the Velázquez room with me one morning, saw that forest of masterpieces and cried, "Impossible! It's a trick of the Spanish government." And then the English woman looked at the beggar and shook her head, "A poor man like this without a peseta to be painted by the most expensive artist in the world!" '

I proposed a toast, saying, 'For three weeks I vainly tracked you through Madrid, and now I find you in a fish restaurant in Bayona,' to which he replied in a soft voice, 'I suppose if one had to pick a single picture it would be Velázquez's "Medici Gardens in Moonlight." '

The second topic concerned a strange, tormented Galician woman about whom Filgueira-Valverde was one of the world's leading authorities, having written several books about her. It was late in the afternoon, with the sun dipping toward the surface of the Atlantic and only husks of percebes on our plates, when the mayor said, 'The older I become, the greater I believe Rosalía de Castro to have been. It has been a great source of pleasure to me to watch Spanish and French critics come around to the view that she was one of the fine poets of the last century. I am additionally proud because of the fact that she wrote her best poems in Galician.' Dr. Sánchez Cantón left off being director of the Prado and became again a Galician from Pontevedra, his home town, and as the two men spoke with animation of the great Rosalía, I understood why the little museum of Pontevedra had such a good collection of master paintings. When you get two Galician cronies like Sánchez Cantón and Filgueira-Valverde, one in charge of the Prado, the other of the museum in their home town, something has got to happen. Galicians are like that.

'She was the soul of our people,' the mayor continued, and as he spoke I reflected that he must be the only mayor in the world who was both a museum director and an expert on imagist poetry. 'She had a tortured and miserable life, but she sublimated it in her poetry.'

Rosalía of the Castros, a name which in her case had special meaning, was born in Santiago de Compostela in 1837, the child of an unmarried daughter of one of the region's important families. She was reared by suspicious relatives who did not hide from her the fact that her father, who continued to live in Compostela, could not marry her mother or acknowledge himself to be her father for a reason so final as to permit no discussion: he had been ordained a priest. Rosalía knew him and followed his career until he died, an inconspicuous padre in Padrón, the port at which the body of St. James had landed eighteen hundred years before.

Rosalía was a heavy, awkward girl who lived her poetry before she wrote it. 'I believe she had an exceptionally wide field of consciousness,' Filgueira-Valverde said. 'She was always interested in thoughts, affections, intimateness, sentiment and the cultivation of one's self and one's philosophical analysis.' She married a dwarf who was equally tortured, a writer who existed only on the fringe of movements without ever directing or understanding them, and the two had an unhappy life, although they did produce six children who shared their anxieties and accomplishments. At forty-eight Rosalía was dead, but she left behind three books of poetry, *Galician Songs*, published in 1863; *New Leaves*, published in 1880 when she was forty-three; and *On the Banks of the Sar*, which appeared in 1884, the year before her death, and it is these poems on which her reputation is founded.

She reminds me of Emily Dickinson, more acquainted with the world than Emily but like her the creator of a personal world which she described with passionate conviction. Her poems are disturbingly simple in construction, depending upon unexpected rhymes and rhythms.

> Dig it with all speed, dig it,
> Thought, you gigantic digger.
> Dig a very deep hole, where we can bury
> Remembrance of what's over.

Rosalía had an intense identification with her natural surroundings and seems always a captive of them.

> Give me your perfumes, loveliest of roses.
> Oh, quench the burning of my thirst, clear fountains,
> For it is scorching me. Clouds made of gossamer
> Like veils of lightest lace now cover over
> The bright beams of the sun at its most burning.
> And you, you temperate and loving breezes,
> Make a beginning of mysterious concerts
> Among the oak trees of the shaded farmland
> Through which the Sar passes with a light murmur.

I, like many pilgrims to Compostela, like especially her poems dedicated to the cathedral or the pilgrim spirit. They have been translated recently, under the direction of Filgueira-Valverde, by the American poet Charles David Ley, who has wisely not attempted to reproduce the almost accidental rhymes which Rosalía sometimes uses. Of the Pórtico de la Gloria she says:

> In highest heaven
> The band of musicians is starting.
> Those who play the concert in Glory
> Are tuning their instruments happily.
> Are they alive? How can those faces

> Which look so genuine be merely stone ones?
> How could stone make those marvelous tunics,
> Those eyes which speak of the life within them?
> You who chiseled them with God to help you,
> Master Mateo, your name's immortal.
> Since you remain kneeling there so humbly,
> Speak to me now and tell me about it.
> With your curly locks around you, you're silent.
> 'Saint they bump their heads against,' I'm praying.

But in Galicia this strange woman is loved primarily for her skill in catching the life of the countryside, and in a series of poems that are at once completely feminine yet hard as the granite of Galicia, she speaks of the most ordinary experiences:

> What's the lad up to?
> What can it be?
> Now he looks at me with a face like winter.
> Up at the mill, he wants me to dance with him
> And won't talk to me down in the village.
> What's the lad up to?
> What can it be?

Occasionally, when she sings of the small incidents of Galician life, she gives her words an unexpected twist which throws them into a universal aspect; she has transmuted Galicia into the whole world, and the expansive horizons of which the mayor speaks when referring to his favorite poet become apparent, as in the longer poem in which she sings of the Feast of the Rock, held beside the sea in one of the Galician rías:

> The quiet little tickles, the humorous tussles,
> The shouts and the leaping, and good-natured tales,
> Everyone tipsy and everyone quite merry
> *And Our Lady is stood there behind the cask.*

As my affection for Galicia has increased, so my interest in this heavy and almost ugly woman has grown. To a newspaperman to whom she refused to give a photograph of herself she said, 'Women such as I, who have not received the splendid gifts of physical beauty from nature, must be excused from exposing their faces to public view.' And now, as the long afternoon waned, I asked Mayor Filgueira-Valverde and Dr. Sánchez Cantón a question which had concerned me for some time: 'I've been studying the lives of your two most famous Galician writers, both women, Rosalía de Castro and the Condesa Emilia Pardo Bazán, whom I read years ago as a student, and I find numerous references to the fact that these two women, both residents of Compostela at one time or another, engaged in a long feud. Some claim that the condesa, who had all good fortune on her side with a great name and a better education, treated Rosalía very shabbily.'

I might have dropped a bomb with less impact than this literary question produced. At first they were astonished that an American wandering through Galicia had come upon this ancient female feud; then they were disgusted that such rumors had persisted; finally they were eager to clear up the matter. It was, of course, the ebullient mayor who led off with a fiery speech which reminded me of how seriously Spaniards take these literary brawls.

'Michener, I give you my solemn word, knowing much about each of these great women, that it was not a feud. Rosalía must be seen as a romantic, a solitary, one who broods incessantly, whose life consists of this tiny corner of Galicia into which she digs with an intensity that most human beings never know.' He spoke of the dead poet with tears in his voice and deep love, but then his voice changed and he became a resonant orator: 'Pardo Bazán, on the other hand, was a complete woman, very intelligent, of suave temperament, sensual, an activist, extremely realistic, a critic of world literature, the translator of Voltaire, but above all a grand aristocrat. She was most erudite, and educated herself a second time in Paris in revolutionary ideals. Remember one fact when you think of the two women. Pardo Bazán never wrote in Galician. Rosalía did.'

'You have explained away the fight,' I said, 'but you speak with such fury that I'm sure one existed. What was it about?'

The mayor placed his large hand on my arm and said, 'As one literary man to another I must tell the truth. It was the age-old case of a husband in a secondary position who fought the whole world in his wife's name, not because he wanted to protect his wife but because he wanted to insult the world which had ignored him. He fought my father. He fought Pardo Bazán. He fought everyone. You can say of him that he was an archivist who filed his fights in neat order, a historian who kept good records of his triumphs and defeats. He survived his wife by thirty-eight years, during which his embattled defense of her became his life's mission.'

'But was there a feud between the two women?' I persisted.

'The family of Emilia Pardo Bazán had a castle in Cambados. They had many castles. Why would their daughter want to fight with a poor countrywoman who had no father? Why? Tell me why?'

I had hoped that these two scholars would tell me why, but like granite-hewn Galicians they hovered protectively over the ghosts of these two fine women, and from them I would learn no more of the passions which once agitated this region. I was haunted, however, by a picture which had somehow been built up in my mind, I do not know how or with what authority: I see the great Condesa Pardo Bazán, rich with honors as one of Spain's leading novelists, sought after by publishers in both Madrid and Paris, a regal and handsome woman somewhat austere in manner. She is attending a dinner being given in her honor and somehow she is brought face to face with a countrywoman, big-boned and awkward and unlovely, fifteen years older than herself, to whom she refuses either a place at table or the ordinary civilities. The novelist is wealthy from her books; the poet so far as we know never gained a peseta from her poems, and between them as I see them in this persistent portrait there is a gulf that life did not permit to be bridged.

I do not invent such things. Obviously I could not have known either Emilia Pardo Bazán or Rosalía de Castro, and so far as I know have never read a complete life of either, but somewhere years ago in my wanderings I picked up this strange story of the feud between the two women and I wish I knew what the facts were.

On my last day in Galicia I did what millions of pilgrims before me had done. I went to land's end at Finisterre, that wild and distant point of rock which had been my introduction to Spain so many years before, and there at the foot of the lighthouse, on a headland looking westward to the New World with which Spain had been so deeply involved, I tried to summarize what I had learned of this contradictory nation in the years that I had known it. So much of what I had wanted to accomplish in Spain had ended in failure. I, who love music so much, had never once since that first night in Valencia witnessed a complete flamenco, and the failure was not in my trying; it is simply that flamenco cannot be ordered; one must be at the right place at the right time when duende is upon all present. The duende I had missed. Nor had I heard one note of Pedrell's music, though I had traveled far to do so.

I had never once, in all my years in Spain, eaten a good paella, even though my wife and I love rice and seek it out in restaurants around the world. At Eliot Elisofon's home in New York I'd had a fine paella, and at a Greenwich Village restaurant I'd had one, but never in Spain. As with flamenco, one must be at the right table at the right moment, for otherwise he is fed dreadful stuff which the cook has the gall to name paella.

Nor had I seen Curro Romero, he of the burning legend, perform even halfway decently. I'd seen him patiently in more than twenty corridas, that is, with forty-odd different bulls, but never once acceptable. At Finisterre, Vavra and Fulton consoled me: 'Come back next year, and go to the feria at Sevilla and then to San Isidro in Madrid and to San Fermín at Pamplona and on to Valencia and Málaga and Vitoria and Bilbao and Barcelona and wind up in Zaragoza, and maybe some afternoon you'll see him good.' The schedule they proposed would require me to attend some eighty corridas on the remote possibility that I might see one acceptable, four hundred and eighty bulls to see the great Curro Romero good in one.

'The odds are against me,' I pointed out.

'Ah, but if you see him great . . . just once . . .'

Much of Spain is like that. If one is willing to come back four hundred and eighty times, he may see something which will forever haunt him, and to those who have seen these things the odds are not excessive, for when duende is upon this land it offers an illumination that cannot be found elsewhere. And of course, the proposal made by my two companions, that I trek back and forth across Spain for months in search of that golden moment, would yield compensations other than the discovery of the moment itself, and this I knew. The search, the renewal of acquaintances with this land and people, would be worthwhile. I am convinced that in Spain I shall never hear good flamenco, nor eat a decent paella, nor see Curro Romero good, but I would always be eager to return for the effort, because we seek duende not to find it but to be assured that it exists at certain times in certain men.

Strangely, it was not until I returned to New York that I appreciated the gracia of the Curro Romero story, for there I met once more Conrad Janis, who had told me of Romero in the first place, and he said, 'I was present in Madrid when something happened regarding Curro which would interest you. His manager told him at the end of 1965 . . . Now understand, this was Curro's greatest season. Fights everywhere. So his manager reports, "Curro, we've had to spend so much money buying off the critics . . . to prevent them from writing the truth about your bad days . . . Well, there's to be no profit this year." Curro asked, "You mean all those fights, all that travel back and forth and nothing left at the end of the year?" The manager said, "Well, we've lived well and you did have that one great afternoon that everyone's still talking about." Tears came into Romero's eyes. I can vouch for this. I was there. And he said, "To think that with the terrible fear I have each time I face the bull . . . the agony . . . the disasters. To face that all year. And at the end to have nothing." '

In the spring of 1967 I returned to Madrid to work with Vanderford on the translations from Spanish used in this book and happened to be in the city when Curro Romero was scheduled to appear on two successive afternoons. On May 25 his first bull looked at him askance; he grew visibly gray with fear; the fight was a disaster. Vanderford, sitting next to me, growled, 'Curro has just enough bravery to dress in the matador's suit. Anything that happens thereafter is immaterial.' His second bull was by any standards a vicious animal, but the president refused to have it returned to the corrals, whereupon Curro did something never before seen in Madrid. He simply refused to fight. The president would not budge. Curro would not budge. So the bull was allowed to chase wildly about the empty ring for the allotted number of minutes, after which the three warnings were sounded on the trumpet and the bull was led off to slaughter and Curro to jail. He was fined twenty-five thousand pesetas, and Madrid was caught up in a frenzy of rumor. Would he be allowed out of jail to fight the second day? Even if he did get out, would the management let him fight? As he left jail next morning Curro made an announcement which seems sure of a place in bullfight history: 'This day I shall be carried from the ring, either on shoulders through the great gate or into the infirmary.'

He was released in time to participate in what has become known as one of the great days in recent Madrid history. Critics were uniformly ecstatic and termed it 'de apoteosis y de antología' (one for the books). It began with a fine performance by Diego Puerta, crisp and magisterial, and continued with a dazzling exhibition by Paco Camino, who fought as if inspired. The plaza was in delirium, and what was most unusual, for the second time in my life I saw a string of six well-matched bulls, each of which gave serious fight, and by curious chance they were from the ranch of Benítez Cubero, who had provided the earlier string of which I have spoken.

And what of Curro Romero? Did he leave the arena through the great gate or through the infirmary? For a moment it looked as if it would be the latter, for the black bull Bastardo, aptly named and twelve hundred pounds of energy, hooked his right horn into Curro's left leg, tore away his uniform and tossed him high in the air. Normally a serious accident like this would have finished Curro for the day, and he would have been forgiven, but on this afternoon something strange happened. He lay flat on the ground while the bull lunged at him several times, just missing his head and chest. Then he leaped up, tied his torn costume about his damaged leg, grabbed his sword and cloth and proceeded to work wonders. He was brave; he was artistic; he was gallant; and in a way which tore at the emotions of the crowd, he was heroic. When the afternoon ended, the three matadors left the arena as Curro had predicted he would, on shoulders through the great gate. Vanderford and my other friends in the stands gathered about me to gloat. 'We told you that one day you'd see him great. Have you ever seen better?' I surrendered. I had seen Curro good, and he was all that Orson Welles and the others had promised. In fact, the experience has given me courage to keep on trying with flamenco and paella.

Throughout this chapter I have spoken of being on a pilgrimage, and now, as I return from Finisterre to Compostela, I think it not inappropriate to speak of this pilgrimage, which was a most real thing. Walter Starkie, in his fine book *The Road to Santiago* when speaking of the four pilgrimages he made between the years 1924 and 1954, offers this cryptic sentence: 'My 1954 pilgrimage bore for me a deep significance, for it marked the time of my retirement from official life, and I wished to perform religiously all the rituals, in order to prepare myself for making my examination of conscience.' This statement perplexed me and I asked various people what it signified; Don Luis Morenés told me, 'After the Spanish Civil War, countries like America and England were studious to send us Catholics as their representatives, and in this spirit England in 1940 sent us as their first director of the new British Institute, the fiddle-playing Irish-Catholic

Starkie. He stayed in Spain during World War II, helping to organize and operate an escape route for British airmen shot down over France. That was his contribution to the grand alliance against Hitler.' An English informant told me, 'After the war Starkie was looked upon with diminished favor by the British but with real love by the Spanish. In 1954 he was retired from his official position, somewhat prematurely, I felt, and Spain lost one of the truest friends it ever had.' It was at this impasse, when he knew nothing of his future—ultimately he landed a good university position in America—that the gypsy-loving Irishman had set out upon his final walk to Compostela.

In one sense my reason for pilgrimage was less dramatic; in another, more so. In early September, 1965, I was stricken with a sizable heart attack, and as I lay in that fitful slumber which is not sleep I thought of the good days I had known in northern Spain with Don Luis, and of the approaches to Santiago de Compostela and of how we had strained to see who would be first to spot those splendid towers rising in the moonlight, and of that portico which I had studied with affection but not carefully. And I thought then that if I ever were to leave that restricted room, which I sometimes doubted, for it seemed unlikely that I would regain sufficient strength to travel, I should like to see Compostela again.

I was lucky in that my doctor was a student of Paul Dudley White, the notable specialist of Boston, whom I had known in Russia. As a courtesy Dr. White flew down from Boston and recited his now-famous theory: 'If a man with a heart attack tries to do anything at all before the passage of three months, he's an idiot; but if at the end of three months he doesn't at least try to do all he did before, he's an even greater one.'

When I returned to Spain my capacity to travel and work was unknown. If I have spoken in this book with a certain regard for the trivial hill city of Teruel it is partly because it was to Teruel that I first went on my return journey, and each step I took in that pregnant place was a test to see whether I could stand the sun, whether I could climb hills, and whether my mind could focus on a specific problem for some hours. Teruel, where I had first seen the true Spain more than three decades ago . . . Teruel, where I had lived and died with the Spanish Republic . . . Teruel, which had been a magnet for years, now became important in another way, and when I discovered that I could negotiate those hilly streets I decided that I was ready for the feria at Pamplona and the long trip across northern Spain.

When I entered the cathedral of Santiago de Compostela for the last time the national celebration of which I spoke earlier was in progress. The great botafumeiro was in full swing, its massive cargo of silver and incense descending perilously toward my head as I slipped through the crowded nave to a point behind the main altar, where the organ seemed to be exploding. There I found the small and narrow flight of stairs which took me upward to a hiding point behind the great stone statue of Santiago Matamoros which occupies the center of the altar. Only the rear of his head and shoulders was visible to me, the latter encased in a metal robe encrusted with jewels, but beyond the saint I could look through the peephole in the altar and out into the vast cathedral where the censer was coming to a halt, where Father Precedo Lafuente was sitting in his red robes, where Admiral Núñez Rodríguez in white uniform was preparing to make his rededication of Spain to the apostle, and where Cardinal Quiroga Palacios waited to make his speech of acknowledgment. It was a dazzling moment, as rich in pageantry and as filled with the spirit of Spain as any that I had witnessed, and there I hid in the darkness as if an interloper with no proper role in the ceremonial except that I had completed my vow of pilgrimage and stood at last with my arm about the stone-cold shoulder of Santiago, my patron saint and Spain's.

Index

*In this index, phrases and titles beginning with *The* and *A* and their Spanish equivalents are alphabetized under the next word. Page numbers in italics refer to maps or illustrations.